THE
VANQUISHED

THE
VANQUISHED

Why the First World War Failed to End

ROBERT GERWARTH

FARRAR, STRAUS AND GIROUX   NEW YORK

Farrar, Straus and Giroux
18 West 18th Street, New York 10011

Copyright © 2016 by Robert Gerwarth
All rights reserved
Printed in the United States of America
Originally published in 2016 by Allen Lane, an imprint
of Penguin Books, Great Britain
Published in the United States by Farrar, Straus and Giroux
First American edition, 2016

Library of Congress Cataloging-in-Publication Data
Names: Gerwarth, Robert, author.
Title: The vanquished : why the First World War failed to end / Robert Gerwarth.
Description: First American edition. | New York : Farrar, Straus and Giroux, 2016. |
    "Originally published in 2016 by Allen Lane, an imprint of Penguin Books, Great
    Britain"—Title page verso. | Includes bibliographical references and index.
Identifiers: LCCN 2016032496 | ISBN 9780374282455 (hardback) |
    ISBN 9780374710682 (ebook)
Subjects: LCSH: World War, 1914–1918—Influence. | World War, 1914–1918—
    Social aspects—Europe. | War and society—Europe—History—20th century. |
    Ethnic conflict—Europe—History—20th century. | Political violence—Europe—
    History—20th century. | Europe—Ethnic relations—History—20th century. |
    Europe—Politics and government—1918–1945. | Europe—Social conditions—
    20th century. | World War, 1939–1945—Causes. | BISAC: HISTORY / Military /
    World War I. | HISTORY / Europe / General. | HISTORY / Modern / 20th century.
Classification: LCC D523 .G478 2016 | DDC 940.5/1—dc23
LC record available at https://lccn.loc.gov/2016032496

Our books may be purchased in bulk for promotional, educational, or business use.
Please contact your local bookseller or the Macmillan Corporate and Premium
Sales Department at 1-800-221-7945, extension 5442, or by e-mail at
MacmillanSpecialMarkets@macmillan.com.

www.fsgbooks.com
www.twitter.com/fsgbooks • www.facebook.com/fsgbooks

1   3   5   7   9   10   8   6   4   2

For Oscar and Lucian

Contents

PART III

Imperial Collapse

List of Maps

List of Illustrations

18. *Minden a mienk!* (Everything Is Ours!), anti-Semitic Hungarian poster by Miltiades Manno, 1919. (Photograph: Budapest Poster Gallery, http://budapestposter.com)

19. *Freikorps* soldiers and government troops march prisoners through the streets of Munich after the fall the 'Soviet Republic', May 1919. (Photograph: Scherl/Süddeutsche Zeitung Photo)

20. The signing of the Neuilly treaty, 27 June 1919. (Photograph: National Library 'Cyril and Methodius', Sofia (C II 1292))

21. Arrest of Stambolijski's man-servant during the anti-BANU putsch, June 1923. (Photograph: Süddeutsche Zeitung Photo)

22. Mussolini and fellow Italian Blackshirts during the 'March on Rome', 1922. (Photograph: BIPs/Getty Images)

23. Romanian military parade in central Budapest, 1919. (Photograph: De Agostini/Getty Images)

24. Anti-Czech demonstration, Vienna, March 1919. (Photograph: Scherl/Süddeutsche Zeitung Photo)

25. Ethnic German refugees from West Prussia, 1920. (Photograph: Scherl/Süddeutsche Zeitung Photo)

26. Greek infantry advances through the Anatolian plateau during the Greco-Turkish War. (Photograph: TopFoto)

27. Mustafa Kemal and his general staff, 1919. (Photograph: Scherl/Süddeutsche Zeitung Photo)

28. Smyrna in flames, September 1922. (Photograph: Alamy)

29. Greek refugees flee Smyrna by sea, September 1922. (Photograph: Getty Images)

30. Demonstration against the Trianon Treaty, Budapest, 1931. (Photograph: Scherl/Süddeutsche Zeitung Photo)

31. The train carriage in which the Germans signed the armistice is removed from a French museum, June 1940. (Photograph: Bundesarchiv, Koblenz (Bild 146-2004-0147))

Europe in March 1918

Central Powers

areas occupied by
Central Powers

Moscow

RUSSIA

Ural

Don

Volga

Kharkov

Dnieper

Caspian Sea

CRIMEA

Black Sea

GEORGIA

AZERBAIJAN

Kars

ARMENIA

PERSIA

OTTOMAN
EMPIRE

Euphrates

Tigris

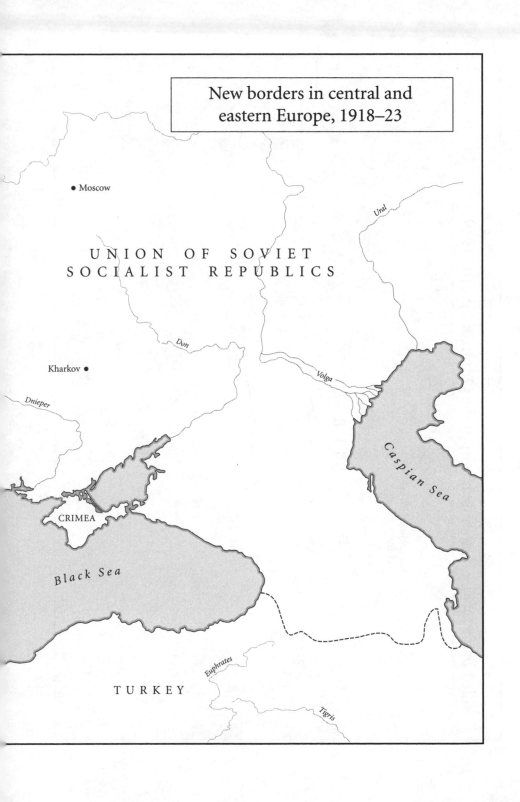

New borders in central and
eastern Europe, 1918–23

• Moscow

Ural

UNION OF SOVIET
SOCIALIST REPUBLICS

Don

Volga

Kharkov •

Dnieper

Caspian Sea

CRIMEA

Black Sea

Euphrates

TURKEY

Tigris

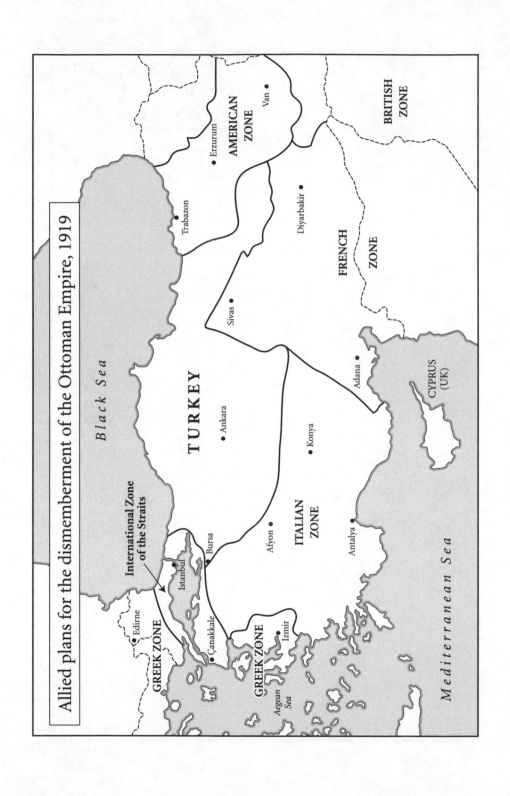

Allied plans for the dismemberment of the Ottoman Empire, 1919

Black Sea

AMERICAN ZONE

Van

Erzurum

BRITISH ZONE

Trabazon

Diyarbakir

FRENCH ZONE

Sivas

Adana

CYPRUS (UK)

TURKEY

Ankara

Konya

International Zone of the Straits

Bursa

Istanbul

Afyon

ITALIAN ZONE

Antalya

Edirne

GREEK ZONE

Çanakkale

GREEK ZONE

Izmir

Aegean Sea

Mediterranean Sea

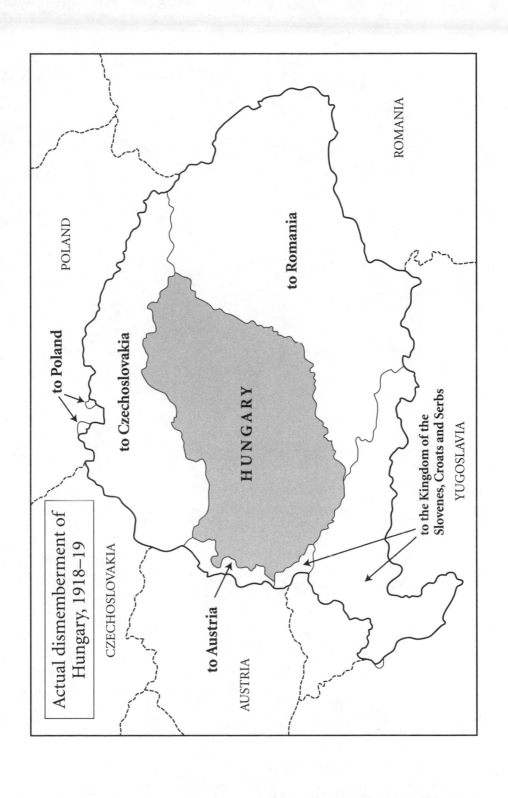

Actual dismemberment of Hungary, 1918–19

Introduction

Both sides, victors and vanquished, were ruined. All the
Emperors or their successors were slain or deposed ... All
were defeated; all were stricken; everything they had given
was in vain. Nothing was gained by any ... Those that survived, the veterans of countless battle-days, returned, whether
with the laurels of victory or tidings of disaster, to homes
engulfed already in catastrophe.

Winston Churchill, The Unknown War *(1931)*

This war is not the end but the beginning of violence. It is the
forge in which the world will be hammered into new borders
and new communities. New molds want to be filled with
blood, and power will be wielded with a hard fist.

Ernst Jünger, Der Kampf als Inneres Erlebnis *(1928)*

It was on 9 September 1922 that the passions aroused by a decade of
war descended on the city of Smyrna. As Turkish cavalry entered what
was once the most prosperous and cosmopolitan city of the Ottoman
Empire, the Christian majority among its population looked on in
nervous anticipation. Smyrna was a city in which Muslims, Jews,
Armenians and Greek Orthodox Christians had lived together more
or less peacefully for centuries. But nearly ten years of war had
changed the city's inter-ethnic relations. After losing nearly all of its
vast European territories in the Balkan Wars of 1912–13, the Ottoman Empire had joined the Great War as Germany's ally in August
1914 – and found itself on the losing side yet again. Stripped of its
Arab domains in what subsequently became known as the 'Middle

East', the defeated Ottoman Empire and its humiliated Muslim Turkish population soon faced another threat: encouraged by the British Prime Minister, David Lloyd George, a Greek invasion army had landed in Smyrna in 1919, determined to carve out a new empire for itself in the partly Christian-populated territories of Asia Minor.[1]

After a brutal three-year conflict that saw extraordinary levels of atrocities against both Muslim and Christian civilians, the fortunes of war had now turned decisively against the Greeks. Lured into the interior of central Anatolia by the capable leader of the Turkish nationalists, Mustafa Kemal, the hopelessly overstretched and incompetently led Greek troops collapsed when Kemal – better known under his future honorific name Atatürk ('Father of the Turks') – launched a major counter-offensive in the summer of 1922. The hasty withdrawal of the ruined Greek army, accompanied by looting, murder and arson against the Muslim population of western Anatolia, led to well-founded fears of reprisals among the Christian population of Smyrna. But deceptive assurances from the city's Greek occupation authorities and the presence of no fewer than twenty-one Allied warships anchored in the harbour of Smyrna lured the Greeks and Armenians into a false sense of security. Given that the Western Allies – most notably Britain – had encouraged Athens' conquest of Smyrna, surely they would intervene to protect the Christian population from Muslim reprisals?

Such hopes soon proved to be misplaced as the great tragedy of the city unfolded. Shortly after the victorious Turkish army had conquered Smyrna, soldiers arrested the Orthodox Archbishop, Chrysostomos, an outspoken supporter of the Greek invasion, and delivered him to their commanding officer, Major General Sakallı Nureddin Pasha. The general released Chrysostomos to a Turkish mob that had gathered outside his quarters, demanding the Metropolitan's head. As one observer, a French sailor, recalled, the 'crowd fell upon Chrysostomos with guttural shrieks and dragged him down the street until they reached a barber's shop where Ismael, the Jewish proprietor, was peering nervously from his doorway. Someone pushed the barber aside, grabbed a white sheet, and tied it around Chrysostomos's neck, shouting, "Give him a shave!" They tore out the Prelate's beard, gouged out his eyes with knives, cut off his ears, his nose, and his

2

hands.' Nobody intervened. Chrysostomos' tormented body was then dragged into a nearby backstreet where he was hurled into a corner and left to die.[2]

The violent death of the Orthodox Metropolitan of Smyrna was no more than an overture to a fortnight of violent orgies reminiscent of the sacking of enemy towns during Europe's religious wars in the seventeenth century. Over the following two weeks an estimated 30,000 Greeks and Armenians were slaughtered. Many more were robbed, beaten, or raped by Turkish soldiers, paramilitaries and local teenage gangs.[3]

The first houses were set alight in the city's Armenian quarter in the late afternoon of 13 September. By the following morning most of the Christian quarters of Smyrna were on fire. Within hours, thousands of men, women and children had taken refuge by the quayside. The British reporter George Ward Price observed the murderous spectacle from the safety of a battleship in the harbour and recorded an 'indescribable' situation:

> What I see as I stand on the deck of the *Iron Guard* is an unbroken wall of fire, two miles long, in which twenty distinct volcanoes of raging flames are throwing up jagged, writhing tongues to a height of a hundred feet . . . The sea glows a deep copper-red, and, worst of all, from the densely packed mob of thousands of refugees huddled on the narrow quay, between the advancing fiery death behind and the deep water in front, comes continuously such frantic screaming of sheer terror as can be heard miles away.[4]

While Turkish troops cordoned off the quay, many of the desperate refugees sought to find ways of getting towards the Allied ships anchored in the harbour. As it became increasingly clear that the Allies would not intervene or make any attempt to rescue them by boat, some terrified Greeks took their own lives by plunging into the water and drowning themselves. Others attempted to swim to safety, frantically trying to reach one of the Allied ships. Children and the elderly were stampeded by a crowd desperate to escape from the unbearable heat of the burning buildings around them. Cattle and horses, impossible to evacuate under the circumstances, had their forelegs broken before being pushed into the water to drown – a scene immortalized in the short story 'On the Quai at Smyrna', written by the then little-known foreign correspondent for the *Toronto Star*, Ernest Hemingway.[5]

Hemingway was only one of many Western reporters documenting the sacking of Smyrna. For several days the city's dire fate made headline news around the world. It prompted the British Secretary of State for the Colonies, Winston Churchill, in a letter he sent to the Dominion Prime Ministers, to condemn the destruction of Smyrna as an 'infernal orgy' with 'few parallels in the history of human crime'.[6]

As the grim fate of Smyrna's Christian population and the preceding massacres of Muslim Turks chillingly illustrate, the Great War was not immediately followed by a period of peace. Churchill was, in fact, wrong about the unique nature of the Smyrna atrocities. On the contrary: violent incidents as harrowing as the ones in western Anatolia were no rarity in what is often (but rather misleadingly) referred to as the 'interwar' years, a neatly framed period that allegedly began with the armistice of 11 November 1918 and ended with Hitler's attack on Poland on 1 September 1939. Yet such a periodization only makes sense for the principal victors of the Great War, namely Britain (with the notable exception of the Irish War of Independence) and France, for whom the cessation of hostilities on the Western Front indeed marked the beginning of a post-war era.

For those living in Riga, Kiev, Smyrna, or many other places in eastern, central and south-eastern Europe in 1919, there was no peace, only continuous violence. 'The world war formally ended with the conclusion of the armistice,' the Russian philosopher and polymath Piotr Struve observed from the vantage point of a contemporary public intellectual who had exchanged his affiliations from the Bolshevik to the White movement in the midst of his country's violent civil war. 'In fact, however, everything from that point onward that we have experienced, and continue to experience, is a continuation and transformation of the world war.'[7]

Struve did not have to look far to prove his point: violence was ubiquitous as armed forces of different sizes and political purposes continued to clash across eastern and central Europe, and new governments came and went amid much bloodshed. Between 1917 and 1920 alone Europe experienced no fewer than twenty-seven violent transfers of political power, many of them accompanied by latent or open civil wars.[8] The most extreme case was, of course, Russia itself, where hostility between the supporters and opponents of Lenin's Bolshevik coup in October 1917 had rapidly escalated into a civil war of historically unprecedented proportions, eventually claiming well over three million lives.

Yet even in places where violence was much more muted, many contemporaries shared Struve's belief that the end of the Great War had not brought stability, but had instead ushered in a highly volatile situation in which peace was at best precarious, if not altogether illusory. In post-revolutionary Austria – no longer the centre of one of the largest land empires in Europe but a tiny and impoverished Republic in the Alps – a widely circulated conservative newspaper made a similar point in a May 1919 editorial, published under the headline 'War in Peace'. Pointing to the continuously high levels of violence in the territories of the vanquished land empires of Europe, the paper observed that an extensive arc of post-war violence now stretched from Finland and the Baltic States through Russia and Ukraine, Poland, Austria, Hungary and Germany, all the way through the Balkans and into Anatolia and the Caucasus.[9]

Curiously, the article did not mention Ireland, the one emerging western European country that, at least during the Irish War of Independence (1919–21) and the subsequent civil war (1922–3), seemed to follow a similar (albeit less violent) course to the central and eastern European states between 1918 and 1923.[10] Yet the similarities between Ireland and central Europe did not escape astute contemporary observers in Dublin, who viewed Ireland's predicament as part of a much wider European malaise, an ongoing conflict that originated in the world crisis of 1914–18, while also being distinct from it. As the Nobel Laureate W. B. Yeats put it in one of his most famous poems, 'The Second Coming' (1919):

> Things fall apart; the centre cannot hold;
> Mere anarchy is loosed upon the world,
> The blood-dimmed tide is loosed . . .
> And what rough beast, its hour come round at last,
> Slouches towards Bethlehem to be born?[11]

Europe's violent transition from world war to a chaotic 'peace' is the subject of this book. Moving beyond the more familiar histories of Britain and France, or the equally well-known story of peace-making on the Western Front in 1918, it aims to reconstruct the experiences of people living in those countries that were on the losing side in the Great War: the Habsburg, Romanov, Hohenzollern and Ottoman empires (and their successor states), as well as Bulgaria. Yet any history of the vanquished also has to include Greece and Italy. Although victors in the autumn of 1918, both states soon found their fortunes declining. For Athens, the Greco-Turkish War (1919–22) turned victory into 'the Great Catastrophe' of 1922, while many Italians felt that their hard-won success over the Habsburg Army in 1918 was not sufficiently rewarded. Dissatisfaction with the compensation received for some 600,000 casualties became an obsessive concern in Italy – most forcibly expressed in the popular notion of the *vittoria mutilata* ('mutilated victory') – generating support for radical nationalism, while serious labour unrest and farm occupations convinced many that a Bolshevik revolution in Italy was imminent. In many ways the country's post-war experience, which culminated in the appointment of the first fascist Prime Minister, Benito Mussolini, in October 1922, resembled that of the defeated empires of eastern and central Europe more closely than that of France or Britain.

By focusing on the defeated land empires of Europe, and the shape they took after the Great War, this book deals with states that have often been portrayed either through the prism of wartime propaganda or from the vantage point of 1918, when the legitimization of new nation states in east-central Europe required the demonization of the empires from which they seceded. This reading allowed some historians in the West to portray the First World War as an epic struggle between the democratic Allies on the one hand and the autocratic Central Powers on the other (while ignoring the fact that the most autocratic empire of all, Imperial Russia, was part of the Triple Entente). In more recent years, however, a growing body of scholarship on the late Ottoman, Hohenzollern and Habsburg empires has disputed the black legend that the Central Powers were simply rogue states and anachronistic 'people's prisons'. This reassessment has been an emphatic one for both Imperial Germany and the Habsburg

Empire, which appear in a much more benign (or at least more ambivalent) light to historians today than they did in the first eight decades after 1918.[12] Even with respect to the Ottoman Empire, where the wartime genocide of the Armenians seemed to confirm the malicious nature of an oppressive empire that violently suppressed its minorities, a more complex picture is gradually emerging. Some historians have recently highlighted that up until 1911–12 there was still some potential for an Ottoman future with equal rights and citizenship for all ethnic and religious groups living within the empire.[13] While the nationalism of the Committee of Unity and Progress (CUP) government, brought to power by the 1908 revolution, stood in stark contrast with the more inclusive civic nationalism of the Ottoman Empire, the CUP had lost a great deal of popular support by 1911.[14] It was the Italian invasion of the Ottoman province of Tripolitania (Libya) that year and the First Balkan War in 1912 that allowed the CUP to establish a dictatorship and which changed inter-ethnic relations profoundly, as up to 300,000 Muslims, including the families of some leading CUP politicians, were violently uprooted from their homes in the Balkans, prompting a refugee crisis and political radicalization in Constantinople.[15]

Even if one deems the recent scholarly 'rehabilitation' of the pre-war land empires exaggerated or overstated, it is difficult to suggest that post-imperial Europe was a better, safer place than it had been in 1914. Not since the Thirty Years War of the seventeenth century had a series of interconnected wars and civil wars in Europe been as inchoate and deadly as in the years after 1917–18. As civil wars overlapped with revolutions, counter-revolutions and border conflicts between emerging states without clearly defined frontiers or internationally recognized governments, 'post-war' Europe between the official end of the Great War in 1918 and the Treaty of Lausanne in July 1923 was the most violent place on the planet. Even if we exclude the millions of people who perished from the Spanish flu pandemic between 1918 and 1920, or those hundreds of thousands of civilians between Beirut and Berlin who died of starvation as a consequence of the Allied decision to keep up the economic blockade beyond the end of hostilities, well over four million people – more than the combined wartime casualties of Britain, France and the United States – died as a result of armed conflicts in post-war Europe. In addition, millions of impoverished refugees from central, eastern and southern Europe roamed the war-torn landscapes of western Europe in search of safety and a better life.[16] It is with good reason that some historians of eastern Europe have classified the years immediately after 1918 as a time of 'extended European civil war'.[17]

Despite the horrific events that took place in large parts of 'post-war' Europe, the numerous conflicts of the years after 1917–18 have not attracted nearly as much attention as the events on the Western Front over the previous four years. Contemporary British observers such as Winston Churchill famously dismissed the post-war conflicts as the 'wars of the pygmies' – a condescending comment that reflects the orientalizing (and implicitly colonial) attitude towards eastern Europe that prevailed in western European textbooks of the period for decades after 1918.[18] It also tapped into an idea, stemming in large part from the years between the Great Eastern Crisis (1875–8) and the two Balkan Wars of 1912–13, that eastern Europe was somehow 'inherently' violent, as opposed to the civilized and peaceful West. These blinkered assumptions and the general degradation of discourse during 1914–18 made the British and French policymakers strikingly myopic about the catastrophes that now unfolded in east-central Europe, even if they occurred in places that prior to the Great War had been for many years deeply law-abiding, culturally sophisticated and peaceful.

While the story of Europe's transition from war to peace remains less familiar to many western European readers than that of the Great War itself, the eventful years between 1917 and 1923 are still very much present in the collective memory of people from eastern, central and southern Europe, as well as those from the Middle East and Ireland. For them the memory of the Great War is often overshadowed, if not fully eclipsed, by foundational stories of independence struggles, national liberation and revolutionary change in and around 1918.[19] In Russia, for example, Lenin's Bolshevik revolution of 1917 – not the 'imperialist war' that preceded it – remained the central historical reference point for decades. In today's Ukraine, national independence in 1918 (however short-lived) is ever-present in public debates about the geopolitical threat posed by Putin's Russia. For some post-imperial states – notably Poland, Czechoslovakia, and the Kingdom of Serbs, Croats and Slovenes (the future Yugoslavia) – a commemorative focus on the triumphal birth (or rebirth) of the nation state in 1918 enabled them to conveniently 'forget' that millions of their citizens had fought in the defeated armies of the Central Powers.

Elsewhere, the years after 1917–18 feature prominently in collective memory because they represent particularly divisive moments in history: in Finland, a non-combatant during the Great War, the shadow of the extremely bloody civil war of 1918 that killed off more than 1 per cent of the country's population within less than six months has haunted political debates ever since, while in Ireland the affiliations and dilemmas of the civil war of 1922–3 continue to shape the country's party-political system to the present day. Within the Middle East, too, the Great War is a topic of marginal interest compared to the Allies' subsequent 'invention of nations' (such as Iraq or Jordan), the mandate regime imposed by the League of Nations, and the still ongoing conflict over Palestine. In the eyes of many Arabs this conflict originated in the pledge of British support for 'the establishment in Palestine of a national home for the Jewish people' by the Foreign Secretary, Arthur Balfour, hence known as the 'Balfour Declaration'.[20]

The complex picture of Europe's emergence from the Great War, a conflict that had left nearly 10 million men dead and over 20 million wounded, defies any easy categorization or definition of the violent convulsions that followed it. At the risk of simplification, however, it is possible to identify at least three distinct, but mutually reinforcing and often overlapping, types of conflict within the ensuing 'European civil war'. First, the European 'post-war' period witnessed the eruption of battles between regular or emerging national armies in inter-state wars, such as the Polish-Soviet War, the Greco-Turkish conflict, or the Romanian invasion of Hungary. These inter-state conflicts, fought with weapons left over from the Great War, tended to occur in the geographical zones where the disintegration of the Habsburg, Romanov, Hohenzollern and Ottoman empires provided the space for the emergence of new and often nervously aggressive nation states, which sought to consolidate or expand their territories through force. One such war, that between Russia and Poland (1919 to 1921), left an estimated 250,000 people dead or missing, while Greek and Turkish military casualties between 1919 and 1922 may have been as high as 200,000.[21]

Secondly, the brief period between 1917 and 1923 saw a massive proliferation of civil wars, as was the case in Russia or Finland, but also in Hungary, Ireland, and parts of Germany. In the former territories of the Romanov Empire, the difference between regular inter-state wars and civil wars was not always easy to decipher, as all kinds of interconnected conflicts fuelled one another. The Red Army was engaged in war with Poland and the repression of breakaway republics in the western borderlands and the Caucasus, but Lenin also sought to secure victory over his White adversaries and a whole host of other real or imagined enemies – from kulaks to anarchists and moderate socialists, suspected of trying to subvert the Bolshevik revolution. The situation in Russia was further complicated by the involvement of outsiders such as Allied intervention troops supporting the Whites, or the tens of thousands of German *Freikorps* soldiers who roamed the Baltic region after 1918 and fought with (and against) Latvian and Estonian nationalists in pursuit of land, glory or adventure.

The civil wars that haunted Europe in this period were generally triggered by a third distinct form of political violence that dominated the years 1917–23, namely social and national revolution. If during the later stages of the Great War many combatant states had witnessed work stoppages and strikes prompted by material deprivation and war-weariness, the end of the war was accompanied by outright revolutions and violent regime changes in all of the vanquished states of Europe. The revolutions that occurred between 1917 and 1923 could be socio-political in nature, pursuing a redistribution of power, land, and wealth, as was the case in Russia, Hungary, Bulgaria and Germany; or they could be 'national' revolutions, as was the case in the shatter-zones of the defeated Habsburg, Romanov, Hohenzollern and Ottoman empires, where new and re-emerging states, inspired by ideas of national self-determination, sought to establish themselves.[22] The simultaneous occurrence and frequent overlap of these two currents of revolution was one of the peculiarities of the years between 1917 and 1923.

Few in 1914 would have anticipated either the length and deadliness of the Great War or the revolutionary upheaval that followed.

Nor could anyone have foreseen that, by 1923, two particularly radical variants of revolutionary ideology, Bolshevism and Fascism, would have emerged triumphant in Russia and Italy respectively. The First World War was, after all, a conflict that many in the West hoped would 'end all wars' and make the world 'safe for democracy'.[23] In the event, the opposite was the case and the issues raised but not solved by the war or the peace treaties of 1919–20 created far more dangerous asymmetries of power than had existed prior to 1914. Before the Great War, the established European order was a great deal more stable than is often assumed. Not all was well within the land empires that dominated continental Europe and the Middle East (as violent incidents such as the Hamidian massacres of 1894–6 or the suppression of the 1905 revolution in Russia exemplify), but few could have imagined revolutionary regime changes and a complete dissolution of the continental land empires when hostilities broke out in August 1914. Although the decline and fall of Europe's continental land empires has often been portrayed as a historical inevitability from the vantage point of 1918, the ruling dynasties of the pre-war world had seemed firmly entrenched and, for the most part, in total control of the vast swathes of territory that belonged to their empires.[24]

The main exception to the general picture of a largely peaceful and economically vibrant Europe before 1914 can be found in the Balkans and the Ottoman Empire. In south-eastern Europe and the Mediterranean, war began not in 1914 but in 1911, when Italy annexed the formerly Ottoman province of Tripolitania (Libya). The following year a coalition of Balkan States expelled the Ottomans from all of Constantinople's European domains, except for a small toehold in eastern Thrace, triggering a wave of extreme violence against Muslim civilians in the region, including mass murder, forced conversions and expulsions.[25]

In western or central Europe, however, no similar escalation of violence occurred, even if the Balkan Wars anticipated forms of violence that would become widespread across the continent over the following decades. Here, it was the outbreak of war in August 1914 – the 'great seminal catastrophe' of the twentieth century, in George Kennan's words – that abruptly ended an unusually long period of peace in European history.[26]

As Kennan and many other historians have argued, it was the Great War that marked the beginning of the 'Age of Extremes' (Eric Hobsbawm's term) and of decades of violent upheavals. The escalation after 1939 of an even more devastating conflict than the First World War raised the question of whether the aggressive dictatorships of Stalin, Hitler, or Mussolini could be traced back to the events of 1914–18. Many were convinced that the Great War had unleashed furies that could not be contained by the Paris peace treaties of 1919–20. This 'brutalization thesis', famously developed for the German case in George Mosse's *Fallen Soldiers* (and extended to all of Europe since), essentially suggested that the trench experience of the First World War generated a brutalization both of war and society by establishing new and unprecedented levels of acceptable violence. These prepared the way for, and were only surpassed by, the horrors of the Second World War, during which the death toll for civilians exceeded that of combatants.[27]

More recently, however, historians have cast doubt on the explanatory value of the 'brutalization thesis', notably because the war experience itself does not account for why politics and society were brutalized in some of the former combatant states but not in others. After all, there was no fundamental difference in the war experiences of Allied soldiers and those of the Central Powers – except for the outcomes of the war. Other critics have pointed out that the vast majority of veterans who had fought for the Central Powers and who survived the Great War returned to peaceful civilian lives in late 1918. Not everyone who fought in the Great War became a proto-fascist or Bolshevik or longed to continue fighting beyond the official end of hostilities in November 1918.[28]

While it is obvious that none of the post-war violence can be explained without reference to the Great War, it might be more appropriate to view that conflict as the unintentional enabler of the social or national revolutions that were to shape Europe's political, social and cultural agenda for decades to come. Notably in its final stages, from 1917 onwards, the Great War changed in nature, as the Bolshevik revolution of 1917 led to Russia's withdrawal from the war while the Western Allies, strengthened by America's entry into the conflict, increasingly endorsed the dismantling of the European land empires as a war aim. Events in Russia in particular had a dual effect: Petro-grad's admission of defeat heightened expectations of imminent victory among the Central Powers (only months before their ultimate defeat led to the search for the 'internal enemies' who had allegedly caused that collapse), while simultaneously injecting powerful new energies into a war-torn continent ripe for revolution after four years of fighting.

It was in this period that a particularly deadly but ultimately con-ventional conflict between states – the First World War – gave way to an interconnected series of conflicts whose logic and purpose was much more dangerous. Unlike World War I, which was fought with the purpose of forcing the enemy to accept certain conditions of peace (however severe), the violence after 1917–18 was infinitely more ungovernable. These were *existential* conflicts fought to anni-hilate the enemy, be they ethnic or class enemies – a genocidal logic that would subsequently become dominant in much of Europe between 1939 and 1945.

What was also noteworthy about the conflicts that erupted after 1917–18 was that they occurred after a century in which European states had more or less successfully managed to assert their monopoly on legitimate violence, in which national armies had become the norm, and in which the fundamentally important distinction between combatants and non-combatants had been codified (even if frequently breached in practice). The post-war conflicts reversed that trend. In the absence of functioning states in the former imperial lands of Europe, militias of various political persuasions assumed the role of the national army for themselves, while the lines between friends and foes, combatants and civilians, became terrifyingly unclear.[29]

In contrast to Mosse's encompassing but misleading 'brutalization thesis', this book makes a number of different arguments about Europe's transition from war to peace. It proposes that in order to understand the violent trajectories that Europe – including Russia and the former Ottoman lands in the Middle East – followed throughout the twentieth century, we must look not so much at war experiences between 1914 and 1917 as at the way in which the war ended for the vanquished states of the Great War: in defeat, imperial collapse and revolutionary turmoil.

While one of these factors – revolution – has been well investigated for individual countries, notably for Russia and Germany, the literature on this topic remains remarkably nation-centric, as if the revolutionary events that shook Europe between 1917 and the early 1920s were completely unconnected.[30] Interwar Germany's 'culture of defeat' has also been the subject of historical investigation, but there is no study in any language that investigates the experiences of all the vanquished states of Europe within the confines of one book.[31] This seems odd because one obvious explanation for the escalation of post-war violence clearly lies in the mobilizing power of defeat in 1918 (or, in the case of Italy, the perception of a 'mutilated victory').[32] In the victorious states of Europe (except Italy and, again, the Irish part of the United Kingdom), there was no substantial increase in political violence post-1918, partly because military victory in the Great War vindicated the sacrifices of the war years and strengthened the legitimacy of the states that emerged triumphant.[33] The same cannot be said about the vanquished. None of the defeated states of the Great War managed to return to anything like pre-war levels of domestic stability and internal peace.

Another major factor for the upsurge in violence after 1918 was the abrupt break-up of Europe's land empires and the difficult birth of their successor states. The Paris peace treaties assigned millions of people – notably ethnic Germans in Czechoslovakia, Italy and Poland, Magyars in Czechoslovakia, Yugoslavia and Romania, and Bulgarians in Romania and Greece – to newly created states that faced a fundamental dilemma: although seeking to be *national* states, Poland, Yugoslavia and Czechoslovakia in particular were multi-national empires in miniature. The main difference between them and their Habsburg predecessor was not the ethnic purity to which they aspired, but merely their size and reversed ethnic hierarchies.[34]

It was no coincidence that the centre of gravity for attempts at territorial revisionism in Europe over the following decades was located in the lands of the old multi-national empires whose break-up created new 'frontiers of violence'.[35] Territorial gains of 'historic' lands and the recovery of populations lost in 1918 played a crucial role in foreign and domestic policies in east-central Europe until the end of the Second World War, and sometimes even beyond 1945, particularly for

Hungary, Bulgaria and Germany. It was also important for the Soviet Union, which found itself shorn of not just its conquests from the Great War but also of Imperial Russia's western borderlands. Moscow's attempts to reimpose itself on 'lost' land, and to cement its influence over east-central Europe more generally, would continue, under unimaginably violent circumstances, until the 1940s and beyond.

Revolutions, the defeat of the Central Powers, and the territorial reorganization of a continent previously dominated by empires, created ideal conditions for new and lasting conflicts – though any explanation for their escalation has to be mindful of the importance of local traditions and conditions, often deriving from much older conflicts, which shaped the violence that emerged after the war. The *chetnik* tradition of guerrilla warfare in the Balkans, for example, Irish Republican activism before 1914, and the pre-war revolutionary tensions in Russia are cases in point.[36] Yet, taken together, the overarching factors mentioned above – revolution, defeat and national 'rebirth' in the imperial wreckage of Europe – were crucial in triggering a transnational wave of armed conflict that in some parts of Europe continued until 1923. A temporary end point came then with the Treaty of Lausanne in July of that year. This defined the territory of the new Turkish Republic and ended Greek territorial ambitions in Asia Minor through a vast forced exchange of populations.

Even if Europe experienced a short-lived period of stabilization between 1924 and 1929, the core issues raised but not solved between 1917 and 1923 would return, with new urgency, to the international and domestic political agenda after the onset of the Great Depression in 1929. As such, the story of Europe in the years between 1917 and 1923 is crucial for understanding the cycles of violence that characterized the continent's twentieth century. And the starting point of that story has to be the cataclysmic events that played out in Russia in early 1917, when the most populous of all combatant states in the Great War became the first to descend into the chaos of revolution and military defeat.

I

Defeat

The peace with Russia ... and the great victory of these days against the English are like two powerfully ringing hammer blows to all German hearts ... Those who timidly doubted the German victory and those who never believed in it now see it as an attainable possibility before them and must bow down to the idea of victory.

Alfred Hugenberg to Paul von Hindenburg, 26 March 1918

A victorious outcome of the war would never have occasioned a revolution, and even a timely peace accord would have prevented it.

Today we are all children of defeat.

Heinrich Mann, 'The Meaning and Idea of the Revolution',
Münchner Neueste Nachrichten, 1 December 1918

I

A Train Journey in Spring

On Easter Sunday 1917 the 'triumphal march' of Bolshevism began with a train journey. In the late afternoon of 9 April the Russian Bolshevik, Vladimir Ilyich Ulyanov, his wife and fellow activist Nadezhda ('Nadya') Krupskaya, and thirty of his closest associates departed from the main railway station in Zurich on a train bound for Germany.[1]

The authorities in Berlin who had approved the secret journey from neutral Switzerland through German territory, and provided the logistics for the onward journey to Russia, placed great hopes in a man that few people outside the Socialist International had heard of at the time, a man who used the pseudonym 'Lenin' for his journalistic articles in left-radical fringe publications with very small print runs. Equipped with significant funds, Lenin was to take charge of the small Bolshevik movement in his home country, radicalize the February Revolution which had toppled the tsarist regime earlier that year, and end Russia's war with the Central Powers.[2]

Ever since the outbreak of war in late July 1914, the German Foreign Office had developed secret plans to destabilize the Allied home fronts by supporting revolutionary movements of different political complexions: Irish republicans aiming to sever ties with London, jihadists in the British and French empires, and Russian revolutionaries conspiring against the tsar's autocratic regime in Petrograd.[3] Although largely indifferent to the political ambitions of each of these movements, Berlin saw them as strategic partners in an effort to weaken the Allies from within.[4] Much to the regret of the strategists in Germany's capital, however, none of their efforts seemed to deliver the desired results. The roughly 3,000 Muslim prisoners of war who were first interned in 1914 in a special 'Half Moon Camp' in Zossen near the German capital, before being dispatched to the Mesopotamian and

Persian fronts for propaganda purposes, never managed to mobilize large numbers of jihadists. In the spring of 1916, Berlin suffered a further setback when the German-backed Easter Rising failed to ignite a general revolution in Ireland, while Roger Casement, who had spent the first two war years in the Reich trying to set up an 'Irish Brigade' from prisoners of war in German captivity, was arrested shortly after disembarking from a German U-boat off the coast of Kerry in April and executed for treason in August.[5]

After the fall of the tsar in February 1917, Berlin decided to revive its strategy of smuggling revolutionaries back to their home countries. In line with Berlin's strategic ambitions to cause upheaval on the Allied home fronts, the German embassies in neutral countries had started to draw up lists of exiled Russian revolutionaries in 1914. Lenin's name first appeared on one of these lists in 1915. After the abdication of the tsar, the German Foreign Ministry informed its government and the Army High Command (Oberste Heeresleitung, or OHL) that they were aware of a number of radical Marxists in neutral Switzerland whose return to Petrograd would strengthen the anti-war Bolshevik faction of the Russian far Left. The political and military decision-makers in Berlin supported the plan.[6]

When Lenin embarked on his train journey in April 1917 he was forty-six years of age and could look back on several decades of revolutionary activism. Originally from Simbirsk (Ulyanovsk) on the Volga river, Vladimir and his family moved to his mother's family estate near Kazan when his father Ilya, a hereditary nobleman and school director, died of a brain haemorrhage in 1886. Shortly thereafter, Vladimir renounced his belief in God. Family disaster struck again the following year when his older brother, Alexander, was arrested and executed for participating in an assassination plot against Tsar Alexander III. Following his brother's death, Vladimir, too, became increasingly involved in Marxist circles. Expelled from Kazan State University for participating in anti-tsarist demonstrations, he kept up his political interest during his days as a law student in the Russian capital. Following his exams, he involved himself intensively in the revolutionary movement as a lawyer and cultivated contacts with leading Russian social democrats. In February 1897, after returning from a trip to Europe, he was banished to Siberia for three years as a political agitator.[7] It was during this period spent in exile, sometime between 1897 and 1900, that he adopted a widespread revolutionary practice by taking an alias, 'Lenin' – probably after the Siberian river Lena – in an attempt to confuse the tsarist police.[8]

From 1900 onwards, Lenin lived in western Europe, first in Switzerland and then in Munich, where he edited the newspaper *Iskra* (*The Spark*), in which he also published his famous programmatic essay 'What Is to Be Done?' (1902). Although firmly based on Karl Marx's analysis of capitalism, Lenin's ideas for the creation of a Communist society differed in at least one important way. For Marx, the final stage of bourgeois society and the capitalist economic order would naturally result in a spontaneous popular uprising caused by class antagonisms. Lenin by contrast did not want to wait for this spontaneous revolutionary moment. It was predicated on an advanced industrial society as well as an equally well-developed class-consciousness among industrial workers, neither of which existed in Russia. Instead, he planned to seize power violently through a coup d'état, executed by a determined and well-trained avant-garde of professional revolutionaries.[9] Soviets (or workers' councils), of the kind that had sprung up spontaneously in many large cities of the Russian Empire over the course of the Revolution of 1905, were to replace the old power structure and accelerate a top-down development of class-consciousness among the still largely illiterate peasants and workers of Russia.[10]

In light of the revolutionary upheavals in Russia in 1905 and the tsar's subsequent concessions in his October Manifesto, Lenin had returned to Russia, but was forced to flee again in December that year. He was to spend the next twelve years in exile again. During that time he lived in various European cities – Geneva, Paris, London, Cracow and, from 1916 onwards, in Zurich. The largest city in Switzerland was a particularly attractive refuge at the time, one of a handful of places in Europe not engaged in the war, but with good communication links and a tradition of sheltering dissenters. Zurich was not only the birthplace of the avant-garde Dadaist art movement surrounding Hugo Ball and Tristan Tzara at the Cabaret Voltaire, but also became the temporary home of numerous radicals of the European Left who were propagating revolution while frequently disagreeing among themselves about how to achieve that objective.[11]

Such disputes among members of the socialist Left were not new. Ever since the formation of the socialist Second International in July 1889, different factions had argued endlessly about how to realize a proletarian utopia. Divisions between those advocating reforms and those insisting on revolution deepened further at the start of the twentieth century. In the case of Russia's Social Democratic Workers' Party, the irreconcilable positions of the two most important factions – Lenin's radical Bolsheviks and the more moderate Mensheviks, who (in line with Marx's theories) advocated a bourgeois-democratic reorganization of Russia before a proletarian revolution could take place – had led to a complete split of the party in 1903.[12]

The outbreak of war in 1914 had further deepened the rifts within the European labour movement. The majority of social democratic parties in 1914 had approved their countries' war credits, thus placing national loyalty above international class solidarity.[13] Lenin was an uncompromising critic of the reformist Left and a fervent advocate of radical revolution, a position that, in Berlin's estimation, made him an ideal candidate for the task of further destabilizing Russia's domestic situation.[14]

Lenin himself, who lived in modest circumstances and spent most of his days writing in Zurich's public libraries, was surprised when the February Revolution against the Romanov dynasty broke out in Petrograd. The Zurich emigrants depended entirely on newspaper reports to keep abreast of the situation in Russia, and it was not until early March 1917 that Lenin learnt about it. On the urging of a Duma delegation and senior generals, the tsar had abdicated, and his brother Mikhail had also renounced the throne. Even if the exact outcome of the revolution was still entirely open at this point, Lenin spotted his chance. Unlike in 1905, when he had missed his opportunity to influence the course of that revolution, this time he did not want to waste any time. Instead, he wished to return to Russia as quickly as possible in order to become involved on the ground.[15]

Lenin was fully aware that in order to cross war-torn Europe he needed German support. It was unthinkable that the Allies would endorse anything that might take Russia out of the war, but the Germans had long tried to weaken their opponents from within. While he knew he was being used by the Germans, Lenin felt that the end – a potentially successful Bolshevik revolution in Russia – justified the means. In negotiation with German representatives he demanded extraterritorial status for his own train compartment and that of his fellow Russian travellers in April 1917; with a piece of chalk, 'German territory' was separated from 'Russian territory', and Lenin successfully insisted that no further contact should occur between the accompanying German officers and the Russian revolutionaries.[16]

Their train soon crossed into German territory. As they sped north and drove through German train stations and cities, the travellers from neutral Switzerland saw emaciated soldiers and exhausted civilians for the first time, raising Lenin's hopes that the war would soon lead to revolution in Germany as well. On the German Baltic Sea island of Rügen, Lenin and his entourage were put on a ship heading for Copenhagen, before continuing their journey to Stockholm and boarding another train bound for Petrograd. Contrary to Lenin's concerns, he and his party had no difficulty crossing into Russian territory. On 16 April 1917 – after twelve years in exile – Lenin arrived back in the Russian capital, where he was welcomed by an enthusiastic crowd of Bolshevik supporters, who played the Marseillaise, waved red flags, and offered flowers as the train entered Petrograd's Finland station.[17] Lenin was home.

2

Russian Revolutions

When Lenin arrived back in Petrograd, Russia was a different country from the one he had left in 1905. Arguably the most authoritarian state in Europe at the turn of the century, Imperial Russia was also a country of major contradictions. Although predominantly agrarian with semi-feudal structures even after the emancipation of the serfs in 1861, the empire had also experienced exceptional rates of industrial growth, albeit from a low base. Notably in sectors such as oil and steel, the economic latecomer was 'leapfrogging' into modernity, with growth rates higher than those of the United States, Germany and Great Britain at the turn of the century.[1]

To be sure, not all was well within the giant empire that stretched from eastern Poland in the West to the coast of Siberia in the East. Large parts of Russia's society did not benefit from rapid economic growth. The empire's social composition 'resembled a pyramid with a large base', comprised mainly of peasants and a growing industrial proletariat in the cities, 'extending gradually to a narrow tip'.[2] At the top stood the emperor, Nicholas II, who followed his father, Alexander III, in reviving the old Muscovite tradition of the tsar as 'merciful father' of his people. The social elite was mainly aristocratic, but the Russian nobility – some 1.9 million people on the eve of the Great War – did not resemble a homogeneous social class with a unified political outlook.[3]

What many landowning aristocrats shared in the decades preceding the outbreak of war in 1914 was a sense of crisis, a belief that the forces of economic modernization would profoundly transform the traditional aristocratic lifestyle. This sense of crisis was not only powerfully captured in Anton Chekhov's famous play *The Cherry Orchard* (1904), in which the tragic protagonist, Lyubov Andreyevna

Ranevskaya, loses the family estate after refusing to turn her orchard into vacation lots.[4] The pre-war world of aristocratic anxiety about the future and perceived decay was also powerfully described by Ivan Bunin, the first Russian writer to win the Nobel Prize for literature (1933). A descendant of an old and once wealthy aristocratic family, whose alcoholic father had gambled away much of the family fortunes, Bunin offered a darkly prophetic vision in his 1912 novella *Sukhodol (Dry Valley)*. The story revolves around the Khrushchevs, a once wealthy noble family whose fortunes decline to the point that, by the end of the story, all traces of the family have disappeared.[5]

Despite the perceived decline of the landed aristocracy, they still fared a lot better than the vastly greater number of Russian peasants who found themselves at the bottom of the social hierarchy. Although serfdom had been abolished, its legacies lingered on. Poverty forced many peasants to look for employment in the cities where new factories required more and more industrial workers. Working conditions in the factories were harsh, and the low pay, coupled with high inflation, meant that many working-class families lived in appalling circumstances.[6] Crammed into tenements rife with crime, prostitution and inadequate sanitary provisions, workers and their families were also highly susceptible to disease such as typhus, cholera and tuberculosis.[7]

By the beginning of the twentieth century, the inability of the state to address social inequality and the tsar's unwillingness to meet popular demands for political reforms had led to a significant escalation of everyday violence. This culminated in the revolution of 1905 when the humiliation of losing a war against Japan in the Far East coalesced with a multitude of internal conflicts ranging from labour unrest to political militancy and ethnic conflict in the western borderlands and the Caucasus.[8] After the tsar's concessions – including the establishment of a Parliament, the State Duma, and the passing of a constitution – the domestic situation in Imperial Russia stabilized somewhat, but revolutionary violence continued unabated, despite the sustained efforts of the tsarist police to re-establish control.[9] Between January 1908 and May 1910 alone, more than 700 government officials and 3,000 ordinary citizens were killed, and a further 4,000 wounded.[10] Two years later, in the spring of 1912, a massive strike in the Lena goldfields of south-eastern Siberia was met with brutal force by government troops, leaving some 500 people dead or wounded, thereby further escalating solidarity strikes across the empire.[11]

Yet without the Great War it is unlikely that social and political unrest or violent acts against state authority would have caused the complete collapse of the tsarist regime.[12] If anything, the Romanov regime on the eve of the Great War seemed more stable than it had been in previous years.[13] In 1913, Tsar Nicholas and his regime ordered public celebrations of the tercentenary of the Romanov dynasty's rule over Russia in order to mark his family's contribution to transforming the once modest eastern European principality of Muscovy into one of the Great Powers of Europe, an empire that covered one sixth of the dry land on earth.[14]

The war that broke out in 1914 was supposed to cement Russia's place among the Great Powers, and a wave of patriotism – similar to that in other combatant nations – momentarily covered up the deep social and political tensions within the empire. Yet nowhere else did the initial euphoria sparked by the outbreak of war disappear as quickly as in Russia. After an initially successful offensive into eastern Prussia and the defeat of Ottoman troops attacking through the Caucasus, the fortunes of war turned against the Russians. The defeats that the tsar's armies suffered at the hands of the Germans in 1914 and 1915 led to the 'Great Retreat' of Russian troops through the empire's western borderlands and prompted domestic unrest and strikes within the textile and metal industries, while there were also major conscription revolts in central Asia in 1916.[15] The decision of Tsar Nicholas to assume for himself the role of Supreme Commander of the Russian armies did not improve the domestic situation. His frequent absences from the capital created the popular perception that political power now rested with his unpopular wife, the German-born tsarina Alexandra Feodorovna and her inner circle, including notably the Siberian monk, Grigori Rasputin. Enraged by Rasputin's growing influence on the tsarina, two Russian aristocrats and a right-wing member of the Duma eventually decided to act: on 30 December 1916 they brutally assassinated the monk. Even among the elites of the empire, so the violent act clearly showed, distrust of the tsarist regime was rapidly increasing.[16]

Meanwhile the military situation continued to deteriorate. Although the Brusilov Offensive of June–September 1916 had inflicted major casualties on the ill-prepared Austro-Hungarian forces in Galicia, effectively forcing the Germans to transfer large numbers of soldiers from Verdun in order to stabilize the Eastern Front, the offensive proved extremely costly for Russia as well: nearly one million Russian soldiers were killed or wounded during the campaign, so that by early 1917 Russian casualties stood at around 2.7 million. In addition, by this point between four and five million Russian soldiers had been captured by the enemy.[17]

The continuous deterioration of the military situation led to an explosive mood in the barracks, where some 2.3 million new recruits, frequently coerced into military service under enormous pressure, encountered the disillusioned and increasingly politicized veterans of previous battles. The garrisons, notably around Petrograd (the patriotically de-Germanized name of St Petersburg since September 1914), would become particular focal points for revolutionary activity over the following months.[18]

Although the lack of military success led to widespread war-weariness in Russia that aggravated an already tense domestic situation, the main causes of the revolution in 1917 were economic. Despite its reputation as a major grain exporter, Russia had the lowest agricultural productivity in all of Europe on the eve of the Great War. The beginning of the war further increased the threat of famine by depriving the country of its agricultural workers and farm animals. Eighteen million Russian men, most of them peasants, were mobilized during the conflict; two million horses were requisitioned. The longer the conflict lasted, the more the food-supply situation deteriorated, and from 1916 onwards the population of Russia's largest cities lived under the permanent threat of malnutrition and outright starvation.[19] In late 1916 a report from the tsarist secret police, the *Okhrana*, warned that the Russian home front was about to collapse. Severe food shortages made the threat of revolution feasible, so the report concluded, and an imminent hunger revolt was likely to be accompanied by 'the most savage excesses'.[20]

The food crisis heightened the social tensions and influenced the revolutionary events that eventually brought down the tsarist regime in the spring of 1917. The immediate spark was provided by protests in the Russian capital over bread shortages. Petrograd, the fifth largest city in Europe, was an ideal breeding ground for revolutionary activity. Seventy per cent of the cities' workers were employed in large factories. The pay was poor, as were the living conditions for workers and their families. Roughly half of the available accommodation had no water supply or sewage system. The contrast between the working-class factory district of Vyborg and the affluent Nevsky Prospect area across the Neva river could not have been greater. To make matters worse, food had become increasingly scarce and expensive as the war dragged on.[21]

On the morning of Thursday, 8 March 1917 (23 February, according to the old Julian calendar that remained in place until the Bolsheviks changed to the Western, Gregorian calendar in February 1918), more than 7,000 female workers from the textile plants in the Vyborg district downed tools to protest against inadequate food provisions. The food shortages and ever-rising prices in early 1917 had devastated the city's workers and left them hungry and desperate. The first two months of the year had seen a surge of strikes and protests in the capital and cities across the empire in response to the mounting crisis. As they marched through the streets on 8 March, women were joined by other workers flooding out of nearby factories. By noon more than 50,000 protesters were marching, and before the day was over between 80,000 and 120,000 people had taken to the streets.[22]

At first the authorities in Petrograd saw no cause for alarm and even failed to report the demonstrations to the tsar at his military headquarters in Mogilev, 800 kilometres to the south. The next morning, however, the number of protesters marching through Petrograd's affluent inner-city neighbourhoods had doubled compared to the previous day. And they continued to grow. On Saturday, 10 March, some 300,000 workers took to the streets.[23] Worse still for the authorities, the demonstrations that had begun with complaints about food shortages quickly took a political turn with demands for democracy, an end to the war, and criticism of the incompetence of the tsarist regime and of Nicholas II himself.[24]

That evening the tsar was finally informed of the disorder in his capital. Deeply unsympathetic to his people's calls for bread and peace, he ordered the commander of the Petrograd military district, General Sergei Khabalov, to end the demonstrations immediately, with force if necessary. After all, Petrograd was a vast military garrison with over 300,000 soldiers in the city and its immediate environs.[25] When, on the morning of Sunday, 11 March, troops loyal to the tsar followed their orders and opened fire on crowds of protesters, dozens of marchers were shot and killed. This proved to be a fatal mistake. Over the course of the day more and more soldiers from other units refused to shoot unarmed protesters and abandoned their loyalty to the regime.[26]

The following day the situation escalated further as rebellious soldiers and workers marched to the city's prisons and released the inmates before raiding police stations, the Ministry of the Interior, and the headquarters of the *Okhrana*. When General Khabalov informed Tsar Nicholas that the situation in the capital could no longer be controlled, the tsar briefly considered dispatching loyal troops to Petrograd.[27] But it was too late. In Petrograd the tsar's ministers resigned and fled, while in Mogilev, Nicholas was eventually persuaded to abdicate in favour of his brother, Grand Duke Mikhail Alexandrovich, who immediately rejected the poisoned chalice out of fear for his own safety.[28]

With Nicholas's abdication, the Romanov dynasty and the thousand-year-old rule of monarchy in Russia thus came to an end. The effects of this regime change were keenly felt in Russia and beyond. The February Revolution introduced a major new dynamic in war-torn Europe, which would, in country after country, raise profound questions about the future nature of political legitimacy. While it was yet unclear which direction the revolution would take, the events of February 1917 marked the first successful overthrow of a major authoritarian regime in Europe since 1789.

As the old order collapsed amid joyous celebrations of crowds in Petrograd, Moscow and other cities across the empire, members of the Duma formed what became known as the Provisional Government with the liberal Prince Georgy Yevgenyevich Lvov as Prime Minister. Other important members of the new executive included the Duma chairman, Mikhail Rodzianko, the historian Pavel Miliukov as leader of the Constitutional Democrats ('Cadets'), and the socialist lawyer Alexander Kerensky as deputy chairman.[29]

As the Provisional Government commenced its work, a rival political power emerged in the form of local Soviets, which – following the model of the 1905 revolution – were created to represent and fight for the interests of people in the streets.[30] While the Provisional Government was dominated by liberal and centre-right politicians striving for democratic reform, the Petrograd Soviet in particular was in the hands of the far Left, namely the Mensheviks, Bolsheviks and Socialist Revolutionaries (SRs). The creation of the Soviets marked a period known as *dvoevlastie*, or 'dual power', until democratic elections to a constituent assembly would determine the country's political future. For the time being, the Provisional Government and the Petrograd Soviet recognized each other's different roles as government and grassroots pressure groups, even if they held fundamentally different views on the future direction of the revolution.[31] To gain the conditional support of the Soviets, the Provisional Government had to agree to eight conditions. They included amnesty for all political prisoners; freedom of speech, press and assembly; and the abolition of all restrictions based on class, religion and nationality. It was within this context that Lenin famously called post-revolutionary Russia 'the freest country in the world'.[32]

The Provisional Government also agreed to abolish the *Okhrana* and the Corps of Gendarmes. This, together with the dissolution of the tsarist provincial bureaucracy, was to have severe consequences. Without new institutions to take their place, the Provisional Government was unable to police or govern the country effectively at the very moment when it was descending into greater disorder.[33]

Yet Russia's problem after the February Revolution did not simply stem from the absence of a state monopoly on violence or the coexistence of two rival power centres. The fate of Russia's democratic February Revolution was also inextricably bound up with the country's involvement in the First World War. The Provisional Government's assurances to Russia's allies that Petrograd would honour its commitments inevitably meant a continuation of the dreaded war. The revolution had aroused expectations of imminent peace and land reform, promises that could not now be fulfilled. The disappointment this caused among significant parts of Russian society damaged the credibility and authority of the new political actors. The Provisional Government's commitment to continuing the war alienated the soldiers from the new regime; the rural population would not forgive it for postponing the promised land reforms until after the end of the war.[34]

When he returned to Russia in early April, Lenin thus benefited both from the regime change that already taken place and from the fact that the Provisional Government was unable to fulfil the high hopes and expectations for change. While the Provisional Government, partly due to Allied pressure, decided to continue Russia's war effort, Lenin took the opportunity to push the discourse into a more radical direction, proclaiming in the very first of his famous 'April Theses' that the Great War was an 'unconditionally predatory imperialist war' that needed to be ended.[35]

Meanwhile in the summer of 1917, Kerensky, the Provisional Government's recently appointed Minister of War, hoped to channel the energy of the revolution into the armed forces and ordered a new offensive. Starting on 1 July 1917, Russian troops attacked the Austro-Hungarian and German forces in Galicia, pushing towards Lemberg. The dual objectives of capturing the city and knocking Austria-Hungary out of the war were similar to those of the Brusilov Offensive of the previous year. Initial Russian successes in July 1917 were the result of powerful artillery bombardment, followed by infantry attacks, during which large numbers of shock troops were deployed. However, stubborn resistance, notably by German forces, prevented a decisive breakthrough and led to heavy casualties among the attacking Russians.[36]

The soaring casualty rates undermined whatever was left of the troops' combat morale. Infantry soldiers of the Seventh and Eleventh Armies refused to move forward after the first enemy defence lines had been broken. Soldiers' committees were formed to discuss what to do next. Even when a division did not flatly refuse to fight, no orders were obeyed without preliminary discussion by the divisional committee. During the first two weeks of July the offensive came to a grinding halt, amid bad weather and food-supply shortages.[37]

The Russian advance collapsed altogether in mid-July when the Germans and Austro-Hungarians counter-attacked. Meeting with little resistance from the Russian forces, their armies quickly advanced through Galicia, Ukraine and the Baltics. Within days the Russians had retreated about 240 kilometres. In August, Riga, the empire's second-largest port city, surrendered to German forces.[38] As the Central Powers advanced, the Russian Imperial Army disintegrated. Units disappeared, fought each other, ransacked towns, burned manor houses, or dispersed towards their homes. By the end of 1917 the number of deserters amounted to as many as 370,000.[39]

Even more problematic for the Provisional Government than the deserters were the over one million soldiers stationed in the hinterland and the garrisons. Since the spring these troops had increasingly refused to be sent to the front. Garrisons in large cities now became a political factor in themselves. As a rule, they sided with the Soviets and increasingly with the Bolsheviks or Social Revolutionaries, while refusing to support the local representatives of the government. The tone was set by the Petrograd garrison, which saw itself as the guardian of the revolution and could only be convinced with great difficulty to send elements to the front.[40]

Military failure not only led to the crumbling of the Russian Army itself but also prompted internal attempts to topple the Provisional Government. In mid-July members of the Bolshevik Red Guards, soldiers of the Petrograd garrison and sailors from the island naval base of Kronstadt attempted a coup in the capital. Fighting between Bolshevik supporters and troops loyal to the Provisional Government left some 400 people dead by the time government forces had stormed Tauride Palace, the meeting place of the Petrograd Soviet. Although the coup was crushed, forcing Lenin and his close associate, Grigory Zinoviev, into a temporary exile in Finland, the Bolsheviks were able to stage a second and successful coup only a few months later.[41]

This time the circumstances were more favourable. Kerensky, who became Prime Minister after the failed Bolshevik putsch in July, lost all remaining support from the military when his summer offensive ended in unmitigated disaster. Six days after German troops had conquered Riga, the army's commander-in-chief, General Lavr Kornilov, attempted a putsch against the Provisional Government. The coup quickly collapsed in the face of armed opposition from the Petrograd and Moscow Soviets and passive resistance from railway and telegraph workers. Kornilov and several other generals were arrested.[42]

The prime beneficiaries of the Kornilov Affair were the Bolsheviks. Kerensky had enlisted their help in 'saving' the revolution from Kornilov. Instead of keeping them locked away, he released their leaders from prison (although Lenin himself remained in Finland) and provided them with arms and ammunition to fend off the alleged counter-revolutionary threat. The Bolsheviks unexpectedly found their fortunes revived, while Kerensky lost all remaining support of the conservatives and liberals, the military leadership and even much of the moderate Left.[43]

The Bolsheviks also benefited from the return of a particularly talented organizer, Leon Trotsky, from exile in America. Born as Lev Davidovich Bronstein in Yanovka, the son of a modestly wealthy Jewish peasant, Trotsky, like Lenin, had spent several years in exile, first in Siberia – where he took his pseudonym from one of his jailers, whose passport he stole to escape in 1902 – then outside Russia. A former left-wing Menshevik, Trotsky had spent his years in New York editing an émigré paper with another prominent Communist, the future General Secretary of Comintern's executive committee, Nikolai Bukharin. As Trotsky gradually moved towards Bolshevism, Lenin had come to value his intellectual abilities and organizational talent, which were coupled with ruthless ambition and a willingness to use excessive force to crush enemies of the doctrine. Trotsky's theory of 'permanent revolution', which he had developed since 1905, underpinned Lenin's belief that revolution could occur in a relatively backward country like Russia, before being 'exported' elsewhere. As soon as he returned to Petrograd from exile, Trotsky became the key figure in building up a Bolshevik paramilitary organization: the Red Guards. Trotsky and his Red Guards were to play a decisive role in the Petrograd coup a few months later.[44]

Lenin himself was still in Finland at this time, penning his programmatic essay *The State and Revolution* (1917), in which he attacked the compromising attitudes of Social Democrats and Mensheviks at home. Calling for a more complete destruction of the state by a revolutionary 'vanguard', he invoked Marx's call for the establishment of a dictatorship of the proletariat that would ultimately lead to a classless society.[45]

Back in Petrograd, Kerensky failed to calm the mood within the country, even when, in late August 1917, long-promised (but repeatedly postponed) elections to the Constituent Assembly were announced for 25 November. As summer gave way to autumn, Russia found itself in an increasingly volatile situation in which the central government could no longer claim a 'monopoly on violence' across the country's enormous territory while simultaneously being confronted by demands for autonomy from territories on the western periphery of the former empire as well as from Central Asia.[46] Unwilling to wait for the promised Constituent Assembly to address the land question, peasants in the countryside began taking matters into their own hands and seizing the estates.[47] The greatest explosion of peasant violence was in the traditionally volatile region of the Volga river, especially in the provinces of Saratov, Samara, Penza and Simbirsk.[48]

Compared to these incidents of peasant violence, the Bolshevik seizure of power that eventually took place on 25–26 October (7–8 November in the Gregorian calendar) was largely bloodless. Nor did it involve large revolutionary crowds, as suggested in Sergei Eisenstein's famous film *October* (1928). Instead the Bolsheviks toppled the Provisional Government in a small-scale coup during which Lenin's supporters took control of the Petrograd garrison and occupied some of the capital's most strategically important points. These included the electric power station, the main post office, the State Bank and the central telegraph exchange, as well as key bridges and railway stations. The October Revolution was a model of revolution that would soon become worryingly familiar in numerous other locations across the rest of vanquished Europe. Supported by sailors from the cruiser *Aurora*, who provided covering cannon fire, pro-Bolshevik troops occupied the Winter Palace, the seat of the now completely isolated Provisional Government. Kerensky, who had disguised himself as a sailor, managed to flee to the American Embassy before leaving the country altogether.[49]

The following morning Lenin issued his famous proclamation 'To the Citizens of Russia':

> The Provisional Government has been deposed. Government has passed into the hands of the organ of the Petrograd Soviet . . . The task for which the people have been struggling has been assured – the immediate offer of a democratic peace, the abolition of the landed property of the landlords, worker control over production, and the

creation of a Soviet Government. Long live the Revolution of Workers, Soldiers and Peasants![50]

Compared with the violent excesses of the ensuing civil war, this was an almost peaceful revolution. The storming of the Winter Palace had left six people dead – the only fatalities of the October Revolution in the Russian capital. The situation in Moscow was different, as officer cadets resisted the Bolsheviks for an entire week, but compared to other revolutions the initial seizure of power by the Bolsheviks was remarkably non-violent.[51] Nevertheless, Lenin was fully aware that the Bolsheviks' grasp on power was tenuous. He had to consolidate his regime throughout the former empire, which, considering the vast lands and populations involved, was no easy task. At this point the core membership of the Bolshevik Party itself was probably no more than 15,000 people, though the number of supporters was growing exponentially. Lenin bought his party time by allowing the promised general elections for the Constituent Assembly to take place in November 1917. Yet, when the more moderate Socialist Revolutionary Party emerged as the big winners with 41 per cent of the vote (as opposed to the Bolsheviks' 23.5 per cent), he lost no time in dissolving the assembly in Petrograd after only one day.[52]

Lenin sought to sweeten the demise of Russia's short-lived democracy by reiterating some of his most popular promises: immediate peace, total democracy in the army, the right of self-determination for all peoples and nationalities, workers' control of the factories, and the transfer of all lands held by the nobility, the bourgeoisie, the Church and the government into the hands of 'the people'. Lenin's manifesto was adopted by the Second Congress of Soviets in Petrograd shortly after the Socialist Revolutionaries and the Mensheviks, disastrously, walked out in protest against the Bolshevik coup.[53]

Lenin's regime quickly enacted legislation to implement these promises, notably with respect to land and property reform. The Decree on Land, adopted by the Congress on 8 November 1917, laid the 'legal' foundation for a massive redistribution of wealth and the abolition of private ownership of land. The dispossessed were not to be compensated for their losses. The only exception would be land worked by peasants, which they would be allowed to keep.[54] The Decree on Land was issued largely in response to growing peasant activism in the countryside, where privately owned land was increasingly seized and handed to poorer peasants as a result of local initiatives. The Decree thus simply sanctioned what was already taking place. By February 1918 some 75 per cent of all estates in Russia had been confiscated.[55] The victims were not just aristocratic landlords, but also 'wealthy' peasants whose property was redistributed.[56] The Bolsheviks also nationalized land owned by the Orthodox Church, including more than 1,000 monasteries. Furthermore, between the middle of November 1917 and early March 1918, Lenin issued some thirty decrees on the nationalization of private industry, banks and manufacturing companies.[57]

Lenin's second and equally popular promise was to withdraw from the war. Coldly pragmatic as always, he knew that Russia's military defeat had become unavoidable at this stage, but he also detected a great opportunity in that defeat: not only had Russia's military misfortunes allowed the Bolsheviks to gain power in the first place, but a complete withdrawal from the conflict was now the only viable option to save the Bolshevik revolution. By taking Russia out of the war, he could concentrate on dealing with his many internal enemies. Simultaneously, he expected that war-weariness and material deprivation in central and western Europe would soon lead to revolution in other combatant nations, paving the way for the pan-European, if not global, triumph of Bolshevism. On 15 December 1917, Lenin's emissaries signed an armistice with the Central Powers.

3

Brest-Litovsk

Only days after the armistice between Russia and the Central Powers had come into force, a peace conference got underway on 22 December 1917 in the fortress city of Brest-Litovsk, then the German military headquarters on the Eastern Front. In an unprecedented move, one designed to spread Bolshevik propaganda and expose German imperialism, the Bolsheviks had successfully insisted that the peace negotiations should be conducted publicly.[1]

The peace conference was also unique in its heterogeneous composition, a clash between the old forces of empire and those of a new revolutionary state. The Central Powers' fourteen delegates (five Germans, four from Austria-Hungary, three Ottomans and two Bulgarians) represented either the splendour and glory of the *ancien régime*, as in the case of the highly strung Austro-Hungarian Foreign Minister, Ottokar Count Czernin, who repeatedly complained about the Bolsheviks' table manners, or the forces of extreme nationalism, such as Talaat Pasha, one of the instigators of the Armenian genocide. The Bolshevik delegation at Brest-Litovsk, first led by Adolph Joffe, then by the newly appointed People's Commissar for Foreign Affairs, Leon Trotsky, made it clear that they represented the exact opposite: Trotsky's delegation, composed to reflect those who had brought the Bolsheviks to power, consisted of twenty-eight members, including casually dressed workers, soldiers, sailors, women and a peasant. The Germans and their allies had never seen anything like it at a formal diplomatic meeting.[2]

The German delegation, headed by the state secretary in the Foreign Ministry, Richard von Kühlmann, sought the quickest possible termination of the war on the Eastern Front, while simultaneously trying to establish an informal empire in east-central Europe, one composed of newly independent nation states on Russia's western periphery whose future could now be controlled by Germany. Both Berlin and Vienna were particularly keen for Ukraine to gain independence in order to ensure grain and ore supplies for the Central Powers' continuing war effort on other fronts.[3] When General Max Hoffmann, Chief of the General Staff on the Eastern Front, revealed Berlin's support for the right to national self-determination of Poland, Lithuania and Courland, Trotsky was outraged by what he rightly saw as ill-disguised German imperialism and threatened to break off the negotiations. The talks resumed ten days later, after the Russian delegation had had an opportunity to consult with the government in Petrograd.[4]

The leading Bolsheviks held different opinions regarding the next steps to take. Lenin assessed the situation pragmatically and favoured a peace agreement at any price in order to stabilize the Bolsheviks' position in Russia and secure the achievements of the revolution. Opposed to Lenin's assessment were those among the Bolshevik leadership who, like Trotsky, were convinced that an outbreak of revolution in other parts of Europe was only a matter of weeks away, so the negotiations with the Central Powers should be drawn out until this happened. When Trotsky returned to Brest-Litovsk after the consultations in Petrograd, he therefore played for time. His impassioned speeches against the Central Powers' plans for annexations, coupled with appeals to the German people's desire for peace, certainly had an impact: on 14 January 1918 the Austrian Social Democrats called for large-scale demonstrations, with strikes quickly spreading to Budapest and Berlin, where more than 500,000 workers downed their tools.[5]

While the massive strikes in January, in Berlin, Vienna and other cities, encouraged Trotsky further to think that the Bolshevik revolution would soon spread westwards, Kühlmann and the other representatives of the Central Powers in Brest-Litovsk were having none of it. Losing patience, they signed a separate treaty with Ukraine on 9 February. Under this so-called 'Bread Peace', Ukraine agreed to supply Germany and Austria-Hungary with a million tons of bread annually in exchange for their recognition of the Ukrainian People's Republic (UNR) that had recently declared its independence from Russia.[6]

Trotsky, on hearing about the separate peace treaty, stormed out of the conference and refused further negotiations. The Central Powers responded by resuming hostilities. As of 18 February, one million German and Austro-Hungarian troops were pushing eastwards. During their rapid advance they made huge conquests, meeting almost no resistance as they conquered Dorpat (Tartu), Reval (Tallinn) and Narva. The rest of Latvia, Livonia, Estonia and Belarus were overrun, as was Ukraine whose capital, Kiev, was occupied on 1 March.[7]

The offensive led to the arrival of new, non-negotiable peace terms in Petrograd. Immediately after the fall of Kiev, on 3 March the Bolsheviks signed the Treaty of Brest-Litovsk after Lenin had threatened to resign as party leader and chairman of the Council of People's Commissars if the government refused to accept peace at any price. The Treaty brought Germany much closer to its initial war aim of becoming the dominant power in Europe than had been the case at any time since 1914. For the Central Powers this was a moment of extraordinary triumph.

Aware that the Bolsheviks possessed no financial resources to pay for reparations, Berlin decided to extract its pound of flesh in the form of territorial annexations, which made those that would be included in the future Treaty of Versailles seem benign by comparison. The Germans demanded that Petrograd allow vast formerly tsarist territories with vital natural resources to achieve 'independence' (an independence that in many cases included the presence of strong German forces), including Finland, Russian Poland, Estonia, Livonia, Courland, Lithuania, Ukraine and Bessarabia. In addition, the Bolsheviks were expected to return the provinces of Ardaham, Kars and Batumi – gained after the Russo-Turkish War of 1877–8 – to the Ottoman Empire. Soviet Russia was thus stripped of nearly all of the western non-Russian territories of the former Romanov Empire: 1.6 million square kilometres of land – twice the size of the German Empire – and a third of its pre-war population. Some 73 per cent of Russia's iron-ore output and a staggering 89 per cent of her coal, together with the major part of her industry, was lost to it.[8] Russia thus became the first vanquished state of the Great War, even though the Bolsheviks never tired of emphasizing that it was the tsarist regime and the Provisional Government that had lost the war.

While opposition to the draconian terms of Brest-Litovsk was strong, even within the Bolshevik movement, Lenin understood that the survival of his regime depended on external peace – a peace that would buy him time to secure the dictatorship of the proletariat from internal enemies. In addition to fulfilling Lenin's domestic promises to end the war, the Treaty of Brest-Litovsk fully exposed Germany's vast imperialist war aims, while the release of Central Power prisoners of war from Russian captivity could only help to speed up the anticipated revolution in central Europe.

Lenin was soon to be proven correct on most of these assumptions. The release of hundreds of thousands of prisoners of war, particularly from the Austro-Hungarian Army, had a deeply radicalizing effect at home.[9] Among those soldiers returning to their homelands there were indeed many who had been influenced by Bolshevik ideology and who were to become future leaders of the Left in central and south-eastern Europe, such as the Austrian socialist Otto Bauer, the Hungarian Béla Kun and the Croatian Sergeant-Major Josip Broz, better known under his future Communist nom de guerre, Tito.[10]

4

The Taste of Victory

Russia's defeat was not the only cause for optimism among the Central Powers' military leadership in late 1917. Although, just before Christmas, the Ottoman Empire had lost the city of Jerusalem to British troops, Lenin's decision to withdraw Russia from the war allowed Constantinople's forces to retake control of all of eastern Anatolia and even encouraged military decision-makers to revive their plans to invade the Caucasus. 'The Russian Revolution,' one Turkish newspaper declared, 'has saved us from an immediate threat. As long as we do not forget the importance of events in Russia for us and follow them attentively, we can now take a deep breath.'[1]

Although the United States had extended its April 1917 declaration of war on Germany to Austria-Hungary that December, no more than 175,000 American troops, many of them inexperienced, had arrived in Europe at this point.[2] Instead, there was good reason to believe that the Central Powers now held the strategic initiative – at least until the Allied lines on the Western Front were replenished with American soldiers. Moreover, Russia's exit from the war had left another Allied power, Romania, isolated and surrounded by strong German, Austro-Hungarian and Bulgarian forces. On 9 December 1917, Bucharest accepted the new realities and signed the draconian armistice of Focsani.[3]

More important, however, were developments on the southern front in the Alpine foothills along the Isonzo river, where Habsburg troops and their mainly Italian adversaries had been engaged in indecisive offensives and counter-offensives throughout 1916 and 1917.[4] Up until then, the war had not gone too well for the Habsburg Empire, which had played a key role in the escalation of the conflict during the July Crisis of 1914. Over the following years Vienna had experienced disastrous setbacks on several fronts. In the war's opening stages Austro-Hungarian forces were humiliatingly repulsed in their attempt to invade a minor power, Serbia, and only managed to defeat Belgrade the following year with substantial German and Bulgarian aid. Furthermore, the Russian Imperial Army succeeded twice in invading Habsburg Galicia, first during the war's opening phase and again during the shattering Brusilov offensive of 1916.[5]

In October 1917, however, in the twelfth battle of the Isonzo, better known as the Battle of Caporetto after the nearby town, the Habsburg army landed a surprise success over its Italian adversaries. Aided by six German divisions, which included a promising young infantry officer called Erwin Rommel, the attackers benefited from misty weather conditions as they launched their offensive, taking the Italians completely by surprise. Initiated by a heavy artillery barrage, the combined force broke through the lines of the Italian Second Army almost immediately, shock troops having advanced a remarkable 25 kilometres by the close of day. Their attack overwhelmed the Italians, who retreated in chaos before eventually establishing a new defensive line north of Venice: 30,000 Italian soldiers were killed or wounded while 265,000 were taken prisoner. Even if the rout of Caporetto, which led to the dismissal of the Italian Chief of Staff, Marshal Luigi Cadorna, and the fall of Prime Minister Paolo Boselli, did not bring about a complete collapse of the Italian Army, in November 1917 it seemed as if the best that Rome could now hope for was the conclusion of an honourable peace treaty without territorial losses.[6]

On 11 November 1917, exactly one year before what proved to be the end of the war on the Western Front, Germany's senior military strategist, Quartermaster General Erich Ludendorff, looked optimistically to a future that could now result in a showdown on the Western Front:

> The situation in Russia and Italy will likely make it possible to strike a blow in the western theatre of war in the New Year. The balance of forces will be approximately equal. Around thirty-five divisions and 1,000 heavy artillery pieces can be made available for an offensive . . . Our overall situation demands that we strike as early as possible, ideally in late February or early March, before the Americans throw powerful forces into the balance.[7]

One of his General Staff officers, Colonel Albrecht von Thaer, shared Ludendorff's optimism, noting in his diary on New Year's Eve 1917:

> Our position was really never so good. The military giant Russia is completely finished and pleads for peace; the same with Romania. Serbia and Montenegro have simply gone. Italy is supported only with difficulty by England and France and we stand in its best province. England and France are still ready for battle but are much exhausted (above all the French) and the English are very much under pressure from the U-boats.[8]

To be sure, the German High Command was well aware that victory had to be attained swiftly.[9] War-weariness and indiscipline were spreading in all combatant nations, including the Central Powers. In late 1917 and early 1918 there were increasing signs of exhaustion and political dissent, culminating in the massive strikes in Vienna, Budapest and Berlin. At the same time, however, the Germans were in the fortuitous position of being able to transfer forty-eight divisions from the east and field them against exhausted Allied soldiers on the Western Front.[10]

This sense of opportunity was not confined to the German military establishment. By the time the Treaty of Brest-Litovsk was signed, Constantinople had already ordered the Ottoman Third Army to begin its offensive to reconquer the whole of eastern Anatolia and take military action against the short-lived Transcaucasian Federation, a state founded by Armenian, Georgian and Azeri separatists who viewed the Bolshevik Revolution of October 1917 as a unique historical opportunity for independence. With Russia defeated, the threat of Ottoman expansion into the Caucasus loomed large, even if the Federation's government in Tbilisi (today in Georgia) was quick to reject Lenin's territorial concessions to Constantinople at Brest-Litovsk. Instead, Tblisi firmly stated its intention to resist militarily any Ottoman advance towards the state's borders.[11]

Despite fierce resistance, Ottoman units advanced into the Federation's territory. By early March 1918 they had reached the gates of Erzurum and then approached the Black Sea port of Trabzon. Although Trabzon was taken by Ottoman troops without much fighting, their conquest of Erzurum was accompanied by gruesome massacres. The killing of some 4,000 local Muslim civilians by Armenian troops retreating from Erzurum led to a wave of indiscriminate revenge killings as Ottoman forces continued their advance through the towns and villages along the former Ottoman border of 1877. In April 1918 they seized the Armenian stronghold of Kars with considerable violence.[12]

Emboldened by these victories, Ottoman generals and the leaders of the ruling nationalist Committee for Union and Progress (CUP) renewed their commitment to imperial expansion in the Caucasus. Instead of moving all available forces to the Mesopotamian front, the Minister of War, Enver Pasha, and the Ottoman High Command clearly felt confident that it was possible to sustain the war effort against the British while simultaneously moving further into the Caucasus. The momentum, or so they believed, was on the side of the Central Powers. 'Now,' one Ottoman minister declared, 'we only travel forward.'[13]

In the capital cities of the Central Powers there was thus sense of misguided optimism and high expectations of a swift and immediate victory as events unfolded during the final year of the war. While the possibility of imminent victory boosted the morale of the troops, the raised hopes also raised the stakes, with the danger of serious disappointment and a subsequent widespread collapse in morale.[14]

Everything now depended on the success or failure of the 1918 Spring Offensive. As Ludendorff was well aware, this was a potentially very costly gamble. The battles of the previous three and a half years had clearly demonstrated that a war fought with industrial firepower gave a decisive advantage to a defensive strategy, whereas an offensive strategy bore the risk of huge losses of manpower. But Field Marshal Paul von Hindenburg and Ludendorff had no serious alternative. Their troops could have remained in their well-fortified positions, probably inflicting enormous losses on newly arrived and inexperienced American recruits, but there was little doubt that the home fronts of all the Central Powers would not tolerate the war for much longer.[15]

The purpose of Ludendorff's Spring Offensive was thus to end the war swiftly by pushing the British Expeditionary Force towards the Channel, where it would be evacuated, before dealing a decisive blow against the French. The main objective of the offensive, codenamed

Operation Michael, was to break through the British lines in the Somme-Arras sector, where the numerical advantage for the German attackers was about 2:1.[16]

The surprise offensive opened in the early morning of 21 March 1918 with a bombardment of unprecedented intensity. For almost five hours German guns fired an uninterrupted artillery barrage of well over a million shells into the British front lines. As the German infantry lieutenant, Ernst Jünger, noted in his diary (subsequently published in 1920 as the international best-seller *Storm of Steel*), the intense shelling caused a 'hurricane' of fire 'so terrible that even the biggest of the battles we had survived seemed like child's play by comparison'. The infantry was then ordered to advance towards enemy lines. 'The great moment had come. A creeping barrage of fire rolled over the trenches. We went on the attack.'[17]

The advancing infantry of thirty-two of the German divisions quickly overran the southern sector of the front. On this first day alone the three attacking German armies took 21,000 men as prisoners, and inflicted more than 17,500 casualties.[18] The Allies were panic-stricken, at least temporarily. On 24 March, Field Marshal Douglas Haig indicated to the French Commander-in-Chief, Philippe Pétain, that the British front line could no longer be held and that he would have to abandon the defence of Amiens. The following day Haig indeed ordered his troops to fall back to the old positions they had held in 1916.[19] Amid a chaotic retreat, plans were made to evacuate the British Expeditionary Force from French ports along the Channel, just as Ludendorff had intended. It was the worst setback suffered by the British in the entire war and forced the Allies on 3 April to overcome their internal rivalries by creating a joint Supreme Command under General Ferdinand Foch.[20]

Germany's early victories seemed to confirm the High Command's hopes and expectations. Everything appeared to be going according to plan. As early as 23 March the Kaiser, Wilhelm II, had been convinced that the 'the battle is won' and that 'the English have been utterly defeated'.[21] The optimistic view that victory was imminent also took hold on the German home front, a critical factor in how Germany later understood its defeat. On 26 March the chairman of the board of the Krupp company, Alfred Hugenberg, sent a congratulatory telegram to

General Hindenburg: 'The peace with Russia ... and the great victory of these days against the English are like two powerfully ringing hammer blows to all German hearts ... Those who timidly doubted the German victory and those who never believed in it now see it as an attainable possibility before them and must bow down to the idea of victory.'[22]

In reality, however, the German advances during Operation Michael – impressive though they were – did not amount to anything decisive. When the operation ended on 5 April, German troops of the Eighteenth Army had advanced well over 50 kilometres into enemy territory – an achievement greater than any seen in the West since 1914. Some 90,000 Allied troops had surrendered and 1,300 artillery pieces had been captured.[23] The strategic gains, however, were marginal. The British were bruised, but not broken. Although the territory gained by the Germans was considerable, it largely consisted of ravaged, worthless wasteland over which they now had to run their grossly overextended supply lines.[24] Worse still, the Germans had lost some 240,000 men during the offensive, with particularly high casualty rates among the irreplaceable elite assault units.[25] The British Army, by contrast, almost immediately replaced most of its losses with new recruits shipped across the Channel – over 100,000 of them had arrived in French ports by the end of April.[26]

It was at this point that Ludendorff, under pressure to deliver success after gambling everything on the Spring Offensive, began to make erratic mistakes. Realizing that Operation Michael had not achieved its main purpose of breaking the British, he decided to try his luck in another sector of the front. When he devised his Spring Offensive in late 1917, he had initially considered a major attack in Flanders, codenamed Operation George, as an alternative to Operation Michael. With Michael's failure, Operation George was back on the table, albeit on a smaller scale that was reflected in the plan's new name: Operation Georgette. Two German armies were ordered to overrun the nine Allied divisions – eight of them British and one Portuguese – that were between the German lines and the strategically important railway junction of Hazebrouck, which controlled vital Allied supply lines. Initially the offensive that began with heavy artillery fire in the early-morning hours of 9 April appeared to be highly successful. German storm troops smashed through the Portuguese defences and had advanced some 10 kilometres by nightfall. The offensive continued over the following days, but ultimately came to a grinding halt, just a few kilometres short of Hazebrouck. Ludendorff's renewed failure was due both to stubborn British resistance and general exhaustion of the German soldiers, many of whom had previously participated in Operation Michael.[27]

With the failure of Operation Georgette, the German offensives became increasingly incoherent and frantic. Abandoning further action against the British, Ludendorff now lashed out against another sector of the front. The Aisne offensive against the French began in late May, preceded by the heaviest German artillery effort of the war with two million shells fired in four and a half hours. It was Germany's final attempt to secure victory and brought the largest advance of the war in the West. After taking Château-Thierry on the Marne, German troops were once again – as in 1914 – within reach of the French capital, where long-range artillery fire killed nearly 900 Parisians.[28]

5

Reversals of Fortune

The military offensives of the German Army in the spring and early summer of 1918 created more problems than they solved. Communication and supply lines were longer than before and it was difficult to bring up reserves to the front. The discovery of Allied food supplies in hastily abandoned enemy trenches – supplies of white bread, corned beef, biscuits and wine – literally gave the deprived German soldiers a taste of their enemies' economic superiority. Moreover, the cost in men was immense, more than at any other time apart from the first two months of the war: a total of 915,000 soldiers had been lost by the end of June 1918. The huge bloodletting caused by Ludendorff's gamble did not pay off. While German losses, often among the best and most experienced fighters, were simply too high to be compensated for with fresh recruits, the Allies were able to increase their armies' strength with 250,000 Americans now arriving in Europe every month.[1]

On top of the military losses, the first wave of the 'Spanish Flu', a particularly aggressive influenza virus, which ultimately killed more than 50 million people worldwide, reached the German lines in the summer. Initially, the virus affected Allied troops less severely than German ones.[2] Normally caused by a virus that affects children and the elderly most of all, this strain of influenza affected all soldiers regardless of age and physical fitness, including the elite assault formations.[3] The German Sixth Army in Alsace alone reported 10,000 new cases per day during the first half of July. In total, over one million German soldiers fell ill between May and July 1918. By contrast, the British Army suffered 50,000 cases of influenza for the months of June and July.[4] Other illnesses – pneumonia, dysentery and even malaria – further undermined the strength of the German Army.[5]

From midsummer, the depleted German troops – weakened by the previous offensives and various illnesses – faced sustained Allied counter-attacks. The French counter-offensive that began the Second Battle of the Marne in July 1918, and the attack launched by the British on 8 August outside Amiens, confirmed that the tide had turned in the Allies' favour. Sixteen German divisions were wiped out during the Allied counter-attack. Although a complete collapse was avoided, German troops were almost universally demoralized and exhausted, increasingly blaming their own leadership for the dire situation in which they found themselves.[6] The Mail Censorship Office of the Sixth Army, for example, reported that during August more and more soldiers had openly turned against 'Prussian militarism' and the 'bloodthirsty Kaiser' himself.[7]

Without reinforcements, overextended and weakened by illness and heavy losses from the offensive, the German troops were in no position to effectively resist Allied forces. Within a short time all German territorial gains during the summer offensive had been lost. One week after the Allies had severely dented the German lines on 8 August (the 'Black Day' of the German Army), Ludendorff told the Kaiser that Germany should seek a negotiated peace – a position he had rejected throughout the war.[8]

Ludendorff at this point was a mere shadow of his former self. His meteoric rise within the German General Staff after 1914 owed much to his central role in expelling the Russians from East Prussia in the Battle of Tannenberg (1914) and the First Battle of the Masurian Lakes (1915), even if Ludendorff's direct superior, Paul von Hindenburg, a formerly retired veteran officer of the Franco-Prussian War of 1870–1, publicly received all of the credit. Hindenburg was smart enough, however, to make the talented Ludendorff his Quartermaster General when he was appointed Chief of the German General Staff in 1916. For the following two years Hindenburg and Ludendorff effectively established a military dictatorship, but it was Ludendorff who essentially ran the entire German war effort. If the defeat of Russia and Romania in 1917 had emboldened his position, the subsequent failure of the offensives in the west in the spring and summer of 1918 fatally undermined his confidence.[9] Although the persistent rumour that Ludendorff suffered a complete nervous breakdown is exaggerated, he was clearly under significant stress.[10]

The situation of the Central Powers did not look much better on other fronts in the late summer and early autumn of 1918. On the Macedonian front, the Allies attacked on 14 September and routed the Bulgarian Army, forcing Bulgaria within a fortnight to seek an armistice. The suddenness of this collapse came as a surprise to many observers. Since Bulgaria's entry into the war in October 1915, its army had fought valiantly and chalked up significant early victories in 1915 (Niš, Ovche Pole, Kosovo, Krivolak) and 1916 (Lerin, Chegan, Bitola, Strumitsa, Cherna, Tutrakan, Dobrich, Kobadin and Bucharest). Before 1918 the Bulgarian Army had not lost any major battles in the war. For example, it repeatedly repelled Allied attacks at Doiran, a small town in Macedonia, where a Bulgarian force built a strong defence line, which withstood systematic assaults by British, French and imperial troops.[11]

Eventually, however, the Entente succeeded in breaking through at another point of the Bulgarian south-western front. During the summer of 1918 the Allies had amassed over thirty-one divisions with 650,000 men on the Macedonian front north of Salonika. The offensive launched by French and Serbian troops on 14 September 1918 completely overwhelmed the Bulgarian defenders. The French and Serbs smashed through enemy lines at Dobro Pole, while British and Greek troops pierced the Bulgarian defences at Lake Doiran. Within a few days most of the Bulgarian Army had collapsed. By 25 September the Bulgarian government decided to ask the Allies for an end to hostilities.[12]

Only four days later Bulgaria, the last country to join the Central Powers, became the first of Germany's allies to exit the war when the Bulgarian delegation signed an armistice at Salonika. In it Bulgaria agreed to the full demobilization of its army (with the exception of a handful of troops to guard the border with Turkey and the railway lines); the occupation of several strategic points by Allied troops; the handover of military equipment to Entente forces; and, most controversially for the government in Sofia, the complete evacuation of all Greek and Serbian territories conquered during the war, including Macedonia, a territory that Bulgaria had laid claim to ever since independence in the late nineteenth century. The armistice also included secret clauses, envisioning the possibility of temporary Allied occupation as a guarantee for Bulgaria's exiting the war. Another serious blow was that, to ensure Sofia's 'good behaviour', a significant number of Bulgarian troops (between 86,000 and 112,000) were to remain interned as prisoners of war for the foreseeable future.[13]

For Bulgaria the war that came to an end in late 1918 had essentially begun six years earlier, in October 1912. Back then, Bulgaria, Serbia, Greece and Montenegro had joined forces in their attack on the Ottoman Empire, driven by the shared desire to end Constantinople's reign in south-eastern Europe once and for all.[14] The Bulgarians, who gained autonomy in 1878 but had effectively lived under Ottoman rule since the fourteenth century, wanted Ottoman Macedonia and Thrace. The First Balkan War, as this conflict soon came to be known, ended in May 1913 with a swift and devastating defeat for the Ottomans, accompanied by a wave of ethnic cleansing in which thousands of Muslim civilians were murdered or expelled.[15] Within weeks, however, the members of the victorious Balkan coalition fell out over the distribution of the spoils and went to war again, in late June. This time, Bulgaria was the loser, whereas Greece, Serbia and Romania further expanded their territory at Sofia's expense while the Ottoman Empire managed to regain eastern Thrace.[16]

Fearful of Ottoman vengeance, large numbers of ethnic Bulgarians sought to escape eastern Thrace in 1913, where Constantinople now implemented a policy of forced expulsions in retaliation for all the massacres directed against Balkan Muslims in 1912 and 1913. According to the report of the Carnegie Commission, charged with the investigation of crimes committed during the Balkan Wars, more than 50,000 people – 20 per cent of the ethnically Bulgarian population in Thrace at the time – were murdered in the process.[17]

The outcome of the Second Balkan War, the first of several 'national catastrophes' suffered by Bulgaria in the twentieth century, temporarily ended Sofia's dream of unifying all 'ethnically Bulgarian' territories. The intensity of feelings of national humiliation and despair in 1913 helps to explain Bulgaria's position at the outbreak of the Great War in August 1914. Although the recovery of the lost territories remained part of the Bulgarian national dream, Sofia initially proclaimed neutrality when hostilities broke out that summer. While King Ferdinand, born in Vienna as a prince of the ducal family of Saxe-Coburg-Gotha, and Prime Minister Vasil Radoslavov, favoured siding with the Central

Powers, many Bulgarians harboured pro-Russian sentiments. Some Bulgarian officers – including eleven generals – actually volunteered for service in the Russian Army.[18]

The political leadership in Bulgaria, however, sensed an opportunity to undo the disastrous provisions of the Treaty of Bucharest of August 1913, but waited until the beginning of October 1915 to see which way the fortunes of war were turning before committing itself to either side. The Bulgarians negotiated with both sides until the summer of 1915. Both the Central Powers and the Entente knew that the price of Bulgaria's participation on either side was the return of at least two of the territories lost in the Second Balkan War – Macedonia and eastern Thrace – giving Sofia control not only of the Aegean coast but also of the railway networks that linked central Europe with southern Europe and the Middle East. The best the Entente could offer was eastern Thrace (then in Ottoman hands), while Serbia was unwilling to surrender one inch of Macedonia. After some calculation, and encouraged by the Allied setbacks in Galicia and Gallipoli, Tsar Ferdinand and his government decided that the Central Powers offered the better deal. In the autumn of 1915, Bulgarian troops aided the Austro-German attack on Serbia under General August von Mackensen, with incursions into Macedonia and Kosovo.[19] This German-led invasion soon overwhelmed the Serbs, who, with the help of their French allies, managed to evacuate some 150,000 of their people across the Albanian mountains to the Adriatic.

In the spring of 1916, presumably in response to the pro-Entente stance of the Greek government, the Germans authorized (and militarily supported) a Bulgarian advance into Greece, leading to the capture of Fort Rupel on the Struma river north-east of Salonika and the occupation of parts of northern Greece.[20] In August 1916, following the Romanian declaration of war against Austria-Hungary, Bulgaria also joined the other Central Powers in an attack on Romania, which had contributed so much to Bulgaria's defeat in the Second Balkan War. Now the time had come to avenge that defeat: in early September, Bulgarian troops advanced into the Dobrudja region, dealing several severe blows to their adversaries, notably in the Battle of Tutrakan – also known as the 'Romanian Verdun'. In attempting to defend the fortress at Tutrakan, over 8,000 Romanian soldiers died in a defeat that severely weakened their country's strategic position.[21]

Despite Bulgaria's military successes, the length of the war began to have a serious effect on it. Mounting losses and dwindling manpower resources to maintain the economy on the home front meant that more and more Bulgarians had become war-weary by 1917, when a food crisis affected the cities and the military. Many Bulgarians were outraged by the fact that during this crisis scarce food and raw materials from Bulgaria continued to be delivered to Germany to sustain Berlin's war effort, leaving a growing number of them seriously malnourished.[22]

In mid-June an alarming report about conditions on the front was sent by Bulgaria's most senior general, Nikola Zhekov, to Tsar Ferdinand, explicitly blaming poor management and organization for the plight of the troops: 'The soldiers struggle for a daily survival . . . Meat is given once a week only. The situation with the clothing is even more awful. The soldiers are poorly dressed and with no shoes. They have to run barefoot on the rocks against the enemy. Instead of army caps they wear kerchiefs made of torn sand-sacks. And the winter is coming . . . The current government created this situation.'[23] Shortly after receiving the report, Tsar Ferdinand replaced Prime Minister Radoslavov with a new government under Alexander Malinov.[24]

Bulgaria's defeat in September 1918 reinforced the impression among the leaders of the Central Powers that the war was lost. Not only did this defeat result in the interruption of the land connection between the Ottoman Empire and the rest of the Central Powers, but it also effectively paved the way for Allied armies to attack Constantinople from the west and Habsburg-occupied Serbia from the east.[25] The Central Powers simply had no additional troops that could deal with the engulfing threat.

Meanwhile, on the Italian front, the tide began to turn against the Central Powers with the so-called Second Battle of Piave, which had begun on 15 June with an ill-advised and poorly prepared Habsburg offensive on an extended 80-kilometre front.[26] The offensive quickly collapsed in the face of stubborn Italian resistance, now coordinated by General Armando Diaz, who had been appointed the Italian supreme commander after Italy's disastrous military defeat at Caporetto the previous year.[27]

Much to the surprise of many observers, the Italian forces had rallied after their rout at Caporetto, not least because of some radical changes in the military and political leadership. The new Prime Minister, Vittorio Emanuele Orlando, an eminent law professor turned politician who had originally advocated Italy's neutrality in 1914, suddenly found himself in a position where changing Italy's military fortunes was the single most important issue of his premiership. Orlando, who was to remain in office as Prime Minister until he resigned in June 1919 in protest over the lack of progress at the Paris Peace Conference, was the right man for the challenge. He embarked on an ambitious remobilization campaign under the slogan 'unione sacra' (deliberately echoing the French 'sacred union'), while also improving welfare provisions for agricultural workers and veterans in an attempt to boost morale. Orlando's efforts paid off. Italian politics had been galvanized by the near collapse of the army in 1917, and new energies were channelled into the war effort. Morale was raised, and with it, fatefully, the expectations of territorial gains that a victory might yield for Italy.[28]

The Second Battle of Piave marked the beginning of the end for the Habsburg Army. It left over 142,000 men dead or wounded, while 25,000 of their soldiers were taken captive by the Allies.[29] The Dual Monarchy could no longer compensate for such losses with new recruits. Even the dismissal in mid-July 1918 of the long-serving Chief of the General Staff, Conrad von Hötzendorf, made no difference at this point.[30] On 14 September the Austrian Emperor Karl I appealed for peace. However, French and British leaders were suspicious that his move might simply be an attempt to divide the Allies, while Washington responded that it had already communicated its peace terms. Any further discussions were thus deemed superfluous.[31]

While the Habsburg Army was weakened by the ill-fated offensive on the Piave, Rome sought to capitalize on its regained strategic advantage and improve its position at the negotiation table after the war's end. On 24 October the Italian Army launched two attacks on the Monte Grappa and across the Piave river at Vittorio Veneto. Within five days a Habsburg army was in full retreat. At least 300,000 men and twenty-four generals were taken captive. On 30 October the Italians took Vittorio Veneto. Against this backdrop the Hungarian government decided on 1 November to recall its own troops, which accelerated the collapse of the rest of the Habsburg Army.[32] On 2 November the Austrian High Command requested an armistice, prompting Armando Diaz to send a jubilant 'bulletin of victory' to his troops: 'The Austro-Hungarian army is vanquished . . . The remnants of what was one of the world's most powerful armies are returning in hopelessness and chaos up the valleys from which they had descended with boastful confidence.'[33]

By the time the armistice with Austria-Hungary came into force on 4 November, another key player among the Central Powers, the Ottoman Empire, had already accepted defeat. The Armistice of Mudros, signed on 30 October 1918, ended a war that, for the Ottoman Empire, had effectively started in September 1911.[34] Back then, Italy – deeming the Ottoman Empire sufficiently weak – had attacked and occupied Ottoman Tripoli and Cyrenaica (today's Libya), as well as the Dodecanese islands in the Mediterranean.[35] A year later, in early October 1912, while still at war with Italy, Constantinople had faced yet another military challenge when a combined force of Bulgarian, Greek, Montenegrin and Serbian troops launched their invasion.[36] Although the Ottomans managed to retake Edirne, once the empire's capital, in the Second Balkan War of 1913, Constantinople had lost almost all of its European territory. In the wake of defeat in the Balkans, the Ottoman government of Mehmed Kamil Pasha was toppled on 23 January 1913, when a group of Young Turk officers, led by Lieutenant-Colonel Enver Bey, forced the Grand Vizier to resign at gunpoint.[37] In the eyes of the Young Turks, Russia posed a threat to the empire's borders from the north and east, and Britain had established strategically vital bases in Cyprus and Egypt, exposing the Ottomans' Arab domains to a potential assault by land and naval forces.[38]

Confronted with this perceived existential threat to its borders, Ottoman leaders tried to enter into an alliance with Britain, but the proposal was rejected by London. Instead they now began to look to Germany, the only European Great Power without vested interests in any of the territories under Constantinople's control. Berlin, or so the CUP leaders believed, would provide security from British and Russian imperialism. An alliance with Germany would thereby provide the stability needed for the internal consolidation and imperial expansion of the Ottoman Empire.[39] The Ottoman leaders decided to go on the attack, without a previous declaration of war, in a spectacular night operation culminating with the sinking of Russian ships in the Black Sea and the naval bombardment of the Russian ports of Sevastopol and Odessa on 29 October 1914.[40]

For all its alleged weakness, the Ottoman Empire was to prove itself a formidable opponent in the Great War. In the short period between the Ottoman defeat in the First Balkan War of 1912–13, the Ottoman government, now totally under the control of the Committee of Union and Progress (CUP), had radically reformed its armed forces. With the help of German military advisers and thanks to a new generation of very capable young officers, the Ottoman Army was transformed into a serious fighting force.[41] Although Constantinople's initial campaign into the Caucasus proved disastrous, the reorganized Ottoman Army performed well elsewhere, repelling their enemies on various fronts, from Eastern Anatolia to Sinai, and from Baghdad to the Dardanelles. As the Western Allies learnt the hard way at Gallipoli and during other campaigns in the Middle East, including the Ottoman victory over Indian forces at Kut in April 1916, the 'sick man of Europe' still had some life in him.[42] The humiliating Allied withdrawal from Gallipoli in January 1916, and the surrender of 13,000 Indian and British troops at Kut, some 160 kilometres south-east of Baghdad, brought serious embarrassment to the Asquith government back in London.[43]

As the war dragged on, however, the Ottoman Empire could not match the Entente's resources and numerical superiority in manpower. Although the empire profited from the Russian Revolution in 1917 and reconquered territory previously lost to Imperial Russia, the fortunes of war eventually turned against it. Constantinople possibly could have lived with the loss of Baghdad and Jerusalem, captured by British troops in March and December 1917 respectively, but a further British offensive on the Palestinian front, launched on 19 September 1918, devastated the defenders north of Jerusalem, routing three Ottoman armies in twelve days. Utter chaos ensued. Ottoman troops were surrendering en masse, deserting in thousands, and retreating in total disorder. By 1 October, Allied forces had advanced into Damascus. On 26 October an Anglo-Indian force accompanied by Arab rebels from the Hijaz, led by Hussein bin Ali, the custodian of the holy cities of Mecca and Medina, captured Aleppo in northern Syria.[44]

A second British army was moving towards the Ottoman capital from the north, after breaking through the Bulgarian lines at Salonika. Its armed forces already depleted by mass desertion and huge military casualties, the Ottoman leadership was simply in no position to fight on yet another front. The CUP leadership that had led the empire into the war resigned in the first week of October and fled on a German warship, while a new, liberal government swiftly appointed by the sultan, Mehmed VI, sent word to the British that it wanted peace. The recently appointed Minister of the Navy, Hüseyin Rauf Orbay, a former war hero who had also served as one of the empire's delegates during the peace talks at Brest-Litovsk, met with British representatives on the Aegean island of Limnos. After four days of discussions aboard HMS *Agamemnon*, on 30 October 1918, Rauf Orbay signed what became known as the Armistice of Mudros (as the Allies called the island) in the presence of the British commander, Admiral Arthur Calthorpe.[45]

The Armistice of Mudros confirmed the Ottomans' worst fears for the future of the empire, harboured since the beginning of the war when the British Prime Minister, Herbert Asquith, had declared that the conflict would lead to the demise of Ottoman rule. These fears were confirmed by the Bolsheviks' gleeful publication, in November 1917, of the secret Sykes-Picot-Sazonov agreement (1916), which proposed parcelling out the Arab lands into zones of interest controlled by the Allies after victory had been achieved. Roughly at the same time the British Foreign Secretary, Arthur Balfour, had pledged his government's support for 'the establishment in Palestine of a national home for the Jewish people' (the Balfour Declaration), while US President Woodrow Wilson (as part of his 'Fourteen Points') called for a dismemberment of the Ottoman Empire along ethnic lines.[46]

By the time the armistice was signed, the Ottoman Empire's Arab provinces – from Mesopotamia (the term the British used loosely to refer to the former Ottoman provinces of Mosul, Baghdad and Basra) to Palestine, from Syria down to the Arabian Peninsula – were already gone. In the east, Armenia had proclaimed itself an independent democratic republic in May 1918, while Kurdish leaders were also demanding a state of their own. Yet the new rulers in Constantinople were hoping that the Wilsonian principle of self-determination would at least be applied to the Turkish-speaking heartlands of Anatolia and eastern Thrace. As it turned out, some of the victorious Allies had other plans.

Under the terms of the armistice, the sultan's government agreed to a complete demobilization as well as to the withdrawal of all remaining troops from the Caucasus and Arabia. The Allies also reserved the right to occupy strategically important points in Anatolia at will – from roads to telegraph stations, railway lines and tunnels. Although the capital, Constantinople, was not officially occupied at first, Allied warships moved into the Straits of Bosphorus within a month of the armistice.[47]

The Ottoman signatory of the armistice, Rauf Orbay, later recalled the sense of betrayal that he felt when he realized there was not going to be an honourable peace: 'There was a general conviction in our country that England and France were countries faithful not only to their written pacts, but also to their promises. And I had this conviction too. What a shame that we were mistaken in our beliefs and convictions!'[48] From his post far away to the south, by the Syrian border, a friend of Rauf's, the thirty-seven-year-old Brigadier Mustafa Kemal, sent stern warnings against hasty demobilization to his government: 'It is my sincere and frank opinion that if we demobilize our troops and give in to everything the British want, without taking steps to end misunderstandings and false interpretations of the armistice, it will be impossible for us to put any sort of brake on Britain's covetous designs.'[49]

Kemal swiftly returned to Constantinople from the Palestinian front where he had commanded the Ottoman Empire's last offensive against the Entente. In Constantinople in late 1918 he found a city that had suffered greatly from the naval blockade. There was no coal and very little food. Grieving widows, orphaned children and crippled veterans roamed the streets. On street corners disabled soldiers were begging for food, while tens of thousands of refugees – Russians fleeing the Bolsheviks, Turks abandoning the Middle East and Europe – were camping on the streets. Kemal also found himself surrounded by non-Muslims – mainly Greeks and Armenians who had survived the genocide – for whom news of the Ottoman defeat was cause for joy, as they welcomed Allied battleships approaching Constantinople by waving Greek and Allied flags.[50]

The armistice not only marked the end of Ottoman participation in the Great War but also effectively signalled the demise of one of the longest-lasting empires in history. The House of Osman had ruled the Ottoman domains since about 1299, expanding into south-eastern Europe in the fourteenth century and conquering the eastern Arab lands in the sixteenth century. At this point the Ottoman sultan also assumed the title of caliph, the political and religious successor to the Islamic prophet, Muhammed, leader of the Muslim world. Although the last sultan of the House of Osman, Mehmed VI, only left Constantinople for exile on 17 November 1922, his empire had already disintegrated. Its enemies for half a century and more had denounced the Ottoman Empire as a corrupt, oppressive relic of the past, and as much a 'prison of peoples' as the Habsburg monarchy. The Ottoman defeat in the Great War, or so it was suggested by many in the West, would now 'liberate' the Christian and Arab populations that Constantinople had allegedly opposed for centuries.[51]

By the beginning of November, the last of the Central Powers remaining at war was Germany. Remarkably enough, despite the increasingly desperate military situation, the German forces on the Western Front continued to hold a 400-kilometre line for almost another month and a half after the collapse of their Bulgarian allies. Nonetheless, very few people doubted the inevitable outcome of the war at this stage. Bulgaria's exit offered a convenient excuse for Ludendorff to end the war without assuming responsibility for the consequences. On 29 September, the day of the armistice in Bulgaria, Ludendorff and Hindenburg offered Kaiser Wilhelm II their assessment of the military situation and its political consequences: 'I have asked His Majesty to bring into government those circles whom we mostly have to thank for getting us into the present situation,' Ludendorff informed high-ranking officers at the Army High Command (OHL) on 1 October. He frankly admitted that the German Army's will to resist had been broken. 'No more reliance could be placed on the troops,' he insisted.[52] Yet Ludendorff was equally sure that it was the representatives of the political Left in the Reichstag, not the army leadership, who were to be blamed for Germany's defeat, which he deemed 'unavoidably imminent': 'I have advised his Majesty to bring those groups into government whom we have to thank for the fact that matters have reached this pass. We shall now see these gentlemen moving into the country's ministries. Let them conclude the peace that must now be made. Let them eat the broth they have cooked for us.'[53] Apart from allowing the OHL to shift responsibility for defeat, the proposed 'revolution from above' was to have an additional advantage: President Wilson would be more inclined to conclude a peace based on his Fourteen Points if he was to negotiate with a democratically sanctioned government in Berlin.[54]

Following the advice of the OHL, Wilhelm II publicly announced on 30 September that 'men who have the confidence of the people should have a broad share in the rights and duties of government'.[55] With this decree the Kaiser initiated an entirely cynical process of democratization, which was also aimed at defusing a potentially revolutionary situation in Germany similar to the one that had brought down the tsarist regime in Russia.

The first consequence of this abrupt reform was the replacement of Chancellor Georg von Hertling – a strong opponent of reforms – with the fifty-one-year-old Maximilian von Baden. Prince Max, an intellectual liberal from southern Germany, differed significantly from his predecessors, as did his government, which was backed by a wide range of political parties.[56] Prince Max could count on the support of the Progressive People's Party, the National Liberals, the Catholic Centre Party and the Social Democrats – representing an overwhelming majority within Parliament. In July 1917 these parties had declared their willingness to enter into peace talks without territorial losses for their enemies or any other acts of political, economic or financial violation. The reversal of military fortunes in 1918 finally brought them to power, while Germany's transformation from constitutional monarchy to parliamentary democracy was finalized on 28 October 1918 when the constitution of 1871 was formally amended by the Reichstag.[57]

By that point the new government had already been in conversation with Washington about a possible truce for several weeks. On the very day of his appointment, and urged by Ludendorff who insisted on the 'speediest possible' conclusion of hostilities, Chancellor von Baden had initiated contact with Wilson's government, requesting an immediate end to hostilities on the basis of the Fourteen Points.[58] Yet the exchange of notes was not as straightforward as von Baden and his new government had hoped. Initially, Wilson's reply of 8 October gave cause for cautious optimism, as it sought clarification on whether the German government was now representative of the people's will and whether it accepted the Fourteen Points. However, following the sinking of a British passenger ship, the *Leinster*, by a German U-boat on 10 October off the Irish coast near Dublin, Wilson issued a second note in which he strongly criticized Berlin for the continuation of 'illegal and inhumane practices' of warfare. Wilson also said that Germany was still controlled by an 'arbitrary power' – presumably the Kaiser and the OHL. Berlin suspended submarine warfare on 20 October and sped up the democratization of the constitution, but the American President's third note of 23 October left no doubt that he considered Berlin's reforms insufficient. Wilson insisted that 'the United States cannot deal with any but veritable representatives of the German people . . . If it must deal with the military masters and the monarchical autocrats of Germany . . . it must demand, not peace negotiations, but surrender.'[59]

The German High Command rejected Wilson's note outright and ordered their troops to prepare for a 'fight to the bloody end' to avoid a shameful capitulation, but Max von Baden was now determined to end the war at all costs. Faced with increasingly louder calls for the Kaiser himself to abdicate to secure better peace terms for Germany, Wilhelm was now prepared to support his new Chancellor against the High Command.[60] On the morning of 26 October, Ludendorff and Hindenburg were summoned to the Bellevue Palace in Berlin for an audience with Wilhelm II. During the meeting Ludendorff was dismissed. Hindenburg, whose departure the government feared might further demoralize the army, was ordered to remain, even if he was effectively sidelined by the OHL's new first Quartermaster General, Wilhelm Groener.[61]

These changes in leadership came too late, however. When the fortunes of war had turned so clearly against Germany, civilian and military morale plummeted. As in Russia the previous year, military disaster and general war-weariness created the conditions for revolution. It was not – as nationalist circles were to claim in the following years – revolution that caused defeat. Just as in Russia, revolutionary events in Germany were sparked by material deprivation, strikes among industrial workers, and discontent among the soldiers. The strains of war undermined the legitimacy of the imperial regime and the 'silent' military dictatorship into which it had degenerated during the last two years of the conflict – a regime that was able neither to mitigate the hardships of the civilian population nor to bring the war to the promised victorious conclusion.[62] With the military collapse in the autumn of 1918, any remaining support for the imperial state evaporated. The deterioration of military discipline, the crumbling of the authoritarian governing system, the external pressure from the Allies (in particular, the Fourteen Points articulated by Wilson), alongside extreme war-weariness at home, and the example of Russia (which inspired the workers' and soldiers' councils that emerged in Germany in late 1918) – all combined to create an overwhelming crisis of legitimacy.[63]

The German Revolution itself began with a revolt by sailors and soldiers stationed within Germany. The immediate spark was the order issued on 28 October 1918 by the Imperial Naval High Command under Admiral Reinhard Scheer to send out the fleet to confront the Royal Navy in a final showdown. 'Even if it is not to be expected that this will bring a decisive turn in the course of events', a naval strategy document noted on 16 October, 'nonetheless it is from a moral perspective a question of the Navy's honour and existence that it does its utmost in the final battle.'[64]

Restoring 'honour' seemed particularly important to the Imperial Naval High Command because the German fleet with its expensive vessels had been largely unsuccessful during the war, being too small to beat the Royal Navy decisively and unable to prevent the British naval blockade designed to starve Germany into submission. Ever since the inconclusive Battle of Jutland, 31 May–1 June 1916, the German navy's activities had been confined to submarine warfare.[65] Now that the war was drawing to a close and defeat seemed inevitable, the admirals felt that dramatic action – a full-blown naval attack on their British opponent – was needed, even if it meant the complete destruction of the German High Seas Fleet.[66]

The sailors took a different view. Instead of obeying orders, they mutinied on a number of ships anchored off the port of Wilhelmshaven. The naval command took drastic countermeasures, but these merely fuelled the protests. Unrest spread to the naval base at Kiel where shipyard workers joined in. The revolt against a 'suicide mission' now took a more overtly political turn, as the revolutionaries began to demand peace at any price and the immediate abdication of the Kaiser – demands that sounded uncomfortably similar to those articulated by Russian protesters in Petrograd in early 1917.[67]

In an attempt to restore order while negotiations with the Allies were ongoing, Chancellor von Baden dispatched his friend Conrad Haussmann, a Reichstag deputy for the liberal Progressive Party, and Gustav Noske, a former basket-maker and now a leading Social Democrat deputy, on a fact-finding mission. He also asked the two parliamentarians to calm the situation. Arriving in Kiel, the deputies immediately realized that the sailors' mutiny would be difficult to contain. They were met at the station by a large crowd of demonstrators who repeated their demands. Noske gave a speech, promising an amnesty for those involved in the mutiny. He also announced that an armistice would be signed in a few days. In the evening he reported back to the cabinet in Berlin about the situation on the ground, informing them that the mutineers were demanding an immediate armistice and the abdication of the Kaiser – and that they had elected him, Noske, governor of the region.[68]

Any hopes that the mutiny at Kiel could be contained were quickly dashed. Within a few days it had become a full-blown revolution as it spread and reached the port cities of Bremen, Lübeck, Wismar, Cuxhaven, Hamburg and Tilsit.[69] On 7 November the revolution moved inland. In Munich thousands of people rallied in a socialist demonstration. The following morning, the Independent Social Democrat, Kurt Eisner, proclaimed a Socialist Republic of Bavaria. Revolutionary sailors and soldiers acted as missionaries for revolution, and workers' and soldiers' councils were formed.[70] In Dresden, the capital of Saxony, the king abdicated after days of mass demonstrations, ending the rule of the House of Wettin over Saxony. In Berlin the ex-diplomat and aristocratic republican, Count Harry

Kessler, noted: 'Reds are streaming in with every train from Hamburg to Berlin. An uprising is expected here tonight.'[71]

The first casualties of the revolution were the royal houses that had ruled Germany's states for so long. Beginning with the ageing King Ludwig III, whose House of Wittelsbach had ruled Bavaria for over a thousand years, Germany's twenty-two kings, princes and dukes were deposed without resistance. By midday on 9 November only the King of Prussia and Emperor of Germany, Wilhelm II, remained.[72]

The government in the meantime attempted to manage the revolution, or at least prevent its radicalization. Friedrich Ebert, co-chairman of the Social Democratic Party (SPD) alongside Philipp Scheidemann, feared a Bolshevik revolution no less than the Chancellor, but he had come to the conclusion that the key demands of the revolutionaries ought to be met. On 7 November, Ebert warned Max von Baden that 'if the Kaiser does not abdicate, the social revolution is inevitable'. This was followed later in the day by an ultimatum to the government stating that the Kaiser and Crown Prince must abdicate by noon the following day. Wilhelm II, however, refused to accept the inevitable. Instead he announced to Prince Max in a telephone conversation on the evening of 8 November that he intended to return to Berlin at the helm of loyal troops to restore order.[73]

At this point, however, Wilhelm was no longer in control of his political destiny. A meeting of thirty-nine middle-ranking front-line commanders on the Western Front, convened on 9 November by General Groener, revealed that the army was highly unlikely to follow the Kaiser's orders if he decided to march on Berlin.[74] In the capital, meanwhile, the Independent Socialist Party (USPD) had called a mass demonstration for the following morning. The Majority Social Democratic Party (MSPD) increased the pressure on Prince Max, who announced the Kaiser's abdication at noon without waiting for Wilhelm's authorization. He then invited Ebert to take over the chancellorship while tens of thousands of people on the streets of Berlin demonstrated against the Kaiser and called for the establishment of a republic.[75]

Ebert's co-chairman of the MSPD, Philipp Scheidemann, responded to these demands that afternoon when he proclaimed the creation of a republic from a balcony of the Reichstag building. Although Scheidemann's declaration was primarily intended to pre-empt a similar announcement by more radical socialists, he assured the ecstatic crowd that the new government would be made up of both of the Reich's Socialist parties. His speech culminated in an attempt to interpret the birth of the republic as a victory in defeat: 'The German people have triumphed everywhere. The old rotten regime has collapsed. Militarism is finished!'[76]

By the evening of 9 November the old regime had been overwhelmed. The Kaiser fled into exile in the Netherlands the following morning, while in Berlin the councils elected the provisional government of the German Republic. With the revolutionary title 'Council of People's Commissars', it consisted of six members: three Majority Social Democrats (Ebert, Scheidemann and Otto Landsberg) and three Independent Socialists (Hugo Haase, Wilhelm Dittmann and Emil Barth). Ebert would lead the government.[77]

His primary aim was to conclude the war as soon as possible and to return the troops home while avoiding a civil war. In the early hours of 11 November 1918 the German delegation headed by the Centre Party parliamentarian Matthias Erzberger signed the armistice agreement in a railway carriage in the forest of Compiègne.[78] The conditions were hard to accept for a country which, only a few months earlier, had assumed that victory would soon vindicate the sacrifices of four long years of deprivation: the German Army was obliged to immediately evacuate all invaded territory on the Western Front, while also surrendering large amounts of weaponry and the High Seas Fleet. Alsace-Lorraine was to be returned to France, which also occupied the left bank of the Rhine. To ensure good behaviour, the British naval blockade would continue, thereby threatening large parts of the German civilian population with starvation. Berlin's delegation warned that the terms of the armistice would lead to a state of chaos in Germany. Despite his protest, Erzberger signed the armistice, which only came into effect six hours later, at 11 a.m. At long last, the guns on the Western Front had fallen silent.[79]

I I

Revolution and Counter-Revolution

When they told us that the war was over, we laughed, because we *were* the war. Its flame continued to burn in us, it lived on in our deeds surrounded by a glowing and frightful aura of destruction. We followed our inner calling and marched on the battlefields of the post-war period ...

Friedrich Wilhelm Heinz, Sprengstoff *(1930)*

All around us madness and danger rules ... a thickening dark cloud is gathering above us, and a great black abyss opens before us.

Solomon Grigorevich Gurevich, Smolensk, 1917

The bourgeois revolution of 1789 – which was revolution and war in one – opened the gates of the world to the bourgeoisie ... The present revolution, which is also a war, seems to open the gates of the future to the masses ...

Benito Mussolini in a speech at Bologna, 19 May 1918

6

No End to War

Two days after hostilities in the West drew to a close on 11 November 1918, the Russian Red Army, with significant support from Latvian Bolsheviks, began a major offensive in the western borderlands of the former Tsarist Empire. Their aim was to seize the opportunity presented by Germany's defeat and to reconquer territories lost as a result of the Treaty of Brest-Litovsk. Simultaneously, the revolutions in Berlin, Munich, Vienna and Budapest encouraged Lenin to think that Bolshevism might be exported westwards after all. The odds were in his favour: mutinous and demoralized German soldiers were streaming back to the Reich from their garrisons in eastern Europe and new national armies in east-central Europe were still in their infancy. Facing weak resistance, the Red Army occupied recently independent Estonia and Latvia, reconquering Riga on 3 January 1919, before pushing into Lithuania and conquering Vilnius five days later.[1]

Lenin wasted no time in advancing revolution in the newly conquered lands. His decision to sign the Treaty of Brest-Litovsk and thus to focus on the survival of socialism in Russia had been forced upon him by the military advances of the Central Powers. Now that Germany and her allies had been defeated, he could return to pursuing his ultimate objective of igniting a global Bolshevik revolution. The Bolshevik-sponsored Latvian and Lithuanian Soviet Republics and their much smaller Estonian equivalent – the Commune of the Working People with headquarters in the city of Narva – swiftly began to introduce radical reforms, including the expropriation and nationalization of property and land in the hands of the middle classes, while suppressing resistance from the starving population with brutal force.[2]

However, none of the improvised Baltic Soviet Republics were to last very long. While the Commune in Narva was terminated within weeks by a counter-revolutionary Estonian People's Force, the Latvian and Lithuanian Soviets could only be toppled with significant external assistance. Faced with these rapid developments, the Western Allies tentatively asked the new German government under Friedrich Ebert to stop the withdrawal of its troops from the Baltics, as neither London nor Paris had any significant forces in the region. Shortly before the fall of Riga, on 29 December 1918, the Latvian government, with the acquiescence of the British, also called for the creation of a Baltic German anti-Bolshevik self-defence force, the *Baltische Landeswehr*, composed of volunteers from the ethnic German minority and reinforcements from the Reich. Together with the remnants of the German Eighth Army still present in the Baltics, volunteers from Germany formed the 'Iron Division', a sizeable fighting force that grew to an overall strength of 16,000 men. The Iron Division was led by the charismatic and highly decorated Major Josef Bischoff, whose long and chequered military career included direct involvement in the genocidal campaign against the Herero and Nama in German South-West Africa in 1904–6 as well as fighting on virtually every front of the Great War.[3]

In order to persuade further volunteers from the Reich to join their new republic, the Latvian government announced that Germans who had served against the Bolsheviks for at least four weeks would be allowed to settle in the country as farmers. Settlement and the promise of land were attractive propositions for ex-soldiers facing a bleak future of unemployment and uncertainty in post-war Germany, while also resonating with long-standing German fantasies of eastern expansion through settlement.[4] When the Latvian government's offer was published in Germany on 9 January 1919, thousands of volunteers reported to the recruitment offices in Berlin and other cities across the Reich.[5]

But the promise of living space and farmland was only one of several reasons why many Germans volunteered for service in the eastern states. Some were attracted by the collapse of law and order in the Baltics. Growing long beards and living off the land, they likened themselves to early modern freebooters or pirates, and thrived on the culture of lawlessness that pervaded the region. Others craved the continuation of their soldierly existence, especially in a fight against

Bolshevism, and believed that the campaign in Latvia could provide a base for a final effort to avenge the defeat and the humiliation of the post-war settlement. It was no coincidence that many of the volunteer formations called themselves '*Freikorps*' – a name coined during the anti-Napoleonic 'Wars of Liberation' (1813–15) when German volunteers, spurred on by Prussia's military humiliation at the hands of the French, made a significant contribution to Napoleon's eventual defeat.

In February 1919, as large numbers of *Freikorps* soldiers arrived in the Baltics with the ostensible mission of protecting the region and Europe against Bolshevism, the Baltic German *Landeswehr* and the Iron Division were placed under the central command of Rüdiger von der Goltz, a former infantry general who had previously helped the Finnish 'Whites' in the spring of 1918 to secure victory over their left-wing adversaries during the Finnish Civil War. The German forces – 30,000–40,000 strong according to Goltz – began to fully engage with the Bolsheviks in mid-February.[6] Goltz's offensive in Latvia initially focused on the capture of the ethnically German towns of Goldingen (Kuldīga), Windau (Ventspils) and Mitau (Jelgava), repelling the Bolsheviks from the Latvian coast in the process. His main objective, however, was the conquest of Latvia's capital and most populous city, Riga.[7]

Throughout these weeks the military campaign differed noticeably from the fighting that had taken place over the previous four years, not least because it was, in essence, a conflict without clearly demarcated battle lines or readily identifiable combatants.[8] Ethnic Russians, Latvians and even former German prisoners of war fought on the side of the Bolsheviks, often in improvised uniforms or disguised as civilians, thus reinforcing the perception among the German troops that this was a guerrilla war, in which the opponent had to be fought ruthlessly and killed without remorse. As one Baltic German volunteer, Alfred von Samson-Himmelstjerna, recalled: 'No one could be left alive.'[9]

Descriptions of unmitigated violence feature prominently in numerous autobiographical accounts of the Baltic campaign, including that of Rudolf Höss, the future commandant of Auschwitz, who served in Latvia as a volunteer after 1918: 'The battles in the Baltic states were more brutal and vicious than anything I had experienced before. There was hardly a front line; the enemy was everywhere. Wherever the opposing forces collided, there was a slaughter until no one was left.'[10]

Höss's account, written shortly before his 1947 execution for war crimes in Nazi-occupied Poland, must, of course, be read with caution, as he sought to explain how his own brutalization had occurred in a time of war and savageness. Yet there can be no doubt that the German Baltic campaign was characterized by extreme violence and a deliberate targeting of civilians suspected of being Bolshevik sympathizers. In Mitau (Jelgava) alone, *Freikorps* soldiers executed some 500 Latvian civilians accused of aiding and abetting the Bolsheviks; a further 325 were killed in the towns of Tuckum (Tukums) and Dünamunde (Daugavgrīva).[11] Although violence against civilians had certainly not been uncommon over the preceding four years, notably on the Eastern Front, it had remained exceptional, at least within the general context of a major war between uniformed combatants. After 1918, the targeting of 'suspect' civilians by troops no longer bound by conventional military laws and regulations became the norm.

The marauding German troops often legitimized their unrestrained violence against enemy soldiers and civilians alike by emphasizing their own exposure to the boundless violence of their opponents. One German volunteer, Erich Balla, gave a graphic description of his experiences shortly after the occupation of a Latvian village by *Freikorps* soldiers in early 1919. While searching a house occupied by two Latvian women, Balla and his men discovered 'the corpses of five brutally mutilated German soldiers. Their eyes, noses, tongues and genitals have been cut off.'[12] Horror over the discovery of the mutilated soldiers quickly turned into rage as 'two or three men, obsessed by the same thought, rush upstairs. One can hear the muffled sound of rifle butt strokes, and the two women lie dead on the floor.'[13]

The unlikely coalition between German volunteer forces and the Latvian government was seriously strained by *Freikorps* violence against Latvian civilians, and it completely fell apart after the objective of the campaign – the expulsion of the Red Army – had been largely achieved by late March 1919. The Latvian People's Council had already declared the country's independence from Russia in November 1918.

But if Karlis Ulmanis, the American-educated strongman of the Council, had assumed that German soldiers might become Latvian land
labourers after the Red Army's expulsion, Goltz and his men had
other plans. When Ulmanis's government requested the withdrawal of
German troops, they responded by staging a coup. On 16 April 1919,
Freikorps soldiers replaced the government with a puppet regime
headed by Pastor Andreas Needra, who Goltz believed was open to
German interests.[14] The coup prompted the Western Allies to demand
the immediate recall of the *Freikorps* to Germany. Ebert's government
in Berlin responded that a German withdrawal would inevitably lead
to a Bolshevik victory in the Baltics, unless the government of London
or Paris was prepared to send in its own troops.[15]

In late May 1919 the German campaign in the Baltics culminated
in the Battle of Riga, a city that had already suffered greatly over the
previous years. Before the war, Riga had been the fourth-largest city
in the Russian Empire, a multicultural Baltic metropolis with more
than half a million inhabitants, including a substantial German minority.[16] In 1915, during the 'Great Retreat' of Russian forces from the
western borderlands, Riga had lost much of its population, as a result
of the forced Russian evacuation of workers in war industries and
their families.[17] In September 1917 the Germans had finally entered
the city, but abandoned it after their defeat in the autumn of 1918. It
was then occupied by Latvian and Russian Bolshevik forces in early
January 1919. Throughout these years of turmoil Riga had lost half
its population.[18]

The German onslaught against the city in late May 1919 did little
to improve matters. Immediately after the German victory over Bolshevik forces in the Battle of Riga, violent retribution was directed
against communist supporters, both men and women, who had allegedly fired as snipers on German troops. Particular hatred was reserved
for communist 'rifle women' (*Flintenweiber*). They featured prominently in the memoirs of *Freikorps* soldiers like Erich Balla, who
participated in the battle:

> The anger of the [Baltic Germans] now rampaged through the streets
> of Riga. It is horrible to admit this, but it was mostly directed against
> young women between the ages of 16 and 20. These were the so-called
> '*Flintenweiber*', mostly beautiful things . . . who spent their nights in

sexual orgies and their days in orgies of violence . . . The Baltic Germans showed no mercy. They did not see their youth or their charm. They saw only the face of the devil as they were beating, shooting, stabbing them to death, wherever they showed. On 22 May 1919, four hundred rifle women were lying in their blood in the streets of Riga. Callously the nailed boots of the marching German volunteers stepped over them.[19]

Violence against women, including murder and rape, was common in this conflict – so common, in fact, that it became a major theme in one of the most famous interwar novels, Marguerite Yourcenar's *Coup de Grâce* (1939). The German-Latvian communist partisan, Sophie von Reval, betrays her former lover, the officer and novel's narrator Erich von Lhomond, before being caught and delivered to him for sentencing:

> I took my revolver and automatically advanced one step . . . Her lips did not move: hardly aware of what she was doing she had begun to unbutton the upper half of her jacket, as if I were about to press the gun against her very heart. I must admit that the few thoughts I had at the moment went out to that body, so alive and warm . . . and I felt pangs of something like regret, absurdly enough, for the children that this woman might have borne, who would have inherited her courage and her eyes. I fired, turning my head away like a frightened child setting off a firecracker on Christmas Eve. The first shot did no more than tear open the face . . . On the second shot everything was over.[20]

Yourcenar's fictional account was more than matched by reality, even if the victims of violence included both men and women. Approximately 3,000 people were killed in the anti-Bolshevik terror that followed the capture of Riga.[21] In the aftermath of their defeat there, the Bolsheviks retreated from the Baltics. Dizzy with success, German troops planned to invade Estonia and defied British demands for *Freikorps* soldiers to be withdrawn. It was at this point, however, that triumph turned to tragedy for the German invaders. Backed by Estonian troops, Latvian forces inflicted a crushing defeat on the *Freikorps* at the Battle of Wenden on 23 June and drove them back in a series of armed clashes that lasted until 3 July. Von der Goltz was forced to sign the Treaty of Strazdumuiža and to withdraw from Riga with the rest of his forces, while Ulmanis, deposed in the Germans' April 1919 coup, was reinstated as Prime Minister.[22]

During their retreat, angered by the reversal of military fortunes and the German government's decision to sign the Versailles Treaty with the Western Allies in late June 1919, the *Freikorps* mutinied and refused to return to Germany.[23] Instead, some 14,000 heavily armed men remained in Latvia and joined forces with the White Russian Army of the West, commanded by the eccentric Colonel Pavel Bermondt-Avalov.[24] For several months the German volunteers continued to fight with Bermondt-Avalov's army against the Latvians. Deprived of material support from Berlin, the *Freikorps* soldiers increasingly lived off the land, requisitioning food from an already starving rural population. This increased the Latvians' determination to fight and they eventually succeeded in forcing the Germans to retreat into Lithuania, where they suffered a further defeat.[25]

Retreating German soldiers felt betrayed by the Baltic people they had allegedly sought to 'liberate' from Bolshevism, and left a trail of tears in their wake. Farms and smaller dwellings were burnt to the ground, civilians murdered in the process. As one German volunteer subsequently recalled: 'Our fists lashed down in destructive lust . . . Yes, our accomplishment was destruction.'[26] Another volunteer, Ernst von Salomon, proudly remembered the rituals of violence that dominated his experience of the retreat:

> We fired into surprised crowds and we raged, we shot and hunted. We chased the Latvians like rabbits over the fields, we burnt every house and destroyed every bridge and every telegraph mast. We flung the bodies into fountains and threw hand grenades on top. We slaughtered whoever fell into our hands; we burned whatever would catch fire . . . There were no human feelings left in our hearts . . . A giant smoke trail marked our path. We had set fire to the stake where we burnt . . . the laws and values of the civilised world . . .[27]

The surviving remnants of the *Freikorps* eventually returned to safety in Germany in late 1919. Some of them continued their violent careers in underground organizations of the extreme Right, being directly involved in the 1921 murder of the signatory of the Versailles Treaty, Matthias Erzberger, or the 1922 assassination of Germany's Jewish Foreign Minister, Walther Rathenau.[28] Others returned to their homes, seeking respite from several years of uninterrupted war. For those living further east, however, the violence continued unabated.

7
The Russian Civil Wars

By the time the German *Freikorps* retreated from the Baltics in late 1919, the territories of the former Russian Empire had descended into complete chaos. What is commonly known as the 'Russian Civil War' was, in fact, a whole series of overlapping and mutually reinforcing conflicts: a rapidly escalating struggle between the armed forces of Lenin's Bolshevik government and its 'counter-revolutionary' opponents; the attempts by several regions on the western border of the former Russian Empire to break away entirely from Petrograd's rule; and peasant insurgencies, triggered by the Communists' forced requisitions of desperately needed foodstuffs. These three distinct but interconnected conflicts were further complicated by outside forces: until their defeat in November 1918, the Central Powers had controlled vast swathes of land on the western periphery of the former Romanov Empire, while the Western Allies had sent troops – some 180,000 men by late 1919 – to various entry points such as Murmansk, Archangelsk (Arkhangelsk), Vladivostok and Odessa shortly after Lenin's decision to withdraw Russia from the war in October 1917. Although initially intended to prevent the Central Powers from taking control of strategically vital places, the purpose of the Allied intervention soon included military aid for the loose confederation of anti-communist forces known as the 'Whites' in their struggle against the 'Red' Bolsheviks.[1]

Within the complex amalgam of violent actors in the post-revolutionary territories of the former Russian Empire, two groups in particular stood out in sheer size: the Red Army – initially composed of scattered groups of soldiers and sailors from the old dissolved army, workers' militias and recently released former Austro-Hungarian prisoners of war – and its much more diverse 'White' adversaries.[2]

While, at least in theory, the Bolshevik forces strove to realize the proletarian utopia set out in the writings of Marx and Lenin, their opponents were highly heterogeneous in political outlook. What they had in common was that they were fiercely anti-Bolshevik or 'anti-Red'.³ Yet, being anti-Bolshevik was something that applied to fundamentally different groups, from monarchists to nationalists. Equally opposed to Lenin's rule were the Mensheviks and Social Revolutionaries, who resented the Bolshevik coup that had disempowered them.

Mutual mistrust and rivalry between these groups prevented them from forming a coherent movement under a nationwide unified military command. As a result, various leaders acted largely independently from each other: Admiral Alexander Kolchak in the east; General Nikolay Yudenich and Colonel Pavel Bermondt-Avalov in the northwest; General Anton Denikin in the North Caucasus and the Don region; General Pyotr Wrangel in the Crimea; warlords or 'Atamans' like Grigory Semenov or Roman von Ungern-Sternberg in Siberia and southern Russia.⁴

The armed conflict between Whites and Reds was further complicated by the involvement of other local actors as chaos and lawlessness in the countryside led to the emergence of a large 'Green' peasant self-defence movement. In Ukraine, one of the most brutally embattled territories during the civil war, Nestor Makhno, a peasant anarchist, who had only been released from a tsarist prison in 1917, commanded sizeable troops that clashed repeatedly with both White and Red armies.⁵

The scale and intensity of the Russian Civil War that ultimately killed well over three million people would have been difficult to predict in the first weeks after the Bolsheviks' seizure of power in Petrograd, Moscow and other major Russian towns and cities in the autumn of 1917. To be sure, the Bolsheviks were well aware that large pockets of potential resistance existed throughout the former Romanov Empire. Areas opposed to Lenin's rule from the start included Mogilev in Belarus to the south-west (where the imperial army's headquarters was based), the Cossack regions of eastern and southern Russia, and significant parts of the German-occupied western borderlands – notably Ukraine and the Baltic region – where the forces of Bolshevism encountered strong opposition from national independence movements.[6] Yet initially, as Trotsky's troops spread out to establish their rule over the Ukrainian capital of Kiev and the Cossack regions, they only encountered sporadic and largely uncoordinated resistance, prompting Lenin to call the first months after the revolution a 'triumphal march' of Bolshevism.[7]

During this period Lenin clearly benefited from having taken Russia out of the war. However humiliating and costly the Treaty of Brest-Litovsk may have been for Russia, it allowed Lenin's party, which renamed itself the Communist Party in late 1917, to focus its energies and resources on fighting domestic enemies instead of continuing a deeply unpopular war. While Lenin moved the capital from Petrograd to the less exposed city of Moscow in early 1918, Trotsky, the new War Commissar, concentrated on organizing the Red Army as an efficient military fighting force, recruiting former tsarist officers to train and command a growing number of peasant conscripts.[8]

Both men were aware, however, that their opponents were numerous and increasingly determined to challenge Bolshevik rule with violence.[9] Lacking broad popular support and surrounded by a host of real and imagined enemies, the Bolsheviks quickly resorted to terror in order to suppress a wide range of opponents: Whites (and their foreign backers), moderate socialists or anarchists unwilling to submit to Bolshevik rule, the bourgeoisie, and the more nebulous 'kulaks' (wealthy peasants), 'marauders', 'speculators', 'hoarders', 'black marketeers' and 'saboteurs' were from now on declared 'enemies of the people'.[10]

The Bolsheviks' prime instrument of terror was the 'All-Russian Extraordinary Commission for Combating Counter-Revolution and Sabotage' – better known by its Russian acronym, 'Cheka'. It was inaugurated by Lenin on 20 December 1917, with the Polish-born revolutionary Felix Dzerzhinsky as its first head. Dzerzhinsky, like many of those who worked for the Cheka, had spent more than half his life in prisons and labour camps that were run as a brutal regime by the *Okhrana*, the tsarist secret police. During his imprisonment Dzerzhinsky had been beaten so severely by his captors that he was left with a permanently disfigured jaw and mouth. Some ten months after his release in the wake of the February Revolution of 1917,

Dzerzhinsky and his ideologically driven fellow Chekists were to start emulating their former captors, exacting a terrible vengeance for their own ill-treatment.[11]

As Lenin introduced a large number of decrees for the nationalization of the economy, the enforced requisitioning of resources, and the banning of any kind of organized opposition, the new state required an instrument like the Cheka for the policing and surveillance of the population. The Bolshevik fear that the revolution might be swept aside by its internal enemies – not because they had committed terror but because they had not committed enough of it – became an almost obsessive leitmotif.[12] As early as January 1918, two months after seizing power, Lenin complained that the Bolsheviks were being too easy on their class enemies. 'If we are guilty of anything,' he argued, 'then it is of the fact that we are being too humane, too decent, with regard to representatives of the bourgeois-imperialist world, monstrous in their betrayal.'[13]

Such sentiments were further reinforced when, in the summer of 1918, the new regime was threatened by an ultimately unsuccessful uprising organized by Socialist Revolutionaries in Moscow and central Russia, and a series of assassination attempts against leading Bolsheviks. First, a young military cadet, Leonid Kannegisser, infuriated by the violent treatment of some tsarist officers by the Bolsheviks, fatally shot Moisei Uritsky, the head of the Petrograd Cheka, on 17 August; the assassin was later executed. On 30 August, Fanya Kaplan, a former anarchist who now supported the Socialist Revolutionaries, fired shots at Lenin as he was leaving a gathering of workers in Moscow. Two of the bullets struck Lenin, nearly killing him. Kaplan, who had spent eleven years in a Siberian labour camp under the tsarist regime for participation in a terrorist act in Kiev in 1906, was executed on 3 September.[14]

The assassination attempts spurred the Bolsheviks into action and marked the beginning of an intensified wave of 'Red Terror'. Within a week of Kaplan's attempt on Lenin's life, the Petrograd Cheka shot 512 hostages, many of them former high-ranking tsarist officials. In Kronstadt, Bolsheviks killed 400 hostages in one night.[15] It would be wrong, however, to suggest that the use of terror was merely reactive or irrational. Instead, the Bolsheviks used terror in a strategic way.

It served a dual purpose on the path towards the realization of a Communist utopia: terror permitted 'surgical operations' against perceived class enemies while also being a deterrent to potential enemies.[16]

As the Red Terror intensified, more and more people were recruited into the ranks of the Cheka. Over the coming years its numbers grew at a remarkable rate, from 2,000 in mid-1918 to some 140,000 by the end of the civil war. An additional 100,000 frontier troops supported the Cheka in suppressing 'counter-revolutionary' activities. Although not as efficient and well organized as its successor organization, the NKVD (People's Commissariat for Internal Affairs), the Cheka quickly established a wide-ranging network of local offices throughout the country, targeting just about anybody suspected of economically or politically sabotaging Bolshevik rule.[17]

Violence escalated further when, in the spring and early summer of 1918, the Bolsheviks deliberately extended the class war to the countryside. After years of war-induced food-supply crises that had triggered the Russian Revolution in the first place, the Bolshevik government, in May 1918, took the decisive step of establishing a far-reaching monopoly on food distribution. Committees of poor peasants were put in charge of requisitioning agricultural surpluses from 'wealthier' peasants. Lenin publicly called for a 'crusade' for bread, announcing a 'merciless and terroristic struggle and war' against those 'concealing grain surpluses'.[18] Military food brigades and requisitioning squads, composed of militant Bolsheviks, workers and demobilized soldiers – nearly 300,000 men by 1920 – tried to enforce the new order, with only limited success.[19]

Lenin's forced requisitions at gunpoint led to an immediate escalation of extreme violence. Villagers who dared to oppose the requisitions were severely punished. The military food brigades threatened them with death, took families hostage, imposed heavy fines, searched houses, and did not hesitate to burn the villages of those who hid part of the harvest.[20]

Refusal to cooperate was met with brutal suppression. Following peasant resistance against requisitions in the Penza region in August 1918, for example, Lenin ordered his local followers to 'mercilessly suppress' those in charge:

The interests of the entire revolution require this, because now 'the last decisive battle' with the kulaks is underway everywhere. One must give an example. 1. Hang (hang without fail, so the people see) no fewer than one hundred known kulaks, rich men, bloodsuckers. 2. Publish their names. 3. Take from them *all* the grain. 4. Designate hostages . . . Do it in such a way that . . . the people will see, tremble, know, shout: they are strangling and will strangle to death the bloodsucker kulaks.[21]

Inevitably, those living in the countryside rose up to resist the requisitions. Resistance took different forms, from the deliberate hiding of part of the harvest to open armed revolt.[22] The Bolshevik response ensured that violent opposition from villagers facing the threat of starvation simply increased. Desperate for scarce grain to feed their families and outraged by the Bolsheviks' attempts to deprive them of their livelihood, peasant insurrectionists often used very expressive – or symbolically charged – forms of violence that conveyed clear messages to their opponents. Bolshevik commissars who tried to requisition grain from infuriated peasants were publicly disembowelled and their stomachs filled with grain to visibly mark them as thieves of foodstuffs. Older forms of execution or punishment for theft, such as quartering or the severing of limbs, were revived. As peasants were short of ammunition, they often used knives or farm instruments normally needed for working the fields – to kill their prisoners. In other cases, members of requisitioning squads had Bolshevik symbols such as hammers and sickles cut into their foreheads. Others were branded with crosses or crucified to impose a Christian identity on the openly atheistic Bolsheviks.[23] 'In Tambov province,' Maxim Gorky (still a supporter of Lenin) noted, 'Communists were nailed with railway spikes by their left hand and left foot to trees a metre above the soil, and [the peasants] watched the torments of these deliberately oddly crucified people.'[24]

The Bolsheviks responded in kind and there were no limits to creative ways of torturing, maiming or killing those deemed to be in opposition to Lenin's decrees. It is estimated that some 250,000 people were killed in these 'bread wars', as the Red Army and the Cheka increasingly turned wartime practices – including the aerial bombing of villages and the use of poison gas – against their own population.[25]

Just as Lenin was beginning to export the terror to the countryside, the Bolshevik hold on power was challenged by yet another actor in the civil war: in May 1918 the Czechoslovak Legion revolted. The Legion had originally been formed from Czechs and Slovaks working in Russia before 1914, men who were keen to fight against the Habsburg monarchy. The Legion grew substantially as its ranks were swelled by deserters or prisoners of war from the Austro-Hungarian Army until it reached an overall strength of two self-contained divisions with a total of 40,000 well-trained and heavily armed men.[26] After the signing of the Treaty of Brest-Litovsk, the majority of its units tried to leave Russia via the Siberian port of Vladivostok. Their aim was to board ships and join the Allied forces in France in order to continue their fight for an independent Czechoslovakia. Initially, the Soviet government had agreed to let them leave the country, but the legionnaires, who had to cross the entire country along the Trans-Siberian railway to get to Vladivostok, increasingly suspected that the Bolsheviks might hand them over to the Germans and Austrians if they refused to fight with the Red Army. They also clashed violently with recently released Hungarian prisoners of war, some 30,000 of whom were indeed joining the Red Army. In May, prompted by fears that they were about to be disarmed by the Soviet authorities, and probably encouraged by the Western Allies, the legionnaires mounted a mutiny along the railway system from the Volga river to the Russian Far East. Their strategy was as simple as it was effective. Aware that in a country the size of Russia the railway lines were militarily critical to moving men and material, they took over the trains, seizing control of one train station after another.[27]

The Bolshevik leaders in Moscow were alarmed and told their local supporters that all Czechs were to be taken from their trains and drafted into the Red Army or labour battalions. Czech soldiers, who controlled the railway station at Chelyabinsk, intercepted this telegram, as well as a further message two days later in which Trotsky himself called for the immediate disarmament of the Czechs and Slovaks. Those who resisted were to be 'shot on the spot'.[28]

Instead of surrendering to the Bolsheviks, the legionnaires decided to resist. Within a climate of generally escalating violence, they quickly adjusted. As one Czech veteran remembered from his days as a legionnaire: 'We chased the Russians from their posts. The order was: no pardon, no prisoners . . . And we pounced on them like beasts. We used bayonets and knives. We sliced their necks as if they were baby geese.'[29] Although boasting about the brutal handling of Bolsheviks became a widespread phenomenon among former legionnaires in the 1920s and 1930s, there can be little doubt about the existence of extensive atrocities committed during their revolt. There are several well-documented cases of public executions at the hands of legionnaires, notably of captured Bolsheviks or German or Hungarian volunteers for the Red Army. Their sacking of the town of Samara in south-western Russia in June 1918, for example, was accompanied by public mass hangings and the burning alive of captured Red Army soldiers.[30]

The mutiny of the Czechoslovak Legion acted as a stimulus for other anti-Bolshevik movements, whose resistance until then had been confined to sporadic local skirmishes. Now they rose and swiftly took control of the central Volga region and Siberia, and set up their own government in Samara on the eastern banks of the Volga.[31] The 'Committee of Members of the Constituent Assembly', or *Komuch*, as it was called, was dominated by the Socialist Revolutionaries. As they had won the elections for the Russian Constituent Assembly before it was dissolved by Lenin, they felt themselves to be the only legitimate government of Russia.[32]

By the summer of 1918 rumours spread that anti-Bolshevik forces were advancing on the Red stronghold of Yekaterinburg in the Urals where the tsar and his family had been held captive for several months. Although Lenin had not yet taken a firm decision on the future of the royal family, the mere possibility of the tsar being freed and handed over to royalist forces made the very existence of Nicholas II a liability for the Bolshevik cause.[33]

After receiving authorization from Moscow on 16 July 1918, a group of Bolsheviks under the leadership of Yekaterinburg's deputy head of the Cheka, Yakov Yurovsky, woke up the royal family and their closest servants in the early-morning hours of 17 July. Nicholas, Alexandra, their five children and four members of their entourage were then led downstairs to an empty room in the basement where Yurovsky, surrounded by a group of armed men, announced that the royal family had been sentenced to death. Yurovsky then pointed his revolver at the tsar and fired. The other family members and their servants were shot and bayoneted until every last one was dead. After the killings, the executioners used explosives to destroy the bodies before dousing them with acid and burning the remains.[34]

The killing of the royal family was greeted with horror in the West and among the Whites, and it did little to improve the Bolsheviks' position. In fact, there were clear indications that Bolshevik power was dwindling in the summer of 1918. In August, *Komuch* forces, supported by the Czechoslovak Legion, took the city of Kazan, 800 kilometres from Moscow. With Russia's western borderlands still under German control, its Caucasian territories claimed by the Ottomans, with Allied intervention troops landed in Murmansk and Archangelsk, and wide swathes of the south and east under the command of various anti-Communist forces and warlords, the Bolsheviks' future seemed highly uncertain.[35]

But the Bolsheviks prevailed. Trotsky was able to rally the still-developing Red Army through a combination of logistical brilliance, revolutionary rhetoric, and draconian punishment for anyone unwilling to engage the enemy. As General Gordon-Finlayson, a British commander at Archangelsk in 1918–19, reported to the General Staff in London, Trotsky had succeeded in turning the Red Army into a serious fighting force: 'There appears to be an impression in Great Britain that the Bolshevik forces are represented by a great rabble of men armed with sticks, stones and revolvers who rush about foaming at the mouth in search of blood and who are easily turned and broken by a few well-directed rifle shots.' Instead, Finlayson found the Red Army to be 'well-equipped, organised and fairly well trained . . .' – in short, a force perfectly capable of facing up to its opponents.[36] His assessment proved accurate. A Bolshevik counter-attack stopped their opponents' advance up the Volga. Kazan was retaken in September 1918, prompting a retreat of the Legion and *Komuch* forces across the Ural Mountains.[37]

However, resistance continued in other parts of the country, notably in the North Caucasus. In the floodplains of the Don, one of the historical settlement areas of the Cossacks, the Germans had supported the consolidation of an anti-Bolshevik government in 1918.[38] Further south, in the lands of Kuban Cossacks, an even more dangerous Russian nationalist force was beginning to take shape: the Volunteer Army, heavily dominated by former tsarist officers. General Mikhail Alekseev, the political figurehead, had been Chief of Staff to Nicholas II from 1915 to 1917, and General Kornilov, the former Supreme Commander-in-Chief, was the Volunteer Army's first military leader until he died attempting to capture the Kuban capital of Ekaterinodar from Red forces in early 1918. Kornilov was succeeded by yet another tsarist officer, General Anton Denikin. Over the course of the summer in 1918, protected from Soviet attacks from the north by the presence of German forces in Ukraine, the Volunteers were able to consolidate their position in the Kuban.[39]

The situation in the late summer and early autumn of 1918 – at the end of the first year of the civil war – was thus bewilderingly complex. Lenin's forces now controlled north-central European Russia as far east as the Ural Mountains. However, in the western and southern borderlands, in Finland, the former Baltic provinces, Poland, Belarus, Ukraine and the Caucasus, the Red Army faced stiff opposition from national independence movements, local warlords and other anti-Bolshevik forces. To the east, an anti-Bolshevik government under the Allied-supported Admiral Kolchak, former commander of the Imperial Black Sea Fleet, overthrew the *Komuch*, dominated by Socialist Revolutionaries, in November 1918. With backing from the Allies who were hoping for a more unified White movement, Kolchak was installed as 'Supreme Leader'. From his main base in the city of Omsk in south-western Siberia, he now commanded all anti-Bolshevik forces between the Volga and Lake Baikal.[40]

The Central Powers' defeat that November radically changed the situation, notably in Russia's western borderlands where the hasty withdrawal of German and Austro-Hungarian troops left a vast power vacuum within which all actors in the civil war sought to capitalize. For much of 1919 and 1920 the western borderlands experienced a three-way struggle involving the Bolsheviks, the Whites, and a host of nationalist movements whose claim to independence was rejected by both Whites and Reds. The situation was further complicated by the presence of Allied intervention troops.[41]

The Allied troops' impact on the outcome of the civil war was limited, however. They were not actively involved in any of the major battles and much of the material aid they provided to the Whites was wasted through inefficiency and corruption. Petty officials behind the lines took the uniforms intended for the soldiers; their wives and daughters wore British nurses' skirts. While Denikin's trucks and tanks seized up in the cold, anti-freeze was sold in the bars as a substitute for liquor.[42]

What the intervention did achieve, however, was to convince Lenin and the Bolsheviks that they were threatened by an international conspiracy to end their rule, strengthening the perception that this was an existential war against a host of internal and external enemies in which all means were permitted to achieve victory. The Allied intervention also reinforced the tendency, present from the February Revolution of 1917 onwards, to view the unfolding events through the prism of the French Revolution of 1789. If Kerensky, the head of the deposed Provisional Government, had been encouraged by the French to view himself as a Russian Danton who could channel the energies of the revolution into the war effort against Germany, the Bolsheviks perceived themselves as the far more radical Jacobins and the Cossack regions as the modern-day equivalent of the Vendée, the centre of royalist opposition to the French Revolution.[43]

Even before October 1917, Lenin had repeatedly referred to Jacobinism as a historical inspiration. Responding to critics who accused the Bolsheviks of being modern-day 'Jacobins', he wrote in July 1917:

> Bourgeois historians see Jacobinism as a fall. Proletarian historians see Jacobinism as one of the highest *peaks* in the emancipation struggle of an oppressed class . . . It is natural for the bourgeoisie to hate Jacobinism. It is natural for the petty bourgeoisie to dread it. The class-conscious workers and working people generally put their trust in the transfer of power to the revolutionary, oppressed class, for *that* is the essence of Jacobinism, the only way out of the present crisis, and the only remedy for economic dislocation and the war.[44]

Learning the lessons of the past meant that Lenin and the Bolsheviks could not allow for another 'Thermidor' – the coup of 27 July 1794 during which Maximilien Robespierre and his Committee of Public Safety were toppled, resulting in the execution of the Jacobin leadership and their replacement first by the conservative Directory, then by the rule of Napoleon. In order to prevent such a scenario from repeating itself in Russia, more terror – not less – was required.[45]

As a result of such reasoning and further food shortages, the civil war became ever more brutal the longer it lasted. The constantly shifting fortunes of war, in which entire regions were subjected to repeatedly changing regimes, triggered a never-ending cycle of retaliatory violence in which neither the Whites nor their Red opponents did anything to restrain their troops.[46] On the contrary: local warlords and generals often encouraged the further escalation of brutality, as the example of one particularly notorious White general, Baron Roman von Ungern-Sternberg, demonstrates. Born in 1882 into an old German-Baltic family from Reval (Tallinn), Ungern-Sternberg had first risen to dubious fame during the Great War when, as a member of a Cossack regiment during the Russian invasion of eastern Prussia, he earned a reputation as a brave but reckless and mentally unstable officer.[47]

A fanatical anti-Bolshevik and anti-Semite, Ungern-Sternberg joined the White forces in Siberia during the civil war and gained notoriety for mindless brutality, having his men slaughter captured Bolshevik commissars and 'suspicious' civilians in a variety of barbarous ways, including skinning them alive.[48] After the defeat and execution of Admiral Kolchak at the hands of the Bolsheviks in February 1920, Ungern-Sternberg formally came under the command of Ataman Grigory Semenov, although in reality he operated independently for most of the time. Commanding a multi-ethnic cavalry division composed of predominantly non-Russian troops and including Tatars, Mongols, Chinese and Japanese troops, Ungern-Sternberg moved across the border into Mongolia in the summer of 1920 where he conquered Chinese-occupied Urga (Ulan Bator) in February 1921. Although initially welcomed by the local population for reconstituting Mongolian autonomy, Ungern-Sternberg and his men acted so barbarously that the general mood towards them swiftly changed.[49]

As a former officer in Ungern-Sternberg's division recalled, the conquest of Urga had been accompanied by unprecedented atrocities during which the men particularly 'turned on the Jews who were tortured to death. The humiliation of the women was terrible: I saw one officer walking into a house with a razor blade and recommending a girl to kill herself before his men could descend on her. She thanked him under tears and slit her own throat . . . The nightmare continued for three days and nights.'[50]

Ungern-Sternberg's rule of terror in Urga was brutal but short-lived. In August 1921, when he ordered a strategic withdrawal to western Mongolia in the face of advancing Bolshevik troops, his officers, who had lost confidence in him, rebelled. Arrested by his own men, the 'White Baron' was handed over to the Red Army, put on trial by the Bolsheviks in Novonikolajevsk, and swiftly executed by a firing squad.[51]

Although extreme in his savagery, Ungern-Sternberg was by no means unique in his views or actions. Anti-Semitic pogroms in particular were a common feature in many of the territories affected by the civil war, notably in the towns and shtetls of the western borderlands.[52] Fanned by the comparatively strong Jewish representation in the Communist leadership, anti-Bolshevik movements were quick to stigmatize the October Revolution as the result of a Jewish conspiracy.[53] Admiral Kolchak, for example, provided his troops with a pamphlet programmatically entitled 'The Jews have killed the Tsar', a suggestion that echoed and reinforced a well-established narrative at the heart of traditional Christian anti-Semitism: that the Jews had been responsible for Jesus's death, thus establishing a tradition of murderous treachery that could be traced throughout the centuries and into the present.[54]

The idea of a Jewish conspiracy at the heart of the revolution became central to the Whites' propaganda as they tried to orchestrate resistance against the Bolsheviks who otherwise had much more appealing promises ('land, bread, liberation') to offer new recruits.[55] The anti-Judeo-Bolshevik card gave the Whites at least something popular with which to identify and it quickly led to outbreaks of anti-Semitic violence throughout the former Romanov Empire. In Kaunas and other Lithuanian towns, and in Latvia, Jews were harassed by counter-revolutionary forces who associated them with the short-lived Bolshevik dictatorship in Riga.[56] In western Russia and Ukraine, the situation was even worse as Jews became one of the primary victim groups of anti-Bolshevism. Between June and December 1918 alone some 100,000 Jews were murdered, notably, but by no means exclusively, by members of General Denikin's Volunteer Army. Ukrainian and Polish nationalist forces and various peasant armies, agitated by rumours about Jews aiding the enemy or hoarding food, also participated in the slaughter of Jews, usually in alcohol-fuelled pogroms of which well over a thousand were recorded in the region between late 1918 and 1920.[57] In the Galician capital of Lemberg (Lwów), once the fourth-largest city in the Austro-Hungarian Empire and now claimed by Polish and Ukrainian nationalists for their emerging states, a terrible pogrom occurred in late November 1918 once Polish troops had chased out their Ukrainian adversaries. Under the pretext of searching for snipers aiding the withdrawal of Ukrainian troops, Polish soldiers cordoned off the city's Jewish quarter before entering it in small units armed with guns and knives. Violence escalated swiftly as the soldiers moved through the quarter, killing men of military age. In the three-day pogrom, seventy-three inhabitants of the quarter were murdered and hundreds more injured, while shops were ransacked and buildings set on fire.[58]

To be sure, the Ukrainians did not treat Jews any better – on the contrary. In February 1919, for example, Cossacks fighting for the Ukrainian National Republic carried out a particularly well-documented pogrom in Proskurov, during which 2,000 Jews were murdered. Following a victorious battle with Bolshevik troops, the Cossacks' commander, Ataman Semosenko exclaimed, according to one of his officers, 'that the worst enemies of the Ukrainian people and of the Cossacks were the Jews, who must all be exterminated to save Ukraine and their own lives'.[59]

The following day Semosenko's men descended on the local Jewish population:

They used not only sabres, but also bayonets. Firearms were only used in the few cases where their victims made attempts to escape . . . The house of Krotchak was visited by eight men, who began breaking all the window panes. Five men entered the house while three remained outside. Those in the house seized the old man Krotchak by his beard, dragged him to the window of the kitchen and threw him out of the window to the other three who killed him. Then they killed the old woman and her two daughters. A young girl who was visiting in the house was dragged by her long hair into another room, then thrown out of the window into the street and there killed. After that the Cossacks re-entered the house and inflicted several wounds on a boy aged 13, who became deaf in consequence. His elder brother received nine wounds in his stomach and in his side, having first been placed on his mother's dead body.[60]

The massacre was only called off after a local representative of the Kiev government intervened, but it resumed a few days later in the nearby town of Felshtin where eyewitnesses reported that 100 people were murdered. Joseph Aptman, a restaurant owner, recalled: 'Nearly all the girls were assaulted and then done to death – cut up by sabres. Blood was flowing in the streets . . . In the house of Monich Brenman there was a Galician Jew and his wife. They were taken outside the house, the woman was stripped and was forced to dance stark naked, after that four bandits assaulted her in the presence of the husband who was made to look on; after that they both were cut up into pieces . . .'[61]

Over time the alleged inseparability of Bolshevism and Jews became a self-fulfilling prophecy. Lenin's language of emancipation and the Bolsheviks' public denunciations of anti-Semitism and pogroms suggested an ethnic and religious 'colour-blindness' that naturally appealed to many Jews, as it did to other ethnic minorities within the empire, such as Georgians, Armenians, Latvians and Poles.[62] Of all these groups, however, Jews responded to the Bolshevik call for support in proportionately the largest numbers, joining the ranks of the Red Army, the Cheka and the party in significant numbers.[63] This did not, however, prevent Red Army units from themselves occasionally participating in anti-Semitic pogroms.[64]

Despite the particular prominence of Jews among the victims of the civil war, the conflict affected people of all ages, social groups and both sexes, prompting a raw struggle for survival and never-ending cycles of retaliatory violence. Neither the Whites nor the Reds could claim a decisive victory by the spring of 1919.[65] The temporary stalemate only ended when, in the spring and summer of that year, White forces launched major offensives against the Red Army with the aim of uniting their widely dispersed troops. In the north, in early March, Kolchak's armies started to advance from Siberia towards Archangelsk, with a second offensive towards the Ural Mountains. In the south, meanwhile, Denikin's 'Armed Forces of South Russia' launched an offensive towards Moscow that summer. By mid-April, Kolchak had succeeded in linking up with a small and beleaguered advance guard in Archangelsk, while his other armies had pushed the Bolsheviks back out of 300,000 square kilometres of territory. Ultimately, however, Kolchak failed to score a decisive victory and to break the stubborn resistance of the Red Army. By mid-summer his armies were thrown back beyond the Urals. During their long retreat east along the Trans-Siberian railway lines Kolchak's troops suffered enormous casualties caused by cold weather, typhus and constant attacks by partisans.[66] His men responded to the reversal in military fortunes and the hostile conditions of the retreat by using even more violence. As they moved eastwards, Kolchak ordered prisoners to be shot, hanged, or buried alive. In the Yekaterinburg region alone Kolchak's men executed an estimated 25,000 people.[67] This final outburst of anti-Bolshevik violence in the north could not, however, conceal that Kolchak and his armies were doomed. Kolchak's capital, Omsk, fell in November 1919. Kolchak himself retreated east to Irkutsk, where he was eventually arrested, put on trial and shot.[68]

Matters were not much better for the Whites in the south. In the summer and autumn of 1919, Denikin's 'Armed Forces of South Russia', composed of the Volunteer Army and strong Cossack troops, had been able to advance as far north as Orel, some 400 kilometres from Moscow, only to be repelled by the Red Army. The failure of the Orel offensive was followed by the collapse of Denikin's forces between November 1919 and January 1920, amid political conflict between the Volunteer Army and the Cossacks.[69]

By the beginning of 1920 it was increasingly clear that the Red Army was winning the civil war. When the remnants of the Volunteer Army found temporary refuge in the Crimean Peninsula, Denikin was replaced by General Pyotr Wrangel, a tsarist career officer with Baltic German family roots who had commanded various cavalry units during the Great War.[70] The Whites' Crimean refuge was easily defensible, the only land access being the narrow isthmus of Perekop, but the Whites were increasingly weak in numbers and lacked sufficient military resources. International support was also waning. The British, who had come to view a White defeat as inevitable, refused to provide any further assistance. The French, who had landed their own troops alongside Greek and Polish contingents in the Black Sea ports of Odessa and Sevastopol in December 1918, only to pull them out the following April amid the threat of mutinies, had no appetite to get involved again. The Red Army, by contrast, was able to increase its troops on the southern front after the Russo-Polish War of 1919–21 had come to an end. Eventually, in late 1921, the Red Army broke the last resistance on the Crimea.[71]

Wrangel's defeat effectively ended the Russian Civil War, even if localized peasant resistance continued until 1922. The reasons for the Red victory were many, but perhaps most important was the fact that the Bolsheviks came to be seen by many as the lesser of two evils, offering a somewhat more compelling and coherent vision of the future than their White adversaries, who could barely agree on any policy aims other than terminating Bolshevik rule. To be sure, the Red Army, too, had huge problems with maintaining discipline and suffered from mass desertions. Yet they always controlled the core of the Russian war economy around Petrograd and Moscow, while their heterogeneous opponents were widely dispersed around the periphery and often divided spatially as well as politically.[72]

Whatever the decisive reason for the Bolshevik victory, Lenin's eventual triumph came at a staggeringly high price for the country. After two revolutions and seven uninterrupted years of armed conflict, Russia in 1921 lay in ruins. In addition to its 1.7 million dead from the Great War, over three million people had perished in the civil war, while the great famine of 1921–2 alone, sparked by years of fighting and back-to-back droughts in the preceding years, killed some two million people through starvation.[73] Overall, as a result of civil war, expulsions, immigration and famine, the population in the territories that formally became the Soviet Union in 1922 had declined by a total of some ten million people, from about 142 million in 1917 to 132 million in 1922.[74]

For those who survived, the future seemed bleak, as Russia's economy had virtually collapsed during the years of war and civil conflict. Already by 1920 industrial production had fallen by some 80 per cent compared to 1914, while only 60 per cent of pre-war agricultural land remained cultivated. Lenin's New Economic Policy (NEP), introduced in 1921 to end the peasant rebellions and put the war-torn country back on its feet, came too late for most people.[75] In the cities severe food shortages caused mass starvation. Hunger was omnipresent, especially affecting children and older people. Intellectuals, too, whose irregular incomes had been further devalued by rampant inflation, were highly vulnerable. A report of the American Relief Administration of 1923 suggested that the entire Russian intelligentsia was threatened with extinction through starvation:

> Death was now more in evidence than life. Before my eyes died Feodor Batiushkov, the famous professor of philology, poisoned from eating uneatably filthy cabbage. Another one to die from hunger was S. Bengerov, professor of history and literature, he who gave to the Russian people entire editions of Shakespeare, of Schiller and of Pushkin . . . At the same period the philosopher V. V. Rosanov succumbed to starvation in Moscow. Before this death the latter roamed the streets in search of cigarette ends with which to appease his hunger . . .[76]

By the end of the civil war Russia was completely devastated. Millions of men and women had died as a consequence of war and famine, and an estimated seven million orphaned children were homeless, begging on the streets and selling their bodies to survive.[77] A good measure of the widespread desperation in Russia at the time were the huge numbers of refugees, a total of 2.5 million of whom had left the former Russian imperial territories by 1922.[78] While a total of 7.7 million people had already been displaced during the Great War, notably (though not exclusively) in eastern Europe, the civil war triggered a new wave of refugees who roamed the devastated landscapes of eastern Europe in search of safety and a better life.[79] By July 1921 550,000 former Russian subjects had fled to Poland.[80] A further 55,000 – including the family of Isaiah Berlin, who was to become one of the leading political thinkers of the twentieth century – had arrived in the Baltic States by 1922, but soon moved further westwards.[81]

Desirable European destinations for Russian refugees included London, Prague and Nice.[82] But the largest number of refugees, among them the political leaders of emigrant communities, made their way to Germany, which, despite the recently lost war, offered better economic prospects than most other central European countries. They numbered 560,000 by the autumn of 1920. Berlin – notably the districts of Schöneberg, Wilmersdorf and Charlottenburg (which then acquired its nickname 'Charlottengrad') – became a major centre of settlement for Russia's exiled community, which had created some seventy-two Russian publishing houses in the German capital by 1922.[83]

While most of the refugees from the western borderlands tried to get to western Europe, the city of Harbin in Manchuria became a major destination for exiled Russians from Siberia, who set up theatres and a music school that was to train, among others, the future Hollywood star Yul Brynner.[84] In addition, there were between 120,000 and 150,000 White Russian survivors of the final battles in the Crimea and their families, who were herded together in camps near Constantinople and Gallipoli.[85] As many of the refugee camps were quickly overcrowded, the Allies had little choice but to keep thousands of the emaciated Russian refugees interned on ships in the Sea of Marmara. 'The ship *Wladimir* that was meant to carry 600 passengers currently has more than 7,000 people aboard!' one member of the International Red Cross reported from Constantinople. 'Most of them live on the open deck, others in the hold, where they are suffocating.'[86]

In recognition of the scale of this human tragedy, the League of Nations eventually created a High Commission for Refugees in 1921, with the legendary Norwegian explorer, Fridtjof Nansen, as its first head. Nansen had qualified himself for the job not so much because of his widely reported polar expeditions of the mid-1890s, but through his experience in repatriating prisoners of war after 1918. His most historically significant achievement, however, was a legal document created in 1922 in response to the Russian refugee crisis: the Nansen Passport, which made it possible for stateless people to circulate and settle abroad under the patronage of the League of Nations and the High Commission for Refugees.[87]

While the future fortunes of the more than two million civil war refugees from Russia differed hugely, depending on circumstances and luck, many of them were – unsurprisingly – united in their staunchly anti-Bolshevik views. Berlin in particular became a hotbed for anti-Bolshevik Russian exile propaganda. Supported in their views by ethnic German refugees from the Baltics, Russian exiles wasted no time spreading horror stories about Lenin's Bolshevik movement, thus injecting new energy into the emerging far Right in Germany and further afield.[88]

As a result the Bolshevik Revolution and the subsequent civil war across the former imperial territories quickly interacted with revolutionary and counter-revolutionary movements further afield, either as a beacon of hope for those longing for violent socio-economic and political change, or as the nightmarish vision of an imminent takeover by the politicized masses.[89] The 'spectre of Communism', which Marx and Engels had identified in Europe in the spring of 1848 in their *Communist Manifesto*, was, in reality, something that was felt much more keenly by everyone in Europe after 1917. Prior to 1914, Marxist-inspired revolutionary violence had been confined to underground movements of the extreme left, which carried out individual assassinations against crowned heads. The Bolshevik Revolution changed everything. For the first time since 1789, a revolutionary movement had taken over a state.

Conservative and liberal politicians in the West, even Social Democrats, reacted with horror to events in Russia, though tellingly, newspaper reports tended to focus on the Red Terror while largely ignoring the atrocities committed by their 'White' opponents. Many of the stories came, of course, from Russian émigrés, who had lost everything and were therefore inclined to portray Bolshevik rule in the bleakest possible way. They found a receptive audience in western and central Europe, where – after a brief moment of shock and apathy on the part of Conservative parties in the autumn of 1918 – anti-Communist movements were gaining momentum, as politicians and businessmen feared that something akin to the Russian Revolution might be repeated in their own countries.[90]

As 1918 drew to a close, Britain's Minister of Munitions, Winston Churchill, told his constituency in an election speech in Dundee that the now defeated evil Hun had been replaced by a new force of moral deprivation in the East, a spectre threatening the values of the free world. 'Russia', he declared, 'is being rapidly reduced by the Bolsheviks to an animal form of barbarism . . . Civilisation is being completely extinguished over gigantic areas, while Bolsheviks hop and caper like troops of ferocious baboons amid the ruins of cities and the corpses of their victims.'[91]

By late 1918 there were few Western diplomats or foreign news-paper correspondents left in Russia to verify rumours or separate fact from fiction. Although the reality of the civil war was so terrible that it hardly needed any embellishment, fantastical stories about Lenin's regime flourished and drifted westwards: of a social order turned upside down, of a never-ending cycle of atrocities and retri-bution amid moral collapse in what had previously been one of the Great Powers of Europe. Several American newspapers reported that the Bolsheviks had introduced an electrically operated guillo-tine in Petrograd designed to decapitate 500 prisoners an hour, while in Britain a variety of publications featured apocalyptic reports from eyewitnesses that underlined the limitless evil of which the Bolshe-viks were apparently capable. The Bolsheviks, or so it was suggested, had 'nationalized' middle- and upper-class women who might now be raped at will by any member of the proletariat. Orthodox churches had been turned into brothels in which aristocratic women were forced to offer sexual services to ordinary workers. Chinese executioners had been recruited by the Bolsheviks for their know-ledge of ancient oriental torture techniques, while inmates in the infamous Cheka prisons had their heads stuck into cages filled with hungry rats in order to extort information.[92]

Furthermore, the internationally reported news of the murder of the tsar and his entire family in the summer of 1918 brought back uncomfortable memories of the escalation of the French Revolution after the execution of King Louis XVI and his wife, Marie Antoinette, in 1793. Unsurprisingly, given the nature of reports emanating from Russia, the Western media competed in painting the bleakest possible image of the Bolshevik leadership and their supporters. *The New York Times* referred to Lenin and his followers as 'human scum', while in London the conservative *Morning Post* described the Bolshe-vik regime as one in which 'emancipated criminals, wild idealists, Jewish Internationalists, all the cranks and most of the crooks, have joined hands in an orgy of passion and unreason'.[93] A German news-paper published a lengthy article on the Bolsheviks' 'unlimited terrorism' against everything considered 'middle class', and reports became even more critical of the situation in Russia after the German ambassador, Count Wilhelm von Mirbach, was shot dead by the

Socialist Revolutionary Yakov Blumkin in his Moscow residence in July 1918.[94] The apocalypse suddenly had a new name: 'Russian conditions', a term commonly used to describe an inversion of all moral values of 'the West'. Political posters of the Right began to portray Bolshevism as a spectral or skeletal figure with a bloody dagger clamped between its teeth. Variations of this poster appeared not only in France and Germany, but also in Poland and Hungary.[95]

Not dissimilar to the situation in the late eighteenth century when Europe's horrified ruling elites feared a Jacobin 'apocalyptic' war, many Europeans after 1917 assumed that Bolshevism would spread to 'infect' the rest of the old world, prompting violent mobilization and action against the supposed menace. What was characteristic of this menace, as it was perceived almost everywhere in Europe, was the seemingly faceless nature of its threat to the established order: from anonymous crowds that assaulted bourgeois notions of property to Jewish-Bolshevik world conspiracies. Such abstract fears were fuelled by the news about Bolshevik atrocities, many of them real, others exaggerated, which circulated widely in western Europe. Those concerned about Bolshevism spreading west had their fears confirmed when they read Lenin's or Trotsky's speeches calling for world revolution, received news of Communist parties being founded across Europe, or learned about Bolshevik-inspired putsches and civil wars taking place.[96]

The first and most immediate case of 'contagion' – or so it was perceived – was Finland in 1918. Due to its status as an autonomous duchy within the Russian Empire, Finland had been a non-combatant in the Great War, even though some 1,500 Finns volunteered to fight on either the Russian or the German side between 1914 and 1918.[97] Despite the lack of 'brutalization' through war, Finland experienced one of the proportionally bloodiest civil wars of the twentieth century: over 36,000 people (1 per cent of the population) died within the little more than three months of the conflict and its immediate aftermath. The prelude to the civil war came in mid-November 1917 when, in the shadow of revolutionary events in Russia, the Finnish trade unions joined forces with the Social Democrats and Otto Kuusinen's Finnish Bolsheviks in calling for a general strike, in which armed Red Guards were pitted against supporters of Finland's independence.[98]

Just seven weeks after the centre-right government of Pehr Evind Svinhufvud had declared his country's breakaway from revolutionary Russia in early December, Red Guards, with the support of Petrograd, toppled the government in Helsinki on 27 January 1918. While Svinhufvud fled on an ice-breaker across the Baltic Sea, a new government – the Council of People's Representatives – was set up. The script of the putsch seemed to follow the familiar trajectory of the Bolshevik Revolution in Petrograd a few months earlier. Yet despite the self-designations of the antagonists in Finland's ensuing civil war as 'Whites' and 'Reds', it would be wrong to conflate the two conflicts, as contemporaries frequently did. In reality, the two civil wars were quite distinct and the often alleged 'Russian involvement' in the Finnish revolution was actually rather marginal, with no more than 5 to 10 per cent of those fighting for the 'Reds' being Russian volunteers. More importantly, the Finnish 'Reds' were not Bolsheviks, at least not the majority. Even if Bolshevik-inspired Red Guards had carried out the coup in Helsinki, thereby triggering the civil war, it was the more moderate Finnish Social Democrats who almost immediately assumed control of the revolutionary movement, which temporarily gained power in the towns and industrial centres of southern Finland. [99]

Meanwhile their opponents, backed by the conservative-dominated Senate, controlled the more rural central and northern parts of the country. With active support from German troops, the military leader of the 'Whites' and former general in the Russian Imperial Army, Carl Mannerheim, defeated his opponents in the decisive battles at Tampere, Viipuri, Helsinki and Lahti in early 1918. Any further resistance was suppressed with the extreme violence typical of civil wars fought between members of the same local communities. When, for example, Mannerheim's counter-revolutionary troops seized the 'red capital' of revolutionary Finland, the southern city of Tampere, in March, they captured and subsequently executed more than 10,000 'Red' troops, while others died of malnutrition in the improvised prisoner camps.[100]

Even though the Finnish Civil War ended with a White victory, observers in the West remained concerned. 'Bolshevism', or so it seemed, was not peculiar to Russia; it was clearly spreading westwards – an impression reinforced by the central European revolutions of 1918–19. Contemporaries frequently perceived and portrayed Bolshevism as a festering wound or a contagious illness – a notion that became even more prominent after Bolshevism appeared to move further west and into the heartlands of central Europe in the spring of 1919.

8

The Apparent Triumph of Democracy

On 10 November 1918, one day after the birth of the first German democracy, the prominent editor-in-chief of the liberal daily *Berliner Tageblatt*, Theodor Wolff, published an enthusiastic commentary eulogizing the events of the previous day that had led to the abdication of Kaiser Wilhelm II:

> Like a sudden driving windstorm, the greatest of all revolutions has toppled the imperial regime together with all it comprised, from top to bottom. One can call it the greatest of all revolutions, since never before was such a solidly built and walled Bastille taken at one go . . . Yesterday morning, at least in Berlin, everything was still there. Yesterday afternoon, all of it had vanished.[1]

Not everyone, of course, shared Wolff's enthusiasm. Reactions to the events of November 1918 in Germany were, in fact, extremely varied. The vast majority of German soldiers, relieved at having survived the war, simply dispersed and returned home as soon as their units crossed back into their homeland. Others, notably sailors and soldiers who had served in the rear areas during the war, actively participated in the revolution that was to topple the German monarchy. Many of the veterans of the Great War became pacifists and were adamant that they never wanted anyone to go through the same experiences to which they had been subjected over the past four years.[2]

Among the front-line soldiers and officers who had maintained discipline throughout the extraordinarily difficult final weeks of the war, attitudes towards the revolution were more hostile. The initial response of arguably the best-known soldier of the Great War, the twenty-nine-year-old private Adolf Hitler, was characteristic of those in the front line. When Hitler, unconscious and temporarily blinded by poison gas in the last weeks of the war, awoke on 12 November 1918 in his military hospital bed in the Prussian town of Pasewalk, he felt that the world around him had changed beyond recognition. The once mighty Imperial German Army, in which he had served as a dispatch runner, had collapsed. The Kaiser had abdicated in the face of revolutionary turmoil. Hitler's homeland, Austria-Hungary, no longer existed. Upon receiving the news of the Central Powers' military defeat, he experienced a meltdown: 'I threw myself on my bed, and buried my burning head in my pillow and the duvet. I had not cried since the day I had stood at my mother's grave. Now I couldn't do anything else.' The perceived humiliation of 1918 remained a central tenet of the rest of Hitler's life until its violent end in the bunker in Berlin. Even in his final orders of April 1945 he insisted that there would be no repeat of 1918, no new version of the 'cowardly' capitulation at the end of the First World War. Germany and its people would burn, he declared, before any retreat or surrender could take place.[3]

On the home front, too, opinions were deeply divided, mostly along party-political lines. The Heidelberg-based medievalist Karl Hampe described the revolution of 9 November from the perspective of a middle-class intellectual, for whom Bismarck's nation state of 1871 had been the high point of Germany's national history. For Hampe, 9 November marked the 'most wretched day of my life! What has become of the Kaiser and the Reich? From the outside, we face mutilation (... and) a sort of debt servitude; internally we face ... civil war, starvation, chaos.'[4] The arch-conservative politician Elard von Oldenburg-Januschau (who would play an unfortunate role in the political events of January 1933, when he advised his old friend, President Paul von Hindenburg, to appoint Hitler as Chancellor) spoke for many German aristocrats when he wrote that he 'could not find words to express my sorrow over the events of November 1918; to describe how shattered I was. I felt the world collapsing, burying under its rubble all that I had lived for and all that my parents had taught me to cherish since I was a child.'[5]

The former Chancellor, Prince Bernhard von Bülow, in his desperation unsuccessfully searched for parallels in the past to express his horror at the events unfolding:

In Berlin on 9 November, I witnessed the beginnings of revolution. Alas, she did not come, as Ferdinand Lassalle had envisaged . . . in the shape of a radiant goddess, her hair flowing in the wind, and shod with sandals of iron. She was like an old hag, toothless and bald, her great feet slipshod and down at the heel . . . It revealed no such figures as the Danton whose statue in bronze stands on the Paris boulevard: erect, with clenched fist, to the left of his plinth a *sans-culotte* with fixed bayonet, to his right a tambour, beating up the *levée en masse*. Our revolution brought us no Gambetta to proclaim war to the knife and prolong our resistance by five months . . . I have never in my life seen anything more brutally vulgar than those straggling lines of tanks and lorries manned by drunken sailors and deserters from reserve formations which trailed through the Berlin streets on 9 November . . . I have seldom witnessed anything so nauseating, so maddeningly revolting and base, as the spectacle of half-grown louts, tricked out with the red armlets of social democracy, who, in bands of several at a time, came creeping up behind any officer wearing the Iron Cross or the order *Pour le mérite*, to pin down his elbows at his side and tear off his epaulettes.[6]

Others went even further in their despair. Distraught at the collapse of Imperial Germany and faced with an uncertain financial future, Albert Ballin, the Jewish shipping magnate and personal friend of Wilhelm II, committed suicide on 9 November 1918. Ballin, the head of HAPAG – once the world's largest shipping company – was simply unable to cope with the perceived bleakness of his country's future.[7]

At the same time, it is worth bearing in mind that – at least in the autumn of 1918 and throughout the spring of 1919 – the revolutionary transformation of Germany from a constitutional monarchy with limited parliamentary participation rights into a modern republic enjoyed the backing of an overwhelming majority of its people. They supported the momentous turn of events either out of conviction or because they felt that the country's internal democratization would be rewarded with more lenient peace terms at the upcoming Paris Peace Conference.[8]

When the monarchy was toppled in Germany on 9 November, decision-making powers were assumed by the Council of People's Deputies (*Rat der Volksbeauftragten*), which briefly reunited the two Social Democratic parties that had split in 1917 over their diverging attitudes towards the war: the moderate Majority Social Democrats (MSPD) and the more radical Independent Social Democrats (USPD). The Council consisted of three members each from both parties and was chaired by Friedrich Ebert, a long-time Social Democratic Party functionary with impeccable working-class credentials. Ebert, the first 'man of the people' to rule Germany since the Reich's foundation in 1871, was to become a central figure in the November revolution. The future first President of the Weimar Republic (a post he held until his premature death in 1925), Ebert came from humble beginnings. Born in the university town of Heidelberg in 1871, the son of a tailor, he had trained as a saddler apprentice while getting involved in the infant trade union movement. He worked on the editorial staff of the Social Democratic newspaper in the north German city of Bremen, but also ran a pub in the 1890s that quickly became a centre for local political activism. Ebert's reputation as a tireless advocate of working-class interests, coupled with his organizational skills, secured his election to the national Parliament in 1912, when the SPD became the strongest political party in the Reichstag.[9]

Ebert was in many ways a typical example of the pragmatism that characterized the second generation of Social Democratic leaders in Germany. While a Marxist, his primary political objective was the day-to-day improvement of working-class life through reforms. In 1913, Ebert was elected joint chairman of the SPD, alongside the more radical Hugo Haase, a well-known German-Jewish lawyer and socialist politician from the East Prussian city of Königsberg.[10]

Haase, a pacifist, had reluctantly maintained party discipline in 1914 and voted in favour of the war loans. But he eventually parted ways with Ebert in 1917 on becoming chairman of the newly founded Independent Social Democrats, who demanded an immediate peace. Meanwhile Ebert felt that it was his and the Majority Social Democrats' 'damned duty and obligation' to co-operate with the government as well as with the more middle-class Centre Party and the left-liberal Progressive Party in order to prevent the descent into chaos that characterized the Russian experience. Despite his Marxist background and beliefs, Germany's transformation into a parliamentary system, not a Bolshevik-style revolution, was Ebert's objective. As he pointed out in conversation with the Kaiser's last Chancellor, Prince Max von

Baden, a Communist revolution was the last thing he desired: 'I don't want that, indeed I hate it like sin.'[11]

Ebert's statement reflected the fact that, by 1918, the MSPD was no longer a revolutionary party in a traditional Marxist sense. Instead, its policies focused on developing a parliamentary democracy, voting rights for women, the improvement of material working conditions, and the expansion of the welfare state. All of this was to be achieved through gradual reforms rather than revolution. Ebert was fully aware that, unlike Tsarist Russia, Imperial Germany was not an auto-cratic state. Despite its semi-authoritarian constitution that reserved the Kaiser, and not the Parliament, the right to appoint and dismiss governments, the Wilhelmine Empire offered the working classes sig-nificant organizational opportunities and a certain degree of political participation through universal male suffrage. It provided a legal sys-tem and a level of social and economic security that most Russians at the time could only dream of. To be sure, glaring socio-economic inequalities persisted within German society, but by 1914 it was widely accepted among a majority of the working classes that more could be gained through reforms than through a revolution. It was this realization that made the 'Ebert Generation' decisively reject a Bolshevik-style bid for power.[12]

Once the Council of People's Deputies had been formed under Ebert's leadership, a temporary calm set in. However, the creation of the Coun-cil merely postponed the burning question of the future direction of Germany's reform and renewal. Unlike the left wing of the USPD, the leaders of the MSPD did not want to embark on any radical socialist experiments that might risk civil war and an Allied invasion. The SPD had advocated a democratic renewal of Germany for many years, and a return to the Orthodox Marxist mantra of 'class war' would have been rightly perceived as a betrayal of that long-standing reformist position. Ebert and other leading Social Democrats were more con-cerned to tackle the most urgent problems of the hour: preparing a peace treaty that would formally bring the war to a close, ensuring adequate food supplies for the starving population, and the demobiliza-tion of several million soldiers.[13] Each of these problems represented an enormous challenge for an inexperienced government. Germany had just lost a war of unprecedented scale and destructiveness – a war in which more than 13 million Germans (nearly 20 per cent of the population in 1914) had served and two million had died. In addition, some 2.7 million German soldiers had been physically injured or psychologically damaged during the war. Unlike in the victorious states of the Great War, the dilemma of how to justify the sacrifices of sons, brothers and fathers after a lost war preoccupied (and divided) the German public for years to come, as it did the populations of all the other European countries that had been defeated in the autumn of 1918.[14]

It was against the background of this dilemma that on 10 December 1918, at the Brandenburg Gate in Berlin, Ebert greeted troops returning from the front with the famous words: 'No enemy has vanquished you.' Ebert's words were not delusionary, but rather born out of a desire to co-opt the army into supporting the new regime in the face of a potential challenge by either right-wing opposition or those advocating a more radical revolution in Germany. For the same reason, Ebert had come to a pragmatic agreement with Ludendorff's successor in the Army High Command, General Wilhelm Groener, an agreement that has often wrongly been criticized as a Faustian pact with the old imperial army. On 10 November, Groener had assured Ebert of the loyalty of the armed forces. In return, Ebert promised that the government would take prompt action against potential leftist uprisings, that he would call elections for a National Assembly, and that the professional officer corps would remain in control of military command.[15]

Negotiated change, not violent upheaval, was thus the hallmark of the initial phase of the German revolution in November 1918. This applied both to the world of politics and to the social arena: on 15 November business leaders and trade unions forged an agreement on wage arbitration, the introduction of the eight-hour day, and workers' representation in companies with more than fifty employees. Known as the Stinnes-Legien Agreement after its two main signatories – the leading industrialist Hugo Stinnes and the chairman of the Free Trade Unions, Carl Legien – the deal pre-empted a potential nationalization from below or radical redistribution of property that would have been in the interest of neither the employers nor the SPD-dominated Free Trade Unions.[16]

The long-term question of Germany's political future, however, was to be decided by a democratically elected constitutive National

Assembly – at least that is what Ebert, the MSPD, and parts of the Independent Socialists intended. For this reason general elections for the Constituent Assembly were conducted as quickly as possible. When the elections were held on 19 January 1919, the electorate returned an overwhelming majority of 76 per cent for the three parties that firmly stood for the democratic renewal of Germany: the Majority Social Democrats, the liberal German Democratic Party (DDP) and the Catholic Centre Party.[17]

The democratic transformation of Germany bore strong similarities with events in neighbouring Austria-Hungary. What made the revolution here more complex, however, was the overlap of national and social revolution.[18] Before the war, the Dual Monarchy had been Europe's third most populous state (after Imperial Russia and the German Reich), and one of its most ethnically diverse empires. Ever since 1918 it has been commonly suggested that the collapse and disintegration of the Austro-Hungarian Empire were due primarily to the centrifugal powers of nationalism – an ideology that grew exponentially in the nineteenth century. According to this now outdated reading, Vienna's military defeat simply provided the different nationalities within the empire with an opportunity to realize the independent statehood that they had long desired.[19]

In more recent years historians have painted a different picture: even if Slavic nationalisms, in particular, had posed a challenge to the existence of the multi-ethnic state, the reasons for the empire's eventual demise are to be found in the years of the Great War itself rather than in the small pre-war nationalist movements.[20] Prominent among the short-term factors that enabled a revolution in Austria-Hungary were the material deprivations of large sections of the population, notably in Austria's cities during the war years. By late 1917 parts of its urban populations were starving, thus significantly increasing the potential for civil unrest.[21] Strikes in Austria initially took the form of protests against high prices and poor food distribution. As in Russia in 1917 and Germany in 1918, demands for 'bread and peace' ultimately ushered in widespread strikes, notably in January 1918. Within days nearly a million workers had downed tools across Austria, Hungary, Galicia and Moravia; demands grew for 'the most speedy end to the war' and for national self-determination.[22] This was followed at the beginning of February by a short-lived sailors' mutiny at the naval bases of Pola and Cattaro, driven by complaints about food shortages and demands for an immediate end to the war.[23]

As in Germany, the strikes and mutinies in Austria-Hungary did not cause the collapse of the regime or the war effort. What mattered more was that the general mood was changing within the army, which had suffered several serious setbacks during the First World War. Notably on the Eastern Front, the Austro-Hungarian Army was under constant pressure and lost enormous numbers of soldiers as prisoners. Increasingly Vienna was dependent on German military assistance, both in Galicia and on the Italian front. These cumulative pressures intensified as the war dragged on; and in the last months of the war the Austro-Hungarian Army, once a main pillar of the multi-ethnic empire, crumbled. By the autumn of 1918 the army was short of supplies and its soldiers were going hungry. Increasing incidents of desertion left it in no position to fight effectively.[24] Once it became apparent, with the failure of the final Austrian offensive in Italy and the German defeats in the west, that the war was lost, the Habsburg Empire's army fell apart as military discipline collapsed.[25] Non-Germans in the Austro-Hungarian Army refused to continue the fight for an empire that now appeared doomed to be replaced by independent nation states. In October 1918, Slav and Hungarian soldiers, unwilling to prolong a lost war, were refusing to obey orders.[26] The end of imperial loyalties in the final weeks of the war was to give rise to an Austrian version of the German 'stab-in-the-back' legend: senior Habsburg officers such as the two wartime Chiefs of Staff of the Habsburg Imperial Army, Conrad von Hötzendorf and Arthur Arz von Straussenburg, were to claim later that the empire had been defeated through the unwillingness of its Slavic population to fight.[27]

The total breakdown of military discipline became evident on 30 October 1918 when even German-speaking Austrian soldiers in the capital took to the streets of Vienna wearing red cockades, while others sported cockades in black, red and gold – the colours of the liberal pan-German revolution of 1848. In ever-increasing numbers, soldiers and junior officers joined the revolutionary movements in the empire's principal cities, Vienna and Budapest.[28]

The demonstrations of 30 October rallied around calls for the proclamation of a republic and the release from prison of Friedrich Adler, the radicalized son of the Austrian Social Democratic Party's founder, Victor Adler. In the first decade of the twentieth century, Friedrich Adler had established for himself a reputation as an outstandingly talented scientist. Yet he rejected the chair of theoretical physics in Zurich (a post subsequently offered to Adler's lifelong friend, Albert Einstein) in order to devote himself to politics full-time. In 1911 he became party secretary of the Austrian Social Democrats, but fell out with his comrades when his party approved the war credits in 1914. Increasingly radicalized, Adler wasted no time in publicly attacking the party leadership (including his father) and the political establishment of Austria-Hungary in a series of newspaper articles and pamphlets. In October 1916 he went further and shot Count Karl von Stürgkh, Minister-President of Cisleithania (the northern and western 'Austrian' parts of the Dual Monarchy), in a deliberate act of protest against the war. Originally sentenced to death for the assassination of von Stürgkh, Adler was pardoned by Kaiser Karl, who commuted his sentence to eighteen years in prison. As one of his last acts as emperor, Karl released Adler from prison in November 1918.[29]

Adler's reappearance on Vienna's political scene further invigorated the demonstrations, which by now included loud demands for the abdication of the emperor. On 3 November an Austrian daily newspaper vividly compared the revolutionary mood in Vienna with the delirium of the Spanish flu:

> Burning fever has befallen many of its inhabitants, raging through their bodies, impairing their senses. Their limbs refuse to obey; their heads are full of the 'painful mass' which suggests wild nightmares and agonizing visions. And just like the individual citizen, the whole 'huge sick body' of the town is smitten by a fever attack, sapping the vigour that enabled it to carry its heavy burden for so long. Like a 'red flag' the feverish blaze is flickering, finding its expression in a cry mouthed by hundreds of thousands: Revolution![30]

So-called 'Red Guards', inspired by events in Russia, marched through the city, attracting left-wing intellectuals like the famous journalist Egon Erwin Kisch and the Expressionist writer Franz Werfel, as well as radicalized soldiers and workers. The Austro-Marxist Otto Bauer, who was to become Vienna's first post-war Minister of Foreign Affairs, commented on the developments in the city with growing concern:

> The wildly agitated homecomers, the desperate unemployed men and women, the militants rejoicing in a romantic revolutionary ideal joined with those disabled by the war, who wanted to take revenge for their personal destiny on a blameworthy social order. They joined with morbidly excited women whose husbands had languished as prisoners of war for years, with intellectuals and writers of all kind, who all of a sudden, confronted with Socialism, were full of the utopian radicalism of the neophyte. They joined with the Bolshevik agitators sent home from Russia.[31]

By this stage the imperial state had little to offer in terms of resistance. Each day thousands of ex-soldiers arrived back in Vienna and other Austrian cities, many of them politicized and heavily armed.[32] To be sure, not all of them were enthusiastic about the empire's defeat and revolution. In their diaries and memoirs, many Austrian ex-officers invoked the horrors of returning from the front in 1918 to an entirely hostile world of political and social upheaval, triggered by the temporary collapse of military hierarchies and public order. The future Higher SS and Police Leader in the occupied Netherlands during the Second World War, Hanns Albin Rauter, who returned to the Styrian city of Graz in 1918, emphasized his first contact with the 'red mob' as an 'eye-opener': 'When I finally arrived in Graz, I found that the Communists had taken the streets.' Confronted by a group of Communist soldiers, 'I pulled my gun and I was arrested. This was how the *Heimat* welcomed me.'[33]

Being arrested by soldiers of lower rank reinforced Rauter's perception of having returned to a 'world turned upside down', a revolutionary world in which hitherto unquestionable norms and values, social hierarchies, institutions and authorities had suddenly become obsolete. Met with public unrest and personal insults, the 'bitter anger' of counter-revolutionaries soon turned into 'a burning desire to return to a soldier's existence as soon as possible, to stand up for the humiliated Fatherland . . .'. Only then could 'the shame of a gloomy present' be forgotten.[34]

In the initial phase of the revolution, however, such voices remained those of a minority, as the political Right in central Europe seemed paralyzed by defeat and revolution. On 11 November, for example, Franz Brandl, Vienna's superintendent of police, noted that in Austria the forces of the Right appeared to have disappeared while the Left dominated the scene: 'One sees and hears nothing of activity on the part of the Christian Social or German Nationalist party leaders. As if the earth has swallowed them up! The Reds hold all the cards!'[35]

Despite the enormous potential for violence, the Austrian revolution – like its German counterpart – remained remarkably peaceful, expressing itself in mass demonstrations rather than a violent coup. Even Friedrich Adler, whose influence on the far Left was crucial, openly opposed a Bolshevik-style revolution.[36] On 11 November, Kaiser Karl finally accepted the inevitable when he issued a carefully worded proclamation in which he recognized the Austrian people's right to determine the future form of their state and renounced his own 'participation in the administration of the State'. He consciously omitted the word 'abdication' in the hope that 'his people' would choose to recall him at some point in the future. Karl and his wife, Zita, left for exile in Switzerland the following spring. He clearly had second thoughts about his decision of November 1918, for in 1921 he made two serious but ultimately unsuccessful attempts to reclaim the throne of Hungary. Following his second failed attempt at restoration in Budapest, the Allies deported him to the isolated Portuguese island of Madeira, where the last Habsburg Emperor died of pneumonia on 1 April 1922 at the age of thirty-four.[37]

The provisional National Assembly that convened in Vienna on 12 November 1918, one day after the emperor's abdication, elected the Social Democrat Karl Renner as Chancellor. As in Germany, the future government was to be decided in general elections, which were held on 16 February 1919, bringing about a grand coalition government of the two main democratic parties, the Social Democratic Party and the conservative Christian Social Party. Despite the difficult circumstances of the Austrian Republic's birth and the inadequate food supplies, amplified by the Allied decision not to lift the economic blockade, many Austrians hoped that the successful introduction of democracy would make the peacemakers in Paris look favourably on the young republic.[38]

Similar hopes were cherished in Hungary where, in late October 1918, the power of government had been handed to a democratic coalition movement headed by Count Mihály Károlyi, a liberal whose political ideas were rooted in the tradition of the 1848 revolution. Károlyi had long promoted a political programme aimed at Hungarian independence, and thus a revocation of the 1867 'Compromise' that established the Dual Monarchy of Austria-Hungary. He also advocated universal suffrage and land reform – an interesting proposition given that Károlyi himself was one of the biggest landowners in Hungary. In order to achieve his goals, Károlyi's United Party of Independence (generally known as the Károlyi Party) struck an alliance with the bourgeois Radicals and the Hungarian Social Democrats, and formed a National Committee. Károlyi proclaimed himself Provisional President, a role that was formalized in January 1919 when the National Council elected him as President. Convinced that the only chance to retain Hungary's territorial integrity in the post-war world consisted in repealing the constitutional union with Austria, Károlyi severed all legal ties with Vienna on 16 November 1918. Hungary, ruled by the Habsburgs since 1526, had become an independent republic.[39]

If the Hungarian secession and democratization process were partly pragmatic events driven by the desire to secure favourable peace terms for Budapest, revolutionary events in Bulgaria, the first of the Central Powers to accept defeat, were initially more chaotic. Unlike Germany or Austria-Hungary, Bulgaria had experienced anti-war protests at home and at the front ever since the country's leadership decided to go to war against the Entente in October 1915. Chronic food-supply problems, war-weariness and popular objection to fighting alongside Germany and Bulgaria's old regional rival, the Ottoman Empire, led to consistently high numbers of disturbances at the front. Between 1915 and the spring of 1918 some 40,000 Bulgarian soldiers were court-martialled, 1,500 of them being sentenced to death and shot.[40]

Unrest was also widespread on the Bulgarian home front and found expression in protests and riots by women across the country over food shortages, notably in 1916 and 1918. The women's riots had a significant impact on the soldiers' morale on the front line, triggering numerous cases of refusal to fight. News of the Russian Revolution of 1917 and the Fourteen Points proposed by President Woodrow Wilson in January 1918 stimulated fresh waves of anti-military propaganda among the soldiers and further increased their desire to end the war.[41]

From the summer of 1918 the situation on the front line became increasingly untenable. Exhausted by years of uninterrupted fighting, undermined by the collapsing morale on the home front, and influenced by the anti-military propaganda of socialists and agrarians, the Bulgarian troops were in a state of revolutionary restlessness. Alarming letters from front-line officers arrived in Sofia, warning that unless a peace treaty was signed by the middle of September the army would collapse. As one soldier put it in a letter from the front: 'I have never in my life seen such a terrible discontent of so many worn-out and suffering people.' Even the commander-in-chief of the Bulgarian Army had to confess in a letter to the government: 'The roles have changed, now the command depends not on the commanders, but on subordinate people; soldiers dictate their will and their understanding to the commanders.'[42]

The social and economic crisis soon affected the government. On 21 June 1918, Prime Minister Vasil Radoslavov resigned. A Bulgarian government led by the more conciliatory Alexander Malinov, who was willing to negotiate a settlement with the Entente, replaced him. Yet time was slipping away for the government. Even before the Salonika armistice was signed on 29 September between Bulgaria and the Allies, following the Allied breakthrough on the Macedonian front, thousands of disillusioned soldiers had started to march on to Sofia. They were determined to topple the government and force the abdication of Tsar Ferdinand, who they held responsible for entering the war on the side of the Central Powers in the first place. Some 15,000 of them gathered at Radomir, a small town south-west of the capital, where they were met by Alexander Stambolijski, Bulgaria's charismatic future Prime Minister. The leading representative of the Bulgarian Agrarian National Union (BANU) and an outspoken republican, Stambolijski had spent the war years in prison after attacking the tsar in a private audience when Ferdinand sided with the Central Powers in 1915, and for publishing the details of their confrontation in his newspaper.

As the growing group of rebels approached the outskirts of Sofia on 30 September, they were met by a highly motivated force of loyal Bulgarian military cadets and German soldiers. Their anger at the rebellious 'traitors' had already been vented two days earlier when the cadets held up a train transporting injured Bulgarian soldiers from the front. Accusing them of defeatism and Bolshevik subversion of the front, the loyalist troops had executed some 500 of the injured. Over the following days they proceeded to crush the Radomir rebellion with heavy artillery, followed by mass arrests and massacres, in which about 3,000 supporters of the uprising were killed and 10,000 wounded.[43]

The surviving supporters of the Radomir rebellion, including Stambolijski, went into hiding. In the eyes of Bulgarians loyal to the old regime, the Radomir rebellion was a reflection of internal betrayal, demonstrating how deeply communist propaganda had infiltrated the army, thereby encouraging ordinary soldiers to lay down their arms and turn on the monarchy. In the decades that followed, the deep internal divisions in Bulgarian politics were reflected in the vastly different interpretations of the Radomir rebellion as either an insurrection of treacherous 'oath-breakers' or as an event that regrettably failed to turn into a revolution resembling the one in Russia.[44]

Despite the defeat of the rebellion, some of its core demands – peace at any price and a democratization of the country – were actually met with the signing of the armistice and the abdication of Tsar Ferdinand on 4 October, one of the Allies' core conditions for peace. Although Ferdinand, who fled the country for one of his vast estates abroad, was replaced by his oldest son, Boris, his departure was rightly celebrated as the beginning of a new era. Real power now lay in the hands of the government, which, after the resignation of Malinov's administration in November, was formed by a coalition of Social Democrats and the Agrarian Party, BANU. Under the leadership of Teodor Teodorov, who had studied law in Odessa and Paris before making a name for himself as a liberal law reformer and pre-war Finance Minister, the new government was now in charge of the unenviable task of bringing peace to a country that had suffered extremely through six years of almost uninterrupted war.[45]

Since the beginning of the Balkan Wars in 1912, southern Dobrudja, Macedonia and eastern Thrace had been gained and lost again, amid unprecedented misery. The Bulgarian Army had suffered some 250,000 casualties, including 150,000 severely wounded. As elsewhere in Europe, those crippled, maimed or blinded in military service remained omnipresent in everyday life in interwar Sofia, and in smaller towns and villages. During 1918 alone some 180,000 people on the home front had perished from hunger and disease. However, the full extent of the Bulgarian national catastrophe is only grasped when the losses of the Balkan Wars of 1912–13 are taken into account. Out of a total population of five million, Bulgaria suffered some 157,000 dead and 154,000 wounded in six years of fighting between 1912 and 1918. In addition, more than 100,000 ethnically Bulgarian refugees had flooded into the country from the now lost territories of Dobrudja, Macedonia and Eastern Thrace, posing almost insurmountable challenges to a bankrupt and defeated state.

At least in this respect, there was some similarity between the Bulgarian case and that of the Ottoman Empire. Although Constantinople experienced no socialist revolution of the sort that took place elsewhere in Europe between 1917 and 1919, military defeat in the Great War brought about the demise of the Committee of Union and Progress (CUP) that had ruled the wartime Ottoman Empire. After the empire's unconditional surrender at Moudros in October 1918 and the flight of the CUP's wartime leadership to Odessa, the formerly oppositional liberal Freedom and Coalition Party stepped onto the political scene and ruled the country during the armistice period (1918–23).[46] With the support of Mehmed VI, who had been crowned sultan only four months earlier, the liberals wasted no time in reversing the wartime policies of the CUP: deported Kurds and displaced survivors of the Armenian genocide were encouraged to return home. After international and public pressure, the new rulers even instigated a formal criminal inquiry in January 1919 into the CUP's wartime policies. Police in Constantinople arrested a large number of prominent Unionists on the basis of official warrants for over three hundred individuals on charges of mass murder and corruption. The arrests continued throughout the spring, after the appointment of the sultan's liberal brother-in-law, Damad Ferid Pasha, as Grand Vizier.[47]

Not dissimilarly to the situation in central Europe, the new government in Constantinople inherited political responsibility for a country that had been devastated by the war in numerous ways: the Ottoman Army had lost some 800,000 soldiers (nearly 25 per cent of its troops).[48] Civilian casualties were even higher. In addition to the more than one million Armenians who had died in the genocidal wartime deportations unleashed by the CUP, the First World War claimed at least two and a half million Ottoman lives. Most of them were civilians, who succumbed to disease or starvation as a result of the combined impact of the Anglo-French naval blockade, mismanagement in the distribution of scarce foodstuffs, and the effects of a severe locust plague that resulted in one out of seven people starving to death in Syria alone.[49]

Despite these terrible legacies, the Ottoman Empire's new liberal rulers at first benefited from public support (at least in the capital). As in the vanquished states of central Europe, this support was based on the vain hope that they could deliver a merciful peace treaty. Although, in hindsight, the initial optimism of what the German theologian and philosopher Ernst Troeltsch called 'the dreamland of the armistice period' must seem naive, it was a powerful sentiment in all of the defeated states of Europe at the time.[50] After all, from the vantage point of late 1918 and early 1919, it looked as if moderate reformers had triumphed in the empires of the former Central Powers, while supporters of a Bolshevik-style revolution had been marginalized. The new rulers conveyed their firm belief to the peacemakers in Paris that their regimes had broken with the autocratic traditions of the past, thus fulfilling the key criteria of Wilson's Fourteen Points for a 'just peace'.

It is easy for us now to dismiss such rhetoric as purely pragmatic or even an opportunistic move in the shadow of defeat. Yet many policymakers in the vanquished states, and notably in central Europe, firmly believed that they had delivered where the liberal revolutionaries of 1848 had failed. It was no coincidence that the Weimar Republic, named after the central German town of Weimar in which the Constituent Assembly convened in January 1919, was to adopt the black, red and golden banner of the 1848 revolution as its national flag. In Austria, meanwhile, democrats celebrated the historical coincidence that the

Republic of German-Austria *(Deutsch-Österreich)* had come to life almost exactly seventy years after Field Marshal Prince Windisch-Graetz's victory over the Viennese revolution of 1848.[51] The meaning of all this was obvious to everyone: the moderate revolutionaries of 1918 were correcting the erroneous political developments since 1848. Liberal democracy, which had failed to come into existence then, had finally emerged triumphant.

9

Radicalization

If, in the late autumn of 1918, it looked as if democracy had become the unchallenged form of state government in central Europe, the situation changed that winter, as unresolved tensions between moderate and radical revolutionaries erupted violently. In Germany, the Majority Social Democrats (MSPD) were adamant that only a democratically elected National Assembly could decide on the future constitution of the country. Yet not everyone was willing to accept this position. The representatives of the left wing of the Independent Social Democratic Party (USPD), the so-called 'Spartacus League' (named after the leader of the largest slave rebellion in ancient Rome), rejected the idea of a National Assembly and preferred a political system in which all power was in the hands of the soldiers' and workers' councils. They eventually joined forces with other radical left-wing splinter groups to become the Communist Party of Germany (KPD) in late 1918.[1]

The two dominant figures of the communist Left in Germany at that point were Rosa Luxemburg and Karl Liebknecht. Liebknecht, arguably the most prominent proponent of radical change outside Russia, was from Germany's most distinguished socialist family. Born in Leipzig in 1871, he was the son of Wilhelm Liebknecht, a close friend and collaborator of Karl Marx and, alongside the SPD's long-serving chairman, August Bebel, one of the founding fathers of Social Democracy. Karl Liebknecht was significantly more radical than his father. Having studied law and political economy at the universities of Leipzig and Berlin, he opened a law practice in Berlin in 1899, and specialized in defending fellow socialists in the German courts.[2]

In 1907, Liebknecht's anti-militarist writings got him into trouble with the courts, which sentenced him to eighteen months in prison. His imprisonment only helped to improve his standing among his followers. Liebknecht was elected to the Reichstag as a Social Democrat in 1912. In 1914 he was the only Member of Parliament to vote against the war credits. Liebknecht and other prominent left-wing critics of the war – including Rosa Luxemburg and Clara Zetkin, a pioneer of the socialist women's movement – soon formed their own organization within the SPD: the 'Group of the International', which renamed itself as the Spartacus League in 1916. In their periodic pamphlets *Spartakusbriefe* (*Spartacus Letters*), Liebknecht and his followers called for a socialist revolution and an immediate end to the war. Unsurprisingly, the *Spartacus Letters* were soon banned, and Liebknecht – despite his ostensible immunity as a Member of Parliament – was arrested and sent to the Eastern Front. Released from active military service in 1915 due to his ill health, he was arrested again on May Day 1916 for leading an illegal anti-war demonstration on Berlin's Potsdamer Platz. This time he was sentenced to four years' imprisonment for high treason. He was released in late October 1918, when political prisoners received an amnesty as part of the general democratization of Imperial Germany, and returned to Berlin. Here Liebknecht led another anti-war demonstration that culminated in a symbolically charged march to the Russian Embassy, where Bolshevik emissaries hosted a reception for him.[3]

Liebknecht's most important ally in the weeks and months after the war was the Polish-born Marxist activist and intellectual, Rosa Luxemburg, with whom he shared the editorship of the flagship communist publication, *Die Rote Fahne* (*The Red Flag*). Born as Róża Luksemburg in the then Russian city of Zamość in 1871, she was the youngest child of a secular Jewish wood merchant who afforded all of his daughters an extensive humanist education. Rosa had become involved in revolutionary activities as a schoolgirl in Warsaw and had to flee the city to escape persecution by the tsarist police. From 1889 she lived in Zurich, one of the centres for socialist refugees from all over Europe. Here her lover, Leo Jogiches, a socialist from Vilnius, supported her materially during her studies at Zurich University. He also backed her in founding the Social Democratic Party of Poland and Lithuania, whose members included the future head of the Cheka in Russia, Felix Dzerzhinsky.[4]

In 1898, Luxemburg obtained German citizenship through marriage to the only son of her Zurich host family, Gustav Lübeck, while continuing her relationship with Jogiches. Moving to Berlin that same year, she immediately joined the SPD and actively engaged in the ongoing controversy between reformist and revolutionary Social Democrats. As a radical proponent of revolution, she was imprisoned three times between 1904 and 1906, and again during the Great War, during which time she continued her political activism for peace and revolution through a series of pamphlets that were smuggled out of her prison cell in Breslau. On her release in early November 1918, she returned to Berlin, where she joined Liebknecht as one of the leaders of the radical Left.[5]

Under the slogan 'All power to the councils!' Luxemburg and Liebknecht constantly demanded 'a second revolution', notably in their articles in *Die Rote Fahne*. On 18 November, ten days after her release from Breslau prison and return to Berlin, Luxemburg demanded a continuation of the revolution beyond the overthrow of the imperial state: 'Scheidemann-Ebert are the appointed leaders of the German Revolution in its current stage. But the Revolution is not standing still. Its law of life is rapid advancement . . .'[6]

Just how tense the relationship between the different factions within Germany's labour movement had grown became evident by Christmas 1918, when a long-smouldering conflict between the left-leaning People's Navy Division (*Volksmarinedivision*) and Berlin's military commander, the Majority Social Democrat Otto Wels, finally escalated. Wels perceived the People's Navy Division as a threat, an armed unit in the capital that appeared to favour a Bolshevik-style revolution. Wels insisted on a significant reduction of the Division and withheld the soldiers' wages as leverage. In response on 23 December the mutinous sailors took Wels prisoner. The Chancellor, Friedrich Ebert, reacted quickly: without conferring with his coalition partner, the USPD, he asked the army for immediate military assistance. The ensuing bloody fighting in the city centre, around the Hohenzollerns' Imperial Castle, ended with an embarrassing military defeat of the government troops.[7]

The 'Battle of Christmas Eve' heightened the relative weakness of Ebert's government and had two immediate consequences. The first was the end of the short-lived pragmatic alliance between the USPD and the MSPD. On 29 December the three USPD representatives left the Council of People's Deputies, strongly protesting against Ebert's unilateral decision to dispatch troops against the sailors. Second, the Prussian Prime Minister, Paul Hirsch (MSPD), decided to dismiss the chief of the Berlin police, Emil Eichhorn (USPD), who had come to the aid of the People's Navy Division by sending out the Berlin Security Guard (*Sicherheitswehr*).[8] The USPD and the more radical Left, including the KPD, reacted to what they regarded as a deliberate provocation by calling for a mass demonstration against the Ebert government on 5 January 1919. The situation quickly escalated. One group of armed demonstrators occupied the building of the Social Democratic newspaper, *Vorwärts*, along with other publishing houses in Berlin's newspaper district. On the evening of 5 January these spontaneous actions were followed by the formation of a 'Revolutionary Committee', while Liebknecht further escalated the situation by once more demanding the 'overthrow of the Ebert-Scheidemann government'. The twofold goal of the ensuing 'Spartacist Uprising' was to prevent the planned election of a National Assembly in late January and to bring into being a 'dictatorship of the proletariat'.[9]

Even if the actual power base of the Spartacus League was small, its very existence raised concerns among the leading Majority Social Democrats. Ebert took the threat very seriously. To him, the Bolshevik Revolution in Russia offered a vivid example of the fact that a determined minority of radicals were capable of wresting control from a more moderate government, even if they did not have anything like the support of the majority of the population. In Ebert's view the communist uprising in Berlin in early January 1919 bore more than a fleeting resemblance to the Bolsheviks' successful bid for power in the autumn of 1917. He was utterly determined to prevent the events in Petrograd from being repeated in Berlin, with force if necessary.[10]

A central figure in the resolution of this situation was the MSPD's military expert, Gustav Noske, who, following the departure of the USPD from government, had assumed responsibility for the army and navy within the Council of People's Deputies. With the famous words '[s]omebody has to be the bloodhound, and I do not shrink from this responsibility', Noske assumed command of the government troops in and around Berlin.[11] His task was to re-establish 'law and order' with all available means. For this purpose, he did not rely on regular troops alone, but also and mainly on *Freikorps* volunteers, some of whom served in Germany in the winter of 1918–19 before joining the military campaign in the Baltic over the following months.[12]

In calling on volunteers to terminate the apparent threat of Bolshevism hanging over the German capital, Noske was enlisting those members of German society who had loathed and opposed the revolution from the very beginning, and who had been waiting for an opportunity to settle scores for the past two months. They were not fighting *for* the Republic, but against 'Bolshevism'. In the *Freikorps*, former front-line soldiers, infuriated by defeat and the subsequent revolution, joined forces with untested cadets and right-wing students, who compensated for their lack of combat experience by often surpassing the war veterans in terms of radicalism, activism and brutality.

For many of these younger volunteers, who had come of age in a bellicose atmosphere saturated with tales of heroic bloodshed but who had missed out on first-hand experience of the 'storms of steel', the militias offered a welcome opportunity to live a romanticized warrior existence. As one militia leader observed, many younger volunteers tried to impress their superiors through 'rough militarist behaviour', which was 'nurtured as a virtue in large parts of the postwar youth', and which deeply affected the general tone and atmosphere within paramilitary organizations after 1918.[13] Once they had joined paramilitary units dominated by former shock-troop officers, younger volunteers were keen to prove their worthiness within a community of often highly decorated warriors and 'war heroes'.[14]

Together the battle-hardened veterans of the Great War and the younger 'romantic' volunteers formed explosive all-male subcultures in which brutal violence was an acceptable, if not a desirable, form of political expression. Action, not ideology, was the defining characteristic of these groups. They were driven forward not by a revolutionary vision of a new political utopia, but by a common rhetoric of restoring order and an interlocking series of social antipathies.[15] In marked contrast to the upheaval that surrounded them, the militias offered clearly defined hierarchies, and a familiar sense of belonging and purpose. The paramilitary groups were bastions of soldierly camaraderie and 'order' in what the activists perceived as a hostile world of democratic egalitarianism and communist internationalism. It was this spirit of defiance, coupled with the desire to be part of a post-war project that would give meaning to what now seemed the pointless experience of mass death and defeat during war, which held these groups together. They perceived themselves to be the nucleus of a 'new society' of warriors, representing both the eternal values of the nation and new authoritarian concepts for a state in which that nation could thrive.[16]

One of them, Ernst von Salomon, who had experienced the post-war revolution of 1918 as a sixteen-year-old cadet, described his perception of the revolution in his autobiographical novel *Die Geächteten* (*The Outlaws*) of 1923:

> Behind the (red) flag tired crowds surged in a disorderly fashion. Women marched in front. They shoved their way ahead with their broad skirts, the grey skin of their faces hanging in wrinkles over sharp bones . . . The men, old and young, soldiers and workers, and many petty bourgeois in-between them, strode with dull, worn faces . . . Thus they marched, the champions of the Revolution. Was it from this black crowd that the glowing flame of revolution was to spring, that the dream of blood and barricades was to be realized? Impossible to capitulate before them . . . I sneered at their claims which knew no pride, no confidence in victory . . . I stood up straight and thought 'rabble', 'pack', 'scum', and squinted as I watched these hollow, destitute figures; like rats, I thought, carrying the dust of the gutter upon their backs . . .[17]

Just like Salomon, many former front-line soldiers bitterly resented the outbreak of revolution in 1918 and felt that their sacrifices had been betrayed by the home front. Units returning from the front were sometimes disarmed, insulted, and deprived of their epaulettes by the supporters of the workers' and soldiers' councils in the towns through which they passed. Others felt no welcome from their families because their long absence and corresponding loss in family income had not been vindicated by victory – a theme explored in Joseph Roth's famous and remarkably perceptive 1923 novel *Das Spinnennetz* (*The Spider's Web*). Roth's novel centres around the post-war upheavals in Berlin: the protagonist of the book, Lieutenant Theodor Lohse, is one of the many demobilized officers of the Central Powers, for whom defeat in the Great War serves as a major source of political mobilization against the post-war order. Forced to earn a meagre living as a private tutor in the household of a wealthy Jewish businessman, Lohse soon despairs over the perceived national humiliation caused by military collapse and the hostility with which his own family greets his return from the battlefields of Flanders:

> They couldn't forgive Theodor – he who had twice been mentioned in dispatches – for having failed to die a hero's death as a lieutenant. A dead son would have been the pride of the family. A demobilized lieutenant, a victim of the revolution, was a burden to his womenfolk . . . He could have told his sisters that he was not responsible for his own misfortune; that he cursed the revolution and was gnawed by hatred for the socialists and the Jews; that he bore each day like a yoke across his bowed neck and felt himself trapped in his epoch as in some sunless prison.[18]

The only escape route for Lohse from the 'sunless prison' of an invalidated existence is the possibility of continuing the war through other means. As a consequence he quickly joins one of the many paramilitary organizations that mushroomed in post-war Europe and which embodied a major problem facing most of the continent in the years immediately after 1918: the inability of many to leave the war behind them and to accept the arrival of peace. As one of the more prominent real-life *Freikorps* men, Friedrich Wilhelm Heinz, put it in his memoirs: 'We laughed when they told us that the war was over, because we *were* the war.'[19]

The absence of Allied soldiers on German soil before the official end of hostilities on 11 November gave rise to powerful conspiracy theories claiming that the Central Powers had not actually been defeated from outside but had only collapsed as a result of a 'stab in the back' by subversive elements or 'fifth columns' on the home front. In Germany, where this sentiment was most widespread, those like the former German Army High Command chief (and future President) Paul von Hindenburg, who promoted the idea of the army having been 'undefeated in the field', could build on older and well-established narratives of betrayal; notable among them was the medieval legend of the Nibelungs, in which the Germanic hero Siegfried is callously stabbed in the back with a spear by the story's villain, Hagen. Its modern, post-1918 version emphasized internationalist conspiracies and betrayal on the home front as the primary cause of Germany's defeat, an idea that was to become a cornerstone of right-wing belief in interwar Germany.[20]

Central to the stab-in-the-back myth was the sometimes implicit, but more often explicit, notion that the betrayal had to be avenged on a 'day of reckoning' when the 'enemy within' would be combated ruthlessly and without mercy. As the notorious German *Freikorps* leader, former naval officer and future Nazi ambassador to Bucharest, Manfred von Killinger, emphasized in a letter to his family: 'I have made a promise to myself, Father. Without armed struggle, I have handed over my torpedo boat to the enemies and watched my flag go down. I have sworn to take revenge against those who are responsible for this.'[21]

Noske's decision to recruit men like Killinger in an attempt to suppress the perceived Bolshevik threat thus offered such men a state-sanctioned opportunity to act on their fantasies of violent retribution. It was in Berlin in January 1919, during the suppression of the 'Spartacist Uprising', that the pent-up hatred towards the November Revolution and its backers exploded. On 11 January the *Freikorps* marched on Berlin, storming the newspaper district that same day. Five communist occupiers of the *Vorwärts* building were captured when trying to negotiate the terms of their surrender and were shot, together with two intercepted couriers. Overall, some 200 people were killed in bitter street fighting, and a further 400 arrested. That afternoon Noske led a military parade through central Berlin to celebrate the victory of his forces of order over their communist adversaries.[22]

Rosa Luxemburg and Karl Liebknecht, the two most prominent members of the Central Committee of the Communist Party, tried to escape the revenge killings by going into hiding and constantly changing their quarters in Berlin. Their last hiding place was in a flat in the affluent suburb of Wilmersdorf. Here they wrote their final articles for the *Rote Fahne*. Liebknecht published his ardent text 'Trotz alledem!' ('Despite it all!'), in which he admitted temporary defeat but called on his followers to persevere. The time had not been ripe for a Communist revolution, he wrote: 'The horrendous counter-revolutionary mudslide from backward elements of the people and the propertied classes drowned it.' And yet: 'The defeated of today will be the victors of tomorrow.'[23] Luxemburg echoed these sentiments in a powerful essay sarcastically entitled 'Order restored in Berlin': 'You stupid henchmen! Your "order" is built on sand. Tomorrow the revolution will once again "raise itself with a rattle" and announce with fanfare, to your terror: "I was, I am, I will be!"'[24]

In the evening hours of 15 January 1919 right-wing paramilitaries broke into the flat. Liebknecht and Luxemburg were arrested and handed over to the Garde-Kavallerie-Schützen-Division, an elite unit of the old imperial army, now under the command of a notorious anti-Bolshevik, Captain Waldemar Pabst.[25] At the division's headquarters in the upmarket Hotel Eden, Liebknecht was assaulted, spat upon, and struck down with rifle butts. At 10.45 that night the unconscious Communist leader was driven to the largest park in central Berlin, the Tiergarten, where he was shot three times at close range.[26]

Luxemburg was sitting in Pabst's temporary office reading Goethe's *Faust* when the soldiers returned to the hotel. She was also struck twice in the face with a rifle butt. Bleeding heavily, she was thrown into a car. After a short drive a lieutenant jumped onto the left running board and killed Luxemburg with a single shot to the head. Her corpse was thrown into the Landwehr Canal, and was only found several weeks later.[27]

Even after the suppression of the 'Spartacist Uprising', the situation in the German capital remained volatile – so much so that the newly elected Constituent National Assembly met in the provincial city of Weimar rather than in Berlin. During the spring of 1919 parts of Germany continued to be affected by revolutionary upheavals. In the industrial heartlands of the Ruhr Valley and central Germany a series of strikes demanded the nationalization of the mining industry. In Dresden the War Minister of Saxony, Gustav Neuring, was thrown into the River Elbe at Dresden, then shot dead as he tried to reach the bank. When, on 9 March 1919, in response to strikes and disorder in Berlin, Noske ordered government troops to shoot on sight anyone holding a weapon, his men caused mayhem in the capital. Using machine guns, tanks and even aeroplanes to drop a few bombs, government forces descended on their opponents, leaving a thousand dead. The March uprising also provided a welcome excuse for a long-anticipated reckoning: government soldiers murdered Leo Jogiches, Luxemburg's former lover and her successor as editor of *Die Rote Fahne*, as well as twenty-nine members of the People's Naval Division, which had caused their humiliating defeat in the Battle of Christmas Eve in 1918.[28]

Unrest also spread to Munich, where the initially bloodless revolution radicalized in the spring of 1919. Back in early November 1918, street demonstrations had forced the Bavarian King, Ludwig III, to abdicate and flee to Austria. A Socialist Council of Workers, Soldiers and Peasants proclaimed an independent Bavarian Republic under the leadership of Kurt Eisner, a Jewish drama critic of the *Münchener Post*. Eisner was a Berliner, who seemed almost like a cliché of the leftist intellectuals that frequented the coffee houses in the Bohemian quarter of Schwabing. He had served as editor of *Vorwärts* in 1899, but was sacked in 1905. Eisner then moved to Bavaria where he continued to work as a journalist. During that time his views moved steadily further to the left. In the spring of 1917, Eisner founded the Bavarian USPD (Independent Social Democratic Party), and he supported the nationwide strike in January 1918.[29] His involvement in the strike brought Eisner a conviction and he spent the next eight and a half months in Stadelheim prison. On 15 October he was suddenly released and quickly became the leader of the revolution in Bavaria.[30]

Eisner was eccentric and committed to furthering revolutionary change. As Prime Minister of Bavaria he leaked state documents which he believed proved that the war in 1914 had been caused by 'a small horde of mad Prussian military' men as well as by 'allied' industrialists, capitalists, politicians and princes.[31] At an international conference of socialists, held in the Swiss city of Berne in February 1919, Eisner attacked Ebert's government for refusing to acknowledge Germany's guilt in starting the war in 1914. Both the message itself and its timing (at the start of the Paris Peace Conference) did not help to endear conservative circles to Eisner's rule.[32]

Although a firm believer in radical reform, Eisner was not opposed to the principles of democracy and called for general elections for the Bavarian Parliament on 12 January 1919, during which his Independent

Social Democrats suffered a crushing defeat, winning no more than three out of a total of 156 seats. As Eisner was walking to Parliament to submit his resignation, he was shot in the back and killed by a twenty-two-year-old nationalist law student, Count Anton Arco-Valley.[33] In response to this attack on the leader of the Bavarian USPD, a socialist radical, Alois Lindner, entered the Bavarian Parliament and opened fire, leaving the Bavarian Majority Social Democratic Party leader, Erhard Auer, severely injured and two other people dead.[34]

Following Eisner's assassination and the attempted murder of Auer, the Bavarian Parliament elected a former schoolteacher and Majority Social Democrat, Johannes Hoffmann, as Minister-President. But the extreme Left was unwilling to accept the new government. On 3 April socialists in the city of Augsburg called for the creation of a Bavarian Council Republic, a move inspired by recent events in Hungary, where, on 22 March, the Communist leader Béla Kun had proclaimed a Soviet Republic, simultaneously calling on Bavarian and Austrian radicals to follow his example.[35]

'The news from Hungary hit Munich like a bomb,' wrote the anarchist essayist and poet Erich Mühsam in the Bavarian capital.[36] Bavaria descended once more into a state of revolutionary unrest. Under the leadership of a former schoolteacher, Ernst Niekisch, the Central Council of the Bavarian Republic announced that the elected government under Johannes Hoffmann had come to an end and instead proclaimed the state a Soviet Republic. From the start, however, the Munich Soviet Republic could build on little support in the largely agrarian, conservative and Catholic state of Bavaria. The new regime's leadership was dominated by urban (and often Jewish) literati from Schwabing, such as the twenty-five-year-old Bohemian poet Ernst Toller or the anarchist writer and translator of Shakespeare, Gustav Landauer. Their revolutionary agenda was as ambitious as it was unrealistic: it could only have been imposed in a far more dislocated and broken state than Bavaria. Banks and large industrial concerns were to be nationalized; 'free money' would be issued to abolish capitalism; universities were to be run by the students. The press was to be subjected to censorship by Landauer's Office of Enlightenment and Public Instruction.[37]

News of the events in Munich was welcomed by Russian Bolsheviks as a sign that a Communist revolution in all of Germany was imminent. From Moscow the Politburo member and chairman of the newly founded Comintern, Grigory Zinoviev, sent an enthusiastic message: 'We are deeply convinced that the time is not far off when the whole of Germany will be a soviet republic. The Communist International is aware that you in Germany are now fighting at the most responsible posts, where the immediate fate of the proletarian revolution throughout Europe will be decided.'[38] Other contemporaries agreed, even if they objected to communism. The politically conservative future Nobel Laureate Thomas Mann, himself living in Munich at the time, was convinced that the Bolshevik revolution was bound to spread: 'It may be assumed that the rest of Germany will follow,' Mann noted in his diary on 7 April 1919.[39]

From Paris and other Western capitals the Allies were observing the unfolding events in eastern and central Europe with growing concern. Robert Lansing, US Secretary of State, stated on 4 April 1919 that 'Central Europe is aflame with anarchy; the people see no hope; the Red Armies of Russia are marching westward. Hungary is in the clutches of the revolutionists; Berlin, Vienna and Munich are turning towards the Bolsheviks . . . It is time to stop fiddling while the world is on fire . . .'[40]

In the meantime the Hoffmann government had fled Munich for the safety of Bamberg in northern Franconia, just as the German National Assembly had fled Berlin for Weimar. However, Hoffmann was not going to accept the putsch in Munich without a fight. On Palm Sunday, 13 April 1919, a Bavarian republican militia loyal to the Hoffmann government attempted to topple the Munich Soviet Republic by force, but failed in the face of stiff resistance from heavily armed Communist soldiers.[41] Hoffmann's attempt to violently reinstate the legitimate Bavarian government had an immediate radicalizing effect. In Munich the Bavarian Councils' Republic moved significantly to the left, as Max Levien and Eugen Leviné, two Russian-born revolutionary activists who had long demanded more radical political change, took over the leadership of what became known as the Second Munich Soviet Republic.[42]

The defeat of Palm Sunday, coupled with another failed military intervention at Dachau on the outskirts of Munich three days later, also led to a radicalization of the anti-Bolshevik forces.[43] Hoffmann, who had been reluctant at first to enlist anti-Republican volunteers or to seek support from the national government in Berlin, now had a change of heart. He publicly appealed to all anti-Bolshevik forces in Bavaria to crush the Councils' Republic:

> Bavarians! Countrymen! In Munich rages a Russian terror, unleashed by foreign elements. This insult to Bavaria cannot be allowed to last another day, not even another hour. All Bavarians must immediately help, regardless of party affiliation . . . Munich calls for your aid. Come on! Step forward! Now! The Munich disgrace must be wiped out.[44]

Hoffmann's call helped to mobilize those who appreciated the opportunity to settle scores with the forces of Bolshevism. Many of them had loyally served the imperial regime and longed for its restoration, like Major General Franz Ritter von Epp, a former commander of the Bavarian Life Guards, who led the *Freikorps* Oberland, or his adjutant, the highly decorated thirty-one-year-old war hero and future head of the Nazi SA, Captain Ernst Röhm. In total, some 15,000 men from Bavaria answered Hoffmann's call to arms.[45]

In addition to locally recruited forces, the government in Berlin sent some 15,000 regular troops, under the command of the Prussian Major General von Oven, to put an end to Communist rule in Munich.[46] As the troops poured into Bavaria from mid-April, rumours spread that the Councils' Republic had released from prison and armed large numbers of criminals as well as having enlisted former Russian prisoners of war to strengthen the ranks of their armed forces.[47] Before government soldiers had reached the city of Munich, a communiqué jointly signed in the name of the military command and Hoffmann's Bavarian government announced: 'Whoever takes up arms against government troops will be punished by death . . . Each member of the Red Army will be treated as an enemy of the Bavarian people and the German Reich.'[48]

The Battle for Munich that began on 1 May allowed anti-Bolsheviks to act on these orders. One day earlier, as the government troops and *Freikorps* surrounded the city, the Red Army rebels unwisely chose to shoot ten hostages, including one woman, in the Luitpold-Gymnasium in Munich. The fact that the woman in question was an aristocratic relative of one of the *Freikorps* commanders, and that she was rumoured to have been subjected to sexual violence before her execution, did not improve the situation. The execution was a grave mistake, since it gave the counter-revolutionaries the ideal pretext for violent revenge.[49]

The German-Jewish literature professor Victor Klemperer, who would later become world famous for his diary account of his own persecution under the Nazis after 1933, observed the end of the Munich Soviet in 1919 first hand in the Bavarian capital:

> ... today, as I'm writing these lines, a veritable battle is raging. A whole squadron of planes is flying over Munich, firing and being shot at, dropping flares ... Infantry fire is rattling. More and more troops march or drive or ride down Ludwig Street with mortars and artillery ... and from the safety of the street corners, where it is safe and the view is good, crowds of spectators watch on, often with opera glasses in hand.[50]

As the army and *Freikorps* troops moved into the city, more than 600 people were killed during the fighting, many of them civilian bystanders. Summary executions of prisoners, including Gustav Landauer and Rudolf Egelhofer, the War Commissar of the Councils' Republic, continued on 2 and 3 May. Fifty-three Russians who had served in the Red Army were tortured and shot in Pasing, an outskirt of Munich. Over the following weeks some 2,200 supporters of the Councils' Republic were sentenced to death or long prison terms, while a total of 5,000 court cases were concerned with crimes committed during the Bavarian Soviet Republic.[51]

The cataclysmic events in and around Munich had a lasting effect on a city that previously prided itself on being a largely peaceful and deeply bourgeois metropolis. Untouched by the Great War – except through economic deprivation and numerous deaths of the city's sons on far-flung fronts – Munich had suddenly experienced revolutionary turmoil, street fighting, and even artillery fire and aerial bombardment. As Thomas Mann recorded in his diary on 1 May, the citizens of Germany's second city were horrified, although middle-class observers tended to attribute blame for the escalation of violence and disorder exclusively to the Reds. Mann, a resident of the affluent residential district of Bogenhausen, was kept abreast about events in the city centre through the mother of his wife, Katia, who lived closer to the government district:

> K's mother called in the morning; apparently a white flag was flying over the Wittelsbach Palais, the Reds had surrendered at 4 a.m. Turns out this was untrue. A handover is not yet on the cards, and the shooting continues intermittently. In the city . . . there is a mighty uproar: during the night, the middle-class and aristocratic hostages interned in the Luitpoldgymnasium . . . have been been mutilated and executed . . . Incredible outrage among the middle-class citizens. All red armbands have suddenly disappeared.[52]

The profound sense of living in a world in which established social orders and hierarchies had been violently overturned prompted a right-wing backlash in Bavaria. Munich in particular was to become the most staunchly nationalist and anti-Bolshevik city in Weimar Germany – and it was no coincidence that the Bavarian capital would emerge as the birthplace of Nazism.

After the fall of the Bavarian Soviet Republic, Lenin's hopes for world revolution were diminished. The only Communist country in Europe outside Russia at this point was Hungary, which was led by the thirty-two-year-old former lawyer and journalist Béla Kun. The son of a secular Jewish notary from rural Transylvania and himself a lawyer by training, Kun had made a name for himself before the war as a radical journalist. After 1914 he fought in the Habsburg Army on the Eastern Front, where he was captured by the Russians and sent to a prisoner-of-war camp. Converted to Bolshevism during his time in Russia, Kun was freed as a result of the October Revolution and returned to Budapest on 17 November 1918.[53]

The timing of Kun's return to Budapest could not have been better. Deprived of necessary food deliveries and humiliated by the ongoing territorial amputation of their country, many Hungarians became increasingly radicalized.[54] When Hungary had parted ways with Austria in the autumn of 1918, many Hungarians had naively assumed that their future independent nation state would comprise the historic lands of the crown of St Stephen. As confirmed in the Austro-Hungarian *Ausgleich* of 1867 and the Croatian-Hungarian Settlement the following year, these lands included today's Hungary, Slovakia, Transylvania, Ukrainian Ruthenia, Vojvodina and Croatia. By late 1918, however, nearly all of these territories were also claimed by rival emerging states. Hungary's Liberal government under Count Mihály Károlyi, backed by the Social Democrats, had focused its energies on preserving the country's territorial integrity while pushing through a number of urgently needed reforms designed to transform it from a semi-feudal oligarchy into a modern, democratic state. Both of these projects failed miserably.[55] By early 1919 roughly half of the country's historical territory, populated by hundreds of thousands of ethnic Magyars, had been lost to secession movements, encouraged by the Western Allies and sponsored by Hungary's neighbours. Domestically, Károlyi focused his energies on a long-overdue land reform and even announced the distribution of all his own landed property to the peasants, in line with the new law he had guided through the National Assembly. For five months Károlyi managed to steer a difficult course between the forces of the Right and the Left, each of which accused him of being too soft on their opponents. Both sides agreed, however, that he was too soft on the Allied peacemakers.

By January 1919, increasingly alarming reports were reaching audiences in the Western world. 'The Russian epidemic of Bolshevism', reported *The New York Times*, 'has reached the virulent stage. Famine and freezing are its active allies. New Year's Eve was celebrated with riot and murder in the city's streets.'[56] The riots had been caused by the government's decision to shut down one of Kun's newspapers. After a number of bloody clashes between his supporters and forces loyal to the government, Kun was eventually arrested on 21 February, alongside other Communist leaders. The government that Kun had tried to overthrow curiously allowed him to establish a Communist Party secretariat in his prison cell. The general mood of dissatisfaction was further exacerbated by a growing resentment at international attitudes towards Hungary and its territories. The Western Allies tolerated and sometimes even encouraged land-grabbing at Budapest's expense. When the peacemakers in Paris decided to give Romania a large swathe of Hungarian territory, and ordered the Hungarians to withdraw all their troops from a 'demilitarized zone' in the border region, Károlyi resigned in protest on 21 March.[57]

That very same day the Social Democrats – fearful of a civil war – agreed to form a coalition government with Kun and released him from prison. The following day he declared Hungary a Soviet Republic. Kun quickly set about putting his revolutionary ideas into practice. During its 133 days in power Kun's Republic announced dramatic and largely unenforceable reforms: all large agricultural estates were to be broken up and redistributed; industrial enterprises that employed more than twenty-five people were to be nationalized; Church property was confiscated; schools were reorganized to emphasize the teaching of science and the principles of socialism. Alcohol consumption became illegal. Titles were abolished. Rural food stores were requisitioned to feed the starving capital. The Soviet political structure of soldiers', sailors' and workers' councils was imposed, and the whole of the judicial power of the state was put into their hands, with special revolutionary tribunals to try political cases.[58]

Emulating Lenin's crusade against class enemies, Kun and his Commissar for Military Affairs, Tibor Szamuely, unleashed a wave of 'revolutionary terror'. Szamuely, like Kun an ideologically driven former POW in Russian captivity, wrote in the pages of the Vörös Újság (Red News): 'Everywhere counter-revolutionaries run about and swagger; beat them down! Beat their heads where you find them! If counter-revolutionaries were to gain the upper hand for even a single hour, there will be no mercy for any proletarian. Before they stifle the revolution, suffocate them in their own blood!'[59] Together with József Cserny, Szamuely organized a detachment of some 500 men known as the 'Lenin Boys'. Dressed in black leather jackets and pants, the Lenin Boys roamed the Hungarian countryside in an armoured train in search of 'counter-revolutionaries'. In Budapest and rural areas such paramilitary groups of the Left arrested putative or real enemies, killing an estimated 600 people in the process.[60]

Kun's regime did enjoy the support of the industrial workforce and Budapest's intelligentsia, but it was less successful in winning the support of those in the countryside. Left-leaning urban intellectuals took it for granted that the peasants – who were often illiterate, exposed to miserable living conditions, and politically apathetic – would acquiesce in the policies decreed by the capital and accept the rule of the proletariat.[61] When agrarian supplies for Budapest diminished, the regime embarked on a campaign of forced requisitioning in the countryside, thereby antagonizing the opponents of Bolshevism further.[62] It did not help the Kun government that some of its members, such as József Pogány, were preaching the values of communism to a starving population while simultaneously hosting decadent parties in the spa town of Siófok.[63]

While maintaining close relations with Moscow, Kun also appealed to radical revolutionaries in Austria to follow his example.[64] Support from Austria was crucial for the Communist regime in Budapest. Its chances for survival depended on the fortunes of war, and Austria possessed sizeable amounts of weaponry formerly belonging to the Austro-Hungarian military. Thus, on 22 March 1919, the Hungarians appealed to the executive committee of the Vienna Workers' Council to proclaim a 'Soviet Republic of Austria' and to enter into an alliance with Hungary.[65] When Vienna's Social Democrats declined, Kun called on the Austrian Communists to stage a coup. In response to Kun's appeal and to the proclamation of the Bavarian Councils' Republic a few days earlier, several hundred Austrian Communists stormed the Austrian Parliament building on 18 April and set it on fire. Police and loyal Social Democratic militias, the *Volkswehr*, were called in to quell the uprising. Six members of the security forces were killed in the shooting that ended the uprising.[66]

About one month later Ernst Bettelheim, an envoy dispatched by Kun, arrived in Vienna. In the name of the Communist International, which he claimed to represent, Bettelheim dismissed the entire leadership of the Austrian Communist Party (KPÖ) and charged a newly appointed executive board with preparations for a second putsch attempt. This time the Communists hoped to recruit former Red Guards and disgruntled members of the *Volkswehr* dissatisfied with the imminent downsizing of the Austrian armed forces. Simultaneously, Hungarian troops would cross the border into Austria.[67] Unfortunately for the conspirators, the government had been tipped off about the Communist conspiracy and mobilized loyal forces. During the night of 14–15 June most Communist leaders were arrested. When, in the course of the following day, several thousand demonstrators marched to the police jail in order to free the prisoners, a city guard detachment opened fire. In the shooting twenty were killed and eighty injured, terminating both the imminent putsch and Kun's dreams of finding a strong ally in the region.[68]

Without international backing and with dwindling domestic support, the future of Hungary's Soviet Republic looked bleak. In implementing a radical agenda and enforcing it violently, Kun's regime alienated almost every section of the population, from Catholics horrified by the murder of at least seven priests and Communist plans to secularize Church property, to liberals appalled by censorship, arbitrary arrests and the secret police.[69] Public opinion condemned the regime above all for its failure to cope with inflation and food shortages, and for its own corruption.[70] A majority of the gentry, now deprived of its pre-war privileged status, formed an unlikely alliance with peasants, who in turn were irritated and embittered by the refusal of the Soviet regime in Budapest to redistribute estate land among them. Claiming to speak for the whole nation, the anti-urban and anti-modern gentry-peasant alliance heaped scorn on the metropolitan elites of Red Budapest.

On 30 May 1919 anti-Communist politicians formed a counter-revolutionary government in the southern city of Szeged, then under French occupation. Its armed forces, the 'National Army', were placed under the command of Miklós Horthy, a decorated hero of the Great War and the last commander-in-chief of the Austro-Hungarian Navy.[71] Not dissimilar to the army of the Russian 'Whites', Horthy's 'National Army' was very top-heavy: of the 6,568 volunteers who followed Horthy's initial recruitment call on 5 June 1919 for the formation of the counter-revolutionary National Army, almost 3,000 were former Habsburg officers and an additional 800 men were from the militarized border guards, the Gendarmerie (Magyar Királyi Csendőrség). Many of them came from rural backgrounds, notably from the new border regions or the lost territories of Transylvania, where issues of embattled ethnicity were much more real than they were in the capital. Given the often rural backgrounds of many activists, there was also a clearly discernible anti-urban animus, as prominent paramilitaries railed against the 'red capital' of Budapest.[72]

Many of these men had experienced similar homecomings to German and Austrian demobilized officers during the revolution of 1918. Upon arrival in Hungary from the front in the winter of 1918, the

Hussar officer Miklós Kozma was one of many veterans 'welcomed' by disorderly crowds shouting abuse at the returning officers or physically attacking them.[73] In Kozma's account revolutionary activists appeared – rather characteristically in such narratives – as an effeminate 'dirty crowd' led by 'Red Amazons', a crowd 'that has not washed in weeks and has not changed their clothes in months; the smell of clothes and shoes rotting on their bodies is unbearable.'[74]

What Kozma and many others described in their autobiographical accounts was to them the manifestation of a nightmare that had haunted Europe's conservative establishment since the French Revolution of 1789: the triumph of a faceless revolutionary crowd over the forces of law and order. The image they invoked was partly influenced by a vulgarized understanding of Gustave Le Bon's *Psychologie des foules* (1895), whose ideas were widely discussed in right-wing circles across Europe from the turn of the century. Le Bon's juxtaposition of the 'barbarian' masses and the 'civilized' individual was also reflected in the ways in which ex-officers described the humiliating experiences of being stripped of their military decorations by agitated crowds or lower-ranked soldiers. Many of the ex-officers who shared these experiences ended up in Horthy's 'National Army'.[75]

What eventually brought down Kun's government, however, was not the Hungarian 'National Army' but rather the country's external enemies. The Western Allies' hostility towards Kun had already become obvious when, in April 1919, he was visited in Budapest by an Allied delegation led by the South African Prime Minister, General Jan Christiaan Smuts. If Kun had hoped that the delegation's visit would bring his regime international recognition, his hopes were quickly dashed. Neither Smuts nor the accompanying senior British diplomat, Harold Nicolson, were impressed by Kun or his regime. Nicolson described Kun's features as that of a 'sulky and uncertain criminal' with a 'puffy white face and loose wet lips – shaven head – impression of red hair – shifty suspicious eyes'. Kun's accompanying foreign-policy adviser did not fare much better in Nicolson's account, which reflected common racial and social stereotypes of his class: 'a little oily Jew – fur-coat rather moth-eaten – stringy tie – dirty collar'.[76] Smuts and Nicolson left Budapest only two days after they had arrived, without having made any concessions to Kun.[77]

Shortly after Smuts's departure, in mid-April 1919, the Romanian Army invaded Hungary with the tacit approval of the French.[78] Bucharest claimed it was acting in self-defence, because the Hungarian government had been organizing and subsidising a Bolshevik propaganda campaign in the villages of (now Romanian) Transylvania, aimed at provoking an uprising. A few days later the Czechs invaded Slovakia from the north, citing similar excuses.[79]

The Hungarians temporarily put aside their internal differences in the face of the foreign threat. With the Romanians threatening Hungary's territorial integrity, Kun toned down his class war rhetoric while the army, including conservative officers with limited symphathies for Bolshevism, rallied to the defence of the country's borders. The Italians, motivated largely by their rivalry with Hungary's other hostile neighbour, Yugoslavia, sold Kun guns and ammunition. By the middle of May, Hungarian forces had driven the Czechs out of Slovakia but they were less successful against the Romanians. An attempt to push the invaders back across the Tisza river that July was met with a clever executed Romanian counter-attack. It was then that many Hungarian officers and soldiers decided to stop fighting after being encouraged to do so by the oppositional Hungarian National Army under Admiral Horthy who wanted the Romanians to finish off Kun's Soviet Republic. Deprived of the support of many of its soldiers, the Hungarian lines collapsed and the Romanians deposed Kun and his regime. Kun fled to Austria and then the Soviet Union, where he was ultimately executed during Stalin's purges.[81]

On 3 August 1919, Romanian troops entered Budapest, where they remained until the beginning of 1920.[82] Several atrocities were committed against the local population and the extensive looting of the Hungarian capital by Romanian troops during the occupation heightened the sense of outrageous injustice shared by many contemporary Hungarians. The fact that these acts were carried out not by the victorious Western Allies but by soldiers of a country defeated by the Central Powers in 1918 made the experience even more humiliating.[83]

When the Romanians eventually withdrew in the autumn of 1919 under Allied pressure, the counter-revolutionary forces of Admiral Horthy saw their opportunity. On 16 November, Horthy entered Budapest on a white horse in front of his 'National Army'. Describing

Budapest as a revolutionary 'city of sin' (a phrase first coined by the nationalist novelist Dezső Szabó), Horthy made it clear that he had come to punish and purify the capital.[84] Many of his men and various paramilitary groups alongside the army were driven by the desire to avenge the crimes of the 'Red Terror'. Already in August, Kozma had written in his diary: 'We shall see to it . . . that the flame of nationalism leaps high . . . We shall also punish. Those who for months have committed heinous crimes must receive their punishment. It is predictable . . . that the compromisers and those with weak stomachs will moan and groan when we line up a few red rogues and terrorists against the wall. The false slogans of humanism and other 'isms' have helped to drive the country into ruin before. This second time they will wail in vain.'[85]

Wherever a temporary power vacuum allowed the militia men to act upon these fantasies of violent retribution, they did. Prominent intellectual critics of the Hungarian White Terror, such as the journalist Béla Bacsó and the editor of the Social Democratic daily *Népszava*, Béla Somogyi, were abducted and murdered by right-wing paramilitaries.[86] Hungarian militias of the Right targeted the supporters of the Left as well as apolitical and middle-class Jews. Political violence in the second half of 1919 and early 1920s took the lives of up to 5000 people.[87] A further 75,000 individuals were imprisoned, and 100,000 went into exile. Given that many leaders of the Hungarian revolution, including Kun himself, had managed to flee the country before they could be arrested, others had to pay for their 'treason'.[88]

Socialists, Jews and trade unionists, when caught, were dragged into the barracks and beaten unconscious. 'On these occasions,' recalled the infamous Hungarian militia leader and temporary head of Horthy's bodyguard, Baron Pál Prónay, descended from a respected family of landed gentry, 'I ordered an additional fifty strokes with the rod for these fanatic human animals, whose heads were drunk with the twisted ideology of Marx.'[89] For Prónay and other militia leaders of the Right, the dehumanized ('human animal') and denationalized ('Bolshevik') enemy could be tortured and killed without remorse, because these acts were legitimized and necessitated by the holiness of the cause: the salvation of the nation threatened by a socialist abyss and territorial amputation. Against the background of war and revolution, the activists were convinced that the internal enemy, who had broken the rules of 'civilized' military conduct, could only be stopped through the use of the same kind of extreme violence that their opponents were – rightly or wrongly – believed to have employed during the brief 'Red Terror' in Bavaria and Hungary.[90]

The post-war project of 'cleansing' the nation of its internal enemies was viewed as a necessary precondition for a national rebirth, a form of violent regeneration that would justify the sacrifices of the war despite defeat and revolution. In some ways this abstract hope for national rebirth out of the ruins of empire was the only thing that held the highly heterogeneous paramilitary groups of Austria and Hungary together. In retrospect, the paramilitary upsurge of the months after November 1918 looks more like an attack on the new political establishments and the territorial amputations confirmed by the Western Allies than a coordinated attempt to create any particular form of authoritarian new order. For despite their common opposition to revolution and their shared hope for national revival, the activists involved in right-wing paramilitary action did not necessarily have the same ideological aims and ambitions. Quite the opposite: paramilitary activists of the political right in Austria and Hungary were in fact deeply divided by their divergent visions of preferable future forms of statehood. For example, there were strong 'legitimist' forces, particularly in the Hungarian community in Vienna, from where two unsuccessful attempts were undertaken to restore Emperor Karl to the throne of St Stephen, but also large numbers of proto-fascist activists, who despised the monarchy nearly as much as they loathed communism. Some royalist paramilitaries in Austria, too, demanded a restoration of the Habsburg monarchy (though not necessarily under the former emperor) and found themselves in direct confrontation with those in favour of Austrian unification with the German Reich.[91]

Such differences in political objectives could and did lead to serious tensions. In October 1921 one of the two failed coup attempts by Emperor Karl helped Horthy to rid himself of some royalist militia leaders such as Colonel Anton Lehár, the younger brother of the composer Franz Lehár. Anton Lehár, who had commanded the largest militia in Hungary in 1919, was forced to leave the country and started a second career as a publisher of light music in Berlin, where he and his more famous brother continued to thrive throughout the Nazi dictatorship, despite the fact that Franz Lehár had a Jewish wife (something the Nazi authorities chose to resolve by making her an 'honorary Aryan').[92]

Yet, even with the sidelining of royalists, there was no consensus among the radical Right in central Europe about what the future should look like. What they could agree on was what they were against. As the pan-German 'Oberland League' phrased it in its pamphlet *The Policy of German Resistance*, a national rebirth was only possible through a thoroughly critical engagement with the ideas of 1789, those of enlightenment, humanism and natural rights. 'The ideas of 1789 are manifest in modern individualism, bourgeois views on the word and economy, parliamentarianism, and modern democracy . . . We members of the Oberland League will continue on our path, marked out by the blood of the German martyrs who have died for the future Reich, and we will continue, then as now, to be the shock troops of the German resistance movement.'[93] Waldemar Pabst, who had been responsible for the murder of Rosa Luxemburg and Karl Liebknecht in Berlin in 1919 before moving to Austria and becoming the chief military organizer of the *Heimwehr*, articulated similarly abstract ideas when he called for 'the replacement of the old trinity of the French Revolution [*liberté, egalité, fraternité*] . . . with a new trinity: authority, order, and justice.'[94]

Both texts demonstrated quite clearly that the paramilitary world of post-Habsburg central Europe was a world of action, not ideas. Against whom these 'actions' should be directed was consequently one of the most widely discussed themes in paramilitary circles. For Alfred Krauss, former commander-in-chief of the Habsburg Empire's eastern armies, the 'enemies of the German people' included 'the French, the English, the Czechs, the Italians' – a clear indication of the continuity of wartime thinking after 1918. More dangerous than the nationalist enemies of other countries, however, were the internationalist enemies: 'the Red International', the 'Black International' (political Catholicism), and, 'above all', the 'Jewish people who aim at mastery of the Germans'. All other enemies, Krauss was certain, stood in the paid service of the Jews.[95]

In Munich the Baltic German refugee (and future Nazi Minister for the Occupied Eastern Territories), Alfred Rosenberg, commented in an article of May 1919:

Lenin is the only non-Jew among the peoples' commissars; he is, so to speak, the Russian storefront of a Jewish business ... But one can observe, and all recent news confirms it, that the hatred against the Jews in Russia is constantly spreading despite all terror ... If the present government falls, no Jew will remain alive in Russia; one can say with certainty that those not killed will be driven out. Where to? The Poles are already keeping them at bay, and so they will all come into old Germany, where we love the Jews so much and keep the warmest seats ready for them.[96]

The notion of Jews as the main drivers and beneficiaries of Bolshevism clearly originated in Russia, most notably from White propaganda, but the idea spread quickly across Europe. The fact that a relatively high number of Jews had played prominent roles in the subsequent central European revolutions of 1918–19 – Rosa Luxemburg in Berlin, Kurt Eisner in Munich, Béla Kun in Hungary, Victor Adler in Vienna – seemed to make such accusations plausible, even for observers in Britain and France. A large number of contemporary French newspapers, for instance, attributed the Bolshevik revolution to Jewish influence.[97] In London policy-makers at the British Foreign Office arrived at similar conclusions. 'The Jews are determined to do everything in their power to prevent the foundation of a great and independent Poland,' wrote one, while another observed: 'There is, I fear, some justification for the suggestion that Jews are the backbone of Bolshevism.'[98] In 1920, Winston Churchill wrote his infamous article attributing blame for the continental European revolutions to the Jews:

From the days of Spartacus-Weishaupt to those of Karl Marx, and down to Trotsky (Russia), Bela Kun (Hungary), Rosa Luxemburg (Germany), and Emma Goldman (United States), this world-wide revolutionary conspiracy for the overthrow of civilization and for the reconstitution of society on the basis of arrested development, of envious malevolence, and impossible equality, has been steadily growing ... It has been the mainspring of every subversive movement during the

Nineteenth Century; and now at last this band of extraordinary per-
sonalities from the underworlds of the great cities of Europe and America have gripped the Russian people by the hair of their heads and have
become practically the undisputed masters of the enormous empire.
There is no need to exaggerate the part played in the creating of Bolshevism and in the actual bringing about of the Russian Revolution by
these international and for the most part atheistic Jews. It is certainly
the very great one; it probably outweighs all others.[99]

Such views were further fuelled by the broad international circulation
of the fabricated *Protocols of the Elders of Zion*, the alleged minutes
of a late nineteenth-century meeting of Jewish leaders to discuss how
to achieve global domination for the Jews. The text of the *Protocols*
was translated into western European languages from 1919 onwards,
often funded by wealthy private individuals such as the American
industrialist Henry Ford, who provided the printing cost for over
500,000 copies to be distributed in the United States. Its exposure as
a forgery in 1921 did not reverse the enormous impact of the *Protocols* on the counter-revolutionary imagination. Yet the unholy
marriage of anti-Semitism and anti-Bolshevism produced very different results in different European settings. It was only east of the River
Rhine (and more dramatically east of the River Elbe) that anti-'Judeo-
Bolshevism' would lead to the pogroms and mass murders of Jews
that were such a terrible feature of the years 1917–23, and again of
the years after 1939.[100]

Unsurprisingly, given such widespread sentiments, the Jews of central Europe – although a small minority of no more than 5 per cent
of the Austrian and Hungarian populations – suffered most from
right-wing paramilitary violence after the Great War. Allegedly representing everything the far Right despised, the Jews could simultaneously (and paradoxically) be portrayed as the embodiment of a
pan-Slavic revolutionary menace from 'the East' that threatened
the traditional order of Christian central Europe, as 'red agents' of
Moscow, and as representatives of an obscure capitalist 'Golden
International' and force of Western democratization. What these
accusations had in common was the assumption that Jews had a
'natural' internationalist hatred for the nation state and their 'host
peoples'.

In Hungary, in contrast to German-Austria, anti-Semitic violence was tolerated by the state authorities and at times applauded by the nationalist press.[101] A report on anti-Semitic violence published by Vienna's Jewish community in 1922 reported that 'more than 3000 Jews were murdered in Transdanubia', the broad region of Hungary west of the Danube.[102] Although these figures are probably exaggerated, there can be no doubt that the White Terror specifically targeted Jews in substantial numbers. A typical case of anti-Semitic violence in Hungary was reported to the police by Ignaz Bing from Bőhőnye in 1919: 'During the night before 1 October, a group of sixty White Guards came to our community and ordered that every Jewish man had to appear immediately on the market square. The Jewish men, seventeen altogether, who were entirely innocent of Communist activity, followed the order.' When they had assembled, 'they were beaten and tortured and – without any interrogation – they [the soldiers] started hanging them'. This act of extreme violence served the dual purpose of eliminating the 'source of Bolshevism' and giving a public demonstration of what would happen to any enemy who fell into the hands of the White Guards.[103]

In Austria anti-Semitism was similarly widespread, even though it never assumed a particularly violent character prior to 1938. Before 1914, anti-Semitism in Austria had been common currency among right-wing politicians, who complained bitterly about the high numbers of Jews from Galicia and the Bukovina who had migrated to Vienna. During the war more Galician Jews fled what was now front-line territory and arrived in the Austrian capital in huge numbers. Simultaneously, wealthier Austrian Jews working in the banking sector or in the armaments and food industries were stigmatized by anti-Semites as 'Jewish profiteers'.[104] When, in 1918, Galicia fell to Poland and the Bukovina to Romania, the number of Jewish migrants further increased, accelerated by large-scale pogroms in Galicia and Ukraine. In 1918 some 125,000 Jews were living in Vienna, although German-Austrian nationalists maintained that the number was as high as 450,000.[105]

The situation was no different in Germany, the destination of choice for many eastern European Jews fleeing from pogroms. The Jews who fled the violence in the western borderlands of the collapsed Romanov

Empire or in formerly Habsburg Galicia after the Great War received at best a lukewarm welcome in their new homelands. Even the Jewish communities that already existed in the Reich or in Vienna viewed Orthodox Jewish refugees as outsiders who lacked social standing and cultural refinement.[106]

The arrival of tens of thousands of *Ostjuden* also fanned anti-Semitism among those Germans who had long regarded their fellow German citizens of Jewish faith as second-class citizens, and who felt their long-standing preconceptions of Jewish 'otherness' confirmed and reinforced when eastern Jews with their different dress, cultural traditions and languages arrived. When Lina von Osten, the future wife of the chief organizer of the Holocaust, Reinhard Heydrich, first encountered Orthodox Jewish refugees, she felt nothing but disgust. Von Osten, who introduced Heydrich to Nazism in the late 1920s, recalled in her memoirs that she had regarded the eastern Jews who arrived in Germany in large numbers after 1918 as 'intruders and unwelcome guests', and had felt so 'provoked' by their mere presence that she just 'had to hate them': 'We compared living with them to a forced marriage, in which one partner literally cannot bear the smell of the other.'[107]

Such views were widespread among many on the Right in Germany and Austria, where the accusation that 'the Jew' had become the 'slaveholder' of a defenceless German people was very prominent after the Great War, when it could build on wartime notions of Jews as 'profiteers'. According to this reading, the Jews were determined 'to exploit our peril in order to make good business . . . and to squeeze out our last drop of blood'.[108] The identification of 'the Jewish people' as the 'wire-pullers' behind revolution and imperial collapse was generally linked to the hope that 'the German giant will rise again one day', and that then 'the day of reckoning must come for all the treason, hypocrisy and barbarism, for all their crimes against the German people and against humanity'.[109]

Like those in Hungary, anti-Semites in Austria usually appealed to Christian principles and linked the notion of Jewish responsibility for the military collapse to older Christian stereotypes of 'Jewish treason'.[110] As a consequence, politicians from the Christian Social Party such as the Tyrolese *Heimwehr* leader, Richard Steidle, argued that 'only a thorough reckoning with the spirit of Jewry and its helpers can save the German Alpine lands'.[111] Anti-Semitism after 1918 was further exacerbated by the widespread perception that a 'Jewish conspiracy' was at the heart of the revolutions of 1918–19. The fact that the intellectual leader of the Austrian Red Guards, Leo Rothziegel, and prominent members of the Social Democratic Party, such as Victor Adler and Otto Bauer, were Jewish, was constantly referred to in the right-wing press.

In Hungary, too, the revolution and the Red Terror of the immediate post-war period were, in the eyes of conservative officers, inextricably linked with Jews, most importantly with the revolutionary leader, Béla Kun, and his chief military adviser, Tibor Szamuely.[112] It mattered little to anti-Semitic nationalists in Hungary or elsewhere that the vast majority of Kun's supporters were, in fact, non-Jewish. Immediately after the fall of the Kun regime in early August 1919, the lawyer Oszkár Szőllősy published a widely circulated newspaper article on 'The Criminals of the Dictatorship of the Proletariat', in which he identified Jewish 'red, blood-stained knights of hate' as the main perpetrators of the Red Terror and the driving force behind communism.[113] In Hungary (as in Austria), Jews were also held directly responsible for the military defeat of the Central Powers. According to Gyula Gömbös, Hungary's subsequent Prime Minister, defeat was a direct consequence of the fact that the Jewish proportion of the Habsburg Empire's population was substantially higher ('1:56') than in the Entente countries ('1:227').[114]

To proclaim one's anti-Semitism publicly, and to pride oneself on having used merciless violence against Jewish civilians, subsequently became a common mark of distinction among the paramilitary activists of central Europe. In Hungary, where paramilitary atrocities against Jews were usually carried out with the tacit acquiescence of the authorities, the situation was particularly extreme. Pál Prónay, for example, collected the chopped-off ears of his Jewish victims as lucky charms.[115] At a dinner party conversation one of Prónay's officers, György Geszay, proudly remarked that he had an excellent appetite that evening as he had spent the afternoon roasting a Jew alive in a train.[116]

In Austria the situation was far less extreme. However, the language of violence used by Austrian paramilitaries certainly foreshadowed the future. When Hanns Albin Rauter expressed his aim to 'get rid of the Jews as soon as possible', and a student leader in Graz and the future *Heimwehr* leader, Ernst Rüdiger Starhemberg, attacked the 'Jewish war profiteers' as 'parasites', the rhetoric of violent anti-Semitism started a tradition on which radical nationalists would build in subsequent years.[117]

While the situation in Austria remained relatively calm, revolutionary and counter-revolutionary violence erupted in Bulgaria, though with a slight delay and without a strong anti-Semitic dimension. Despite its numerous internal problems, the country managed to hold democratic elections in 1919. The principal choice was on the one hand between the recently founded Communist Party, which closely followed the political line of Lenin's Bolsheviks, and on the other hand the Bulgarian Agrarian National Union (BANU). The Communists enjoyed considerable popular backing, notably in the cities. But the agrarians, under the charismatic leadership of Alexander Stambolijski, emerged as the stronger party.[118] Stambolijski secured a parliamentary majority by having several Communist candidates disqualified on procedural grounds. He remained in power for the next four years, using increasingly dictatorial and violent means to suppress any kind of dissent. Curiously, he made no move to abolish the monarchy.[119]

Despite having studied in Germany, Stambolijski cultivated his image as a peasant leader from a humble background. An imposing figure with wild black hair and a bushy moustache, he was vividly compared by a contemporary British observer to 'a brigand, moving through a blackberry bush'.[120] Using simple language that could be understood by peasant audiences, Stambolijski was not a communist but rather a peasant socialist – an appealing combination in a country where there were many small farmers. In particular, Stambolijski articulated the peasants' suspicions of townspeople and the upper classes. 'Who sent you to the trenches?' he asked. 'They did. Who made you lose Macedonia, Thrace and Dobrudja? They did.'[121]

His rhetorical skills and pro-agrarian policies may have secured him the loyalty of many small farmers, but Stambolijski was quick to alienate almost everyone else. Nationalists grudgingly forgave him for signing the devastating Treaty of Neuilly of November 1919 after the resignation of the former Prime Minister Teodor Teodorov, for it was obvious that the government had little choice but to accept the Allies' terms. What was more difficult for many to swallow was Stambolijski's willingness to come to terms with Bulgaria's neighbouring enemies, the most powerful of which was the Kingdom of Serbs, Croats and Slovenes. In March 1923, in an attempt to overcome Bulgaria's international isolation, Stambolijski and the Yugoslav government concluded an agreement at Niš, which provided for co-operation on border security to stamp out terrorist activities carried out by Macedonian extremists. The agreement was perceived as a second 'stab in the back' (after the acceptance of the Neuilly Treaty) for Macedonian nationalists, who had aspired to become part of an independent Bulgarian nation state ever since the waning days of Ottoman rule over the Balkans.[122] After the Great War, Macedonian nationalists had continued their activism through the IMRO (Internal Macedonian Revolutionary Organization, or *Vatreshna makedonska revolyutsionna organizatsia*), which declared as its major goal the autonomy of Macedonia and the protection of its Bulgarian population. In February 1920 guerrilla units (the so-called 'cheta') revived their pre-war activity in both Vardar and Aegean Macedonia – territories now controlled by Greece and the Kingdom of Serbs, Croats and Slovenes. They also began to target and assassinate politicians in Bulgaria, including representatives of Stambolijski's Agrarian Party. The Nish agreement hoped to put an end to the activities of IMRO.[123]

Stambolijski made further enemies at home when he pursued a radical political agenda in the area of land redistribution – an important subject in a nation of peasant proprietors. Stambolijski's administration declared a maximum holding of 30 hectares, thus enabling the government to confiscate land from the Church, local authorities and the state. The main objective was to make all agrarians into owners of relatively equal properties. However, this reform broke private property rights as guaranteed by the constitution and – although supported by many peasants – agrarian reform became, not surprisingly, a bone of major contention among other sectors of the population.[124]

Similar policies were followed in other spheres of the economy, most notably in the measures that aimed to limit the concentration of large capital in industry, trade and finance. Stambolijski also introduced the concept of maximum property holdings in urban centres and established a compulsory labour service, which required all citizens, men and women, to work for several months on public projects such as road construction and the building of schools. Although the initiative was conceived as a means of securing labour for important infrastructure projects in the post-war reconstruction, it was deeply unpopular. Radical ideas were also expressed with regards to the restructuring of Bulgaria's political system. Stambolijski promoted the idea of abolishing all parties and leaving only three political organizations based on the principle of labour affiliation: the Agrarian Union, the Working-Class Organization and the Craftsman's Union.[125] These steps indicated to the other political parties that Stambolijski was planning to introduce a peasant dictatorship through the back door.

In July 1922 the major Liberal, Conservative and Social Democratic parties in Bulgaria overcame their differences and formed the so-called *Konstitutsionen blok* (Constitutional Bloc). Driven primarily by their shared animosity towards the agrarians, representatives of the Bloc publicly denounced Stambolijski's rule as a dictatorship run by the worst scum of the Bulgarian peasantry and one that had to be fought with all means available.[126]

Stambolijski also managed to alienate the military elites, already humiliated by the dual military defeats of 1913 and 1918. Not only were they deprived of access to political power and social prestige, but they were also targets of the regime's apparent disdain for the traditional military establishment. Military elites were concerned, too, about the growth of Stambolijski's own paramilitary organization, the 'Orange Guard', which consisted of militarized peasants loyal only to BANU and its political leader.[127] The Orange Guard was dedicated exclusively to the maintenance of 'domestic order' and the intimidation of political opponents. Although Stambolijski's party was never close to establishing a real peasant dictatorship, the very existence of the Orange Guard threatened the government's opponents, the conservative establishment and the military elite, the latter of which formed itself into the so-called Military League, an increasingly powerful organization founded in 1919 and led by a professor of law, Alexander Tsankov. From the time of its establishment, the Military League, which included the majority of Bulgarian officers, waited for an opportune moment to end the agrarians' rule.[128]

Ironically, the opportunity arose when Stambolijski's Agrarian Party won the parliamentary elections on 1 April 1923, a victory greatly aided both by the government's ban on opposition rallies and by the abolition of proportional representation, which would have worked against the Agrarian Party. In response to the increased marginalization of all opposition to Stambolijski's government, the conspirators struck on 9 June 1923. Overnight the army occupied all strategically vital points in the capital before arresting the ministers of Stambolijski's government and other prominent members of the agrarian movement. Alexander Tsankov, the leader of the Military Union (which had been crucial in the coup), replaced Stambolijski as Prime Minister with the blessing of Tsar Boris, whose relationship with the republican Stambolijski had always been tense.[129]

In order to capture Stambolijski, who at the time of the coup was visiting relatives in his native village of Slavovitsa, the conspirators blocked all escape routes from Bulgaria and distributed leaflets that declared Stambolijski a wanted criminal. 'It is a duty of everybody – whether city dweller or peasant – to capture or shoot him. Whoever does not fulfil this order will be arrested.'[130] Within days the agrarian leader was caught by members of IMRO, who brutally tortured him and eventually killed him and his brother. The hand that had signed the treaties of Neuilly and Nish was cut off and Stambolijski's severed head sent back to Sofia in a large biscuit box.[131]

The brutal nature of Stambolijski's death prompted a violent and immediate response from his supporters. Throughout the countryside mass riots erupted, with peasant associations and Orange Guard members mobilizing to fend off the coup. If the agrarians had hoped for Communist support, they were to be disappointed. The Communist Party took the view that the conflict was one between two sections of the bourgeoisie (one 'rural' and one 'urban') and decided to stay out if it. Isolated and insufficiently armed, the peasant riots were swiftly suppressed with the utmost brutality by the armed forces. Meanwhile Tsankov assured the alarmed Western Allies that his government would adhere to the terms of the Neuilly Treaty and re-establish democratic rule in Bulgaria.[132]

Tsankov kept the first part of his promise but not the second. Democratic rule was not easily re-established and, for the remainder of the 1920s, violence remained a constant issue in Bulgarian political life. The communists, who had chosen not to fight the military in June while Bulgarian peasants were slaughtered in the countryside, were ordered by Moscow to stage a revolution. This produced an abortive rising of communists, anarchists and peasants against the Tsankov government in September 1923. Spreading mainly in north-western and central Bulgaria, the rising ended in disaster. Between 1,200 and 1,500 communist supporters were murdered and many of those who survived were imprisoned with harsh sentences, starting a period in Bulgarian history known as the 'White Terror'. The brutality with which the uprising was crushed by army and police units inspired a whole wave of novels and poems, none more famous than Geo Milev's poem 'September', written in 1924:

> Village squares once more stained scarlet with blood
> Death shrieks from throats cruelly cut.
> The ill-boding clanking of chains
> Jails crowded again
> From barracks and prison yards
> Echo commands
> Volleys ring out
> Doors are locked
> Dark visitors hammer at them
> The son with pistol cocked
> Lies dead on the threshold
> Father hanged
> Sister defiled
> Peasants driven from villages
> Escorted by troops:
> A dismal convoy
> Bound for the firing squad . . .

One year after writing the poem, Milev himself was murdered in police custody along with other left-leaning Bulgarian intellectuals.

As a further direct consequence of the uprising, the Communist Party and all associated organizations were banned. In retaliation, an underground group of communist activists detonated a bomb on 16 April 1925 in the roof of Sofia's Sveta Nedelya Cathedral during a public funeral service for General Konstantin Georgiev, who had been assassinated by communists a few days earlier. The explosion led to the collapse of the cathedral's roof, killing over 130 mourners, including many senior army officers and politicians, and wounding another 500. This bomb attack act was followed by yet another round of mass arrests of Communist Party members, their supporters, and many ordinary citizens. The arrested suffered torture and imprisonment, and around one thousand of them disappeared without a trace within the first month of the bombing, most of them killed in police custody.[133]

IO

Fear of Bolshevism and the Rise of Fascism

The revolutionary upheavals in the vanquished states of central, eastern and south-eastern Europe soon threatened to spread to the victor states and even to formerly neutral countries further west. Spain, which had remained neutral in the Great War, came close to an open civil war during its *Trienio Bolchevique* ('three Bolshevik years') from 1918 to 1920, when serious labour unrest, already common before the war, spread across the rural south and flared up in the cities, leading to more than 750 deaths in the struggles between union supporters, employers and the police forces of the state.[1] In Catalonia, most notably in Barcelona, the Confederation of Labour (CNT) aimed to create a Catalan Workers' Republic that would sever all links with the unloved capital, Madrid. Already in August 1917 they had joined the Socialist General Union of Labour (UGT) in calling for a general strike in Barcelona, a strike that was put down with brutal force, leaving seventy dead and thousands of suspected 'revolutionaries' in prison. In the spring of 1919, encouraged by the revolutions in Russia and central Europe, the CNT called for yet another general strike, prompting some 100,000 workers in Barcelona to down their tools for an entire month.[2] The strike failed to deliver a permanent solution that would have satisfied all sides involved. Within weeks solidarity strikes were held in other parts of Spain, notably in the south. There were major work stoppages in Andalusia, notably in Seville and Granada, while impoverished land labourers working on the large semi-feudal estates in Spain's deep south felt inspired by the radicalism with which Lenin and the Bolsheviks had resolved the land question in Russia. As one Anarcho-Syndicalist newspaper from Cordoba, *La Voz del Cantero* (*The Voice of the Quarry*), put it:

Prepare yourselves, workers of Spain, for the fact that at any moment the clarion of justice may sound! Oppressed and desperate people, the hour has arrived to demand accounting from our enemies for all the crimes they have committed against the labouring and productive classes.[3]

Confronted with an increasingly volatile situation and agitated landless labourers, estate owners abandoned their country homes.[4] Meanwhile the fear of Bolshevism went far enough for the government to round up some 800 Russian citizens and other suspected foreign communists living in Spain at the time and forcibly send them to Odessa on board the steamer *Manuel Calvo*, which left Spain in the spring of 1919.[5] Amid growing economic instability and internal strife, fifteen governments came and went between 1917 and 1923, while in 1921 the far Left founded the Spanish Communist Party (PCE). Eventually, Spain was to follow a very central European pattern when General Miguel Primo de Rivera seized power in September 1923, transforming the country into a conservative dictatorship endorsed by King Alfonso XIII.[6]

The threat of revolution was a great deal less serious in the principal European victor states of the war – Britain and France – than it was elsewhere. The short-lived 'Limerick Soviet', established in western Ireland in the second half of April 1919 at the beginning of the Irish War of Independence, was motivated by Republicanism rather than Bolshevism, and, in any event, it was terminated by British troops within two weeks. Yet despite the absence of any serious Communist bid for power in either Britain or France, contemporaries in both countries were obsessed with the perceived threat of Bolshevik contagion. While the attempted assassination of the French Prime Minister Georges Clemenceau, by an anarchist, Eugène Cottin, in February 1919, could be dismissed as an isolated incident, policymakers in France had not forgotten the serious waves of strikes that had occurred in the country in the last two years of the Great War.

Several serious work stoppages had occurred in the French metallurgical industry in July 1916 and again in May 1918. In the spring of 1917 the strikes spread and led to general calls for higher wages and an end to the war. Worse still were the mutinies in the French Army: in May and June 1917 nearly half of the French divisions on the Western

Front were affected.[7] While the mutinies and work stoppages never escalated into a revolution, the memories of 1917 lingered on, amplified by revolutionary events in Russia. When, in the spring of 1920, France was again beset by a series of strikes, supported by the General Confederation of Labour (CGT), fears of Bolshevik contagion spread quickly within the country's political establishment and middle classes. The founding of the French Section of the Workers' International (soon renamed as the Communist Party of France) in mid-December of that year did little to decrease their suspicion. While the Germans were not fully replaced as the main threat to the geopolitical status quo, the new political message of the conservative establishment in France was that there were now *two* threats emanating from east of the French border: German revisionism and Russian Bolshevism.[8]

Britain, too, suffered recurring labour unrest during the 1920s, including a national miners' strike in October 1920, which lasted for two and a half weeks and brought the country to a temporary standstill. Labour unrest culminated in the great General Strike of 1926, which involved workers from all areas of British industry. The causes of the strikes, however, were mainly economic, and not driven by any desire for a revolutionary overthrow of the existing system. The only party openly advocating radical change, the Communist Party of Great Britain founded in July 1920, never received significant public support. Nevertheless, at least between the autumn of 1918 and the early 1920s, many people in Britain believed that events in Russia and central Europe might be replicated at home. In London the social reformer and intellectual Beatrice Webb, co-founder with her husband of the London School of Economics, wrote in her diary on 11 November 1918, the day that hostilities on the Western Front came to an end:

> Peace! Thrones are everywhere crashing and the men of property everywhere secretly trembling. How soon will the tide of revolution catch up with the tide of victory? That is the question which is exercising Whitehall and Buckingham Palace and causing anxiety even among the more thoughtful democrats.[9]

As Russia was drowning in her citizens' blood amid civil war, and revolution spread westwards, anxiety turned into fear the following spring. In his Fontainebleau Memorandum of late March 1919, written under the shadow of the recent establishment of the Hungarian and Bavarian Soviet Republics, Prime Minister David Lloyd George urged that 'the greatest danger that I see in the present situation is that Germany may throw in her lot with Bolshevism and place her resources, her brains, her vast organizing power at the disposal of the revolutionary fanatics whose dream it is to conquer the world for Bolshevism by force of arms'.[10]

Such fears quickly infused the popular imagination, as communism gradually eclipsed Britain's wartime enemy, the evil Hun, as the prime threat of the future. When, in 1924, the highly popular author, John Buchan, published the fourth of his five best-selling thrillers about Richard Hannay, the upper-class hero who protects Britain, the empire and the English class system from the underhand enemies who menace it on every side, communism featured prominently. Whereas the threat in the three previous novels had been Germany, the villain of *The Three Hostages* was Dominick Medina, ostensibly the very picture of the urbane English conservative politician but in fact *déraciné* Irish 'with a far-away streak of Latin . . . and that never makes a good cross'. Medina symbolized a new kind of nihilism that seemed to threaten the established order: Bolshevism.[11]

Concerns about the brewing threat of Bolshevism even extended to the United States, where a series of bomb attacks were carried out by Italian-American anarchists in 1919–20. They culminated in a lethal bomb attack on New York's Wall Street at midday on 16 September 1920, killing thirty-eight people and injuring hundreds more. The authorities never apprehended the culprits, but it was widely assumed that the bombing had been carried out by anarchists, prompting a 'Red Scare' and fears of further unrest, which helped to establish an extreme anti-communist mentality.[12]

In the victorious states of the Great War the threat of a Bolshevik revolution was probably greatest in the least of the Great Powers of Europe: Italy. Even during the war, in the spring and summer of 1917, northern Italy had witnessed mass protests against insufficient food supplies and the continuation of the war.[13]

The reversal of military fortunes after Italy's disastrous setback at the Battle of Caporetto in 1917, with the surprisingly swift 'victory

of Vittorio Veneto' over Austro-Hungarian forces in 1918, temporarily eased internal tensions and wiped out the tragic memories
of the previous autumn, when Italy had appeared to be on the brink
of almost certain collapse. Austria-Hungary's defeat marked the first
major military victory in the history of the Italian nation state and
it inspired the wildest dreams and aspirations.[14] In the newly
'redeemed' territories, notably in the former Austro-Hungarian city
of Trieste, ethnic Italians greeted the victory of the Italian Army
with boundless joy: 'For four days, 130,000 people of all ages, of
every sex, of every political party, have taken to the streets and
squares of Trieste . . . Everybody cries with joy, hugging and kissing
others as if they were all born to the same mother. This mother is
Italy. Her name is on everyone's lips . . .'[15]

In reality, Italy emerged from the war deeply divided, as astute contemporary observers were well aware. The famous Italian philosopher
Benedetto Croce, for example, wrote to his friend, the German literary scholar Karl Vossler, on the day of the armistice with Vienna, that
'Italy comes out of this war with a serious and deadly disease, with
open sores, with dangerous weaknesses in the flesh . . .'[16]

Croce was right, of course, in observing that military victory was
unlikely to heal the deep rifts in Italian society that dated back to
1914, when a fierce public controversy had erupted between those
Italians who advocated going to war and those who preferred neutrality. Although Italy was still part of the Triple Alliance (with
Germany and Austria-Hungary), interventionists urged the government to enter the war against the Central Powers to redeem what they
perceived as Italian territories from Habsburg rule, namely Trentino
and the city of Trieste. Other Italians remained sceptical and the Italian Socialist Party (Partito Socialista Italiano, or PSI) opposed the
war. Unsurprisingly, the government's decision in the spring of 1915
to enter the war on the Allies' side proved deeply divisive.[17]

In late 1917 and early 1918, Prime Minister Vittorio Orlando further deepened these divisions when – in response to the Italian army's
rout at Caporetto in 1917 – his government tightened censorship,
criminalized peace activism, and launched a major nationalist mobilization campaign, in which socialists, trade unionists, priests and
pacifists were singled out as 'enemies within' and held responsible for

the collapse in military morale.[18] Orlando's campaign undoubtedly exacerbated the 'climate of ideological civil war', which originated in the fierce controversy between 'neutralists' and 'interventionists' in 1914 and which had gained new urgency after Caporetto.[19] Socialists and Catholic critics of the war bemoaned the huge death tolls caused by their country's involvement, while the 'interventionists' blamed them for Italy's military misfortunes, branding them as traitors who had 'stabbed the nation in the back' by undermining support for the troops on the home front.[20]

The deep rifts caused by such accusations were not the only internal problems that Italy faced, even after victory had been secured in late 1918. Arguably the poorest of the victorious states, Italy emerged from the war with an unsustainable national debt due to heavy wartime borrowing from Britain and the United States. Riddled with debt and burdened by social and political conflicts, Italy's post-war government remained extremely unstable. Returning soldiers put additional pressures on the already volatile job market, while high inflation wiped out family savings. Despite victory in the war, food supplies remained severely disrupted while the government delayed long-overdue land reform.

During the war the ruling classes had offered a tempting promise to the millions of landless young farm labourers, who were now risking life and limb for their country: a post-war reform would give them access to, and ownership of, hitherto uncultivated land. When the war ended in victory, this promise was not kept, exacerbating pre-war social conflicts, notably in the Italian countryside. In response, and inspired by events in Russia in 1917–18, the Socialist Party adopted a programme advocating social revolution along Bolshevik lines during its national congress of October 1919, while also pledging its allegiance to Lenin's Third International. Motivated by the belief that the time for the long-anticipated collapse of the capitalist order had come, and, inspired by events in eastern Europe, the party's new political programme insisted that a 'dictatorship of the proletariat' could only be achieved through a 'violent seizure of power', thus widening a pre-existing internal rift between the reformist and the revolutionary wings of the party.[21]

The party's radicalization seemed to capture the mood of large segments of the population. In the general election of November 1919, the Socialists won more than a third of all the votes and became the largest party in the Chamber of Deputies, followed by the conservative Catholic Popular Party (Partito Popolare Italiano, or PPI), which won one-fifth of the total vote on a platform of social reform. The former ruling parties, the Liberals and the Democrats, lost heavily.

With the creation of a Socialist-led central government, and socialist election successes in the local elections of October and November 1919 (notably in the Po Valley), party leaders felt it was time to implement radical reforms. Meanwhile bourgeois fears of 'Russian conditions' were heightened by actual acts of violence and expropriation. In the Lombardian countryside around Crema, for example, the trade union organizations in June 1920 stirred up violent protests against those landowners who were deemed to have breached previous labour agreements. Hundreds of peasants went on strike, occupied farms, and confiscated foodstuffs, occasionally taking over the private residences of landowners, as the alarmed local prefect reported back to Rome.[22]

Similar events occurred elsewhere in the Italian countryside and they often turned violent. When, in April 1920, farm workers in the small Apulian town of Nardò attacked the local police station, they also cut telegraph wires, blew up some railway tracks, and erected barricades before plundering the town's warehouses. The arrival of army troops the following day led to violent clashes that resulted in many injuries as well as the deaths of three peasants and a soldier.[23]

Violent class struggle, including continuous strikes in the state and private sectors, reached a climax in September 1920, when workers occupied more than six hundred factories, and set up governing bodies of workers' councils in industrial towns and cities, leaving the impression that Italy was on the brink of Bolshevik rule. The unrest, coupled with ineffective law enforcement and the apparent unwillingness of the government of Giovanni Giolitti to get involved in labour disputes, caused great alarm among industrialists and estate owners, who looked around with increasing desperation for a saviour to protect them from the Red menace. They eventually found him in Benito Mussolini and his nascent Fascist movement.

Mussolini at this point had only recently completed his personal journey from being a prominent socialist in pre-war Italy to becoming a radical nationalist. This journey had started in November 1914, when – against the official line of the Italian Socialist Party – he had advocated Italy's entry into the war.²⁴ Before the war, he had been a leader of the maximalist wing of the Italian Socialist Party and, from 1912 to 1914, the editor of the party's official paper, *Avanti!* Mussolini's rejection of the official party line, which advocated neutrality in a 'capitalist' war, led to his expulsion from the party in November 1914. That same month he founded his own newspaper, *Il Popolo d'Italia*. Through a combination of funding from like-minded businessmen and his rhetorical gifts, Mussolini soon emerged as the leader of the 'interventionist' campaign, which was in favour of joining the war against the Central Powers.

When Italy eventually entered the war on the Allied side in May 1915, Mussolini served as a soldier on the Isonzo front until February 1917, when he contracted syphilis (rather than being wounded by a mortar bomb, as official history books in Fascist Italy suggested).²⁵ He observed the last year of the war from the desk of his paper, *Il Popolo d'Italia*, redefining his views on the future of Italy. The main target of his polemical attacks were his former socialist comrades. Branding the Socialist Party 'a more dangerous enemy than the Austrian army', he urged his readers to fight it with 'sword and fire'.²⁶ Mussolini's rhetoric became even more radical after the Bolshevik Revolution in Russia, which he considered no more than a first step in a global Communist bid for power that could only be contained through violence: 'It is not a time for angels, it is a time for devils. It requires ferocity, not humility . . . It requires a long sword and a great deal of fire . . . Either that or defeat. Either that or Russia.'²⁷ With his pre-war activism in the socialist movement no more than a distant memory, he now aspired to a 'nationalist revolution'. The future state would be run by the *'trincerocrazia'* ('trenchocracy'), a new aristocracy born out of the blood and mud of the trenches.²⁸

In March 1919, Mussolini founded the *Fasci di Combattimento* ('Combat Leagues') in Milan. Initially, however, his movement was not particularly successful in attracting new supporters. By the end of the year it still only had a total of 800 members, many of them former *arditi*, the Italian shock troops of the Great War, for whom

Mussolini's rhetoric of fire and sword had a particular appeal.[29] The movement only began to grow exponentially from 1920 onwards, partly in response to the perceived threat of Bolshevik revolution. It was at this time that Mussolini's supporters launched their violent campaign against organized labour, socialist councils and newspapers, notably in the regions of the Po Valley dominated by the Socialist Party.[30] As in the German *Freikorps*, Mussolini's Fascist *squadristi* attracted men who had been too young to fight in the Great War. To them, the squads were a surrogate for that missing experience.[31]

On 16 October 1920, Mussolini's official newspaper openly called for a violent campaign against fascism's socialist adversaries: 'If civil war is unavoidable, then so be it!' Mussolini's rhetoric was equally belligerent, referring to Bolshevism and the intended fight against it with medical metaphors: if Bolshevism was a 'gangrene', 'infection', or 'cancer' that required rooting out, he described fascism as the 'scalpel' that would be used with surgical precision to cure the national 'body politic'.[32]

Inflammatory words were quickly followed by violent deeds. In Bologna, which was governed by the Socialists, Fascist squads began to assault the local government buildings, and on 21 November 1920, when thousands of people celebrated the election of a socialist mayor in Piazza Maggiore, a group of Fascists opened fire on the crowds. Socialist paramilitaries, the 'Red Guards', returned fire and threw grenades. The incident left ten people dead and approximately sixty wounded, leaving the Socialist city council with little choice but to resign. For Mussolini and the Fascists, it provided an important lesson: violence paid.[33]

In rural areas the Fascists contributed decisively to the suppression of all other political and trade union organizations, particularly those affiliated to the Socialist Party and, to a lesser extent, the Popular Party (Partito Popolare). Thousands of *squadristi* spread terror through the countryside, destroying the premises of 'subversive' parties, occupying whole towns, and beating up or humiliating political opponents – often with the knowledge and tacit support of the police, many of whom looked favourably upon Mussolini's 'forces of order'. In what seemed increasingly like an open civil war, the number of people killed in violent clashes soared. All in all, it is estimated that about 3,000 people were killed in Italy between 1919 and 1922.[34] The main victims of political violence were socialists and militants of non-Fascist parties. In 1920 alone 172 socialists were killed, as were ten members of the Popular Party, four Fascists, fifty-one innocent bystanders, and fifty-one law-enforcement officers, while the number of those seriously injured in that year stood at around 1,600.[35]

Amid continuing violence the following spring, Mussolini's movement, now rebranded as the Partito Nazionale Fascista (PNF), emerged as the strongest political party in Italy, with almost a tenfold increase in membership.[36] In response to the rapid growth of Mussolini's party, the liberal Prime Minister, Giovanni Giolitti, made the fateful decision to include the PNF in his 'National Bloc' for the May 1921 general elections. Rather than containing the Fascists, Giolitti's decision helped to enhance Mussolini's standing as a 'respectable' politician. Meanwhile his squads continued their campaign, now enjoying near immunity from police intervention. Having reduced their opponents to impotence, the Fascists ruled without opposition in many regions of the north and centre of the peninsula.[37]

Mussolini could thus take advantage of both the widespread fear of Bolshevism and the instability of Italy's central government. Between 1919 and 1922 a succession of five governments propped up by unsteady majorities exacerbated the crisis of the parliamentary regime, and lent credit to Fascist anti-democratic propaganda that 'the century of democracy is over' by confirming the inability of the state to uphold order. Ironically, Mussolini's Fascists, the political movement that was responsible for much of the violent chaos that prevailed in the country, began to seem like the only force that could restore order, whereas the democratic government appeared powerless.[38]

In this situation the Fascist Party decided that the time was ripe to make a bid for power. On the evening of 27 October 1922, Mussolini ordered his paramilitary troops to 'march on Rome'. The Prime Minister at the time, the liberal Luigi Facta, asked the king, Victor Emanuel III, to declare a state of emergency in response. Victor Emanuel initially agreed, but had second thoughts and refused to sign the order the following morning. It was only after the king had accepted Mussolini's demand to become Prime Minister that the fascist leader, choosing to take the train rather than 'marching' on Rome, joined up with his roughly 25,000 paramilitary troops who had camped outside the Italian capital. By that time, however, the Fascists had effectively taken control of many provincial towns across Italy.[39]

Mussolini's dualistic strategy – his attempts to win over supporters in Parliament and the social elites while simultaneously endorsing *squadristi* violence against the state – had clearly paid off: it forced the king to invite him to form a coalition government of Fascists, liberals, nationalists and Catholics.[40] Mussolini had learnt more from Lenin and the Bolsheviks than he would have cared to admit, notably the lesson that parliamentary majorities were far less important than the ability and determination to instil fear in opponents and to act ruthlessly when an opportunity presented itself. Following on from Lenin's dissolution of the democratically elected Russian Parliament in 1918, Mussolini's appointment as Prime Minister was the second time within five years that power had been handed over to the head of a militia party which had imposed its authority by means of violence.[41]

Most historians agree today that the armed forces of the Italian state could easily have defeated the paramilitary forces of fascism. 'But neither the king nor the government nor the country's political and economic elites had the political will or the courage to impose a state of order that might have saved the parliamentary regime. Rather, they feared that repression of the Fascist onslaught would breathe new life into the socialist revolution and they nurtured the illusion that the responsibilities of government would suffice to convince the Fascists to renounce their violent paramilitary organization.'[42] Very few people fully understood the long-term consequences of the events of October 1922 and the new form of politics they ushered in. The liberal bourgeoisie believed in the possibility of domesticating fascism by involving it in government, while the majority of anti-Fascist parties were of the view that fascism was merely an ephemeral movement destined to fizzle out once it had failed in its function as the armed guard of the bourgeois state. These illusions prevailed even after the 'March on Rome'. In reality, Mussolini set out from the start to abolish parliamentary democracy and build a dictatorship, which he eventually achieved in 1925.[43]

The lesson that violence could trump democracy was not lost on other leaders of the extreme Right in Europe, or indeed on astute observers of the liberal Left, who feared that Mussolini's example could be followed by others. As the German liberal journalist and former diplomat Count Harry Kessler noted in his diary on 29 October 1922:

> The Fascists have mounted a coup in Italy and seized power. If they are able to hold on to it, this will be a historic event that may have incalculable consequences, not just for Italy but for the whole of Europe. It is the first step in the victorious march of the counter-revolution . . . In a certain sense Mussolini's coup can be compared with Lenin's in October 1917, albeit as its antithesis. Perhaps it will usher in a period of renewed turmoil and war in Europe.[44]

In contrast to Kessler, the far Right saw Mussolini's example as one to emulate. On 9 November 1923, after proclaiming a 'national revolution' the previous night, the leader of the infant Nazi Party in Germany, Adolf Hitler, tried to match Mussolini's 'March on Rome' the previous year when his supporters staged a 'March on the Feldherrnhalle' in Munich, which was to be followed by a 'March on Berlin'.[45]

Few in Germany at the time would have considered Hitler a likely 'second Mussolini' who could bring about a successful 'national revolution'. He was not even a German citizen. The impoverished son of a customs inspector from the Austrian town of Braunau am Inn, Hitler had spent his early years in Vienna as an aimless drifter and failed artist, carrying out a string of poorly paid jobs, including the painting of postcards. In May 1913 he moved from Vienna to Munich in order to avoid military service in Austria-Hungary, but joined the Bavarian Army as a volunteer when war broke out in 1914. After serving on the Western Front as a dispatch runner, rising to the rank of corporal and being awarded an Iron Cross, his immediate post-war years were characterized by ideological confusion. The war or, more specifically, the Central Powers' defeat in November 1918 had radicalized Hitler, but he was not quite sure whether his extremism tended to the Left or the Right.[46] Indeed, when he was demobilized and returned to Munich, he briefly served in the propaganda department of Kurt Eisner's revolutionary government, charged with training fellow soldiers in democracy, before being elected in April 1919 to a soldiers' council of the Munich Soviet Republic. But Hitler's interest in socialism was short-lived and soon he converted to the extreme Right.[47]

Employed by the German Reichswehr as an educator and confidential informant, Hitler first attended a beer-hall meeting of the radical right-wing German Workers' Party (Deutsche Arbeiterpartei, or DAP) in September 1919. He soon took control of the party that renamed itself the National Socialist German Workers' Party (NSPD) in February 1920. Hitler's unique worldview of later years, with its distinct emphasis on racial doctrine, biological anti-Semitism and violent expansionism, was not fully articulated at this point, even if he identified the Jews as Germany's main enemy in his early speeches of 1919. What shaped Hitler at this time was the experience of perpetual crisis, from war to defeat and revolution, from the peace treaties of 1919 to the common contemporary assumption that Germany was on the verge of civil war.[48]

Such perceptions were not unfounded, as revolutionary and counter-revolutionary turmoil in Germany continued after the fall of the Munich Soviet in 1919. The following year, prompted by the Versailles Treaty's stipulation of a reduction of the German armed forces to 100,000 men and the German government's subsequent order to *Freikorps* units to disband, the German Right staged a coup in Berlin. One of the key figures behind the putsch of March 1920, General Walther von Lüttwitz, refused to obey the orders to disband the *Freikorps* and demobilize the army, and was dismissed by the Defence Minister, Gustav Noske. Lüttwitz, however, had the support of many *Freikorps* soldiers, especially that of the notorious Ehrhardt Brigade, named after its leader the naval captain Hermann Ehrhardt. Assured of their loyalty, Lüttwitz sent an ultimatum to Friedrich Ebert, now the German President, threatening to overthrow the government with force if the demobilization of the army and *Freikorps* was not stopped immediately. The putschists also demanded new general elections, which they assumed would return a majority against the Ebert government.[49] When Ebert rejected the ultimatum, the Ehrhardt Brigade marched on Berlin. On 13 March, Lüttwitz and Dr Wolfgang Kapp, an East Prussian civil servant and co-founder of the extreme-right wartime Fatherland Party, proclaimed that the Reich government had ceased to exist.[50]

Ebert and his government fled Berlin for Dresden before moving on to Stuttgart. The future of the democratically elected government was hanging in the balance, as the Social Democrats did not have the unambivalent support of the army. The Reichswehr's senior commander, General Hans von Seeckt, was conflicted between his oath to uphold the Weimar Constitution and his loyalty towards fellow officers. In any case, he refused to let 'troops shoot on troops'. Without military assistance, Ebert decided to call a general strike, which was supported by the two socialist parties and the unions. In an impressive demonstration of social democracy's grassroots strength, the strike brought life in Germany to an abrupt standstill. After four and a half days the putsch collapsed.[51]

Calling off the strike proved difficult, however. Emboldened by their victory over the supporters of the Kapp Putsch, the left-wing advocates of radical change saw their opportunity. They assumed that the temporary power vacuum created by the Kapp Putsch and its collapse offered the possibility of realizing some of the revolutionary demands that had not been met in 1918. To that end, the far Left re-established workers' council governments within socialist strongholds in central Germany. This led to fighting between retreating Kapp putschists and socialist insurgents on the one hand, and between regular Reichswehr troops trying to restore order and self-appointed Red Guards supporting the councils on the other. As Harry Kessler noted in his diary on 19 and 20 March, fierce fighting occurred in Berlin[52] and revenge killings were frequent: 'At various points in Berlin, the mob has captured officers of the retreating putschist forces and murdered them. The bitterness of the working classes against the military seems to be boundless; and the successful general strike has greatly increased their sense of power.'[53]

The situation was even more tense in central Germany and in the industrial heartland of the Ruhr Valley. During the so-called March Rising socialist militants joined forces with industrial workers and miners in demanding the nationalization of industries and the reintroduction of workers' councils. Ebert and his government responded with force and found a willing ally in the Reichswehr and the *Freikorps*. Unlike during the Kapp Putsch, the army leadership had no reservation about opening fire on striking workers. In the event, some

1,000 'Red Army' insurgents were killed before the March Rising was finally put down by government troops.

Fears of further left-wing revolutionary threats like those of 1919 and 1920 became particularly entrenched in Munich, which became the most staunchly right-wing city in Weimar Germany. It was no coincidence that this was the city where Hitler converted to the extreme Right and found susceptible audiences for his radical messages of anti-Bolshevism and national renewal. Yet his premature attempt to follow Mussolini's example and seize power in 1923 failed miserably. At midday on 9 November, Bavarian police opened fire on his supporters as they marched through Munich, killing sixteen of them. Hitler himself managed to escape, but was arrested two days later on charges of treason and put in Landsberg prison.[54] What he had overlooked in his attempt to emulate Mussolini's 'March on Rome' was that the Duce's success in Italy was largely owed to a dual strategy that oscillated between legality and illegality: the use of brutal violence on the streets combined with parliamentary promises to restore order and national values.[55] By the time Hitler was pardoned by the Bavarian Supreme Court and released from prison, just over eight months later, he knew that he and his party would have to pursue a course of legality if they were to have any hope of ever coming close to the halls of power. This realization was of critical importance for his second, and successful, bid for power in January 1933.

III

Imperial Collapse

The recent Treaties which regulate, or are supposed to regulate, the relations among peoples are, as a matter of fact, nothing but a terrible regress . . .
  Francesco Saverio Nitti (Italian Prime Minister during the signing of the Paris peace treaties), Peaceless Europe *(1921)*

As soon as the emperor says goodnight, we'll break up into a hundred pieces . . . All the peoples will set up their own dirty little statelets . . . Nationalism is the new religion.
  Joseph Roth, Radetzky March *(1932)*

II

Pandora's Box: Paris and the
Problem of Empire

Amid the revolutionary and counter-revolutionary turmoil in central and eastern Europe, the Paris Peace Conference convened in mid-January 1919 to decide on the future of the vanquished. As the British Prime Minister, David Lloyd George, acknowledged retrospectively, the nature of this peace conference differed fundamentally from the great European peace conference of the previous century: the Congress of Vienna of 1814–15. First, and most importantly, the vanquished imperial powers and their successor states – Germany, Austria, Hungary, Bulgaria and the Ottoman Empire – were excluded from the negotiations in Paris, whereas France had been a central actor in the Vienna discussions about the creation of a new international order. The defeated powers in the Great War were to be summoned only when the various peace treaties to be imposed on them had been finalized. Russia – Britain and France's key ally between 1914 and 1917 – was also not represented in Paris, largely because Britain and France were still actively involved in trying to bring down Lenin's Bolshevik government by offering logistical and military assistance to its White opponents. A second difference lay in the sheer size and composition of the Paris Peace Conference. Whereas the Vienna Congress had been an exclusively European affair with merely five participating countries, the Paris Peace Conference was attended by more than thirty Allied and associated states.[1] Obviously, not all participants had equal rights and say in the discussions. At the top of the hierarchical pyramid stood the 'Council of Ten', which from late March 1919 was replaced by the 'Council of Four', with the conference's host, French Prime Minister Georges Clemenceau, as chairman. Apart from Clemenceau, US President Woodrow Wilson and the British Prime Minister David Lloyd George were the key actors, even if

Italy's head of government, Vittorio Emanuele Orlando, also sat on the 'Council of Four'. From late April, as Italy temporarily withdrew from the conference in anger over Rome's unresolved territorial claims on the Adriatic port of Fiume, it was essentially the 'Big Three' – Clemenceau, Wilson and Lloyd George – who made the decisions. During their deliberations they were advised by a total of fifty-two expert commissions dealing with complex issues such as reparations and new borders.[2]

Soon after the opening of the Peace Conference, it became clear that each delegation leader had come to Paris with his own objectives, which often proved incompatible with those of other Allied leaders. For France, the future of its intrinsically powerful eastern neighbour, Germany, was the single most important issue on the agenda. Clemenceau deliberately decided to open the conference on 18 January, the anniversary of the founding of the German Reich in Versailles after France's humiliating defeat in the Franco-Prussian War of 1870–1. Finding a solution to the 'German problem' that had haunted Paris ever since was considered a matter of both collective security and justice: during the Great War ten French *départements* had suffered directly from battle or occupation, leaving vast areas in the north-east of the country in ruins. Even worse, France had lost a quarter of its male population between the ages of eighteen and twenty-seven. Of all the Western Allies, it was the country most profoundly and directly affected by the conflict. Clemenceau knew all too well that the overwhelming majority of his people demanded punishment for the vanquished and due compensation for the victors (notably for France). In order to ensure that Germany would never threaten France again, various plans were contemplated by Clemenceau and his advisers: a complete break-up of the Reich, the occupation of much of the Rhineland, and the creation of strong allied states on Germany's eastern border.[3]

For the British – then, as before the war, concerned about the 'balance of power' on the continent – the prospect of French hegemony was as menacing as had been the pre-war threat of German dominance. Instead of backing all of the French demands, Lloyd George ultimately wanted to re-establish trading links with Germany, even if public pressure back home demanded some sort of punishment of the Reich. Germany's global importance was to be minimized (by taking away her overseas colonies and scuppering the fleet), but not to the extent that bilateral trade would cease altogether. Germany had been a major trading partner for Britain before the war, therefore a completely impoverished, potentially even Bolshevik, Germany was simply not in London's best interest. At the same time, however, and against the backdrop of general elections to be held in December 1918, Lloyd George found himself under significant domestic pressure to impose a harsh peace on Germany, notably from conservative newspapers such as Lord Northcliffe's *Daily Mail* and *The Times*, which demanded substantial reparations as well as the trial and execution of Kaiser Wilhelm II for war crimes. Britain's interests also clashed with those of France in the Middle East, where vital strategic and economic interests were at stake.[4]

The American President Wilson, by contrast, had always maintained that the result of the conference should be a 'just peace', leading to a redesigned system of international relations based on a radically new interpretation of popular sovereignty with global application. Rational, morally accountable individuals would elect sovereign governments everywhere. The subjects closest to Wilson's heart – the realization of the principle of national 'self-determination' (by which he meant government derived from popular sovereignty) and the creation of a League of Nations that would make future wars unlikely, if not impossible, by guaranteeing collective security and international peace – featured particularly prominently on his agenda.[5] Wilson had the example of the United States in mind, which he sought to universalize and apply to Europe in particular. Within the successor states to Europe's empires, religious and ethnic differences were to be preserved and protected, even if minorities had to adhere to the overall values of the national community in which they lived.[6] Behind Wilson's apparent idealism, however, lay a calculated aim: if the Great War and the Allied victory had shifted the global balance of power away from Europe and towards the US, the new world order he promoted would cement his country's global dominance, both politically and economically.[7]

Reconciling the Allies' conflicting positions while also keeping the delegations of smaller countries in Paris happy was an almost impossible task. Even if the Western Allies' political leaders were reluctant to admit it, they were fully aware from the start of the deliberations in Paris that the final versions of the peace treaties were going to be a compromise – not between the victors and the vanquished, but between the key actors among the victorious Allies.[8]

Set against the complex backdrop of contemporary expectations, the Paris peace treaties almost inevitably disappointed everyone involved. With the benefit of hindsight, historians have been somewhat kinder than contemporaries in their assessment of the treaties, acknowledging that the peacemakers in Paris were often forced to accept new realities that had already been created on the ground, confining their role to adjudicating between conflicting ambitions of various parties.[9] Yet not all historians are persuaded that the peacemakers made the best of a bad job, emphasizing instead that the Paris Peace Conference fell short of its ultimate objective: the creation of a secure, peaceful and lasting world order.[10]

The unravelling of the order established in Paris within less than two decades owed much to the rise of strong revisionist and nationalist forces in the vanquished states of Europe; not least in Germany, where the economic turmoil in the wake of the Great Depression after 1929 played into the hands of Hitler's Nazi movement, which had always been adamant that it would tear apart the 'dictated peace' of Versailles, with force if necessary. Precisely because of the rise of Nazism, historians and the general public alike have devoted far greater attention to the Versailles Treaty than to any other aspect of the peace-making process. Yet it could be argued that the focus on Versailles (and notably on the reparations question and the 'war guilt' clause, attributing sole responsibility for the outbreak of hostilities to Berlin) has narrowed our understanding of the Paris Peace Conference and somewhat marginalized the single biggest issue at stake at the time: the transformation of an entire continent previously dominated by land empires into one composed of 'nation states'. This issue had only become central to the Great War in the final stages of the conflict. Neither London nor Paris had gone to war in 1914 with the aim of creating a 'Europe of nations', and it was only from early 1918 onwards that the destruction of the land empires became an explicit war aim.[11]

It is worth recalling the scale of this transformation: when the First World War formally ended with an Allied victory, three vast and

1. Following a failed Bolshevik putsch against the Provisional Government in the summer of 1918, Lenin fled Petrograd and crossed the border into Finland with this forged passport.

2. German and Russian soldiers celebrate the armistice between their countries at the end of the Great War with a dance. This cordial moment differed sharply from the general mood during the war and in the subsequent conflicts.

3. Victory on the Eastern Front allowed the German Army High Command to carry out their all-or-nothing Spring Offensive in 1918. Initially, the German army, led by specially trained shock troops, advanced rapidly.

4. The ultimate failure of the Spring Offensive and Allied counter-attacks that summer led to a collapse in the morale of the German troops. Tens of thousands surrendered without resistance, finding themselves in Allied POW camps.

5. Italian troops at Vittorio Veneto. The Battle culminated in an Italian victory, effectively ending the war for the Habsburg Empire. The armistice was signed on 3 November.

6. Like their German counterparts, tens of thousands of former Habsburg subjects ended in Allied captivity towards the end of the war, here in a camp in Trento in November 1918.

7. (*above*) German *Freikorps* troops in the Baltic region in 1919. Germany's defeat in November 1918 triggered Soviet military intervention in the newly independent Baltic States. *Freikorps* formations fought against both Bolsheviks and Baltic nationalists.

8. (*below*) Finland experienced one of the most brutal civil wars in modern European history, killing 1 percent of the population. Fighting culminated in the Battle of Tampere, where this picture of victorious White Guards was taken in 1918.

9. The Russian Civil War was fought with savagery by all sides involved. This was particularly the case in the so-called peasant wars, in which villagers violently resisted Lenin's collectivization. Hanging captured enemies was common practice.

10. (*below*) The Bolshevik government tries to find foster parents for Russian orphans. Years of war and civil war, coupled with severe famines, left tens of thousands of children as destitute orphans.

11. On 9 November 1918, the co-chairman of the German Majority Social Democrats, Philipp Scheidemann, proclaims the German Republic from a balcony on the Reichstag building in Berlin.

12. The so-called Aster Revolution in Budapest on 31 October 1918, named after the flowers that replaced the Habsburg cap roses, transformed Hungary into an independent state and a short-lived Democratic Republic under Mihály Károlyi.

13. Austria was also transformed through revolution into a parliamentary democracy. In mid-June 1919 the new republic was challenged by a Communist putsch which, although ultimately defeated, saw violent clashes.

14. (*above*) During the Spartacist
Rising in Berlin in January 1919,
supporters of the Communist
Party and the Independent Social
Democrats exchange fire with
government troops, here in the
newspaper district of the
German capital.

15. The Spartacist Rising was
brutally suppressed by *Freikorps*
soldiers and government troops,
pictured here near Berlin Cathedral
in the city centre.

16. (*above*) The Hungarian
revolutionary leader Béla Kun
addresses a gathering of students
and workers in 1919. His
short-lived regime was
overthrown by a Romanian
invasion that same year.

17. During the 'Red Terror'
of the Kun regime, hundreds of
suspected 'counter-revolutionaries'
were killed, as shown here in
May 1919. After Kun's fall,
counter-revolutionary troops
would retaliate in kind.

18. 'Everything Is Ours!' An anti-Semitic Hungarian poster circulated after the fall of the Kun regime shows a Jewish Soviet Republic Commissar stealing the possessions of a disabled Hungarian veteran.

19. After the fall of the Munich 'Soviet Republic', arrested supporters of the bygone regime are marched through the streets of the city by *Freikorps* soldiers and government troops.

20. (*above*) Victors and vanquished: Bulgarian Prime Minister Stambolijski (*centre*) during the signing of the Neuilly treaty, with Clemenceau to his left and Lloyd George to the right.

21. (*below*) Counter-revolution in Bulgaria: after the anti-BANU putsch, supporters of the brutally murdered Stambolijski – including his man-servant pictured here – were arrested en masse and often killed.

22. (*above*) An iconic, if staged, image of leading Italian Blackshirts – notably Benito Mussolini and his close associates Emilio de Bono and Italo Balbo – during the 'March on Rome' in 1922.

23. (*below*) Romanian military parade in central Budapest, 1919. Hungarians were outraged by the occupation and pillaging of their capital by a country they had helped defeat militarily the previous year.

Nieder mit der tschechischen Tyrannei

24. (*above*) 'Down with the Czech tyranny': protestors in Vienna in March 1919 demonstrate against the newly independent Czechoslovak state after its government's decision to ban the Sudeten Germans from participating in the Austrian general elections of 1919.

25. (*below*) Ethnic German refugees from West Prussia on their way to Germany following the 1920 plebiscite.

26. Greek infantry advances through the Anatolian plateau during the Greco-Turkish War. Despite initial successes, the invaders were facing stiff Turkish resistance.

27. Mustafa Kemal and his general staff deliberating on their strategy. In response to the Greek landings in Western Anatolia, the Turkish nationalists' resistance, led by Kemal, intensified greatly.

28. Soon after the Turkish re-conquest of Smyrna, violence against Christian civilians escalated, while the burning of the Armenian quarters soon spread to other parts of the city.

29. The failure of the Greeks to defeat Mustafa Kemal had further catastrophic consequences, eventually leading to the forced 'population exchange' of well over 1 million Ottoman Christians and Muslim Greeks.

30. (*above*) Outrage over the terms of the Paris peace treaties persisted in all of the defeated states of Europe for many years – nowhere more so than in Hungary. Here, a demonstration is held in Budapest in 1931, more than ten years after the signing of the Treaty.

31. (*below*) The humiliation of defeat in the Great War also remained a prominent theme in Hitler's speeches. After the fall of France in 1940, German troops witness the removal from a museum of the train carriage in which the Germans had signed the armistice in 1918. The French delegation would now be forced to accept defeat in the same train carriage.

centuries-old dynastic land empires – the Ottoman, Habsburg and Roma-nov empires – vanished from the map. A fourth, Imperial Germany, which had become a major land empire during the Great War when it gained enormous territories in east-central Europe, was significantly reduced in size, stripped of its overseas colonies, and transformed into a parliamentary democracy with what Germans across the political spec-trum referred to as a 'bleeding frontier' towards the east.[12] Nor were the victorious western European empires unaffected by the cataclysm of war: Ireland had experienced an unsuccessful nationalist uprising in 1916, but eventually gained independence in 1922 after a bloody guer-rilla war against British forces.[13] Elsewhere, from India to Egypt, nascent nationalist movements felt inspired by the public discourse over 'autonomous development' and 'national self-determination', as prompted (with very different intentions) both by Woodrow Wilson and Lenin, leader of the Russian Bolsheviks.[14] Spokesmen for those seeking recognition of their right to a state, including Zionists, Armeni-ans and Arabs, travelled to Paris to promote their claim to 'self-determination'. Other new actors, such as the first Pan-African Congress, demanded the same, while a young Vietnamese *sous-chef* at the Ritz in Paris, Nguyễn Sinh Cung (better known under his future *nom de guerre*, Hô Chi Minh), wrote to Woodrow Wilson to demand independence for his country.[15]

Ultimately, these small non-European decolonization movements were to be disappointed by the results of the Paris Peace Conference, as 'national self-determination' was granted to some of the central European successor states favoured by the Allies, but denied to everyone else. Disappointment soon turned into violent activism: in Egypt, India, Iraq, Afghanistan and Burma, Britain responded to imperial unrest with considerable force, while, over the following decades, France fought back against resistance to its imperial ambi-tions in Algeria, Syria, Indochina and Morocco.[16] But it was in east-central Europe and in the former territories of the defeated Ottoman Empire that the effects of the lost war and the implosion of imperial structures were felt most keenly and most immediately. As the continental empires disintegrated, ten new states emerged from their ruins: Finland, Estonia, Latvia, Lithuania, Poland, Czechoslova-kia, German-Austria, Hungary, Yugoslavia and Turkey, now firmly based in Asia. Meanwhile, in the Arab Levant, which had been ruled for centuries by the Ottomans, Britain and France invented new 'states': Palestine, Transjordan (Jordan), Syria, Lebanon and Mesopotamia (Iraq) were to become League of Nations' 'mandates' administered by London and Paris until an uncertain point in the future when they were to be released into independent statehood.[17] Yet while in theory the Paris Peace Conference prescribed the self-determining nation state as the only legitimate political form of organization, the victor states were all empires of one form or another. This was not only true for Britain and France whose blue-water empires expanded further through the mandates, but also for the aspiring Mediterranean and Asian empires of Italy, Greece and Japan, all of which were playing catch-up in the great imperial game of land-grabbing in the years after 1918. Even the United States was an empire, exercising various forms of sovereignty over lands as diverse as Alaska, Hawaii, Puerto Rico, Panama and the Philippines, to say nothing of its powerful informal influence over independent states such as Cuba, Haiti and Mexico.[18]

In late 1918, even before any decisions were made on the future shape of the Middle East, the future Italian dictator Benito Mussolini famously commented on the disintegration of the great European land empires in a surprisingly apocalyptic tone: neither the fall of ancient Rome nor the defeat of Napoleon, he insisted in an article for his newspaper *Il Popolo d'Italia*, could compare in its impact on history with the current reshuffling of Europe's political map. 'The whole earth trembles . . . In old Europe, men disappear, systems break, institutions collapse.'[19] For once, Mussolini had a point. For centuries, European history had been a history of empires. On the eve of the Great War much of the landmass of the inhabited world was divided into European empires or economically dependent territories, and there was little to suggest that the age of land empires was about to end.

To be sure, the earlier 'awakening of peoples' in Europe due to nineteenth-century nationalist movements posed a challenge to the future of imperial rule, notably in the Balkans, where competing national and imperial interests had a history pre-dating the Great War. From the First Serbian Uprising of 1804–13, the Greek Revolution of 1821, the Great Eastern Crisis of the mid-1870s, and the

Greek-Ottoman War of 1897, to the Macedonian uprising of 1903, the Young Turks' revolution of 1908, and the Albanian insurgencies of 1909–12, the Balkans could look back over a long century of violent disorder as they transitioned from imperial Ottoman rule to nationhood and independence.[20] Balkan nationalism had exploded violently during the Balkan Wars of 1912–13, when Serbia, Montenegro, Greece and Bulgaria had joined forces and expelled the Ottomans from their remaining European territories, before turning on each other over the spoils of war.[21] The subsequent influx into Anatolia of huge numbers of penniless and brutalized Muslim refugees was to have a profound impact on the rapidly deteriorating Christian-Muslim relations within the shrinking Ottoman Empire.[22]

Yet the situation in the Balkans in 1912–13 differed significantly from that elsewhere. While there were calls for more autonomy within imperial structures, notably in Austria-Hungary and Russia, few in 1914 would have predicted (or indeed demanded) a complete dissolution of the continental land empires until hostilities broke out that August. Reform, not national revolution, had been on the minds of those who openly articulated criticism of the existing imperial structures. Although the decline and fall of Europe's continental land empires after 1918 has often been portrayed as a historical inevitability, it is important to remember that from the vantage point of 1914 the ruling dynasties of the pre-war world seemed firmly entrenched and confidently in control of the vast swathes of territory that belonged to their empires.[23]

The complexity of the world of empires that existed in 1914 can be illustrated by the example of Austria-Hungary. Before the war, the Dual Monarchy had been Europe's third most populous state (after Imperial Russia and the German Reich), and one of its most ethnically and linguistically diverse empires. According to the official census of 1910, over 23 per cent of the empire's population spoke German as their first language, while almost 20 per cent put down Hungarian as their mother tongue. If German and Hungarian were the most commonly spoken languages, they were by no means the only ones: some 16 per cent of Habsburg citizens spoke Czech or Slovak, nearly 10 per cent Polish, close to 9 per cent Serbian, Croatian or Bosnian, while 8 per cent spoke Ukrainian, 6 per cent Romanian, 2 per cent Slovene and 1.5 per cent Italian. The remaining 2.3 million people spoke a variety of other languages.[24] The allegiance of these different ethno-linguistic communities was essentially dynastic, namely to the Dual Monarchy's long-serving Kaiser. Following Vienna's catastrophic defeat at the hands of Prussia in 1866, Franz Joseph instigated a number of reforms, most notably the 1867 *Ausgleich*, which turned Hungary into a sovereign kingdom with a separate Parliament within the empire and several nationalities under its control. The special concessions to Budapest evoked jealousies and political desires for greater autonomy among other ethnic groups, especially among Czech, Polish and Croatian elites, but calls for complete independence from within the empire were rare. Those Croat and Slovene intellectuals who wrote about sharing a common, South Slav (Yugoslav) identity with the Serbs were a tiny minority.[25]

It was the outbreak of war in 1914 that undermined an increasingly complex system of regional compromises, and an overall strategy of imperial divide and rule within the Austro-Hungarian Empire. In December 1914, in the so-called Niš Declaration, Serbia proclaimed an independent South Slav state as its official war aim.[26] Initially, however, few of the Slovenes or Croats fighting in the Austro-Hungarian Army seem to have paid any attention to this proclamation. For much of the war, imperial loyalties (undoubtedly mixed with fears of repression and reprisals) trumped national loyalties, as Poles, Czechs, Croats, and even Serbs and Italians, fought in the Habsburg Army. The often repeated tale that Czechs in particular were reluctant supporters of the imperial war effort – an idea reflected in Jaroslav Hašek's internationally best-selling novel, *The Good Soldier Švejk* (1921–3) – is mainly a post-war creation, a myth adopted both by Czech nationalists to underline long-standing hatred of Habsburg 'oppression' and by Austrian nationalists to explain the Austro-Hungarian Army's defeat.[27]

The internal cohesion of the Dual Monarchy was undoubtedly weakened by the change of imperial leadership after the death of the popular and long-serving Kaiser Franz Joseph on 21 November 1916. He had ruled the empire for almost six decades, symbolizing the unity of the ethnically complex state. As the Hungarian politician and novelist Miklós Bánffy, author of the magnificent *Transylvanian Trilogy* (1934–40), noted in his diary that day:

On most evenings the people of Budapest, sick of the monotonous sameness of war news, would hurry past the depressing news stands – but tonight they stopped to look and read ... Today they put aside their daily anxiety for those on the front line, their fears and worry for husbands, sons, and brothers who were prisoners of war, their anguish for the dead. Today all were overcome by the sense of a great national disaster, by the fear of what was to come and the terror of an unknown future. What was drawing everyone to those brightly lit newsstands was the announcement of the death of Franz Joseph.[28]

With the death of the Kaiser, the embodiment of continuity and stability since the 1848 Revolution, the empire lost its integrative figurehead. His death caused uncertainty as the Habsburg Empire entered the third year of the war.[29] Yet without the eventual defeat of the Central Powers, the Dual Monarchy would have undoubtedly survived the transfer of power from Franz Joseph to his twenty-nine-year-old nephew and heir, Karl. What was decisive for the fate of the Habsburg Empire was the outcome of the war, and the fact that French, British and American decision-makers gradually moved towards the war aim of dismantling the empire. From the very start of the war exiled Czech(oslovak) and South Slav citizens of the Habsburg monarchy had lobbied for this aim, making contact with a number of influential experts on central Europe in Britain and France, such as the well-connected *Times* journalist Henry Wickham Steed (who had served as a correspondent in Vienna before the war), Robert Seton-Watson (publisher of the weekly *The New Europe* from 1916), and the Sorbonne historian Ernest Denis (who advised the French government on war aims in relation to the Bohemian lands). All three men played a key role in shaping Allied public perception that the Dual Monarchy was a 'people's prison', whose non-German and non-Magyar peoples should be liberated.[30]

Their highly agenda-driven writings played into the hands of Tomáš Garrigue Masaryk, a Czech philosophy professor and nationalist politician, who had fled Prague in late 1914. Masaryk moved to London, where he taught Slavonic studies at London University while simultaneously engaging in high-powered conversations about the future of central Europe. In early 1918 he also travelled to the United States where he met President Wilson in an attempt to secure his approval for an independent Czechoslovak state.[31] As the historian Andrea Orzoff has pointed out, the essence of the narrative spread by Masaryk was this:

> Czechs were as Western in their values and in their political inclinations as the Westerners themselves: they were Enlightenment rationalists yearning to be free from Austrian repression. They ought to be joined with their fellow Slavs, the Slovaks, to lead an East European state that was dedicated to tolerance, egalitarianism, and human rights, and was capable of joining with the West. Not coincidentally, this same state, with Western support, might help withstand German aggression and contain Bolshevik social radicalism.[32]

Until the beginning of 1918, however, Entente decision-makers were reluctant to officially embrace the break-up of the Dual Monarchy as a war aim. Allied plans for the post-war future of the Habsburg monarchy focused on the transformation of the empire's constitutional composition without questioning its very existence.[33] In January 1918, President Wilson had advocated in his famous 'Fourteen Points' speech a federal Austria-Hungary, whose peoples 'should be accorded the freest opportunity to autonomous development'. But Czechoslovak and South Slav autonomy was not the same as independence, as promised to Poland in the very same speech. By June, however, Wilson's position had hardened and he now advocated that 'all branches of the Slav race should be completely free from German and Austrian rule'. To be sure, not everyone on the Allied side was equally enthusiastic about Slavic independence. As late as August 1918 the British Under-Secretary of State, Robert Cecil, stated in a Foreign Office memorandum: 'Whether a new Europe with two or three additional Slav states will be more peaceful than the old seems to me, I confess, very doubtful.'[34] However, when on 3 September the Allies formally recognized Masaryk's dissident Czechoslovak National Committee in Paris as the legal representatives of a Czechoslovak nation, it was clear that the last days of the Austro-Hungarian Empire were approaching, even if South Slavic calls for independence were initially ignored: unlike Poland and Czechoslovakia, the Kingdom of Serbs, Croats and Slovenes was not recognized by the Allies until 1919, and its borders were to be determined at the Paris Peace Conference.[35]

During the war an alternative concept for a future multi-ethnic state had been proposed by Austro-Marxists such as Karl Renner, who was to serve as the first Chancellor of the Austrian Republic from 1918 to 1920. Renner advocated a Habsburg 'state of nationalities' in order 'to offer an example for the future national order of men'.[36] On 16 October 1918, Emperor Karl himself attempted to counter the threat of national revolutions (and gain Wilson's favour) with the publication of his 'Peoples' Manifesto', in which he promised to reorganize the Austrian half of the empire on a federal basis. Karl envisaged a loose imperial superstructure in which German, Czech, South Slav and Ukrainian territories would be ruled autonomously, each with their own parliaments. The Habsburg Polish territories would be permitted to secede to the independent Polish state that Wilson had demanded in his Fourteen Points.[37]

Yet it was clear that both the 'Peoples' Manifesto' and Austro-Marxist proposals for serious federal reform would not satisfy those who longed to sever their ties with Vienna once and for all. Czech, Slovak and South Slav politicians left no room for doubt that complete independence was the only option for them, and from the summer of 1918 their position was endorsed by Allied leaders.[38] In July, Czech and Slovak politicians had formed a Czechoslovak National Committee in Paris.[39] Between 5 and 11 October other groups had taken similar steps: a National Council of Serbs, Croats and Slovenes was formed in Zagreb, while its Polish counterpart proclaimed a 'free and independent Poland' that was to include Habsburg-ruled Galicia.[40]

From the Allied point of view, matters were somewhat more clear-cut when it came to the Ottoman Empire, despite the fact that its ethnic and religious composition was no less complex than that of east-central Europe. Long dismissed by Western diplomats and statesmen as 'the sick man of Europe' and the oppressor of Christian minorities, the Ottoman Empire's entry into the war on the side of the Central Powers and its genocidal policies towards the Armenians further encouraged those (like Lloyd George) who were determined to break it up. Geostrategic, economic, as well as cultural and religious interests played a significant role in attitudes towards the Ottomans. Some of the empire's Arab provinces contained large reserves of oil in the Mosul region and elsewhere, while the Bosphorus Straits and the Suez Canal were considered strategically vital, notably by the British, eager to secure safe passage to India by sea and land.[41] Moreover, French claims on Syria and Lebanon had much to do with France's self-perception as the protector of the local Christian minorities, and the dream of a 'Mediterranean' France.[42]

During the war the Allies had held a number of discussions about the future of the Ottoman Empire. In the spring of 1915, Petrograd had been assured by London that its interests in the Straits, Constantinople and Armenia would be safeguarded. One year later, in May 1916, the diplomats Mark Sykes and François Georges-Picot conducted secret negotiations about British and French post-war ambitions in the Middle East. The Sykes-Picot agreement gave London control of today's southern Iraq, including Baghdad and Basra, and Paris most of present-day Lebanon and the coast of Syria, extending northwards into Cilicia (the southern coastal region of Asia Minor). Palestine would have an international administration. The rest of the Ottoman's Arab provinces – a huge area that included what is now eastern Syria, northern Iraq and Jordan – would be left to local Arab chiefs under the supervision of the French in the north and the British in the south. The agreement was remarkably ambitious at the time, given Britain's recent setbacks at the Gallipoli Peninsula and on the Mesopotamian front in 1916. Yet from Britain's and France's point of view, it was important to stake out areas of interest for a future peace settlement, whenever that would be agreed and signed.[43]

Even before the Sykes-Picot agreement – and in contrast to its content – Britain had been meddling in the muddy waters of 'Arab nationalism' to encourage an indigenous revolt against Ottoman rule. In 1915, Sir Henry McMahon, the British High Commissioner in Egypt, made written promises about post-war 'independence of the Arabs' to Hussein bin Ali, the Sharif of Mecca, in return for an Arab revolt that would aid Britain's war effort on the Mesopotamian front. Exempted from that future Arab state were the coastlines of Syria and Lebanon, roughly from Aleppo to Damascus, and the old Ottoman provinces of Baghdad and Basra. In return for these promises, the Arab revolt began in June 1916.[44] Over the following two years irregular Arab forces under the command of Hussein bin Ali's ambitious third son, Faisal, and his British liaison officer, Thomas Edward Lawrence ('Lawrence of Arabia'), fought Ottoman troops in what was to become Saudi Arabia, Jordan and Syria.[45]

When the Bolsheviks published the Allied secret treaties and other diplomatic documents from the tsarist regime in late 1917 in a deliberate attempt to embarrass the 'imperialist states' and discredit their secret diplomacy, it became obvious to everyone that the promises made to Arab insurgents contradicted the provisions of both the Sykes-Picot agreement and the Balfour Declaration of November 1917, in which the British government had pledged support for 'the establishment in Palestine of a national home for the Jewish people', with the proviso 'that nothing shall be done which may prejudice the civil and religious rights of the existing non-Jewish communities in Palestine or the rights and political status enjoyed by Jews in any other country'.[46]

The Balfour Declaration was the result of many years of lobbying, notably by Chaim Weizmann, the future first President of the State of Israel (1949–52), who had emerged during the Great War as the leading figure of the Zionist movement in Britain. Born in 1874 in the remote Russian shtetl of Motal, some 30 kilometres west of Pinsk, he had followed the example of tens of thousands of Jews from the Pale by migrating west to escape economic deprivation and Russian anti-Semitism. In Germany, where he studied chemistry, he had his first encounters with Theodor Herzl's programmatic book, *Der Judenstaat* (*The Jewish State*), the bible of Zionism published in 1896, and became actively involved in the movement to realize Herzl's utopia.[47]

In July 1904, Weizmann left Switzerland, where he held his first teaching job, and worked as a senior lecturer in biochemistry at the University of Manchester, without giving up on his political ambitions. On the contrary: two years after arriving in Manchester, he first met the former British Prime Minister, Arthur Balfour, through a mutual acquaintance. Balfour was sympathetic to Weizmann's quest for a Jewish homeland and the two remained in touch after Balfour returned to a cabinet position. Weizmann's ability to quickly connect with Britain's social and political establishment was remarkable for a foreigner. He cultivated contacts with influential Jewish families in Britain, such as the Rothschilds, senior journalists from important papers such as the *Manchester Guardian*, and even met with David Lloyd George and Herbert Asquith at the height of their power. His lobbying efforts eventually paid off when, in November 1917, Lord Balfour pledged London's support for a 'National Home for the Jewish people' in Palestine. The British government's support for the Zionist cause seems to have been genuine – it would have made far more sense from a purely strategic point of view to come to an agreement with the Arabs instead. To be sure, a 'National Home' was not an independent state such as the one the Western Allies envisaged for Poland. It was more akin to the 'greatest possible autonomy' that Woodrow Wilson promised the Czechs, Slovaks and South Slavs in January 1918. But it was a crucially important foundation on which Zionism could build to realize Herzl's vision.[48]

There were some serious problems with this promise, however. Despite several waves of immigration, from Europe, the Jews remained a small minority in the region, no more than 6 per cent of the population of Palestine in 1914. The vast majority of Palestine's 700,000-strong population was Arab, most of them Muslim but some Christian.[49] Moreover, at least until 1917, the overwhelming majority of the Jewish population in Palestine was not propagating an independent state. Instead, many supported Jewish autonomy rights within the Ottoman Empire. Loyalty to the empire was expressed, for example, in the newspaper *ha-Herut*, which printed the patriotic speech of a Jewish soldier in the Ottoman Army in 1914: 'From this moment we are not separate people [individuals]. All the people of this country are as one man, and we all want to protect our country and respect our empire.'[50] Another supporter of Ottomanism at this time was the future first Prime Minister of Israel, David Ben-Gurion, who had studied in Constantinople (alongside the future President of Israel, Yitzhak Ben-Zvi) and who recruited a Jewish volunteer force to aid the Ottoman Empire at the start of the Great War. It was the course of the war and Balfour's promise of a 'National Home' for the Jews that encouraged Ben-Gurion and others to switch sides and join the Jewish Legion in 1918, thus supporting the Allied war effort.[51]

The Palestinian Arabs, by contrast, were outraged by the Balfour Declaration. From December 1917, after General Edmund Allenby's conquest of Jerusalem, the question of how and by whom newly 'liberated' Palestine would be governed became even more pressing. Much to the annoyance of those Palestinian Arabs who hoped for future independence, the British administration facilitated the arrival of a Zionist commission, chaired by Weizmann himself, in now British-occupied Palestine in the spring of 1918.[52] The Arab population of Palestine could not help but gain the impression that Ottoman rule, destroyed by the war, was being replaced by a new imperial superstructure, its future shape yet uncertain. The American intelligence officer in the region, William Yale, reported as early as April 1918:

> It is rather significant that in Palestine, where there has been so much suffering and privation, and where the disaffection with the Turkish regime was so great in 1916 and 1917, that nearly every Arab talked open treason against the Ottoman government and longed for the deliverance of their country from the Turks, there should be in the spring of 1918, soon after the British occupation, a party, which, according to British political agents, wished to live in the future under the suzerainty of Turkey. The sentiments of this party cannot be altogether explained by an inherent dislike of Europeans and the very natural Muslim desire of wishing to be under a Muslim ruler. There undoubtedly enters into the sentiments of this party the belief that under Turkish rule the Zionists would not be allowed to gain a stronger foothold in Palestine than they now have.[53]

Less than a year later, Yale's assessment was supported by an American fact-finding mission to Syria and Palestine. The so-called King-Crane Commission, named after its two American leaders, the Christian higher-education reformer Henry Churchill King and the wealthy Democratic Party supporter and foreign-policy entrepreneur Charles R. Crane, reported back in August 1919 that the Arabs in Palestine were 'emphatically against the entire Zionist program'. The King-Crane Commission thus recommended that the Paris Peace Conference limit Jewish immigration and give up the idea of making Palestine a Jewish homeland.[54] The recommendations of the King-Crane Commission were ignored, however. Instead, in April 1920, Britain and France agreed at a conference in the Ligurian coastal city of San Remo that Britain would receive the Palestine mandate, thereby implementing the Balfour Declaration (a decision that was endorsed by the League of Nations in July 1922). The Palestinian Arabs were not represented in San Remo, but they had left Western observers in no doubt about their feelings towards further Jewish migration, let alone a Jewish state: on 4 April 1920 anti-Jewish riots broke out in the streets and alleys of Jerusalem, lasting three days and leaving five people dead and hundreds injured.[55]

Over the following decades Palestine was to serve as a painful reminder that the promises made to various invested parties between 1915 and 1917 had been fatally contradictory and often made in bad faith. During the war they were designed as short-term expedients for the mobilization of indigenous support rather than as statements of long-term intent, as Arabs in particular had assumed. The consequences of this wartime strategy still haunt the Middle East today.

12

Reinventing East-Central Europe

On 31 October 1918 the commander of the Adriatic-based Habsburg fleet, Miklós Horthy, sent a final telegram to Emperor Karl I, assuring him of his 'unshakable loyalty'. Minutes later, he surrendered the flagship of his fleet, the SMS *Viribus Unitis*, and released the remaining Czech, Croatian, Polish and German-Austrian sailors and officers around him into an uncertain future as post-imperial subjects.[1]

By that point the national revolutions within the empire had already taken place. Somewhat ironically, it was the Germans and the Hungarians, the peoples who had thrived most under the Dual Monarchy, who first made the transition to independent statehood. In Vienna a Provisional National Assembly of German-Austria was created on 21 October. On 11 November, Emperor Karl made a general proclamation in which he 'relinquish[ed] every participation in the administration of the State' without actually abdicating. The next day the Provisional National Assembly proclaimed the Republic of German-Austria, with the Social Democrat, Karl Renner, as its first Chancellor and head of a grand coalition government composed of Social Democrats, Christian Socials and German Nationalists. In line with the Wilsonian rhetoric of national self-determination, the new Republic claimed all German-speaking territories of the former Habsburg Empire, including Austrian Silesia, parts of South Tyrol, and the German-speaking Bohemian territories. Most importantly, the new rulers of the Republic announced that Austria ought to become part of the German Reich – a demand entirely in line with Wilson's principles.[2]

In Hungary the national revolution was more turbulent. The conservative wartime government under Sándor Wekerle announced on 16 October 1918 that the Austro-Hungarian compromise of 1867, which had established the Dual Monarchy in the first place, was no longer legally binding for Budapest. However, this was not enough of a stand against the empire in the eyes of opposition parties. On 23 October the Hungarian Social Democrats and the Radicals founded a National Committee under the liberal Count Mihály Károlyi. The National Committee insisted it was the only legitimate representative of the Hungarian people. Its twelve-point programme demanded the complete independence of Hungary, the introduction of universal male and female suffrage, the immediate end of the war, the abolition of censorship, and agrarian reform. Demands for reform and independence, so the National Committee naively hoped, might aid the new Hungarian state in its quest to retain all historically Hungarian territories.[3]

Such demands were supported by tens of thousands of protesters on the streets of Budapest and by striking workers, who clashed violently with police forces on 28 October, leaving three protesters dead and fifty wounded.[4] By this point it was obvious that Hungary would become a fully independent state and that the old regime of Habsburg loyalists would be replaced by a National Committee which could count on the support of large numbers of nationalist officers and soldiers. On 30 October they publicly renounced their loyalty to the emperor. The following morning Károlyi was appointed Minister-President and the executive of the National Committee became the government. For some this was not enough: only hours after the new government had taken over a number of soldiers broke into the villa of the former Minister-President, Count István Tisza, widely seen as the personification of now unfashionable loyalty to Vienna and held responsible for Hungary's suffering over the previous years. Tisza was murdered in front of his family.[5] Otherwise, Hungary's national revolution was relatively peaceful. The national red, white and green tricolour replaced that of the Dual Monarchy on public buildings throughout Budapest, and hundreds of thousands celebrated in the city's squares.[6]

By the time the Hungarian Republic was born, national revolution had spread across the empire, promoted by the decisive defeat of the imperial army in late October. The inevitability of that defeat had become clear to everyone after the imperial army had failed to halt the major Italian offensive that started on 24 October 1918 near Vittorio Veneto. Instead, the Habsburg army was routed. Faced with the refusal of soldiers to continue the fight, Vienna requested an armistice on 28 October.[7]

Encouraged by the Habsburg request for an armistice, the Czechoslovak National Committee took control of matters in Prague on 28 October. People came out into the streets carrying the red-and-white flag of Bohemia and destroyed symbols of the now villified Habsburg state, while the Allies formally recognized Tomáš Garrigue Masaryk as head of state – a position he would hold for seventeen years.[8]

As in Budapest and Prague, all of the former territories of the Habsburg Empire initially experienced revolutions that were far less 'Bolshevik' in nature than had been the case in Russia the previous year. Instead, these were national and indeed remarkably peaceful revolutions aimed at political independence from Vienna. In the Croatian capital of Zagreb, where the National Committee of South Slavs proclaimed its independence from Vienna in late October 1918, revolutionaries celebrated the birth of their new state and the triumph of Wilsonianism. As one of the Croatian leaders, Stjepan Radić, proudly remarked one day after independence had been won: 'The peoples rise in order to deliver freedom with their blood and over the whole world Wilson's principles enjoy victory.'[9]

To be sure, not everyone shared these sentiments. As Ante Pavelić, secretary of the Croatian Party of Rights in 1918 and the future leader of the Croatian Ustashe, recalled in his memoirs: '1 December [1918 – the day Prince Regent Alexander officially proclaimed the Kingdom of Serbs, Croats and Slovenes] was a sad and blurry day. People passed by the streets with nausea, without expression and with a bitter taste in their mouths ... That day Croatia was put to the grave by the policy of Greater Serbia and there was deep conviction that she would never exist again.'[10]

As elsewhere in the former Habsburg lands, the initial national revolution in Zagreb was relatively bloodless. But this did not mean that the replacement of a multi-national empire with nation states was without risks. Given the territories' complex ethnic composition and the likelihood that the region's ethnic groups would use Wilson's notion of self-determination to justify territorial claims, the outbreak of violence should have been predictable.[11] The initially non-violent national revolutions within the Dual Monarchy soon morphed into violent upheavals in the form of both inter-state and civil wars, notably in the eastern borderlands. In the early hours of 1 November, for example, former Habsburg troops loyal to the Ukrainian National Committee in the Galician capital of Lemberg (Polish: Lwów; Ukrainian: L'viv) occupied public buildings and interned the Habsburg governor of the region. Nine days later the National Committee proclaimed the West Ukrainian People's Republic, with Lemberg as its capital. As a consequence war broke out between the newly established West Ukrainian state and the Polish Republic, which also laid claim to Lemberg and East Galicia. Both sides were aware that military control over the disputed territory would create realities on the ground that the peacemakers in Paris would be unable to ignore. After two weeks of fighting, Polish troops conquered Lemberg, but the war itself continued until July 1919 when it ended with a Ukrainian defeat.[12]

The Polish case more generally proves the point that the abrupt break-up of Europe's land empires, and the inability of the successor states to peacefully settle territorial disputes with their neighbours, played a major role in triggering violence after the First World War. France had endorsed the idea of an independent Poland in the autumn of 1917 and Woodrow Wilson had promised, in the thirteenth of his Fourteen Points, that a reconstituted Poland should receive territory that was 'indisputably' Polish while also gaining 'free and secure access to the sea'.[13] The impossibility of simultaneously fulfilling both of these promises, given the size of the German communities settled all along the Baltic coast, illustrates the challenge of creating a new functioning successor state with undisputed borders in east-central Europe. This challenge was further complicated by other factors: four years of armed conflict on the Eastern Front had ravaged the lands that were to become Poland. Hundreds of thousands of its inhabitants had been killed or deported far to the east and west by occupying Germans, Austrians and Russians. Epidemics and famine plagued the rural and urban population in late 1918. The future US President, Herbert Hoover, who was heading the American Relief Administration at the time, noted in 1919 that significant parts of Poland had witnessed no fewer than seven invasions and retreats by different armies during the war, each accompanied by mass destruction and hundreds of thousands of casualties.[14]

The country was also deeply divided internally with different ethnicities competing for the same territory: Germans in the west, Lithuanians in the north, Ukrainians and Belarusians to the east, and Czechs and Slovaks to the south. With hostile neighbours all around it, the army of the emerging Polish nation state had to be built from scratch with soldiers who had fought in three different imperial armies during the Great War, often against each other. While the Czech leadership was united in its political representation at the Paris Peace Conference, the Polish leadership was divided between its new head of state and commander-in-chief, Józef Piłsudski, and the Polish National Committee in Paris under Roman Dmowski.[15]

Piłsudski was to emerge triumphant from that power struggle, not least because he focused on realities on the ground while the peacemakers in Paris were still discussing the future borders of east-central Europe. The son of an impoverished Polish-Lithuanian nobleman from Vilnius (Polish: Wilno) in the Russian part of Poland, Piłsudski had been politically active from an early age. This was largely in response to Russian rule, which made it mandatory for him, a practising Catholic, to attend Orthodox services and to speak Russian rather than Polish. He was arrested for the first time in 1887 for participating in a failed plot organized by Lenin's elder brother to assassinate Tsar Alexander III, and was sent to Siberia for five years. In 1900 he was arrested again but escaped. He spent the years before the war in the socialist underground, robbing banks and trains to procure desperately needed funds for his political causes.[16]

When the Great War started in 1914, large numbers of ethnic Poles fought in three different imperial armies, some for Austria-Hungary and Germany, others for Russia. Piłsudski initially supported the Central Powers and even raised volunteers, the Polish Legions, to assist in the war against Russia, the chief obstacle in the way of Polish hopes for national independence. Germany and Piłsudski were thus united in their desire to defeat the Russian Army. Yet when Russia collapsed in 1917, he grew increasingly concerned that a victorious Germany might be too powerful a neighbour. His increasingly tense relationship with the Germans who had occupied the formerly Russian Polish territories since 1915 eventually landed him in prison, where he remained until the very end of the Great War.[17] On his release and return to the old Polish capital of Warsaw in November 1918, Piłsudski was acclaimed 'first marshal of Poland' by his legionnaires. It was obvious to him and anyone else that the near simultaneous collapse of Russia, Germany and Austria-Hungary provided a unique historical opportunity to recreate a state that had been swallowed up in the late eighteenth century. But where exactly were the borders of Poland? The borders of the old state had repeatedly changed, and since the partitions of the late eighteenth century, Poland had completely vanished from the map. Ethnic Poles had lived under Russian, German and Austro-Hungarian rule since the partitions, and the population patterns, urban structures and economy of resurrected Poland had little in common even with the eighteenth-century Polish-Lithuanian Commonwealth.[18]

Under Piłsudski's military leadership, Poland remained in a constant state of open or undeclared war between 1918 and 1921, fighting against Russians, Ukrainians and Belarusians to the east, Lithuanians to the north, Germans to the west, Czechs to the south, and Jews (as 'internal enemies') on territory it already controlled.[19] In the east, Poland's military engagement against Ukrainian troops in Galicia began at the very beginning of November 1918, even before the official conclusion of hostilities on the Western Front and the proclamation of the Second Polish Republic on 11 November.[20] Here, as elsewhere, territorial ambitions in ethnically divided regions were at the heart of the conflict. While Galicia's western half, including the city of Kraków, had a clear Polish majority, matters were more complicated further east, where – with the exception of the cities of Lemberg and Tarnopol (Ukrainian: Ternopil) – ethnic Poles were vastly outnumbered by Ruthenians (Catholic Ukrainians), who, after gaining independence from the Habsburg Empire in November 1918, now sought unification with the Ukrainian Republic. The Poles, however, were entirely unsympathetic to such aspirations and resisted with force.[22]

By the spring of 1919, Piłsudski's reorganized Polish armed forces were also engaged in Upper Silesia against a strong force of German volunteer troops in the west and in the north against Lithuanian Bolsheviks, who had recently captured the disputed city of Vilnius.[23] However, the most existentially threatening of conflicts for the newly reconstituted Polish nation state was the war against Soviet Russia between the spring of 1919 and the autumn of 1920. It began with a Polish thrust into Belarus in 1919 and a second advance towards Kiev in April 1920. In bitter fighting the Poles advanced east, capturing Kiev in May, but lacking the hoped-for local support to sustain their position. Leon Trotsky's Red Army held firm. In June the Red Army drove the Poles out of the Ukrainian capital, before starting parallel offensives through Minsk in Belarus, and across western Ukraine. Lenin seized the opportunity to overthrow what he perceived as a bourgeois Polish government and to export the revolution further west, ordering his troops to advance on Warsaw. In the summer of 1920 he even set up a puppet government – the 'Polish Soviet Socialist Republic' under Felix Dzerzhinsky – to administer the territories they had already conquered. During its brief existence of merely three weeks the 'Polish Soviet Socialist Republic' was governed from an armoured train commuting between Smolensk and Białystok.[24]

Throughout the campaign, both sides committed countless atrocities against enemy soldiers and civilians, notably Jews.[25] As the German Jewish war veteran and novelist Arnold Zweig noted in 1920, presumably in response to a particularly well-documented pogrom in Pinsk: 'Poles and pogroms have befallen the eastern Jewish people who live piled together in the big cities and scattered through towns and villages. From the big cities comes shocking news, but the towns and villages, without railroads, without telegraph offices, have long been mute. Slowly one hears what is happening there: murder and massacre.'[26]

By August the Soviet troops were closing in on the suburbs of Warsaw. The Poles were largely cut off from Allied support, with the exception of a small French contingent under General Maxime Weygand, who had been accompanied to Poland by a young and talented staff officer, Charles de Gaulle.[27] As foreign diplomats began to evacuate the Polish capital, a masterfully executed counter-attack by Piłsudski, celebrated in national mythology as the 'Miracle on the Vistula', gave the Poles the upper hand and led to the rout of the Red

Army. In September, Lenin sued for peace. The Treaty of Riga, signed on 18 March 1921, left Poland with the western parts of Belarus and Ukraine. These territories would remain contested for many years to come, not least because they added more minorities – some four million Ukrainians, two million Jews and a million Belarusians – to Poland's ethnic make-up.[28]

In the south of the new Polish state, the Allies acted as mediator between the rival interests of two 'victor states'. The small former Habsburg duchy of Teschen (Polish: Cieszyn; Czech: Těšín), for example, was claimed by both Poland and Czechoslovakia. According to the Habsburg census of 1910, ethnic 'Czechs' were outnumbered two to one by 'Poles' in Teschen, while another considerable percentage of the population was 'German'.[29] Despite its tiny size, the former Habsburg duchy had significant coalfields, which added an economic dimension to its perceived strategic importance as a major railway junction in central Europe. Czechoslovakia, the favourite successor state of the Western Allies, claimed that the territory was vital for its economic and strategic future, but Polish speakers constituted a majority of the population. In January 1919, Prague and Warsaw dispatched troops to address the situation on the ground before a decision was made in Paris. Unsure as to how to appease their two key allies in central Europe, the peacemakers in Paris partitioned the duchy in July 1920 without holding a referendum, a solution with grim results for the inhabitants.[30]

The practice of land-grabbing with the aim of creating new realities before the Allies in Paris could make up their minds was by no means unique to the Polish. Up until the summer of 1919, and in some cases even later than that, all victorious successor states of the defunct Habsburg Empire tried to expand their borders through paramilitary action, in order to establish fresh 'realities'. Notably in the disputed borderlands, irregular militias or emerging armies – 'nationalized' through imperial implosion and newly imposed border changes – created new realities by force. The emerging Czechoslovak state, too, had sent troops into the heavily German-populated Sudetenland after the war's end. Here, armed intervention with the purpose of securing territory culminated in a massacre on 4 March 1919, during which fifty-four ethnic Germans, including women and children, were killed and over a thousand injured when Czech soldiers opened fire on unarmed crowds of protesters.[31] Altogether, between 1918 and 1920 roughly 150 civilians were killed in the ethnic and political turmoil in the Czech lands alone, while the war that Prague waged against the Hungarian Soviet Republic during the spring and summer of 1919 cost more than one thousand lives.[32]

Many of the perpetrators of irregular violence against civilians were former Czech legionnaires who had gradually returned home from Russia, before forming the nucleus of Prague's new republican army.[33] Given their active role in the war and in the fight against Russian Bolshevism, former legionnaires felt that it was their 'duty' to defend the new state against communists, German and Hungarian 'separatists', and Jews.[34] In May 1919, for example, legionnaires played a prominent role in the public lootings of Jewish and German property in the streets of Prague.[35] More dramatic incidents of violence occurred in the borderlands. During the Czechoslovak invasion of Slovakia, and notably after the repulsion of Prague's troops by the Hungarian Red Army and the introduction of the short-lived Slovak Soviet Republic, Czech troops resorted to terror against civilians, notably Jews, Catholic priests and suspected communists.[36] In another border region, near Uzhgorod, a Catholic priest was assaulted and eventually stabbed to death with bayonets in front of terrified villagers.[37]

From the moment of Austria-Hungary's defeat, the Serbian Army, too, had moved into Habsburg territory, first to the north and south and then, by November, into Croatia and Slovenia.[38] Serbia had good reasons to push its claims through land-grabbing: in total the country had lost some 400,000 soldiers during the Great War, notably after the German-led attack in 1915 when approximately 240,000 soldiers and civilians perished in the 'great retreat' across Albania.[39] Compared to the beginning of the Balkan Wars in 1912, the country by 1918 had lost 28 per cent of its population (some 1.2 million people) within six years, two-thirds of them civilians. And this figure does not account for the more than 72,000 disabled veterans or 180,000 war widows at the end of the war. The Serbian government estimated that the country had lost half of its national wealth as a consequence of the violent upheavals in the region.[40]

Now the time had come to reap the rewards for years of suffering.

Reinforced by other South Slav troops, mainly Croatian and Slovenian ex-Habsburg soldiers, newly formed Yugoslav units occupied territories that were in the main (though not exclusively) former parts of the Kingdom of Hungary, and were now subsumed within the Kingdom of Serbs, Croats and Slovenes. These included the Banat, Backa, Baranja, southern Hungary, Bosnia and Herzegovina, Dalmatia, Montenegro, Croatia and Slovenia.[41] Some 10,000 Serbian and Slovene soldiers were also militarily engaged in the Austrian state of Carinthia in the autumn of 1918 and the spring of 1919, where they fought against Austrians resisting the prospect of being annexed with force.[42] Carinthia, with its ethnically mixed population of 150,000 Germans and Slovenes, was eventually awarded to German-Austria following a referendum in October 1920, but until then the region saw considerable violence as resistance to Serbian and Slovene occupation flared up repeatedly. As an example of 'victory in defeat,' the return of Carinthia to German-Austria soon played a crucial role in Austrian paramilitary memory culture, because it testified to the paramilitary activists' unbroken spirit of defiance against both external enemies and the 'weak' central government in Vienna. A popular poem of 2 May 1919 celebrated the day of the 'liberation' of the village of Völkermarkt, as a triumph of Austrian determination over 'Slavic treason': 'You, Slav, should remember the important lesson that Carinthian fists are hard as iron.'[43]

Despite its territorial consolidation, the new South Slav state (the Kingdom of Serbs, Croats and Slovenes) emerged weaker from the post-war troubles than the other major winners in east-central Europe, namely Poland, Czechoslovakia and Romania. One of the reasons for this was that the Kingdom of Serbs, Croats and Slovenes had fewer friends in Paris than the other successor states (and a very outspoken regional rival in the form of Italy). The peacemakers also found the Balkans and its complex demographic mix of Serbs, Croats, Slovenes, Bulgarians, Macedonians, Greeks, Romanians, Jews, Albanians, and other Muslim groups deeply confusing.[44] Although Serbia had featured prominently in Allied propaganda as a 'victim' of Austro-Hungarian aggression during the war, most Western commentators and decision-makers simultaneously held essentialist views about the Balkans as a troubled and troublesome realm of violence, featuring continuous crises from the 1870s through to the First World War.[45]

Yet the main reason for the new South Slav state's relative weakness was uncertainty about its future internal shape. The different conceptions of the future were embodied by the two key players in the kingdom's formation: the Serb Nikola Pašić and the Croat Ante Trumbić.[46] Pašić, the dominant figure in Serbian politics for decades, hailed from the small town of Zaječar on the Bulgarian border, where he had been born in 1845. Before the Great War he had been a founding member of the Serbian People's Radical Party, which advocated the unification of all ethnic Serbs (including those living in Habsburg-controlled Bosnia) in one country, the preservation of the traditional local autonomy of the Serbian peasantry, and the limitation of the authority of the Serbian monarchy. In 1904 he had risen through Serbian politics to become Prime Minister, a post he was to occupy for another twenty years. In his mid-seventies at the time of the collapse of the Austro-Hungarian Empire, Pašić primarily conceived of the future South Slav state as just a significantly enlarged Serbia.[47]

Trumbić was in many ways the antithesis of everything Pašić represented. He was eighteen years younger and came from the cosmopolitan Dalmatian town of Split on the Adriatic. Trumbić had studied law in Zagreb before moving on to graduate studies in Vienna. At the age of thirty-three he had joined the Lower House of the Habsburg Parliament.[48] Even if he came to support a federal South Slav state in the later war years, he regarded the Serbs as culturally inferior, not least because of their long subjugation to Ottoman rule. 'You are not going to compare, I hope,' he famously commented in an interview with the French media, 'the Croats, the Slovenes, the Dalmatians whom centuries of artistic moral and intellectual communion with Austria, Italy, and Hungary have made pure occidentals, with these half-civilized Serbs, the Balkan hybrids of Slavs and Turks.'[49]

The Great War and the exhilarating prospect of a South Slav state outside of imperial structures brought Pašić and Trumbić together. With the outbreak of hostilities, Trumbić fled to Italy, and then to Paris and London. He and Pašić worked together closely on the Yugoslav National Committee founded in Paris in April 1915.[50] In July 1917 the two men agreed on the Corfu Declaration, which envisaged Serbia, Croatia and Slovenia as a united post-war state – a parliamentary monarchy with a king from the ruling Serbian House of Karadjordjević. The new state was to guarantee equal rights to all religious denominations. What Trumbić and Pašić failed to settle was the thorny issue of whether the future Yugoslavia would be a federal state with far-reaching local autonomy for its constituent peoples or a centralized unitary state. While Trumbić believed that he had signed up for a federal model, Pašić clearly aspired to a unitary state that would best serve Serbian interests. This issue was to reassert itself quickly after the end of the war.[51]

Other regions within the South Slav state also seemed unhappy with the situation after 1918. In Montenegro a civil war erupted between the 'Greens', who refused to be absorbed into a Greater Serbian state and see their own royal family deposed, and the 'Whites', who favoured unconditional unification with Serbia.[52] Italy, determined to undermine the new South Slav state wherever possible, facilitated the unrest and helped to organize armed resistance. Some 300 supporters of King Nicholas of Montenegro were shipped on Italian vessels to the Montenegrin port of Bar. They rallied 3,000 insurgents and went to attack the Montenegrin capital, Cetinje, but were repelled and forced to retreat to Italy by their 'White' opponents.[53]

Ultimately, the South Slav state would prove unable to bridge the gulf between the different visions invested in the Yugoslav project.[54] Even if the inevitability of Yugoslavia's failure to survive as a nation state has perhaps been exaggerated, the inability of politicians to compromise over the centralization of state power doomed the inter-war South Slav state, which explains much about the repeated explosion of inter-ethnic violence in the region.[55]

13

Vae Victis

At 3 p.m. on 28 June 1919 the two German government ministers chosen for the unenviable task of signing the peace treaty – Foreign Minister Hermann Müller and Johannes Bell, the Minister for Transport – entered the great Hall of Mirrors in Versailles. The venue had been carefully chosen by the elderly French Prime Minister and host of the Paris Peace Conference, Georges Clemenceau: it was the very same place where, after France's defeat in the Franco-Prussian War of 1870–1, Wilhelm I had been proclaimed Kaiser of a unified German nation state. Normally more level-headed, the then Prussian Prime Minister and soon-to-be Chancellor of the Reich, Otto von Bismarck, had consciously chosen the Palace of Louis XIV as the stage for a symbolic humiliation of a recently defeated France.[1]

Now, almost half a century later, the opportunity had arisen for France to avenge the humiliation. The two German emissaries chosen to sign the peace treaty had first to proceed past a long line of permanently disfigured French veterans, who had been brought to the signing ceremony as living reminders of the damage inflicted by Germany.[2] 'The whole affair was elaborately staged and made as humiliating to the enemy as it well could be,' noted Colonel Edward House, the key American diplomatic adviser to President Woodrow Wilson.[3] According to a British observer, the German dignitaries looked like 'prisoners led in to hear the reading of their sentence'.[4] Having signed the treaty, Müller and Bell immediately returned to Berlin, while in Paris people celebrated in the streets.

The terms of the treaty were greeted with disbelief in the Reich: Germany had lost 13 per cent of its territory (roughly 43,000 square kilometres) and thus a tenth of its population (some 6.5 million people). In the west, Alsace-Lorraine was handed back to France after nearly half a century under German rule, along with the border territories of Eupen and Malmedy, which were ceded to Belgium. Between 200,000 and 300,000 ethnic Germans left Alsace and Lorraine as a consequence, either voluntarily or as a result of expulsions.[5] At least temporarily, Germany also lost sovereignty over a 50-kilometre-wide strip of land east of the Rhine, a territory that was to be demilitarized and 'secured' through three Allied bridgeheads across the river, largely to appease French security concerns. The bridgeheads were to be removed in the future if Germany fulfilled its treaty obligations. The Saar region, a major coal-mining and manufacturing area on the Franco-German border, fell under the administration of the League of Nations, with special permission given to France to exploit the region's coal mines for fifteen years in compensation for German devastation to northern France.[6]

The largest and most contested territorial transfers, however, were to the east. The creation of a new Polish state meant the loss to Germany of Posen (Poznan), much of West Prussia, and parts of the coalfields of Upper Silesia. Danzig, the Baltic port at the mouth of the Vistula with an overwhelmingly German population, became a 'Free City' under the nominal control of the newly founded League of Nations. In order to give Poland access to the Baltic Sea, as promised in Wilson's Fourteen Points, the Allies created a 'corridor' of land separating East Prussia from the rest of Germany. Some 575,000 of the 1.1 million Germans who had resided in the Polish Corridor in 1919 had six years later moved to the new German Republic.[7]

In some disputed cases the Allies allowed for plebiscites, calling on the inhabitants of regions in question to decide to which state they wished to belong. The most important of these was held in the coal-rich region of Upper Silesia, one of three disputed ethnically mixed German border regions in which plebiscites were prescribed by the Versailles Treaty (the others being North Schleswig and the small districts of Allenstein and Marienwerder, where Poles and Germans lived side by side).[8] Upper Silesia mattered to both Berlin and Warsaw because of its mines, and iron and steel mills. The Silesian mines were the source of almost a quarter of Germany's annual output of coal, 81 per cent of its zinc, and 34 per cent of its lead. The German government argued that the people of Upper Silesia were overwhelmingly

German; that the territory had been German for centuries; and that its prosperity owed everything to German industry and German capital. If Germany lost Upper Silesia, the German note concluded, it would not be able to fulfil its other obligations under the Treaty.[9]

- After the Upper Silesia referendum held on 20 March 1921, which was preceded and accompanied by significant outbursts of violence, the final delineation of the new Polish-German frontier was decided in October of that year. The Supreme Council of the Paris Peace Conference adopted a partition that gave Poland a third of the Upper Silesian territory and 43 per cent of the population; this included the cities of Kattowitz (Katowice) and Königshütte (Chorzow), both of which had overwhelmingly voted to remain within Germany, as well as four-fifths of the industrial triangle in the east – a result widely decried in Germany as an act of 'victor's justice'.[10]

Compared to the territorial losses in the east, few Germans cared that the Reich's overseas colonies (territories with a combined size of 1.6 million square kilometres) were redistributed between the victor states under mandates from the League of Nations. The loss of German Kamerun (Cameroon), Togoland (the western part of which now forms the Volta region of Ghana), Ruanda-Urundi, German South-West Africa (Namibia), and the German South Pacific Islands meant that Germany was stripped of all of her oversees territories, a bluewater empire built in the late nineteenth century – but other concerns were more pressing to Germans at the time.[11]

At the heart of contemporary German indignation stood Articles 231 and 232 of the Versailles Treaty. Article 231 assigned sole responsibility for the outbreak of war in 1914 to Germany and her allies, while Article 232 stipulated that a guilty Germany owed reparations for the damage that it had caused. If Articles 231 and 232 were seen by the Germans as a form of moral condemnation that added to the humiliation of defeat, and accompanying territorial and material losses, the real purpose of Article 231, was to legitimize the imposition by the Allies of punitive financial reparations on Germany in order to compensate the French and the Belgians for the damage caused by over four years of German occupation. Germany's 'war guilt' and responsibility for atrocities in Belgium in 1914 and in France – particularly during the German strategic retreat in the spring of 1917 to the heavily fortified

'Siegfried Line' between Arras, St Quentin and Vailly, when the army implemented a scorched-earth policy – made the country liable for 'all losses and damages' suffered during the war. The Allies realized that such a broad definition of financial liability, which theoretically encompassed the cost for every bullet and every orphan pension, was likely to lead to unrealistic claims beyond Germany's ability to pay. Yet they were also aware that any concession on the reparations issue would outrage their domestic electorates, still reeling from the devastations of the war. The French public in particular had also not forgotten about Berlin's imposition of vast indemnities in 1871 (which did not even have the justification of immense property damage). As it proved impossible to agree on a definitive sum, the exact amount of reparations to be paid by Germany was deferred to a later point in time.[12]

The final reparations figure agreed on in the 1921 London Schedule of Payments was 132 billion gold marks, structured in three types of bonds ('A', 'B' and 'C' bonds). However, a large share of this seemingly enormous sum, the so-called 'C' bonds that amounted to 82 billion gold marks, was never expected to be repaid. C bonds were mainly included to appease Allied public opinion. Instead, the Germans would pay reparations by servicing the so-called 'A' and 'B' bonds, which together totalled 50 billion gold marks, to be paid over thirty-six years. German experts were secretly convinced that these payments were manageable, even if they would never have admitted this in public.[13]

The Allies further sought to ensure that Germany would not be in a position to wage war again by seizing huge amounts of weaponry. The Versailles Treaty obliged the German Army to be restricted to a maximum strength of 100,000 men and banned it from having tanks, aeroplanes and submarines.[14] The German Navy, reduced to a total of 15,000 men, was effectively dismantled and barred from building any large new ships. The great high-seas fleet, whose expansion before 1914 had contributed significantly to the rise of Anglo-German tensions, had been interned in Scapa Flow in the British Orkneys since November 1918. Eleven days before the German emissaries in Paris signed the Treaty, the German commander of the fleet, Admiral Ludwig von Reuter, decided to scuttle his seventy-four vessels, from battleships to destroyers, to prevent them from being distributed among the victorious Allies.[15]

The provisions of the Treaty were condemned as outright criminal by most Germans from the moment the draft was handed to the government in Berlin in May 1919. Post-imperial Germany, internally divided over almost everything else, was united in its shared hatred of the Treaty of Versailles. Philipp Scheidemann's speech in the German National Assembly on 12 May 1919 was indicative of the general mood: 'Which hand would not wither that binds itself and us in these chains?' According to the minutes, the speech of Germany's first democratically elected head of government was greeted 'with several minutes of emphatic applause' from fellow parliamentarians across the political divide.[16]

Scheidemann and the other parliamentarians had good reason to feel that their reform efforts had been in vain. Many of them felt betrayed, notably by President Wilson, on whom they had placed their high hopes for a 'just peace'. Wilson had repeatedly suggested before November 1918 that the Central Powers could expect an honourable peace based on negotiations if they rid themselves of their autocratic rulers. Now, in May 1919, a democratically elected German government had to accept a dictated peace without the slightest pretence of 'negotiations'. The German delegation attempted to soften some of the conditions for peace, while back in Berlin some politicians and generals contemplated the possibility of resuming hostilities against the Western Allies.[17] In the end, however, Germany had no alternative but to accept the peace treaty. The Allied ultimatum of 22 June to accept the terms or face a continuation of war intimidated the Germans sufficiently, and they agreed to sign the treaty under protest.[18]

The general population in Berlin and elsewhere, regardless of political affiliation, was outraged. Spontaneous demonstrations were held across the Reich to protest the injustices of a peace treaty that seemed intent on permanently expelling Germany from the ranks of the Great Powers. The fact that Britain and the United States had gone to considerable lengths to preserve German unity and independence, notably in opposing French efforts to detach the Rhineland, was generally overlooked. Instead, the enthusiasm with which so many Germans had welcomed the advent of democracy in 1918 turned into a sense of fundamental betrayal and resentment at the terms of the peace treaty less than a year later.[19] A significant proportion of the population came to associate the Versailles Treaty with the revolution of 1918 and its outcome, the Weimar Republic. Some, notably on the far Right, referred to the Treaty as 'the real constitution' of Weimar – an externally enforced 'un-German' form of state, whose sole purpose was to enslave the German people for generations.[20]

Such views were reinforced by John Maynard Keynes's polemical attack on the Treaty, articulated in his best-selling book *The Economic Consequences of the Peace*, published in December 1919. Keynes, who had been a British Treasury expert during the Paris Peace Conference, portrayed the Versailles Treaty as a Carthaginian peace, intent on ruining Germany as effectively as Rome had destroyed Carthage in 146 BC.[21] What was generally ignored, then and since, was that Germany had actually fared better in Paris than all of the other Central Powers.[22] In the Treaty of St Germain-en-Laye, signed in September 1919, for example, the German-Austrian rump state was forced to cede South Tyrol to Italy, southern Styria to the Kingdom of Serbs, Croats and Slovenes, and Feldsberg and Böhmzell to Czechoslovakia. Habsburg Galicia had already been claimed by Poland, while Bohemia, with its three million German speakers, had become part of Czechoslovakia. The Treaty also stipulated that Austria (along with Hungary) would have to carry most of the old empire's war debt, as well as paying reparations. Setting the figures for reparations was eventually turned over to the reparations commission (which, two years later, concluded that Austria could not pay anything at all).[23]

If many in German-Austria had hoped for *Anschluss* – the voluntary union of Austria with the German Reich – as a realization of liberal nationalists' aspirations during the 1848 Revolution, they were to be bitterly disappointed.[24] Ever since the military defeat and the disintegration of the empire, the Austrian Left (and their German counterparts) had promoted the idea that a union between the two states would comply with Wilson's ideal of self-determination while also offering a major boost of legitimacy to the emerging Weimar Republic. There was also a clear economic rationale for such a move: hardly anybody considered that the Austrian state, now stripped of its breadbaskets in the fertile lands of Hungary and Bohemia, would be able to feed its six-million-strong population. Agrarian production in

Austria immediately after the war's end only reached half of the pre-war levels, while domestic coal production could only meet one-quarter of the demand during the icy winter of 1918–19.[25]

The effects of depleted resources were felt most keenly in Vienna, which had been transformed overnight from being the capital of Europe's third-largest state to a city that was now inhabited by one-third of the country's population. Even before the war, Vienna had been entirely dependent on food supplies from the countryside. As these supplies quickly dried up, the city's population lived under the daily threat of starvation, dramatically intensifying a trend that had already begun during the war.[26] 'In that winter it seemed a city of the dead, a huge and silent mausoleum,' recalled the humanitarian activist Francesca Wilson, who spent several years in post-war Vienna working as a volunteer:

> It was not that one saw children dead in the street or death-carts piled with corpses as one saw in the Russian famine. Nothing so dramatic. Its wounds were hidden. The silence struck me. The streets were deserted, except for queues of people waiting for rations of wood and sour bread, all of them, women and children as well as men, huddled in old patched army coats: all of them pale, hungry, cold, silent, and waiting. This was defeat: this was how a great Empire ends, not with a bang, not even it seemed with a whimper. Nothing here but hunger, cold, and hopelessness.[27]

The British pacifist Ethel Snowden painted a similarly bleak picture of despair, when she reported back from post-war Vienna that 'uniformed officers sold roses in the cafés. Delicate women in faded finery begged with their children at street corners . . . Gallant doctors struggled in clinic and hospital with puny children covered with running sores, with practically no medicines, no soap, no disinfectants.'[28] Alarming reports about conditions in Austria were also sent to the peacemakers in Paris. In January 1919, William Beveridge, a British civil servant (and later the father of the welfare state in the UK), who had been sent to Vienna to assess the situation on the ground, warned that, without immediate relief, there was likely to be complete social collapse.[29]

Despite this very serious economic deprivation, many Austrians in late 1918 and early 1919 had remained hopeful that the peace treaty would be along Wilsonian lines. When the Social Democratic Chancellor, Karl Renner, left for Paris to receive Austria's peace terms, optimistic crowds at Vienna's railway station shouted, 'Bring us a good peace.'[30] In Paris, Renner made the case that the revolution had transformed Austria into a democratic state. It should not be held accountable for the misdeeds of the bygone Habsburg Empire. 'We stand before you,' Renner emphasized 'as one of the parts of the vanquished and fallen Empire . . . In the same way as the other national States, our new Republic too has sprung to life, consequently she can no more than the former be considered the successor to the late Monarchy.'[31]

He was soon to be disappointed. When the Austrian delegation first received the draft treaty, they responded with indignation: as one of them noted, we were 'very sad, bitter and depressed when we realized that Austria had received harsher terms than Germany while we had hoped they would be more favourable'.[32] In Austria itself, where there were three days of mourning, the shock and disillusionment following the Versailles Treaty were profound.[33] As the Foreign Minister, Otto Bauer, noted in the Austrian capital: 'No less than two-fifths of our people are to be subjected to foreign domination, without any plebiscite and against their indisputable will, being thus deprived of their right of self-determination.'[34] For Bauer and many other Austrians, the key issue was the Allied prohibition of *Anschluss*. From the Allies' perspective, however, the veto on Austria's union with Germany made perfect sense. It would have been impossible to communicate to domestic audiences in Britain, France, or Italy why the Allies had fought and suffered for many years when the outcome of the conflict was a significantly enlarged and more populous German state. Yet at the same time it was clear to everyone involved that the prohibition of *Anschluss* was a blatant violation of the principle of national self-determination. The fact that the Allies forbade union was to have disastrous consequences. If, in 1918–19, *Anschluss* had been a democratic project of the Left, its non-realization was soon used by the extreme Right in both Austria and Germany as 'proof' of the inability of the republican state to deliver on promises.[35]

Similarly to Germany, Austria did get some minor concessions: a plebiscite in the area around Klagenfurt in the south of Carinthia, also being claimed by Yugoslavia, was eventually held in October 1920 and returned a majority of votes in favour of remaining within Austria. The Allies further agreed to the transfer of the Burgenland, a strip of territory from the western edge of Hungary, predominantly inhabited by German speakers, from Hungary to the Republic of German-Austria. Most of the area went to Austria, producing major tensions with the government in Budapest. These tensions violently erupted in 1920–1 when Hungarian militias clashed with Austrian police forces, leaving dozens of people dead. A referendum held in December 1921 in the city of Ödenburg returned the city to Hungary amid Austrian accusations that the Budapest government had pressurized the population and forged the plebiscite results. The rest of the Burgenland remained Austrian.[36]

The loss of the Burgenland was not the worst thing that happened to Hungary as a result of the lost war. Altogether the country lost two-thirds of its pre-war territory and more than 73 per cent of its population, according to the provisions of the Treaty of Trianon, which – due to political upheaval in Budapest and the Romanian invasion of Hungary – was only signed in June 1920.[37] Wrecked by four years of war, revolution and counter-revolution, as well as foreign invasion in 1919, the country was economically in ruins even before it signed the Treaty, with production levels in Hungary's consumer-goods industry at about 15 per cent of pre-war levels.[38]

In Paris the Hungarian delegation waiting to receive the terms of peace had made a case similar to that of the Austrians: Budapest should not be held accountable for the sins of the Habsburgs. After the fall of the Bolshevik regime in Budapest, Hungary was no longer a threat. The leader of its delegation, Count Albert Apponyi, also rightly pointed out that Hungary was being punished more severely than any of the other defeated Central Powers. His plea fell on deaf ears. Allied leaders and their advisers had long viewed the Hungarians as culpable of oppressing the minorities in the Hungarian half of the Dual Monarchy through stringent policies of Magyarization.[39]

On 4 June 1920, at the Trianon Palace on the outskirts of Paris, Hungary's representatives signed the Treaty under protest. Back in Budapest, the flags on public buildings flew at half-mast, where they remained until two decades later, when northern Transylvania was returned to Hungary under the Second Vienna Award of August 1940. A year later, Hungarian troops plunged deep into the Soviet Union alongside the Wehrmacht in what was widely perceived as a 'just war' for the revision of Trianon and the global defeat of Bolshevism. Until that day (and again since 1990), 'Trianon' was a shorthand phrase in Hungary for Allied injustice, fuelling an almost universal desire to undo its provisions the moment an opportunity presented itself.[40]

Compared to Hungary's staggering territorial losses, those of Bulgaria, the one Balkan nation to have fought alongside the Germans, Habsburgs and Ottomans, were slightly less dramatic, even if the Bulgarians did not see it that way. Like the other vanquished powers, Bulgaria was not represented at the Paris Peace Conference. Similarly to other leaders of the Central Powers, the new government in Sofia had initially hoped that the principle of self-determination would be applied after the country's new borders were settled in Paris, as Bulgarians were in a majority in three areas outside its new notional borders: in the southern Dobrudja along the west coast of the Black Sea, in Western Thrace at the top of the Aegean, and in parts of Macedonia. The problem was that all three territories were also claimed by other states – states that were considered friends of the Allies: Romania insisted on the southern Dobrudja (even if there were fewer than 10,000 Romanians living there, out of a population of almost 300,000); Greece demanded Western Thrace; and the Kingdom of Serbs, Croats and Slovenes claimed Macedonia.[41]

The Bulgarian delegation was summoned to Paris in July 1919 but only received the draft treaty two and a half months later.[42] The Allies met them with hostility. Harold Nicolson, more familiar with the Balkans than most others in Paris after serving in the British Embassy in Constantinople before the war, felt particularly vengeful towards Bulgaria: 'Their traditions, their history, their actual obligations should have bound them to the cause of Russia and the Entente. They had behaved treacherously in 1913 and in the Great War they had repeated this act of perfidy. Inspired by the most material motives of acquisition they had joined with Germany, and by so doing lengthened the War by two whole years.'[43]

The Bulgarian Prime Minister until October 1919, Teodor Teodorov, tried to dispel such sentiments by pointing out that the Bulgarian people themselves had always opposed the wartime alliance with Germany, and that the elites who had been in favour of it were no longer in power. Teodorov also emphasized that many Bulgarian officers had sympathized with the Allies or actively supported them: 'If other nations were happily rewarded only because of their sympathies and friendship with the Entente . . . why should one not acknowledge that similar feelings were demonstrated by our nation – as confirmed in the thousands of sentences and executions that were issued against soldiers who refused to fight, and in the fact of 11 generals and more than 100 Bulgarian officers who fought as volunteers with the Russians against the Germans?'⁴⁴

When the draft treaty was finally delivered in September, its content surpassed even the gloomiest predictions. In relative terms the Treaty of Neuilly of November 1919 was certainly harsher than the Versailles Treaty imposed on Germany. The treaty forced Sofia to cede a total of 11,000 square kilometres of territory, including Western Thrace (handed over to Greece), and four border areas, including the strategically important towns of Strumica, Caribrod and Bosilegrad with their surroundings (amounting to 2,500 square kilometres), to the new Kingdom of Serbs, Croats and Slovenes. The treaty also presented Bulgaria with a staggering reparations bill of 2,250 million gold francs, to be paid over thirty-seven years. In addition, Sofia had to agree to the transfer of large quantities of livestock and railroad equipment to Greece, Romania, and the Kingdom of Serbs, Croats and Slovenes, which also was to receive annual deliveries of 50,000 tons of coal from Sofia. Proportionate to its size and GDP, Bulgaria faced the highest reparations bill of all the Central Powers.⁴⁵

Finally, the armed forces were severely slashed; the army was to be reduced from roughly 700,000 men to a pitiful force of 20,000. When the details of the treaty were transmitted to Sofia, some generals and politicians wanted to resume hostilities, but realists like the successor to Teodorov as Bulgarian Prime Minister, Alexander Stambolijski, said that he would sign 'even a bad peace' for lack of alternatives.⁴⁶ On 27 November 1919 he did this, during a brief ceremony in the old town hall in Neuilly. It looked, said an American present that day, 'as if the office boy had been called in for a conference with the board of directors'. Among the observers was the Greek Prime Minister,

Eleftherios Venizelos, 'endeavouring not to look too pleased' at having gained Western Thrace for his country.[47]

In the eyes of most Bulgarians, and not without reason, the Treaty of Neuilly symbolized the lowest point of their national existence as an independent state. The redrawing of borders left Bulgaria without agriculturally fertile areas (such as Dobrudja and Thrace) and without access to the Aegean Sea – a major issue as trade via ships was a decisive factor for whole sectors of the Bulgarian economy.[48] Prompted by the redrawing of borders, Bulgaria experienced yet another massive influx of refugees from Macedonia, Thrace and Dobrudja (as well as from the ceded western borderlands), the second wave of refugees since 1913. Between 1912 and the mid-1920s, Bulgaria had to accommodate roughly 280,000 refugees, which now made up to 5 per cent of the overall population. Around half of these people came from territories that were ceded to Greece (Aegean Macedonia and Western Thrace) and 25 per cent from the Ottoman Empire (Eastern Thrace). Smaller in number, but no less dramatic, was the influx of refugees from territories that now belonged to the Kingdom of Serbs, Croats and Slovenes (12.5 per cent) and Romania (11 per cent).[49] Accommodating such a massive population intake at a time of severe economic and social crisis posed one of the most significant challenges to the Bulgarian state for years to come.[50] As Stambolijski put it in a desperate letter to the unsympathetic French Prime Minister, Clemenceau, on 22 November 1919: 'The population of Bulgaria now lives in a truly disturbed state. Its disasters are made even worse by the sufferings of the numerous refugees . . . These countless refugees, homeless people without any possessions . . . will always be a bleeding wound in the relationships in the Balkans.'[51] Stambolijski was right, even if he did not live to see developments after 1923. For much of the interwar period, Bulgaria struggled to come to terms with the human and financial costs of a lost war, economic crisis and international isolation, leading to deep internal divisions and violent clashes between supporters of different political camps, and rapidly changing governments, often disposed of through putsches.[52]

For Bulgaria's long-time colonial master and wartime ally until 1918, the Ottoman Empire, the process of disintegration had begun well before the armistice, when the great retreat of Ottoman forces and the advance of British troops and local auxiliaries 'liberated' all of its Arab territories. Even before the convening in January 1919 of the Paris Peace Conference – at which the Turks were the only representatives of the Ottoman Empire's peoples excluded from the deliberations – it had become clear that the fate of the empire lay in the hands of Britain and France, as US President Woodrow Wilson displayed little interest in getting involved in implementing a post-war order in the Middle East. The United States had never declared war on the Ottoman Empire, and Wilson's departure from Paris on the very day of the signing of the Versailles Treaty was indicative of his lack of interest in the peace settlement with Constantinople. Britain and France, by contrast, were intent on dividing most of the Ottoman Empire's Arab provinces between them.[53]

Yet while realists in Constantinople had long given up on the Arab territories in the Middle East, there were some Ottoman statesmen who optimistically hoped for a strict application of the twelfth of Wilson's Fourteen Points. This advocated 'a secure sovereignty' to the 'Turkish portion of the present Ottoman Empire', namely Anatolia in Asia Minor and Eastern Thrace in Europe.[54] On 17 June 1919 the liberal Turkish Grand Vizier, Damad Ferid, argued along similar lines as his counterparts in the other defeated states when he assured Clemenceau, Lloyd George and Wilson in Paris that his government had nothing in common with the wartime rulers of the Committee of Union and Progress (CUP) who were to blame for the Ottoman Empire's entry into the war and the terrible fate of the Armenian Christians. If the Wilsonian principle of self-determination was to be applied, Anatolia in particular had to remain Turkish. The problem was that parts of Anatolia were now also claimed by others. Thanks to vague promises made in early 1915 by Sir Edward Grey, the British Foreign Secretary, Greece, which went on to fight on the Allied side for the last eighteen months of the war, felt entitled to make claims on western Anatolia, which was home to substantial Greek communities. The Greeks enjoyed traditional sympathies in the West as fellow Christians, whereas the Ottomans could expect little support in either Britain or France. Lloyd George famously dismissed the Turks as 'a human cancer, a creeping agony in the flesh of the lands which they misgovern, rotting away every fibre of life'.[55]

Other existing or emerging states also had their designs on parts of

Anatolia. Italy sought to establish a permanent foothold in western Anatolia, after previously occupying the formerly Ottoman Dodecanese Islands in 1912. Having received vague assurances in the 1915 London Treaty that if the Ottoman Empire was to be broken up, Rome would receive its 'fair share', Italian diplomats further pushed for a sphere of influence in Anatolia. Meanwhile, the Kurds – dreading the prospect of minority status under Armenian, Arab, or Turkish rule – also demanded independence or autonomy with foreign protection. Likewise, former Russian Armenia, which had become the Democratic Republic of Armenia in May 1918, pressed for the annexation of a number of Ottoman provinces in the East. Violence here had escalated in the spring of 1918, when survivors of the *Aghet* exacted revenge against local Muslim civilians, notably in massacres in Erzinjan and Erzurum from late January to mid-February 1918, where close to 10,000 Muslim Turks were estimated to have been butchered.[56]

Territorial demands and violence further exacerbated the situation in a country already devastated by the Great War, as British fact-finding missions clearly demonstrated. One of the officers dispatched into the interior from Constantinople, Lieutenant Clarence Palmer (who had spent most of the war in an Ottoman prisoner-of-war camp), visited various towns and villages in north-western Anatolia, from where he reported back to his superiors. As he travelled from Eskişehir to Konya, he came across towns and villages ravaged by hunger, sickness and material shortages. Displaced Armenians, he noted, had sold their children for food, while the absence of men killed in the war and the requisitioning of farm animals meant that agricultural production and manufacturing had come to a standstill.[57]

In August 1920, more than a year after the conclusion of the Treaty of Versailles, the victorious Allies finally signed a peace treaty with the sultan's government under Damad Ferid. It was to be the last of the Paris peace treaties. The Treaty of Sèvres, signed in the showroom of a porcelain factory in August, radically reduced the territory that would be left under Constantinople's rule. Only one third of Anatolia was deemed indisputably Turkish. Greece was allocated Smyrna and its environs, subject to a plebiscite within five years. The Armenians received vast areas of eastern Anatolia, stretching from Trabzon on the Black Sea coast to Lake Van, and Kurdistan was to become an autonomous region. The Straits of Bosphorus were placed under international administration. France and Italy each retained spheres of influence in Anatolia.[58] As elsewhere in the vanquished states, the terms of the treaty were greeted with horror in Anatolia. Yet unlike the other peace treaties, the Treaty of Sèvres was never ratified and was replaced with a very different peace treaty within two and a half years – for reasons we will return to.

The Allies' apparently vengeful attitude towards the vanquished in 1918–20 owed much to the passions of nationalism aroused by the Great War.[59] The lingering memory of German atrocities in Belgium in 1914, the damage caused by the German troops during their strategic withdrawal in 1917, the offensives of 1918, and the despair and anger over lost relatives and friends killed in the field, were still very present in 1919. The passions of war had not yet subsided and the Allied leaders, dependent on popular support, were aware that soldiers, as well as their families, were looking for compensation from the enemy in order to validate their sacrifices. In the eyes of the Allies, the Central Powers had also done themselves great damage by suddenly talking about a 'just peace' when – only a few months earlier – they had imposed draconian terms on Russia and Romania in the 1918 treaties of Brest-Litovsk and Bucharest. And then there was, of course, the issue of collective security: the victorious Allies feared a military revival of their defeated opponents, especially that of a resurgent Germany. Depriving Berlin of the means to wage a revenge war was central to the maintenance of a general peace, and to France's territorial integrity in particular.

The perception among the vanquished was, of course, fundamentally different. Resentment against the peace treaties of Paris in the vanquished states of Europe was not only fuelled by the perceived humiliation of defeat. There was also the issue of perceived hypocrisy, as Wilson's idea of self-determination was clearly applied to peoples considered allies of the Entente (Poles, Czechs, south Slavs, Romanians and Greeks), but not to those viewed as enemies (Austrians, Germans, Hungarians, Bulgarians and Turks). Worse still, the application of the principle of national self-determination to territories of mind-boggling ethnic complexity was at best naive and, in practice, an invitation to transform the violence of the First World War into a multitude of border conflicts and civil wars. Ethnic rivalries in central Europe turned violent as older antagonisms, such as that between the Czechs and Germans of Bohemia, were joined by new national struggles such as those between Czechs and Poles in Teschen.[60]

All of the new states, supposedly founded on the principle of national self-determination, had within their borders large and vocal national minorities, which (most notably after the onset of the Great Depression) began to demand reunification with their 'homelands'. The Allies' violation of the principle of self-determination left 13 million Germans (including German Austrians) beyond the Reich's borders. Meanwhile, Budapest bemoaned the loss of over 3.2 million ethnic Hungarians to new neighbouring states, while some 420,000 refugees from territories taken by Czechoslovakia, Yugoslavia, Romania and Austria were a radicalizing presence in interwar Hungary, demanding a return of their native lands to Budapest's control.[61]

The problem of irredentism continued to haunt European politics for decades, not least because many of the successor states of east-central Europe were, in fact, mini-empires themselves and every bit as multi-ethnic as the vanquished land empires they had replaced (with the added problem that pre-war ethnic tensions had been exacerbated by years of brutal fighting).[62] Those who now found themselves as a minority in ethnically mixed successor states often succumbed to nationalist agitation. In contested Silesia, for example, the Friedrich Wilhelms University in Breslau became a centre of German nationalist agitation. Reflecting the city's multi-ethnic composition, the university had traditionally been one of Germany's most cosmopolitan educational institutions, and throughout the nineteenth century its student body included a significant proportion of Poles, as well as large numbers of Jewish students.[63] After 1918, however, the atmosphere was deeply hostile to inter-ethnic cohabitation. Young German nationalists were particularly attracted by right-wing intellectuals such as Walter Kuhn, a self-proclaimed expert in the increasingly fashionable field of *Ostforschung* ('Research of the East'), give lectures on the need to reverse the Versailles Treaty and recover 'lost' German populations in Poland and east-central Europe more generally.[64] Such ideas fell on fertile ground. Generally speaking, Germans who lived in ethnically mixed border areas were disproportionately more likely to support parties of the radical Right, and eventually end up in one form of Nazi affiliation or another, than those who inhabited the urban centres further west.[65] Nazi Germany and its overtly exterminationist imperial project of the later 1930s and early 1940s owed much to the logic of ethnic conflict and irredentism created by the Great War and the redrawing of borders in 1918–19.[66]

The only ethnically homogeneous states in post-war eastern-, central-, or south-eastern Europe were the core states of the vanquished land empires: the Weimar Republic, Austria, Hungary, Bulgaria and the Turkish Republic (founded in October 1923). Each of these new states contained small minorities (notably Jews in central Europe and remnants of the Orthodox Christian community in Constantinople) that would be harassed or subjected to violence over the following decades, but the minority question in the 1920s and early 1930s was quantitatively far more significant in the victorious successor states. The new Polish nation state, for example, contained a population that was roughly 35 per cent non-Polish, including sizeable Ukrainian, Belarusian, Lithuanian and German minorities. The Kingdom of Serbs, Croats and Slovenes did not reflect in its name that some two million of its inhabitants belonged to none of these groups, mainly Bosnian Muslims (9.6 per cent), Hungarians (4 per cent), Albanians (3 per cent) and ethnic Germans (14 per cent). Czechoslovakia contained more ethnic Germans (23 per cent of the overall population) than Slovaks, plus sizeable communities of Ruthenes and Magyars. And some three million Hungarians lived in Romania, a state that doubled its pre-war size by absorbing Transylvania, Bessarabia, Bukovina and a large part of the Banat.[67]

The large ethnic minorities in these new nation states made it abundantly clear that 'self-determination' was only granted to peoples considered allies of the Entente, and not to their wartime enemies. Nor were the Allies willing to consider 'self-determination' for non-Europeans. As colonial nationalists lobbied the peace conference demanding autonomy rights, Woodrow Wilson did not live up to their high expectations, failing to challenge the imperial ambitions of Britain and France, whose empires expanded further after 1918, notably through the League of Nations' mandates in the Middle East and elsewhere.[68] Wilson's lack of support for colonial self-determination should not have come as a major surprise to anyone. For all his liberal talk about self-determination and moral pacts, the American President – an otherwise progressive academic intellectual from Virginia – overtly supported racial segregation in the United States, permitting segregation within federal institutions soon after taking office.[69]

Within an international context, Wilson clearly believed (as did most Westerners at the time) that race mattered when it came to deciding whether a given community merited 'self-determination' or not. The Covenant of Wilson's pet project, the League of Nations, which was published as a preamble to all five treaties produced by the Paris Peace Conference, never mentioned the colonial peoples of the victorious empires.[70] Instead, the Covenant established the former imperial domains of Ottoman Turkey as so-called 'Class A' mandates or territories 'inhabited by peoples not yet able to stand by themselves under the strenuous conditions of the modern world'. They were to be released into independent statehood after being guided to administrative maturity by their mandatory power. Britain and France eventually divided the Class A mandates – Mesopotamia (now Iraq), Palestine (including Jordan) and Syria (including Lebanon) – between them, while the Hijaz (Saudi Arabia) became independent. The so-called 'Class B' mandates, most of the former German colonies in Africa, required firmer guidance by their mandatory power, but would be released into independence at some indefinite point in the future. Still other territories, notably the former German South-West Africa (today's Namibia) and the South Pacific Islands formerly occupied by Germany, became 'Class C' Mandates. The 'C mandates' were in essence colonies in all but name, 'best administered under the laws of the Mandatory as integral portions of its territory'.[71] Unlike the territories of the former Austro-Hungarian Empire inhabited by White Europeans – so ran the emphatically racist rationale that guided the entire mandate system of the Paris peace treaties – the colonial peoples of colour were not ready to look after their own affairs.[72]

Within Europe, the peacemakers in Paris clearly recognized that the problems arising from contested multi-ethnicity in the emerging nation states had to be addressed. Although by some accounts Europe's territorial reorganization in 1918–19 actually halved the total number of people deemed minorities, from 60 million to between

25 and 30 million, the new successor states initially had no legal framework in place to secure their rights.[73] The Allies thus drew up the so-called Minorities Treaties, a series of bilateral agreements signed by each of the new states as a precondition for their international recognition.[74]

Post-imperial Poland was supposed to provide the model. The Polish Minorities Treaty, or 'Little Versailles' Treaty, signed on the same day as its better-known namesake, would guide all subsequent statements from the conference on the subject, and similar agreements would bind no fewer than seven additional successor states.[75] The Minorities Treaties sought to protect the collective rights of all ethnic or religious minorities now living inside the successor states of east-central Europe.[76] The new nation states had to guarantee the rights of political organization and representation, and the use of minority languages in courtrooms and schools, as well as compensation for land transfers. In Czechoslovakia, for example, international treaties guaranteed minority groups collective rights. In areas where they made up at least 20 per cent of the population, Germans had the right to obtain an education and deal with state authorities in their own language. As ethnic Germans tended to be clustered in certain regions, this effectively meant that 90 per cent of them were able to avail themselves of this concession.[77]

Alleged violations of the treaties could be brought to the League Council and the International Court of Justice. Significantly, parties outside the national boundaries could make representations on behalf of beleaguered minorities. The Hungarian government, for example, might sue on behalf of Magyars in Slovakia, or Weimar Germans on behalf of the Sudeten Germans. It was one of the peace conference's most significant achievements, as it provided a legal framework through which aggrieved minorities could (and did) seek redress against treaty violations.[78]

The situation was less clear when it came to minorities that had no national state to fend for their interests, such as the roughly six million Jews living in the Pale of Settlement in the western borderlands of the collapsed Romanov Empire and in the eastern half of the former Habsburg Empire (notably in Western Galicia and Hungary). Whereas the Jews of the Romanov Empire had been periodically subjected to pogroms before 1914, those living in the Habsburg lands were relatively safe from violence. They had rightly perceived the Dual Monarchy as a guarantor of their rights and status as citizens and subjects of the empire. It was thus no coincidence that many of the nostalgic Habsburg novels of the 1920s and 1930s were written by Jewish authors such as Stefan Zweig or Joseph Roth. As Count Chojnicki, a Polish aristocrat from Galicia and a key figure in Roth's famous *Radetzky March* (1932), puts it in one of his angry, prophetic comments: 'As soon as the emperor says goodnight, we'll break up into a hundred pieces . . . All the peoples will set up their own dirty little statelets . . . Nationalism is the new religion.'[79]

To Jews like Roth, it had been much more preferable to live in a large multi-ethnic empire that afforded legal protection to its minorities than in smaller nation states based on the idea of ethnic or religious exclusivity. Soon after the implosion of empires in central Europe, the Jewish populations of Ukraine, the Baltic States, Poland, Galicia, the Bukovina, Bohemia and Moravia were suddenly confronted with the dual accusation of being both loyal subjects of the bygone empires (and thus patriotically unreliable) and supporters of Bolshevism.[80]

Overall, the treaties designed to allow ethnic minorities a certain degree of cultural autonomy and legal protection proved ineffective. Even Czechoslovakia, generally considered the most tolerant and democratic of the successor states, soon displayed an ambivalent attitude towards its non-Czech subjects. At least in theory, or so Tomáš Masaryk, the son of a Czech mother and a Slovak father, assumed, the cultural differences between Czechs and Slovaks could easily be bridged. But while the Reformation had turned the majority of Czechs into Protestants, the Slovaks, who had lived under Hungarian rule since the tenth century, were staunchly Catholic. And if the Slovaks had hoped that Masaryk would keep his promise, made in the Pittsburgh Agreement of 1918, that they would be granted far-reaching cultural autonomy within the new state, they were soon proven wrong.[81]

Masaryk's attitude towards the sizeable German minority was even more problematic, even if the 'Sudeten' enjoyed a considerable degree of cultural freedom in areas where they constituted a majority.

Simultaneously, however, he led the grassroots pressure for land reform, when he decided to break up the large (mostly German-owned) estates – a move that also allowed Czechs to 'colonize' the German-inhabited western borderlands of Czechoslovakia.[82] As Masaryk's Foreign Minister, Edvard Beneš, freely admitted in conversation with a British diplomat, the end of Austro-Hungarian rule had led to a reversal of ethnic hierarchies: 'Before the war, the Germans were here' (pointing to the ceiling) and 'we were there' (pointing to the floor). 'Now,' he declared, reversing his gestures, 'we are here and they are there.' Land reform, Beneš insisted, was 'necessary' to 'teach the Germans a lesson'.[83]

From the perspective of the vanquished states of Europe, the Minorities Treaties were merely a fig leaf to cover up the blatant breach of the fundamental principle of self-determination, which they had wrongly assumed would underpin the new world order. The defeated states agreed that their 'lost' minorities had to be 'returned' at all cost, putting treaty revisionism high up on the political agenda long before the Nazis entered the scene. It was not a good foundation for a lasting peace.[84]

14

Fiume

Resentment at the new world order forged in Paris over the period 1919–20 was not confined to the defeated powers. It was also keenly sensed by those who believed they had won the war but lost the peace. Japan – the one Asian member of the Supreme War Council and theoretically one of the Great Powers at the heart of decision-making in Paris – felt increasingly marginalized. Although Japan gained some territories, notably the former German concession in Shandong and the German Pacific islands north of the equator, no advances were made in recognizing Japan as a fully equal partner of the Western Allies. The Japanese proposal for a 'racial equality' clause in the Covenant of the League of Nations was a particularly thorny issue. It was primarily intended to put Japan on an equal footing with the 'white' Western Allies (rather than establish racial equality between Whites and Asians more generally), but it created a rift within the British Empire delegation, based on strident opposition in the Dominions to Japanese immigration. The Australian representatives, determined to maintain their country as a 'white' dominion, blocked the Japanese quest for racial equality in the international system and managed to win the debate within the delegation. Infuriated by their treatment, Japanese politicians increasingly turned their backs on the West, while their expansion in Shandong and the Pacific islands encouraged over-ambitious dreams of dominance over a Great East Asia.[1]

The sentiment of a lost or 'mutilated' victory was even more prominent in Italy, a country that had lost more men in the war than Britain, and whose population felt that the territorial promises made by London and Paris in exchange for Rome's entry into the conflict were no longer taken seriously. Back in 1915, in exchange for an Italian declaration of war against its former allies, the Central Powers, the country had indeed received sweeping promises from its new allies. In the secret Treaty of London it was agreed that Italy would gain substantial territories: not only was Rome going to keep control over the formerly Ottoman Dodecanese Islands (occupied since 1912) and gain a 'protectorate' over Albania, but it was also promised Habsburg-controlled Trentino and the heavily German-populated South Tyrol up to the Brenner Pass, northern Dalmatia, and the entire Austrian Littoral, including the port city of Trieste. One problem with this generous offer was that it had been made at a point in time when there was no thought of creating an independent Yugoslavia, and no talk of 'national self-determination'. The other problem was that by late 1918, Rome's appetite for imperial expansion had grown beyond the territories that were promised in 1915: it now also wanted the Adriatic port of Fiume (Rijeka), which had been administered by Hungary until the end of the war.[2]

Rome did not wait for the Paris Peace Conference to convene to claim some of the land promised in 1915. As soon as the armistice with Austria-Hungary was signed on 3 November 1918, Italian troops marched into Istria and Dalmatia. The question of Fiume's future was more difficult to resolve, as Belgrade staked a counter-claim to the city for the emerging South Slav state, prompting Italian diplomats in Paris to launch their ultimately futile campaign to prevent the Great Powers from recognizing the Kingdom of Serbs, Slovenes and Croats altogether.[3]

Italy's often criticized uncompromising position in 1918–19 warrants some explanation. Like other heads of governments of formerly combatant states, the Italian Prime Minister, Vittorio Emanuele Orlando, had to justify the extraordinary wartime suffering of the Italian people over the previous three years as well as the deaths of some 600,000 Italian soldiers. The population, here as in other victorious countries, demanded maximum compensation, financial as well as territorial.[4] At the same time, however, Orlando's demands in Paris must be understood within a longer tradition of Italian liberal imperialism.[5] Ever since the foundation of the Italian nation state between 1861 and 1870, the reconquest of parts of the bygone Roman Empire – notably around the *mare nostrum* ('our sea'), as nationalists called the Mediterranean – had played an important part in public discussions about Italy's future place in the world. In 1911 it moved to implementing these ideas and started imperial expansion through its attack on the Ottoman Empire's north African *vilayets* of Tripolitania and Cyrenaica, which Italian imperialists – mindful of their Roman heritage – commonly referred to as 'Libya' (the name of ancient Rome's north African province).[6] The new colony across the Mediterranean, or so it was hoped, would finally establish Italy as a European Great Power with an empire to prove it – an ambition that had been thwarted fifteen years earlier with Italy's defeat at Adowa (1896) at the hands of the Ethiopians.[7]

In reality, the military intervention in Libya turned out to be extremely costly, not least because of stubborn Ottoman and local resistance against the Italian aggression. Commanded by capable officers like Enver Bey – a future member of the Young Turk triumvirate – and involving other notable figures such as the young Mustafa Kemal, the Turkish forces tenaciously resisted the Italians, soon to be joined by local Arabs, whose loyalty towards their alleged Ottoman 'oppressors' proved stronger than the Italian invaders had hoped.[8] The conflict dragged on for months and ultimately ended with an incomplete victory for Italy: by the time the war came to an end in October 1912, around 10,000 Italian soldiers had died, almost double those lost at the Battle of Adowa, yet Italy only controlled some coastal cities and not the entire country as originally intended.[9] Furthermore, following the peace treaty with the Ottomans, local guerrilla groups continued to fight the new colonial masters for almost two decades. It would take the Italian Army until 1931 to gain full control over its new territories in north Africa.[10]

Vittorio Orlando could thus draw on a longer tradition of Italian expansionism when, in 1918–19, he pursued a policy of liberal imperialism. The dissolution of the Austro-Hungarian Empire offered a historically unique opportunity. In his view (and that of many other Italian contemporaries) the time had come to realize the dream of Giuseppe Mazzini, Giuseppe Garibaldi and the Risorgimento: the consolidation of all Italian-inhabited territories in a unified nation state, thereby overcoming the deep frictions within Italian society that had existed ever since Rome had decided to enter the war in May 1915.[11]

Italy's entry into the war and the decision to turn against its former allies of the Triple Alliance – Germany and Austria-Hungary – in favour of the Entente, had been anything but uncontroversial.[12] It created one of the most lasting cleavages in Italian society and politics: that between advocates of neutrality and those who favoured an armed intervention on the side of the Entente.[13] Italy's declaration of war in the spring of 1915 had been preceded by nine months of heated (and at times violent) debate in which unusual alliances were formed. Nationalists and radical democrats, for example, came together in urban squares to demonstrate in favour of war, although with different purposes: the nationalists to make Italy a truly Great Power; the radical democrats to defeat Prussian militarism. The call to arms was supported by parts of the otherwise pro-neutral Socialist Party, which did not want to be involved in an imperialist war and took the catchphrase of international working-class solidarity more seriously than its European counterparts; this led in November 1914 to the expulsion of the pro-war wing, led by Benito Mussolini, from the Socialist Party.[14] 'Interventionist' propaganda fostered a powerful narrative that was to divide the nation for years to come: the myth of 'two Italys' – one virile, forward-looking, young, and thus pro-war; the other decaying, backward-looking and cowardly. If, from the perspective of the 'interventionists', war would bring out the best of the 'true Italy', those who tried to prevent it had to be eradicated from the national body politic.[15]

Orlando was of course well aware of this when he pursued his maximalist agenda in Paris and added Fiume to Italy's imperial shopping list. What began as an exercise in prestige politics for a domestic audience soon gained a dynamic of its own.[16] For Fiume not only inspired the fantasies of nationalists like the flamboyant warrior-poet Gabriele D'Annunzio, who coined the term 'mutilated victory', but also those with revolutionary aspirations, who hoped for avant-garde political and social values to replace the pre-war bourgeois and conservative order.[17]

Staunch opposition to Italy's claims to Fiume came from the Kingdom of Serbs, Croats and Slovenes, which had its own designs on the city. Belgrade was backed by Woodrow Wilson, albeit for different reasons. Wilson generally objected to secret diplomacy, epitomized in his view by Britain and France's dealings with Italy. He also doubted that Italy had a legitimate claim to the city on the basis of 'national self-determination', as only half the population could reasonably claim to be Italian, while the other half identified themselves with other ethnic groups.[18] But the Italian diplomats in Paris were unwilling to back off and insisted on the Allies honouring the terms of the Treaty of London *and* accepting Italy's claims to Fiume. Infuriated by Rome's unwillingness to compromise, Wilson published a statement in which he directly appealed to the Italian people to forego unjustified territorial claims. His self-congratulatory reference to his own Fourteen Points as 'sacred obligations' did not help his cause. The following day, 24 April, the Italians walked out of the Paris Peace Conference and returned to Rome, where large-scale anti-American demonstrations greeted them, while an editorial in the newspaper *L'Epoca* asked: 'How could he for a moment think that at his bidding the Italian people would rise against their government and force it to accept a program dictated by a foreigner shut up in an ivory tower of his own abstractions?'[19]

Wilson's statement further outraged the forces of extreme Italian nationalism that Orlando sought to contain with his insistence on adding Fiume to the Italian wish-list. Even after the signing of the Versailles Treaty with Germany in the summer of 1919, the issue remained unresolved and provided a rallying point for all Italians dissatisfied with the peace settlement. One of them was D'Annunzio, whose name is inseparably linked with the inter-Allied conflict over Fiume. The most famous Italian poet of his time, D'Annunzio had a national as well as an international reputation, even among the likes of James Joyce, Marcel Proust and Henry James, who ranked him among the leading *fin-de-siècle* writers. D'Annunzio was also politically active, namely as a prominent spokesman for the irredentist movement, which called for an inclusion of all those 'Italian' territories that had been left *irredenti* (unredeemed) when Italy was unified as a nation state in the second half of the nineteenth century.[20] In 1915, at the age of fifty-two, D'Annunzio had returned to Italy from France to enlist in the war against the Central Powers.[21] He served with distinction during the war, cultivating his reputation as Italy's great poet-warrior with a number of aviation stunts, including an air raid on Habsburg-controlled Trieste and the dropping of propaganda leaflets over Vienna.[22]

After the war D'Annunzio, like many other veterans, expected Italy to be rewarded for its sacrifices. But following Woodrow Wilson's public appeal to the Italians to soften their territorial demands in April 1919, rumours spread through the army that the government in Rome was about to succumb to American pressure. This suspicion was strengthened further when Francesco Saverio Nitti, an economist and leader of the radical wing of the Liberal Party, replaced Orlando as Prime Minister on 23 June 1919 after the latter's resignation.[23] Nitti's appointment was especially welcomed by the other delegations of the Great Powers at Paris, who believed him to be more reasonable than Orlando. They were to be disappointed, however. Facing public pressure, notably from the Right, Nitti and his government were unwilling to give up Italy's claim on Fiume. The nationalist Right, however, remained unconvinced that Nitti would deliver on the Fiume question.[24]

And so D'Annunzio decided to act. On 11 September he began his famous 'March on Fiume' from Ronchi dei Legionari (Ronke), some 300 kilometres further to the north-west. He had fewer than two hundred soldiers, but was soon joined by others. When D'Annunzio reached the outskirts of Fiume in a bright red Fiat, his army had grown to 2,000 men, most of them former Italian shock troops or *arditi*. The largely Italian inter-Allied garrison in the city handed over power to D'Annunzio without firing a shot.[25]

Over the next fifteen months D'Annunzio ruled as the undisputed leader (*Duce*) of what was now called the Regency of Carnaro, with its own constitution and currency. He himself was not a fascist in any meaningful sense and Fiume remained a remarkably non-violent place by the standards of the time, but the new city-state was to become a central reference point for Italian nationalists.[26] Mussolini, initially cautious about the Fiume adventure, was later to draw heavily on D'Annunzio's political experiments and rituals, borrowing from him elements of imperial, secular nationalism and symbolic gestures (including the March on Rome, which was partly modelled on D'Annunzio's March on Fiume).[27]

Throughout the existence of the Regency of Carnaro, the government in Rome tried to end D'Annunzio's rule by upholding a naval blockade of Fiume. Yet the Italian government shied away from a direct military assault on Fiume, partly because it feared a likely nationalist backlash driven by widespread sympathies for D'Annunzio's insubordination. It was only in December 1920, shortly after the signing of the Rapallo Treaty (which turned Fiume into a Free State), that Rome decided to act. On Christmas Eve, after Italian naval bombardment, D'Annunzio and his supporters surrendered the city. Yet even after D'Annunzio's retirement to a villa on the shores of Lake Garda, his legacy in politics lived on and Fiume remained on the nationalists' agenda. Mussolini, who publicly celebrated D'Annunzio's 'defiance' and emulated his populist style, soon revoked parts of the Treaty of Rapallo, and from September 1923 onwards the city was once again Italian.[28]

15

From Smyrna to Lausanne

Italy's imperial ambitions after 1918 went beyond Fiume. The London Treaty of 1915 had made vague promises about a 'just share' of the Ottoman Empire for Rome, should the empire be dismantled at the end of the war. In early May 1919, to make clear that these promises had not been forgotten, the Italians landed troops at the ports of Adalia (Antalya) and Marmaris in southern Anatolia, without consulting their allies. There were also rumours in Paris of Italian vessels approaching Smyrna, the heavily Christian-populated port on the western Anatolian coast that was also being claimed by Greece.[1]

On 6 May, Lloyd George suggested that in order to end Italy's imperial aspirations in Asia Minor, Greece should be allowed to occupy Smyrna and its environs. Even Woodrow Wilson, normally opposed to imperial land-grabbing, approved of the idea, if only to put the increasingly annoying Italian government in its place. Lloyd George then summoned the Greek Prime Minister, Eleftherios Venizelos, and asked him to prepare for the landing at Smyrna.[2] Venizelos seemed like an inspired choice for the role of re-establishing a Byzantine Empire with close links to London. Born in Ottoman-ruled Crete in 1864, Venizelos' wealthy merchant family had been forced to flee to mainland Greece as a consequence of his father's involvement in the Cretan insurrection of 1886. A lawyer by training, Prime Minister since 1910, and founder of the Liberal Party, Venizelos had favoured his country joining the Allies ever since 1914. This belief brought him into direct conflict with his king, Constantine I. Constantine was a Germanophile who had spent some of his earlier years studying in Germany. He was married to Sophia of Prussia, a sister of Kaiser Wilhelm II, who accorded him the honorary rank of Field Marshal of the German Army. Although he made no secret of his affection for

Germany, Constantine advocated neutrality for his country when hostilities began in 1914. In defiance of the wishes of his king, however, Venizelos invited the British and French governments to send armies to Greece's recently acquired former Ottoman port of Salonika (Thessaloniki). This led to Venizelos's dismissal and, in early 1916, the king granted permission for German and Bulgarian forces to enter eastern Macedonia and Thrace.[3]

Venizelos and his supporters were appalled and publicly voiced their anger at the king's pro-German attitude during a mass rally in Athens on 16 August 1916. The confrontation between Constantine and Venizelos ultimately led to the formation of two rival governments, with Athens and Salonika becoming the respective capitals of a de facto divided Greece in August 1916. Venizelos ultimately emerged triumphant from the power struggle when the Allies imposed a punitive naval blockade on southern Greece, causing great economic hardship among the civilian population. Constantine eventually succumbed to the external pressure in June 1917 and abdicated in favour of his younger son, Alexander, who had been the Allies' choice because of his pro-Western stance. Alexander's accession to the throne paved the way for Venizelos' return to Athens and Greece's full military participation in the war against the Central Powers. Now, following victory over the Central Powers, Venizelos expected to be rewarded for his support of the Allied cause. Lloyd George assured him in Paris that a Greek conquest of Smyrna would not be opposed by the other victor states. The Greek Prime Minister thus had every reason to believe that he enjoyed the unqualified support of the British government in this matter. However, Venizelos ignored the stern warning of Field Marshal Henry Wilson, also present at their meeting, that the occupation of Smyrna would result in another war with an uncertain outcome, as the Turkish Army was beaten but not altogether destroyed. This assessment was echoed by Lord Curzon, Arthur Balfour's right-hand man in the Foreign Office, who sent several memoranda warning the Greek Prime Minister not to underestimate the ability of Turkish troops to remobilize against an external threat.[4]

Wilson and Lord Curzon were not the only senior strategists who strongly objected to the idea of a Greek occupation of Smyrna. When Venizelos had first contemplated the idea of joining the Entente in exchange for extensive territorial gains in Anatolia in early 1915, he sought the advice of Colonel Ioannis Metaxas, one of the military masterminds behind Greece's success in the First Balkan War of 1912 and the country's future military dictator between 1936 and 1941. Metaxas' response was not what Venizelos had hoped for. He emphasized that the coastal areas inhabited by Ottoman Greeks were not readily defensible. The envisaged occupation area contained large numbers of Muslims who might rise up against foreign rule, while the fertile valleys of western Anatolia were dangerously exposed to any Turkish counter-attack from the Anatolian hinterland. Any invasion could easily lead to something similar to Napoleon's disastrous campaign in Russia, as Turkish defenders would surely attempt to lure their attackers into the interior of central Anatolia with its extreme climate in both summer and winter.[5]

Venizelos chose to ignore these warnings. Like all those on the winning side in 1918, he seemed to be driven by a sense of unique historical opportunity. Normally a realist, he must have felt that the re-establishment of an ancient Greek Mediterranean Empire was finally within reach. The Megali Idea – the 'Great Idea' of Greek territorial expansion into Asia Minor, reuniting the mainland with the various irredentist populations under Ottoman rule – had been a prominent recurrent theme in Greek political discourse ever since the revolution of 1843, which had led to the establishment of an independent constitutional monarchy. Since then, the constant expansion of Greece's borders and the gradual assimilation of previously irredentist Greek minorities within the nation state had created high expectations for the future inclusion of the sizeable Orthodox minority within the Ottoman Empire, largely concentrated on the western and northern Anatolian coastline and its hinterland as well as in the Pontus on the southern shore of the Black Sea. With roots stretching back to the Byzantine period, the Greek Orthodox community had expanded significantly in the nineteenth century, when an economic boom in and around Smyrna drew large numbers of penniless immigrants from mainland Greece and the islands of the eastern Aegean. Although this trend had reversed due to growing inter-communal tensions in the wake of the First Balkan War of 1912, the Greek Orthodox population of Smyrna in 1914 still stood at 200,000 out of a total population of 350,000.[6] The Pontian Greeks also formed a sizeable community, notably in and around the Black Sea cities of Sampson (Samsun) and Trapezous (Trabzon), but they never constituted a majority in the predominantly Muslim-populated region.[7] According to official Ottoman statistics, the Christian population in Pontus stood at 530,000, while the Muslims numbered just under one million.[8]

Just over a week after Venizelos' fateful conversation with Lloyd George, on 15 May, the Greek invasion troops arrived in Smyrna by boat, sparking excitement among the Christian population and outrage among the Muslims, some of whom spontaneously founded the National Committee of Refusal of the Annexation (Redd-i İlhak Heyt-i Milliyesi), calling on the Turkish population to resist the invaders.[9]

It did not take long for tensions to erupt violently. As Greek troops disembarked and marched into the city, a shot was fired on them by a Turkish refugee from Salonika, Hasan Tahsin, who had served in the CUP's 'Special Organization' during the war.[10] The Greek troops responded by storming the nearby Turkish barracks, arresting the soldiers inside and force-marching them towards the harbour – a procession during which the prisoners 'were made to go through no end of humiliation', as a Smyrna-based British businessman recalled.[11] As one of the prisoners fell out of line, he was bayoneted to death, a murder that was followed by several others. British officers in the harbour reported that they witnessed several bodies of killed Turks being thrown into the sea. Local Greek thugs and gangs of nationalists took their cue from the behaviour of the soldiers. Recalling the suppression of Ottoman Christians during the war, they started a riot in the Turkish quarter, killing, maiming, looting and raping at will. In the chaos throughout the day, between 300 and 400 Muslim civilians and soldiers were killed. The Greek troops suffered just two casualties.[12]

Despite the imposition of martial law and the Greek military commander's public appeal 'to respect the personal freedom and the religious beliefs of your (Muslim) fellow countrymen', violence continued unabated, notably in the rural areas of the Erythraia Peninsula, where, during the war, many Christian inhabitants of the region had been deported.[13] As a local Christian from Vourla (Urla) detailed in his diary, he and his fellow Greeks 'poured out into the Turkish villages around Vourla and began to loot them', before setting fire to some of them.[14] The atrocities in Smyrna and the Greek-occupied hinterland raised serious concerns among the Allies about an escalating cycle of violence and retribution. 'The events of Smyrna,' one Allied general reported back to Paris from Anatolia, 'have undoubtedly cheapened every Christian life in Turkey, the landing of the Greeks there being looked upon by the Turks as deliberate violation by the Allies of the terms of their armistice and the probable forerunner of further unwarranted aggression.'[15]

Concerned that the Allies might withdraw their support for the Greek annexation of Smyrna, Venizelos ordered the recently appointed High Commissioner of Smyrna, Aristides Stergiadis, to restore order. Stergiadis only arrived in the city four days after the mid-May landings, and immediately court-martialled some of those responsible for the atrocities committed against Muslims. Although Stergiadis' reputation in Greece remains tainted to this day by the fact that he fled the city one day before the Turkish army reconquered Smyrna in 1922, his record in maintaining a balanced administration for the preceding three years was laudable. Throughout his time as High Commissioner, he tried to ensure that the city's Muslim population were not treated as second-class citizens. He resisted, for example, pressures from the Orthodox Church and the Smyrna Council of Elders to introduce anti-Muslim legislation, insisted on equality before the law, and retained Muslim employees in lower administrative positions.[16]

Yet, while the state of affairs in Smyrna itself stabilized somewhat after Stergiardis' arrival, the situation escalated in the surrounding area as Greek troops sought to gain control over the hinterland. Throughout the summer of 1919 the Allies received repeated reports of civilian atrocities by Greek soldiers and Turkish irregulars, and of widespread killing and raping, notably during the Battle of Aidini (Aydin) in June and July 1919, when the city changed hands several times. Shortly after the initial Greek conquest of Aidini, irregular Turkish bands (*çete*) staged a concerted counter-attack, forcing a Greek retreat during which the Greeks set fire to the Turkish quarter, and slaughtered large numbers of Muslims.[17] The Turks responded in kind, murdering Christian civilians and setting fire to the Greek quarter.[18] The subsequent recapture of the city by a Greek army led to a new cycle of violence and reprisals. As one Greek soldier recalled:

We surrounded the city and the closer we got, the more we heard shouts and the noise of rifles and grenades. It was hell. The regular Turkish army was in retreat, but the *çete* had remained and were slaughtering, plundering, and torturing Greeks and Armenians, and were rounding up females for their harems ... In one Greek neighbourhood, whole families had been slaughtered in their homes, together with the children. Greek flags had been torn and defecated on. Flagpoles had been pushed up the backsides of some of the dead Greeks. The wells were full of corpses ... Then reprisals began – mosques set alight, the beards of *hodjas* set fire to; trousers were pulled down, followed by shots in the buttocks ... A priest came out with a sabre in his hand and slaughtered like sheep anyone he encountered on the road. The Turks had killed his wife and one of his daughters ... He left no-one, not even a dog, alive ...[19]

An international special investigative committee, established in July 1919 to examine Turkish allegations of Greek atrocities and composed of high-ranking military personnel from Britain, France, Italy and the United States, found many of the Turkish charges confirmed. It placed the blame upon the Greek side much more than on the Turkish, undermining international support for the Greek intervention.[20] Simultaneously, Greek atrocities in Asia Minor galvanized and united the previously fragmented and localized Turkish resistance, which increasingly operated independently from the sultan's unloved government in Constantinople. The government's apparent inability and unwillingness to defend the shores of Anatolia militarily gave prominent nationalist officers a reason to return to their soldierly existences. Fighting the Greeks along the Aegean finally offered them an opportunity to overcome the painful memories of the lost war by winning this conflict in the name of a newborn 'Muslim and Turkish' nation.[21]

Only four days after the Greek occupation of Smyrna, the future leader of the Turkish resistance, Mustafa Kemal, had arrived by boat in the Black Sea port of Samsun, officially as an army inspector in the service of the sultan. His real intentions were different, as Kemal was hoping to rally Turkish nationalist resistance against the Greek invasion. Later generations of Turks would celebrate the day of his arrival in Samsun as Atatürk Commemoration Day (reflecting Mustafa

Kemal's honorary name as Atatürk, or 'Father of the Turks', bestowed on him in November 1934).

Kemal was anything but an unknown figure in his country at the time. Before 1914 few people had heard of the young officer from then Ottoman Salonika, but the Great War had transformed him into a national hero.[22] His fame was based on the pivotal role he had played in the defence of the empire in April 1915, when the Allies began their ill-fated landing on the shores of the Gallipoli Peninsula.[23] On the day that the first Allied soldiers disembarked on the barren terrain of the peninsula, Ottoman troops initially retreated in disarray. Observing the panic-stricken soldiers streaming inland, Kemal left his command spot in an adjacent sector of the front and led his troops back into battle. His bold counter-offensive halted the Allied assault, prompting a bloody stand-off for several months that would ultimately lead to more than 360,000 casualties among both the invaders and the defenders.[24]

Kemal's central role in the defence of Gallipoli had not gone unnoticed, and he rose to become a brigadier general and commander of the Seventh Army in Syria by the end of the Great War. Although his army was routed by the Allied offensive in mid-September 1918, he was widely credited for the Ottoman victory at Gallipoli. In the eyes of his admirers, he had saved the empire again the following year when he repelled a Russian offensive into eastern Anatolia in August 1916. Many of his fellow countrymen shared that view, even those who had not been supporters of the wartime regime of the Committee of Union and Progress (CUP). What helped Kemal gain widespread popularity was that he was not too closely associated with the now discredited CUP leadership. Although he was a member of the CUP and promoted a post-war vision of a Turkish nation state that was entirely compatible with Young Turk aspirations, Kemal had stayed out of politics and played no role in the military blunders and civilian massacres committed by the CUP leadership after 1914.[25]

When he returned to Constantinople in late November 1918, Kemal found the capital of his homeland utterly transformed. The Entente's occupation of Anatolia had begun within a month of the armistice, and small garrisons were set up in Constantinople. Rather than land legions of troops, the war's victors dispatched a flotilla of fifty-five British, French, Italian and Greek warships through the Bosphorus Straits. The clear implication behind the presence of these ships was that non-compliance with the terms of the armistice would result in serious naval bombardment. Much to the disgust of many Muslim Ottomans, large crowds of Orthodox Christians had enthusiastically greeted the fleet, and notably the arrival of the Greek flagship *Georgios Averof*.[26]

Meanwhile, following the flight of leading CUP politicians from the capital, the political leadership was now in the hands of the sultan's new government, led by the CUP's liberal archenemies, the Freedom and Coalition Party, which ruled the empire during the armistice period (1918–23) and reversed many CUP policies, notably by encouraging deported Armenians and Kurds to return home in an ultimately ill-fated attempt to revive Ottomanism. Kemal and many other nationalists were convinced that the sultan's government was doing nothing to stop the violent dismantlement of the Turkish core of the Ottoman Empire. The largely unopposed landing of Greek troops in Smyrna and the unanswered simultaneous threat in eastern Anatolia posed by Armenian and Kurdish demands for national independence only seemed to confirm such sentiments.

At the same time, however, the nationalist resistance was still highly fragmented in the late spring of 1919. Local warlords, former Young Turk paramilitaries of the wartime 'Special Organization', demobilized Ottoman officers, social bandits, professional criminals and others made up the decentralized and locally operating national resistance groups, whose knowledge of the local terrain and support from the local Muslim population made it possible for them to inflict serious damage on the Greek invaders.[27] It was in this context that Kemal demonstrated his indisputable talent for organization and networking. As soon as he arrived in Samsun, he reached out to his old comrades who now commanded the remnants of the Ottoman Army in eastern and northern Anatolia, attending meetings organized by local nationalists, backing Muslim bandit activity, and issuing statements publicly criticizing the sultan's government.[28]

As reports about Kemal's activities started to arrive in Constantinople, the British pressed the sultan's government to recall him. When he received the order on 23 June 1919 to return to Constantinople,

Kemal resigned his commission and instead called a congress of nationalists at Erzurum, which convened on 23 July (not coincidentally the eleventh anniversary of the Young Turk Revolution of 1908).[29] The schism between the nationalist resistance movement and the sultan's government in Constantinople was now too wide to be bridged. When general elections were called for a new Ottoman Parliament in late 1919, Kemal's Defence of National Rights movement won a landslide victory. The new Ottoman Parliament in January 1920 passed a daring resolution that challenged both the victorious Allies and the sultan's government: the so-called 'National Pact' (Misak-i Millî). The National Pact stipulated that Anatolia and Eastern Thrace formed the indisputable homeland of all Muslim Turks. Furthermore, the National Pact demanded that plebiscites should be held in all former Ottoman territories to determine whether or not they wished to remain part of the empire.[30]

No other Parliament of the defeated states of the Great War had articulated its revisionist policy in such bold terms, prompting the British, in March 1920, to occupy Constantinople and arrest a number of leading nationalist parliamentarians. The sultan dissolved Parliament. Kemal, however, did not bow to such pressure and instead moved the Parliament to a new capital, Ankara, comfortably remote from Allied troops and naval vessels. He also arrested every Allied soldier within the territory controlled by him, including Lieutenant-Colonel Alfred Rawlinson, who had been dispatched to Anatolia by Lord Curzon in a secret mission to sound out what peace terms Kemal might accept.[31]

More important for the acceleration of nationalist sentiment than even the occupation of Constantinople was the signing of the draconian Treaty of Sèvres on 10 August 1920. In this last treaty of the Paris Peace Conference, the representatives of the now largely isolated sultan's government agreed to cede a substantial portion of the lands claimed in Kemal's 'National Pact' to Greeks, Armenians and Kurds, while allowing foreign spheres of influence and domination in much of the rest.[32] Post-imperial Turkey would also lose control over its finances. According to Article 231 of the Treaty, Turkey had caused 'losses and sacrifices of all kinds for which she ought to make complete reparation'. As with the German *Kriegsschuld* clause, the Allies recognized it would be well beyond the capacity of post-imperial Turkey to pay these kinds of reparations, particularly given the loss of the Arabic-speaking lands. Accordingly, the Treaty set up a Financial Commission comprising one representative each from France, the British Empire and Italy, with a Turkish representative serving in a consultative capacity. This commission had vast powers, including complete control over the government budget and authority over future government loans. No other defeated Central Power had to subject itself to such a compromise of its sovereignty, and for Turkish nationalists it continued in an even more extreme form the humiliating European interference in Ottoman affairs during the nineteenth century.[33]

The daunting prospect of further territorial dismemberment and decades of debt servitude gave the Turkish nationalists around Kemal a major boost, as the nationalist Parliament in Ankara rejected both the terms of the Treaty of Sèvres and the sultan's government's claim to represent the Turkish nation.[34] Defying the notion that peace had been established, Kemal and his men simply fought on. In September 1920, less than a month after the Treaty of Sèvres had promised an independent Armenia incorporating part of Turkey, Kemal's forces attacked from the south. Despite fierce resistance, the Armenians were gradually pushed back and forced to surrender on 17 November.[35]

Simultaneously, and with remarkable skill, Kemal managed to overcome his country's political isolation by securing assistance from the equally friendless government in Moscow. Even though he had little sympathy for communism, Kemal was shrewd enough to ascertain that the Bolsheviks were the enemies of his enemy: Britain. As he recognized, only the small republics that had declared their independence in 1918 – Armenia, Georgia and Azerbaijan – kept the Turks and the Bolsheviks from linking up to form a common front against Western aggression. The Bolsheviks responded with enthusiasm. Negotiations with the Bolsheviks' new Commissar for Nationalities, the young Joseph Stalin, ultimately led to the Treaty of Moscow, signed between the Turkish nationalists and the Soviet government in March 1921. According to its provisions, the territory of the short-lived independent Armenian Republic, proclaimed in the spring of 1918, was to be divided between Turkey and the Soviet Union. Moscow also recognized the new borders of Turkey, which would include the provinces of Kars and Ardahan. In addition, the Russians secretly pledged to provide 10 million gold rubles, as well as sufficient weaponry and ammunition to arm two divisions, in order to help the nationalist government fight Western imperialism and the Greek invaders.[36]

In south-eastern Anatolia, too – occupied by French troops since December 1918 – Kemal sought a military decision.[37] In early 1920 his troops won several decisive battles against the French Armenian Legion and smaller colonial contingents in the southern cities of Maraş, Anteb and Urfa. When the French chose to retreat from Maraş, abandoning the city's Armenian population, Turkish troops entered the city on 10 February, and massacred some 10,000 Armenians.[38] The French retreat dragged on over the course of the year, but by late 1920 Kemal's southern army controlled most of this region, prompting the French government to agree to a complete withdrawal of their troops the following year.[39]

By early 1921, Mustafa Kemal had thus succeeded in transforming a military struggle on various fronts into a more manageable war with the Greeks in western Anatolia. An attempt by the British to negotiate with Ankara's government at the London Conference in the spring of 1921 failed, prompting Lloyd George to encourage a renewed Greek offensive in Anatolia with the explicit ambition of bringing down Kemal's rival government in Ankara. While the initial success of this campaign brought the Greeks some 400 kilometres into the interior, they failed to achieve a decisive victory. When the numerically superior Greek forces attempted to take Ankara, the defenders, now under Mustafa Kemal's personal command, held firm. Despite staggering casualties, including 80 per cent of the officer corps, Turkish troops continued to fight on with dogged resistance, forcing the Greeks, after three bloody weeks of slaughter in September 1921, to retreat and form a defensive line of their own to the west of the Sakarya river. A stalemate now lasted for almost a year.[40]

By this point the Greek home front was no longer unequivocally in favour of the war. Initially, the Greek campaign had been largely funded by Allied loans, but with the growing duration of the conflict Athens had to rely on increased taxes and an inflationary monetary policy to pay for the war. Direct war expenses now accounted for 56 per cent of government spending, while the extra printing of money led to dramatic inflation with the cost of basic foodstuffs increasing by almost 600 per cent when compared to 1914.[41] Growing disillusionment with Venizelos had led to a landslide defeat for his Liberal Party in the general elections of November 1920, prompting the return from exile of King Constantine, and Venizelos' temporary withdrawal from politics. Contrary to pre-election promises to bring the campaign in Asia Minor to an end, the new government under Prime Minister Dimitrios Gounaris responded to the Turkish refusal to negotiate in the spring of 1921 with an intensified military engagement. On 11 June (29 May according to the Julian calendar, the highly symbolic anniversary of the fall of Constantinople to Islamic forces in 1453), the king and his Prime Minister set sail for Smyrna, where Constantine would assume the supreme command of his army. The supporters of the 'Great Idea' within Greece placed high hopes on Constantine, who bore the same name as the last Byzantine Emperor (Constantine XI Palaiologos) and was often referred to as 'Constantine XII'. Yet contrary to the high hopes invested in him, the king's presence in Asia Minor had little effect on the outcome of the military campaign. By the end of 1921, when Constantine returned to Athens, his troops had failed to deliver a military breakthrough.

Instead, frustrated Greek soldiers vented their anger against Muslim civilians in increasingly systematic acts of ethnic cleansing. A 1921 International Red Cross investigation found that:

> ... elements of the Greek army of occupation have been employed in the extermination of the Muslim population ... The facts established – burnings of villages, massacres, terror of the inhabitants, coincidences of place and date – leave no room for doubt in regard to this. The atrocities which we have seen, or of which we have seen the material evidence, were the work of irregular bands of armed civilians (*tcheti*) and of organised units of the regular army. No cases have come to our knowledge in which these misdeeds have been prevented or punished by the military command. Instead of being disarmed and broken up, the bands have been assisted in their activities and have collaborated hand in hand with organised units of regulars.[42]

As the Red Cross was reporting about the razing of Muslim villages on the Izmit Peninsula, revenge killings were being carried out by Muslim paramilitaries in the unoccupied Pontus region on the Black Sea. Here atrocities against Pontic Greeks had been prompted by ill-advised Greek naval bombardments of Trabzon and Samsun in early August 1921, an attack that heightened Turkish fears of a second Greek front being opened up. In response, the Kemalists decided to clear the area of 'unreliable' Christians. Militia units commanded by the notorious warlord 'Topal' Osman descended on the Greek-inhabited villages along the coast, murdering some 11,000 inhabitants.[43]

Osman was a veteran volunteer of the Balkan Wars, during which he was injured (earning him the nickname 'Topal' Osman – 'limping Osman'). During the Great War he had played a key role in the CUP's 'Special Organization', with direct responsibility for countless Armenian deaths. The post-war conflict in the region offered him and his men the opportunity to continue their ethnic-cleansing operations. As one Pontic Greek survivor recalled, his village was attacked in 1921 by Osman and his men, armed with guns and axes. 'They gathered people in the middle of the village. They separated off the children. They stripped them and threw them into wells. Then they threw stones on top of them. The wells groaned. They filled the church, the school, and the barns with the old people and set fire to them.'[44] Elsewhere in the region special squads under the command of Major Emin and Colonel Kemal Bey committed similar atrocities, notably in Bafra in July 1921.[45]

Although the government in Ankara expressly ordered 'the slaughter to cease' and to focus on (non-murderous) deportations instead, violence continued unabated for several weeks.[46] The Near East Relief Committee in a contemporary report assumed that out of the 30,000 Pontic deportees some 8,000 died as a result of maltreatment.[47] Greek guerrillas formed from the local communities responded in kind, hiding in the mountains and frequently raiding villages where they killed Muslim civilians.[48] As Greek resistance stiffened and Turkish losses mounted, a truce was agreed that allowed the Pontic Greeks safe passage to the harbours from where they departed to Greece, bringing to an end a community that had existed in the Black Sea region since at least 700 BC.[49]

Meanwhile in Athens and Smyrna, Greek military planners were united in the view that the expedition into Anatolia had to be brought to a swift conclusion if it was to end in success. Even if the Greek Army controlled large tracts of territory in the late summer of 1921 – a triangle between Smyrna, Eskişehir and Afyonkarahişar – the supply lines now extended over hundreds of kilometres of barren land. Furthermore, the occupied area was impossible to defend against incursions from attacks by both the regular Turkish Army and irregular insurgents. Worse still, the military leadership's failure to deliver a decisive blow against Kemal's troops led to rapid disillusionment among ordinary Greek soldiers. As one of them succinctly noted in his diary during the military stalemate between the summer of 1921 and August 1922: 'Instead of capturing Ankara, we are now digging our own graves in Anatolia.'[50]

While the Greek generals were still contemplating how to defeat the Turks, Kemal succeeded in further isolating the Greeks politically. In March 1921, and again in October that year, peace treaties were signed between the government in Paris and the Turkish National Movement, ending the conflict in Cilicia and allowing Kemal to transfer some 80,000 troops from Cilicia to fight the Greek invaders.[51] France's de facto withdrawal from Anatolia meant that Athens could no longer rely on unequivocal support from the Western Allies. Although Britain continued to send warm words of encouragement to Athens, it stopped any provision of material support. In early 1922 the fortunes of war were thus gradually turning against Greece. Although Athens still had a sizeable fighting force of 177,000 soldiers in Anatolia, it lacked both the means and the will to continue the war for much longer.[52]

Kemal's rejuvenated army, bolstered by troops from southern and eastern Anatolia, Soviet weapons and new recruits enlisted through general mobilization, attacked on 26 August 1922. Four days later the Greek defences around Afyon (Afyonkarahişar) collapsed after sustained Turkish attacks with over 260 artillery pieces, infantry and cavalry. Unable to establish a new defensive position, chaos ensued while the incompetent Greek commander of the forces in Asia Minor, Georgios Hatzanestis, insisted on issuing instructions to his widely overstretched troops from his far-away base in Smyrna. Panic spread among the Greek soldiers in central Anatolia. Ignoring their orders, many of them retreated in panic. The breakdown of military discipline during the long retreat to the western Anatolian coast found expression in wild acts of retribution against the Turkish civilian population. Greek soldiers razed villages to the ground, including Uşak, Alaşehir and Manisa, prompting a Catholic missionary in the region to comment that 'the Greeks have lost any right now to speak of Turkish barbarism'.[53]

Hastily improvised evacuation schemes were put in place as tens of thousands of Greek soldiers now rushed back towards the coast to reach the ships that could bring them to safety. Their evacuation ended a military campaign that had cost Greece more men than all its previous wars between 1897 and 1918 taken together. The losses suffered by the Greek Army during the Asia Minor campaign amounted to 23,000 dead and 50,000 wounded, in addition to 18,000 soldiers captured as prisoners of war. It was the worst military defeat in modern Greek history.[54]

While the soldiers were evacuated, the Christian civilians in Anatolia were not. In the wake of the retreating army, tens of thousands of refugees from villages throughout western Anatolia were arriving in Smyrna. By the beginning of September the city resembled an enormous refugee camp, with thousands of ethnic Greeks camping in the streets and parks. Their hopes for protection from Turkish vengeance rested on the presence of Allied ships and soldiers off the city's shores. What they did not know was that the Allies had no intention to intervene militarily in the Greco-Turkish conflict.

The Greek authorities were also reluctant to facilitate a mass exodus of Christian civilians from western Anatolia. While on 1 September the High Commissioner in Smyrna, Aristeidis Stergiadis, in a confidential edict requested all Greek administrators in the city to pack up and prepare for evacuation, he publicly assured the Christians of Smyrna that they had nothing to fear. One reason for the refusal to evacuate at least parts of the civilian population from Smyrna was the fear of impoverished and politicized refugees arriving in Athens en masse, potentially triggering a revolution. As Stergiadis remarked days before the Turkish army captured Smyrna: 'Better for them to stay here and be slaughtered by Kemal, than for them go to Athens and turn everything upside down.'[55] Stergiadis himself departed from Smyrna on a British vessel in the morning hours of 8 September.

Smyrna had been abandoned, its Christian inhabitants and refugees left to hope for mercy from the advancing Turkish regular and irregular forces. As described in the introduction to this book, such hopes soon proved to be misplaced.[56]

While Smyrna was descending into chaos, with estimates of the dead ranging from 12,000 to 30,000 murdered Christians, the evacuated Greek troops on the islands of Mytilene and Chios mutinied in protest against their own government in Athens, which was perceived as responsible for their defeat. On 24 September 1922 a coup was carried out under the leadership of Colonels Stylianos Gonatas, the commanding officer of the First Army Group, and Nikolas Plastiras, who had been in charge of an elite Evzone regiment nicknamed 'Satan's Army' by the Turks. Sailing into Athens in a mixed convoy of merchant vessels and warships, the putschists demanded the abdication of King Constantine, the dissolution of Parliament, and the immediate reinforcement of the front in Eastern Thrace, where fighting with the Turkish Army continued. On 27 September, Constantine did indeed abdicate in favour of his son, George II, and left for Sicily, where he died the following January. The Venizelists regained power while six leading royalists deemed responsible for the Asia Minor disaster, including the former Prime Minister, Dimitrios Gounaris, and the incompetent last commander of the Greek forces in Asia Minor, General Hatzanestis, were sentenced to death and executed.[57]

The new Greek government signed an armistice with Kemal's government at Mudanya on 11 October 1922.[58] The terms of the armistice secured Eastern Thrace for Turkey and mandated that the remnants of the Greek Army as well as the local Orthodox population had to evacuate within two weeks – a process documented by the foreign correspondent for the *Toronto Daily Star*, Ernest Hemingway:

> Twenty miles of carts drawn by cows, bullocks and muddy-flanked water buffalo, with exhausted, staggering men, women and children, blankets over their heads, walking blindingly along in the rain besides their worldly goods . . . All day long I have been passing them, dirty, tired, unshaven, wind-bitten soldiers, hiking along the trails across the brown, rolling, barren Thrace countryside . . . They are the last of the glory that was Greece. This is the end of their second siege of Troy.[59]

The failure of Greece's military campaign had ramifications beyond the region and brought down Venizelos' greatest supporter among the Allies, Lloyd George. In September 1922, as Kemal's forces closed in on the neutral zone in the Dardanelles, direct military confrontation between British and Turkish forces had seemed likely. Lloyd George was prepared to go to war but remained largely isolated politically, both at home and internationally. When Great Britain requested military support from the Dominions, Canada and Australia declined while South Africa did not issue any official response. In London the Conservatives bowed to public opinion, which was staunchly against the war, and declared their intention to withdraw from government. The big loser of the so-called 'Chanak crisis' was thus Lloyd George, the last of the great wartime leaders still in office, whose coalition government fell on 19 October 1922.⁶⁰ It was left to the succeeding Conservative government under Andrew Bonar Law to finally bring hostilities in Asia Minor to a close. His reappointed Foreign Secretary, Lord Curzon, faced the first major challenge of the new administration when he convened a conference in the Swiss city of Lausanne, where a lasting peace with the new government in Ankara was at last to be concluded.

At Lausanne, Curzon and his French colleague Raymond Poincaré represented the victorious powers of the Great War, but unlike in Paris in 1919 they were now negotiating directly with representatives of Turkey. They were also joined by other revisionist politicians such as Bulgaria's Prime Minister, Alexander Stambolijski, Benito Mussolini as the newly appointed Italian Prime Minister, and Georgi Chicherin, the Soviet Commissar of Foreign Affairs. The line-up clearly reflected drastic new political realities in Europe.

The Treaty of Lausanne that emerged from the negotiations was widely welcomed in Turkey as a diplomatic triumph, as it completely overturned the draconian terms of the Treaty of Sèvres. Anatolia and Eastern Thrace were to remain Turkish, while earlier plans to establish an independent Armenia or Kurdish autonomy were shelved.⁶¹ The Greek delegation and the Turkish representatives, led by Kemal's trusted general (and future successor as President of the Turkish Republic), Ismet Inönü, also agreed that peace between them would be accompanied by a 'population exchange', which, in fact, was already well on its way when the conference had first convened. In total some 1.2 million Orthodox Anatolians were transferred from Turkey to Greece, while nearly 400,000 Muslims were resettled the other way. Religion was the sole criterion for the 'exchanges', according to the 'Convention on the Compulsory Exchange of Populations' that was signed in Lausanne on 30 January 1923.

This was a radical reversal of the logic guiding the Minorities Treaties of 1919, which had sought to legally protect minorities in multi-ethnic states. Yet it was not completely without precedent: it was first suggested by Venizelos in the context of the Balkan Wars and again during the negotiations for the Neuilly Treaty when Sofia and Athens agreed on a 'voluntary' population swap of some 100,000 people to resolve their long-term dispute over the control of Western Thrace.[62] Although in reality many Bulgarian refugees had no choice in the matter, the openly mandatory character of the transfer sanctioned at Lausanne differentiated the Treaty from any previous agreements.[63] In the eyes of some it confirmed the now increasingly popular idea that a 'true' nation state could only be founded on the principle of ethnic or religious homogeneity, and that this had to be achieved at almost any human price.

When the Treaty of Lausanne was signed, most of the Greek Orthodox Ottomans had already left their homes in Asia Minor under extremely difficult circumstances. Back in mid-September 1922 the military governor of Smyrna, Nureddin Pasha, had set a deadline of two weeks, later extended to 8 October, for the complete evacuation of the Orthodox population in western Anatolia. The only exemptions were men between the ages of eighteen and forty-five. They were to remain and serve in labour battalions to rebuild the towns and villages destroyed by the Greek army during its retreat. Many of these forced labourers died during the course of the marches into the hinterland, and systematic revenge was particularly directed towards former Ottoman subjects who had served in the Greek invasion army as well as towards priests and teachers, who were deemed staunch supporters of the Megali Idea. As recalled by Evripides Lafazanis, a Turkish-speaking Greek Orthodox villager from Horoskioi (Horoz-Kōy), who ended up in one of the forced-labour battalions, priests and teachers were targeted as apparent ringleaders of Greek nationalism within Anatolia:

'We had six male teachers, six lady teachers from Axos and from Vourla, two priests and two psalm-singers ... They poured petrol over them and burned them alive.'[64]

Even for those fortunate enough to be allowed to leave, the future was highly uncertain. Some of the refugees escaped to Salonika, others to Athens or the Greek islands. Many died during the journey. One ten-year-old boy who had fled to Salonika later remembered: 'We starved. The boat stopped in Cavala for water only. Older people and younger ones, about four or five of them, died. Their bodies were thrown into the sea.'[65] Those who survived found themselves in the most difficult of circumstances. The American Red Cross representative in Greece, Lane Ross Hill, was shocked by the terrible conditions in Salonika:

> [There are] 70,000 refugees in the city and 70,000 more in the surrounding districts. Nearly a hundred refugees are dying daily. Malaria is widespread in the camps and there are no food, no clothing, no medical hospital supplies. Whoever gets sick, dies ... Every day big riots occur at the only soup kitchen in Salonica, which dispenses 7500 portions of soup to refugees. In order to get soup people fight each other by pulling hair and knocking each other down ... One of the greatest tragedies is frequent suicides of those who can no longer endure the awful conditions. The city is choked with refugees who are in schools, churches, mosques, warehouses, cafes, cinemas, ruins, corridors of public schools, railway stations, quays.[66]

The situation was not much better in Athens, which doubled its population as a result of the influx of refugees from Anatolia. 'The city had been almost somnolent before this irruption,' wrote Henry Morgenthau, then the director of the Greek Refugee Resettlement Commission. 'Now the streets were thronged with new faces. Strange dialects of Greek assailed the ear. The eye was caught by outlandish peasant costumes from interior Asia Minor ...'[67]

The 1923 Treaty of Lausanne sanctioned these expulsions retrospectively. The remaining Orthodox Christians in central Anatolia – 192,356 in total – were transported to Greece over the following months, while some 400,000 Rumelian ('Balkan') Muslims crossed the Aegean in the opposite direction. Behind these statistics lay incredible individual and collective stories of hardship. In Greece the land formerly inhabited by Muslims was handed over to the Anatolian refugees, increasing local animosity towards them. Some 30,000 of them spoke Turkish as their first language. Many refugees were discriminated against in terms of employment opportunities and social status. The Rumelian Muslims' fate was no better. Set apart from the majority population of Anatolia by different lifestyles, accents and customs, they were not welcomed with open arms by their new neighbours. Many of the new arrivals spoke Greek or Albanian as their first language.[68]

The expulsions thus fundamentally altered both countries. Multiethnic Salonika became Greek Thessaloniki. The province of Macedonia was now overwhelmingly Greek (89 per cent in 1923 compared to 43 per cent in 1912), while in Anatolia the predominantly Christian-inhabited city of Smyrna became the entirely Muslim port of Izmir. The Greek state, whose 4.5 million population grew by a quarter as a consequence of the 'Asia Minor catastrophe', thus became the last of the vanquished states of the 'post-war' period. Hopelessly overstretched in financial terms for years to come, the government in Athens could provide neither proper housing nor sanitation for destitute families, many of whom continued to die of curable diseases well into the 1920s.[69] Greece required two successive emergency loans from the Bank of England just to keep its refugee-inundated state from total collapse. The dream of the Megali Idea had turned into the nightmare of the *mikrasiatiki katastrofi*, or Great Catastrophe.[70]

Yet the Lausanne Convention also had a significance that went well beyond the Greek and Turkish context to which it ostensibly applied. The Convention effectively established the legal right of state governments to expel large parts of their citizens on the grounds of 'otherness'. It fatally undermined cultural, ethnic and religious plurality as an ideal to which to aspire and a reality with which – for all their contestations – most people in the European land empires had dealt with fairly well for centuries.[71] Lausanne signalled that the West's prior commitment through the Minorities Treaties to the defence of vulnerable ethnic minorities had been fatefully reversed.[72] If, in 1919, ethnic coexistence had still been seen as something worth protecting, the future now seemed to belong to ethnic homogeneity as a kind of precondition for nation states to live in peace. Although the Lausanne

Convention had been drawn up to prevent mass violence between different religious groups, the application of this logic to eastern Europe would prove to be catastrophic: for in the multi-ethnic territories of the vanquished central European land empires, the utopia of a mono-ethnic or mono-religious community could only be achieved through extreme violence. This was indeed the case in the following two and a half decades, ending in the later 1940s, when the forced expulsion of millions of ethnic Germans from east-central Europe was completed.[73]

Few politicians observed the developments in Anatolia between 1918 and 1923 with greater interest than Adolf Hitler, who would later profess that in the aftermath of the Great War he and Mussolini had looked up to Mustafa Kemal as a model of how defiance and will power could triumph over Western 'aggression'. Hitler not only admired Kemal's uncompromising resistance to Allied pressure, but also sought to imitate his means of constructing a radically secular, nationalist and ethnically homogeneous nation state after a crushing military defeat. The CUP's genocidal wartime policies towards the Armenians and Kemal's ruthless expulsion of Christian Ottomans featured prominently in the Nazi imagination. They became a source of inspiration and a model for Hitler's plans and dreams in the years leading up to the invasion of Poland on 1 September 1939.[74]

Epilogue: The 'Post-War' and Europe's Mid-Century Crisis

'As long as they stood united, the German people have never been defeated in their history. Only disunity in 1918 led to the collapse. Therefore, whoever betrays this unity now can expect nothing but annihilation as an enemy of the nation.'

Adolf Hitler, 'Proclamation to the German People', 3 September 1939

'We were maltreated at Trianon, losing 72 per cent of our thousand-year-old country; everybody who owned something lost his property; and when all decent men were on the front, the Jews engineered a revolution here and made Bolshevism.'

Miklós Horthy in a letter to Hitler, July 1940

Was 1923 the year that peace finally arrived in Europe? The end of inter-state and civil wars, coupled with relative economic stabilization, suggests that this was indeed the case. From late 1923, after the signing of the Lausanne Treaty that ended conflict in Anatolia and Eastern Thrace, Europe as a whole entered a period of relative political and economic stability.[1] Internationally, a new spirit of rapprochement was quickly embodied in agreements such as the 1924 Dawes Plan, designed to make German reparations payments more manageable; the Locarno Treaty of 1925, in which Germany acknowledged its new western borders, thereby improving Berlin's previously tense relationship with Paris; and the Kellogg-Briand Pact of 1928, which effectively banned war as an instrument of foreign policy, except in self-defence.[2] Highlighting the significance of this sea change in international relations, the principal architects of the Locarno Treaty – the British Foreign Secretary, Austen Chamberlain, and his German and French colleagues, Gustav Stresemann and Aristide Briand – were awarded the Nobel Peace Price in 1925 and 1926 respectively. The general climate of international rapprochement also allowed for a symbolic reconciliation between Ankara and Athens during Venizelos' penultimate term as Prime Minister (1928–32), culminating in the Treaty of Friendship (1930) that settled the contentious issue of compensation for the destruction and confiscation of property during the Greco-Turkish War of 1919–22. Venizelos, who had started that war, even proposed Atatürk for the Nobel Peace Prize.[3]

In tandem with these developments, the most important international organization of the 1920s and 1930s, the League of Nations, worked tirelessly towards resolving the effects of the post-war refugee crises, while also making substantial contributions, through its various agencies, to the fields of healthcare, drug control, economic co-operation, labour legislation, disarmament, and the prevention of 'white slave' trafficking.[4]

Yet despite all of these encouraging signs, by 1929, Europe was already plunging back once again into crisis and violent disorder. The Great Depression, which began with the stock-market crash on Wall Street in October 1929, did more than any other event to end Europe's brief era of economic recovery and improved international relations. The Wall Street crash had an immediate knock-on effect on Europe, as American banks withdrew the loans with which the modest economic recovery of previous years had been financed. This was particularly true for Germany, the recipient of significant US loans, which now had to be recalled from businesses, prompting many of them to either go bankrupt or lay off their employees. By 1931 one-third of the German workforce was unemployed, and millions more were on precarious short-term contracts.[5]

Neighbouring Austria, still far from fully recovered from the effects of the Great War, was also badly hit. The country had staggered from one economic crisis to the next in the 1920s, dependent for its survival on financial assistance from the Western Powers. Even before the Depression, unemployment ran at well over 10 per cent a year, and this increased further during the slump when the collapse of one of Austria's largest banks, the Creditanstalt, sent shock waves through the banking system in all of central Europe. Bulgaria and Hungary, already weak economically, were also deeply affected by the Wall Street crash.[6]

The economic and political crisis in Europe after 1929 fatally undermined any remaining faith in democracy and prompted an intensified search for New Orders that could cure the ills of Western capitalism and reverse the injustices imposed on the defeated states of Europe in the period 1918–20. Parties of the extreme Left and Right, which had long denounced democracy as a 'foreign' and involuntarily adopted political system, enjoyed growing support for their populist promises to resolve their countries' economic and political crises by radical means.[7] This particularly applied to Germany, where the slump catapulted Hitler's Nazi Party from the fringes of politics to its very centre. In the general elections of 1928, Hitler had received no more than 2.8 per cent of the popular vote, a figure that would increase to over 37 per cent in the federal elections of July 1932. Although the Nazis did not create Germany's economic and political crisis, they proved to be its main beneficiary. Many voters increasingly viewed them as the only viable alternative to the Communist Party, whose support had also grown steadily in response to the same sense of crisis. The apparent inability of liberal democracy to manage economic crisis and bitter social conflict were crucial to Hitler's election successes between 1929 and 1932.[8]

In other parts of Europe, too, the slump pushed voters towards extremist parties and created excuses for politicians to bypass Parliament in the name of 'stability' and 'order'. Against Woodrow Wilson's optimistic predictions that the post-war world would be 'safe for democracy', most of the democracies established in Europe in 1918 were eventually replaced by authoritarian regimes of one kind or another.[9] In Bulgaria the right-wing Italian- and German-inspired People's Social Movement under Aleksander Tzankov grew in strength, while on the Left, the Communist Bulgarian Workers' Party (BWP) enjoyed significant support in the cities.[10] In May 1934 a small elitist organization of anti-royalist nationalists, 'Zveno', executed a successful coup, supported by other right-wing groups.[11] The new government abolished political parties and trade unions, introduced censorship, and centralized the administration in pursuit of a corporate state along the lines of the Italian Fascist model. Within less than a year, however, the *Zvenari* were forced out of office and their government was replaced by a de facto royal dictatorship under Boris III and his obedient Prime Minister, Georgi Kioseivanov.[12]

In Austria, in early 1933, Chancellor Engelbert Dollfuss shut down Parliament and assumed dictatorial powers, suppressing the Left and banning the Austrian Nazis. When Dollfuss was murdered during an attempted putsch by the Austrian Nazis in July 1934, he was succeeded by Kurt Schuschnigg, who continued to rule by decree until Hitler decided to absorb Austria into the German Reich by force in the *Anschluss* of 1938.[13]

By the mid-1930s authoritarian regimes or outright dictatorships of various forms had become the norm across central and eastern Europe, and appeared to hold the keys to the continent's future.[14] Their common denominator was a fundamental opposition to parliamentary democracy and Western capitalism on the one hand, and anti-Bolshevism on the other. Yet profound differences also existed between them. In Poland, for example, Józef Piłsudski, who had led his country to democracy and independence in 1918, staged a military coup in 1926 and remained in power until his death in 1935. Unlike many other states in central Europe, Piłsudski's Poland never became a fascist dictatorship but certainly more authoritarian than it had been prior to 1926.[15] This would become a common pattern in many of the successor states of eastern Europe, sometimes through military putsches, as in Estonia and Latvia in 1934, or through royal imposition, as in Bulgaria and Yugoslavia. In January 1929, following the shooting of several leaders of the Croatian Peasant Party in Parliament, Yugoslavia's King Alexander dissolved Parliament and proclaimed a royal dictatorship, only to be assassinated in Marseille five years later in what quickly transpired to be a joint IMRO and Ustashe operation.[16]

The chaotic years after 1929 were generally accompanied by significant outbursts of violence, often committed by individuals or groups that had already played a prominent role between 1917 and 1923. Although physical violence was much less widespread between 1923 and 1929, a broader culture of violent rhetoric, uniformed politics and street fighting persisted throughout the 1920s. On the Left, fantasies of exporting the Bolshevik revolution beyond the Soviet

Union were nurtured by the various Communist parties of Europe, which Moscow controlled through the Comintern or Third International (1919–43). On the extreme Right, by contrast, paramilitary movements as diverse as the Nazi storm troopers (*Sturmabteilung*, or SA), the Hungarian Arrow Cross, the Austrian *Heimwehr*, the Croation *Ustashe*, and Baltic Home Guards such as the Lithuanian Riflemen Union, the Latvian *Aizsargi*, and the Estonian *Kaitseliit*, all thrived on the idea of violently opposing the lingering threat of a communist revolution, a fear that dated back to 1917.

In the wake of the Great Depression, these simmering conflicts escalated into frequent clashes between political militants, as many countries returned to the conditions similar to civil war that had prevailed during the immediate post-war years. In the last phase of the Weimar Republic, for example, street-fighting resulted in some 400 casualties, while in Austria the murder in 1934 of Chancellor Dollfuss was indicative of a more general surge in politically motivated violence.[17] Worse still was the situation in Bulgaria, where levels of violence had remained extremely high throughout the 1920s and continued to escalate in the 1930s. In addition to communist and anti-communist cycles of violence and repression, the country was haunted during the entire interwar period by the unresolved Macedonian question. The Macedonian IMRO, emboldened by its prominent role in the brutal murder of Prime Minister Stambolijski in 1923, and supported by Mussolini, further intensified its operations, carrying out more than 460 armed operations in Yugoslavia before 1934, including hundreds of assassinations and kidnappings of members of the armed services and the gendarmerie.[18]

Further west, Portugal and Spain also abandoned democracy and descended into violence. Already in 1926 a coup in Lisbon established first the *Ditadura Nacional* and then the *Estado Nuevo* under António de Oliveira Salazar, who ruled Portugal from 1932 to 1968.[19] In Madrid, General Miguel Primo de Rivera imposed a military dictatorship in 1923, which lasted until 1930. Following the overthrow of the monarchy in 1931, Spain returned to democracy for six troubled years before its Popular Front coalition of Socialists and Communists, in power from February 1936, was challenged by an army coup that July. The Left, soon supported by International Brigades composed of volunteers from around the world, rallied in defence of the Republic and fought the nationalist putschists under General Francisco Franco for the next three years. Matters were made worse by international meddling in the conflict, with Nazi Germany and fascist Italy backing Franco while the Spanish Left received some support from the Soviet Union. The civil war killed more than half a million people, and eventually ended in Franco's victory.[20]

By the later 1930s only two of the new states invented on the continent of Europe in 1918 – Finland and Czechoslovakia – had survived as liberal democracies. However, Czechoslovakia was destroyed when Hitler annexed the Sudetenland in 1938, and then occupied the rest of the Czech territories in March 1939, giving the occupied lands their pre-1918 Habsburg names of Bohemia and Moravia.[21] Finland, meanwhile, managed to defend its independence against the invading Red Army in the extremely violent Winter War of 1939–40, but had to accept reduced territory in the Treaty of Moscow (1940).[22]

On the eve of the Second World War there were thus many fewer democracies in Europe than there had been before the Great War. Even in the two principal European victor states of the Great War, France and Britain, economic instability had given rise to extremist movements. Although it was never a real contender for power, Oswald Mosley's British Union of Fascists claimed to have some 50,000 members at the peak of its popularity in 1934.[23] In France, both the extreme Left and the Right were becoming increasingly militant. Paramilitary organizations such as the royalist *Action française* and the right-wing veterans' organization *Croix de Feu*, proliferated, the latter growing to a membership of nearly half a million in the mid-1930s.[24] Both Britain and France survived the radicalization of politics as democracies, but the international situation they were facing in 1938–9 was bleak. Resurgent revisionist powers such as Germany and Italy in Europe and Japan in the Far East were determined to tear apart whatever was left of the ailing international system established in Paris in 1919.

Although there was nothing inevitable about the war that began in September 1939 and transformed into a global conflict of unprecedented scale in 1941, many of the key issues at its heart – and the way in which it was fought – can be traced back to the final phase of the

Great War and its immediate aftermath. Much of Europe before 1914 had prided itself on the relative legal security and stability that many of its states provided for their citizens. Oddly, even during the First World War, the states' monopoly on force, upheld by the police, continued to prevail in the huge swathes of territory away from the fighting fronts. One of the novelties of the February Revolution in Russia in 1917 was that the pressures of war led to the first major crack in this system, soon to be followed by its complete implosion. As we have seen, it was defeat in the Great War, and the collapse of the pre-war system, that allowed new actors to compete violently for power, generally without the relative restraint that had characterized social and political conflicts prior to 1914.

The first fateful legacy of these years lay in a new logic of violence that permeated domestic as well as international conflicts, and culminated in the war on the Eastern Front during the Second World War. The purpose of Nazi Germany's Operation Barbarossa, launched in June 1941, was no longer to militarily defeat an opposing army and to impose harsh conditions of peace on a defeated Soviet Union, but rather to destroy a regime and annihilate significant proportions of the civilian population in the process. Entire countries in central and eastern Europe were to be purged of those deemed racially or politically undesirable.[25] This logic, which had a longer tradition in relation to the allegedly 'inferior' populations of the colonial world and which also underpinned the Balkan Wars and the Armenian genocide, experienced a pan-European breakthrough in the various conflicts between 1917 and 1923. This was a radical reversal of the long-standing ambition of European policymakers since the Wars of Religion in the sixteenth and seventeenth centuries to tame armed conflict by distinguishing between combatants and non-combatants, and by decriminalizing the enemy as a *iustus hostis*.[26] In the internal and international armed conflicts discussed in this book, and again in the civil wars and inter-state wars from the mid-1930s onwards, by contrast, opponents were often portrayed and perceived as criminalized and dehumanized enemies undeserving of mercy or military restraint. The distinctions between civilians and combatants, already blurred during the First World War, completely vanished in this type of conflict. It is no coincidence that both during the period between 1918 and 1923 and again from the 1930s, the number of civilians murdered in armed conflicts generally exceeded those of soldiers killed.

The criminalization and dehumanization of the enemy was not only reserved for external foes. It also applied to internal enemies of different guises. Central to this new attitude towards 'enemy civilians' was the widely perceived need to cleanse communities of their 'alien' elements before a utopian new society could emerge, and to root out those who were perceived to be harmful to the balance of the community. On the political Right, the belief that only an ethnically homogeneous national community, cleansed of internal enemies, was capable of winning the war of the future – which many considered inevitable – constituted a powerful component of the common currency of radical politics and action in Europe between 1917 and the 1940s; this was especially so in those countries frustrated with the outcomes of both the Great War and post-war conflicts. On the radical Left, the idea of the 'purified community' had a different meaning, and violence was primarily directed against real or perceived class enemies. Yet political persecution in the Soviet Union (which culminated in the Great Purge of 1937–8 that eventually killed off 1 per cent of the Soviet Union's adult population) was also more generally directed against suspect population groups and potential 'fifth columns' in a future war with Nazi Germany, which Stalin anticipated would take place in the mid- to late 1940s.[27]

In the vanquished states of the Great War, the direction and purpose of internal violence was further guided by the widely held belief that the outcome of that war had remained open until 1918, and that the defeat of the Central Powers was nothing but the result of treason on the home front. References to this 'betrayal' and to 'unfinished business' were common.[28] In Nazi Germany in particular, those groups allegedly responsible for the events of November 1918 (communists, Jews, pacifists) featured prominently as victims of Nazi terror from the moment of Hitler's appointment as Chancellor. From the mid-1930s the terror became more systematic, as Hitler began preparing the nation for war. He was determined to prevent a repeat of November 1918 when – in his view and that of many other Germans – a small minority of revolutionaries and Jews on the home front had betrayed the war effort and caused military collapse.

The Nazis' obsession with the idea of internal betrayal loomed large until the spring of 1945, when thousands of deserters or alleged 'defeatists' were shot or strung up on lamp posts and trees along German roads as the Allies crossed the border into the Reich. Most German soldiers, however, did not require such gruesome reminders. Driven on by fear of Red Army retribution and the belief that death with honour intact was preferable to a repeat of 1918, the Wehrmacht fought on futilely until the bitter end, thereby causing the deaths of a further 1.5 million soldiers in the last three months of the war.[29]

In Italy, too, an obsession with internal divisions dating back to the Great War played out violently, as Mussolini's regime subjected real or potential dissenters to arrests, intimidation through violence, and forced resettlement to remote parts of southern Italy. The Gestapo's Italian equivalent, the political police or 'PolPol', formed in 1926, worked hand in hand with the Organisation for Vigilance and Repression of Anti-Fascism (OVRA), whose job it was to monitor the correspondence of dissidents. Similar to the Gestapo, the PolPol and OVRA employed a large number of informers, some of them former socialists or communists either coerced into collaboration or persuaded to work for the regime through financial incentives.[30]

The continuation of a logic of violence was also traceable in the former Habsburg lands in which crude notions of violently 'un-mixing' the region's ethnic complexity, coupled with militant anti-Bolshevism and radicalized anti-Semitism, created fateful legacies. The Hungarian White Terror of 1919–20 had given an indication of the widespread chauvinist and racist mood in the country at the end of the Great War, notably through the widespread pogroms against Jews. It revived with added fury (and on an even broader popular basis) between the early 1930s and the mid-1940s, culminating in the active collaboration of some Hungarians with the Nazis in the systematic mass murder of the Hungarian Jews.[31] The same attitudes were also felt in Austria, where traditional anti-Semitism and anti-Slav sentiments, reinforced during the Great War and through Jewish migration from east-central Europe to Vienna in its wake, would resurface with renewed intensity after the brief moment of relative stabilization in the mid-1920s gave way to economic depression and political turmoil.[32]

This kind and level of violence was not in itself particularly surprising as the violent actors of 1917–23 were often identical with those who would unleash a new cycle of violence in the 1930s and early 1940s. For many German, Austrian and Hungarian fascists of the 1930s, the experiences of 1918–19 provided a decisive catalyst for political radicalization and a catalogue of political agendas, whose implementation was merely postponed during the years of relative stability between 1923 and 1929. Some of the most prominent paramilitary activists of the immediate post-war period would resurface in the central European dictatorships of the Right, not only in Italy, where the veterans of fascist squads were given prominent positions in Mussolini's dictatorship.[33] In Hungary, too, leading Arrow Cross members such as Ferenc Szálasi and others repeatedly pointed to the period between November 1918 and the signing of the Trianon Treaty in June 1920 as the moment of their 'political awakening'. In 1932 the most notorious Hungarian paramilitary leaders of the post-war years, Pal Prónay and Gyula Ostenburg, founded the short-lived Hungarian National Fascist Party (*Magyar Országos Fascist Párt*). When Hitler handed power to Szálasi's Arrow Cross in Hungary in 1944, Prónay helped to put together a new militia, which fought against the Red Army between December 1944 and February 1945 during the Battle of Budapest.[34]

In Austria, too, personal continuities between the armed conflicts of the immediate post-First World War period and their sequel from 1939 are easy to identify. Robert Ritter von Greim, for example, once the leader of the Tyrolese branch of the paramilitary Oberland League, briefly became Hermann Göring's successor as commander of the German Luftwaffe. Other Austrian paramilitaries from the period following the First World War also enjoyed high-powered careers during the Second World War: Hanns Albin Rauter, who had contributed decisively to the radicalization of the Styrian Heimwehr, became Higher SS and Police Chief in the Nazi-occupied Netherlands, while his compatriot and friend, Ernst Kaltenbrunner, succeeded Reinhard Heydrich as head of the Nazis' major terror agency, the Reich Security Main Office (RSHA), in 1943. For all of these men, fascist dictatorships provided the opportunity to settle old scores and 'solve' some of the issues that the inglorious defeat of 1918, coupled with the perceived threat of Bolshevik revolution and imperial collapse, had raised.

To be sure, the relationship between post-1918 paramilitarism and the various fascist movements of the 1930s and early 1940s was not always that straightforward. Many prominent paramilitaries of the immediate post-war period were dedicated anti-Bolsheviks and committed anti-Semites in 1918, but eventually found their own political ambitions to be at odds with those of the Nazis. The former Heimwehr leader, Ernst Rüdiger Starhemberg, who had entertained close personal relations with Hitler after 1919 (and indeed participated in the Nazis' unsuccessful Munich putsch of November 1923), opposed the Austrian Nazi movement in the 1930s, rejected his own post-war anti-Semitism as 'nonsense', advocated Austrian independence in 1938, and even served in the British and Free French forces as a fighter pilot during the Second World War.[35] Starhemberg was not the only prominent paramilitary who came to realize that his vision for a national Austrian 'rebirth' was incompatible with that of Nazism. Captain Karl Burian, founder and head of the monarchist underground organization 'Ostara' after the end of the Great War, paid for his continued royalist beliefs with his arrest by the Gestapo and his execution in 1944.[36] Even in Germany the ranks of former *Freikorps* leaders were purged, notably during the Night of the Long Knives in June 1934 when several of them, now within the SA leadership, were killed.

This did not, of course, prevent the Nazis from celebrating the *Freikorps* as their spiritual predecessors, who had heroically and violently defied the peacemakers in Paris in 1919. Prominent figures such as Heinrich Himmler and Reinhard Heydrich emphasized their *Freikorps* past, even if they had themselves only seen limited military action after 1918. It is also telling that one of the largest monuments ever to be built in the Third Reich was the Annaberg memorial in Upper Silesia, celebrating the May 1921 victory of *Freikorps* soldiers over Polish insurgents in the battle that raged over Silesia's 'Holy Mountain'. Through their 'victory in defeat' at the Battle of Annaberg the *Freikorps* embodied the kind of violent revisionism that the Nazis implemented from the later 1930s onwards.[37]

It is precisely this treaty revisionism, driven by the desire to 'redeem' lost territory and populations, that forms a second enduring legacy of the immediate post-war period. The Lausanne Conference of 1923 had demonstrated that it was possible for a defeated state to become a victorious one, as Mustafa Kemal succeeded in tearing up the Treaty of Sèvres while also achieving his aim to transform the 'Turkic core' of the Ottoman Empire into a homogeneous, secular nation state. Both Hitler and Mussolini were impressed and inspired by Kemal's 'success' and his willingness to wage war, if necessary, to confront Western imperialism. It was their shared determination to challenge the international system established in 1919 that eventually brought Berlin and Rome together, starting with their intervention in the Spanish Civil War and the Pact of Friendship (1936) that was to form the basis of the wartime 'Axis'.[38] In Italian and German propaganda the Pact of Friendship was celebrated as the joining of forces between two long-suppressed but now re-emerging states with common foes who had long sought to prevent them from assuming their rightful place among the world's Great Powers.[39]

The alliance became global when Hitler entered into a further pact with Japan, which was soon to be known as the 'Anti-Comintern Pact'. Despite Hitler's racial prejudices against the Japanese, he viewed the country as having complementary geopolitical interests with Germany, notably in its mutual quest to overcome the constraints of the international system established in Paris. Although Japan was never ruled by a regime that could be described as 'fascist' in any meaningful sense, leading politicians in Tokyo came to share some common ground with Nazi Germany and Fascist Italy in the 1930s. Most importantly, perhaps, there was a common ideological rejection of the liberal political order on the one hand and Soviet-style Bolshevism on the other, as well as the ambition to provide a non-communist authoritarian alternative to both.[40] Furthermore, politicians in Tokyo had not forgotten that the United States and the British Dominions prevented the inclusion of a 'racial equality' clause in the Covenant of the League of Nations, one of the key demands of Japanese diplomats in Paris in 1919. Racial equality had been high up on Tokyo's political agenda ever since Japan emerged as the Far East's economic and military powerhouse in the second half of the nineteenth century, and even more so after the country's stunning victories over Chinese forces in the Sino-Japanese War of 1894–5, and over the Russian Empire ten years later. Still being denied recognition as a racially equal partner after emerging victorious from the First World War had left many in Japan feeling deeply offended.[41]

Even if the full military alliance between Berlin, Tokyo and Rome was yet to be formalized through the Tripartite Pact of September 1940 (subsequently joined by other revisionist states such as Hungary and Bulgaria), it was the Pact of Friendship and the Anti-Comintern Pact that first sent a very clear and alarming message to the rest of the world's Great Powers: the most staunchly revisionist powers in the world were now working together in their attempts to overcome the remnants of the Paris peace treaties.[42]

The likelihood of a general war in Europe had increased significantly since the mid-1930s, and neither Hitler nor Mussolini had ever made a secret of their firm belief that this would be something positive, a way of bringing out the 'racial essence' of their people. Both agreed that a great reckoning with the West and Soviet Russia was inevitable in the long run. Mussolini himself described Italy's intervention against the Western Allies from 1940 as a war against 'the plutocratic and reactionary democracies of the West who have invariably hindered the progress and often threatened the very existence of the Italian people'.[43]

Hitler's initial step towards the undoing of the Paris peace settlement of 1919 had been to start Germany's rearmament, thereby defying the provisions of the Versailles Treaty. In March 1936, German troops entered the previously demilitarized Rhineland, without prior consultation with Paris or London. Two years later, Hitler annexed his native Austria, a move greeted by many Austrians with outright enthusiasm over this 'correction' of the Treaty of St Germain. Hitler received a triumphal welcome when he visited his birthplace of Braunau am Inn just over the Austrian border and again in Vienna, as thousands of Austrians celebrated the *Anschluss* on the capital's Heldenplatz.

Up until the *Anschluss* of 1938, Hitler got away with undoing the provisions of the Versailles Treaty, as many contemporaries, even in western Europe, regarded his moves as a not altogether unreasonable correction of some of the injustices built into the Paris peace settlements. It was only from the summer of 1938 onwards, as Hitler began his assaults on other successor states founded in 1918 and 1919, that this mood began to change. At the Munich Conference in September 1938, London and Paris permitted Nazi Germany to absorb the Sudetenland on the periphery of Czechoslovakia, where some three million ethnic Germans lived, but they also made it clear that they would not tolerate further expansion. Although a more general war was only narrowly avoided in September 1938, Hitler had no intention of abandoning his aggressive foreign policy. Instead, he stepped up the pace of military preparation and increased pressure on the states of east-central Europe to join the Axis. By that stage Hungary had already drawn closer to Germany and Mussolini's Italy. In the wake of the Munich settlement and Hitler's occupation of the rest of the Czech lands in March 1939, Hungary successfully demanded the return of a slice of Slovakia and the whole of Ruthenia. More territorial gains were made by Budapest when, following Hitler's decision to wage a more general war in the East, the Hungarian head of state Miklós Horthy secured Hitler's support for regaining two-fifths of Transylvania and part of the Banat, at the expense of Romania and Yugoslavia. This revisionism gave Berlin a uniquely strong hand as the Western Allies (until their betrayal of Czechoslovakia) had by definition to stand by the borders established after the Great War. Both Mussolini and Horthy to different degrees feared Hitler and were suspicious of German military power, but by building their regimes on the basis of post-war injustices, there was an unstoppable logic to their falling into the Nazi orbit.

Bulgaria, too, fell in line with the other revisionist powers of Europe. Up until 1938, Tsar Boris had tried to keep Bulgaria neutral, even if he agreed with the Nazi aim of destroying the post-war peace-treaty system. But after the *Anschluss* of Austria in March 1938 and the Munich Agreement in November, the government in Sofia suddenly found itself under considerable domestic pressure from the pro-Axis lobby, which rightly noted that Bulgaria was the only defeated power of the Great War that had not yet benefited from territorial revisions of the Paris peace treaties. After the outbreak of the Second World War in September 1939, Bulgaria increasingly moved into the German camp. In September 1940, Sofia regained the southern Dobrudja after Germany had pressurized Romania into signing the Treaty of Craiova. In the spring of 1941, Bulgaria officially joined the Axis and dispatched occupation forces to Macedonia, Western Thrace, and parts of eastern Serbia to free up Wehrmacht troops for the war further east.[44]

At the heart of the European war that began in 1939 and turned global two years later, there was thus not only a violent clash between incompatible political regimes but also an attempt to regain lost territories and minorities living under 'foreign rule' after 1918. For Hitler and the Nazis, the return of these minorities was imperative, and the same was true for governments in Budapest and Sofia.[45] For Hungary – Germany's past and future wartime ally – the loss of almost three million Magyars now living under Romanian, Czechoslovak and Yugoslav rule was an injustice that needed to be redeemed. Sofia felt the same way about the one million ethnic Bulgarians 'lost' to other territories in 1919. Yet at the same time, expansionism – notably in the German, Italian and Soviet cases, but also in that of Japan – went further and amounted to nothing less than competing neo-imperial projects. Within Europe this clash of neo-imperial projects played out violently in the former imperial territories of east-central Europe that had become independent in 1918–19.[46]

In the case of Japan, leading businessmen and army circles had for some time called for territorial conquests in northern China to provide Japan with secure areas for colonization and economic exploitation. For years, large Japanese conglomerates (the *zaibatsu*) had operated the coal-mines and iron deposits of Manchuria, protected by strong military forces, the so-called Kwantung Army. Deteriorating relations with China and the growing Soviet threat from the north endangered Tokyo's interests in Manchuria at the same time as the Great Depression hit the Japanese economy hard. At the instigation of right-wing leaders of the Kwantung Army, Japanese forces seized the whole of Manchuria in September 1931, establishing the puppet state of Manchukuo in February 1932.[47]

The Manchurian crisis and the League of Nations' lack of determination in its response to a Chinese plea for help offered an important lesson that was not lost on the other revisionist states. They made events seemingly far away part of the same network of challenges to the international order established between 1918 and 1920. Mussolini viewed the West's reaction (or lack thereof) to the Manchurian crisis as an invitation to follow Tokyo's example and adopted a more aggressive foreign policy aimed at increasing Italian influence in the Mediterranean and northern Africa, as well as enlarging Italy's small colonial inheritance (Libya, Somalia, Eritrea) into a second Roman

Empire.[48] In 1932 the Italian Foreign Ministry began planning for the conquest of Ethiopia (Abyssinia), one of the few countries in Africa that had not come under colonial administration during the late nineteenth-century imperialist Scramble for Africa. In October 1935, Italian troops invaded and victory was secured the following spring, after Rome's forces made indiscriminate use of poison gas and aerial bombing against both military and civilian targets.[49]

Japan's violent expansion into northern China and Mussolini's dreams of a *spazio vitale* in northern Africa and the Mediterranean, had its functional equivalent in Hitler's ambitions to carve out a *Lebensraum* in east-central Europe.[50] Hitler's imperial project of creating an 'ethnically cleansed' living space for his people in the territories between Warsaw and the Ural Mountains had roots that pre-dated the First World War. 'The East' had long been seen as a priority area for economic domination and even colonization.[51] The Treaty of Brest-Litovsk that established Imperial Germany as a major (though short-lived) European land empire in 1918 further reinforced the perception of eastern Europe as a realm of possibilities. Hitler's view of the East as a living space for Germany's growing population was a particularly extreme form of this widely discussed idea, notably in its wartime implementation that saw the deliberate killing or starving to death of millions of unwanted inhabitants. But even his obsession with violently establishing a new racial order in the wide spaces of east-central Europe was a direct response to Hitler's reading of the events of the past: if Imperial Germany had failed to 'civilize' and permanently subjugate eastern Europe before and during the Great War, it was because the means chosen at the time had not been radical enough. The war of the future would have to be a 'total war', as Erich Ludendorff had called it in his book of that name (*Der Totale Krieg*), first published in 1935. In Hitler's understanding of the term, that total war could only be won if it was waged against both domestic and international enemies.[52]

Racism was at the core of the expansionism and empire-building of all three Axis powers as it legitimized the conquest of territories inhabited by 'inferior' races – be they Slavs, Chinese, or African – and the killing or rape of enemy civilians. Despite the rhetoric about its ambition to create a pan-Asian 'sphere of co-prosperity', the Japanese regime allowed its soldiers to sexually abuse and massacre Korean and Chinese civilians en masse.[53] Even before the outbreak of the Second World War, Mussolini had adopted a policy of liquidating large sections of Ethiopia's intellectual and professional community as a means of 'pacifying' the newly conquered territory. Biological racism certainly went furthest in Germany, where Nazi anti-Semitism under conditions of war posed a unique case in its ambition to murder each and every Jew in German-occupied Europe.[54]

After Hitler's surprise attack on the Soviet Union in June 1941, his vision for an ethnically cleansed eastern European empire was to clash violently with both indigenous quests for national independence and Soviet imperial ambitions for east-central Europe that also dated back to 1918. Immediately after the end of the Great War, Lenin's dream of recapturing the recently lost western territories of the former Tsarist Empire had to be temporarily abandoned when, in 1920, the Soviet government was forced to sign peace treaties with Estonia, Lithuania and Latvia, effectively renouncing Moscow's territorial claims in the Baltic region. A few months later, in March 1921, the Soviet-Polish Treaty of Riga had assigned western Belorussia, East Galicia and Volhynia to Warsaw's direct control.[55]

Elsewhere, however, the Bolshevik regime had been more successful in regaining vast territories temporarily lost in the final months of the Great War. By the time Soviet Russia emerged from the civil war, Moscow had already regained control over Armenia, Azerbaijan, Georgia and Ukraine.[56] But the Bolsheviks' ambitions did not end there. By late 1939, in line with the secret clauses of the German-Soviet Nonaggression Pact signed in August, Stalin re-established control over the Baltic States and eastern Poland, leaving Finland as the only territory once ruled by the Romanovs to permanently maintain its independence. Hitler's eventual failure to carve out an empire between Warsaw and the Urals after 1941, when he attacked the Soviet Union in violation of the provisions of the German-Soviet Pact, gave Stalin an opportunity to expand the Soviet Empire even further, by setting up clientele states in what was to become the Eastern Bloc. Just thirty years after the Romanov Empire had collapsed for good in 1918, the Soviet Union was larger and more powerful than Imperial Russia had ever been.[57]

Contemporaries who lived through the period saw the continuities between the years 1917–23 and the Second World War more clearly than many scholars have since. Leading politicians before and during the Second World War continually referred back to the 'post-war' period in their attempts to make sense of the world around them or to historically contextualize and justify their geopolitical ambitions. In a famous 1939 speech to mark the twentieth anniversary of the founding of the *Fasci Italiani di Combattimento*, Benito Mussolini, for example, emphasized both the centrality of the post-war years for the rise of fascism and the need to honour through deeds the memory of those who had died in the post-war struggles:

> On 23 March 1919 we raised the black flag of the fascist revolution, the forerunner of European renewal. Veterans of the trenches and young men gathered around this flag, forming squads that wished to march against cowardly governments and against fatal Eastern ideologies, in order to free the people from the evil influence of 1789. Thousands of comrades fell around this flag, fighting like heroes, in the truest meaning of the Roman word, in the streets and squares of Italy, in Africa and in Spain. Their memory is always alive and present in our hearts. Some people may have forgotten the hardships of the post-war years [someone from the crowd shouts: 'Nobody!'], but the squadristi have not forgotten, they cannot forget [someone from the crowd shouts: 'Never!'].[58]

Little over a year later, in June 1940, just as Italy joined the Axis in a war that would see Italian troops deployed in the Mediterranean, north Africa, the Balkans and Russia, Mussolini returned to this theme, suggesting that the Fascists' national 'revolution' was soon to be completed through a reckoning with Italy's external enemies. The war Italy was about to join, he claimed, was 'nothing but a logical stage in the development of our revolution'.[59]

Hitler, too, repeatedly referred back to the 'post-war' years in his speeches and through symbolic gestures. His decision, for example, to have the June 1940 armistice with France signed in the same railway carriage in Compiègne Forest in which the Germans had acknowledged defeat in November 1918 was a heavily charged act, whose meaning was as widely understood and appreciated as the annexation of Danzig and West Prussia the previous year: the *Führer* was correcting the historical injustices brought upon Germany at the end of the Great War.

In the Baltic States and Ukraine, too, the Second World War brought back memories of the wars fought against the Red Army twenty years earlier. At least initially, many nationalists in the region welcomed the German offensive against the Soviet Union in June 1941 as the beginning of a return to independent nationhood first established in 1918. To the north, in Finland, during the 1939 attack by the Red Army, the reappointed commander-in-chief, Carl Mannerheim, emphasized in his very first order to the Finnish Defence Forces that the war ahead of them was nothing but the continuation of a conflict that had begun in 1918: 'Brave soldiers of Finland! As in 1918 our hereditary enemy is once again attacking our country . . . This war is nothing other than the final act of our War of Independence.'[60] In the event, the Winter War was not 'the final act' of the story, as it was followed, between 1941 and 1944, by the brutal Continuation War. Up to this day, many Finnish nationalists maintain that their country never participated in the Second World War, but in a conflict for national independence that played out violently in several interconnected episodes between 1918 and 1944.

As the quotations from Mussolini and Mannerheim make abundantly clear, contemporaries felt the lingering presence of the conflicts that had been fought so violently at end of the Great War and during its immediate aftermath, a period in European history that had destroyed old structures and created new ones, simultaneously ending and expediting or initiating historical developments. In the collective memory of the peoples of Europe this period featured prominently either as one of revolutionary turmoil, national triumph, or perceived national humiliation to be redeemed through yet another war. As such, the period helps us to understand the logic and purpose of subsequent cycles of violence that often extended beyond 1939. In the case of Yugoslavia their legacies could still be felt in the 1990s when the multi-ethnic state, which hitherto had been held together largely due to Josip Broz Tito, descended into a brutal civil war during which all parties replayed, in their attempts at self-justification, the horrors and injustices of the first half of the century.

Beyond Europe's shores, the legacies of the Great War and its immediate aftermath could also be felt for decades. Back in 1918, Lenin's and Wilson's talk of self-determination and the rights of small nations had inspired the enemies of empire everywhere, from the Far East to northern Africa, where nascent decolonization movements demanded racial equality, autonomy, or outright independence. Such demands were generally met with violence, and there was hardly a year in the interwar period when Paris or London was not involved in quelling some form of colonial unrest within their respective empires. Even if it was to take another and yet more murderous war between 1939 and 1945 to usher the process of global imperial dissolution towards completion in the 1950s and 1960s, its origins coincide with the 'Wilsonian moment' of 1918 and the further expansion of the British and French empires shortly thereafter.[61] The most durable of these post-imperial conflicts proved to be those that haunted the Arab lands once ruled by the Ottomans. Here violence has erupted with great regularity for nearly a century. It is not without grim historical irony that the centenary of the Great War was accompanied by civil war in Syria and Iraq, revolution in Egypt, and violent clashes between Jews and Arabs over the Palestinian question, as if to offer proof that at least some of the issues raised but not solved by the Great War and its immediate aftermath are still with us today.

Notes

INTRODUCTION

1. On the Greek occupation of Smyrna, see Evangelia Achladi, 'De la guerre à l'administration grecque: la fin de la Smyrne cosmopolite', in Marie-Carmen Smyrnelis (ed.), *Smyrne, la ville oubliée? 1830–1930: Mémoires d'un grand port ottoman* (Paris: Editions Autrement, 2006), 180–95; Michael Llewellyn Smith, *Ionian Vision: Greece in Asia Minor 1919–1922* (London: Allen Lane, 1973).
2. Quoted in Marjorie Housepian Dobkin, *Smyrna 1922: The Destruction of a City* (New York: Newmark Press, 1998), 133–4.
3. For a detailed account of the sacking of Smyrna, see also Giles Milton, *Paradise Lost: Smyrna 1922: The Destruction of Islam's City of Tolerance* (London: Sceptre, 2008).
4. *Daily Mail*, 16 September 1922.
5. Ernest Hemingway, 'On the Quai at Smyrna', in idem, *In Our Time* (New York: Boni and Liveright, 1925). Hemingway was based in Constantinople at the time. Matthew Stewart, 'It Was All a Pleasant Business: The Historical Context of "On the Quai at Smyrna"', in *Hemingway Review* 23 (2003), 58–71.
6. Martin Gilbert, *Winston Churchill*, vol. IV, part 3: April 1921–November 1922 (London: Heinemann, 1977), 2,070.
7. Struve, as quoted in Peter Holquist, *Making War, Forging Revolution: Russia's Continuum of Crisis, 1914–1921* (Cambridge, MA: Harvard University Press, 2002), 2.
8. Peter Calvert, *A Study of Revolution* (Oxford and New York: Oxford University Press, 1970), 183–4.
9. 'Krieg im Frieden', *Innsbrucker Nachrichten*, 25 May 1919.
10. On parallels between Ireland and Poland, see Julia Eichenberg, 'The Dark Side of Independence: Paramilitary Violence in Ireland and Poland after the First World War', in *Contemporary European History* 19 (2010), 231–48; Tim Wilson, *Frontiers of Violence: Conflict and Iden-*

tity in Ulster and Upper Silesia, 1918–1922 (Oxford and New York: Oxford University Press, 2010).

11. I am very grateful to Yeats' biographer, Roy Foster, for alerting me to how prominently the wider European crisis of 1917–23 featured on Yeats' mind and in his work, not just in 'The Second Coming' but also in his poem-sequence 'Nineteen Hundred and Nineteen' (1921, originally titled 'Thoughts on the Present State of the World').

12. See, among others: Pieter M. Judson, *The Habsburg Empire: A New History* (Cambridge, MA: Harvard University Press, 2016); John Boyer, 'Boundaries and Transitions in Modern Austrian History', in Günter Bischof and Fritz Plasser (eds), *From Empire to Republic: Post-World War I Austria* (New Orleans, LA: University of New Orleans Press, 2010), 13–23; Gary B. Cohen, 'Nationalist Politics and the Dynamics of State and Civil Society in the Habsburg Monarchy 1867–1914', in *Central European History* 40 (2007), 241–78. Tara Zahra, *Kidnapped Souls: National Indifference and the Battle for Children in the Bohemian Lands, 1900–1948* (Ithaca, NY: Cornell University Press, 2008); Laurence Cole and Daniel L. Unowsky (eds), *The Limits of Loyalty: Imperial Symbolism, Popular Allegiances, and State Patriotism in the late Habsburg Monarchy* (New York and Oxford: Berghahn Books, 2007); John Deak, 'The Great War and the Forgotten Realm: The Habsburg Monarchy and the First World War', in *The Journal of Modern History* 86 (2014), 336–80; Maureen Healy, *Vienna and the Fall of the Habsburg Empire: Total War and Everyday Life in World War I* (Cambridge and New York: Cambridge University Press, 2004). On Imperial Germany, see the now classic revisionist book by David Blackbourn and Geoff Eley, *The Peculiarities of German History: Bourgeois Society and Politics in Nineteenth-Century Germany* (Oxford and New York: Oxford University Press, 1984), as well as Christopher Clark, *Iron Kingdom: The Rise and Downfall of Prussia, 1600–1947* (London: Allen Lane, 2006); and the essays in Dominik Geppert and Robert Gerwarth (eds), *Wilhelmine Germany and Edwardian Britain: Essays on Cultural Affinity* (Oxford and New York: Oxford University Press, 2008).

13. Michelle U. Campos, *Ottoman Brothers: Muslims, Christians, and Jews in Early Twentieth-Century Palestine* (Stanford, CA: Stanford University Press, 2011), 1–19.

14. M. Sükrü Hanioğlu, *A Brief History of the Late Ottoman Empire* (Princeton, NJ: Princeton University Press, 2006), 187–8.

15. Nicholas Doumanis, *Before the Nation: Muslim-Christian Coexistence and its Destruction in Late Ottoman Anatolia* (Oxford and New York: Oxford University Press, 2013), 152.

16. On the Spanish influenza, see Howard Phillips and David Killingray (eds), *The Spanish Influenza Pandemic of 1918–19: New Perspectives* (London and New York: Routledge, 2003). On the blockade and its effects, see, for example: Nigel Hawkins, *The Starvation Blockades: Naval Blockades of World War I* (Barnsley: Leo Cooper, 2002); Eric W. Osborne, *Britain's Economic Blockade of Germany, 1914–1919* (London and New York: Frank Cass, 2004); C. Paul Vincent, *The Politics of Hunger: The Allied Blockade of Germany, 1915–1919* (Athens, OH: Ohio University Press, 1985); N. P. Howard, 'The Social and Political Consequences of the Allied Food Blockade of Germany, 1918–19', in *German History* 11 (1993), 161–88.

17. Peter Holquist, 'Violent Russia, Deadly Marxism? Russia in the Epoch of Violence, 1905–21', in *Kritika: Explorations in Russian and Eurasian History* 4 (2003), 627–52, here 645.

18. Churchill as quoted in Norman Davies, *White Eagle, Red Star: The Polish-Soviet War, 1919–20*, 2nd edition (London: Pimlico, 2004), 21. For a more recent exploration of revolutionary, counter-revolutionary and ethnic conflicts from a systematically comparative or transnational angle, see, for example, Robert Gerwarth and John Horne (eds), *War in Peace: Paramilitary Violence after the Great War* (Oxford and New York: Oxford University Press, 2012). A notable exception is the pioneering study by Sven Reichardt, *Faschistische Kampfbünde: Gewalt und Gemeinschaft im italienischen Squadrismus und in der deutschen SA* (Cologne, Weimar and Vienna: Böhlau Verlag, 2002).

19. Michael Provence, 'Ottoman Modernity, Colonialism, and Insurgency in the Arab Middle East', in *International Journal of Middle East Studies* 43 (2011), 206; Dietrich Beyrau and Pavel P. Shcherbinin, 'Alles für die Front: Russland im Krieg 1914–1922', in Horst Bauerkämper and Elise Julien (eds), *Durchhalten! Krieg und Gesellschaft im Vergleich 1914–1918* (Göttingen: Vandenhoeck and Ruprecht, 2010), 151–77, here 151.

20. Balfour to Lord Walter Rothschild, 2 November 1917. On the context: Provence, 'Ottoman Modernity', 206, and most recently, Eugene Rogan, *The Fall of the Ottomans: The Great War in the Middle East, 1914–1920* (London: Allen Lane, 2015).

21. Estimates for these wars are notoriously difficult, but for an approximation see Davies, *White Eagle, Red Star*, 247, who assumes that 50,000 Polish soldiers died and 200,000 were wounded or went missing. Davies estimates that Soviet casualties were even higher.

22. Michael A. Reynolds, *Shattering Empires: The Clash and Collapse of the Ottoman and Russian Empires, 1908–1918* (Cambridge and New

York: Cambridge University Press, 2011); Alexander V. Prusin, *The Lands Between: Conflict in the East European Borderlands, 1870–1992* (Oxford and New York: Oxford University Press, 2010), 72–97; Piotr Wróbel, 'The Seeds of Violence: The Brutalization of an East European Region, 1917–1921', *Journal of Modern European History* 1 (2003), 125–49. Peter Gatrell, 'Wars after the War: Conflicts, 1919–1923', in John Horne (ed.), *A Companion to World War I* (Chichester: Wiley-Blackwell, 2010), 558–75; Richard Bessel, 'Revolution', in Jay Winter (ed.), *The Cambridge History of the First World War*, vol. 2 (Cambridge and New York: Cambridge University Press, 2014), 126–44, here 138.

23. On these discourses, see William Mulligan, *The Great War for Peace* (New Haven, CT, and London: Yale University Press, 2014).

24. Richard Bessel, 'Revolution', 127.

25. Richard C. Hall, *The Balkan Wars, 1912–1913: Prelude to the First World War* (London and New York: Routledge, 2000).

26. George F. Kennan, *The Decline of Bismarck's European Order: Franco-Russian Relations, 1875–1890* (Princeton, NJ: Princeton University Press, 1981).

27. George L. Mosse, *Fallen Soldiers: Reshaping the Memory of the World Wars* (Oxford and New York: Oxford University Press, 1990). Similar arguments were made for the case of Italy and Europe as a whole. On Italy, see Adrian Lyttleton, 'Fascism and Violence in Post-War Italy: Political Strategy and Social Conflict', in Wolfgang J. Mommsen and Gerhard Hirschfeld (eds), *Social Protest, Violence and Terror* (London: Palgrave Macmillan, 1982), 257–74, here 262–3. On Europe more generally, see Enzo Traverso, *Fire and Blood: The European Civil War, 1914–1945* (New York: Verso, 2016).

28. For a critical discussion of George Mosse's book, see Antoine Prost, 'The Impact of War on French and German Political Cultures', in *The Historical Journal* 37 (1994), 209–17. See also: Benjamin Ziemann, *War Experiences in Rural Germany, 1914–1923* (Oxford and New York: Berg, 2007); Dirk Schumann, 'Europa, der Erste Weltkrieg und die Nachkriegszeit: Eine Kontinuität der Gewalt?', in *Journal of Modern European History* 1 (2003), 24–43. See also Antoine Prost and Jay Winter (eds), *The Great War in History: Debates and Controversies, 1914 to the Present* (Cambridge and New York: Cambridge University Press, 2005).

29. Robert Gerwarth and John Horne (eds), 'Vectors of Violence: Paramilitarism in Europe after the Great War, 1917–1923', in *The Journal of Modern History* 83 (2011), 489–512.

30. Robert Gerwarth and John Horne, 'Bolshevism as Fantasy: Fear of Revolution and Counter-Revolutionary Violence, 1917–1923', in Gerwarth and Horne (eds), *War in Peace*, 40–51.
31. Wolfgang Schivelbusch, *The Culture of Defeat: On National Trauma, Mourning and Recovery* (New York: Holt, 2003).
32. Gerwarth and Horne, 'Vectors of Violence', 493.
33. On Britain, Jon Lawrence, 'Forging a Peaceable Kingdom: War, Violence, and Fear of Brutalization in Post-First World War Britain', in *Journal of Modern History* 75 (2003), 557–89. On France, John Horne, 'Defending Victory: Paramilitary Politics in France, 1918–26', in Gerwarth and Horne (eds), *War in Peace*, 216–33.
34. Hannah Arendt, *The Origins of Totalitarianism* (New York: Harcourt, Brace and Company, 1951), 260.
35. On this theme, see Wilson, *Frontiers of Violence*; Annemarie H. Sammartino, *The Impossible Border: Germany and the East, 1914–1922* (Ithaca, NY, and London: Cornell University Press, 2010). Eric D. Weitz and Omer Bartov (eds), *Shatterzones of Empires: Coexistence and Violence in the German, Habsburg, Russian, and Ottoman Borderlands* (Bloomington, IN: Indiana University Press, 2013); Gerwarth and Horne (eds), *War in Peace*; Reynolds, *Shattering Empires*.
36. John Paul Newman, 'Serbian Integral Nationalism and Mass Violence in the Balkans 1903–1945', in *Tijdschrift voor Geschiedenis*, 124 (2011), 448–63, and idem, *Yugoslavia in the Shadow of War: Veterans and the Limits of State Building, 1903–1945* (Cambridge and New York: Cambridge University Press, 2015). On Russia, see Holquist, 'Violent Russia', 627–52. On Ireland, see Matthew J. Kelly, *The Fenian Ideal and Irish Nationalism, 1882–1916* (Woodbridge: Boydell and Brewer, 2006).

1. A TRAIN JOURNEY IN SPRING

1. Robert Service, *Lenin: A Biography* (London: MacMillan, 2000), 256–64.
2. Ibid.
3. On German support for Irish Republicans in 1916, see Jerome aan de Wiel, *The Irish Factor 1899–1919: Ireland's Strategic and Diplomatic Importance for Foreign Powers* (Dublin: Irish Academic Press, 2008); Matthew Plowman, 'Irish Republicans and the Indo-German Conspiracy of World War I', in *New Hibernia Review* 7 (2003), 81–105. On support for jihad, see Tilman Lüdke, *Jihad Made in Germany: Ottoman*

and German Propaganda and Intelligence Operations in the First World War (Münster: Lit Verlag, 2005), 117–25; Rudolf A. Mark, *Krieg an Fernen Fronten: Die Deutschen in Zentralasien und am Hindukusch 1914–1924* (Paderborn: Ferdinand Schöningh, 2013), 17–42.

4. Jörn Leonhard, *Die Büchse der Pandora: Geschichte des Ersten Weltkriegs* (Munich: C. H. Beck, 2014), 654. Gerd Koenen, *Der Russland-Komplex: Die Deutschen und der Osten, 1900–1945* (Munich: C. H. Beck, 2005), 63ff.

5. Reinhard R. Doerries, *Prelude to the Easter Rising: Sir Roger Casement in Imperial Germany* (London and Portland: Frank Cass, 2000); Mary E. Daly (ed.), *Roger Casement in Irish and World History* (Dublin: Royal Irish Academy, 2005).

6. Willi Gautschi, *Lenin als Emigrant in der Schweiz* (Zürich: Benziger Verlag, 1973), 249–56; Helen Rappaport, *Conspirator: Lenin in Exile* (New York: Basic Books, 2010), 286–98.

7. Christopher Read, *Lenin: A Revolutionary Life* (Abingdon and New York: Routledge, 2005), 30; Hélène Carrère d'Encausse, *Lenin: Revolution and Power* (New York and London: Longman, 1982); Service, *Lenin,* 109.

8. Service, *Lenin,* 137.

9. Ibid., 135–42; Leonhard, *Pandora,* 652; Read, *Lenin,* 56ff.

10. Leonhard, *Pandora,* 652.

11. Ibid. On Zurich and Switzerland in this period, see Georg Kreis, *Insel der unsicheren Geborgenheit: die Schweiz in den Kriegsjahren 1914–1918* (Zürich: NZZ, 2014); Roman Rossfeld, Thomas Buomberger and Patrick Kury (eds), *14/18. Die Schweiz und der Grosse Krieg* (Baden: hier + jetzt, 2014).

12. On this debate, see David Priestland, *The Red Flag: A History of Communism* (London: Penguin, 2009), 52–60; Robert Service, *Comrades! World History of Communism* (Cambridge, MA: Harvard University Press, 2007), 36–57.

13. On socialism in 1914, see the classic work of Georges Haupt, *Socialism and the Great War: The Collapse of the Second International* (Oxford: Clarendon Press, 1972).

14. Read, *Lenin,* 36–42.

15. Leonhard, *Pandora,* 654; Service, *Lenin,* 254ff.

16. Leonhard, *Pandora,* 655.

17. Ibid; Service, *Lenin,* 260.

2. RUSSIAN REVOLUTIONS

1. On 'leapfrogging', see the classic book by Alexander Gerschenkron, *Economic Backwardness in Historical Perspective: A Book of Essays* (Cambridge, MA: Belknap Press of Harvard University Press, 1962), notably chapter 2. Hans Rogger, *Russia in the Age of Modernization and Revolution, 1881–1917* (London: Longman, 1983), 102–7; Malcolm E. Falkus, *The Industrialization of Russia, 1700–1914* (London: Macmillan, 1972), 61–74.

2. Douglas Smith, *Former People: The Final Days of the Russian Aristocracy* (London: Macmillan, 2012), 21. See, too: W. Bruce Lincoln, *In War's Dark Shadow: The Russians Before the Great War* (London: Dial Press, 1983), 35; Orlando Figes, *A People's Tragedy: The Russian Revolution, 1891–1924* (London: Jonathan Cape, 1996), 88.

3. Smith, *Former People*, 25. On the Russian aristocracy, see too Dominic Lieven, *Russian Rulers under the Old Regime* (London and New Haven, CT: Yale University Press, 1989). Elise Kimerling Wirtschafter, *Social Identity in Imperial Russia* (DeKalb, IL: Northern Illinois Press, 1997), 21–37; Andreas Grenzer, *Adel und Landbesitz im ausgehenden Zarenreich* (Stuttgart: Steiner, 1995); Roberta Thompson Manning, *The Crisis of the Old Order in Russia: Gentry and Government* (Princeton, NJ: Princeton University Press, 1983); Manfred Hildermeier (ed.), *Der russische Adel von 1700 bis 1917* (Göttingen: Vandenhoeck and Ruprecht, 1990); Seymour Becker, *Nobility and Privilege in Late Imperial Russia* (DeKalb, IL: Northern Illinois Press, 1985).

4. Anton Chekhov, *The Cherry Orchard*, in idem, *Four Great Plays by Anton Chekhov*, trans. Constance Garnet (New York: Bantam Books, 1958); Smith, *Former People*, 27.

5. On Bunin's *Dry Valley*, see Katherine Bowers and Ani Kokobobo, *Russian Writers and the Fin de Siècle: The Twilight of Realism* (Cambridge and New York: Cambridge University Press, 2015), 154ff; Smith, *Former People*, 57ff.

6. Rogger, *Russia*, 109–11; Smith, *Former People*, 29ff; Carsten Goehrke, *Russischer Alltag: Geschichte in neun Zeitbildern*, vol. 2 (Zürich: Chronos, 2003), 365–8.

7. Lincoln, *War's Dark Shadow*, 103–34; Smith, *Former People*, 29ff.

8. Dietrich Beyrau, 'Brutalization Revisited: The Case of Bolshevik Russia', in *Journal of Contemporary History* 50 (2015), 15–37, here 20. On the different layers of the 1905 revolution, see too Toivo U. Raun, 'The Revolution of 1905 in the Baltic Provinces and Finland', in *Slavic Review* 43 (1984), 453–67; Jan Kusber, *Krieg und Revolution in Russ-*

land 1904–1906: Das Militär im Verhältnis zu Wirtschaft, Autokratie und Gesellschaft (Stuttgart: Franz Steiner, 1997).

9. On police violence in Moscow during this period, see Felix Schnell, *Ordnungshüter auf Abwegen? Herrschaft und illegitime polizeiliche Gewalt in Moskau, 1905–1914* (Wiesbaden: Harrassowitz, 2006).

10. Anna Geifman, *Thou Shalt Kill: Revolutionary Terrorism in Russia, 1894–1917* (Princeton, NJ: Princeton University Press 1993), 18–21; Peter Holquist, 'Violent Russia, Deadly Marxism? Russia in the Epoch of Violence, 1905–1921', in *Kritika* 4 (2003), 627–52.

11. Leopold Haimson, 'The Problem of Stability in Urban Russia, 1905–1917', in *Slavic Review* 23 (1964), 619–42; and 24 (1965), 1–22. Michael S. Melancon, *The Lena Goldfields Massacre and the Crisis of the Late Tsarist State* (College Station, TX: Texas A&M University Press, 2006); Ludmilla Thomas, *Geschichte Sibiriens: Von den Anfängen bis zur Gegenwart* (Berlin: Akademie-Verlag 1982), 115ff.

12. Beyrau, 'Brutalization Revisited', 21; David Saunders, 'The First World War and the End of Tsarism', in Ian D. Thatcher (ed.), *Reinterpreting Revolutionary Russia: Essays in Honour of James D. White* (Basingstoke: Palgrave Macmillan, 2006), 55–71.

13. Figes, *People's Tragedy*, 3–6. Wayne Dowler, *Russia in 1913* (DeKalb, IL: Northern Illinois University Press, 2010).

14. Beyrau, 'Brutalization Revisited', 15–37.

15. On the latter, see Joshua Sanborn, *Drafting the Russian Nation: Military Conscription, Total War, and Mass Politics, 1905–1925* (DeKalb, IL: Northern Illinois University Press, 2003).

16. Heinrich August Winkler, *The Age of Catastrophe: A History of the West 1914–1945* (New Haven, CT, and London: Yale University Press, 2015), 19. On the tsarina, see Detlef Jena, *Die Zarinnen Rußlands (1547–1918)* (Graz: Styria, 1999), 326–7.

17. David Stone, *The Russian Army in the Great War: The Eastern Front, 1914–1917* (Lawrence, KS: University of Kansas Press, 2015); on casualty figures, see Rüdiger Overmans, 'Kriegsverluste', in Gerhard Hirschfeld, Gerd Krumeich and Irina Renz (eds), *Enzyklopädie Erster Weltkrieg*, 2nd revised edition (Paderborn: Schoeningh, 2004), 663–6; on the number of POWs: Reinhard Nachtigal, *Kriegsgefangenschaft an der Ostfront 1914–1918: Literaturbericht zu einem neuen Forschungsfeld* (Frankfurt: Peter Lang, 2003), 15–19.

18. Beyrau, 'Brutalization Revisited', 22.

19. Peter Holquist, *Making War, Forging Revolution: Russia's Continuum of Crisis* (Cambridge, MA: Harvard University Press, 2002), 30, 44.

20. Secret police report, as quoted in Smith, *Former People*, 65.

21. Stephen Smith, *Red Petrograd: Revolution in the Factories, 1917–1918* (Cambridge: Cambridge University Press, 1983); Reynolds, *Long Shadow*, 43.

22. On the February Revolution, see Helmut Altrichter, *Rußland 1917: Ein Land auf der Suche nach sich selbst* (Paderborn: Schöningh, 1997), 110–40; Manfred Hildermeier, *Geschichte der Sowjetunion 1917–1991: Entstehung und Niedergang des ersten sozialistischen Staates* (Munich: C. H. Beck, 1998), 64–80; Peter Gatrell, *Russia's First World War, 1914–1917: A Social and Economic History* (London: Pearson, 2005), 197–220; Rex A. Wade, *The Russian Revolution, 1917* (Cambridge and New York: Cambridge University Press, 2000); Stephen Smith, *The Russian Revolution: A Very Short Introduction* (Oxford and New York: Oxford University Press, 2002), chapter 1; Christopher Read, *From Tsar to Soviets: The Russian People and their Revolution, 1917–1921* (Oxford and New York: Oxford University Press, 1996); Tsuyoshi Hasegawa, 'The February Revolution', in Edward Acton, Vladimir Iu. Cherniaev and William G. Rosenberg (eds), *Critical Companion to the Russian Revolution 1914–1921* (London: Arnold, 1997), 48–61; Barbara Alpern Engel, 'Not by Bread Alone: Subsistence Riots in Russia during World War I', in *Journal of Modern History*, 69 (1997), 696–721; Allan K. Wildman, *The End of the Russian Imperial Army*, vol. 1: *The Old Army and the Soldiers' Revolt (March–April 1917)* (Princeton, NJ: Princeton University Press, 1980).

23. W. Bruce Lincoln, *Passage through Armageddon: The Russians in War and Revolution* (New York: Simon and Schuster, 1986), 321–5; Richard Pipes, *The Russian Revolution 1899–1919* (London: Harvill Press, 1997), 274–5; Rogger, *Russia*, 266–7.

24. Dominic Lieven, *Nicholas II: Emperor of all the Russians* (London: Pimlico, 1994), 226.

25. Wildman, *End of the Russian Imperial Army*, vol. 1, 123–4.

26. Lincoln, *Passage*, 327–31; Rogger, *Russia*, 266–7; Figes, *People's Tragedy*, 311–20.

27. Smith, *Former People*, 72; Lincoln, *Passage*, 331–3; Pipes, *Russian Revolution*, 279–81; Figes, *People's Tragedy*, 320–1.

28. Pipes, *Russian Revolution*, 307–17; Lincoln, *Passage*, 337–45.

29. Lincoln, *Passage*, 334–44; Figes, *People's Tragedy*, 327–49. Robert Paul Browder and Alexander F. Kerensky (eds), *The Russian Provisional Government 1917: Documents*, 3 vols (Stanford, CA: Stanford University Press, 1961); William G. Rosenberg, *The Liberals in the Russian Revolution: The Constitutional Democratic Party, 1917–1921* (Princeton, NJ: Princeton University Press, 1974), 114–16.

30. Marc Ferro, *October 1917: A Social History of the Russian Revolution* (London: Routledge and Kegan Paul, 1980).

31. Figes, *People's Tragedy*, 323–31; Smith, *Former People*, 73.

32. Lenin, as quoted in Service, *Lenin*, 268.

33. Figes, *People's Tragedy*, 334–5; Pipes, *Russian Revolution*, 320–3.

34. Figes, *People's Tragedy*, 361–84.

35. Lincoln, *Passage*, 346–71; Altrichter, *Rußland 1917*, 166–70.

36. Joshua Sanborn, *Imperial Apocalypse: The Great War and the Destruction of the Russian Empire* (Oxford and New York: Oxford University Press, 2014), 205–11.

37. Ibid, 209.

38. Andrejs Plakans, *The Latvians: A Short History* (Stanford, CA: Stanford University Press, 1995), 108.

39. Wildman, *End of the Russian Imperial Army*, 369; Mark von Hagen, *War in a European Borderland: Occupations and Occupation Plans in Galicia and Ukraine, 1914–1918* (Seattle, WA: University of Washington Press, 2007), 84–5.

40. Allan K. Wildman, *The End of the Russian Imperial Army*, vol. 2: *The Road to Soviet Power and Peace* (Princeton, NJ: Princeton University Press, 1987), 225–31; Sanborn, *Drafting the Russian Nation*, 173–4.

41. Figes, *People's Tragedy*, 423–35; Ronald G. Suny, 'Toward a Social History of the October Revolution', in *American Historical Review* 88 (1983), 31–52.

42. George Katkov, *The Kornilov Affair: Kerensky and the Breakup of the Russian Army* (London and New York: Longman, 1980); Harvey Ascher, 'The Kornilov Affair: A Reinterpretation', in *Russian Review* 29 (1970), 286–300.

43. Ibid; Smith, *Former People*, 105.

44. On Trotsky, see Isaac Deutscher, *The Prophet Armed: Trotsky, 1879–1921* (Oxford: Oxford University Press, 1954); Robert Service, *Trotsky: A Biography* (Cambridge, MA: Harvard University Press, 2009); Geoffrey Swain, *Trotsky and the Russian Revolution* (London and New York, 2014); Joshua Rubenstein, *Leon Trotsky: A Revolutionary's Life* (New Haven, CT, and London: Yale University Press, 2006).

45. Vladimir Ilyich Lenin, 'The State and Revolution', in Lenin, *Collected Works*, 45 vols (Moscow, 1964–74), vol. 25, 412ff. Winkler, *Age of Catastrophe*, 26–7.

46. Pipes, *Russian Revolution*, 439–67. On the challenge of autonomy demands, see Andreas Kappeler, *Rußland als Vielvölkerreich: Entstehung – Geschichte – Zerfall* (Munich: C. H. Beck, 1993); Mark, *Krieg an fernen Fronten*, 131–4.

47. Figes, *People's Tragedy*, 462–3.
48. Orlando Figes, *Peasant Russia, Civil War: The Volga Countryside in Revolution, 1917–21* (Oxford and New York: Oxford University Press, 1989), 21–2; Graeme J. Gill, *Peasants and Government in the Russian Revolution* (New York: Barnes and Noble, 1979), 157–8; Altrichter, *1917*, 330–58.
49. Lincoln, *Passage*, 463–8.
50. Pipes, *Russian Revolution*, 492.
51. Leonhard, *Pandora*, 679; Hildermeier, *Geschichte*, 117; Rex A. Wade, 'The October Revolution, the Constituent Assembly, and the End of the Russian Revolution', in Ian D. Thatcher, *Reinterpreting Revolutionary Russia: Essays in Honour of James D. White* (London: Palgrave Macmillan, 2006), 72–85.
52. Pipes, *Russian Revolution*, 541–55.
53. Figes, *People's Tragedy*, 492–7; Alexander Rabinowitch, *The Bolsheviks in Power: The First Year of Soviet Rule in Petrograd* (Bloomington, IN: Indiana University Press, 2007), 302–4.
54. Smith, *Former People*, 118; Lincoln, *Passage*, 458–61; Pipes, *Russian Revolution*, 499.
55. Figes, *Peasant Russia*, 296–7.
56. Smith, *Former People*, 134; Gill, *Peasants*, 154.
57. Sean McMeekin, *History's Greatest Heist: The Looting of Russia by the Bolsheviks* (New Haven, CT, and London: Yale University Press, 2009), 12–13, 24–5, 73–91. For a local case study, see Donald J. Raleigh, *Experiencing Russia's Civil War: Politics, Society and Revolutionary Culture in Saratov, 1917–1922* (Princeton, NJ: Princeton University Press, 2002).

3. BREST-LITOVSK

1. On Brest-Litovsk, see Vejas Gabriel Liulevicius, *War Land on the Eastern Front: Culture, National Identity and German Occupation in World War I* (Cambridge and New York: Cambridge University Press, 2000), 204–7; Sanborn, *Imperial Apocalypse*, 232ff; and the classic account by Winfried Baumgart, *Deutsche Ostpolitik 1918: Von Brest-Litovsk bis zum Ende des Ersten Weltkriegs* (Vienna and Munich: Oldenbourg, 1966), 13–92.
2. Baumgart, *Deutsche Ostpolitik 1918*, 16.
3. See Hoffmann's account in Karl Friedrich Nowak (ed.), *Die Aufzeichnungen des Generalmajors Max Hoffmann*, 2 vols (Berlin: Verlag für

Kulturpolitik, 1929), here vol. 2, 190. See also the account of another senior German diplomat involved in drafting the Treaty of Brest-Litovsk, Frederic von Rosenberg: Winfried Becker, *Frederic von Rosenberg (1874–1937): Diplomat vom späten Kaiserreich bis zum Dritten Reich, Außenminister der Weimarer Republik* (Göttingen: Vandenhoeck and Ruprecht, 2011), 26–40; Baumgart, *Deutsche Ostpolitik 1918*, 14.

4. Richard von Kühlmann, *Erinnerungen* (Heidelberg: Schneider, 1948), 523ff; Leon Trotsky, *My Life: The Rise and Fall of a Dictator* (New York and London: Butterworth, 1930); Nowak (ed.), *Die Aufzeichnungen des Generalmajors*, 207ff; Werner Hahlweg, *Der Diktatfrieden von Brest-Litowsk 1918 und die bolschewistische Weltrevolution* (Münster: Aschendorff, 1960); Christian Rust, 'Self-Determination at the Beginning of 1918 and the German Reaction', in *Lithuanian Historical Studies* 13 (2008), 43–6.

5. Ottokar Luban, 'Die Massenstreiks fuer Frieden und Demokratie im Ersten Weltkrieg', in Chaja Boebel and Lothar Wentzel (eds), *Streiken gegen den Krieg: Die Bedeutung der Massenstreiks in der Metallindustrie vom Januar 1918* (Hamburg: VSA-Verlag, 2008), 11–27.

6. Oleksii Kurayev, *Politika Nimechchini i Avstro-Uhorshchini v Pershii svitovij vijni: ukrayinskii napryamok* (Kiev: Inst. Ukraïnskoi Archeohrafiï ta Džereloznavstva Im. M. S. Hrusevskoho, 2009), 220–46; Wolfdieter Bihl, *Österreich-Ungarn und die Friedensschlüsse von Brest-Litovsk* (Vienna, Cologne and Graz: Böhlau, 1970), 60–2; Caroline Milow, *Die ukrainische Frage 1917–1923 im Spannungsfeld der europäischen Diplomatie* (Wiesbaden: Harrassowitz, 2002), 110–15; Stephan M. Horak, *The First Treaty of World War I: Ukraine's Treaty with the Central Powers of February 9, 1918* (Boulder, CO: East European Monographs, 1988); Frank Golczewski, *Deutsche und Ukrainer 1914–1939* (Paderborn: Schöningh, 2010), 240–6.

7. Olch S. Fedyshyn, *Germany's Drive to the East and the Ukrainian Revolution, 1917–1918* (New Brunswick, NJ: Rutgers University Press, 1971); Peter Borowsky, 'Germany's Ukrainian Policy during World War I and the Revolution of 1918–19', in Hans-Joachim Torke and John-Paul Himka (eds), *German-Ukrainian Relations in Historical Perspective* (Edmonton: Canadian Institute of Ukrainian Studies, 1994), 84–94; Golczewski, *Deutsche und Ukrainer*, 289–306; Olavi Arens, 'The Estonian Question at Brest-Litovsk', in *Journal of Baltic Studies* 25 (1994), 309; Rust, 'Self-Determination'; Gert von Pistohlkors (ed.), *Deutsche Geschichte im Osten Europas. Baltische Länder* (Berlin: Siedler, 1994), 452–60; Hans-Erich Volkmann, *Die deutsche Baltikumpolitik zwischen*

Brest-Litowsk und Compiègne (Cologne and Vienna: Böhlau, 1970).

8. Baumgart, *Deutsche Ostpolitik 1918*, 14ff; Dietmar Neutatz, *Träume und Alpträume: Eine Geschichte Russlands im 20. Jahrhundert* (Munich: C. H. Beck, 2013), 158–60; Hahlweg, *Der Diktatfrieden von Brest-Litowsk*, 50–2.

9. Hannes Leidinger and Verena Moritz, *Gefangenschaft, Revolution, Heimkehr. Die Bedeutung der Kriegsgefangenproblematik für die Geschichte des Kommunismus in Mittel- und Osteuropa 1917–1920* (Vienna, Cologne and Weimar: Böhlau, 2003); Reinhard Nachtigal, *Russland und seine österreichisch-ungarischen Kriegsgefangenen (1914–1918)* (Remshalden: Verlag Bernhard Albert Greiner, 2003); Alan Rachaminow, *POWs and the Great War: Captivity on the Eastern Front* (Oxford and New York: Berg, 2002).

10. On the estimated two million Habsburg POWs in Russian captivity, see Nachtigal, *Kriegsgefangenen (1914–1918)*; Lawrence Sondhaus, *World War One: The Global Revolution* (Cambridge and New York: Cambridge University Press, 2011), 421. On Tito in particular, see Vladimir Dedijer, *Novi prilozi za biografiju Josipa Broza Tita 1* (Zagreb and Rijeka: Mladost i Spektar; Liburnija, 1980), 57–9 (reprint of the original 1953 edition).

4. THE TASTE OF VICTORY

1. As quoted in Michael Reynolds, 'The Ottoman-Russian Struggle for Eastern Anatolia and the Caucasus, 1908–1918: Identity, Ideology and the Geopolitics of World Order', PhD Dissertation: Princeton University, 2003, 308.

2. David Kennedy, *Over Here: The First World War and American Society* (Oxford and New York: Oxford University Press, 1980), 169.

3. Keith Hitchins, *Rumania, 1866–1947* (Oxford and New York: Oxford University Press, 1994), 273ff.

4. On Austria-Hungary during the Great War, see Manfried Rauchensteiner, *Der Tod des Doppeladlers: Österreich-Ungarn und der Erste Weltkrieg* (Graz: Styria, 1993).

5. Ibid; on the Brusilov offensive, see Alexander Watson, *Ring of Steel: Germany and Austria-Hungary at War, 1914–18* (London: Allen Lane, 2014), 300–10.

6. Nicola Labanca, 'La guerra sul fronte italiano e Caporetto', in Stéphane Audoin-Rouzeau and Jean-Jacques Becker (eds), *La prima guerra mondiale*, vol. 1 (Turin: Einaudi, 2007), 443–60.

7. Ludendorff, as quoted in Manfred Nebelin, *Ludendorff: Diktator im Ersten Weltkrieg* (Munich: Siedler, 2010), 404.

8. Diary entry for 31 December 1917, in Albrecht von Thaer, *Generalstabsdienst an der Front und in der OHL: Aus Briefen und Tagebuchaufzeichnungen, 1915–1919* (Göttingen: Vandenhoeck and Ruprecht, 1958), 150–1; Watson, *Ring of Steel*, 514.

9. Watson, *Ring of Steel*, 514ff.

10. Michael S. Neiberg, *The Second Battle of the Marne* (Bloomington, IN: Indiana University Press, 2008), 34; Michael Geyer, *Deutsche Rüstungspolitik 1860–1980* (Frankfurt am Main: Suhrkamp, 1984), 83–96; Richard Bessel, *Germany after the First World War* (Oxford and New York: Clarendon Press, 1993), 5. On the transfer of German troops, see Giordan Fong, 'The Movement of German Divisions to the Western Front, Winter 1917–1918', in *War in History* 7 (2000), 225–35, here 229–30.

11. Eugene Rogan, *The Fall of the Ottomans: The Great War in the Middle East, 1914–1920* (London: Allen Lane, 2015), 356–7; Ryan Gingeras, *Fall of the Sultanate: The Great War and the End of the Ottoman Empire, 1908–1922* (Oxford and New York: Oxford University Press, 2016), 244–5.

12. Rogan, *The Fall of the Ottomans*, 356; Gingeras, *Fall of the Sultanate*, 244.

13. Gingeras, *Fall of the Sultanate*, 244–5; Rudolf A. Mark, *Krieg an Fernen Fronten: Die Deutschen in Zentralasien und am Hindukusch 1914–1924* (Paderborn: Ferdinand Schöningh, 2013), 164ff.

14. Jörn Leonhard, *Die Büchse der Pandora: Geschichte des Ersten Weltkriegs* (Munich: C. H. Beck, 2014), 805.

15. David Stevenson, *With our Backs to the Wall: Victory and Defeat in 1918* (London: Allen Lane, 2011), 7 (on the human cost of offensives) and 35 (on lack of alternatives).

16. A very detailed account of the offensive is offered in David T. Zabecki, *The German 1918 Offensives: A Case Study in the Operational Level of War* (New York: Routledge, 2006), 126–33. For a more concise and recent analysis, see Watson, *Ring of Steel*, 517ff.

17. Ernst Jünger, *In Stahlgewittern: Ein Kriegstagebuch*, 24th edition (Berlin: Mittler 1942), 244ff. The edited version is not fundamentally different from the original diary entry: Ernst Jünger, *Kriegstagebuch 1914–1918*, ed. Helmuth Kiesel (Stuttgart: Klett-Cotta, 2010), 375ff (diary entry of 21 March 1918). On Jünger's life, see Helmuth Kiesel, *Ernst Jünger: Die Biographie* (Munich: Siedler, 2007).

18. Watson, *Ring of Steel*, 519ff; Martin Middlebrook, *The Kaiser's Battle: The First Day of the German Spring Offensive* (London: Viking, 1978).

19. J. Paul Harris, *Douglas Haig and the First World War* (Cambridge and New York: Cambridge University Press, 2008), 454–6.

20. Alan Kramer, *Dynamic of Destruction: Culture and Mass Killing in the First World War* (Oxford and New York: Oxford University Press, 2007), 269–71; Holger Herwig, *The First World War: Germany and Austria-Hungary, 1914–1918* (London: Edward Arnold, 1997), 400–16. On the overcoming of Franco-British rivalries, see Elizabeth Greenhalgh, *Victory through Coalition: Politics, Command and Supply in Britain and France, 1914–1918* (Cambridge and New York: Cambridge University Press, 2005).

21. Georg Alexander von Müller, *The Kaiser and his Court: The Diaries, Notebooks, and Letters of Admiral Alexander von Müller* (London: Macdonald, 1961), 344.

22. Hugenberg as quoted in Nebelin, *Ludendorff*, 414–15.

23. Watson, *Ring of Steel*, 520.

24. Zabecki, *German 1918 Offensives*, 139–73; David Stevenson, *With Our Backs to the Wall: Victory and Defeat in 1918* (London: Allen Lane, 2011), 67.

25. Wilhelm Deist, 'Verdeckter Militärstreik im Kriegsjahr 1918?', in Wolfram Wette (ed.), *Der Krieg des kleinen Mannes: Eine Militärgeschichte von unten* (Munich and Zürich: Piper, 1998), 146–67, here 149–50.

26. Alexander Watson, *Enduring the Great War: Combat Morale and Collapse in the German and British Armies, 1914–1918* (Cambridge and New York: Cambridge University Press, 2008), 181.

27. Zabecki, *German 1918 Offensives*, 184–205; Watson, *Ring of Steel*, 521; Robert Foley, 'From Victory to Defeat: The German Army in 1918', in Ashley Ekins (ed.), *1918: Year of Victory* (Auckland and Wollombi, NSW: Exisle, 2010), 69–88, here 77.

28. Stevenson, *With Our Backs to the Wall*, 78–88.

5. REVERSALS OF FORTUNE

1. Holger Herwig, *The First World War: Germany and Austria-Hungary, 1914–1918* (London: Bloomsbury, 1996), 414; Leonard V. Smith, Stéphane Audoin-Rouzeau and Annette Becker, *France and the Great War, 1914–1918* (Cambridge and New York: Cambridge University Press, 2003), 151; David Stevenson, *With Our Backs to the Wall: Victory and Defeat in 1918* (London: Allen Lane, 2011), 345.

2. Scott Stephenson, *The Final Battle: Soldiers of the Western Front and the German Revolution of 1918* (Cambridge and New York: Cambridge University Press, 2009), 25.

3. Ibid, 25.

4. Oliver Haller, 'German Defeat in World War I, Influenza and Postwar Memory', in Klaus Weinhauer, Anthony McElligott and Kirsten Heinsohn (eds), *Germany 1916–23: A Revolution in Context* (Bielefeld: Transcript, 2015), 151–80, here 173ff. See also Eckard Michels, 'Die "Spanische Grippe" 1918/19: Verlauf, Folgen und Deutungen in Deutschland im Kontext des Ersten Weltkriegs', in *Vierteljahrshefte für Zeitgeschichte* (2010), 1–33; Frieder Bauer and Jörg Vögele, 'Die "Spanische Grippe" in der deutschen Armee 1918: Perspektive der Ärzte und Generäle', in *Medizinhistorisches Journal* 48 (2013), 117–52; Howard Phillips and David Killingray (eds), *The Spanish Influenza Pandemic of 1918–19: New Perspectives* (London and New York: Routledge, 2003).

5. Stephenson, *Final Battle*, 25.

6. For the state of front-line units in the last weeks, see the reports in A. Philipp (ed.), *Die Ursachen des Deutschen Zusammenbruches im Jahre 1918. Zweite Abteilung: Der innere Zusammenbruch*, vol. 6 (Berlin: Deutsche Verlagsgesellschaft für Politik, 1928), 321–86.

7. Bernd Ulrich and Benjamin Ziemann (eds), *Frontalltag im Ersten Weltkrieg: Wahn und Wirklichkeit. Quellen und Dokumente* (Frankfurt am Main: Fischer, 1994), 94 (report of 4 September 1918).

8. Stevenson, *With Our Backs to the Wall*, 112–69.

9. Manfred Nebelin, *Ludendorff: Diktator im Ersten Weltkrieg* (Munich: Siedler, 2010), 423–4.

10. Wolfgang Foerster, *Der Feldherr Ludendorff im Unglück: Eine Studie über seine seelische Haltung in der Endphase des ersten Weltkrieges* (Wiesbaden: Limes Verlag, 1952), 73–4.

11. On the battles for Doiran and the commemorations of World War I in Bulgaria, see Nikolai Vukov, 'The Memory of the Dead and the Dynamics of Forgetting: "Post-Mortem" Interpretations of World War I in Bulgaria', in Oto Luthar (ed.), *The Great War and Memory in Central and South-Eastern Europe* (Leiden: Brill, 2016); see also Ivan Petrov, *Voynata v Makedonia (1915–1918)* (Sofia: Semarsh, 2008); Nikola Nedev and Tsocho Bilyarski, *Doyranskata epopeia, 1915–1918* (Sofia: Aniko/ Simolini, 2009).

12. On the breakthrough at Dobro Pole, see Richard C. Hall, *Balkan Breakthrough: The Battle of Dobro Pole 1918* (Bloomington, IN: Indiana University Press, 2010); Dimitar Azmanov and Rumen Lechev, 'Probivatna Dobropoleprezsptemvri 1918 godina', in *Voennoistoricheski sbornik* 67 (1998), 154–75.

13. See full details in Bogdan Kesyakov, *Prinos kym diplomaticheskata istoriya na Bulgaria (1918–1925): Dogovori, konventsii, spogodbi, pro-*

tokoli i drugi syglashenia i diplomaticheski aktove s kratki belejki (Sofia: Rodopi, 1925); Petrov, *Voynata v Makedonia*, 209–11.

14. On Bulgaria's involvement in the Balkan Wars, see Mincho Semov, *Pobediteliat prosi mir: Balkanskite voyni 1912–1913* (Sofia: Universitetsko izdatelstvo 'Sv. Kliment Ohridski', 1995); V. Tankova et al., *Balkanskite voyni 1912–1913: pamet i istoriya* (Sofia: Akademichno izdatelstvo 'Prof. Marin Drinov', 2012); Georgi Markov, *Bulgaria v Balkanskia sayuz sreshtu Osmanskata imperia, 1911–1913* (Sofia: Zahariy Stoyanov, 2012).

15. Richard Hall, 'Bulgaria in the First World War', http://russiasgreatwar. org/media/arc/bulgaria.shtml (last accessed 24 February 2016).

16. Ibid.

17. On refugees to Bulgaria after the Second Balkan war, see: Delcho Poryazov, *Pogromat nad trakijskite bălgari prez 1913 g.: razorenie i etnichesko iztreblenie* (Sofia: Akademichno izdatelstvo 'Prof. Marin Drinov', 2009); Carnegie Endowment for International Peace (ed.), *Report of the International Commission to Inquire into the Causes and Conduct of the Balkan Wars* (reprint, Washington D.C.: Carnegie, 2014), esp. 123–135.

18. Richard C. Hall, 'Bulgaria', in Ute Daniel et al. (eds), *1914–1918 online. International Encyclopedia of the First World War*.

19. On Bulgaria's participation in the Great War, see esp. Georgi Markov, *Golyamata voina i bulgarskiat klyuch kym evropeiskiat pogreb (1914–1916)* (Sofia: Akademichno izdatelstvo 'Prof. Marin Drinov', 1995); Georgi Markov, *Golyamata voyna i bulgarskata strazha mezhdu Sredna Evropa i Orienta, 1916–1919* (Sofia: Akademichno izdatelstvo 'Prof. Marin Drinov', 2006).

20. Hall, 'Bulgaria in the First World War'.

21. On the northern front and particularly on the battle for Tutrakan, see Petar Boychev, *Tutrakanska epopeia* (Tutrakan: Kovachev, 2003); Petar Boychev and Volodya Milachkov, *Tutrakanskata epopeya i voynata na Severnia front, 1916–1918* (Silistra: Kovachev, 2007). See also the publications on the battles for Dobrich, known in Bulgarian historiography as the 'Dobrich epic': Radoslav Simeonov, Velichka Mihailova and Donka Vasileva, *Dobrichkata epopeia, 1916* (Dobrich: Ave fakta, 2006); Georgi Kazandjiev et al., *Dobrichkata epopeia, 5–6 septemvri 1916* (Dobrich: Matador, 2006).

22. Hall, 'Bulgaria in the First World War'.

23. Kanyo Kozhuharov, *Radomirskata republika, 1918–1948* (Sofia: BZNS, 1948), 11.

24. Ibid, 12.

25. Andrej Mitrović, *Serbia's Great War, 1914–1918* (London: Hurst, 2007), 312–19.

26. Gunther Rothenberg, *The Army of Francis Joseph* (West Lafayette, IN: Purdue University Press, 1997), 212–13.

27. Alexander Watson, *Ring of Steel: Germany and Austria-Hungary at War, 1914–18* (London: Allen Lane, 2014), 538.

28. Mario Isnenghi and Giorgio Rochat, *La Grande Guerra 1914–1918* (Milan: La Nuova Italia, 2000), 438–52.

29. Mark Thompson, *The White War: Life and Death on the Italian Front 1915–1919* (London: Faber and Faber, 2009), 344–6; Mark Cornwall, *The Undermining of Austria-Hungary: The Battle for Hearts and Minds* (Basingstoke: Macmillan, 2000), 287–99.

30. Watson, *Ring of Steel*, 538.

31. Ibid, 540; Arthur May, *The Passing of the Habsburg Monarchy*, vol. 2 (Philadelphia, PA: University of Pennsylvania Press, 1966), 760–3.

32. Rudolf Neck (ed.), *Österreich im Jahre 1918: Berichte und Dokumente* (Vienna: Oldenbourg, 1968), 104–13.

33. Quoted in Isnenghi and Rochat, *La Grande Guerra 1914–1918*, 463–4.

34. Erik Jan Zürcher, 'The Ottoman Empire and the Armistice of Moudros', in Hugh Cecil and Peter H. Liddle (eds), *At the Eleventh Hour: Reflections, Hopes, and Anxieties at the Closing of the Great War, 1918* (London: Leo Cooper, 1998), 266–75.

35. Timothy W. Childs, *Italo-Turkish Diplomacy and the War over Libya, 1911–1912* (New York: Brill, 1990), 36.

36. Carnegie Endowment for International Peace (ed.), *Report of the International Commission to Inquire into the Causes and Conduct of the Balkan Wars* (reprint, Washington DC: Carnegie, 2014).

37. M. Şükrü Hanioğlu, *A Brief History of the Late Ottoman Empire* (Princeton, NJ: Princeton University Press, 2006), 165.

38. Mustafa Aksakal, 'The Ottoman Empire', in Jay Winter (ed.), *The Cambridge History of the First World War*, vol. 1 (Cambridge and New York: Cambridge University Press, 2014), 459–78, here 470.

39. Mustafa Aksakal, *The Ottoman Road to War in 1914: The Ottoman Empire and the First World War* (Cambridge and New York: Cambridge University Press, 2008), 93–118.

40. Ibid, 178–87.

41. Edward J. Erickson, *Ordered to Die: A History of the Ottoman Army in the First World War* (Westport, CT, and London: Greenwood Press, 2001); Carl Alexander Krethlow, *Generalfeldmarschall Colmar Freiherr von der Goltz Pascha: Eine Biographie* (Paderborn: Ferdinand Schöningh, 2012).

42. Aksakal, *The Ottoman Road to War*, 94.
43. Hanioğlu, *Brief History of the Late Ottoman Empire*, 180–1; David Reynolds, *The Long Shadow: The Great War and the Twentieth Century* (London: Simon and Schuster, 2013), 88.
44. *A Brief Record of the Advance of the Egyptian Expeditionary Force under the Command of General Sir Edmund H. H. Allenby, G.C.B., G.C.M.G. July 1917 to October 1918* (London: His Majesty's Stationery Office, 1919), 25–36; James Kitchen, *The British Imperial Army in the Middle East* (London: Bloomsbury, 2014).
45. Ryan Gingeras, *Fall of the Sultanate: The Great War and the End of the Ottoman Empire, 1908–1922* (Oxford and New York: Oxford University Press, 2016), 248; Gwynne Dyer, 'The Turkish Armistice of 1918. 2: A Lost Opportunity: The Armistice Negotiations of Moudros', in *Middle Eastern Studies* 3 (1972), 313–48.
46. Eugene Rogan, *The Fall of the Ottomans: The Great War in the Middle East, 1914–1920* (London: Allen Lane, 2015), 285–7 and 359–60.
47. 'Turquie: Convention d'armistice 30 Octobre 1918', in *Guerre Européenne: Documents 1918: Conventions d'armistice passées avec la Turquie, la Bulgarie, l'Autriche-Hongrie et l'Allemagne par les puissances Alliées et associées* (Paris: Ministère des Affaires Étrangères, 1919), 7–9. See also Gingeras, *Fall of the Sultanate*, 249.
48. Dyer, 'The Turkish Armistice of 1918', 319.
49. Quoted in Patrick Kinross, *Atatürk: A Biography of Mustafa Kemal, Father of Modern Turkey* (London: Weidenfeld and Nicolson, 1964), 15.
50. Ryan Gingeras, *Mustafa Kemal Atatürk: Heir to an Empire* (Oxford and New York: Oxford University Press, 2015); Irfan Orga and Margarete Orga, *Atatürk* (London: Michael Joseph, 1962), 164.
51. Elie Kedourie, 'The End of the Ottoman Empire', in *Journal of Contemporary History of the Ottoman Empire* 2 (1968), 19–28, here 19. For a comprehensive history, see Caroline Finkel, *Osman's Dream: The Story of the Ottoman Empire, 1300–1923* (London: John Murray, 2005).
52. Albrecht von Thaer, *Generalstabsdienst an der Front und in der OHL: Aus Briefen und Tagebuchaufzeichnungen, 1915–1919* (Göttingen: Vandenhoeck and Ruprecht, 1958), 234 (diary entry for 1 October 1918).
53. Ibid.
54. Herbert Michaelis, Ernst Schraepler and Günter Scheel (eds), *Ursachen und Folgen*, vol. 2: *Der militärische Zusammenbruch und das Ende des Kaiserreichs* (Berlin: Verlag Herbert Wendler, 1959), 319–20.
55. Harry Rudolph Rudin, *Armistice 1918* (New Haven, CT, and London: Yale University Press, 1944), 53–4.

56. Lothar Machtan, *Prinz Max von Baden: Der letzte Kanzler des Kaisers* (Berlin: Suhrkamp, 2013).

57. Heinrich August Winkler, *The Age of Catastrophe: A History of the West 1914–1945* (New Haven, CT, and London: Yale University Press, 2015), 61–2. On the October reforms, see most recently Anthony McElligott, *Rethinking the Weimar Republic: Authority and Authoritarianism, 1916–1936* (London: Bloomsbury, 2014), 19–26.

58. Rudin, *Armistice 1918*, 53 and 56–80; Watson, *Ring of Steel*, 547–8.

59. Quoted in Rudin, *Armistice 1918*, 173, and Watson, *Ring of Steel*, 550–1.

60. Nebelin, *Ludendorff*, 493.

61. Ibid, 497–8; Watson, *Ring of Steel*, 551.

62. Martin Kitchen, *The Silent Dictatorship: The Politics of the German High Command under Hindenburg and Ludendorff, 1916–1918* (New York: Holmes and Meier, 1976); Richard Bessel, 'Revolution', in Jay Winter (ed.), *The Cambridge History of the First World War*, vol. 2 (Cambridge and New York: Cambridge University Press, 2014), 126–44.

63. West German historians have been particularly interested in the soldiers' councils created within Germany. For years they debated whether these councils might have served as the basis for a 'third path' for Germany's political destiny, offering an alternative to both the Weimar Republic (and its fatal compromises with the old elites) and an extremist Bolshevik-style regime. Reinhard Rürup, 'Demokratische Revolution und der "dritte Weg": Die deutsche Revolution von 1918/19 in der neueren wissenschaftlichen Diskussion', in *Geschichte und Gesellschaft 9* (1983), 278–301.

64. Wilhelm Deist, 'Die Politik der Seekriegsleitung und die Rebellion der Flotte Ende Oktober 1918', in *Vierteljahrshefte für Zeitgeschichte 14* (1966), 341–68; quotation in English translation from Watson, *Ring of Steel*, 552.

65. Gerhard Groß, 'Eine Frage der Ehre? Die Marineführung und der letzte Flottenvorstoß? 1918', in Jörg Duppler and Gerhard P. Groß (eds), *Kriegsende 1918: Ereignis, Wirkung, Nachwirkung* (Munich: Oldenbourg, 1999), 349–65, here 354–65; Watson, *Ring of Steel*, 552.

66. Holger Herwig, *'Luxury Fleet': The Imperial German Navy 1888–1918*, revised edition (London: Ashfield Press, 1987), 247 and 250; Watson, *Ring of Steel*, 552.

67. Hannes Leidinger, 'Der Kieler Aufstand und die deutsche Revolution', in idem and Verena Moritz (eds), *Die Nacht des Kirpitschnikow. Eine andere Geschichte des Ersten Weltkriegs* (Vienna: Deuticke, 2006), 220–35; Daniel Horn, *Mutiny on the High Seas: Imperial German*

Naval Mutinies of World War One (London: Leslie Frewin, 1973), 234–46; Watson, *Ring of Steel*, 553.

68. Watson, *Ring of Steel*, 554.

69. Ulrich Kluge, 'Militärrevolte und Staatsumsturz. Ausbreitung und Konsolidierung der Räteorganisation im rheinisch-westfälischen Industriegebiet', in Reinhard Rürup (ed.), *Arbeiter- und Soldatenräte im rheinisch-westfälischen Industriegebiet* (Wuppertal: Hammer, 1975), 39–82.

70. Ulrich Kluge, *Soldatenräte und Revolution: Studien zur Militärpolitik in Deutschland 1918/19* (Göttingen: Vandenhoeck and Ruprecht, 1975), 48–56.

71. Harry Graf Kessler, *Das Tagebuch 1880–1937*, eds Roland Kamzelak and Günter Riederer, vol. 6: *1916–1918* (Stuttgart: Klett-Cotta, 2006), 616.

72. For a detailed account of the end of the German dynasties, see Lothar Machtan, *Die Abdankung: Wie Deutschlands gekrönte Häupter aus der Geschichte fielen* (Berlin: Propyläen Verlag, 2008).

73. Rudin, *Armistice 1918*, 327–9 and 349–51.

74. Stephenson, *The Final Battle*, 83–90.

75. Rudin, *Armistice 1918*, 345–59; Kluge, *Soldatenräte*, 82–7.

76. Manfred Jessen-Klingenberg, 'Die Ausrufung der Republik durch Philipp Scheidemann am 9. November 1918', in *Geschichte in Wissenschaft und Unterricht* 19 (1968), 649–56, here 653.

77. Winkler, *Age of Catastrophe*, 67.

78. Watson, *Ring of Steel*, 55ff.

79. Rudin, *Armistice 1918*, 427–32; Watson, *Ring of Steel*, 556.

6. NO END TO WAR

1. On this see Annemarie H. Sammartino, *The Impossible Border: Germany and the East, 1914–1922* (Ithaca, NY, and London: Cornell University Press, 2010), chapter 2; Timothy Snyder, *The Reconstruction of Nations: Poland, Ukraine, Lithuania, Belarus, 1569–1999* (New Haven, CT, and London, 2004), 62–3; Vejas Gabriel Liulevicius, *War Land on the Eastern Front: Culture, National Identity and German Occupation in World War I* (Cambridge and New York: Cambridge University Press, 2000), 228ff. On Baltic paramilitaries fighting for national independence, see Tomas Balkelis, 'Turning Citizens into Soldiers: Baltic Paramilitary Movements after the Great War', in Robert Gerwarth and John Horne (eds), *War in Peace: Paramilitary Violence after the Great War* (Oxford and New York: Oxford University Press, 2012), 126–44.

2. This was particularly true for Estonia and Latvia. James D. White, 'National Communism and World Revolution: The Political Consequences of German Military Withdrawal from the Baltic Area in 1918–19', in *Europe-Asia Studies* 8 (1994), 1,349–69. For good general histories of the Baltics, see Andres Kasekamp, *A History of the Baltic States* (New York: Palgrave Macmillan, 2010); Andrejs Plakans, *A Concise History of the Baltic States* (Cambridge and New York: Cambridge University Press, 2011); and the classic work by Georg von Rauch, *The Baltic States: The Years of Independence: Estonia, Latvia, Lithuania, 1917–1940* (Berkeley, CA: University of California Press, 1974).

3. On Bischoff and the 'Iron Division', see Tanja Bührer, *Die Kaiserliche Schutztruppe für Deutsch-Ostafrika: Koloniale Sicherheitspolitik und transkulturelle Kriegführung, 1885 bis 1918* (Munich: Oldenbourg, 2011), 211; Bernhard Sauer, 'Vom "Mythos eines ewigen Soldatentums". Der Feldzug deutscher Freikorps im Baltikum im Jahre 1919', in *Zeitschrift für Geschichtswissenschaft* 43 (1995), 869–902; and the autobiographical account: Josef Bischoff, *Die letzte Front: Geschichte der Eisernen Division im Baltikum 1919* (Berlin: Buch- und Tiefdruck Gesellschaft, 1935).

4. Liulevicius, *War Land on the Eastern Front*, 56ff.

5. John Hiden, *The Baltic States and Weimar Ostpolitik* (Cambridge and New York: Cambridge University Press, 1987), 16; Sammartino, *The Impossible Border*, 48.

6. Rüdiger von der Goltz, *Meine Sendung in Finnland und im Baltikum* (Leipzig: Koehler, 1920), 156 (for the numbers).

7. Hagen Schulze, *Freikorps und Republik, 1918–1920* (Boppard am Rhein: Boldt, 1969), 143.

8. Sammartino, *The Impossible Border*, 53.

9. Alfred von Samson-Himmelstjerna, 'Meine Erinnerungen an die Landwehrzeit', Herder Institut, Marburg, DSHI 120 BR BLW 9, p. 20.

10. Rudolf Höss, *Death Dealer: The Memoirs of the SS Kommandant at Auschwitz*, ed. Steven Paskuly (Buffalo, NY: Prometheus Books, 1992), 60.

11. Robert G. L. Waite, *Vanguard of Nazism: The Free Corps Movement in Postwar Germany, 1918–1923* (Cambridge, MA: Harvard University Press, 1952), 118–19.

12. Erich Balla, *Landsknechte wurden wir: Abenteuer aus dem Baltikum* (Berlin: W. Kolk, 1932), 111–12. Balla's embellished account was specifically designed to shock his audience and justify violent retaliation.

13. Ibid.

14. John Hiden and Martyn Housden, *Neighbours or Enemies? Germans,*

the Baltic, and Beyond (Amsterdam and New York: Editions Rodopi, 2008), 21.

15. Sammartino, *The Impossible Border*, 55.

16. Plakans, *The Latvians*, 108.

17. Julien Gueslin, 'Riga, de la métropole russe à la capitale de la Lettonie 1915–1919', in Philippe Chassaigne and Jean-Marc Largeaud (eds), *Villes en guerre (1914–1945)* (Paris: Amand Colin, 2004), 185–95; Suzanne Pourchier-Plasseraud, 'Riga 1905–2005: A City with Conflicting Identities', in *Nordost-Archiv* 15 (2006), 175–94, here 181.

18. Uldis Ģērmanis, *Oberst Vācietis und die lettischen Schützen im Weltkrieg und in der Oktoberrevolution* (Stockholm: Almqvist and Wiksell, 1974), 147, 155.

19. Balla, *Landsknechte*, 180–1.

20. Marguerite Yourcenar, *Coup de Grâce* (Paris: Éditions Gallimard, 1939).

21. Waite, *Vanguard of Nazism*, 118–19.

22. Sammartino, *The Impossible Border*, 59.

23. Charles L. Sullivan, 'The 1919 German Campaign in the Baltic: The Final Phase', in Stanley Vardys and Romuald Misiunas, *The Baltic States in Peace and War, 1917–1945* (London: Pennsylvania State University Press, 1978), 31–42.

24. Schulze, *Freikorps und Republik*, 184; Liulevicius, *War Land on the Eastern Front*, 232; Sammartino, *Impossible Border*, 63.

25. On the end of the Baltic campaign, see the extensive press coverage collated in the Herder Institut, Marburg, DSHI 120 BLW/BR 1/2.

26. Friedrich Wilhelm Heinz, *Sprengstoff* (Berlin: Frundsberg Verlag, 1930), 8–9.

27. Ernst von Salomon, *Die Geächteten* (Berlin: Rowohlt, 1923), 144–5.

28. On the Organisation Consul, responsible for these acts of terrorism, see in particular the files in the Institut für Zeitgeschichte (Munich), Fa 163/1 and MA 14412. See also Martin Sabrow, *Die verdrängte Verschwörung: Der Rathenau-Mord und die deutsche Gegenrevolution* (Frankfurt am Main: Fischer, 1999).

7. THE RUSSIAN CIVIL WARS

1. Evan Mawdsley, *The Russian Civil War* (Boston, MA, and London: Allen and Unwin, 1987), 45ff (ch. 4: 'The Allies in Russia, October 1917–November 1918, Archangelsk/Murmansk'); Alexandre Sumpf, 'Russian Civil War', in Ute Daniel, Peter Gatrell, Oliver Janz, Heather Jones, Jennifer Keene, Alan Kramer and Bill Nasson (eds), *1914–1918*

online. International Encyclopedia of the First World War; Jonathan D. Smele, *The 'Russian' Civil Wars 1916–1926: Ten Years that Shook the World* (Oxford: Oxford University Press, 2015); Peter Holquist, *Making War, Forging Revolution: Russia's Continuum of Crisis, 1914–1921* (Cambridge, MA: Harvard University Press, 2002).

2. On the Red Guards, see Rex Wade, *Red Guards and Workers' Militias in the Russian Revolution* (Palo Alto, CA: Stanford University Press, 1984); on the emerging Red Army, see Mark von Hagen, *Soldiers in the Proletarian Dictatorship: The Red Army and the Soviet Socialist State, 1917–1930* (Ithaca, NY: Cornell University Press, 1990).

3. William G. Rosenberg, 'Paramilitary Violence in Russia's Civil Wars, 1918–1920', in Robert Gerwarth and John Horne (eds), *War in Peace: Paramilitary Violence after the Great War* (Oxford and New York: Oxford University Press, 2012), 21–39, 37.

4. Nikolaus Katzer, 'Der weiße Mythos: Russischer Antibolschewismus im europäischen Nachkrieg', in Robert Gerwarth and John Horne (eds), *Krieg im Frieden. Paramilitärische Gewalt in Europa nach dem Ersten Weltkrieg* (Göttingen: Wallstein, 2013), 57–93; and idem, *Die weiße Bewegung: Herrschaftsbildung, praktische Politik und politische Programmatik im Bürgerkrieg* (Cologne, Weimar and Vienna: Böhlau, 1999).

5. Viktor P. Danilov, Viktor V. Kondrashin and Teodor Shanin (eds), *Nestor Makhno: M. Kubanin, Makhnovshchina. Krestyanskoe dvizhenie na Ukraine 1918–1921 gg. Dokumenty i Materialy* (Moscow: ROSSPEN, 2006); Felix Schnell, *Räume des Schreckens. Gewalt und Gruppenmilitanz in der Ukraine 1905–1933* (Hamburg: Hamburger Edition, HIS Verlag, 2012), 325–31; Serhy Yekelchyk, 'Bands of Nation-Builders? Insurgency and Ideology in the Ukrainian Civil War', in Gerwarth and Horne (eds), *War in Peace*, 107–25, here 120. For a survey of peasant insurgencies in Ukraine during 1918–20, see Andrea Graziosi, *The Great Soviet Peasant War: Bolsheviks and Peasants, 1917–1933* (Cambridge, MA: Harvard University Press, 1996), 11–37.

6. Sumpf, 'Russian Civil War', *1914–1918 online*.

7. Lenin, 'The Chief Task of Our Day', 12 March 1918, in Vladimir Ilyich Lenin, *Collected Works*, 45 vols, 4th English Edition, vol. 27 (Moscow: Progress Publishers, 1964–74), 15.

8. Geoffrey Swain, 'Trotsky and the Russian Civil War', in Ian D. Thatcher (ed.), *Reinterpreting Revolutionary Russia: Essays in Honour of James D. White* (Basingstoke: Palgrave, 2006), 86–104.

9. Evan Mawdsley, 'International Responses to the Russian Civil War (Russian Empire)', in *1914–1918 online. International Encyclopedia of the First World War.*

10. Mark Levene, *The Crisis of Genocide*, vol.1, 203.

11. Edward Hallett Carr, 'The Origins and Status of the Cheka', in *Soviet Studies* 10 (1958), 1–11; George Leggert, *The Cheka: Lenin's Political Police, the All-Russian Extraordinary Commission for Combating Counter-Revolution and Sabotage (December 1917 to February 1922)* (Oxford: Clarendon Press, 1981); Semen S. Chromow, *Feliks Dzierzynski: Biographie*, 3rd edition (East Berlin: Dietz, 1989).

12. Edward Hallett Carr, *The Bolshevik Revolution 1917–1923* (London: Macmillan, 1950), vol. 1, ch. 7 ('Consolidating the Dictatorship').

13. Lenin as quoted in Julie Fedor, *Russia and the Cult of State Security: The Chekist Tradition, from Lenin to Putin* (London: Routledge, 2011), 186, n. 12.

14. Douglas Smith, *Former People: The Final Days of the Russian Aristocracy* (London: Macmillan, 2012), 143.

15. Ibid; W. Bruce Lincoln, *Red Victory: A History of the Russian Civil War* (New York: Simon and Schuster, 1989), 159–61; Vladimir Petrovich Anichkov, *Ekaterinburg – Vladivostok, 1917–1922* (Moscow: Russkiĭ put', 1998), 155.

16. Orlando Figes, *Peasant Russia, Civil War: The Volga Countryside in Revolution, 1917–21* (Oxford and New York: Oxford University Press, 1989), 332, 351–3; Jonathan Aves, *Workers against Lenin: Labour Protest and Bolshevik Dictatorship* (London: Tauris Publishers, 1996); Felix Schnell, 'Der Sinn der Gewalt: Der Ataman Volynec und der Dauerpogrom von Gajsyn im russischen Bürgerkrieg', in *Zeithistorische Forschung* 5 (2008), 18–39; idem, *Räume des Schreckens*, 245–365.

17. Arno J. Mayer, *The Furies: Violence and Terror in the French and Russian Revolutions* (Princeton, NJ: Princeton University Press, 2000), 135, 272–4, 279–80.

18. Lenin, as quoted in Bertrand M. Patenaude, *The Big Show in Bololand: The American Relief Expedition to Soviet Russia in the Famine of 1921* (Stanford, CA: Stanford University Press, 2002), 20.

19. Katzer, *Die weiße Bewegung*, 269–70; Martin, '*Für ein freies Russland . . .': Die Bauernaufstände in den Gouvernements Tambov und Tjumen 1920–1922* (Heidelberg: Winter, 2010), 168; James E. Mace, *Communism and the Dilemmas of National Liberation: National Communism in Soviet Ukraine 1918–1933* (Cambridge, MA: Harvard University Press, 1983), 65ff.

20. Bruno Cabanes, *The Great War and the Origins of Humanitarianism 1918–1924* (Cambridge and New York: Cambridge University Press, 2014), 197. On the food brigades in the southern Volga region, see Figes, *Peasant Russia*, 262–7.

21. Lenin's letter to V. V. Kuraev, E. B. Bosh and A. E. Minkin, 11 August 1918, as quoted in Ronald Grigor Suny, *The Structure of Soviet History: Essays and Documents* (Oxford and New York: Oxford University Press, 2014), 83.

22. Taisia Osipova, 'Peasant Rebellions: Origins, Scope, Dynamics, and Consequences', in Vladimir N. Brovkin (ed.), *The Bolsheviks in Russian Society* (New Haven, CT, and London: Yale University Press, 1997), 154–76.

23. Dietrich Beyrau, 'Brutalization Revisited: The Case of Bolshevik Russia', in *Journal of Contemporary History* 50 (2015), 36; Figes, *Peasant Russia*, 319–28, 333–46; Krispin, *'Für ein freies Russland . . .'*, 181–97, 400–2; Vladimir N. Brovkin, *Behind the Front Lines of the Civil War: Political Parties and Social Movements in Russia, 1918–1922* (Princeton, NJ: Princeton University Press, 1994), 82–5; Holquist, *Making War*, 166–205; Orlando Figes, *A People's Tragedy: The Russian Revolution, 1891–1924* (London: Jonathan Cape, 1996), 757.

24. Maxim Gorky, 'On the Russian Peasantry', in Robert E. F. Smith (ed.), *The Russian Peasant, 1920 and 1984* (London: Routledge, 1977), 11–27, here 16ff.

25. Rudolph Joseph Rummel, *Lethal Politics: Soviet Genocide and Mass Murder since 1917* (Piscataway, NJ: Transaction Publishers, 1990), 38. On the use of poison gas, see Richard Pipes, *Russia under the Bolshevik Regime* (New York: Knopf, 1993), 387–401. Nicolas Werth, 'L'ex-Empire russe, 1918–1921: Les mutations d'une guerre prolongée', in Stéphane Audoin-Rouzeau and Christophe Prochasson (eds), *Sortir de la Grande Guerre: Le monde et l'après-1918* (Paris: Tallandier, 2008), 285–306.

26. David Bullock, *The Czech Legion, 1914–20* (Oxford: Osprey, 2008), 17–24; John F. N. Bradley, *The Czechoslovak Legion in Russia, 1914–1920* (Boulder, CO: East European Monographs, 1991), 156; Gerburg Thunig-Nittner, *Die Tschechoslowakische Legion in Rußland: Ihre Geschichte und Bedeutung bei der Entstehung der 1. Tschechoslowakischen Republik* (Wiesbaden: Harrassowitz, 1970), 73ff; Victor M. Fic, *The Bolsheviks and the Czechoslovak Legion: The Origins of their Armed Conflict (March–May 1918)* (New Delhi: Shakti Malik, 1978).

27. Thunig-Nittner, *Tschechoslowakische Legion*, 61–90. On their heroization in interwar Czechoslovakia, see Natali Stegmann, *Kriegsdeutungen, Staatsgründungen, Sozialpolitik: Der Helden- und Opferdiskurs in der Tschechoslowakei, 1918–1948* (Munich: Oldenbourg, 2010), 69–70.

28. Fic, *The Bolsheviks and the Czechoslovak Legion*, 284ff.

29. Gustav Habrman, *Mé vzpomínky z války* (Prague: Svěcený, 1928), 46–7. On the increasing willingness to use ultra-violence against prisoners and unarmed civilians, see Thunig-Nittner, *Tschechoslowakische Legion*, 46–57.

30. Manfred Hildermeier, *Geschichte der Sowjetunion 1917–1991: Entstehung und Niedergang des ersten sozialistischen Staates* (Munich: C. H. Beck, 1998), 137–9; Heinrich August Winkler, *The Age of Catastrophe: A History of the West 1914–1945* (New Haven, CT, and London: Yale University Press, 2015), 59.

31. John Channon, 'Siberia in Revolution and Civil War, 1917–1921', in Alan Wood (ed.), *The History of Siberia: From Russian Conquest to Revolution* (London and New York: Routledge, 1991), 158–80, here 165–6; Brovkin, *Behind the Front Lines of the Civil War*, 300ff.

32. Thunig-Nittner, *Tschechoslowakische Legion*, 57ff; Jonathan D. Smele, *Civil War in Siberia: The Anti-Bolshevik Government of Admiral Kolchak, 1918–1920* (Cambridge: Cambridge University Press, 1996), 33ff; Norman G. O. Pereira, *White Siberia: The Politics of Civil War* (Montreal: McGill-Queen's University Press, 1996), 67ff.

33. Hélène Carrère d'Encausse, *Nikolaus II.: Das Drama des letzten Zaren* (Vienna: Zsolnay, 1998), 471; Edvard Radzinsky, *The Last Tsar: The Life and Death of Nicholas II* (New York: Doubleday, 1992), 304.

34. Dominic Lieven, *Nicholas II: Emperor of all the Russians* (London: Pimlico, 1994), 244–6.

35. Mawdsley, *The Russian Civil War*, 70.

36. Finlayson report, as quoted in Catherine Margaret Boylan, 'The North Russia Relief Force: A Study of Military Morale and Motivation in the Post-First World War World', unpublished PhD thesis, King's College London, 2015, here 252.

37. Sumpf, 'Russian Civil War', *1914–1918 online*.

38. Winfried Baumgart, *Deutsche Ostpolitik 1918: Von Brest-Litovsk bis zum Ende des Ersten Weltkriegs* (Vienna and Munich: Oldenbourg, 1966), 140ff; Mawdsley, 'International Responses', *1914–1918 online*.

39. On Denikin, see Dimitry V. Lehovich, *White against Red: The Life of General Anton Denikin* (New York: W. W. Norton, 1974); Yu. N. Gordeev, *General Denikin: Voenno-istoricheski ocherk* (Moscow: TPF 'Arkaiur', 1993).

40. Mawdsley, 'International Responses', *1914–1918 online*; Peter Flemming, *The Fate of Admiral Kolchak* (London: Hart-Davis, 1964); K. Bogdanov, *Admiral Kolchak: Biograficheskaia povest-khronika* (St Petersburg: Sudostroenie, 1993).

41. Apart from the older literature on the Allied intervention, a host of recent PhD theses have been devoted to the British intervention in particular. See Lauri Kopisto, 'The British Intervention in South Russia 1918–1920', unpublished PhD thesis, University of Helsinki, 2011; Boylan, 'North Russia Relief Force'; Steven Balbirnie, 'British Imperialism in the Arctic: The British Occupation of Archangel and Murmansk, 1918–1919', unpublished PhD thesis, University College Dublin, 2015.

42. Margaret MacMillan, *Peacemakers: The Paris Conference of 1919 and its Attempt to End War* (London: John Murray, 2001), 81.

43. John Keep, '1917: The Tyranny of Paris over Petrograd', in *Soviet Studies* 20 (1968), 22–35.

44. 'Can "Jacobinism" Frighten the Working Class?' (7 July 1917), in Lenin, *Collected Works*, vol. 25, 121–2.

45. Winkler, *Age of Catastrophe*, 165.

46. Rosenberg, 'Paramilitary Violence in Russia's Civil Wars', in Gerwarth and Horne (eds), *War in Peace*, 21–39. For an overview and concrete examples, see Figes, *People's Tragedy*. Several excellent studies exist on different geographical areas. On Transcaucasia, see Jörg Baberowski, *Der Feind ist überall: Stalinismus im Kaukasus* (Munich: Deutsche Verlags-Anstalt, 2003); on central Asia, see Hélène Carrère d'Encausse, *Islam and the Russian Empire: Reform and Revolution in Central Asia* (Berkeley, CA, and London: University of California Press, 1988); on the West and Ukraine, see Christoph Mick, 'Vielerlei Kriege: Osteuropa 1918–1921', in Dietrich Beyrau et al. (eds), *Formen des Krieges von der Antike bis zur Gegenwart* (Paderborn: Schöningh, 2007), 311–26; Piotr J. Wróbel, 'The Seeds of Violence: The Brutalization of an East European Region 1917–1921', in *Journal of Modern European History* 1 (2003), 125–49; Schnell, *Räume des Schreckens*.

47. Williard Sunderland, *The Baron's Cloak: A History of the Russian Empire in War and Revolution* (Ithaca, NY, and London: Cornell University Press, 2014), 133ff.

48. Katzer, *Die weiße Bewegung*, 285; Anthony Reid, *The World on Fire: 1919 and the Battle with Bolshevism* (London: Pimlico, 2009), 23.

49. James Palmer, *The Bloody White Baron: The Extraordinary Story of the Russian Nobleman who Became the Last Khan of Mongolia* (New York: Basic Books, 2014), 153–7 (on the conquest of Urga), 179 (Mongolian independence from China), and 196 (changing attitudes towards Ungern).

50. D. D. Aleshin, 'Aziatskaya Odisseya', in S. L. Kuz'min (ed.), *Baron Ungern v dokumentach i memuarach* (Moscow: Tovariščestvo Naučnych Izd. KMK, 2004), 421.

51. Udo B. Barkmann, *Geschichte der Mongolei oder Die 'Mongolische Frage': Die Mongolen auf ihrem Weg zum eigenen Nationalstaat* (Bonn: Bouvier Verlag, 1999) 192–6, 202–5; Canfield F. Smith, 'The Ungernovščina – How and Why?' in *Jahrbücher für Geschichte Osteuropas* 28 (1980), 590–5.

52. Hiroaki Kuromiya, *Freedom and Terror in the Donbas: A Ukrainian-Russian Borderland 1870s–1990s* (Cambridge and New York: Cambridge University Press, 1998), 95–114; Katzer, *Die weiße Bewegung*, 284–91; Oleg Budnitskii, *Russian Jews between the Reds and Whites, 1917–1920* (Philadelphia, PA: University of Pennsylvania Press, 2011), 123ff.

53. Budnitskii, *Russian Jews between the Reds and Whites.*

54. Greg King and Penny Wilson, *The Fate of the Romanovs* (Hoboken, NJ: John Wiley and Sons, 2003), 352–3; Léon Poliakov, *The History of Anti-Semitism*, vol. 4: *Suicidal Europe, 1870–1933* (Philadelphia, PA: University of Pennsylvania Press, 2003), 182; Mark Levene, *Crisis of Genocide*, vol. 1: *The European Rimlands 1912–1938* (Oxford and New York: Oxford University Press, 2014), 191.

55. Norman Cohn, *Warrant for Genocide: The Myth of the Jewish World Conspiracy and the Protocols of the Elders of Zion* (London: Serif, 1996).

56. Tomas Balkelis, 'Turning Citizens into Soldiers: Baltic Paramilitary Movements after the Great War', in Gerwarth and Horne (eds), *War in Peace*, 136; Aivars Stranga, 'Communist Dictatorship in Latvia: December 1918–January 1920: Ethnic Policy', in *Lithuanian Historical Studies* 13 (2008), 161–78, 171ff.

57. Levene, *Crisis of Genocide*, vol. 1, 187–8.

58. On the infamous 1918 pogrom in Lwów, for example, see Hagen, 'The Moral Economy of Ethnic Violence'; Wehrhahn, *Die Westukrainische Volksrepublik*, 154–6; Mroczka, 'Przyczynek do kwestii żydowskiej w Galicji', 300ff. See also Christoph Mick, *Lemberg – Lwów – L'viv, 1914–1947: Violence and Ethnicity in a Contested City* (West Lafayette, IN: Purdue University Press, 2015). Mark Mazower, 'Minorities and the League of Nations in Interwar Europe', in *Daedulus* 126 (1997), 47–63, here 50. Frank Golczewski, *Polnisch-jüdische Beziehungen, 1881–1922: Eine Studie zur Geschichte des Antisemitismus in Osteuropa* (Wiesbaden: Steiner, 1981), 205–13.

59. The pogrom of Proskurov, along with several others, was investigated by delegates of the 'All-Ukrainian Relief Committee for the Victims of Pogroms' under the auspices of the International Red Cross. The Committee carried out its fieldwork during 1919 and

· prepared a report that was published for the Jewish People's Relief Committee of America: Elias Heifetz, *The Slaughter of the Jews in the Ukraine in 1919* (New York: Thomas Seltzer, 1921). They also exist as individual reports. The eyewitness accounts quoted here are extracts from the report of A. I. Hillerson in the Committee of the Jewish Delegations, *The Pogroms in the Ukraine under the Ukrainian Governments (1917–1920)*, ed. I. B. Schlechtmann (London: Bale, 1927), 176–80.

60. Hillerson, *The Pogroms in the Ukraine*, 176–80.

61. Ibid ('evidence of Joseph Aptman, restaurant keeper at Felshtin'), annex no. 30, p. 193ff.

62. Mayer, *The Furies*, 524.

63. See Leonard Schapiro, 'The Role of Jews in the Russian Revolutionary Movement', in *The Slavonic and East European Review* 40:94 (1961), 148–67; Zvi Y. Gitelman, *Jewish Nationality and Soviet Politics: The Jewish Sections of the CPSU 1917–1930* (Princeton, NJ: Princeton University Press, 1972), 114–19, 163–8.

64. Budnitskii, *Russian Jews between the Reds and Whites*, 397.

65. Baberowski, *Der Feind ist überall*, 158–60.

66. Mawdsley, 'International Responses', *1914–1918 online*.

67. Beyrau, 'Brutalization Revisited', 33.

68. Sumpf, 'Russian Civil War', *1914–1918 online*.

69. Mawdsley, 'International Responses', *1914–1918 online*.

70. Sumpf, 'Russian Civil War', *1914–1918 online*.

71. Mawdsley, 'International Responses', *1914–1918 online*.

72. Mawdsley, *The Russian Civil War*, 377–86; Sumpf, 'Russian Civil War', *1914–1918 online*; MacMillan, *Peacemakers*, 90.

73. On the Russian famine, see Patenaude, *The Big Show in Bololand*. See also the classic work of Robert Conquest, *The Harvest of Sorrows: Soviet Collectivization and the Terror-Famine* (Oxford and New York: Oxford University Press, 1986); and the local study by Mary McAuley, *Bread and Justice: State and Society in Petrograd, 1917–1922* (Oxford: Clarendon Press, 1991), 397. For demographic development, see Sergueï Adamets, *Guerre civile et famine en Russie: Le pouvoir bolchevique et la population face à la catastrophe démographique, 1917–1923* (Paris: Institut d'études slaves, 2003).

74. For these estimates, see Dietrich Beyrau, 'Post-War Societies (Russian Empire)', in *1914–1918 online. International Encyclopedia of the First World War*; Jurij Aleksandrovič Poljakov et al., *Naselenie Rossii v XX veke: istoričeskie očerki*, vol. 1 (Moscow: ROSSPEN, 2000), 94–5.

75. Conquest, *Harvest of Sorrows*, 54ff.

76. *American Relief Administration Bulletin*, December 1923, as quoted in Cabanes, *Origins of Humanitarianism*, 202ff.

77. Mawdsley, *The Russian Civil War*, 399–400; Nicholas Riasanovsky and Mark Steinberg, *A History of Russia* (Oxford and New York: Oxford University Press, 2005), 474–5; Donald J. Raleigh, 'The Russian Civil War 1917–1922', in Ronald Grigor Suny (ed.), *The Cambridge History of Russia*, vol. 3 (Cambridge: Cambridge University Press, 2006), 140–67; Alan Ball, 'Building a New State and Society: NEP, 1921–1928', in Ronald Grigor Suny (ed.), *The Cambridge History of Russia*, vol. 3 (Cambridge: Cambridge University Press, 2006), 168–191; Smith, *Former People*, 213.

78. Estimates of the exact number of refugees vary. See Poljakov et al., *Naselenie*, vol. 1, 134; Boris Raymond and David R. Jones, *The Russian Diaspora 1917–1941* (Lanham, MD: Scarecrow, 2000), 7–10; Michael Glenny and Norman Stone (eds), *The Other Russia: The Experience of Exile* (London: Faber and Faber, 1990), xx; Raleigh, 'The Russian Civil War', 166.

79. On wartime refugees, see especially Peter Gatrell, *A Whole Empire Walking: Refugees in Russia during World War I* (Bloomington, IN: Indiana University Press, 1999); Nick Baron and Peter Gatrell, 'Population Displacement, State-Building and Social Identity in the Lands of the Former Russian Empire, 1917–1923', in *Kritika: Explorations in Russian and Eurasian History* 4 (2003), 51–100; Alan Kramer, 'Deportationen', in Gerhard Hirschfeld, Gerd Krumeich and Irina Renz (eds), *Enzyklopädie Erster Weltkrieg* (Paderborn: Schöningh, 2009), 434–5. Joshua A. Sanborn, 'Unsettling the Empire: Violent Migrations and Social Disaster in Russia during World War I', in *The Journal of Modern History* 77 (2005), 290–324, 310; Mark von Hagen, *War in a European Borderland: Occupations and Occupation Plans in Galicia and Ukraine, 1914–1918* (Seattle, WA: University of Washington Press, 2007). On displacement on the Western Front, see Philippe Nivet, *Les réfugiés français de la Grande Guerre, 1914–1920: Les 'boches du nord'* (Paris: Institut de stratégie comparée, 2004); Pierre Purseigle, '"A Wave on to Our Shores": The Exile and Resettlement of Refugees from the Western Front, 1914–1918', in *Contemporary European History* 16 (2007), 427–44.

80. Catherine Goussef, *L'Exil russe: La fabrique du réfugié apatride (1920–1939)* (Paris: CNRS Editions, 2008), 60–3.

81. On Berlin, see Michael Ignatieff, *Isaiah Berlin: A Life* (London: Chatto and Windus, 1998).

82. Marc Raef, *Russia Abroad: A Cultural History of the Russian Emigra-*

tion, 1919–1939 (Oxford and New York: Oxford University Press, 1990). On France, see Goussef, *L'Exil russe.* On Prague, see Catherine Andreyev and Ivan Savicky, *Russia Abroad: Prague and the Russian Diaspora 1918–1938* (New Haven, CT, and London: Yale University Press, 2004).

83. Robert C. Williams, *Culture in Exile: Russian Emigrés in Germany, 1881–1941* (Ithaca, NY: Cornell University Press, 1972), 114; Fritz Mierau, *Russen in Berlin, 1918–1933* (Berlin: Quadriga, 1988), 298; Karl Schlögel (ed.), *Chronik russischen Lebens in Deutschland, 1918 bis 1941* (Berlin: Akademie Verlag, 1999).

84. See Viktor Petrov, 'The Town on the Sungari', in Stone and Glenny (eds), *The Other Russia,* 205–21.

85. Paul Robinson, *The White Russian Army in Exile, 1920–1941* (Oxford and New York: Oxford University Press, 2002), 41; Cabanes, *Origins of Humanitarianism,* 141ff.

86. International Red Cross Report on Russian Refugees in Constantinople, as quoted in Cabanes, *Origins of Humanitarianism,* 142.

87. Ibid, 155ff. On Nansen, see Roland Huntford, *Nansen: The Explorer as Hero* (New York: Barnes and Noble Books, 1998); Martyn Housden, 'When the Baltic Sea was a Bridge for Humanitarian Action: The League of Nations, the Red Cross and the Repatriation of Prisoners of War between Russia and Central Europe, 1920–22', in *Journal of Baltic Studies* 38 (2007), 61–83.

88. Michael Kellogg, *The Russian Roots of Nazism: White Russians and the Making of National Socialism, 1917–1945* (Cambridge and New York: Cambridge University Press, 2005).

89. Robert Gerwarth and John Horne (eds), 'Vectors of Violence: Paramilitarism in Europe after the Great War, 1917–1923', in *The Journal of Modern History* 83 (2011), 497.

90. Robert Gerwarth and John Horne, 'Bolshevism as Fantasy: Fear of Revolution and Counter-Revolutionary Violence, 1917–1923', in Gerwarth and Horne (eds), *War in Peace,* 40ff.

91. Churchill as quoted in MacMillan, *Peacemakers,* 75.

92. For a whole catalogue of reported horrors, see George Pitt-Rivers, *The World Significance of the Russian Revolution* (London: Blackwell, 1920); Read, *The World on Fire,* 23.

93. *The New York Times,* as quoted in David Mitchell, *1919: Red Mirage* (London: Jonathan Cape, 1970), 20ff.

94. Quoted in Mark William Jones, 'Violence and Politics in the German Revolution, 1918–19', unpublished PhD thesis, European University Institute, 2011, 89–90.

95. Gerwarth and Horne, 'Bolshevism as Fantasy', 46–8.
96. Robert Gerwarth and Martin Conway, 'Revolution and Counter-Revolution', in Donald Bloxham and Robert Gerwarth (eds), *Political Violence in Twentieth-Century Europe* (Cambridge and New York: Cambridge University Press, 2011), 140–75.
97. David Kirby, *A Concise History of Finland* (Cambridge and New York: Cambridge University Press, 2006), 152ff.
98. Pertti Haapala and Marko Tikka, 'Revolution, Civil War and Terror in Finland in 1918', in Gerwarth and Horne (eds), *War in Peace*, 71–83.
99. On the Finnish Civil War in English, see Anthony Upton, *The Finnish Revolution, 1917–18* (Minneapolis, MN: University of Minnesota Press, 1980); Risto Alapuro, *State and Revolution in Finland* (Berkeley, CA: University of California Press, 1988); Tuomas Hoppu and Pertti Haapala (eds), *Tampere 1918: A Town in the Civil War* (Tampere: Tampere Museums, 2010); Jason Lavery, 'Finland 1917–19: Three Conflicts, One Country', in *Scandinavian Review* 94 (2006), 6–14; Mawdsley, *The Russian Civil War*, 27–9.
100. Ibid.

8. THE APPARENT TRIUMPH OF DEMOCRACY

1. *Berliner Tageblatt*, 10 November 1918.
2. Adam Seipp, *The Ordeal of Demobilization and the Urban Experience in Britain and Germany, 1917–1921* (Farnham: Ashgate, 2009); Scott Stephenson, *The Final Battle: Soldiers of the Western Front and the German Revolution of 1918* (Cambridge and New York: Cambridge University Press, 2009), 187; Richard Bessel, *Germany after the First World War* (Oxford and New York: Oxford University Press, 1993).
3. Ian Kershaw, *Hitler*, vol. 1: *Hubris, 1889–1936* (London: Allen Lane, 1998), 102.
4. Karl Hampe, *Kriegstagebuch 1914–1919*, ed. Folker Reichert and Eike Wolgast, 2nd edition (Munich: Oldenbourg, 2007), 775 (entry of 10 November 1918).
5. Elard von Oldenburg-Januschau, *Erinnerungen* (Berlin: Loehler and Amelang, 1936), 208; see also Elard von Oldenburg-Januschau, as quoted in Stephan Malinowski, *Vom König zum Führer: Sozialer Niedergang und politische Radikalisierung im deutschen Adel zwischen Kaiserreich und NS-Staat* (Frankfurt am Main: Fischer, 2003), 207.
6. Bernhard von Bülow, *Denkwürdigkeiten* (Berlin: Ullstein, 1931), 305–12.

7. Eberhard Straub, *Albert Ballin: Der Reeder des Kaisers* (Berlin: Siedler, 2001), 257–61.
8. Heinrich August Winkler, *Weimar 1918–1933: Die Geschichte der ersten deutschen Demokratie* (Munich: C. H. Beck, 1993), 25ff and 87ff.
9. Walter Mühlhausen, *Friedrich Ebert, 1871–1925: Reichspräsident der Weimarer Republik* (Bonn: Dietz Verlag, 2006), 42ff. See also Dieter Dowe and Peter-Christian Witt, *Friedrich Ebert 1871–1925: Vom Arbeiterführer zum Reichspräsidenten* (Bonn: Friedrich-Ebert-Stiftung, 1987).
10. Dieter Engelmann and Horst Naumann, *Hugo Haase: Lebensweg und politisches Vermächtnis eines streitbaren Sozialisten* (Berlin: Edition Neue Wege, 1999).
11. Quoted in Heinrich Winkler, *Von der Revolution zur Stabilisierung: Arbeiter und Arbeiterbewegung in der Weimarer Republik, 1918 bis 1924* (Berlin: Dietz, 1984), 39. On Ebert's life, see Dowe and Witt, *Friedrich Ebert*; Mühlhausen, *Friedrich Ebert*.
12. See Bernd Braun, 'Die "Generation Ebert"', in idem and Klaus Schönhoven (eds), *Generationen in der Arbeiterbewegung* (Munich: Oldenbourg, 2005), 69–86.
13. Klaus Hock, *Die Gesetzgebung des Rates der Volksbeauftragten* (Pfaffenweiler: Centaurus, 1987); Friedrich-Carl Wachs, *Das Verordnungswerk des Reichsdemobilmachungsamtes* (Frankfurt am Main: Peter Lang, 1991); Bessel, *Germany after the First World War.*
14. For this concept, see Wolfgang Schivelbusch, *The Culture of Defeat: On National Trauma, Mourning and Recovery* (New York: Holt, 2003). On the trauma of defeat and collective memory, see Jay Winter, *Sites of Memory, Sites of Mourning: The Great War in European Cultural History* (Cambridge and New York: Cambridge University Press, 1995); Stefan Goebel, 'Re-Membered and Re-Mobilized: The "Sleeping Dead" in Interwar Germany and Britain', in *Journal of Contemporary History* 39 (2004), 487–501; Benjamin Ziemann, *Contested Commemorations: Republican War Veterans and Weimar Political Culture* (Cambridge and New York: Cambridge University Press, 2013); Claudia Siebrecht, *The Aesthetics of Loss: German Women's Art of the First World War* (Oxford and New York: Oxford University Press, 2013).
15. Heinz Hürten (ed.), *Zwischen Revolution und Kapp-Putsch: Militaer und Innenpolitik, 1918–1920* (Düsseldorf: Droste, 1977).
16. Gerald D. Feldman, 'Das deutsche Unternehmertum zwischen Krieg und Revolution: Die Entstehung des Stinnes-Legien-Abkommens', in idem, *Vom Weltkrieg zur Weltwirtschaftskrise: Studien zur deutschen*

Wirtschafts- und Sozialgeschichte 1914–1932 (Göttingen: Vandenhoeck and Ruprecht, 1984), 100–27; idem and Irmgard Steinisch, *Industrie und Gewerkschaften 1918–1924: Die überforderte Zentralarbeitsgemeinschaft* (Stuttgart: DVA, 1985), 135–7.

17. Winkler, *Weimar*, 69.

18. On Austria-Hungary's final years and revolution, see Holger Herwig, *The First World War: Germany and Austria-Hungary, 1914–1918* (London: Bloomsbury, 1996), and, more recently, Alexander Watson, *Ring of Steel: Germany and Austria-Hungary at War, 1914–18* (London: Allen Lane, 2014). A detailed classic account can also be found in Richard G. Plaschka, Horst Haselsteiner and Arnold Suppan, *Innere Front. Militärassistenz, Widerstand und Umsturz in der Donaumonarchie 1918*, 2 vols (Vienna: Verlag für Geschichte und Politik, 1974); and in Manfried Rauchensteiner, *Der Tod des Doppeladlers: Österreich-Ungarn und der Erste Weltkrieg* (Graz: Styria, 1993). A perceptive recent study of the effects of the war in Vienna is offered by Maureen Healy, *Vienna and the Fall of the Habsburg Empire: Total War and Everyday Life in World War I* (Cambridge and New York: Cambridge University Press, 2004). See also the essay collection in Günther Bischof, Fritz Plasser and Peter Berger (eds), *From Empire to Republic: Post-World War I Austria* (Innsbruck: Innsbruck University Press, 2010).

19. For a good discussion of this position and its deconstruction, see Clifford F. Wargelin, 'A High Price for Bread: The First Treaty of Brest-Litovsk and the Break-up of Austria-Hungary, 1917–1918', in *The International History Review* 19 (1997), 757–88.

20. Ibid.

21. Ibid, 762.

22. Reinhard J. Sieder, 'Behind the Lines: Working-Class Family Life in Wartime Vienna', in Richard Wall and Jay Winter (eds), *The Upheaval of War: Family, Work and Welfare in Europe, 1914–1918* (Cambridge and New York: Cambridge University Press, 1988), 125–8; Wargelin, 'A High Price for Bread', 777. For the strikes, see Plaschka et al., *Innere Front*, vol. 1, 59–106, 251–74.

23. Otto Bauer, *Die österreichische Revolution* (Vienna: Wiener Volksbuchhandlung, 1923), 66; Plaschka et al., *Innere Front*, vol. 1, 107–48; Wargelin, 'A High Price for Bread', 783.

24. Bauer, *Die österreichische Revolution*, 71–2; Plaschka et al., *Innere Front*, vol. 1, 62–103. For a more positive view on the performance of the Habsburg Army, see István Deák, *Beyond Nationalism: A Social and Political History of the Habsburg Officer Corps, 1848–1918*

(Oxford and New York: Oxford University Press, 1990); Greyton A. Tunstall, *Blood on the Snow: The Carpathian Winter War of 1915* (Lawrence, KS: University Press of Kansas, 2010).

25. Karel Pichlík, 'Der militärische Zusammenbruch der Mittelmächte im Jahre 1918', in Richard Georg Plaschka and Karlheinz Mack (eds), *Die Auflösung des Habsburgerreiches: Zusammenbruch und Neuorientierung im Donauraum* (Munich: Verlag für Geschichte und Politik, 1970), 249–65.

26. Bauer, *Die österreichische Revolution*, 79, 82, 90–2, 97; Rauchensteiner, *Tod des Doppeladlers*, 612–14.

27. Patrick J. Houlihan, 'Was There an Austrian Stab-in-the-Back Myth? Interwar Military Interpretations of Defeat', in Bischof et al. (eds), *From Empire to Republic*, 67–89, here 72. Other histories of Austrian authoritarian movements and anti-Semitism in the twentieth century only briefly mention the existence of an Austrian 'stab-in-the-back' myth but do not explore it in detail. See Steven Beller, *A Concise History of Austria* (Cambridge: Cambridge University Press, 2006), 209. See also Francis L. Carsten, *Fascist Movements in Austria: From Schönerer to Hitler* (London: Sage, 1977), 95; Bruce F. Pauley, *From Prejudice to Persecution: A History of Austrian Anti-Semitism* (Chapel Hill, NC: University of North Carolina Press, 1992), 159. For a more in-depth analysis on how the myth was disseminated through memoirs of former military officers, see Gergely Romsics, *Myth and Remembrance: The Dissolution of the Habsburg Empire in the Memoir Literature of the Austro-Hungarian Political Elite* (New York: Columbia University Press, 2006), 37–43.

28. Wolfgang Maderthaner, 'Utopian Perspectives and Political Restraint: The Austrian Revolution in the Context of Central European Conflicts', in Bischof et al. (eds), *From Empire to Republic*, 52–66, 53; Francis L. Carsten, *Die Erste Österreichische Republik im Spiegel zeitgenössischer Quellen* (Vienna: Böhlau, 1988), 11ff.

29. On Adler, see Douglas D. Alder, 'Friedrich Adler: Evolution of a Revolutionary', in *German Studies Review* 1 (1978), 260–84; John Zimmermann, *'Von der Bluttat eines Unseligen': Das Attentat Friedrich Adlers und seine Rezeption in der sozialdemokratischen Presse* (Hamburg: Verlag Dr. Kovač, Hamburg, 2000); on his relationship with Einstein, see Michaela Maier and Wolfgang Maderthaner (eds), *Physik und Revolution: Friedrich Adler – Albert Einstein: Briefe, Dokumente, Stellungnahmen* (Vienna: Locker, 2006).

30. *Neues Wiener Tagblatt*, 3 November 1918, as quoted in Maderthaner, 'Utopian Perspectives and Political Restraint', 52ff.

31. Bauer, *Die österreichische Revolution*, 121.

32. Maderthaner, 'Utopian Perspectives and Political Restraint', 55.

33. Netherlands Institute for War, Holocaust and Genocide Studies, Amsterdam: Rauter Papers, Doc I 1380, H, 2.

34. Oberösterreichisches Landesarchiv (Linz), Ernst Rüdiger Starhemberg Papers, Aufzeichnungen, 20–2.

35. Franz Brandl, *Kaiser, Politiker, und Menschen: Erinnerungen eines Wiener Polizeipräsidenten* (Vienna and Leipzig: Günther, 1936), 265–6.

36. Maderthaner, 'Utopian Perspectives and Political Restraint', 61.

37. Peter Broucek, *Karl I. (IV.): Der politische Weg des letzten Herrschers der Donaumonarchie* (Vienna: Böhlau, 1997); Pieter M. Judson, *The Habsburg Empire: A New History* (Cambridge, MA: Harvard University Press, 2016), 338–442.

38. Margaret MacMillan, *Peacemakers: The Paris Conference of 1919 and Its Attempt to End War* (London: John Murray, 2001), 261.

39. Maderthaner, 'Utopian Perspectives and Political Restraint', 57.

40. Lyubomir Ognyanov, *Voynishkoto vastanie 1918* [*The Soldiers' Uprising*] (Sofia: Nauka i izkustvo, 1988), 74.

41. Nikolai Vukov, 'The Aftermaths of Defeat: The Fallen, the Catastrophe, and the Public Response of Women to the End of the First World War in Bulgaria', in Ingrid Sharp and Matthew Stibbe (eds), *Aftermaths of War: Women's Movements and Female Activists, 1918–1923* (Leiden: Brill, 2011), 29–47.

42. Letters quoted in Ognyanov, *Voynishkoto vastanie 1918*, 84 and 89.

43. On the soldiers' uprising and the violence in Bulgaria during the postwar years, see Ognyanov, *Voynishkoto vastanie 1918*; Boyan Kastelov, *Ot fronta do Vladaya: Dokumentalen ocherk* (Sofia: BZNS, 1978); idem, *Bulgaria – ot voyna kam vastanie* (Sofia: Voenno izdatelstvo, 1988); Ivan Draev, *Bulgarskata 1918: Istoricheski ocherk za Vladayskoto vastanie* (Sofia: Narodna prosveta, 1970); Tsvetan Grozev, *Voynishkoto vastanie, 1918: Sbornik dokumenti i spomeni* (Sofia: BKP, 1967).

44. About these interpretations in the historiography of the Communist period and after 1989, see Georgi Georgiev, *Propusnata pobeda – Voynishkoto vastanie, 1918* (Sofia: Partizdat, 1989); Nikolay Mizov, *Vliyanieto na Velikata oktomvriyska sotsialisticheska revolyutsia varhu Vladayskoto vaorazheno vastanie na voynishkite masi u nas prez septembri 1918 godina* (Sofia: NS OF, 1957); Kanyu Kozhuharov, *Radomirskata republika, 1918–1948* (Sofia: BZNS, 1948); Kosta Nikolov, *Kletvoprestapnitsite: Vladayskite sabitiya prez septemvri 1918* (Sofia: AngoBoy, 2002).

45. Richard C. Hall, 'Bulgaria in the First World War', in russiasgreatwar .org.

46. Ryan Gingeras, *Fall of the Sultanate: The Great War and the End of the Ottoman Empire, 1908–1922* (Oxford and New York: Oxford University Press, 2016), 236ff.

47. Ibid, 253.

48. Edward J. Erickson, *Ordered to Die: A History of the Ottoman Army in the First World War* (Westport, CT, and London: Greenwood Press, 2001), 237–43. On the number of soldiers who died as a consequence of disease, see Erik J. Zürcher, 'The Ottoman Soldier in World War I', in idem, *The Young Turk Legacy and Nation Building: From the Ottoman Empire to Atatürk's Turkey* (London: I. B. Tauris, 2010), 167–87.

49. Mustafa Aksakal, 'The Ottoman Empire', in Robert Gerwarth and Erez Manela (eds), *Empires at War, 1911–1923* (Oxford and New York: Oxford University Press, 2014), 17–33. On the Armenian genocide, see Donald Bloxham, 'The First World War and the Development of the Armenian Genocide', in Ronald Grigor Suny, Fatma Müge Göçek and Norman M. Naimark (eds), *A Question of Genocide: Armenians and Turks at the End of the Ottoman Empire* (Oxford and New York: Oxford University Press, 2011), 260–75; Ronald Grigor Suny, 'Explaining Genocide: The Fate of the Armenians in the Late Ottoman Empire', in Richard Bessel and Claudia Haake (eds), *Removing Peoples: Forced Removal in the Modern World* (Oxford and New York: Oxford University Press, 2009), 209–53, here 220. On wartime casualties in the Middle East, the locust plague and its dire consequences, see Salim Tamari (ed.), *Year of the Locust: A Soldier's Diary and the Erasure of Palestine's Ottoman Past* (Berkeley, CA: University of California Press, 2011); Elizabeth F. Thompson, *Colonial Citizens: Republican Rights, Paternal Privilege, and Gender in French Syria and Lebanon* (New York: Columbia University Press, 2000).

50. James Sheehan, *Where Have All the Soldiers Gone? The Transformation of Modern Europe* (New York: Houghton Mifflin, 2008), 94.

51. On the German case, see Kathleen Canning, 'The Politics of Symbols, Semantics, and Sentiments in the Weimar Republic', in *Central European History* 43 (2010), 567–80. On Austria, see Wolfgang Maderthaner, 'Die eigenartige Größe der Beschränkung. Österreichs Revolution im mitteleuropäischen Spannungsfeld', in Helmut Konrad and Wolfgang Maderthaner (eds), ... *der Rest ist Österreich: Das Werden der Ersten Republik*, vol. 1 (Vienna: Gerold's Sohn, 2008), 187–206, here 192.

9. RADICALIZATION

1. Heinrich August Winkler, *Von der Revolution zur Stabilisierung: Arbeiter und Arbeiterbewegung in der Weimarer Republik, 1918 bis 1924* (Berlin: Dietz, 1984), 122–3; idem, *Weimar 1918–1933. Die Geschichte der ersten deutschen Demokratie* (Munich: C. H. Beck, 1993), 58.

2. On Karl Liebknecht, see Helmut Trotnow, *Karl Liebknecht: Eine Politische Biographie* (Cologne: Kiepenheuer and Witsch, 1980); Heinz Wohlgemuth, *Karl Liebknecht: Eine Biographie* (East Berlin: Dietz, 1975); Annelies Laschitza and Elke Keller, *Karl Liebknecht: Eine Biographie in Dokumenten* (East Berlin: Dietz, 1982); Annelies Laschitza, *Die Liebknechts: Karl und Sophie, Politik und Familie* (Berlin: Aufbau, 2009); Anthony Read, *The World on Fire: 1919 and the Battle with Bolshevism* (London: Pimlico, 2009), 29.

3. Read, *World on Fire*, 29; Mark William Jones, 'Violence and Politics in the German Revolution, 1918–19', unpublished PhD thesis, European University Institute, 2011, 91.

4. Peter Nettl, *Rosa Luxemburg* (Frankfurt am Main: Büchergilde Gutenberg, 1968), 67 (on her deformity); Annelies Laschitza, *Im Lebensrausch, trotz alledem. Rosa Luxemburg: Eine Biographie* (Berlin: Aufbau, 1996/2002), 25; Jason Schulman (ed.), *Rosa Luxemburg: Her Life and Legacy* (New York: Palgrave Macmillan, 2013); Mathilde Jacob, *Rosa Luxemburg: An Intimate Portrait* (London: Lawrence and Wishart, 2000); Read, *World on Fire*, 29ff.

5. Laschitza, *Rosa Luxemburg*, 584.

6. Rosa Luxemburg, *Gesammelte Werke*, vol. 4: *August 1914–Januar 1919* (East Berlin: Dietz, 1974), 399; Karl Egon Lönne (ed.), *Die Weimarer Republik, 1918–1933: Quellen zum politischen Denken der Deutschen im 19. und 20. Jahrhundert* (Darmstadt: Wissenschaftliche Buchgesellschaft, 2002), 79–82.

7. Ulrich Kluge, *Soldatenräte und Revolution: Studien zur Militärpolitik in Deutschland 1918/19* (Göttingen: Vandenhoeck and Ruprecht, 1975), 241–3; Winkler, *Von der Revolution*, 109–10; Scott Stephenson, *The Final Battle: Soldiers of the Western Front and the German Revolution of 1918* (Cambridge and New York: Cambridge University Press, 2009), 262–71. On violence in this phase of the revolution, see Jones, 'Violence and Politics', 177–96.

8. Eduard Bernstein, *Die deutsche Revolution*, vol. 1: *Ihr Ursprung, ihr Verlauf und ihr Werk* (Berlin: Verlag Gesellschaft und Erziehung, 1921), 131–5; Winkler, *Von der Revolution*, 120.

9. Winkler, *Weimar*, 58.
10. Winkler, *Von der Revolution*, 122.
11. Andreas Wirsching, *Vom Weltkrieg zum Bürgerkrieg: Politischer Extremismus in Deutschland und Frankreich 1918–1933/39. Berlin und Paris im Vergleich* (Munich: Oldenbourg, 1999), 134; Winkler, *Von der Revolution*, 124; Gustav Noske, *Von Kiel bis Kapp: Zur Geschichte der deutschen Revolution* (Berlin: Verlag für Politik und Wirtschaft, 1920), 68.
12. On the *Freikorps*, see Hagen Schulze, *Freikorps und Republik, 1918–1920* (Boppard am Rhein: Boldt, 1969); Hannsjoachim W. Koch, *Der deutsche Bürgerkrieg: Eine Geschichte der deutschen und österreichischen Freikorps 1918–1923* (Berlin: Ullstein, 1978); Wolfram Wette, *Gustav Noske: Eine politische Biographie* (Düsseldorf: Droste, 1987); Bernhard Sauer, 'Freikorps und Antisemitismus', in *Zeitschrift für Geschichtswissenschaft* 56 (2008), 5–29; Klaus Theweleit, *Male Fantasies*, 2 vols (Minneapolis, MN: University of Minnesota Press, 1987); Rüdiger Bergien, 'Republikschützer oder Terroristen? Die Freikorpsbewegung in Deutschland nach dem Ersten Weltkrieg', in *Militärgeschichte* (2008), 14–17; idem, *Die bellizistische Republik: Wehrkonsens und Wehrhaftmachung in Deutschland, 1918–1933* (Munich: Oldenbourg, 2012), 64–9.
13. Starhemberg, 'Aufzeichnungen', in Starhemberg Papers, Oberösterreichisches Landesarchiv, 26.
14. Robert Gerwarth, 'The Central European Counter-Revolution: Paramilitary Violence in Germany, Austria and Hungary after the Great War', in *Past & Present* 200 (2008), 175–209.
15. Ibid.
16. Jürgen Reulecke, *'Ich möchte einer werden so wie die ...': Männerbünde im 20. Jahrhundert* (Frankfurt am Main: Campus, 2001), 89ff.
17. Ernst von Salomon, *Die Geächteten* (Berlin: Rowohlt, 1923), 10–11. On the autobiographical *Freikorps* literature, see, in particular, Matthias Sprenger, *Landsknechte auf dem Weg ins Dritte Reich? Zu Genese und Wandel des Freikorps-Mythos* (Paderborn: Schöningh, 2008).
18. Joseph Roth, *Das Spinnennetz* (first serialized in 1923, first book edition: Cologne and Berlin: Kiepenheuer and Witsch, 1967), 6.
19. Friedrich Wilhelm Heinz, *Sprengstoff* (Berlin: Frundsberg Verlag, 1930), 7.
20. Boris Barth, *Dolchstoßlegenden und politische Disintegration: Das Trauma der deutschen Niederlage im Ersten Weltkrieg* (Düsseldorf: Droste, 2003); see also Gerd Krumeich, 'Die Dolchstoß-Legende', in

Etienne François and Hagen Schulze (eds), *Deutsche Erinnerungsorte*, vol. 1 (Munich: C. H. Beck, 2001), 585–99; Wolfgang Schivelbusch, *The Culture of Defeat: On National Trauma, Mourning and Recovery* (New York: Holt, 2003), 203–47.

21. Manfred von Killinger, *Der Klabautermann: Eine Lebensgeschichte*, 3rd edition (Munich: Eher, 1936), 263. On Killinger, see Bert Wawrzinek, *Manfred von Killinger (1886–1944): Ein politischer Soldat zwischen Freikorps und Auswärtigem Amt* (Preussisch Oldendorf: DVG, 2004).

22. See the report of the Prussian Parliament in *Sammlung der Drucksachen der Verfassunggebenden Preußischen Landesversammlung, Tagung 1919/21*, vol. 15 (Berlin: Preußische Verlagsanstalt, 1921), 7,705; see also Dieter Baudis and Hermann Roth, 'Berliner Opfer der Novemberrevolution 1918/19', in *Jahrbuch für Wirtschaftsgeschichte* (1968), 73–149, here 79.

23. Karl Liebknecht, *Ausgewählte Reden, Briefe und Aufsätze* (East Berlin: Dietz, 1952), 505–20.

24. Rosa Luxemburg, *Politische Schriften*, ed. Ossip K. Flechtheim, vol. 3 (Frankfurt am Main: Europäische Verlags-Anstalt, 1975), 203–9, here 209.

25. On their discovery and arrest, see Klaus Gietinger, *Eine Leiche im Landwehrkanal: Die Ermordnung Rosa Luxemburgs* (Hamburg: Edition Nautilus, 2008), 18. On Pabst, see Klaus Gietinger, *Der Konterrevolutionär: Waldemar Pabst – eine deutsche Karriere* (Hamburg: Edition Nautilus, 2009).

26. On the treatment of Liebknecht, see the summary of evidence contained in BA-MA PH8 v/2 Bl. 206–20: 'Schriftsatz in der Untersuchungsache gegen von Pflugk-Harttung und Genossen. Berlin, den 15 März 1919', and further Bl. 221–7.

27. For the description of how Luxemburg was murdered in the Tiergarten (as told to Weizsäcker by Pflugk-Harttung the following day), see Leonidas E. Hill (ed.), *Die Weizsäcker-Papiere 1900–1934* (Berlin: Propyläen, 1982), 325; see also Gietinger, *Leiche im Landwehrkanal: Die Ermordung Rosa Luxemburgs* (Hamburg: Edition Nautilus, 2008), 37 and 134 (annex document 1). See further the file contained in BA-MA PH8 v/10, esp. Bl.1–3, 'Das Geständnis. Otto Runge, 22 Jan. 1921'.

28. Winkler, *Von der Revolution*, 171–82; Jones, 'Violence and Politics', 313–50, esp. 339–40.

29. On Eisner, see Bernhard Grau, *Kurt Eisner, 1867–1919: Eine Biografie* (Munich: C. H. Beck, 2001); Allan Mitchell, *Revolution in Bavaria*

1918–19: The Eisner Regime and the Soviet Republic (Princeton, NJ: Princeton University Press, 1965), 66–7; Read, *World on Fire*, 33–7.

30. Heinrich Hillmayr, 'München und die Revolution 1918/1919', in Karl Bosl (ed.), *Bayern im Umbruch. Die Revolution von 1918, ihre Voraussetzungen, ihr Verlauf und ihre Folgen* (Munich and Vienna: Oldenbourg, 1969), 453–504; Grau, *Eisner*, 344; Mitchell, *Revolution in Bavaria*, 100; David Clay Large, *Where Ghosts Walked: Munich's Road to the Third Reich* (New York: W. W. Norton, 1997), 78–9; Read, *World on Fire*, 35.

31. Holger Herwig, 'Clio Deceived: Patriotic Self-Censorship in Germany after the Great War', in *International Security* 12 (1987), 5–22, quotation on p. 9.

32. Grau, *Eisner*, 397ff.

33. Susanne Miller, *Die Bürde der Macht: Die deutsche Sozialdemokratie 1918–1920* (Düsseldorf: Droste, 1978), 457; Grau, *Eisner*, 439; Hans von Pranckh, *Der Prozeß gegen den Grafen Anton Arco-Valley, der den bayerischen Ministerpräsidenten Kurt Eisner erschossen hat* (Munich: Lehmann, 1920).

34. Mitchell, *Revolution in Bavaria*, 271; Winkler, *Weimar*, 77; Pranckh, *Der Prozeß gegen den Grafen Anton Arco-Valley*.

35. Wilhelm Böhm, *Im Kreuzfeuer zweier Revolutionen* (Munich: Verlag für Kulturpolitik, 1924), 297; Maderthaner, 'Utopian Perspectives and Political Restraint: The Austrian Revolution in the Context of Central European Conflicts', in Günter Bischof, Fritz Plasser and Peter Berger (eds), *From Empire to Republic: Post-World War I Austria* (New Orleans, LA, and Innsbruck: UNO Press and Innsbruck University Press, 2010), 58.

36. Mühsam as quoted in Read, *World on Fire*.

37. Read, *World on Fire*, 152.

38. Zinoviev as quoted in David Mitchell, *1919: Red Mirage* (London: Jonathan Cape, 1970), 165.

39. Thomas Mann, *Diaries 1919–1939*, trans. Richard and Clare Winston (London: André Deutsch, 1983), 44.

40. Lansing as quoted in Alan Sharp, 'The New Diplomacy and the New Europe', in Nicholas Doumanis, *The Oxford Handbook of Europe 1914–1945* (Oxford and New York: Oxford University Press, 2016).

41. On the flight to Bamberg see Wette, *Noske*, 431. On the events of Palm Sunday, see Heinrich Hillmayr, *Roter und Weißer Terror in Bayern nach 1918* (Munich: Nusser, 1974), 43; Wette, *Noske*, 434; Mitchell, *Revolution in Bavaria*, 316–17.

42. Mitchell, *Revolution in Bavaria*, 304–31.

43. Ernst Toller, *I Was a German: The Autobiography of Ernst Toller* (New York: Paragon House, 1934), 180–9; Mitchell, *Revolution in Bavaria*, 320.

44. Wolfgang Zorn, *Geschichte Bayerns im 20. Jahrhundert* (Munich: C. H. Beck, 1986), 194.

45. Read, *World on Fire*, 154; Mitchell, *Revolution in Bavaria*, 322.

46. Mitchell, *Revolution in Bavaria*, 322; Read, *World on Fire*, 155.

47. On these rumours, see Jones, 'Violence and Politics', 377–8; Hillmayr, *Roter und Weißer Terror in Bayern*, 136–7.

48. As quoted in Wette, *Noske*, 440.

49. Hillmayr, *Roter und Weißer Terror in Bayern*, 108–10.

50. Victor Klemperer, *Man möchte immer weinen und lachen in einem: Revolutionstagebuch 1919* (Berlin: Aufbau, 2015).

51. Mitchell, *Revolution in Bavaria*, 331, n. 51.

52. Thomas Mann, *Thomas Mann: Tagebücher 1918–1921*, ed. Peter de Mendelsohn (Frankfurt am Main: S. Fischer, 1979), 218.

53. György Borsányi, *The Life of a Communist Revolutionary: Béla Kun* (Boulder, CO: Social Science Monographs, 1993), 45 (release from POW camp), and 77 (arrival in Budapest).

54. On food shortages and political radicalization during the war, Péter Bihari, *Lövészárkok a hátországban. Középosztály, zsidókérdés, Antiszemitizmus az első világháború Magyarországán* (Budapest: Napvilág Kiadó, 2008), esp. 94–5.

55. On the failure of land reform under Károlyi, see József Sipos, *A pártok és a földrefom 1918–1919* (Budapest: Gondolat, 2009), 200–9.

56. *The New York Times*, 5 January 1919, as quoted in Read, *World on Fire*, 157.

57. Miklós Molnár, *From Béla Kun to János Kádár: Seventy Years of Hungarian Communism* (New York: St Martin's Press, 1990), 2–4.

58. For the place of the Council Republic in Hungarian and European history, see Tamás Krausz and Judit Vértes (eds), *1919. A Magyarországi Tanácsköztársaság és a kelet-európai forradalmak* (Budapest: L'Harmattan-ELTE BTK Kelet-Európa Története Tanszék, 2010).

59. *Vörös Újság*, 11 February 1919.

60. For a contemporary account of the Crown Attorney who prosecuted communists, see Albert Váry, *A Vörös Uralom Áldozatai Magyarországon* (Szeged: Szegedi Nyomda, 1993). The account was first published in 1922. See also Gusztáv Gratz (ed.), *A Bolsevizmus Magyarországon* (Budapest: Franklin-Társulat, 1921); Ladislaus Bizony, *133 Tage Ungarischer Bolschewismus. Die Herrschaft Béla Kuns und Tibor Szamuellys: Die Blutigen Ereignisse in Ungarn* (Leipzig and

Vienna: Waldheim-Eberle, 1920). For a recent account, see Konrád Salamon, 'Proletárditarúra és a Terror', *Rubicon* (2011), 24–35.

61. Wolfgang Maderthaner, 'The Austrian Revolution', 59.

62. The best study on peasant reactions remains Ignác Romsics, *A Duna-Tisza Köze Hatalmi Viszonyai 1918–19-ben* (Budapest: Akadémiai Kiadó, 1982).

63. Thomas Sakmyster, *A Communist Odyssey: The Life of József Pogány* (Budapest and New York: Central European University Press, 2012), 44–6.

64. See Peter Pastor, *Hungary between Wilson and Lenin: The Hungarian Revolution of 1918–1919 and the Big Three* (New York: Columbia University Press, East European Monograph, 1976).

65. Julius Braunthal, *Geschichte der Internationale*, vol. 2 (Hanover: J. H. W. Dietz, 1963), 160.

66. Maderthaner, 'The Austrian Revolution', 60ff.

67. Ibid, 61.

68. For a detailed account see Hans Hautmann, *Die Geschichte der Rätebewegung in Österreich 1918–1924* (Vienna: Europaverlag, 1987), 329ff.

69. On the Catholic Church's rejection of Kun's regime, see Gabriel Adriányi, *Fünfzig Jahre Ungarische Kirchengeschichte, 1895–1945* (Mainz: v. Hase and Koehler Verlag, 1974), 53–9.

70. Frank Eckelt, 'The Internal Policies of the Hungarian Soviet Republic', in Iván Völgyes (ed.), *Hungary in Revolution, 1918–1919* (Lincoln, NB: University of Nebraska Press, 1971), 61–88.

71. Thomas Sakmyster, *Hungary's Admiral on Horseback: Miklós Horthy, 1918–1944* (Boulder, CO: Eastern European Monographs, 1994).

72. Béla Kelemen, *Adatok a szegedi ellenforradalom és a szegedi kormány történetéhez* (Szeged: Szerzö Kiadása, 1923), 495–6.

73. Miklós Kozma, *Makensens Ungarische Husaren: Tagebuch eines Frontoffiziers, 1914–1918* (Berlin and Vienna: Verlag für Kulturpolitik, 1933), 459. On the counter-revolution in Budapest, see also Eliza Ablovatski, '"Cleansing the Red Nest": Counter-Revolution and White Terror in Munich and Budapest', 1919, unpublished PhD Dissertation, New York, 2004.

74. Kozma, *Makensens Ungarische Husaren*, 461. On the 'Red Amazons' see also *Innsbrucker Nachrichten*, 23 March 1919, 2.

75. Starhemberg, 'Aufzeichnungen', 16–17. See also Emil Fey, *Schwertbrüder des Deutschen Ordens* (Vienna: Lichtner, 1937), 218–20.

76. Harold Nicolson, *Peacemaking, 1919* (London: Grosset and Dunlap, 1933), 298 (diary entry for April 1919).

77. Ibid, 293.

78. Francis Deák, *Hungary at the Peace Conference: The Diplomatic History of the Treaty of Trianon* (New York: Columbia University Press, 1942), 78.

79. Read, *World on Fire*, 192–3.

80. Deák, *Hungary at the Peace Conference*, 78.

81. Rudolf Tokes, 'Bela Kun: The Man and Revolutionary', in Ivan Völgyes (ed.), *Hungary in Revolution* (Lincoln, NB: University of Nebraska Press), 170–207, here 202–3.

82. Deák, *Hungary at the Peace Conference*, 112–28.

83. On the behaviour of the Romanian soldiers and the pillage of the city, see Krisztián Ungváry, 'Sacco di Budapest, 1919. Gheorghe Mârdârescu tábornok válasza Harry Hill Bandholtz vezérőrnagy nem diplomatikus naplójára', in *Budapesti Negyed* 3–4 (2000), 173–203.

84. Miklós Lackó, 'The Role of Budapest in Hungarian Literature 1890–1935', in Tom Bender (ed.), *Budapest and New York: Studies in Metropolitan Transformation, 1870–1930* (New York: Russell Sage Foundation, 1994), 352–66, 352ff.

85. Miklós Kozma, *Az összeomlás 1918–1919* (Budapest: Athenaeum, 1933), 380. On Kozma's war experience, see Kozma, *Makensens Ungarische Husaren*. On the White Terror more generally, see Béla Bodó, 'The White Terror in Hungary, 1919–21: The Social Worlds of Paramilitary Groups', in *Austrian History Yearbook* 42 (2011), 133–63; Gerwarth, 'The Central European Counter-Revolution', 175–209.

86. On the assassination of Somogyi and Bacsó, see Ernő Gergely and Pál Schönwald, *A Somogyi-Bacsó-Gyilkosság* (Budapest: Kossuth, 1978).

87. See Rolf Fischer, 'Anti-Semitism in Hungary 1882–1932', in Herbert A. Strauss (ed.), *Hostages of Modernization: Studies of Modern Antisemitism 1870–1933/39*, vol. 2: *Austria, Hungary, Poland, Russia* (Berlin and New York: de Gruyter, 1993), 863–92, 883–4; Nathaniel Katzburg, *Zsidópolitika Magyarországon, 1919–1943* (Budapest: Bábel, 2002), 36–9.

88. Rudolf Tokes, *Béla Kun and the Hungarian Soviet Republic: The Origins and Role of the Communist Party of Hungary in the Revolutions of 1918–1919* (New York and Stanford, CA: Praeger, 1967), 159. See also Borsányi, *The Life of a Communist Revolutionary*.

89. Pál Prónay, *A határban a halál kaszál: fejezetek Prónay Pál feljegyzéseiből*, eds Ágnes Szabó and Ervin Pamlényi (Budapest: Kossuth, 1963), 90. On the man himself, see Béla Bodó, *Pál Prónay: Paramilitary Violence*

and Anti-Semitism in Hungary, 1919–1921 (Pittsburgh, PA: University of Pittsburgh Press, 2011).

90. Gerwarth, 'Central European Counter-Revolution', 175–209. On the context, see also Bruno Thoss, _Der Ludendorff-Kreis: München als Zentrum der mitteleuropäischen Gegenrevolution zwischen Revolution und Hitler-Putsch_ (Munich: Wölfle, 1978); Lajos Kerekes, 'Die "weiße" Allianz: Bayerisch-österreichisch-ungarische Projekte gegen die Regierung Renner im Jahre 1920', in Österreichische Osthefte 7 (1965), 353–66; Ludger Rape, _Die österreichischen Heimwehren und die bayerische Rechte 1920–1923_ (Vienna: Europa-Verlag, 1977); Horst G. Nusser, _Konservative Wehrverbände in Bayern, Preussen und Österreich mit einer Biographie von Georg Escherich 1870–1941_, 2 vols (Munich: Nusser, 1973).

91. See Hans Jürgen Kuron, 'Freikorps und Bund Oberland', unpublished PhD thesis, Munich 1960, 134; Sabine Falch, 'Zwischen Heimatwehr und Nationalsozialismus. Der "Bund Oberland" in Tirol', in _Geschichte und Region_ 6 (1997), 51–86; Verena Lösch, 'Die Geschichte der Tiroler Heimatwehr von ihren Anfängen bis zum Korneuburger Eid (1920–1930)', unpublished PhD thesis, Innsbruck 1986, 162.

92. On the life of Anton Lehár, see Anton Broucek (ed.), _Anton Lehár. Erinnerungen. Gegenrevolution und Restaurationsversuche in Ungarn 1918–1921_ (Munich: Oldenbourg, 1973). On Franz Lehár, see Norbert Linke, _Franz Lehár_ (Reinbek bei Hamburg: Rowohlt, 2001).

93. Österreichisches Staatsarchiv (ÖStA), B 1477: 'Die Politik des deutschen Widerstands' (1931).

94. Bundesarchiv (Berlin), Pabst Papers, NY4035/6, 37–9. On Pabst, see also Doris Kachulle, _Waldemar Pabst und die Gegenrevolution_ (Berlin: Organon, 2007).

95. Alfred Krauss, _Unser Deutschtum!_ (Salzburg: Eitel, 1921), 7–13.

96. Alfred Rosenberg, 'Die russisch-jüdische Revolution', in _Auf gut Deutsch_, 24 May 1919.

97. Léon Poliakov, _The History of Anti-Semitism_, vol. 4: _Suicidal Europe, 1870–1933_ (Philadelphia, PA: University of Pennsylvania Press, 2003), 274–6.

98. Mark Levene, _War, Jews, and the New Europe: The Diplomacy of Lucien Wolf, 1914–1919_ (Oxford and New York: Oxford University Press, 1992), 212; idem, _Crisis of Genocide_, vol. 1: _The European Rimlands 1912–1938_ (Oxford and New York: Oxford University Press, 2014), quote on p. 184.

99. Winston Churchill, 'Zionism versus Bolshevism', _Illustrated Sunday Herald_, 8 February 1920.

100. Norman Cohn, *Warrant for Genocide: The Myth of the Jewish World Conspiracy and the Protocols of the Elders of Zion* (London: Serif, 1996).

101. On Hungarian anti-Semitism after 1918, see Robert M. Bigler, 'Heil Hitler and Heil Horthy! The Nature of Hungarian Racist Nationalism and its Impact on German-Hungarian Relations 1919–1945', in *East European Quarterly* 8 (1974), 251–72; Béla Bodó, '"White Terror", the Hungarian Press and the Evolution of Hungarian Anti-Semitism after World War I', in *Yad Vashem Studies* 34 (2006), 45–86; Nathaniel Katzburg, *Hungary and the Jews: Policy and Legislation, 1920–1943* (Ramat-Gan: Bar-Ilan University Press, 1981); and Rolf Fischer, *Entwicklungsstufen des Antisemitismus in Ungarn, 1867–1939: Die Zerstörung der magyarisch-jüdischen Symbiose* (Munich: Oldenbourg, 1998).

102. Josef Halmi, 'Akten über die Pogrome in Ungarn', in Jakob Krausz, *Martyrium. Ein jüdisches Jahrbuch* (Vienna: self-published, 1922), 59–66. See also Oszkár Jászi, *Magyariens Schuld: Ungarns Sühne. Revolution und Gegenrevolution in Ungarn* (Munich: Verlag für Kulturpolitik, 1923), 168–79; Josef Pogány, *Der Weiße Terror in Ungarn* (Vienna: Neue Erde, 1920); British Joint Labour Delegation to Hungary, *The White Terror in Hungary. Report of the British Joint Labour Delegation to Hungary* (London: Trade Union Congress and Labour Party, 1920); and The National Archives (TNA), London: FO 371/3558/206720: 'The Jews in Hungary: Correspondence with His Majesty's Government, presented to the Jewish Board of Deputies and the Council of the Anglo-Jewish Association', October 1920.

103. Halmi, 'Akten über die Pogrome in Ungarn', 64.

104. On the history of anti-Semitism up to the Great War, see Peter Pulzer, *The Rise of Political Anti-Semitism in Germany and Austria*, 2nd revised edition (Cambridge, MA: Harvard University Press, 1988); and John W. Boyer, 'Karl Lueger and the Viennese Jews', in *Yearbook of the Leo Baeck Institute* 26 (1981), 125–44. On the image of the 'Jewish profiteer' in wartime Vienna, see Maureen Healy, *Vienna and the Fall of the Habsburg Empire: Total War and Everyday Life in World War I* (Cambridge and New York: Cambridge University Press, 2004). On anti-Semitism in Austrian universities, see Michael Gehler, *Studenten und Politik: Der Kampf um die Vorherrschaft an der Universität Innsbruck 1919–1938* (Innsbruck: Haymon-Verlag, 1990), 93–8.

105. See Bruce F. Pauley, 'Politischer Antisemitismus im Wien der Zwischenkriegszeit', in Gerhard Botz et al. (eds), *Eine zerstörte Kultur: Jüdisches Leben und Antisemitismus in Wien seit dem 19. Jahrhundert* (Buchloe: Obermayer, 1990), 221–3.

106. Steven E. Aschheim, *Brothers and Strangers: The East European Jew in German and German-Jewish Consciousness, 1800–1923* (Madison, WI, and London: University of Wisconsin Press, 1982).

107. Lina Heydrich, *Leben mit einem Kriegsverbrecher* (Pfaffenhofen: Ludwig, 1976), 42ff.

108. Krauss, *Unser Deutschtum!*, 20.

109. Ibid, 16–17.

110. See, for example, the article series on 'The Racial-Political Causes of the Collapse', *Neue Tiroler Stimmen*, 9, 10 and 30 December 1918, and 2 January 1919, as quoted in F. L. Carsten, *Revolution in Central Europe, 1918–1919* (London: Temple Smith, 1972), 261. See also *Innsbrucker Nachrichten*, 8 April 1919. On the broader context, see Paul Rena, *Der christlichsoziale Antisemitismus in Wien 1848–1938*, unpublished PhD thesis, Vienna, 1991; and Christine Sagoschen, *Judenbilder im Wandel der Zeit: die Entwicklung des katholischen Antisemitismus am Beispiel jüdischer Stereotypen unter besonderer Berücksichtigung der Entwicklung in der ersten Republik*, unpublished PhD thesis, Vienna, 1998.

111. *Tagespost* (Graz), 27 May 1919.

112. Thomas Lorman, 'The Right-Radical Ideology in the Hungarian Army, 1921–23', in *Central Europe* 3 (2005), 67–81, esp. 76.

113. Oszkár Szőllősy, 'The Criminals of the Dictatorship of the Proletariat', as printed in Cecile Tormay, *An Outlaw's Diary*, 2 vols (London: Allan, 1923), vol. 2, 226.

114. Thomas Sakmyster, 'Gyula Gömbös and the Hungarian Jews, 1918–1936', in *Hungarian Studies Review* 8 (2006), 156–68, here 161.

115. Bodó, *Paramilitary Violence*, 134.

116. Bundesarchiv (Koblenz), Bauer Papers, NL 22/69: memoirs of Max Bauer's secretary, 33.

117. NIOD, Rauter Papers, Doc I-1380 Pr 6-12-97, 46–7; Oberösterreichisches Landesarchiv (OÖLA), Starhemberg Papers: Starhemberg, 'Meine Stellungnahme zur Judenfrage'.

118. On Stambolijski and BANU, see, for example, Kanyu Kozhuharov, *Reformatorskoto delo na Aleksandar Stambolijski* (Sofia: Fond 'Aleksandar Stambolijski', 1948); Mihail Genovski, *Aleksandar Stambolijski – otblizo i daleko: dokumentalni spomeni* (Sofia: BZNS, 1982); Evgeni Tanchev, *Darzhavno-pravnite vazgledi na Alexandar Stambolijski* (Sofia: BZNS, 1984).

119. Richard J. Crampton, 'The Balkans', 251; Stephane Groueff, *Crown of Thorns: The Reign of King Boris III of Bulgaria, 1918–1943* (Lanham, MD: Madison Books, 1987), 61ff.

120. Margaret Fitzherbert, *The Man Who Was Greenmantle: A Biography of Aubrey Herbert* (London: John Murray, 1983), 235; Margaret Mac-Millan, *Peacemakers: The Paris Conference of 1919 and its Attempt to End War* (London: John Murray, 2001), 148.
121. Groueff, *Crown of Thorns*, 75; MacMillan, *Peacemakers*, 148.
122. Crampton, 'The Balkans', 251; Tsocho Bilyarski, *BZNS, Aleksandar Stambolijski i VMRO: nepoznatata voyna* (Sofia: Aniko, 2009).
123. Stefan Troebst, *Das makedonische Jahrhundert: Von den Anfängen der nationalrevolutionären Bewegung zum Abkommen von Ohrid 1893–2001* (Munich: Oldenbourg, 2007), 85–110.
124. Richard Crampton, 'Bulgaria', in Robert Gerwarth (ed.), *Twisted Paths: Europe, 1914–1945* (Oxford and New York: Oxford University Press, 2007), 237–70, here 251.
125. Doncho Daskalov, *1923 – Sadbonosni resheniya i sabitiya* (Sofia: BZNS, 1983), 24.
126. Ibid, 18.
127. John D. Bell, *Peasants in Power: Alexander Stamboliski and the Bulgarian Agrarian National Union 1899–1923* (Princeton, NJ: Princeton University Press, 1977), 149.
128. Daskalov, *1923*, 25.
129. For details of the coup and the abolition of the agrarian rule, see Yono Mitev, *Fashistkiyat prevrat na deveti yuni 1923 godina i Yunskoto antifashistko vastanie* (Sofia: BZNS, 1973); Nedyu Nedev, *Aleksandar Stambolijski i zagovorat* (Sofia: BZNS, 1984); Daskalov, *1923*.
130. *Izvestia na darzhavnite arhivi* 15 (1968), 99.
131. Richard J. Crampton, *Bulgaria* (Oxford and New York: Oxford University Press, 2007), 96–8; John Paul Newman, 'The Origins, Attributes, and Legacies of Paramilitary Violence in the Balkans', in Gerwarth and Horne (eds), *War in Peace*, 145–63, here 153.
132. Simeon Damyanov, 'Dokumenti za devetoyunskia prevrat i Septemvriyskoto vastanie prez 1923 g. vav Frenskia diplomaticheski arhiv', in *Izvestia na darzhavnite arhivi* 30 (1975), 167–82, here 172.
133. Andreya Iliev, *Atentatat v 'Sveta Nedelya' i teroristite* (Sofia: Ciela, 2011).

10. FEAR OF BOLSHEVISM AND THE RISE OF FASCISM

1. On the cultural impact of the Great War on Spain, see Maximiliano Fuentes Codera, *España en la Primera Guerra Mundial: Una movilización cultural* (Madrid: Akal, 2014), and Francisco J. Romero Sal-

vadó, *Spain, 1914–1918: Between War and Revolution* (London: Routledge, 1999). On labour unrest, see Edward E. Malefakis, *Agrarian Reform and Peasant Revolution in Spain: Origins of the Civil War* (New Haven, CT, and London: Yale University Press, 1970); Gerald H. Meaker, *The Revolutionary Left in Spain 1914–1923* (Stanford, CA: Stanford University Press, 1974). Fernando del Rey Reguillo, 'El empresario, el sindicalista y el miedo', in Manuel Pérez Ledesma and Rafael Cruz (eds), *Cultura y movilización en la España contemporánea* (Madrid: Alianza, 1997), 235–72, and Rafael Cruz, '¡Luzbel vuelve al mundo!: las imágenes de la Rusia soviética y la acción colectiva en España', in Ledesma and Cruz (eds), *Cultura y movilización*, 273–303.

2. Anthony Read, *The World on Fire: 1919 and the Battle with Bolshevism* (London: Pimlico, 2009), 166ff. On the reception of the Bolshevik revolution in Spain, see Juan Avilés Farré, *La fe que vino de Rusia. La revolución bolchevique y los españoles (1917–1931)* (Madrid: Biblioteca Nueva, 2009), and Francisco J. Romero Salvadó, *The Foundations of Civil War: Revolution, Social Conflict and Reaction in Liberal Spain, 1916–1923* (London: Routledge, 2008).

3. *La Voz del Cantero*, 11 March 1918, as quoted in Meaker, *The Revolutionary Left*, 137. See also Juan Díaz del Moral, *Historia de las agitaciones campesinas andaluzas. Córdoba. Antecedentes para una reforma agraria* (Madrid: Alianza, 1995); idem: 'Historia de las agitaciones campesinas andaluzas', in Isidoro Moreno Navarro (ed.), *La identidad cultural de Andalucía, aproximaciones, mixtificaciones, negacionismo y evidencias* (Seville: Fundación Pública Andaluza Centro de Estudios Andaluces, 2008).

4. Del Rey Reguillo, 'El empresario', 235–72, and Cruz, '¡Luzbel vuelve al mundo!, 273–303.

5. For the background to the process of expulsion, see Mikel Aizpuru, 'La expulsión de refugiados extranjeros desde España en 1919: exiliados rusos y de otros países', in *Migraciones y Exilios* 11 (2010), 107–26; James Matthews, 'Battling Bolshevik Bogeymen', *Journal of Military History*, 80 (2016), 725–55.

6. On Primo de Rivera, see Shlomo Ben-Ami, *Fascism from Above: The Dictatorship of Primo de Rivera in Spain 1923–1930* (Oxford: Clarendon Press, 1983); Alejandro Quiroga, *Making Spaniards: Primo de Rivera and the Nationalization of the Masses, 1923–30* (London and New York: Palgrave Macmillan, 2007). More generally, see Raymond Carr, *Modern Spain, 1875–1980* (Oxford: Clarendon Press, 1980); and, more recently, Julián Casanova, *Twentieth-Century Spain: A*

History (Cambridge and New York: Cambridge University Press, 2014).

7. Guy Pedroncini, *Les Mutineries de 1917*, 3rd edition (Paris: Presses universitaires de France, 1996); Leonard V. Smith, Stéphane Audoin-Rouzeau and Annette Becker, *France and the Great War, 1914–1918* (Cambridge and New York: Cambridge University Press, 2003), 113–45.

8. John Horne, 'Defending Victory: Paramilitary Politics in France, 1918–26', in Robert Gerwarth and John Horne (eds), *War in Peace: Paramilitary Violence after the Great War* (Oxford and New York: Oxford University Press, 2012).

9. Beatrice Potter Webb, *Diaries 1912–1924*, ed. Margaret Cole (London: Longmans, Green and Company, 1952), 136 (entry of 11 November 1918).

10. Lloyd George, as quoted in Margaret MacMillan, *Peacemakers: The Paris Conference of 1919 and its Attempt to End War* (London: John Murray, 2001), 208.

11. John Buchan, *The Three Hostages* (London: Nelson, 1948), 210.

12. Read, *World on Fire*, 317; Beverly Gage, *The Day Wall Street Exploded: A Story of America in its First Age of Terror* (Oxford and New York: Oxford University Press, 2008).

13. Richard Bessel, 'Revolution', in Jay Winter (ed.), *The Cambridge History of the First World War*, vol. 2 (Cambridge and New York: Cambridge University Press, 2014), 135.

14. Antonio Gibelli, *La Grande Guerra degli italiani 1915–1918* (Milan: Sansoni, 1998), 221. On the Battle of Vittorio Veneto, see Piero del Negro, 'Vittorio Veneto e l'armistizio sul fronte italiano', in Stéphane Audoin-Rouzeau and Jean-Jacques Becker (eds), *La prima guerra mondiale*, vol. 2 (Torino: Einaudi, 2007), 333–43.

15. Rino Alessi, *La luminosa visione di Trieste redenta*, 'Il Secolo', 6 November 1918, reprinted in Franco Contorbia (ed.), *Giornalismo italiano*, vol. 2: *1901–1939* (Milan: Arnoldo Mondadori, 2007), 908–9.

16. Benedetto Croce, *Carteggio con Vossler (1899-1949)* (Bari: Laterza, 1951), 106.

17. Mark Thompson, *The White War: Life and Death on the Italian Front 1915–1919* (London: Faber and Faber, 2009); Fulvio Cammarano (ed.), *Abbasso la Guerra. Neutralisti in Piazza alla vigilia della Prima Guerra mondiale* (Florence: Le Monnier, 2015).

18. Giovanna Procacci, *Warfare-welfare: Intervento dello Stato e diritti dei cittadini 1914–18* (Rome: Carocci, 2013), 128–9. Andrea Fava, 'Il "fronte interno" in Italia. Forme politiche della mobilitazione patriottica e delegittimazione della classe dirigente liberale', in *Ricerche*

storiche 27 (1997), 503–32. On the birth of a 'totalitarian temptation' during WWI, in reference to the Italian case, see Angelo Ventrone, *La seduzione totalitaria. Guerra, modernità, violenza politica (1914–1918)* (Rome: Donzelli, 2003). On the propaganda campaign, see Gian Luigi Gatti, *Dopo Caporetto. Gli ufficiali P nella Grande Guerra: propaganda, assistenza, vigilanza* (Gorizia: LEG, 2000). Barbara Bracco, 'L'Italia e l'Europa da Caporetto alla vittoria nella riflessione degli storici italiani', in Giampietro Berti and Piero Del Negro (eds), *Al di qua e al di là del Piave. L'ultimo anno della Grande Guerra* (Milan: Franco Angeli, 2001), 531–2; Fava, 'Il "fronte interno" in Italia', 509–21.

19. Giovanna Procacci, *Dalla rassegnazione alla rivolta. Mentalità e comportamenti popolari nella Grande Guerra* (Rome: Bulzoni, 1999).

20. Mussolini, as quoted in MacGregor Knox, *To the Threshold of Power, 1922/23: Origins and Dynamics of the Fascist and National Socialist Dictatorship* (New York: Cambridge University Press, 2007), 222.

21. See Emilio Gentile, *Fascismo e antifascismo: I partiti italiani fra le due guerre* (Florence: Le Monnier, 2000), 40–6; Simonetta Ortaggi, 'Mutamenti sociali e radicalizzazione dei conflitti in Italia tra guerra e dopoguerra', in *Ricerche storiche* 27 (1997), 673–89; Elio Giovannini, *L'Italia massimalista: Socialismo e lotta sociale e politica nel primo Dopoguerra* (Rome: Ediesse 2001); Roberto Bianchi, *Pace, pane, terra. Il 1919 in Italia* (Rome: Odradek, 2006).

22. Guido Crainz, *Padania. Il mondo dei braccianti dall'Ottocento alla fuga dalle campagne* (Rome: Donzelli, 1994), 159.

23. Fabio Fabbri, *Le origini della Guerra civile: L'Italia dalla Grande Guerra al fascismo (1918–1921)* (Turin: Utet, 2009), 191–2.

24. Two classic works on Mussolini's 'metamorphosis' are Renzo de Felice, *Mussolini il rivoluzionario, 1883–1920* (Turin: Einaudi, 1965); Zeev Sternhell, *Naissance de l'idéologie fasciste* (Paris: Fayard, 1989). For a more recent account, see Richard Bosworth, *Mussolini* (London: Arnold, 2002), 100–22.

25. Paul O'Brien, *Mussolini in the First World War: The Journalist, the Soldier, the Fascist* (London: Bloomsbury, 2005).

26. Benito Mussolini, 'Col ferro e col fuoco', in *Il Popolo d'Italia*, 22 November 1917.

27. Benito Mussolini, 'Una politica', in *Il Popolo d'Italia*, 23 February 1918.

28. On Mussolini's ideological realignment, see Sternhell, *Naissance de l'idéologie fasciste*; Emilio Gentile, *The Origins of Fascist Ideology, 1918–1925* (New York: Enigma, 2005).

29. On the social composition, see Emilio Gentile, *The Sacralization of Politics in Fascist Italy* (Cambridge, MA: Harvard University Press, 1996), 364–6, 556–8; Roberta Suzzi Valli, 'The Myth of Squadrismo in the Fascist Regime', in *Journal for Contemporary History* 35 (2000), 131–50.

30. See Alberto Aquarone, 'Violenza e consenso nel fascismo Italiano', in *Storia contemporanea* 10 (1979), 145–55; Adrian Lyttleton, 'Fascism and Violence in Post-War Italy: Political Strategy and Social Conflict', in Wolfgang J. Mommsen and Gerhard Hirschfeld (eds), *Social Protest, Violence and Terror* (London: Palgrave Macmillan, 1982), 257–74; Jens Petersen, 'Il problema della violenza nel fascismo italiano', in *Storia contemporanea* 13 (1982), 985–1,008; and Paolo Nello, 'La rivoluzione fascista ovvero dello squadrismo nazional rivoluzionario', in *Storia contemporanea* 13 (1982), 1,009–25.

31. See, for example, the diary of the squadrista Mario Piazzesi, *Diario di uno Squadrista Toscano: 1919–1922* (Rome: Bonacci, 1981), 73–4, 77–8. See also Salvatore Lupo, *Il fascismo: La politica in un regime totalitario* (Rome: Donzelli, 2000), 85; Antonio Gibelli, *Il popolo bambino. Infanzia e nazione dalla Grande Guerra a Salò* (Turin: Einaudi, 2005), 187–90. On the context, see Sven Reichardt, *Faschistische Kampfbünde: Gewalt und Gemeinschaft im italienischen Squadrismus und in der deutschen SA* (Cologne, Weimar and Vienna: Böhlau Verlag, 2002).

32. Mussolini himself used these metaphors in his famous speech in Ferrara in April 1920. *Opera Omnia*, vol. 16, 239–46. See also Francesca Rigotti, 'Il medico-chirurgo dello Stato nel linguaggio metaforico di Mussolini', in Civiche Raccolte Storiche Milano (ed.), *Cultura e società negli anni del fascismo* (Milan: Cordani, 1987); David Forgacs, 'Fascism, Violence and Modernity', in Jana Howlett and Rod Mengham (eds), *The Violent Muse: Violence and the Artistic Imagination in Europe, 1910–1939* (Manchester: Manchester University Press, 1994), 5–6.

33. Brunella Dalla Casa, 'La Bologna di Palazzo d'Accursio', in Mario Isnenghi and Giulia Albanese (eds), *Gli Italiani in guerra: Conflitti, identità, memorie dal Risorgimento ai nostri giorni*, vol. 4/1: *Il ventennio fascista: Dall'impresa di Fiume alla Seconda Guerra mondiale (1919–1940)* (Turin: Utet, 2008), 332–8.

34. Fabbri, *Le origini della Guerra civile*, 349–58; and idem, 'Paramilitary Violence in Italy: The Rationale of Fascism and the Origins of Totalitarianism', in Gerwarth and Horne (eds), *War in Peace*, 85–106, here 92.

35. Statistics according to Emilio Gentile, *Storia del partito fascista*, vol. 1: *1919–1922, movimento e milizia* (Rome: Laterza, 1989), 472–5.

36. Lupo, *Il fascismo*, 86–98.

37. See, for example, Benito Mussolini, 'Il "Pus" a congresso', in *Il Popolo d'Italia*, 14 January 1921, reprinted in Benito Mussolini, *Opera Omnia*, vol. 16 (Florence: La Fenice, 1955), 116–17.

38. Richard Bosworth and Giuseppe Finaldi, 'The Italian Empire', in Robert Gerwarth and Erez Manela (eds), *Empires at War 1911–1923* (Oxford: Oxford University Press, 2014), 34–51.

39. On the March on Rome, see Giulia Albanese, *La marcia su Roma* (Rome and Bari: Laterza, 2006).

40. Adrian Lyttelton, *The Seizure of Power: Fascism in Italy 1919–1929* (London: Weidenfeld and Nicolson, 1973); Phillip Morgan, *Italian Fascism, 1919–1945* (London: Macmillan, 1995), 51.

41. Cf. the introduction in Emilio Gentile, *E fu subito regime: Il fascismo e la marcia su Roma* (Rome and Bari: Laterza, 2012).

42. Gentile, 'Paramilitary Violence', 98.

43. See, among others, Matteo Millan, *Squadrismo e squadristi nella dittatura fascista* (Rome: Viella, 2014); Emilio Gentile, 'Fascism in Power: the Totalitarian Experiment', in Adrian Lyttelton (ed.), *Liberal and Fascist Italy 1900–1945* (Oxford and New York: Oxford University Press, 2002), 139–42.

44. Harry Graf Kessler, *Das Tagebuch 1880–1937*, eds Roland Kamzelak and Günter Riederer, vol. 7: *1919–1923* (Stuttgart: Klett-Cotta, 2007), 564 (diary entry of 29 October 1922).

45. Ernst Deuerlein (ed.), *Der Hitler-Putsch: Bayerische Dokumente zum 8./9. November 1923* (Stuttgart: DVA, 1962); Hans Mommsen, 'Adolf Hitler und der 9. November 1923', in Johannes Willms (ed.), *Der 9. November. Fünf Essays zur deutschen Geschichte*, 2nd edition (Munich: C. H. Beck, 1995), 33–48.

46. Thomas Weber, *Hitler's First War: Adolf Hitler, the Men of the List Regiment, and the First World War* (Oxford and New York: Oxford University Press, 2010).

47. Othmar Plöckinger, *Unter Soldaten und Agitatoren. Hitlers prägende Jahre im deutschen Militär 1918–1920* (Paderborn: Schöningh, 2013).

48. Peter Longerich, *Hitler: Biographie* (Munich: Siedler, 2015); Plöckinger, *Hitlers prägende Jahre*.

49. Johannes Erger, *Der Kapp-Lüttwitz-Putsch: Ein Beitrag zur deutschen Innenpolitik, 1919–20* (Düsseldorf: Droste, 1967); Erwin Könnemann and Gerhard Schulze (eds), *Der Kapp-Lüttwitz-Putsch: Dokumente* (Munich: Olzog, 2002); Read, *World on Fire*, 319ff.

50. Read, *World on Fire*, 320.

51. Ibid, 321.

52. Kessler, *Tagebuch*, vol. 7: *1919–1923*, 294 (diary entry of 19 March 1920).

53. Ibid, 295 (diary entry of 20 March 1920).
54. Deuerlein (ed.), *Hitler-Putsch*; Mommsen, 'Adolf Hitler und der 9. November 1923', 33–48.
55. This is an interpretative approach that dates back to the 1930s, supported in particular by Angelo Tasca in his famous book, published during his exile in France, *La Naissance du fascisme* (Paris: Gallimard, 1938). For a more recent play on this theme, see Roberto Vivarelli, *Storia delle origini del fascismo: L'Italia dalla Grande Guerra alla marcia su Roma* (Bologna: il Mulino, 2012).

11. PANDORA'S BOX:
PARIS AND THE PROBLEM OF EMPIRE

1. David Lloyd George, *The Truth About the Peace Treaties*, 2 vols (London: Gollancz, 1938), vol. 1, 565; Margaret MacMillan, *Peacemakers: The Paris Conference of 1919 and its Attempt to End War* (London: John Murray, 2001), 5; Bruno Cabanes, '1919: Aftermath', in Jay Winter (ed.), *Cambridge History of the First World War*, vol. 1 (Cambridge and New York: Cambridge University Press, 2014), 172–97.
2. MacMillan, *Peacemakers*, 7; on the Fiume crisis, ibid, 302–21.
3. Bruno Cabanes, *La victoire endeuillée: La sortie de guerre des soldats français (1918–1920)* (Paris: Éditions du Seuil, 2004).
4. Robert E. Bunselmeyer, *The Cost of War 1914–1919: British Economic War Aims and the Origins of Reparation* (Hamden, CT: Archon Books, 1975), 141; MacMillan, *Peacemakers*, 100; David Reynolds, *The Long Shadow: The Great War and the Twentieth Century* (London: Simon and Schuster, 2013), 93; Heinrich August Winkler, *The Age of Catastrophe: A History of the West 1914–1945* (New Haven, CT, and London: Yale University Press, 2015), 125.
5. Leonard V. Smith, 'The Wilsonian Challenge to International Law', in *The Journal of the History of International Law* 13 (2011), 179–208. See also idem, 'Les États-Unis et l'échec d'une seconde mobilisation', in Stéphane Audoin-Rouzeau and Christophe Prochasson (eds), *Sortir de la Guerre de 14–18* (Paris: Tallandier, 2008), 69–91; Manfred F. Boemeke, 'Woodrow Wilson's Image of Germany, the War-Guilt Question and the Treaty of Versailles', in idem, Gerald D. Feldman and Elisabeth Glaser (eds), *The Treaty of Versailles: A Reassessment after 75 Years* (Cambridge and New York: Cambridge University Press, 1998), 603–14. See also Alexander Sedlmaier, *Deutschlandbilder und Deutschlandpolitik Studien zur Wilson-Administration (1913–1921)* (Stuttgart: Steiner, 2003).

6. Leonard V. Smith, 'Empires at the Paris Peace Conference', in Robert Gerwarth and Erez Manela (eds), *Empires at War, 1911–1923* (Oxford and New York: Oxford University Press, 2014), 254–76.
7. Adam Tooze, *The Deluge: The Great War and the Re-Making of Global Order* (London: Allen Lane, 2014).
8. See, in particular, Boemeke, Feldman and Glaser (eds), *The Treaty of Versailles*; David A. Andelman, *A Shattered Peace: Versailles 1919 and the Price We Pay Today* (Hoboken, NJ: Wiley, 2008); MacMillan, *Peacemakers*; Alan Sharp, *The Versailles Settlement: Peacemaking after the First World War, 1919–1923*, 2nd edition (London: Palgrave, 2008).
9. Boemeke, Feldman and Glaser (eds), *The Treaty of Versailles*, 11–20; Zara Steiner, 'The Treaty of Versailles Revisited', in Michael Dockrill and John Fisher (eds), *The Paris Peace Conference 1919: Peace without Victory?* (Basingstoke: Palgrave Macmillan, 2001), 13–33; Mark Mazower, 'Two Cheers for Versailles', in *History Today* 49 (1999); Alan Sharp, *Consequences of the Peace: The Versailles Settlement – Aftermath and Legacy 1919–2010* (London: Haus, 2010), 1–40; Sally Marks, 'Mistakes and Myths: The Allies, Germany and the Versailles Treaty, 1918–1921', in *Journal of Modern History* 85 (2013), 632–59.
10. See, for example, Andelman, *A Shattered Peace*; Norman Graebner and Edward Bennett, *The Versailles Treaty and Its Legacy: The Failure of the Wilsonian Vision* (Cambridge and New York: Cambridge University Press, 2011).
11. Aviel Roshwald, *Ethnic Nationalism and the Fall of Empires: Central Europe, Russia and the Middle East, 1914–1923* (London: Routledge, 2001).
12. On this, see the introduction and chapter contributions to Gerwarth and Manela (eds), *Empires at War, 1911–23*; on the German case in particular, see Annemarie H. Sammartino, *The Impossible Border: Germany and the East, 1914–1922* (Ithaca, NY, and London: Cornell University Press, 2010); Vejas G. Liulevicius, 'Der Osten als apokalyptischer Raum: Deutsche Fronterfahrungen im und nach dem Ersten Weltkrieg', in Gregor Thum (ed.), *Traumland Osten: Deutsche Bilder vom östlichen Europa im 20. Jahrhundert* (Göttingen: Vandenhoeck and Ruprecht, 2006), 47–65.
13. On the Irish case, see the recent accounts of Diarmaid Ferriter, *A Nation and not a Rabble: The Irish Revolution 1913–1923* (London: Profile Books, 2015); Charles Townshend, *The Republic: The Fight for Irish Independence 1918–1923* (London: Allen Lane, 2013).
14. Erez Manela, *The Wilsonian Moment: Self-Determination and the International Origins of Anticolonial Nationalism* (Oxford and New York: Oxford University Press, 2007), 37–43; Woodrow Wilson, 'Four-

teen Points, January 8 1918', in Michael Beschloss (ed.), *Our Documents: 100 Milestone Documents from the National Archives* (Oxford and New York: Oxford University Press, 2006), 149–51. On the different visions offered by Lenin and Wilson, see also Arno Mayer, *Wilson vs. Lenin: Political Origins of the New Democracy, 1917–1918* (Cleveland, OH: World, 1964), and Eric D. Weitz, 'From the Vienna to the Paris System: International Politics and the Entangled Histories of Human Rights, Forced Deportations, and Civilizing Missions', in *The American Historical Review* 113 (2008), 313–43.

15. MacMillan, *Peacemakers*, 67; Sharp, *The Versailles Settlement*.

16. For case studies, see Gerwarth and Manela (eds), *Empires at War*; David M. Anderson and David Killingray (eds), *Policing and Decolonisation: Politics, Nationalism and the Police, 1917–1965* (Manchester: Manchester University Press, 1992); Derek Sayer, 'British Reaction to the Amritsar Massacre, 1919–1920', in *Past & Present* 131 (1991), 130–64; Jon Lawrence, 'Forging a Peaceable Kingdom: War, Violence and Fear of Brutalization in Post-First World War Britain', in *Journal of Modern History* 75 (2003), 557–89; Susan Kingsley Kent, *Aftershocks: Politics and Trauma in Britain, 1918–1931* (Basingstoke and New York: Palgrave Macmillan, 2009), 64–90.

17. Ian Kershaw, *To Hell and Back: Europe, 1914–1949* (London: Allen Lane, 2015), 122.

18. See a number of essays in Gerwarth and Manela (eds), *Empires at War*, notably Leonard Smith, 'Empires at the Paris Peace Conference', 254–76, Christopher Capozzo, 'The United States Empire', 235–53, and Frederick R. Dickinson, 'The Japanese Empire', 197–213.

19. Mussolini as quoted in Richard J. B. Bosworth, *Mussolini* (London: Arnold, 2002), 121.

20. See Béla Király, 'East Central European Society and Warfare in the Era of the Balkan Wars', in idem and Dimitrije Đorđević, *East Central European Society and the Balkan Wars* (Boulder, CO: Social Science Monographs, 1987), 3–13; Peter Bartl, *Albanci, od Srednjeg veka do danas* (Belgrade: CLIO, 2001), 124–38.

21. Richard C. Hall, *The Balkan Wars, 1912–1913: Prelude to the First World War* (London and New York: Routledge, 2000).

22. Uğur Ümit Üngör, 'Mass Violence against Civilians during the Balkan Wars', in Dominik Geppert, William Mulligan and Andreas Rose (eds), *The Wars Before the Great War: Conflict and International Politics Before the Outbreak of the First World War* (Cambridge and New York: Cambridge University Press, 2015).

23. Richard Bessel, 'Revolution', in Winter (ed.), *The Cambridge History of the First World War*, vol. 2, 127. See also Jeffrey R. Smith, *A People's War: Germany's Political Revolution, 1913–1918* (Lanham, MD: University Press of America, 2007), 25–49.

24. Robert A. Kann, *Geschichte des Habsburgerreiches 1526 bis 1918* (Vienna and Cologne: Böhlau, 1990), 581; Peter Haslinger, 'Austria-Hungary', in Gerwarth and Manela (eds), *Empires at War*, 73–90.

25. Haslinger, 'Austria-Hungary', 74.

26. Andrej Mitrović, *Serbia's Great War: 1914–1918* (London: Hurst, 2007), 96. For the general context, see also Frédéric Le Moal, *La Serbie: Du martyre à la victoire 1914–1918* (Paris: Soteca, 2008).

27. See Bela K. Király and Nandor F. Dreisiger (eds), *East Central European Society in World War I* (New York: East European Monographs, 1985), 305–6, and, more generally, Jonathan E. Gumz, *The Resurrection and Collapse of Empire in Habsburg Serbia, 1914–1918* (Cambridge and New York: Cambridge University Press, 2009). See also Pieter M. Judson, *The Habsburg Empire: A New History* (Cambridge, MA: Harvard University Press, 2016), 406.

28. Miklós Bánffy, *The Phoenix Land: The Memoirs of Count Miklós Bánffy* (London: Arcadia Books, 2003), 3–4.

29. Maureen Healy, *Vienna and the Fall of the Habsburg Empire: Total War and Everyday Life in World War I* (Cambridge and New York: Cambridge University Press, 2004), 279–99; Mark Cornwall, 'Morale and Patriotism in the Austro-Hungarian Army, 1914–1918', in John Horne (ed.), *State, Society, and Mobilization in Europe during the First World War* (Cambridge: Cambridge University Press, 1997), 173–91. See also John W. Boyer, *Culture and Political Crisis in Vienna: Christian Socialism in Power, 1897–1918* (Chicago, IL: University of Chicago Press, 1995), 369–443; Laurence Cole and Daniel L. Unowsky (eds), *The Limits of Loyalty: Imperial Symbolism, Popular Allegiances and State Patriotism in the Late Habsburg Monarchy* (New York and Oxford: Berghahn Books, 2007).

30. Mark Cornwall, *The Undermining of Austria-Hungary: The Battle for Hearts and Minds* (Basingstoke: Macmillan, 2000). See Kenneth J. Calder, *Britain and the Origins of the New Europe, 1914–1918* (Cambridge and New York: Cambridge University Press, 1976). Twentieth-century central European historiography (in the English language) was long grounded in this wartime propaganda. Influential historians such as Oszkár Jászi and C. A. Macartney built on the work of the historians mentioned above and argued that national conflict had rendered the

Habsburg monarchy moribund even before the beginning of hostilities in August 1914. Oszkár Jászi, *The Dissolution of the Habsburg Monarchy* (Chicago, IL: University of Chicago Press, 1929); Carlile A. Macartney, *The Habsburg Empire, 1790–1918* (London: Weidenfeld and Nicolson, 1969). For examples of the subsequent generation of historians who agreed that the war was merely a catalyst for the empire's fall, see Robert A. Kann, *The Multinational Empire: Nationalism and National Reform in the Habsburg Monarchy, 1848–1918*, 2 vols (New York: Columbia University Press, 1950); A. J. P. Taylor, *The Habsburg Monarchy, 1809–1918: A History of the Austrian Empire and Austria-Hungary* (London: Hamish Hamilton, 1948).

31. Reynolds, *The Long Shadow*, 15.
32. Andrea Orzoff, *Battle for the Castle* (Oxford and New York: Oxford University Press, 2009), 24.
33. Haslinger, 'Austria-Hungary'.
34. Mark Levene, *War, Jews, and the New Europe: The Diplomacy of Lucien Wolf, 1914–1919* (Oxford and New York: Oxford University Press, 1992), 181. See also Alan Sharp, '"The Genie that Would Not Go Back into the Bottle": National Self-Determination and the Legacy of the First World War and the Peace Settlement', in Seamus Dunn and T. G. Fraser (eds), *Europe and Ethnicity: The First World War and Contemporary Ethnic Conflict* (London and New York: Routledge, 1996), 10–29, 18–19.
35. The United States officially recognized the new state on 7 February 1919; France and Britain in June when the Versailles Treaty had been finalized. Andrej Mitrović, *Jugoslavija na Konferenciji mira 1919–1920* (Belgrade: Zavod za izdavanje udžbenike SR Srbije, 1969), 62–3.
36. As quoted in Mark Mazower, *Dark Continent: Europe's Twentieth Century* (New York: Vintage Books, 1998), 46.
37. For the background to the manifesto, see Manfried Rauchensteiner, *Der Tod des Doppeladlers: Österreich-Ungarn und der Erste Weltkrieg* (Graz: Styria, 1993), 603–8; Edmund Glaise-Horstenau, *The Collapse of the Austro-Hungarian Empire* (London and Toronto: J. M. Dent, 1930), 107–9; Judson, *The Habsburg Empire*, 432; Alexander Watson, *Ring of Steel: Germany and Austria-Hungary at War, 1914–18* (London: Allen Lane, 2014), 541.
38. Jörn Leonhard, *Die Büchse der Pandora: Geschichte des Ersten Weltkriegs* (Munich: C. H. Beck, 2014), 896ff.
39. Jan Křen, *Die Konfliktgemeinschaft: Tschechen und Deutsche, 1780–1918* (Munich: Oldenbourg, 1996), 371–2.
40. Macartney, *The Habsburg Empire*, 831.

41. For the larger context, see Eugene Rogan, *The Fall of the Ottomans: The Great War in the Middle East, 1914–1920* (London: Allen Lane, 2015).

42. For a contemporary justification of the French attachment to the region, see Comte Roger de Gontaut-Biron, *Comment la France s'est installée en Syrie, 1918–1919* (Paris: Plon, 1922), esp. 1–10.

43. On the Sykes-Picot Agreement, see David Fromkin, *A Peace to End All Peace: The Fall of the Ottoman Empire and the Creation of the Modern Middle East* (New York: Henry Holt and Company, 1989), 188–99; David Stevenson, *The First World War and International Politics* (Oxford: Oxford University Press, 1988), 129–30.

44. Gudrun Krämer, *A History of Palestine: From the Ottoman Conquest to the Founding of the State of Israel* (Princeton, NJ: Princeton University Press, 2008), 146; Malcolm E. Yapp, *The Making of the Modern Near East: 1792–1923* (London: Longman, 1987), 281–6.

45. On Faisal, see Ali A. Allawi, *Faisal I of Iraq* (New Haven, CT, and London: Yale University Press, 2014); on Lawrence, see Scott Anderson, *Lawrence in Arabia: War, Deceit, Imperial Folly and the Making of the Modern Middle East* (New York: Doubleday, 2013).

46. Jonathan Schneer, *The Balfour Declaration: The Origins of Arab-Israeli Conflict* (London and Basingstoke: Macmillan, 2014). See also John Darwin, *Britain, Egypt and the Middle East: Imperial Policy in the Aftermath of War, 1918–1922* (London and Basingstoke: Macmillan, 1981), 156.

47. On Weizmann, see Jehuda Reinharz, *Chaim Weizmann: The Making of a Statesman*, 2nd edition (Oxford and New York: Oxford University Press, 1993).

48. For a detailed account, see Schneer, *The Balfour Declaration.*

49. Malcolm E. Yapp, *The Near East Since the First World War: A History to 1995* (London: Longman, 1996), 116.

50. *ha-Herut*, as quoted in Mustafa Aksakal, 'The Ottoman Empire', in Winter (ed.), *The Cambridge History of the First World War*, vol. 1, 459–78, here 477. See also Abigail Jacobson, *From Empire to Empire: Jerusalem between Ottoman and British Rule* (Syracuse, NY: Syracuse University Press, 2011), 27.

51. On Ben-Gurion, see Shabtai Teveth, *Ben-Gurion and the Palestinian Arabs: From Peace to War* (Oxford and New York: Oxford University Press, 1985); idem, *The Burning Ground: A Biography of David Ben-Gurion* (Tel Aviv: Schoken, 1997); Anita Shapira, *Ben-Gurion: Father of Modern Israel* (New Haven, CT, and London: Yale University Press,

2014). On the Jewish Legion, see Martin Watts, *The Jewish Legion and the First World War* (London and New York: Palgrave, 2004).

52. Ryan Gingeras, *Fall of the Sultanate: The Great War and the End of the Ottoman Empire, 1908–1922* (Oxford and New York: Oxford University Press, 2016), 230.

53. Quoted in Jacobson, *From Empire to Empire*, 145; and Aksakal, 'Ottoman Empire', in Winter (ed.), *First World War*, 477.

54. United States Department of State, *Papers relating to the Foreign Relations of the United States. The Paris Peace Conference, 1919* (U.S. Government Printing Office, 1919), vol. XII, 793–5.

55. Bernard Wasserstein, *The British in Palestine: The Mandatory Government and the Arab-Jewish Conflict 1917–1929* (Oxford: Blackwell, 1991).

12. REINVENTING EAST-CENTRAL EUROPE

1. Thomas Sakmyster, *Hungary's Admiral on Horseback: Miklós Horthy, 1918–1944* (Boulder, CO: Eastern European Monographs, 1994), 11.

2. Alexander Watson, *Ring of Steel: Germany and Austria-Hungary at War, 1914–18* (London: Allen Lane, 2014), 542; Pieter M. Judson, *The Habsburg Empire: A New History* (Cambridge, MA: Harvard University Press, 2016), 437.

3. József Galántai, *Hungary in the First World War* (Budapest: Akad. Kiadó, 1989), 315–22; Judson, *The Habsburg Empire*, 438–9; Watson, *Ring of Steel*, 542.

4. Richard G. Plaschka, Horst Haselsteiner and Arnold Suppan, *Innere Front: Militärassistenz, Widerstand und Umsturz in der Donaumonarchie 1918*, 2 vols (Vienna: Verlag für Geschichte und Politik, 1974), vol. 2, 247–59; Watson, *Ring of Steel*, 543.

5. On the murder of Tisza, see Ferenc Pölöskei, *A rejtélyes Tisza-gyilkosság* (Budapest: Helikon Kiadó, 1988).

6. Plaschka, Haselsteiner and Suppan, *Innere Front*, vol. 2, 260–77. For Tisza's death, see Arthur May, *The Passing of the Habsburg Monarchy*, vol. 2 (Philadelphia, PA: University of Pennsylvania Press, 1966), 789; Watson, *Ring of Steel*, 543.

7. Manfried Rauchensteiner, *Der Tod des Doppeladlers: Österreich-Ungarn und der Erste Weltkrieg* (Graz: Styria, 1993), 614–15; Watson, *Ring of Steel*, 543.

8. Zbyněk Zeman, *The Masaryks: The Making of Czechoslovakia* (London: I. B. Tauris, 1976), 115.

9. Plaschka, Haselsteiner and Suppan, *Innere Front*, vol. 2, 143–58, 184–5 and 217; Watson, *Ring of Steel*, 544.

10. Ante Pavelić, *Doživljaji*, reprint (Zagreb: Naklada Starčević, 1996), 459. On his position in 1918 and his subsequent role in the Ustashe, see Fikreta Jelić-Butić, *Ustaše i Nezavisna država Hrvatska 1941–1945* (Zagreb: Školska Knjiga, 1977), 13–14; Mario Jareb, *Ustaško-domobranski pokret od nastanka do travnja 1941* (Zagreb: Hrvatski institut za povijest – Školska Knjiga, 2006), 33–4.

11. Watson, *Ring of Steel*, 544; Alexander V. Prusin, *The Lands Between: Conflict in the East European Borderlands, 1870–1992* (Oxford and New York: Oxford University Press, 2010), 72–97; Piotr J. Wróbel, 'The Seeds of Violence: The Brutalization of an East European Region 1917–1921', in *Journal of Modern European History* 1 (2003), 125–49.

12. Timothy Snyder, *The Reconstruction of Nations: Poland, Ukraine, Lithuania, Belarus 1569–199* (New Haven, CT, and London: Yale University Press, 2003), 137–41; Judson, *Habsburg Empire*, 438.

13. Margaret MacMillan, *Peacemakers: The Paris Conference of 1919 and its Attempt to End War* (London: John Murray, 2001), 217.

14. Włodzimierz Borodziej, *Geschichte Polens im 20. Jahrhundert* (Munich: C. H. Beck, 2010), 97; on the American Relief Administration in Poland, see Matthew Lloyd Adams, 'When Cadillacs Crossed Poland: The American Relief Administration in Poland, 1919–1922', PhD thesis, Armstrong Atlantic State University, 2005; Paul Niebrzydowski, *The American Relief Administration in Poland after the First World War, 1918–1923* (Washington DC: IARO Scholar Research Brief, 2015); William Remsburgh Grove, *War's Aftermath: Polish Relief in 1919* (New York: House of Field, 1940).

15. Piotr Stefan Wandycz, *The Lands of Partitioned Poland, 1795–1918* (Seattle, WA: University of Washington Press, 1974), 291–3; Norman Davies, *God's Playground*, vol. 2: *1795 to the Present* (Oxford and New York: Oxford University Press, 2005), 52–3; MacMillan, *Peacemakers*, 219ff; see also Jochen Böhler, 'Generals and Warlords, Revolutionaries and Nation State Builders: The First World War and its Aftermath in Central and Eastern Europe', in idem, Włodzimierz Borodziej and Joachim von Puttkamer (eds), *Legacies of Violence: Eastern Europe's First World War* (Munich: Oldenbourg, 2014), 51–66.

16. On Piłsudski, see, among other books, Peter Hetherington, *Unvanquished: Joseph Pilsudski, Resurrected Poland, and the Struggle for Eastern Europe*, 2nd edition (Houston, TX: Pingora Press, 2012);

Wacław Jędrzejewicz, *Pilsudski: A Life for Poland* (New York: Hippo-crene Books, 1990); Holger Michael, *Marschall Józef Piłsudski 1867–1935: Schöpfer des modernen Polens* (Bonn: Pahl-Rugenstein, 2010).

17. Davies, *God's Playground*, vol. 2, 385.

18. Ibid, 5ff.

19. Jochen Böhler, 'Enduring Violence. The Post-War Struggles in East-Central Europe 1917–1921', in *Journal of Contemporary History* 50 (2015), 58–77; idem, 'Generals and Warlords, Revolutionaries and Nation State Builders'.

20. On the Polish-Ukrainian conflict, see Torsten Wehrhahn, *Die West-ukrainische Volksrepublik: Zu den polnisch-ukrainischen Beziehungen und dem Problem der ukrainischen Staatlichkeit in den Jahren 1918 bis 1923* (Berlin: Weißensee Verlag, 2004), 102–12; Mykola Lytvyn, *Ukrayins'ko-pol's'ka viyna 1918–1919rr* (L'viv: Inst. Ukraïnoznavstva Im. I. Krypjakevyča NAN Ukraïny; Inst. Schidno-Centralnoï Jevropy, 1998); Michał Klimecki, *Polsko-ukraińska wojna o Lwów i Wschodnią Galicję 1918–1919 r. Aspekty polityczne I wojskowe* (Warsaw: Wojskowy Instytut Historyczny, 1997).

21. MacMillan, *Peacemakers*, 235.

22. Kay Lundgreen-Nielsen, *The Polish Problem at the Paris Peace Conference: A Study in the Policies of Great Powers and the Poles, 1918–1919* (Odense: Odense University Press, 1979), 222–3, 279–88.

23. On Upper Silesia, see Timothy Wilson, *Frontiers of Violence: Conflict and Identity in Ulster and Upper Silesia 1918–1922* (Oxford and New York: Oxford University Press, 2010). On the Polish-Lithuanian conflict, see Andrzej Nowak, 'Reborn Poland or Reconstructed Empire? Questions on the Course and Results of Polish Eastern Policy (1918–1921)', in *Lithuanian Historical Studies* 13 (2008), 134–42; Snyder, *Reconstruction of Nations*, 57–65.

24. Norman Davies, *White Eagle, Red Star: The Polish-Soviet War, 1919–1920 and 'the Miracle on the Vistula'* (London: Pimlico, 2003), 152–9; Jerzy Borzęcki, *The Soviet-Polish Peace of 1921 and the Creation of Interwar Europe* (New Haven, CT, and London: Yale University Press, 2008), 92.

25. Adam Zamoyski, *Warsaw 1920: Lenin's Failed Conquest of Europe* (London: Harper Press, 2008), 67; Davies, *White Eagle, Red Star*, 141, 152ff. On the atrocities, see Jerzy Borzęcki, 'German Anti-Semitism à la Polonaise: A Report on Poznanian Troops' Abuse of Belarusian Jews in 1919', in *East European Politics and Cultures* 26 (2012), 693–707.

26. Arnold Zweig, *Das ostjüdische Antlitz* (Berlin: Welt Verlag, 1920), 9–11.

27. On French involvement in the war, see Frédéric Guelton, 'La France et la guerre polono-bolchevique', in *Annales: Académie Polonaise des Sciences, Centre Scientifique à Paris* 13 (2010), 89–124; idem, 'Le Capitaine de Gaulle et la Pologne (1919–1921)', in Bernard Michel and Józef Łaptos (eds), *Les Relations entre la France et la Pologne au XXe siècle* (Cracow: Eventus, 2002), 113–27.

28. Davies, *White Eagle, Red Star*, 261ff; Borzęcki, *The Soviet-Polish Peace of 1921*.

29. See Piotr Stefan Wandycz, *France and her Eastern Allies, 1919–25: French-Czechoslovak-Polish Relations from the Paris Peace Conference to Locarno* (Minneapolis, MN: University of Minnesota Press, 1962), 75–91.

30. Robert Howard Lord, 'Poland', in Edward M. House and Charles Seymour (eds), *What Really Happened at Paris: The Story of the Peace Conference by American Delegates* (London: Hodder and Stoughton, 1921), 67–86, 82–3; on the dispute, see Harold Temperley (ed.), *A History of the Peace Conference of Paris*, 6 vols (London: Frowde and Hodder and Stoughton, 1921–4), vol. 4, 348–63.

31. On the Czech-German clashes in the first interwar years, see Karl Braun, 'Der 4. März 1919. Zur Herausbildung Sudetendeutscher Identität', in *Bohemia* 37 (1996), 353–80; Johann Wolfgang Brügel, *Tschechen und Deutsche 1918–1938* (Munich: Nymphenburger Verlagshandlung, 1967), 75–78; Rudolf Kučera, 'Exploiting Victory, Sinking into Defeat: Uniformed Violence in the Creation of the New Order in Czechoslovakia and Austria 1918–1922', in *Journal of Modern History* (forthcoming).

32. On the international context of the war, see Miklos Lojko, *Meddling in Middle Europe: Britain and the 'Lands Between', 1918–1925* (Budapest and New York: Central European University Press, 2006), 13–38; Dagmar Perman, *The Shaping of the Czechoslovak State: Diplomatic History of the Boundaries of Czechoslovakia* (Leiden: Brill, 1962); Wandycz, *France and Her Eastern Allies*, 49–74.

33. On the returnees, see Gerburg Thunig-Nittner, *Die Tschechoslowakische Legion in Rußland: Ihre Geschichte und Bedeutung bei der Entstehung der 1. Tschechoslowakischen Republik* (Wiesbaden: Harrassowitz, 1970), 112–23. On the special position of the Czechoslovak Legion members in the Czechoslovak republic, see Natali Stegmann, *Kriegsdeutungen, Staatsgründungen, Sozialpolitik: Der Helden- und Opferdiskurs in der Tschechoslowakei, 1918–1948* (Munich: Oldenbourg, 2010), 63–116.

34. Ivan Šedivý, 'Zur Loyalität der Legionäre in der ersten Tschecho-

slowakischen Republik', in Martin Schulze Wessel (ed.), *Loyalitäten in der Tschechoslowakischen Republik 1918–1938: Politische, nationale und kulturelle Zugehörigkeiten* (Munich: Oldenbourg, 2004), 141–52; Kučera, 'Exploiting Victory, Sinking into Defeat'. For a comparative perspective on Alsace-Lorraine and the Czechoslovak borderlands, see Tara Zahra, 'The "Minority Problem": National Classification in the French and Czechoslovak Borderlands', in *Contemporary European Review* 17 (2008), 137–65.

35. Kučera, 'Exploiting Victory, Sinking into Defeat'.

36. Peter A. Toma, 'The Slovak Soviet Republic of 1919', in *American Slavic and East European Review* 17 (1958), 203–15; Ladislav Lipscher, 'Die Lage der Juden in der Tschechoslowakei nach deren Gründung 1918 bis zu den Parlamentswahlen 1920', in *East Central Europe* 1 (1989), 1–38. On the broader central European context, see Eliza Ablovatski, 'The 1919 Central European Revolutions and the Judeo-Bolshevik Myth', in *European Review of History* 17 (2010), 473–49; Paul Hanebrink, 'Transnational Culture War: Christianity, Nation and the Judeo-Bolshevik Myth in Hungary 1890–1920', in *Journal of Modern History* (2008), 55–80; Kučera, 'Exploiting Victory, Sinking into Defeat'.

37. Kučera, 'Exploiting Victory, Sinking into Defeat'.

38. Andrej Mitrović, *Serbia's Great War: 1914–1918* (London: Hurst, 2007), 320; Mile Bjelajac, *Vojska Kraljevine Srba, Hrvata i Slovenaca 1918–1921* (Belgrade: Narodna knjiga, 1988), 28–9.

39. Milorad Ekmečić, *Stvaranje Jugoslavije 1790–1918*, vol. 2 (Belgrade: Prosveta, 1989), 838; Holm Sundhaussen, *Geschichte Serbiens: 19.–21. Jahrhundert* (Vienna: Böhlau, 2007).

40. John Paul Newman, *Yugoslavia in the Shadow of War: Veterans and the Limits of State Building, 1903–1945* (Cambridge and New York: Cambridge University Press, 2015), 189.

41. Mile Bjelajac, '1918: oslobođenje ili okupacija nesrpskih krajeva?', in Milan Terzić, *Prvi svetski rat i Balkan – 90 godina* (Belgrade: Institut za strategijska istraživanja, 2010), 201–23.

42. On Carinthia, see Bjelajac, *Vojska Kraljevine Srba*, 56; Siegmund Knaus, *Darstellungen aus den Nachkriegskämpfen deutscher Truppen und Freikorps*, vols 7 and 8 (Berlin: Mittler and Sohn, 1941–2); Wilhelm Neumann, *Abwehrkampf und Volksabstimmung in Kärnten, 1918–1920: Legenden und Tatsachen*, 2nd edition (Klagenfurt: Kärntner Landesarchiv, 1985); and the autobiographical account by Jaromir Diakow, in ÖStA, Kriegsarchiv B727, Diakow Papers.

43. On Carinthia and a reprint of the poem, see the anonymous text, 'Der

Sturm auf Völkermarkt am 2. Mai 1919', in ÖStA, Kriegsarchiv, B694, Knaus Papers, 31.

44. MacMillan, *Peacemakers*, 125.

45. Christopher Clark, *Sleepwalkers: How Europe Went to War in 1914* (London: Allen Lane, 2012), 7 and 367–76; MacMillan, *Peacemakers*, 120ff.

46. On the leading Serb and the leading Croat politician during Yugoslavia's formative period and their relationship, see Dejan Djokić, *Pašić and Trumbić: The Kingdom of Serbs, Croats, and Slovenes* (London: Haus, 2010).

47. Ibid.

48. Ibid.

49. Trumbić, as quoted in MacMillan, *Peacemakers*, 123.

50. Mitrović, *Serbia's Great War*, 94–5; Branko Petranović, *Istorija Jugoslavije*, vol. 1 (Belgrade: Nolit, 1988), 12.

51. MacMillan, *Peacemakers*, 124.

52. Srdja Pavlović, *Balkan Anschluss: The Annexation of Montenegro and the Creation of a Common South Slav State* (West Lafayette, IN: Purdue University Press, 2008), 153; Novica Rakočević, *Crna Gora u Prvom svetskom ratu 1914–1918* (Cetinje: Obod, 1969), 428–9.

53. Djordje Stanković, 'Kako je Jugoslavija počela', in Milan Terzić, *Prvi svetski rat i Balkan – 90 godina kasnije* (Belgrade: Institut za strategijska istraživanja, 2010), 242.

54. Newman, *Yugoslavia*.

55. Dejan Djokić, *Elusive Compromise: A History of Interwar Yugoslavia* (Oxford and New York: Oxford University Press, 2007).

13. VAE VICTIS

1. Bruno Cabanes, '1919: Aftermath', in Jay Winter (ed.), *Cambridge History of the First World War*, vol. 1 (Cambridge: Cambridge University Press, 2014), 172–98, here 174.

2. Stéphane Audoin-Rouzeau, 'Die Delegation der "Gueules cassées" in Versailles am 28. Juni 1919', in Gerd Krumeich et al. (eds), *Versailles 1919: Ziele, Wirkung, Wahrnehmung* (Essen: Klartext Verlag, 2001), 280–7.

3. Edward M. House, *The Intimate Papers of Colonel House Arranged as a Narrative by Charles Seymour*, vol. IV (Boston, MA, and New York: Houghton Mifflin, 1926–8), 487.

4. As quoted in Cabanes, '1919: Aftermath', 172–98.

5. Laird Boswell, 'From Liberation to Purge Trials in the "Mythic Provinces": Recasting French Identities in Alsace and Lorraine, 1918–1920', in *French Historical Studies* 23 (2000), 129–62, here 141.

6. Alan Sharp, 'The Paris Peace Conference and its Consequences', in *1914–1918 online. International Encyclopedia of the First World War.*

7. Gotthold Rhode, 'Das Deutschtum in Posen und Pommerellen in der Zeit der Weimarer Republik', in Senatskommission für das Studium des Deutschtums im Osten an der Rheinischen Friedrich-Wilhelms-Universität Bonn (ed.), *Studien zum Deutschtum im Osten* (Cologne and Graz: Böhlau, 1966), 99. Other estimates are higher. See Richard Blanke, *Orphans of Versailles: The Germans in Western Poland, 1918–1939* (Lexington, KY: University Press of Kentucky, 1993), 32–4.

8. For the full story of Upper Silesia's dramatic yet profoundly ambivalent nationalization, see James E. Bjork, *Neither German Nor Pole: Catholicism and National Indifference in a Central European Borderland, 1890–1922* (Ann Arbor, MI: University of Michigan Press, 2008); T. Hunt Tooley, 'German Political Violence and the Border Plebiscite in Upper Silesia, 1919–1921', in *Central European History* 21 (1988), 56–98, and idem, *National Identity and Weimar Germany: Upper Silesia and the Eastern Border, 1918–22* (Lincoln, NB, and London: University of Nebraska Press, 1997). See also Tim K. Wilson, 'The Polish-German Ethnic Dispute in Upper Silesia, 1918–1922: A Reply to Tooley', in *Canadian Review of Studies in Nationalism* 32 (2005), 1–26.

9. Margaret MacMillan, *Peacemakers: The Paris Conference of 1919 and its Attempt to End War* (London: John Murray, 2001), 230.

10. Waldemar Grosch, *Deutsche und polnische Propaganda während der Volksabstimmung in Oberschlesien 1919–1921* (Dortmund: Forschungsstelle Ostmitteleuropa, 2003).

11. Britain and France divided German Kamerun (Cameroon) and Togoland. Belgium gained Ruanda-Urundi in north-western German East Africa, while German South-West Africa (Namibia) was taken under mandate by South Africa. In the Pacific, Japan gained Germany's islands north of the equator (the Marshall Islands, the Carolines, the Marianas, the Palau Islands) and Kiautschou in China. German Samoa was assigned to New Zealand; German New Guinea, the Bismarck Archipelago and Nauru to Australia. Alan Sharp, *The Versailles Settlement: Peacemaking after the First World War, 1919–1923*, 2nd edition (London: Palgrave, 2008), 109–38.

12. Wolfgang Elz, 'Versailles und Weimar', in *Aus Politik und Zeitgeschichte*, 50/51 (2008), 31–8.

13. Sally Marks, 'The Myths of Reparations', in *Central European History*

11 (1978), 231–9; Niall Ferguson, *The Pity of War: Explaining World War I* (London: Allen Lane, 1998), 399–432. The London Schedule of Payments was also to be revised twice, in 1924 (Dawes Plan) and 1929 (Young Plan), before being temporarily suspended during the Great Depression. When Hitler came to power, he cancelled all further payments. Between 1919 and 1932, Germany paid just over 20 billion marks (out of 50 billion gold marks agreed on in 1921 as A and B bonds) in reparations. See Manfred F. Boemeke, Gerald D. Feldman and Elisabeth Glaser (eds), *The Treaty of Versailles: A Reassessment after 75 Years* (Cambridge and New York: Cambridge University Press, 1998), 424.

14. Richard J. Evans, *The Coming of the Third Reich* (London: Penguin, 2004), 65; Alan Sharp, 'The Paris Peace Conference and its Consequences', in *1914–1918 online. International Encyclopedia of the First World War*; MacMillan, *Peacemakers*, 186.

15. Andreas Krause, *Scapa Flow: Die Selbstversenkung der Wilhelminischen Flotte* (Berlin: Ullstein, 1999).

16. *Verhandlungen der verfassunggebenden Deutschen Nationalversammlung. Stenographische Berichte*, vol. 327 (Berlin: Norddeutsche Buchdruckerei u. Verlagsanstalt, 1920), 1,082ff.

17. Alexander Watson, *Ring of Steel: Germany and Austria-Hungary at War, 1914–18* (London: Allen Lane, 2014), 561; MacMillan, *Peacemakers*, 475–81. For Wilson's note of 23 October 1918, see Harry Rudolph Rudin, *Armistice 1918* (New Haven, CT, and London: Yale University Press, 1944), 173.

18. Sharp, *Versailles*, 37–9.

19. Evans, *Coming of the Third Reich*, 66.

20. Heinrich August Winkler, *The Age of Catastrophe: A History of the West 1914–1945* (New Haven, CT, and London: Yale University Press, 2015), 888.

21. John Maynard Keynes, *The Economic Consequences of the Peace* (London: Macmillan, 1919).

22. Elz, 'Versailles und Weimar', 33.

23. On the Treaty of St Germain, see Nina Almond and Ralph Haswell Lutz (eds), *The Treaty of St. Germain: A Documentary History of its Territorial and Political Clauses* (Stanford, CA: Stanford University Press, 1935); Isabella Ackerl and Rudolf Neck (eds), *Saint-Germain 1919: Protokoll des Symposiums am 29. und 30. Mai 1979 in Wien* (Vienna: Verlag für Geschichte und Politik, 1989); Fritz Fellner, 'Der Vertrag von St. Germain', in Erika Weinzierl and Kurt Skalnik (eds), *Österreich 1918–1938*, vol. 1 (Vienna: Böhlau, 1983), 85–106; Lorenz

Mikoletzky, 'Saint-Germain und Karl Renner: Eine Republik wird diktiert', in Helmut Konrad and Wolfgang Maderthaner (eds), *Das Werden der Ersten Republik ... der Rest ist Österreich*, vol. 1 (Vienna: Carl Gerald's Sohn, 2008), 179–86. Erich Zöllner, *Geschichte Österreichs: Von den Anfängen bis zur Gegenwart*, 8th edition (Vienna: Verlag für Geschichte und Politik, 1990), 499.

24. S. W. Gould, 'Austrian Attitudes toward Anschluss: October 1918–September 1919', in *Journal of Modern History* 22 (1950), 220–31; Walter Rauscher, 'Die Republikgründungen 1918 und 1945', in Klaus Koch, Walter Rauscher, Arnold Suppan and Elisabeth Vyslonzil (eds), *Außenpolitische Dokumente der Republik Österreich 1918–1938. Sonderband: Von Saint-Germain zum Belvedere: Österreich und Europa 1919–1955* (Vienna and Munich: Verlag für Geschichte und Politik, 2007), 9–24. On the Anschluss debate in Germany, see Robert Gerwarth, 'Republik und Reichsgründung: Bismarcks kleindeutsche Lösung im Meinungsstreit der ersten deutschen Demokratie', in Heinrich August Winkler (ed.), *Griff nach der Deutungsmacht: Zur Geschichte der Geschichtspolitik in Deutschland* (Göttingen: Wallstein, 2004), 115–33.

25. Ivan T. Berend, *Decades of Crisis: Central and Eastern Europe before World War II* (Berkeley, CA: University of California Press, 1998), 224–6.

26. Maureen Healy, *Vienna and the Fall of the Habsburg Empire: Total War and Everyday Life in World War I* (Cambridge and New York: Cambridge University Press, 2004), 309; Manfried Rauchensteiner, 'L'Autriche entre confiance et résignation, 1918–1920', in Stéphane Audoin-Rouzeau and Christophe Prochasson (eds), *Sortir de la Grande Guerre* (Paris: Tallandier, 2008), 165–85.

27. Francesca M. Wilson, *Rebel Daughter of a Country House: The Life of Eglantyne Jebb, Founder of the Save the Children Fund* (Boston, MA, and London: Allen and Unwin, 1967), 198.

28. Ethel Snowden, as quoted in Ian Kershaw, *To Hell and Back: Europe, 1914–1949* (London: Allen Lane, 2015), 99.

29. Almond and Lutz (eds), *St. Germain*, 92.

30. Karl Rudolf Stadler, *Birth of the Austrian Republic 1918–1921* (Leyden: Sijthoff, 1966), 41–2.

31. Renner as quoted in MacMillan, *Peacemakers*, 258.

32. Stadler, *Birth of the Austrian Republic*, 48.

33. MacMillan, *Peacemakers*, 261.

34. Bauer, as quoted in ibid, 259.

35. Evans, *Coming of the Third Reich*, 62ff; Gerwarth, 'Republik und Reichsgründung'.

36. MacMillan, *Peacemakers*, 264; Stadler, *Birth of the Austrian Republic*, 136–41; József Botlik, *Nyugat-Magyarország sorsa, 1918–1921* (Vasszilvány: Magyar Nyugat Könyvkiadó, 2008); Jon Dale Berlin, 'The Burgenland Question 1918–1920: From the Collapse of Austria-Hungary to the Treaty of Trianon', unpublished PhD dissertation, Madison, WI, 1974; Gerald Schlag, 'Die Grenzziehung Österreich-Ungarn 1922/23', in Burgenländisches Landesarchiv (ed.), *Burgenland in seiner pannonischen Umwelt: Festgabe für August Ernst* (Eisenstadt: Burgenländisches Landesarchiv, 1984), 333–46.

37. For a general account of the effects of Trianon, see Robert Evans, 'The Successor States', in Robert Gerwarth (ed.), *Twisted Paths: Europe 1914–45* (Oxford and New York: Oxford University Press, 2007), 210–36; Raymond Pearson, 'Hungary: A State Truncated, a Nation Dismembered', in Seamus Dunn and T. G. Fraser, *Europe and Ethnicity: World War I and Contemporary Ethnic Conflict* (London and New York: Routledge, 1996), 88–109, here 95–6. Ignác Romsics, *A trianoni békeszerződés* (Budapest: Osiris, 2008); Dániel Ballabás, *Trianon 90 év távlatából: Konferenciák, műhelybeszélgetések* (Eger: Líceum Kiadó, 2011).

38. Berend, *Decades of Crisis*, 224–6.

39. MacMillan, *Peacemakers*, 277; Francis Deák, *Hungary at the Peace Conference: The Diplomatic History of the Treaty of Trianon* (New York: Columbia University Press, 1942), 539–49.

40. Jörg K. Hoensch, *A History of Modern Hungary, 1867–1994* (London and New York: Longman, 1995), 103–4.

41. Georgi P. Genov, *Bulgaria and the Treaty of Neuilly* (Sofia: H. G. Danov and Co., 1935), 31; MacMillan, *Peacemakers*, 248–50.

42. Genov, *Neuilly*, 25 and 49; MacMillan, *Peacemakers*, 150.

43. Harold Nicolson, *Peacemaking, 1919* (London: Grosset and Dunlap, 1933), 34.

44. Letter from Teodor Teodorov to Mr Dutaste, Secretary of the Peace Conference, Neuilly sur Seine, 2 September 1919; Tsocho Bilyarski and Nikola Grigorov (eds), *Nyoiskiyat pogrom i terorat na bulgarite: Sbornik dokumenti i materiali* (Sofia: Aniko, 2009), 90.

45. Richard J. Crampton, *Aleksandur Stamboliiski: Bulgaria* (Chicago, IL: Haus Publishing and University of Chicago Press, 2009), 75–109; Nejiski Mir, *Vojna enciklopedija* (Belgrade: Vojno-izdavački zavod, 1973), 19.

46. MacMillan, *Peacemakers*, 151.

47. Ibid.

48. Doncho Daskalov, *1923 – Sadbonosni resheniya i sabitiya* (Sofia: BZNS, 1983), 23.

49. Theodora Dragostinova, 'Competing Priorities, Ambiguous Loyalties: Challenges of Socioeconomic Adaptation and National Inclusion of the Interwar Bulgarian Refugees', in *Nationalities Papers* 34 (2006), 549–74, here 553. For a detailed early analysis and insightful interpretation of the refugee crisis in interwar Bulgaria, see Dimitar Popnikolov, *Balgarite ot Trakiya i spogodbite na Balgaria s Gartsia i Turtsia* (Sofia: n.p., 1928).

50. For details of the social and economic difficulties with the accommodation of refugees after the First World War in Bulgaria, see Georgi Dimitrov, *Nastanyavane i ozemlyavane na balgarskite bezhantsi* (Blagoevgrad: n.p., 1985); Karl Hitilov, *Selskostopanskoto nastanyavane na bezhantsite 1927–1932* (Sofia: Glavna direktsiya na bezhantsite, 1932).

51. Letter of Alexander Stambolijski to Georges Clemenceau, 22 November 1919. See Bilyarski and Grigorov (eds), *Nyoiskiyat pogrom*, 312.

52. Richard J. Crampton, 'The Balkans', in Gerwarth (ed.), *Twisted Paths*, here 250–2.

53. MacMillan, *Peacemakers*, 386–7.

54. Erik Jan Zürcher, 'The Ottoman Empire and the Armistice of Moudros', in Hugh Cecil and Peter H. Liddle (eds), *At the Eleventh Hour: Reflections, Hopes, and Anxieties at the Closing of the Great War, 1918* (London: Leo Cooper, 1998), 266–75.

55. Quoted in George Goldberg, *The Peace to End Peace: The Paris Peace Conference of 1919* (London: Pitman, 1970), 196.

56. Michael A. Reynolds, 'Ottoman-Russian Struggle for Eastern Anatolia and the Caucasus, 1908–1918: Identity, Ideology and the Geopolitics of World Order', PhD thesis, Princeton University, 2003, 377. From a nationalist perspective, see Justin McCarthy, *Death and Exile: The Ethnic Cleansing of Ottoman Muslims 1821–1922* (Princeton, NJ: Darwin Press, 2004), 198–200; Salahi Sonyel, *The Great War and the Tragedy of Anatolia: Turks and Armenians in the Maelstrom of Major Powers* (Ankara: Turkish Historical Society, 2000), 161–3.

57. Ryan Gingeras, *Fall of the Sultanate: The Great War and the End of the Ottoman Empire, 1908–1922* (Oxford and New York: Oxford University Press, 2016), 255.

58. Hasan Kayali, 'The Struggle for Independence', in Reşat Kasaba (ed.), *The Cambridge History of Turkey*, vol. 4: *Turkey in the Modern World* (Cambridge and New York: Cambridge University Press, 2008), 118ff.

59. Gerd Krumeich (ed.), *Versailles 1919: Ziele, Wirkung, Wahrnehmung* (Essen: Klartext Verlag, 2001).

60. Henryk Batowski, 'Nationale Konflikte bei der Entstehung der Nachfolgestaaten', in Richard Georg Plaschka and Karlheinz Mack (eds),

Die Auflösung des Habsburgerreiches: Zusammenbruch und Neuorientierung im Donauraum (Munich: Oldenbourg, 1970), 338–49.

61. Dudley Kirk, *Europe's Population in the Interwar Years* (Geneva and New York: League of Nations, 1946); Pearson, 'Hungary', 98–9; István I. Mócsy, *The Effects of World War I: The Uprooted: Hungarian Refugees and their Impact on Hungary's Domestic Politics, 1918–1921* (New York: Columbia University Press, 1983), 10.

62. Hannah Arendt, *The Origins of Totalitarianism* (New York: Harcourt, Brace and Company, 1951), 260; On this general theme, see also Karen Barkey and Mark von Hagen (eds), *After Empires: Multiethnic Societies and Nation-Building: The Soviet Union, and the Russian, Ottoman, and Habsburg Empires* (Boulder, CO: Westview Press, 1997), and Leonard V. Smith, 'Empires at the Paris Peace Conference', in Gerwarth and Manela (eds), *Empires at War*, 254–276.

63. Norman Davies, *Microcosm: A Portrait of a Central European City* (London: Pimlico, 2003), 337.

64. Ibid, 389–90.

65. As Michael Mann has pointed out, those who in addition lost their homes as frontiers moved at the conflict's end were six times overrepresented among Holocaust perpetrators. Michael Mann, *The Dark Side of Democracy: Explaining Ethnic Cleansing* (Cambridge and New York: Cambridge University Press, 2005), 223–8.

66. See Mark Mazower, *Hitler's Empire: How the Nazis Ruled Europe* (New York: Penguin Press, 2008).

67. Statistics according to M. C. Kaser and E. A. Radice (eds), *The Economic History of Eastern Europe, 1919–1975*, vol. 1: *Economic Structure and Performance Between the Two Wars* (Oxford: Clarendon Press, 1985), 25. See also the detailed discussion of the issue in Alexander V. Prusin, *The Lands Between: Conflict in the East European Borderlands, 1870–1992* (Oxford and New York: Oxford University Press, 2010), 11–124.

68. Erez Manela, *The Wilsonian Moment: Self-Determination and the International Origins of Anticolonial Nationalism* (Oxford and New York: Oxford University Press, 2007), esp. 60–1 and 145–7. On the May Fourth Movement, see Rana Mitter, *A Bitter Revolution: China's Struggle with the Modern World* (Oxford and New York: Oxford University Press, 2004).

69. Eric Yellin, *Racism in the Nation's Service: Government Workers and the Color Line in Woodrow Wilson's America* (Chapel Hill, NC: University of North Carolina Press, 2016). For a more sympathetic life of Wilson, see John Milton Cooper, *Woodrow Wilson: A Biography* (New York: Random House, 2009).

70. Leonard V. Smith, 'The Wilsonian Challenge to International Law', in *The Journal of the History of International Law* 13 (2011), 179–208. See also idem, 'Les États-Unis et l'échec d'une seconde mobilisation', in Stéphane Audoin-Rouzeau and Christophe Prochasson (eds), *Sortir de la Guerre de 14–18* (Paris: Tallandier, 2008), 69–91.

71. Smith, 'Empires at the Paris Peace Conference'.

72. On the mandate system, see Susan Pedersen, 'The Meaning of the Mandates System: An Argument', in *Geschichte und Gesellschaft* 32 (2006), 1–23; Susan Pedersen, *The Guardians: The League of Nations and the Crisis of Empire* (Oxford and New York: Oxford University Press, 2015), 17–44. See also Nadine Méouchy and Peter Sluglett (eds), *The British and French Mandates in Comparative Perspective* (Leiden: Brill, 2004); and David K. Fieldhouse, *Western Imperialism in the Middle East, 1914–1958* (Oxford and New York: Oxford University Press, 2006), 3–20; See also Lutz Raphael, *Imperiale Gewalt und Mobilisierte Nation: Europa 1914–1945* (Munich: C. H. Beck, 2011), 74–5.

73. Alan Sharp, '"The Genie that Would Not Go Back into the Bottle": National Self-Determination and the Legacy of the First World War and the Peace Settlement', in Seamus Dunn and T. G. Fraser (eds), *Europe and Ethnicity: The First World War and Contemporary Ethnic Conflict* (London and New York: Routledge, 1996), 25; Raymond Pearson, *National Minorities in Eastern Europe: 1848–1945* (London: Macmillan, 1983), 136.

74. Mark Levene, *Crisis of Genocide*, vol. 1: *The European Rimlands 1912–1938* (Oxford and New York: Oxford University Press, 2014), 230–40.

75. For the text, see 'Treaty of Peace between the United States of America, the British Empire, France, Italy, and Japan and Poland', in *American Journal of International Law* 13, Supplement, Official Documents (1919), 423–40. Carole Fink, 'The Minorities Question at the Paris Peace Conference: The Polish Minority Treaty, June 28, 1919', in Manfred Boemeke, Gerald Feldman and Elisabeth Glaser, (eds), *The Treaty of Versailles: A Reassessment after 75 Years* (Cambridge: Cambridge University Press, 1998), 249–74.

76. Ibid.

77. Jaroslav Kucera, *Minderheit im Nationalstaat: Die Sprachenfrage in den tschechisch-deutschen Beziehungen 1918–1938* (Munich: Oldenbourg, 1999), 307.

78. Carole Fink, *Defending the Rights of Others: The Great Powers, the Jews, and International Minority Protection* (Cambridge and New York: Cambridge University Press, 2004), 260; Zara Steiner, *The Lights*

that Failed: European International History 1919–1933 (Oxford and New York: Oxford University Press, 2005), 86.

79. Joseph Roth, *Radetzky March* (New York: Viking Press, 1933), 148–9. On the cultural context, see Adam Kozuchowski, *The Afterlife of Austria-Hungary: The Image of the Habsburg Monarchy in Interwar Europe* (Pittsburgh, PA: University of Pittsburgh Press, 2013).

80. Levene, *Crisis of Genocide*, vol. 1.

81. Mary Heimann, *Czechoslovakia: The State that Failed* (New Haven, CT, and London: Yale University Press, 2009), 33–4 (Pittsburgh Agreement) and 61–2 (on broken promises).

82. On land reform, see Daniel E. Miller, 'Colonizing the Hungarian and German Border Areas during the Czechoslovak Land Reform, 1918–1938', in *Austrian History Yearbook* 34 (2003), 303–17.

83. As quoted in Mark Cornwall, 'National Reparation? The Czech Land Reform and the Sudeten Germans 1918–38', in *Slavonic and East European Review* 75 (1997), 280. On Czech-German relations in interwar Czechoslovakia more broadly, see Jaroslav Kucera, *Minderheit im Nationalstaat*; Jörg Hoensch and Dusan Kovac (eds), *Das Scheitern der Verständigung: Tschechen, Deutsche und Slowaken in der Ersten Republik (1918–1938)* (Essen: Klartext, 1994).

84. On revisionism, see the following collection of essays: Marina Cattaruzza, Stefan Dyroff and Dieter Langewiesche (eds), *Territorial Revisionism and the Allies of Germany in the Second World War: Goals, Expectations, Practices* (New York and Oxford: Berghahn Books, 2012).

14. FIUME

1. On Japan and the First World War, the post-war settlement and Japan's quest for racial equality, see Frederick R. Dickinson, *War and National Reinvention: Japan in the Great War, 1914–1919* (Cambridge, MA, and London: Harvard University Press, 1999); Thomas W. Burkman, *Japan and the League of Nations: Empire and World Order, 1914–1938* (Honolulu: University of Hawai'i Press, 2008); Naoko Shimazu, *Japan, Race and Equality: The Racial Equality Proposal of 1919* (London: Routledge, 1998), 117–36.

2. Glenda Sluga, *The Problem of Trieste and the Italo-Yugoslav Border: Difference, Identity, and Sovereignty in Twentieth-Century Europe* (Albany, NY: SUNY Press, 2001).

3. Misha Glenny, *The Balkans, 1804–1999* (London: Granta Books, 1999), 307–92, especially 370–7.

4. See Mario Isnenghi, *L'Italia in piazza. I luoghi della vita pubblica dal 1848 ai giorni nostri* (Milan: Arnoldo Mondadori, 1994), 231–6.

5. On the continuity of the Italian expansionist ambitions, see Claudio G. Segré, 'Il colonialismo e la politica estera: variazioni liberali e fasciste', in Richard J. B. Bosworth and Sergio Romano (eds), *La politica estera italiana 1860–1985* (Bologna: il Mulino, 1991), 121–46.

6. See, for example, Giuseppe Piazza, *La nostra terra promessa: lettere dalla Tripolitania marzo-maggio 1911* (Rome: Lux, 1911). For background, see R. J. B. Bosworth, *Italy: The Least of the Great Powers: Italian Foreign Policy before the First World War* (Cambridge: Cambridge University Press, 1979), and Gianpaolo Ferraioli, *Politica e diplomazia in Italia tra XIX e XX secolo: vita di Antonino di San Giuliano (1852–1914)* (Soveria Mannelli: Rubbettino, 2007).

7. Richard J. B. Bosworth and Giuseppe Finaldi, 'The Italian Empire', in Robert Gerwarth and Erez Manela (eds), *Empires at War, 1911–1923* (Oxford: Oxford University Press, 2014), 34–51; Claudio G. Segré, 'Il colonialismo e la politica estera: variazioni liberali e fasciste', in Richard Bosworth and Romano (eds), *La politica estera italiana 1860–1985*, 123. See also the volumes of Nicola Labanca: *Oltremare* (Bologna: il Mulino, 2002), and idem, *La guerra italiana per la Libia, 1911–1931* (Bologna: il Mulino, 2012).

8. Angelo Del Boca, *Gli Italiani in Libia, Tripoli bel Suol d'Amore* (Milan: Arnoldo Mondadori, 1993), 110. William Stead, *Tripoli and the Treaties* (London: Bank Buildings, 1911), 59–81; Rachel Simon, *Libya Between Ottomanism and Nationalism* (Berlin: Klaus Schwarz, 1987).

9. Labanca, *Oltremare*, 121; Angelo del Boca, *A un passo dalla forca* (Milan: Baldini Castoli Dalai, 2007), 80.

10. Labanca, *La guerra italiana per la Libia*.

11. Glenny, *The Balkans*, 370.

12. Gian Enrico Rusconi, *L'azzardo del 1915: Come l'Italia decide la sua guerra* (Bologna: il Mulino, 2005); Luca Riccardi, *Alleati non amici: le relazioni politiche tra l'Italia e l'Intesa durante la prima guerra mondiale* (Brescia: Morcelliana, 1992).

13. For an introduction to this theme, see Antonio Gibelli, 'L'Italia dalla neutralità al Maggio Radioso', in Stéphane Audoin-Rouzeau and Jean-Jacques Becker (eds), *La prima guerra mondiale*, vol. 1 (Turin: Einaudi, 2007), 185–95.

14. See Matteo Pasetti, *Tra classe e nazione. Rappresentazioni e organizzazione del movimento nazional-sindacalista, 1918–1922* (Rome: Carocci, 2008).

15. See Emilio Gentile, *La Grande Italia: Ascesa e declino del mito della*

nazione nel ventesimo secolo (Milan: Arnoldo Mondadori, 1997); Angelo Ventrone, *La seduzione totalitaria: Guerra, modernità, violenza politica, 1914–1918* (Rome: Donzelli, 2003), 233–55.

16. Michael A. Ledeen, *The First Duce: D'Annunzio at Fiume* (Baltimore, MD, and London: Johns Hopkins University Press, 1977), 13; Glenny, *The Balkans*, 371.

17. See Claudia Salaris, *Alla festa della rivoluzione. Artisti e libertari con D'Annunzio a Fiume* (Bologna: il Mulino, 2002). On Alceste De Ambris, see Renzo De Felice (ed.), *La Carta del Carnaro nei testi di Alceste De Ambris e di Gabriele D'Annunzio* (Bologna: il Mulino, 1973).

18. Glenny, *The Balkans*, 371–2.

19. Quoted in George Goldberg, *The Peace to End Peace: The Paris Peace Conference of 1919* (London: Pitman, 1970), 170.

20. Lucy Hughes-Hallett, *The Pike: Gabrielle D'Annunzio: Poet, Seducer and Preacher of War* (New York: Fourth Estate, 2013), 267.

21. Ibid, 369.

22. Ledeen, *The First Duce*, 2; Glenny, *The Balkans*, 372–3.

23. On Nitti, see Francesco Barbagallo, *Francesco Saverio Nitti* (Turin: Utet, 1994).

24. Glenny, *The Balkans*, 374.

25. Surprisingly, there are no recent studies on the Arditi. The best 'classic' study remains Giorgio Rochat, *Gli arditi della grande guerra: origini, battaglie e miti* (Milan: Feltrinelli, 1981).

26. Hughes-Hallett, *The Pike*, 4 and 546.

27. Leeden, *The First Duce*, vii. Others have since argued that during the fifteen months of occupation, Fiume became a place of political experiments (e.g. the 'Charter of Carnaro'), of artistic and cultural innovation, as well as the birthplace of 'show politics'. See Salaris, *Alla festa della rivoluzione*.

28. Glenny, *The Balkans*, 376.

15. FROM SMYRNA TO LAUSANNE

1. Margaret MacMillan, *Peacemakers: The Paris Conference of 1919 and its Attempt to End War* (London: John Murray, 2001), 298ff.

2. Ibid, 364ff.

3. On Venizelos, see Thanos Veremis and Elias Nikolakopoulos (eds), *O Eleftherios Venizelos ke I epochi tou* (Athens: Ellinika Grammata, 2005).

4. Misha Glenny, *The Balkans, 1804–1999* (London: Granta Books, 1999), 380; MacMillan, *Peacemakers*, 443 and 449.

5. Glenny, *The Balkans*, 380; Alexandros A. Pallis, *Greece's Anatolian Venture – and After: A Survey of the Diplomatic and Political Aspects of the Greek Expedition to Asia Minor (1915–1922)* (London: Methuen and Company, 1937), 22–5.

6. Figures according to Dimitris Stamatopoulos, 'I mikrasiatiki ekstratia. I anthropogheografia tis katastrofis', in Antonis Liakos (ed.), *To 1922 ke i prosfighes, mia nea matia* (Athens: Nefeli, 2011), 57.

7. Ibid, 58.

8. Dimitri Pentzopoulos, *The Balkan Exchange of Minorities* (Paris and The Hague: Mouton, 1962), 29–30.

9. Michalis Rodas, *I Ellada sti Mikran Asia* (Athens: n.p., 1950), 60–1. Rodas served as head of the press and censorship office at the Smyrna High Commission from 1919 until 1922. See also Evangelia Achladi, 'De la guerre à l'administration grecque: la fin de la Smyrne cosmopolite', in Marie-Carmen Smyrnelis (ed.), *Smyrne, la ville oubliée? 1830–1930: Mémoires d'un grand port ottoman* (Paris: Éditions Autrement, 2006), 180–95.

10. Michael Llewellyn Smith, *Ionian Vision: Greece in Asia Minor 1919–1922* (London: Allen Lane, 1973), 89–91. A statue of Hasan Tahsin, who was killed in the subsequent exchange of fire, is still on display in Izmir today; it is called 'İlk Kurşun Anıtı' (First Bullet Monument).

11. Quoted in Llewellyn Smith, *Ionian Vision*, 89; Glenny, *The Balkans*, 382–3.

12. The reported number of victims varies, depending on the source. The report by the Allied Commission of Investigation that came to Smyrna with the aim of looking into the events recorded two dead Greek soldiers and six wounded, and sixty wounded Greek citizens. The report mentions 300 to 400 Turkish victims, although it does not distinguish between dead and wounded. Llewellyn Smith, *Ionian Vision*, 180.

13. Tasos Kostopoulos, *Polemos ke ethnokatharsi, I ksehasmeni plevra mias dekaetous ethnikis eksormisis, 1912–1922* (Athens: Vivliorama, 2007), 99.

14. Extract from the unpublished diary of Epaminondas Kaliontzis, as printed in the newspaper *Kathimerini* 20/5/2007. See also Ioannis A. Gatzolis, *Ghioulbaxes. Vourlas. Erithrea. Anamnisis. Perigrafes. Laografika. Katastrofi 1922* (Chalkidiki: Nea Syllata, 1988), 45–6.

15. Quoted in Harold M. V. Temperley, (ed.), *A History of the Peace Conference of Paris*, vol. 6 (London: Frowde and Hodder and Stoughton, 1921–4), 72.

16. Giorgos Giannakopoulos, 'I Ellada sti Mikra Asia: To chroniko tis Mikrasiatikis peripetias', in Vassilis Panagiotopoulos (ed.), *Istoria tou*

Neou Ellinismou, 1770–2000, vol. 6, 84–6; Efi Allamani and Christa Panagiotopoulou, 'I Ellada sti Mikra Asia', in *Istoria tou ellinikou ethnous*, vol. 15 (Athens: Ekdotiki Athinon, 1978), 118–32.

17. Report of the Allied Committee of Inquiry, in Rodas, *I Ellada sti Mikran Asia*, 152.

18. The commander of the Greek occupation army put the number of victims at 1,000 and the number of those taken to the hinterland of Asia Minor at 500. Turkish sources, by contrast, speak of 4,000 murdered Muslims and 400 dead Christians. See Kostopoulos, *Polemos ke ethnokatharsi*, 100.

19. Extract from Christos Karagiannis, *I istoria enos stratioti (1918–1922)*, ed. Filippos Drakontaeidis (Athens: Kedros 2013), 117–21.

20. Llewellyn Smith, *Ionian Vision*, 111–14.

21. Ryan Gingeras, *Fall of the Sultanate: The Great War and the End of the Ottoman Empire, 1908–1922* (Oxford and New York: Oxford University Press, 2016), 262.

22. Vamik D. Voltan and Norman Itzkowitz, *The Immortal Atatürk: A Psychobiography* (Chicago, IL: Chicago University Press, 1984), 152.

23. Victor Rudenno, *Gallipoli: Attack from the Sea* (New Haven, CT, and London: Yale University Press, 2008), 162ff.

24. M. Sükrü Hanioğlu, *Atatürk: An Intellectual Biography* (Princeton, NJ: Princeton University Press, 2011), 77.

25. Ibid, 82.

26. Gingeras, *Fall of the Sultanate*, 249.

27. Ryan Gingeras, *Sorrowful Shores: Violence, Ethnicity, and the End of the Ottoman Empire 1912–1923* (Oxford and New York: Oxford University Press, 2009), 68ff.

28. Hanioğlu, *Atatürk*, 97ff; see also Ryan Gingeras, *Mustafa Kemal Atatürk: Heir to an Empire* (Oxford and New York: Oxford University Press, 2015).

29. Hanioğlu, *Atatürk*, 95–7.

30. Ibid.

31. Ibid.

32. A. E. Montgomery, 'The Making of the Treaty of Sèvres of 10 August 1920', in *The Historical Journal* 15 (1972), 775–87.

33. Leonard V. Smith, 'Empires at the Paris Peace Conference', in Robert Gerwarth and Erez Manela (eds), *Empires at War, 1911–1923* (Oxford and New York: Oxford University Press, 2014). See also Paul C. Helmreich, *From Paris to Sèvres: The Partition of the Ottoman Empire at the Paris Peace Conference of 1919–1920* (Columbus, OH: Ohio State University Press, 1974).

34. Briton Cooper Busch, *Madras to Lausanne: Britain's Frontier in West Asia, 1918–1923* (Albany, NY: State University of New York Press, 1976), 207.

35. Christopher J. Walker, *Armenia: The Survival of a Nation*, 2nd edition (London: Routledge, 1990), 315–16.

36. Gingeras, *Fall of the Sultanate*, 279.

37. Vahé Tachjian, *La France en Cilicie et en Haute-Mésopotamie: aux confins de la Turquie, de la Syrie et de l'Irak, 1919–1933* (Paris: Éditions Karthala, 2004).

38. For an eyewitness account see Stanley E. Kerr, *The Lions of Marash: Personal Experiences with American Near East Relief, 1919–1922* (Albany, NY: State University of New York Press, 1973), 99–142.

39. Erik Jan Zürcher, *Turkey: A Modern History* (London and New York: I. B. Tauris, 2004), 154.

40. Peter Kincaid Jensen, 'The Greco-Turkish War, 1920–1922', in *International Journal of Middle East Studies* 10 (1979), 553–65.

41. Giorgos Mitrofanis, 'Ta dimosia ikonomika. Ikonomiki anorthossi ke polemi, 1909–1922', in Vassilis Panagiotopoulos (ed.), *Istoria tou Neou Ellinismou, 1770–2000*, vol. 6 (Athens: Ellinika Grammata, 2003), 124–7.

42. Quoted in Arnold J. Toynbee, *The Western Question in Greece and Turkey: A Study in the Contact of Civilisations* (Boston, MA: Constable, 1922), 285.

43. Konstantinos Fotiadis, 'Der Völkermord an den Griechen des Pontos', in Tessa Hofmann (ed.), *Verfolgung, Vertreibung und Vernichtung der Christen im Osmanischen Reich 1912–1922*, 2nd edition (Berlin: LIT-Verlag, 2010), 193–228.

44. See the testimony of Stylianos Savvides from Neokaisareia, near Katerini, in Paschalis M. Kitromilides (ed.), *Exodos*, vol. 3 (Athens: Centre for Asia Minor Studies, 2013), 220–3.

45. Nicholas Doumanis, *Before the Nation: Muslim-Christian Coexistence and its Destruction in Late Ottoman Anatolia* (Oxford and New York: Oxford University Press, 2013), 161.

46. Kostopoulos, *Polemos ke ethnokatharsi*, 241.

47. Ibid, 240.

48. See the testimony of Savvas Papadopoulos from Vathylakkos, near Kozani, in Kitromilides (ed.), *Exodos*, vol. 3, 206–7.

49. See the testimony of Stylianos Savvides from Neokaisareia, near Katerini, in ibid, 220–3.

50. Extract from Karagiannis, *I istoria enos stratioti*, 215.

51. Giorgos Margaritis, 'I polemi', in Christos Hadjiiosif (ed.), *Istoria tis Elladas tou Ikostou eona*, vol. A (Athens: Vivliorama, 2002), 149–87, here 182, n. 26.

52. Glenny, *The Balkans*, 388.

53. Quoted in Doumanis, *Before the Nation*, 162.

54. Margaritis, 'I polemi', 186.

55. Kostopoulos, *Polemos ke ethnokatharsi*, 138.

56. Victoria Solomonidis, *Greece in Asia Minor: The Greek Administration of the Vilayet of Aidin, 1919–1922*, unpublished PhD thesis, King's College, University of London, 1984, 248–9; Llewellyn Smith, *Ionian Vision*, 520.

57. George Mavrogordatos, 'Metaxi dio polemon. Politiki Istoria 1922–1940', in Vassilis Panagiotopoulos (ed.), *Istoria tou Neou Ellinismou*, vol. 7 (Athens: Ellinika Grammata, 2003), 9–10.

58. Yiannis Yianoulopoulos, 'Exoteriki politiki', in Christos Chatziiosif (ed.), *Istoria tis Elladas tou Ikostou eona*, vol. 2, 140–1.

59. *Toronto Star*, 22 October 1922.

60. Zara Steiner, *The Lights that Failed: European International History 1919–1933* (Oxford and New York: Oxford University Press, 2005), 114–19.

61. MacMillan, *Peacemakers*, 464.

62. Mark Mazower, *Dark Continent: Europe's Twentieth Century* (New York: Vintage Books, 1998), 53; Mark Levene, *Crisis of Genocide*, vol. 1: *The European Rimlands 1912–1938* (Oxford and New York: Oxford University Press, 2014), 230–40. See also Theodora Dragostinova, *Between Two Motherlands: Nationality and Emigration among the Greeks of Bulgaria, 1900–1949* (Ithaca, NY: Cornell University Press, 2011).

63. Levene, *Crisis of Genocide*, vol. 1, 230–40.

64. Testimony of Evripides Lafazanis, in F. D. Apostolopoulos (ed.), *Exodos*, vol. 1 (Athens: Centre for Asia Minor Studies, 1980), 131–6. The famous Greek novelist, Elias Venezis, was a young man of eighteen when he was forced into a labour battalion of 3,000 men at the end of the Greco-Turkish war, and was one of only twenty-three who survived. Venezis' novel *The Number 31,328* recounts his experiences in the labour battalions, but interestingly, like other novels by famous Greek expellees, the story is told without nationalist or anti-Turkish sentiments and focuses on the tragedy of civilians who previously enjoyed good inter-communal relations. Elias Venezis, *To noumero 31328* (1931), and, on the cold reception of refugees from Asia Minor, his novel *Galini* (1939).

65. Quoted in Mark Mazower, *Salonica, City of Ghosts: Christians, Muslims and Jews, 1430–1950* (New York: Harper Perennial, 2005), 335.

66. From Lane Ross Hill in Athens to American Red Cross headquarters in

Washington, 8 November 1922. Records of the Department of State Relating to Internal Affairs of Greece, 1910–1929, National Archives and Records Administration (NARA), M 44, 868.48/297. I am grateful to Ayhan Aktar for providing me with this reference.

67. Henry Morgenthau, *I Was Sent to Athens* (Garden City, NY: Doubleday, 1929), 50. See also Bruce Clark, *Twice a Stranger: How Mass Expulsion Forged Greece and Turkey* (London: Granta Books, 2006).

68. Anastasia Karakasidou, *Fields of Wheat, Hills of Blood: Passages to Nationhood in Greek Macedonia, 1870–1990* (Chicago, IL: University of Chicago Press, 1997), 147; Nikos Marantzidis, 'Ethnic Identity, Memory and Political Behavior: The Case of Turkish-Speaking Pontian Greeks', in *South European Society and Politics* 5 (2000), 56–79, here 62–4.

69. Stathis Gauntlett, 'The Contribution of Asia Minor Refugees to Greek Popular Song, and its Reception', in Renée Hirschon (ed.), *Crossing the Aegean: An Appraisal of the 1923 Compulsory Population Exchange between Greece and Turkey* (New York: Berghahn Books, 2003), 247–60.

70. Renée Hirschon, 'Consequences of the Lausanne Convention: An Overview', in idem (ed.), *Crossing the Aegean: An Appraisal of the 1923 Compulsory Population Exchange between Greece and Turkey* (New York: Berghahn Books, 2003), 14–15; Justin McCarthy, *Death and Exile: The Ethnic Cleansing of Ottoman Muslims 1821–1922* (Princeton, NJ: Darwin Press, 2004), 302.

71. Levene, *Crisis of Genocide*, vol. 1, 236ff.

72. Ibid.

73. Ibid, 233ff. See also Norman M. Naimark, *Fires of Hatred: Ethnic Cleansing in Twentieth-Century Europe* (Cambridge, MA: Harvard University Press, 2002), esp. chapter 1: 'The Armenians and Greeks of Anatolia', 17–56.

74. Stefan Ihrig, *Atatürk in the Nazi Imagination* (Cambridge, MA: Harvard University Press, 2014).

EPILOGUE

1. On this theme, see the essays in Robert Gerwarth (ed.), *Twisted Paths: Europe 1914–1945* (Oxford and New York: Oxford University Press, 2007). On economic recovery and relative political stability through cooperation between American financial power and Britain's political leverage, see also Patrick Cohrs, *The Unfinished Peace after World War*

1: America, Britain and the Stabilisation of Europe, 1919–1932 (Cambridge and New York: Cambridge University Press, 2006).

2. Zara Steiner, *The Lights that Failed: European International History 1919–1933* (Oxford and New York: Oxford University Press, 2005).

3. Paschalis M. Kitromilides (ed.), *Eleftherios Venizelos: The Trials of Statesmanship* (Edinburgh: Edinburgh University Press, 2008), 223.

4. Patricia Clavin, 'Europe and the League of Nations', in Gerwarth (ed.), *Twisted Paths*, 325–54; Pedersen, *The Guardians*; Steiner, *The Lights that Failed*. See also Alan Sharp, *Consequences of the Peace: The Versailles Settlement – Aftermath and Legacy 1919–2010* (London: Haus, 2010), 217.

5. For a general survey of the Great Depression and its effects, see Patricia Clavin, *The Great Depression in Europe, 1929–1939* (Basingstoke and New York: Palgrave, 2000). On Germany in particular, see the classic account by Harold James, *The German Slump: Politics and Economics 1924–1936* (Oxford and New York: Oxford University Press, 1986).

6. On Austria, see Eduard März, 'Die große Depression in Österreich 1930–1933', in *Wirtschaft und Gesellschaft* 16 (1990), 409–38. On Bulgaria and Hungary, see M. C. Kaser and E. A. Radice (eds), *The Economic History of Eastern Europe 1919–1975*, vol. 2: *Interwar Policy, the War and Reconstruction* (Oxford: Clarendon Press, 1986); and Richard J. Crampton, *Eastern Europe in the Twentieth Century and After* (London and New York: Routledge, 1997).

7. On the dual economic and political crisis in interwar Europe, see Robert Boyce, *The Great Interwar Crisis and the Collapse of Globalization* (Basingstoke: Palgrave Macmillan, 2009).

8. Richard J. Evans, *The Coming of the Third Reich* (London: Penguin, 2004), 232–308.

9. Richard J. Overy, *The Interwar Crisis, 1919–1939* (Harlow: Pearson, 1994), 44ff; Woodrow Wilson's quotation is from his speech to the US Congress on 2 April 1917: http://wwi.lib.byu.edu/index.php/Wilson%27s_War_Message_to_Congress, last accessed 9 January 2016.

10. Dimitrina Petrova, *Aleksandar Tzankov i negovata partia: 1932–1944* (Sofia: Dio Mira, 2011); Georgi Naumov, *Aleksandar Tzankov i Andrey Lyapchev v politikata na darzhavnoto upravlenie* (Sofia: IF 94, 2004).

11. See Valentina Zadgorska, *Kragat 'Zveno' (1927–1934)* (Sofia: 'Sv. Kliment Ohridski', 2008), 8.

12. On King Boris III and his rule, see Georgi Andreev, *Koburgite i katastrofite na Bulgaria* (Sofia: Agato, 2005); Nedyu Nedev, *Tsar Boris III: Dvoretsat i tayniyat cabinet* (Plovdiv: IK 'Hermes', 2009); Stefan Gruev, *Korona ot trani* (Sofia: Balgarski pisatel, 2009).

13. On Austria in this period, see, for example, Emmerich Tálos, *Das austrofaschistische Herrschaftssystem: Österreich 1933–1938* (Berlin, Münster and Vienna: LIT, 2013); Jill Lewis, 'Austria: Heimwehr, NSDAP and the Christian Social State', in Aristotle A. Kalis (ed.), *The Fascism Reader* (London and New York: Routledge, 2003), 212–22. On violence in this period, see in particular Gerhard Botz: *Gewalt in der Politik: Attentate, Zusammenstöße, Putschversuche, Unruhen in Österreich 1918 bis 1938* (Munich: Fink, 1983).

14. Mark Mazower, *Dark Continent: Europe's Twentieth Century* (New York: Vintage Books, 1998), 140–1. See also Charles S. Maier, *Leviathan 2.0: Inventing Modern Statehood* (Cambridge, MA: Harvard University Press, 2014), 273.

15. Christoph Kotowski, *Die 'moralische Diktatur' in Polen 1926 bis 1939: Faschismus oder autoritäres Militärregime?* (Munich: Grin, 2011); on the cult surrounding his persona, see Heidi Hein-Kircher: *Der Piłsudski-Kult und seine Bedeutung für den polnischen Staat 1926–1939* (Marburg: Herder-Institut, 2001).

16. Dmitar Tasić, 'The Assassination of King Alexander: The Swan Song of the Internal Macedonian Revolutionary Organization', in *Donau. Tijdschrift over Zuidost-Europa* (2008), 30–9.

17. Gerhard Botz, 'Gewaltkonjunkturen, Arbeitslosigkeit und gesellschaftliche Krisen: Formen politischer Gewalt und Gewaltstrategien in der ersten Republik', in Helmut Konrad and Wolfgang Maderthaner (eds), *Das Werden der ersten Republik . . . der Rest ist Österreich*, vol. 1 (Vienna: Carl Gerold's Sohn, 2008), 229–362, here 341.

18. Archive of Yugoslavia (Belgrade), 37 (Papers of Prime Minister Milan Stojadinović), 22/326. On the context, see Stefan Troebst, *Mussolini, Makedonien und die Mächte 1922–1930. Die 'Innere Makedonische Revolutionäre Organisation', in der Südosteuropapolitik des faschistischen Italien* (Cologne and Vienna: Böhlau, 1987).

19. Filipe de Meneses, *Salazar: A Political Biography* (New York: Enigma Books, 2009).

20. The literature on this subject is extensive. For some recent work, see Julián Casanova and Martin Douch, *The Spanish Republic and Civil War* (Cambridge and New York: Cambridge University Press, 2010); Nigel Townson, *The Crisis of Democracy in Spain: Centrist Politics under the Second Republic, 1931–1936* (Brighton: Sussex University Press, 2000); Helen Graham, *The Spanish Civil War: A Very Short Introduction* (Oxford and New York: Oxford University Press, 2005); Stanley Payne, *Franco and Hitler: Spain, Germany, and World War II* (New Haven, CT, and London: Yale University Press, 2008); Paul Pres-

ton, *The Spanish Civil War: Reaction, Revolution, and Revenge* (New York: W. W. Norton and Company, 2006).

21. Chad Bryant, *Prague in Black: Nazi Rule and Czech Nationalism* (Cambridge, MA: Harvard University Press, 2007).

22. Robert Edwards, *White Death: Russia's War on Finland 1939–40* (London: Weidenfeld and Nicolson, 2006).

23. Andrzej Olechnowicz, 'Liberal Anti-Fascism in the 1930s: The Case of Sir Ernest Barker', in *Albion: A Quarterly Journal Concerned with British Studies* 36 (2004), 636–60, here 643. On the BUF more generally, see Martin Pugh, *'Hurrah for the Blackshirts!': Fascists and Fascism in Britain between the Wars* (London: Pimlico, 2006).

24. Philippe Bernard and Henri Dubief, *The Decline of the Third Republic, 1914–1958* (Cambridge and New York: Cambridge University Press, 1985), 290.

25. Christian Gerlach, *Krieg, Ernährung, Völkermord: Deutsche Vernichtungspolitik im Zweiten Weltkrieg* (Zürich and Munich: Pendo, 1998), 11–53.

26. Jörn Leonhard, *Die Büchse der Pandora: Geschichte des Ersten Weltkriegs* (Munich: C. H. Beck, 2014), 955; David Reynolds, *The Long Shadow: The Great War and the Twentieth Century* (London: Simon and Schuster, 2013).

27. Robert Conquest, *The Great Terror: A Reassessment* (Oxford and New York: Oxford University Press, 1990); Nicolas Werth, 'The NKVD Mass Secret Operation no. 00447 (August 1937–November 1938)', *Online Encyclopedia of Mass Violence*, published 24 May 2010, last accessed 22 January 2016, http://www.massviolence.org/The-NKVD -Mass-Secret-Operation-no-00447-August-1937.

28. Hans-Christof Kraus, *Versailles und die Folgen: Außenpolitik zwischen Revisionismus und Verständigung 1919–1933* (Berlin: be.bra, 2013), 15–33.

29. Michael Geyer, '"Endkampf" 1918 and 1945: German Nationalism, Annihilation, and Self-Destruction', in Richard Bessel, Alf Lüdtke and Bernd Weisbrod (eds), *No Man's Land of Violence: Extreme Wars of the 20th Century* (Göttingen: Wallstein, 2006), 37–67. See also Ian Kershaw, *The End: The Defiance and Destruction of Hitler's Germany, 1944–1945* (London and New York: Allen Lane, 2011).

30. Christopher Duggan, *Fascist Voices: An Intimate History of Mussolini's Italy* (London: The Bodley Head, 2012), 151ff.

31. Christian Gerlach and Götz Aly, *Das letzte Kapitel: Der Mord an den ungarischen Juden 1944–1945* (Frankfurt am Main: Fischer, 2004).

32. For a good survey of the history of Jewish life and anti-Semitism in

Vienna, see Gerhard Botz, Nina Scholz, Michael Pollak and Ivar Oxaal (eds), *Eine zerstörte Kultur. Jüdisches Leben und Antisemitismus in Wien seit dem 19. Jahrhundert* (Vienna: Czernin, 2002).

33. Matteo Millan, 'The Institutionalization of Squadrismo: Disciplining Paramilitary Violence in the Fascist Dictatorship', in *Contemporary European History* 22 (2013).

34. On Prónay's role in the defence of Budapest, see Krisztián Ungváry, *A magyar honvédség a második világháborúban* (Budapest: Osiris Kiadó, 2004), 418–20; Béla Bodó, *Pál Prónay: Paramilitary Violence and Anti-Semitism in Hungary, 1919–1921* (Pittsburgh, PA: University of Pittsburgh Press, 2011).

35. In the 1930s, Starhemberg rejected the myth of a Jewish world conspiracy as 'nonsense' and 'scientific' racism as a propagandistic 'lie'. Ernst Rüdiger Starhemberg, 'Aufzeichnungen des Fürsten Ernst Rüdiger Starhemberg im Winter 1938/39 in Saint Gervais in Frankreich', in Starhemberg Papers, Oberösterreichisches Landesarchiv Linz.

36. See the Gestapo file on Burian, in ÖStA, B 1394, Burian Papers.

37. James Bjork and Robert Gerwarth, 'The Annaberg as a German-Polish *lieu de mémoire*', in *German History* 25 (2007), 372–400.

38. Elizabeth Wiskemann, *The Rome-Berlin Axis: A History of the Relations between Hitler and Mussolini* (New York and London: Oxford University Press, 1949), 68. See also Jens Petersen, *Hitler-Mussolini: Die Entstehung der Achse Berlin-Rom 1933–1936* (Tübingen: De Gruyter Niemeyer, 1973), 60.

39. Ian Kershaw, *Hitler*, vol. 2: *Nemesis, 1936–1945* (London: Penguin, 2001), 26.

40. Robert Gerwarth, 'The Axis: Germany, Japan and Italy on the Road to War', in Richard J. B. Bosworth and Joe Maiolo (eds), *The Cambridge History of the Second World War*, vol. 2: *Politics and Ideology* (Cambridge and New York: Cambridge University Press, 2015), 21–42.

41. Naoko Shimazu, *Japan, Race and Equality: The Racial Equality Proposal of 1919* (London: Routledge, 1998); Frederick R. Dickinson, 'Commemorating the War in Post-Versailles Japan', in John W. Steinberg, Bruce W. Menning, David Schimmelpenninck van der Oye, David Wolff and Shinji Yokote (eds), *The Russo-Japanese War in Global Perspective: World War Zero* (Leiden and Boston, MA: Brill, 2005), 523–43. See also Mark Mazower, *Governing the World: The History of an Idea* (London: Penguin, 2013), 252–5; and Frederick R. Dickinson, *War and National Reinvention: Japan in the Great War, 1914–1919* (Cambridge, MA, and London: Harvard University Press, 1999).

42. On the Axis, see, for example, Shelley Baranowski, 'Making the Nation:

Axis Imperialism in the Second World War', in Nicholas Doumanis, *The Oxford Handbook of Europe 1914–1945* (Oxford and New York: Oxford University Press, 2016); MacGregor Knox, *Common Destiny: Dictatorship, Foreign Policy, and War in Fascist Italy and Nazi Germany* (Cambridge and New York: Cambridge University Press, 2000); Lutz Klinkhammer, Amedeo Osto Guerrazzi, and Thomas Schlemmer (eds), *Die 'Achse' im Krieg: Politik, Ideologie und Kriegführung 1939–1945* (Paderborn, Munich, Vienna, and Zurich: Schöningh, 2010).

43. Knox, *Common Destiny*, 124.

44. Marshall Lee Miller, *Bulgaria during the Second World War* (Stanford, CA: Stanford University Press, 1975).

45. On the German case, see Mark Mazower, *Hitler's Empire: How the Nazis Ruled Europe* (New York and London: Allen Lane, 2008).

46. Timothy Snyder, *Bloodlands: Europe between Hitler and Stalin* (New York: Basic Books, 2010).

47. Rana Mitter, *China's War with Japan, 1937–1945: The Struggle for Survival* (London: Allen Lane, 2014); Edward L. Dreyer, *China at War, 1901–1949* (London: Longman, 1995); Louise Young, *Japan's Total Empire: Manchuria and the Culture of Wartime Imperialism* (Berkeley, CA: University of California Press, 1998); Prasenjit Duara, *Sovereignty and Authenticity: Manchukuo and the East Asian Modern* (Lanham, MD: Rowman and Littlefield, 2003). On Manchukuo, see also Yoshihisa Tak Matsusaka, *The Making of Japanese Manchuria, 1904–1932* (Cambridge, MA: Harvard University Press, 2001).

48. Dennis Mack Smith, *Mussolini's Roman Empire* (London: Longman, 1976). On international politics in this period, see Zara Steiner, *The Triumph of the Dark: European International History, 1933–1939* (Oxford and New York: Oxford University Press, 2011); Anthony D'Agostino, *The Rise of Global Powers: International Politics in the Era of the World Wars* (Cambridge: Cambridge University Press, 2012), 295–302.

49. Alberto Sbacchi, *Ethiopia under Mussolini: Fascism and the Colonial Experience* (London: Zed Books, 1985); Angelo Del Boca, *The Ethiopian War 1935–1941* (Chicago, IL: University of Chicago Press, 1969); David Nicolle, *The Italian Invasion of Abyssinia 1935–1936* (Westminster, MD: Osprey, 1997); George W. Baer, *The Coming of the Italo-Ethiopian War* (Cambridge, MA: Harvard University Press, 1967); idem, *Test Case: Italy, Ethiopia and the League of Nations* (Stanford, CA: Hoover Institution Press, 1976); H. James Burgwyn, *Italian Foreign Policy in the Interwar Period 1918–1940* (Westport, CT: Praeger, 1997).

50. Knox, *Common Destiny*; Davide Rodogno, *Fascism's European Empire: Italian Occupation during the Second World War* (Cambridge: Cambridge University Press, 2008); Gustavo Corni, 'Impero e spazio vitale nella visione e nella prassi delle dittature (1919–1945)', in *Ricerche di Storia Politica* 3 (2006), 345–57; Aristotle Kallis, *Fascist Ideology: Territory and Expansionism in Italy and Germany, 1922–1945* (London: Routledge, 2000).

51. Philipp Ther, 'Deutsche Geschichte als imperiale Geschichte: Polen, slawophone Minderheiten und das Kaiserreich als kontinentales Empire', in Sebastian Conrad und Jürgen Osterhammel (eds), *Das Kaiserreich transnational: Deutschland in der Welt 1871–1914* (Göttingen: Vandenhoeck and Ruprecht, 2004), 129–48.

52. Vejas Gabriel Liulevicius, *War Land on the Eastern Front: Culture, National Identity and German Occupation in World War I* (Cambridge and New York: Cambridge University Press, 2000); Gregor Thum (ed.), *Traumland Osten: Deutsche Bilder vom östlichen Europa im 20. Jahrhundert* (Göttingen: Vandenhoeck and Ruprecht, 2006).

53. Peter Duus, Ramon H. Myers and Mark R. Peattie, *The Japanese Wartime Empire, 1931–1945* (Princeton, NJ: Princeton University Press, 1996). On Korea, Alexis Dudden, *Japan's Colonization of Korea: Discourse and Power* (Honolulu: University of Hawai'i Press, 2005).

54. Paul Brooker, *The Faces of Fraternalism: Nazi Germany, Fascist Italy, and Imperial Japan* (Oxford and New York: Oxford University Press, 1991). On Japanese racism, see John Dower, *War Without Mercy: Race and Power in the Pacific War* (New York: Pantheon, 1986).

55. Steiner, *The Lights that Failed*, notably chapter 5 (The Primacy of Nationalism: Reconstruction in Eastern and Central Europe).

56. Terry Martin, *The Affirmative Action Empire: Nations and Nationalism in the Soviet Union, 1923–1939* (Ithaca, NY: Cornell University Press, 2001).

57. Joshua Sanborn, *Imperial Apocalypse: The Great War and the Destruction of the Russian Empire* (Oxford and New York: Oxford University Press, 2014).

58. Benito Mussolini, *Opera omnia*, vol. 29 (Florence: La Fenice, 1955–9), 249–50.

59. Ibid, 404.

60. Mannerheim, as quoted in Eyal Lewin, *National Resilience during War: Refining the Decision-Making Model* (Lanham, MD, Boulder, CO, and New York: Lexington Books, 2012), 166. On Mannerheim's life and career, see Stig Jägerskiöld, *Mannerheim: Marshal of Finland* (London: Hurst, 1986).

61. Erez Manela, *The Wilsonian Moment: Self-Determination and the International Origins of Anticolonial Nationalism* (Oxford and New York: Oxford University Press, 2007); Robert Gerwarth and Erez Manela (eds), *Empires at War, 1911–1923* (Oxford and New York: Oxford University Press, 2014).

Bibliography

ARCHIVES

Austria

Oberösterreichisches Landesarchiv (Linz)
Österreichisches Staatsarchiv, Kriegsarchiv (Vienna)

Bulgaria

Archive of the Regional History Museum, Pazardjik (Pazardjik)
Bulgarian State Archives (Sofia)
National Library 'Cyril and Methodius' (Sofia)

Germany

Bundesarchiv (Berlin)
Bundesarchiv (Koblenz)
Bundesarchiv- Militärarchiv (Freiburg)
Herder Institut (Marburg)
Institut für Zeitgeschichte (Munich)
Staatsarchiv Freiburg (Freiburg)

Hungary

Hungarian Military Archive (Budapest)
Hungarian National Archives (Budapest)

Serbia

Archive of Yugoslavia (Belgrade)

The Netherlands

Netherlands Institute for War, Holocaust and Genocide Studies (Amsterdam)

United Kingdom

Imperial War Museum (London)
The National Archives (London)

United States

National Archives and Record Administration (NARA)

NEWSPAPERS AND PERIODICALS

Berliner Tageblatt, Daily Mail, Illustrated Sunday Herald, Innsbrucker Nachrichten, Il Popolo d'Italia, Münchner Neueste Nachrichten, Neue Tiroler Stimmen, Neues Wiener Tagblatt, Die Rote Fahne, Tagespost (Graz), *Vörös Újság, Toronto Star, Vorwärts*

PRINTED PRIMARY SOURCES

A Brief Record of the Advance of the Egyptian Expeditionary Force under the Command of General Sir Edmund H. H. Allenby, G.C.B., G.C.M.G. July 1917 to October 1918 (London: His Majesty's Stationery Office, 1919).

Almond, Nina, and Ralph Haswell Lutz (eds), *The Treaty of St. Germain: A Documentary History of its Territorial and Political Clauses* (Stanford, CA: Stanford University Press, 1935).

Balla, Erich, *Landsknechte wurden wir: Abenteuer aus dem Baltikum* (Berlin: W. Kolk, 1932).

Bánffy, Miklós, *The Phoenix Land: The Memoirs of Count Miklós Bánffy* (London: Arcadia Books, 2003).

Beschloss, Michael (ed.), *Our Documents: 100 Milestone Documents from the National Archives* (Oxford and New York: Oxford University Press, 2006).

Bischoff, Josef, *Die letzte Front: Geschichte der Eisernen Division im Baltikum 1919* (Berlin: Buch- und Tiefdruck Gesellschaft, 1935).

Bizony, Ladislaus, *133 Tage Ungarischer Bolschewismus. Die Herrschaft Béla Kuns und Tibor Szamuellys: Die Blutigen Ereignisse in Ungarn* (Leipzig and Vienna: Waldheim-Eberle, 1920).

Böhm, Wilhelm, *Im Kreuzfeuer zweier Revolutionen* (Munich: Verlag für Kulturpolitik, 1924).

Brandl, Franz, *Kaiser, Politiker, und Menschen: Erinnerungen eines Wiener Polizeipräsidenten* (Vienna and Leipzig: Günther, 1936).

British Joint Labour Delegation to Hungary, *Report of the British Joint Labour Delegation to Hungary* (London: Trades Union Congress and Labour Party, 1920).

Browder, Robert Paul, and Alexander F. Kerensky (eds), *The Russian Provisional Government 1917: Documents*, 3 vols (Stanford, CA: Stanford University Press, 1961).

Buchan, John, *The Three Hostages* (London: Nelson, 1948).

Bülow, Bernhard von, *Denkwürdigkeiten* (Berlin: Ullstein, 1931).

Carnegie Endowment for International Peace (ed.), *Report of the International Commission to Inquire into the Causes and Conduct of the Balkan Wars* (reprint, Washington DC: Carnegie, 2014).

Chekhov, Anton, *The Cherry Orchard*, in idem, *Four Great Plays by Anton Chekhov*, trans. Constance Garnet (New York: Bantam Books, 1958).

Committee of the Jewish Delegations, *The Pogroms in the Ukraine under the Ukrainian Governments (1917–1920)*, ed. I. B. Schlechtmann (London: Bale, 1927).

Croce, Benedetto, *Carteggio con Vossler (1899–1949)* (Bari: Laterza, 1951).

Deuerlein, Ernst (ed.), *Der Hitler-Putsch: Bayerische Dokumente zum 8./9. November 1923* (Stuttgart: DVA, 1962).

Fey, Emil, *Schwertbrüder des Deutschen Ordens* (Vienna: Lichtner, 1937).

Genov, Georgi P., *Bulgaria and the Treaty of Neuilly* (Sofia: H. G. Danov and Co., 1935).

Glaise-Horstenau, Edmund, *The Collapse of the Austro-Hungarian Empire* (London and Toronto: J. M. Dent, 1930).

Goltz, Rüdiger von der, *Meine Sendung in Finnland und im Baltikum* (Leipzig: Koehler, 1920).

Gontaut-Biron, Roger, Comte de, *Comment la France s'est installée en Syrie, 1918–1919* (Paris: Plon, 1922).

Gorky, Maxim, 'On the Russian Peasantry', 16–18, in Robert E. F. Smith (ed.), *The Russian Peasant, 1920 and 1984* (London: Routledge, 1977), 11–27.

Habrman, Gustav, *Mé vzpomínky z války* (Prague: Svěcený, 1928).

Halmi, Josef, 'Akten über die Pogrome in Ungarn', in Jakob Krausz, *Martyrium. Ein jüdisches Jahrbuch* (Vienna: self-published, 1922), 59–66.

Hampe, Karl, *Kriegstagebuch 1914–1919*, ed. Folker Reichert and Eike Wolgast, 2nd edition (Munich: Oldenbourg, 2007).

Heifetz, Elias, *The Slaughter of the Jews in the Ukraine in 1919* (New York: Thomas Seltzer, 1921).

Hemingway, Ernest, *In Our Time* (New York: Boni and Liveright, 1925).

Heydrich, Lina, *Leben mit einem Kriegsverbrecher* (Pfaffenhofen: Ludwig, 1976).

Höss, Rudolf, *Death Dealer: The Memoirs of the SS Kommandant at Auschwitz*, ed. Steven Paskuly (Buffalo, NY: Prometheus Books, 1992).

Jünger, Ernst, *In Stahlgewittern: Ein Kriegstagebuch*, 24th edition (Berlin: Mittler 1942).

——, *Kriegstagebuch 1914–1918*, ed. Helmuth Kiesel (Stuttgart: Klett-Cotta, 2010).

Kerr, Stanley E., *The Lions of Marash: Personal Experiences with American Near East Relief, 1919–1922* (Albany, NY: State University of New York Press, 1973).

Kesyakov, Bogdan, *Prinos kym diplomaticheskata istoriya na Bulgaria (1918–1925): Dogovori, konventsii, spogodbi, protokoli i drugi syglashenia i diplomaticheski aktove s kratki belejki* (Sofia: Rodopi, 1925).

Kessler, Harry Graf, *Das Tagebuch 1880–1937*, eds Roland Kamzelak and Günter Riederer, vols 5–7 (Stuttgart: Klett-Cotta, 2006–8).

Keynes, John Maynard, *The Economic Consequences of the Peace* (London: Macmillan, 1919).

Killinger, Manfred von, *Der Klabautermann: Eine Lebensgeschichte*, 3rd edition (Munich: Eher, 1936).

Klemperer, Victor, *Man möchte immer weinen und lachen in einem: Revolutionstagebuch 1919* (Berlin: Aufbau, 2015).

Knaus, Siegmund, *Darstellungen aus den Nachkriegskämpfen deutscher Truppen und Freikorps*, vols 7 and 8 (Berlin: Mittler and Sohn, 1941–2).

Könnemann, Erwin, and Gerhard Schulze (eds), *Der Kapp-Lüttwitz-Ludendorf-Putsch: Dokumente* (Munich: Olzog, 2002).

Kozma, Miklós, *Az összeomlás 1918–1919* (Budapest: Athenaeum, 1933).

——, *Makensens Ungarische Husaren: Tagebuch eines Frontoffiziers, 1914–1918* (Berlin and Vienna: Verlag für Kulturpolitik, 1933).

Krauss, Alfred, *Unser Deutschtum!* (Salzburg: Eitel, 1921).

Krausz, Jakob (ed.), *Martyrium: ein jüdisches Jahrbuch* (Vienna: self-published, 1922).

Kühlmann, Richard von, *Erinnerungen* (Heidelberg: Schneider, 1948).

Lenin, Vladimir Ilyich, *Collected Works*, 45 vols, 4th English edition (Moscow: Progress Publishers, 1964–74).

Liebknecht, Karl, *Ausgewählte Reden, Briefe und Aufsätze* (East Berlin: Dietz, 1952).

Lloyd George, David, *The Truth About the Peace Treaties*, 2 vols (London: Gollancz, 1938).

Lord, Robert Howard, 'Poland', in Edward M. House and Charles Seymour (eds), *What Really Happened at Paris: The Story of the Peace Conference by American Delegates* (London: Hodder and Stoughton, 1921), 67–86.

Luxemburg, Rosa, *Gesammelte Werke*, vol. 4: *August 1914–Januar 1919* (East Berlin: Dietz, 1974).

———, *Politische Schriften*, ed. Ossip K. Flechtheim, vol. 3 (Frankfurt am Main: Europäische Verlags-Anstalt, 1975).

Mann, Thomas, *Thomas Mann: Tagebücher 1918–1921*, ed. Peter de Mendelsohn (Frankfurt am Main: S. Fischer, 1979).

Michaelis, Herbert, Ernst Schraepler and Günter Scheel (eds), *Ursachen und Folgen*, vol. 2: *Der militärische Zusammenbruch und das Ende des Kaiserreichs* (Berlin: Verlag Herbert Wendler, 1959).

Müller, Georg Alexander von, *The Kaiser and His Court: The Diaries, Notebooks, and Letters of Admiral Alexander von Müller* (London: Macdonald, 1961).

Nicolson, Harold, *Peacemaking, 1919* (London: Grosset and Dunlap, 1933).

Nowak, Karl Friedrich (ed.), *Die Aufzeichnungen des Generalmajors Max Hoffmann*, 2 vols (Berlin: Verlag für Kulturpolitik, 1929).

Pavelić, Ante, *Doživljaji*, reprint (Zagreb: Naklada Starčević, 1996).

Philipp, Albrecht (ed.), *Die Ursachen des Deutschen Zusammenbruches im Jahre 1918. Zweite Abteilung: Der innere Zusammenbruch*, vol. 6 (Berlin: Deutsche Verlagsgesellschaft für Politik, 1928).

Piazzesi, Mario, *Diario di uno Squadrista Toscano: 1919–1922* (Rome: Bonacci, 1981).

Pogány, Josef, *Der Weiße Terror in Ungarn* (Vienna: Neue Erde, 1920).

Potter Webb, Beatrice, *Diaries 1912–1924*, ed. Margaret Cole (London: Longmans, Green and Company, 1952).

Pranckh, Hans von, *Der Prozeß gegen den Grafen Anton Arco-Valley, der den bayerischen Ministerpräsidenten Kurt Eisner erschossen hat* (Munich: Lehmann, 1920).

Prónay, Pál, *A határban a halál kaszál: fejezetek Prónay Pál feljegyzéseiből*, eds Ágnes Szabó and Ervin Pamlényi (Budapest: Kossuth, 1963).

Report of the International Commission to Inquire into the Causes and Conduct of the Balkan Wars (Washington, DC: Carnegie Endowment for International Peace, 1914).

Roth, Joseph, *Das Spinnennetz* (Cologne and Berlin: Kiepenheuer and Witsch, 1967).

——, *Radetzky March* (New York: Viking Press, 1933).

Salomon, Ernst von, *Die Geächteten* (Berlin: Rowohlt, 1923).

Sammlung der Drucksachen der Verfassunggebenden Preußischen Landesversammlung, Tagung 1919/21, vol. 15 (Berlin: Preußische Verlagsanstalt, 1921).

Thaer, Albrecht von, *Generalstabsdienst an der Front und in der OHL: Aus Briefen und Tagebuchaufzeichnungen, 1915–1919* (Göttingen: Vandenhoeck and Ruprecht, 1958).

Toller, Ernst, *I Was a German: The Autobiography of Ernst Toller* (New York: Paragon House, 1934).

'Treaty of Peace between the United States of America, the British Empire, France, Italy, and Japan and Poland', in *American Journal of International Law* 13, Supplement, Official Documents (1919), 423–40.

Trotsky, Leon, *My Life: The Rise and Fall of a Dictator* (New York and London: Butterworth, 1930).

'Turquie: Convention d'armistice 30 Octobre 1918', *Guerre Européenne: Documents 1918: Conventions d'armistice passées avec la Turquie, la Bulgarie, l'Autriche-Hongrie et l'Allemagne par les puissances Alliées et associées* (Paris: Ministère des Affaires Étrangères, 1919).

Ulrich, Bernd, and Benjamin Ziemann (eds), *Frontalltag im Ersten Weltkrieg: Wahn und Wirklichkeit. Quellen und Dokumente* (Frankfurt am Main: Fischer, 1994).

Verhandlungen der verfassunggebenden Deutschen Nationalversammlung. Stenographische Berichte, vol. 327 (Berlin: Norddeutsche Buchdruckerei u. Verlagsanstalt, 1920).

Wilson, Francesca M., *Rebel Daughter of a Country House: The Life of Eglantyne Jebb, Founder of the Save the Children Fund* (Boston, MA, and London: Allen and Unwin, 1967).

Woodrow Wilson's speech to the US Congress on 2 April 1917: http://wwi.lib.byu.edu/index.php/Wilson%27s_War_Message_to_Congress.

Yourcenar, Marguerite, *Le Coup de grâce* (Paris: Éditions Gallimard, 1939).

Zweig, Arnold, *Das ostjüdische Antlitz* (Berlin: Welt Verlag, 1920).

SECONDARY SOURCES

Ablovatski, Eliza, '"Cleansing the Red Nest': Counter-Revolution and White Terror in Munich and Budapest', 1919, unpublished PhD Dissertation, New York, 2004.

——, 'The 1919 Central European Revolutions and the Judeo-Bolshevik Myth', in *European Review of History* 17 (2010), 473–89.

Achladi, Evangelia, 'De la guerre à l'administration grecque: la fin de la Smyrne cosmopolite', in Marie-Carmen Smyrnelis (ed.), *Smyrne, la ville oubliée? 1830–1930: Mémoires d'un grand port ottoman* (Paris: Éditions Autrement, 2006), 180–95.

Ackerl, Isabella, and Rudolf Neck (eds), *Saint-Germain 1919: Protokoll des Symposiums am 29. und 30. Mai 1979 in Wien* (Vienna: Verlag für Geschichte und Politik, 1989).

Adamets, Serguëi, *Guerre civile et famine en Russie: Le pouvoir bolchevique et la population face à la catastrophe démographique, 1917–1923* (Paris: Institut d'études slaves, 2003).

Adams, Matthew Lloyd, 'When Cadillacs Crossed Poland: The American Relief Administration in Poland, 1919–1922', unpublished PhD thesis, Armstrong Atlantic State University, 2005.

Adriányi, Gabriel, *Fünfzig Jahre Ungarische Kirchengeschichte, 1895–1945* (Mainz: v. Hase and Koehler Verlag, 1974).

Aizpuru, Mikel, 'La expulsión de refugiados extranjeros desde España en 1919: exiliados rusos y de otros países', in *Migraciones y Exilios* 11 (2010), 107–26.

Aksakal, Mustafa, 'The Ottoman Empire', in Jay Winter (ed.), *Cambridge History of the First World War*, vol. 1 (Cambridge: Cambridge University Press, 2014), 459–78.

——, 'The Ottoman Empire', in Gerwarth and Manela (eds), *Empires at War*, 17–33.

——, *The Ottoman Road to War in 1914: The Ottoman Empire and the First World War* (Cambridge and New York: Cambridge University Press, 2008).

Alapuro, Risto, *State and Revolution in Finland* (Berkeley, CA: University of California Press, 1988).

Albanese, Giulia, *La marcia su Roma* (Rome and Bari: Laterza, 2006).

Alder, Douglas D., 'Friedrich Adler: Evolution of a Revolutionary', in *German Studies Review* 1 (1978), 260–84.

Aleshin, D. D., 'Aziatskaya Odisseya', in Sergej L. Kuz'min (ed.), *Baron Ungern v dokumentach i memuarach* (Moscow: Tovariščestvo Naučnych Izd. KMK, 2004).

Allamani, Efi, and Christa Panagiotopoulou, 'I Ellada sti Mikra Asia', in *Istoria tou ellinikou ethnous* (Athens: Ekdotiki Athinon, 1978), vol. 15, 118–32.

Allawi, Ali A., *Faisal I of Iraq* (New Haven, CT, and London: Yale University Press, 2014).

Alpern Engel, Barbara, 'Not by Bread Alone: Subsistence Riots in Russia during World War I', in *Journal of Modern History*, 69 (1997), 696–721.

Altrichter, Helmut, *Rußland 1917: Ein Land auf der Suche nach sich selbst* (Paderborn: Schöningh, 1997).

Andelman, David A., *A Shattered Peace: Versailles 1919 and the Price We Pay Today* (Hoboken, NJ: Wiley, 2008).

Anderson, David M., and David Killingray (eds), *Policing and Decolonisation: Politics, Nationalism and the Police, 1917–1965* (Manchester: Manchester University Press, 1992).

Anderson, Scott, *Lawrence in Arabia: War, Deceit, Imperial Folly and the Making of the Modern Middle East* (New York: Doubleday, 2013).

Andreev, Georgi, *Koburgite i katastrofite na Bulgaria* (Sofia: Agato, 2005).

Andreyev, Catherine, and Ivan Savicky, *Russia Abroad: Prague and the Russian Diaspora 1918–1938* (New Haven, CT, and London: Yale University Press, 2004).

Anichkov, Vladimir Petrovich, *Ekaterinburg – Vladivostok 1917–1922* (Moscow: Russkiĭ put', 1998).

Apostolopoulos, F. D. (ed.), *Exodos*, vol. 1 (Athens: Centre for Asia Minor Studies, 1980).

Aquarone, Alberto, 'Violenza e consenso nel fascismo Italiano', in *Storia contemporanea* 10 (1979), 145–55.

Arendt, Hannah, *The Origins of Totalitarianism* (New York: Harcourt, Brace and Company, 1951).

Arens, Olavi, 'The Estonian Question at Brest-Litovsk', in *Journal of Baltic Studies* 25 (1994), 305–30.

Ascher, Harvey, 'The Kornilov Affair: A Reinterpretation', in *Russian Review* 29 (1970), 286–300.

Aschheim, Steven E., *Brothers and Strangers: The East European Jew in German and German-Jewish Consciousness, 1800–1923* (Madison, WI, and London: University of Wisconsin Press, 1982).

Audoin-Rouzeau, Stéphane, 'Die Delegation der "Gueules cassées" in Versailles am 28. Juni 1919', in Gerd Krumeich et al. (eds), *Versailles 1919: Ziele, Wirkung, Wahrnehmung* (Essen: Klartext Verlag, 2001), 280–7.

Audoin-Rouzeau, Stéphane, Annette Becker and Leonard V. Smith, *France and the Great War, 1914–1918* (Cambridge and New York: Cambridge University Press, 2003).

Audoin-Rouzeau, Stéphane, and Jean-Jacques Becker (eds), *La prima guerra mondiale*, vols 1 and 2 (Turin: Einaudi, 2007).

Audoin-Rouzeau, Stéphane, and Christophe Prochasson (eds), *Sortir de la Grande Guerre: Le monde et l'après-1918* (Paris: Tallandier, 2008).

Aves, Jonathan, *Workers against Lenin: Labour Protest and Bolshevik Dictatorship* (London: I. B. Tauris, 1996).

Avilés Farré, Juan, *La fe que vino de Rusia. La revolución bolchevique y los españoles (1917–1931)* (Madrid: Biblioteca Nueva, 2009).

Azmanov, Dimitar, and Rumen Lechev, 'Probivatna Dobropoleprezsptemvri 1918 godina', in *Voennoistoricheskisbornik* 67 (1998), 154–75.

Baberowski, Jörg, *Der Feind ist überall: Stalinismus im Kaukasus* (Munich: Deutsche Verlags-Anstalt, 2003).

Baer, George W., *The Coming of the Italo-Ethiopian War* (Cambridge, MA: Harvard University Press, 1967).

——, *Test Case: Italy, Ethiopia and the League of Nations* (Stanford, CA: Hoover Institution Press, 1976).

Balbirnie, Steven, 'British Imperialism in the Arctic: The British Occupation of Archangel and Murmansk, 1918–1919', unpublished PhD thesis, University College Dublin, 2015.

Balkelis, Tomas, 'Turning Citizens into Soldiers: Baltic Paramilitary Movements after the Great War', in Gerwarth and Horne (eds), *War in Peace*, 126–44.

Ball, Alan, 'Building a New State and Society: NEP, 1921–1928', in Ronald Grigor Suny (ed.), *The Cambridge History of Russia*, vol. 3 (Cambridge: Cambridge University Press, 2006), 168–91.

Ballabás, Dániel, *Trianon 90 év távlatából: Konferenciák, műhelybeszélgetések* (Eger: Líceum Kiadó, 2011).

Baranowski, Shelley, 'Making the Nation: Axis Imperialism in the Second World War', in Nicholas Doumanis, *The Oxford Handbook of Europe 1914–1945* (Oxford and New York: Oxford University Press, 2016).

Barbagallo, Francesco, *Francesco Saverio Nitti* (Turin: Utet, 1994).

Barkey, Karen, and Mark von Hagen (eds), *After Empires: Multiethnic Societies and Nation-Building: The Soviet Union, and the Russian, Ottoman, and Habsburg Empires* (Boulder, CO: Westview Press, 1997).

Barkmann, Udo B., *Geschichte der Mongolei oder Die 'Mongolische Frage': Die Mongolen auf ihrem Weg zum eigenen Nationalstaat* (Bonn: Bouvier Verlag, 1999).

Baron, Nick, and Peter Gatrell, 'Population Displacement, State-Building and Social Identity in the Lands of the Former Russian Empire, 1917–1923', in *Kritika: Explorations in Russian and Eurasian History* 4 (2003), 51–100.

Barth, Boris, *Dolchstoßlegenden und politische Disintegration: Das Trauma der deutschen Niederlage im Ersten Weltkrieg* (Düsseldorf: Droste, 2003).

Batowski, Henryk, 'Nationale Konflikte bei der Entstehung der Nachfolgestaaten', in Richard Georg Plaschka and Karlheinz Mack (eds), *Die Auflösung des Habsburgerreiches: Zusammenbruch und Neuorientierung im Donauraum* (Munich: Oldenbourg, 1970), 338–49.

Baudis, Dieter, and Hermann Roth, 'Berliner Opfer der Novemberrevolution 1918/19', in *Jahrbuch für Wirtschaftsgeschichte* (1968), 73–149.

Bauer, Frieder, and Jörg Vögele, 'Die "Spanische Grippe" in der deutschen Armee 1918: Perspektive der Ärzte und Generäle', in *Medizinhistorisches Journal* 48 (2013), 117–52.

Bauer, Otto, *Die österreichische Revolution* (Vienna: Wiener Volksbuchhandlung, 1923).

Baumgart, Winfried, *Deutsche Ostpolitik 1918: Von Brest-Litovsk bis zum Ende des Ersten Weltkriegs* (Vienna and Munich: Oldenbourg, 1966).

Becker, Seymour, *Nobility and Privilege in Late Imperial Russia* (DeKalb, IL: Northern Illinois Press, 1985).

Becker, Winfried, *Frederic von Rosenberg (1874–1937): Diplomat vom späten Kaiserreich bis zum Dritten Reich, Außenminister der Weimarer Republik* (Göttingen: Vandenhoeck and Ruprecht, 2011).

Bell, John D., *Peasants in Power: Alexander Stamboliski and the Bulgarian Agrarian National Union 1899–1923* (Princeton, NJ: Princeton University Press, 1977).

Beller, Steven, *A Concise History of Austria* (Cambridge: Cambridge University Press, 2006).

Ben-Ami, Shlomo, *Fascism from Above: The Dictatorship of Primo de Rivera in Spain 1923–1930* (Oxford: Clarendon Press, 1983).

Berend, Ivan T., *Decades of Crisis: Central and Eastern Europe before World War II* (Berkeley, CA: University of California Press, 1998).

Bergien, Rüdiger, *Die bellizistische Republik: Wehrkonsens und Wehrhaftmachung in Deutschland, 1918–1933* (Munich: Oldenbourg, 2012).

——, 'Republikschützer oder Terroristen? Die Freikorpsbewegung in Deutschland nach dem Ersten Weltkrieg', in *Militärgeschichte* (2008), 14–17.

Berlin, Jon Dale, 'The Burgenland Question 1918–1920: From the Collapse of Austria-Hungary to the Treaty of Trianon', unpublished PhD dissertation, Madison, WI, 1974.

Bernard, Philippe, and Henri Dubief, *The Decline of the Third Republic, 1914–1958* (Cambridge and New York: Cambridge University Press, 1985).

Bernstein, Eduard, *Die deutsche Revolution*, vol. 1: *Ihr Ursprung, ihr Verlauf und ihr Werk* (Berlin: Verlag Gesellschaft und Erziehung, 1921).

Bessel, Richard, *Germany after the First World War* (Oxford: Clarendon Press, 1993).

———, 'Revolution', in Jay Winter (ed.), *The Cambridge History of the First World War*, vol. 2 (Cambridge and New York: Cambridge University Press, 2014), 126–44.

Beyrau, Dietrich, 'Brutalization Revisited: The Case of Bolshevik Russia', in *Journal of Contemporary History* 50 (2015), 15–37.

———, 'Post-War Societies (Russian Empire)', in *1914–1918 online. International Encyclopedia of the First World War*.

Beyrau, Dietrich, and Pavel P. Shcherbinin, 'Alles für die Front: Russland im Krieg 1914–1922', in Horst Bauerkämper and Elise Julien (eds), *Durchhalten! Krieg und Gesellschaft im Vergleich 1914–1918* (Göttingen: Vandenhoeck and Ruprecht, 2010), 151–77.

Bianchi, Roberto, *Pace, pane, terra. Il 1919 in Italia* (Rome: Odradek, 2006).

Bigler, Robert M., 'Heil Hitler and Heil Horthy! The Nature of Hungarian Racist Nationalism and its Impact on German-Hungarian Relations 1919–1945', in *East European Quarterly* 8 (1974), 251–72.

Bihari, Péter, *Lövészárkok a hátországban. Középosztály, zsidókérdés, Antiszemitizmus az első világháború Magyarországán* (Budapest: Napvilág Kiadó, 2008).

Bihl, Wolfdieter, *Österreich-Ungarn und die Friedensschlüsse von Brest-Litovsk* (Vienna, Cologne and Graz: Böhlau, 1970).

Bilyarski, Tsocho, *BZNS, Aleksandar Stambolijski i VMRO: nepoznatata voyna* (Sofia: Aniko, 2009).

Bilyarski, Tsocho, and Nikola Grigorov (eds), *Nyoiskiyat pogrom i terorat na bulgarite: Sbornik dokumenti i materiali* (Sofia: Aniko, 2009).

Bischof, Günther, Fritz Plasser and Peter Berger (eds), *From Empire to Republic: Post-World War I Austria* (Innsbruck: Innsbruck University Press, 2010).

Bjelajac, Mile, '1918: oslobođenje ili okupacija nesrpskih krajeva?', in Milan Terzić, *Prvi svetski rat i Balkan – 90 godina* (Belgrade: Institut za strategijska istraživanja, 2010), 201–23.

———, *Vojska Kraljevine Srba, Hrvata i Slovenaca 1918–1921* (Belgrade: Narodna knjiga, 1988).

Bjork, James E., *Neither German Nor Pole: Catholicism and National Indifference in a Central European Borderland, 1890–1922* (Ann Arbor, MI: University of Michigan Press, 2008).

Bjork, James E., and Robert Gerwarth, 'The Annaberg as a German-Polish *lieu de mémoire*', in *German History* 25 (2007), 372–400.

Blackbourn, David, and Geoff Eley, *The Peculiarities of German History: Bourgeois Society and Politics in Nineteenth-Century Germany* (Oxford and New York: Oxford University Press, 1984).

Blanke, Richard, *Orphans of Versailles: The Germans in Western Poland, 1918–1939* (Lexington, KY: University Press of Kentucky, 1993).

Bloxham, Donald, 'The First World War and the Development of the Armenian Genocide', in Ronald Grigor Suny, Fatma Müge Göçek and Norman M. Naimark (eds), *A Question of Genocide: Armenians and Turks at the End of the Ottoman Empire* (Oxford and New York: Oxford University Press, 2011), 260–75.

Bodó, Béla, *Pál Prónay: Paramilitary Violence and Anti-Semitism in Hungary, 1919–1921* (Pittsburgh, PA: University of Pittsburgh Press, 2011).

———, '"White Terror", the Hungarian Press and the Evolution of Hungarian Anti-Semitism after World War I', in *Yad Vashem Studies* 34 (2006), 45–86.

———, 'The White Terror in Hungary, 1919–21: The Social Worlds of Paramilitary Groups', in *Austrian History Yearbook* 42 (2011), 133–63.

Boemeke, Manfred F., 'Woodrow Wilson's Image of Germany, the War-Guilt Question and the Treaty of Versailles', in idem, Gerald D. Feldman and Elisabeth Glaser (eds), *The Treaty of Versailles: A Reassessment after 75 Years* (Cambridge and New York: Cambridge University Press, 1998), 603–14.

Boemeke, Manfred F., Gerald D. Feldman and Elisabeth Glaser (eds), *The Treaty of Versailles: A Reassessment after 75 years* (Cambridge and New York: Cambridge University Press, 1998).

Bogdanov, K., *Admiral Kolchak: Biograficheskaia povest-khronika* (St Petersburg: Sudostroenie, 1993).

Böhler, Jochen, 'Enduring Violence: The Post-War Struggles in East-Central Europe 1917–1921', in *Journal of Contemporary History* 50 (2015), 58–77.

———, 'Generals and Warlords, Revolutionaries and Nation State Builders: The First World War and its Aftermath in Central and Eastern Europe', in idem, Wlodzimierz Borodziej and Joachim von Puttkamer (eds), *Legacies of Violence: Eastern Europe's First World War* (Munich: Oldenbourg, 2014), 51–66.

Borodziej, Włodzimierz, *Geschichte Polens im 20. Jahrhundert* (Munich: C. H. Beck, 2010).

Borowsky, Peter, 'Germany's Ukrainian Policy during World War I and the Revolution of 1918–19', in Hans-Joachim Torke and John-Paul Himka (eds), *German-Ukrainian Relations in Historical Perspective* (Edmonton: Canadian Institute of Ukrainian Studies, 1994), 84–94.

Borsányi, György, *The Life of a Communist Revolutionary: Béla Kun* (Boulder, CO: Social Science Monographs, 1993).

Borzęcki, Jerzy, 'German Anti-Semitism à la Polonaise: A Report on Poznanian Troops' Abuse of Belarusian Jews in 1919', in *East European Politics and Cultures*, 26 (2012), 693–707.

————, *The Soviet-Polish Peace of 1921 and the Creation of Interwar Europe* (New Haven, CT, and London: Yale University Press, 2008).

Boswell, Laird, 'From Liberation to Purge Trials in the "Mythic Provinces": Recasting French Identities in Alsace and Lorraine, 1918–1920', in *French Historical Studies* 23 (2000), 129–62.

Bosworth, Richard J. B., *Italy: The Least of the Great Powers: Italian Foreign Policy before the First World War* (Cambridge: Cambridge University Press, 1979).

————, *Mussolini* (London: Arnold, 2002).

Bosworth, Richard J. B., and Giuseppe Finaldi, 'The Italian Empire', in Robert Gerwarth and Erez Manela (eds), *Empires at War, 1911–1923* (Oxford: Oxford University Press, 2014), 34–51.

Botlik, József, *Nyugat-Magyarország sorsa, 1918–1921* (Vasszilvány: Magyar Nyugat Könyvkiadó, 2008).

Botz, Gerhard, *Gewalt in der Politik: Attentate, Zusammenstöße, Putschversuche, Unruhen in Österreich 1918 bis 1938* (Munich: Fink, 1983).

————, 'Gewaltkonjunkturen, Arbeitslosigkeit und gesellschaftliche Krisen: Formen politischer Gewalt und Gewaltstrategien in der ersten Republik', in Helmut Konrad and Wolfgang Maderthaner (eds), *Das Werden der ersten Republik ... der Rest ist Österreich*, vol. 1 (Vienna: Carl Gerold's Sohn, 2008), 229–362.

Botz, Gerhard, Nina Scholz, Michael Pollak and Ivar Oxaal (eds), *Eine zerstörte Kultur: Jüdisches Leben und Antisemitismus in Wien seit dem 19. Jahrhundert* (Vienna: Czernin, 2002).

Bowers, Katherine, and Ani Kokobobo, *Russian Writers and the Fin de Siècle: The Twilight of Realism* (Cambridge and New York: Cambridge University Press, 2015).

Boyce, Robert, *The Great Interwar Crisis and the Collapse of Globalization* (Basingstoke: Palgrave Macmillan, 2009).

Boychev, Petar, *Tutrakanska epopeia* (Tutrakan: Kovachev, 2003).

Boychev, Petar, and Volodya Milachkov, *Tutrakanskata epopeya i voynata na Severnia front, 1916–1918* (Silistra: Kovachev, 2007).

Boyer, John W., 'Boundaries and Transitions in Modern Austrian History', in Günter Bischof and Fritz Plasser (eds), *From Empire to Republic: Post-World War I Austria* (New Orleans, LA: University of New Orleans Press, 2010), 13–23.

————, *Culture and Political Crisis in Vienna: Christian Socialism in Power, 1897–1918* (Chicago: University of Chicago Press, 1995).

————, 'Karl Lueger and the Viennese Jews', in *Yearbook of the Leo Baeck Institute* 26 (1981), 125–44.

Boylan, Catherine Margaret, 'The North Russia Relief Force: A Study of Military Morale and Motivation in the Post-First World War World', unpublished PhD thesis, King's College London, 2015.

Bracco, Barbara, 'L'Italia e l'Europa da Caporetto alla vittoria nella riflessione degli storici italiani', in Giampietro Berti and Piero del Negro (eds), *Al di qua e al di là del Piave: L'ultimo anno della Grande Guerra* (Milan: Franco Angeli, 2001).

Bradley, John F. N., *The Czechoslovak Legion in Russia, 1914–1920* (Boulder, CO: East European Monographs, 1991).

Braun, Bernd, Die 'Generation Ebert', in idem and Klaus Schönhoven (eds), *Generationen in der Arbeiterbewegung* (Munich: Oldenbourg, 2005), 69–86.

Braun, Karl, 'Der 4. März 1919. Zur Herausbildung Sudetendeutscher Identität', in *Bohemia* 37 (1996), 353–80.

Braunthal, Julius, *Geschichte der Internationale*, vol. 2 (Hanover: J. H. W. Dietz, 1963).

Brooker, Paul, *The Faces of Fraternalism: Nazi Germany, Fascist Italy, and Imperial Japan* (Oxford and New York: Oxford University Press, 1991).

Broucek, Anton (ed.), *Anton Lehár: Erinnerungen. Gegenrevolution und Restaurationsversuche in Ungarn 1918–1921* (Munich: Oldenbourg, 1973).

Broucek, Peter, *Karl I. (IV.): Der politische Weg des letzten Herrschers der Donaumonarchie* (Vienna: Böhlau, 1997).

Brovkin, Vladimir N., *Behind the Front Lines of the Civil War: Political Parties and Social Movements in Russia, 1918–1922* (Princeton, NJ: Princeton University Press, 1994).

Brown, Archie, *The Rise and Fall of Communism* (New York: Harper Collins, 2009).

Brügel, Johann Wolfgang, *Tschechen und Deutsche 1918–1938* (Munich: Nymphenburger Verlagshandlung, 1967).

Bryant, Chad, *Prague in Black: Nazi Rule and Czech Nationalism* (Cambridge, MA: Harvard University Press, 2007).

Budnitskii, Oleg, *Russian Jews between the Reds and Whites, 1917–1920* (Philadelphia, PA: University of Pennsylvania Press, 2011).

Bührer, Tanja, *Die Kaiserliche Schutztruppe für Deutsch-Ostafrika: Koloniale Sicherheitspolitik und transkulturelle Kriegführung, 1885 bis 1918* (Munich: Oldenbourg, 2011).

Bullock, David, *The Czech Legion, 1914–20* (Oxford: Osprey, 2008).

Bunselmeyer, Robert E., *The Cost of War 1914–1919: British Economic War Aims and the Origins of Reparation* (Hamden, CT: Archon Books, 1975).

Burgwyn, H. James, *Italian Foreign Policy in the Interwar Period 1918–1940* (Westport, CT: Praeger, 1997).

Burkman, Thomas W., *Japan and the League of Nations: Empire and World Order, 1914–1938* (Honolulu: University of Hawai'i Press, 2008).

Burleigh, Michael, *The Third Reich: A New History* (London: Pan Macmillan, 2001).

Busch, Briton Cooper, *Madras to Lausanne: Britain's Frontier in West Asia, 1918–1923* (Albany, NY: State University of New York Press, 1976).

Cabanes, Bruno, '1919: Aftermath', in Jay Winter (ed.), *Cambridge History of the First World War*, vol. 1 (Cambridge: Cambridge University Press, 2014), 172–98.

——, *The Great War and the Origins of Humanitarianism 1918–1924* (Cambridge and New York: Cambridge University Press, 2014).

——, *La victoire endeuillée: La sortie de guerre des soldats français (1918–1920)* (Paris: Éditions du Seuil, 2004).

Calder, Kenneth J., *Britain and the Origins of the New Europe, 1914–1918* (Cambridge and New York: Cambridge University Press, 1976).

Calvert, Peter, *A Study of Revolution* (Oxford and New York: Oxford University Press, 1970).

Cammarano, Fulvio (ed.), *Abbasso la Guerra. Neutralisti in Piazza alla vigilia della Prima Guerra mondiale* (Florence: Le Monnier, 2015).

Campos, Michelle U., *Ottoman Brothers: Muslims, Christians, and Jews in Early Twentieth-Century Palestine* (Stanford, CA: Stanford University Press, 2011).

Canning, Kathleen, 'The Politics of Symbols, Semantics, and Sentiments in the Weimar Republic', in *Central European History* 43 (2010), 567–80.

Capozzola, Christopher, 'The United States Empire', in Gerwarth and Manela (eds), *Empires at War*, 235–53.

Carr, Edward Hallett, *The Bolshevik Revolution 1917–1923* (London: Macmillan, 1950).

——, 'The Origins and Status of the Cheka', in *Soviet Studies* 10 (1958), 1–11.

Carr, Raymond, *Modern Spain, 1875–1980* (Oxford: Clarendon Press, 1980).

Carrère d'Encausse, Hélène, *Islam and the Russian Empire: Reform and Revolution in Central Asia* (Berkeley, CA, and London: University of California Press, 1988).

——, *Lenin: Revolution and Power* (New York and London: Longman, 1982).

——, *Nikolaus II.: Das Drama des letzten Zaren* (Vienna: Zsolnay, 1998).

Carsten, Francis L., *Die Erste Österreichische Republik im Spiegel zeitgenössischer Quellen* (Vienna: Böhlau, 1988).

————, *Fascist Movements in Austria: From Schönerer to Hitler* (London: Sage, 1977).

————, *Revolution in Central Europe, 1918–1919* (London: Temple Smith, 1972).

Casa, Brunella Dalla, 'La Bologna di Palazzo d'Accursio', in Mario Isnenghi and Giulia Albanese (eds), *Gli Italiani in guerra: Conflitti, identità, memorie dal Risorgimento ai nostri giorni*, vol. 4/1: *Il ventennio fascista: Dall'impresa di Fiume alla Seconda Guerra mondiale (1919–1940)* (Turin: Utet, 2008), 332–8.

Casanova, Julián, *Twentieth-Century Spain: A History* (Cambridge and New York: Cambridge University Press, 2014).

Casanova, Julián, and Martin Douch, *The Spanish Republic and Civil War* (Cambridge and New York: Cambridge University Press, 2010).

Cattaruzza, Marina, Stefan Dyroff and Dieter Langewiesche (eds), *Territorial Revisionism and the Allies of Germany in the Second World War: Goals, Expectations, Practices* (New York and Oxford: Berghahn Books, 2012).

Channon, John, 'Siberia in Revolution and Civil War, 1917–1921', in Alan Wood (ed.), *The History of Siberia: From Russian Conquest to Revolution* (London and New York: Routledge, 1991) 158–80.

Chickering, Roger, *Imperial Germany and the Great War, 1914–1918* (Cambridge and New York: Cambridge University Press 1998).

Childs, Timothy W., *Italo-Turkish Diplomacy and the War over Libya, 1911–1912* (New York: Brill, 1990).

Chromow, Semen S., *Feliks Dzierzynski: Biographie*, 3rd edition (East Berlin: Dietz, 1989).

Clark, Bruce, *Twice a Stranger: How Mass Expulsion Forged Greece and Turkey* (London: Granta Books, 2006).

Clark, Christopher, *Iron Kingdom: The Rise and Downfall of Prussia, 1600–1947* (London: Allen Lane, 2006).

————, *The Sleepwalkers: How Europe Went to War in 1914* (London: Allen Lanc, 2012).

Clavin, Patricia, 'Europe and the League of Nations', in Robert Gerwarth (ed.), *Twisted Paths: Europe 1914–1945* (Oxford and New York: Oxford University Press, 2007), 325–54.

————, *The Great Depression in Europe, 1929–1939* (Basingstoke and New York: Palgrave, 2000).

Codera, Maximiliano Fuentes, *España en la Primera Guerra Mundial: Una movilización cultural* (Madrid: Akal, 2014).

Cohen, Gary B., 'Nationalist Politics and the Dynamics of State and Civil Society in the Habsburg Monarchy 1867–1914', in *Central European History* 40 (2007), 241–78.

Cohn, Norman, *Warrant for Genocide: The Myth of the Jewish World Conspiracy and the Protocols of the Elders of Zion* (London: Serif, 1996).

Cohrs, Patrick, *The Unfinished Peace after World War I: America, Britain and the Stabilisation of Europe, 1919–1932* (Cambridge and New York: Cambridge University Press, 2006).

Cole, Laurence, and Daniel L. Unowsky (eds), *The Limits of Loyalty: Imperial Symbolism, Popular Allegiances and State Patriotism in the Late Habsburg Monarchy* (New York and Oxford: Berghahn Books, 2007).

Conquest, Robert, *The Great Terror: A Reassessment* (Oxford and New York: Oxford University Press, 1990).

———, *The Harvest of Sorrows: Soviet Collectivization and the Terror-Famine* (Oxford and New York: Oxford University Press, 1986).

Contorbia, Franco (ed.), *Giornalismo italiano*, vol. 2: *1901–1939* (Milan: Arnoldo Mondadori, 2007).

Cooper, John Milton, *Woodrow Wilson: A Biography* (New York: Random House, 2009).

Corni, Gustavo, 'Impero e spazio vitale nella visione e nella prassi delle dittature (1919–1945)', in *Ricerche di Storia Politica* 3 (2006), 345–57.

Cornwall, Mark, 'National Reparation? The Czech Land Reform and the Sudeten Germans 1918–38', in *Slavonic and East European Review* 75 (1997), 259–80.

———, 'Morale and Patriotism in the Austro-Hungarian Army, 1914–1918', in John Horne (ed.), *State, Society, and Mobilization in Europe during the First World War* (Cambridge: Cambridge University Press, 1997), 173–92.

———, *The Undermining of Austria-Hungary: The Battle for Hearts and Minds* (Basingstoke: Macmillan, 2000).

Crainz, Guido, *Padania: Il mondo dei braccianti dall'Ottocento alla fuga dalle campagne* (Rome: Donzelli, 1994).

Crampton, Richard J., *Aleksandur Stamboliiski: Bulgaria* (Chicago, IL: Haus Publishing and University of Chicago Press, 2009).

———, 'The Balkans', in Robert Gerwarth (ed.), *Twisted Paths: Europe 1914–1945* (Oxford and New York, 2007), 237–70.

———, *Bulgaria* (Oxford and New York: Oxford University Press, 2007).

———, *Eastern Europe in the Twentieth Century and After* (London and New York: Routledge, 1997).

Cruz, Rafael, '¡Luzbel vuelve al mundo!: las imágenes de la Rusia soviética y la acción colectiva en España', in Manuel Ledesma Pérez and Rafael Cruz (eds), *Cultura y movilización en la España contemporánea* (Madrid: Alianza, 1997), 273–303.

Ciuljat, Tomislav, 'Nejiski mir', in *Vojna enciklopedija*, vol. 6: *Nauloh–Podvodni*, 2nd edition (Belgrade: Izd. Redakcije vojne Enciklopedije, 1973).

D'Agostino, Anthony, *The Rise of Global Powers: International Politics in the Era of the World Wars* (Cambridge: Cambridge University Press, 2012).

Daly, Mary E. (ed.), *Roger Casement in Irish and World History* (Dublin: Royal Irish Academy, 2005).

Damyanov, Simeon, 'Dokumenti za devetoyunskia prevrat i Septemvriyskoto vastanie prez 1923 g. vav Frenskia diplomaticheski arhiv', in *Izvestia na darzhavnite arhivi* 30 (1975), 167–82.

Danilov, Viktor P., Viktor V. Kondrashin and Teodor Shanin (eds), *Nestor Makhno: M. Kubanin, Makhnovshchina. Krestyanskoe dvizhenie na Ukraine 1918–1921 gg. Dokumenty i Materialy* (Moscow: ROSSPEN, 2006).

Darwin, John, *Britain, Egypt and the Middle East: Imperial Policy in the Aftermath of War, 1918–1922* (London and Basingstoke: Macmillan, 1981).

Daskalov, Doncho, *1923 – Sadbonosni resheniya i sabitiya* (Sofia: BZNS, 1983).

Davies, Norman, *God's Playground*, vol. 2: *1795 to the Present* (Oxford and New York: Oxford University Press, 2005).

———, *Microcosm: A Portrait of a Central European City* (London: Pimlico, 2003).

———, *White Eagle, Red Star: The Polish-Soviet War, 1919–1920 and 'the Miracle on the Vistula'* (London: Pimlico, 2003).

Deak, John, 'The Great War and the Forgotten Realm: The Habsburg Monarchy and the First World War', in *The Journal of Modern History* 86 (2014), 336–80.

Deák, Francis, *Hungary at the Peace Conference: The Diplomatic History of the Treaty of Trianon* (New York: Columbia University Press, 1942).

Deák, István, *Beyond Nationalism: A Social and Political History of the Habsburg Officer Corps, 1848–1918* (Oxford and New York: Oxford University Press, 1990).

Dedijer, Vladimir, *Novi prilozi za biografiju Josipa Broza Tita 1* (Zagreb and Rijeka: Mladost i Spektar; Liburnija, 1980); reprint of the original 1953 edition.

De Felice, Renzo, *Mussolini il rivoluzionario, 1883–1920* (Turin: Einaudi, 1965).

De Felice, Renzo (ed.), *La Carta del Carnaro nei testi di Alceste De Ambris e di Gabriele D'Annunzio* (Bologna: il Mulino, 1973).

Deist, Wilhelm, 'Die Politik der Seekriegsleitung und die Rebellion der Flotte

Ende Oktober 1918', in *Vierteljahrshefte für Zeitgeschichte* 14 (1966), 341–68.

——, 'Verdeckter Militärstreik im Kriegsjahr 1918?', in Wolfram Wette (ed.), *Der Krieg des kleinen Mannes: Eine Militärgeschichte von unten* (Munich and Zürich: Piper, 1998), 146–67.

Del Boca, Angelo, *A un passo dalla forca* (Milan: Baldini Castoli Dalai, 2007).

——, *The Ethiopian War 1935–1941* (Chicago, IL: University of Chicago Press, 1969).

——, *Gli Italiani in Libia, Tripoli bel Suol d'Amore* (Milan: Arnoldo Mondadori, 1993).

Deliyski, Bozhan, *Doyranskata epopeia – zabravena i nezabravima* (Sofia: BolTenInKo, 1993).

Deutscher, Isaac, *The Prophet Armed: Trotsky, 1879–1921* (Oxford: Oxford University Press, 1954).

Dickinson, Frederick R., 'Commemorating the War in Post-Versailles Japan', in John W. Steinberg, Bruce W. Menning, David Schimmelpenninck van der Oye, David Wolff and Shinji Yokote (eds), *The Russo-Japanese War in Global Perspective: World War Zero* (Leiden and Boston, MA: Brill, 2005), 523–43.

——, 'The Japanese Empire', in Gerwarth and Manela (eds), *Empires at War*, 197–213.

——, *War and National Reinvention: Japan in the Great War, 1914–1919* (Cambridge, MA, and London: Harvard University Press, 1999).

Dimitrov, Georgi, *Nastanyavane i ozemlyavane na balgarskite bezhantsi* (Blagoevgrad: n.p., 1985).

Djokić, Dejan, *Elusive Compromise: A History of Interwar Yugoslavia* (Oxford and New York: Oxford University Press, 2007).

——, *Pašić and Trumbić: The Kingdom of Serbs, Croats, and Slovenes* (London: Haus, 2010).

Dobkin, Marjorie Housepian, *Smyrna 1922: The Destruction of a City* (New York: Newmark Press, 1988).

Doerries, Reinhard R., *Prelude to the Easter Rising: Sir Roger Casement in Imperial Germany* (London and Portland: Frank Cass, 2000).

Doumanis, Nicholas, *Before the Nation: Muslim-Christian Coexistence and its Destruction in Late Ottoman Anatolia* (Oxford and New York: Oxford University Press, 2013).

Doumanis, Nicholas (ed.), *The Oxford Handbook of Europe 1914–1945* (Oxford and New York, 2016).

Dowe, Dieter, and Peter-Christian Witt, *Friedrich Ebert 1871–1925: Vom Arbeiterführer zum Reichspräsidenten* (Bonn: Friedrich-Ebert-Stiftung, 1987).

Dower, John, *War Without Mercy: Race and Power in the Pacific War* (New York: Pantheon, 1986).

Dowler, Wayne, *Russia in 1913* (DeKalb, IL: Northern Illinois University Press, 2010).

Draev, Ivan, *Bulgarskata 1918: Istoricheski ocherk za Vladayskoto vastanie* (Sofia: Narodna prosveta, 1970).

Dragostinova, Theodora, *Between Two Motherlands: Nationality and Emigration among the Greeks of Bulgaria, 1900–1949* (Ithaca, NY: Cornell University Press, 2011).

——, 'Competing Priorities, Ambiguous Loyalties: Challenges of Socioeconomic Adaptation and National Inclusion of the Interwar Bulgarian Refugees', in *Nationalities Papers* 34 (2006), 549–74.

Dreyer, Edward L., *China at War, 1901–1949* (London: Longman, 1995).

Duara, Prasenjit, *Sovereignty and Authenticity: Manchukuo and the East Asian Modern* (Lanham, MD: Rowman and Littlefield, 2003).

Dudden, Alexis, *Japan's Colonization of Korea: Discourse and Power* (Honolulu: University of Hawai'i Press, 2005).

Duggan, Christopher, *Fascist Voices: An Intimate History of Mussolini's Italy* (London: The Bodley Head, 2012).

Duus, Peter, Ramon H. Myers and Mark R. Peattie, *The Japanese Wartime Empire, 1931–1945* (Princeton, NJ: Princeton University Press, 1996).

Dyer, Gwynne, 'The Turkish Armistice of 1918. 2: A Lost Opportunity: The Armistice Negotiations of Moudros', in *Middle Eastern Studies* 3 (1972), 313–48.

Eckelt, Frank, 'The Internal Policies of the Hungarian Soviet Republic', in Iván Völgyes (ed.), *Hungary in Revolution, 1918–1919* (Lincoln, NB: University of Nebraska Press, 1971), 61–88.

Edwards, Robert, *White Death: Russia's War on Finland 1939–40* (London: Weidenfeld and Nicolson, 2006).

Eichenberg, Julia, 'The Dark Side of Independence: Paramilitary Violence in Ireland and Poland after the First World War', in *Contemporary European History* 19 (2010), 231–48.

Ekmečciće, Milorad, *Stvaranje Jugoslavije 1790–1918*, vol. 2 (Belgrade: Prosveta, 1989).

Elz, Wolfgang, 'Versailles und Weimar', in *Aus Politik und Zeitgeschichte*, 50/51 (2008), 31–8.

Engelmann, Dieter, and Horst Naumann, *Hugo Haase: Lebensweg und politisches Vermächtnis eines streitbaren Sozialisten* (Berlin: Edition Neue Wege, 1999).

Erger, Johannes, *Der Kapp-Lüttwitz-Putsch: Ein Beitrag zur deutschen Innenpolitik, 1919–20* (Düsseldorf: Droste, 1967).

Erickson, Edward J., *Ordered to Die: A History of the Ottoman Army in the First World War* (Westport, CT, and London: Greenwood Press, 2001).

Evans, Richard J., *The Coming of the Third Reich* (London: Allen Lane, 2004).

Evans, Robert, 'The Successor States', in Robert Gerwarth (ed.), *Twisted Paths: Europe 1914–45* (Oxford and New York: Oxford University Press, 2007), 210–36.

Fabbri, Fabio, *Le origini della Guerra civile: L'Italia dalla Grande Guerra al fascismo (1918–1921)* (Turin: Utet, 2009).

Falch, Sabine, 'Zwischen Heimatwehr und Nationalsozialismus. Der "Bund Oberland" in Tirol', in *Geschichte und Region* 6 (1997), 51–86.

Falkus, Malcolm E., *The Industrialization of Russia, 1700–1914* (London: Macmillan, 1972).

Fava, Andrea, 'Il "fronte interno" in Italia. Forme politiche della mobilitazione patriottica e delegittimazione della classe dirigente liberale', in *Ricerche storiche* 27 (1997), 503–32.

Fedor, Julie, *Russia and the Cult of State Security: The Chekist Tradition, from Lenin to Putin* (London: Routledge, 2011).

Fedyshyn, Oleh S., *Germany's Drive to the East and the Ukrainian Revolution, 1917–1918* (New Brunswick, NJ: Rutgers University Press, 1971).

Feldman, Gerald D., 'Das deutsche Unternehmertum zwischen Krieg und Revolution: Die Entstehung des Stinnes-Legien-Abkommens', in idem, *Vom Weltkrieg zur Weltwirtschaftskrise: Studien zur deutschen Wirtschafts- und Sozialgeschichte 1914–1932* (Göttingen: Vandenhoeck and Ruprecht, 1984), 100–27.

Feldman, Gerald D., and Irmgard Steinisch, *Industrie und Gewerkschaften 1918–1924: Die überforderte Zentralarbeitsgemeinschaft* (Stuttgart: DVA, 1985).

Fellner, Fritz, 'Der Vertrag von St. Germain', in Erika Weinzierl and Kurt Skalnik (eds), *Österreich 1918–1938*, vol. 1 (Vienna: Böhlau, 1983), 85–106.

Ferguson, Niall, *The Pity of War: Explaining World War I* (London: Allen Lane, 1998).

Ferraioli, Gianpaolo, *Politica e diplomazia in Italia tra XIX e XX secolo: vita di Antonino di San Giuliano (1852–1914)* (Soveria Mannelli: Rubbettino, 2007).

Ferriter, Diarmaid, *A Nation and not a Rabble: The Irish Revolution 1913–1923* (London: Profile Books, 2015).

Ferro, Marc, *October 1917: A Social History of the Russian Revolution* (London: Routledge and Kegan Paul, 1980).

Fic, Victor M., *The Bolsheviks and the Czechoslovak Legion: The Origins of their Armed Conflict (March–May 1918)* (New Delhi: Shakti Malik, 1978).

Fieldhouse, David K., *Western Imperialism in the Middle East, 1914–1958* (Oxford and New York: Oxford University Press, 2006).

Figes, Orlando, *Peasant Russia, Civil War: The Volga Countryside in Revolution, 1917–21* (Oxford and New York: Oxford University Press, 1989).

———, *A People's Tragedy: The Russian Revolution, 1891–1924* (London: Jonathan Cape, 1996).

Fikreta Jelić-Butić, *Ustaše i Nezavisna država Hrvatska 1941–1945* (Zagreb: Sveučilišna naklada Liber and Školska knjiga, 1977).

Fink, Carole, *Defending the Rights of Others: The Great Powers, the Jews, and International Minority Protection* (Cambridge and New York: Cambridge University Press, 2004).

———, 'The Minorities Question at the Paris Peace Conference: The Polish Minority Treaty, June 28, 1919', in Manfred Boemeke, Gerald Feldman and Elisabeth Glaser (eds), *The Treaty of Versailles: A Reassessment after 75 Years* (Cambridge: Cambridge University Press, 1998), 249–74.

Fischer, Rolf, 'Anti-Semitism in Hungary 1882–1932', in Herbert A. Strauss (ed.), *Hostages of Modernization: Studies of Modern Antisemitism 1870–1933/39*, vol. 2: *Austria, Hungary, Poland, Russia* (Berlin and New York: de Gruyter, 1993), 863–92.

———, *Entwicklungsstufen des Antisemitismus in Ungarn, 1867–1939: Die Zerstörung der magyarisch-jüdischen Symbiose* (Munich: Oldenbourg, 1998).

Fitzherbert, Margaret, *The Man Who Was Greenmantle: A Biography of Aubrey Herbert* (London: John Murray, 1983).

Flemming, Peter, *The Fate of Admiral Kolchak* (London: Hart-Davis, 1963).

Foerster, Wolfgang, *Der Feldherr Ludendorff im Unglück. Eine Studie über seine seelische Haltung in der Endphase des ersten Weltkrieges* (Wiesbaden: Limes Verlag, 1952).

Foley, Robert, 'From Victory to Defeat: The German Army in 1918', in Ashley Ekins (ed.), *1918: Year of Victory* (Auckland and Wollombi, NSW: Exisle, 2010), 69–88.

Fong, Giordan, 'The Movement of German Divisions to the Western Front, Winter 1917–1918', in *War in History* 7 (2000), 225–35.

Forgacs, David, 'Fascism, Violence and Modernity', in Jana Howlett and Rod Mengham (eds), *The Violent Muse: Violence and the Artistic Imagination in Europe, 1910–1939* (Manchester: Manchester University Press, 1994), 5–21.

Fotiadis, Konstantinos, 'Der Völkermord an den Griechen des Pontos', in Tessa Hofmann (ed.), *Verfolgung, Vertreibung und Vernichtung der Chris-*

ten im Osmanischen Reich 1912–1922, 2nd edition (Berlin: LIT-Verlag, 2010), 193–228.

Fromkin, David, *A Peace to End All Peace: The Fall of the Ottoman Empire and the Creation of the Modern Middle East* (New York: Henry Holt and Company, 1989).

Gage, Beverly, *The Day Wall Street Exploded: A Story of America in its First Age of Terror* (Oxford and New York: Oxford University Press, 2008).

Galántai, József, *Hungary in the First World War* (Budapest: Akad. Kiadó, 1989).

Gatrell, Peter, *Russia's First World War, 1914–1917: A Social and Economic History* (London: Pearson, 2005).

———, 'Wars after the War: Conflicts, 1919–1923', in John Horne (ed.), *A Companion to World War I* (Chichester: Wiley-Blackwell, 2010), 558–75.

———, *A Whole Empire Walking: Refugees in Russia during World War I* (Bloomington, IN: Indiana University Press, 1999).

Gatti, Gian Luigi, *Dopo Caporetto. Gli ufficiali P nella Grande Guerra: propaganda, assistenza, vigilanza* (Gorizia: LEG, 2000).

Gatzolis, Ioannis A., *Ghioulbaxes. Vourlas. Erithrea. Anamnisis. Perigrafes. Laografika. Katastrofi 1922* (Chalkidiki: Nea Syllata, 1988).

Gauntlett, Stathis, 'The Contribution of Asia Minor Refugees to Greek Popular Song, and its Reception', in Renée Hirschon (ed.), *Crossing the Aegean: An Appraisal of the 1923 Compulsory Population Exchange between Greece and Turkey* (New York: Berghahn Books, 2003), 247–60.

Gautschi, Willi, *Lenin als Emigrant in der Schweiz* (Zürich: Benziger Verlag, 1973).

Gehler, Michael, *Studenten und Politik: Der Kampf um die Vorherrschaft an der Universität Innsbruck 1919–1938* (Innsbruck: Haymon-Verlag, 1990).

Geifman, Anna, *Thou Shalt Kill: Revolutionary Terrorism in Russia, 1894–1917* (Princeton, NJ: Princeton University Press 1993).

Genovski, Mihail, *Aleksandar Stambolijski – otblizo i daleko: dokumentalni spomeni* (Sofia: BZNS, 1982).

Gentile, Emilio, *E fu subito regime: Il fascismo e la Marcia su Roma* (Rome and Bari: Laterza, 2012).

———, 'Fascism in Power: The Totalitarian Experiment', in Adrian Lyttelton (ed.), *Liberal and Fascist Italy 1900–1945* (Oxford and New York: Oxford University Press, 2002).

———, *Fascismo e antifascismo: I partiti italiani fra le due guerre* (Florence: Le Monnier, 2000).

——, *La Grande Italia: Ascesa e declino del mito della nazione nel ventesimo secolo* (Milan: Arnoldo Mondadori, 1997).

——, *The Origins of Fascist Ideology, 1918–1925* (New York: Enigma, 2005).

——, 'Paramilitary Violence in Italy: The Rationale of Fascism and the Origins of Totalitarianism', in Gerwarth and Horne (eds), *War in Peace*, 85–106.

——, *The Sacralization of Politics in Fascist Italy* (Cambridge, MA: Harvard University Press, 1996).

——, *Storia del partito fascista*, vol. 1: *1919–1922, movimento e milizia* (Rome: Laterza, 1989).

Georgiev, Georgi, *Propusnata pobeda – Voynishkoto vastanie, 1918* (Sofia: Partizdat, 1989).

Geppert, Dominik, and Robert Gerwarth, (eds), *Wilhelmine Germany and Edwardian Britain: Essays on Cultural Affinity* (Oxford and New York: Oxford University Press, 2008).

Gergely, Ernő, and Pál Schönwald, *A Somogyi-Bacsó-Gyilkosság* (Budapest: Kossuth, 1978).

Gerlach, Christian, *Krieg, Ernährung, Völkermord: Deutsche Vernichtungspolitik im Zweiten Weltkrieg* (Zürich and Munich: Pendo, 1998).

Gerlach, Christian, and Götz Aly, *Das letzte Kapitel: Der Mord an den ungarischen Juden 1944–1945* (Frankfurt am Main: Fischer, 2004).

Ģērmanis, Uldis, *Oberst Vācietis und die lettischen Schützen im Weltkrieg und in der Oktoberrevolution* (Stockholm: Almqvist and Wiksell, 1974).

Gerschenkron, Alexander, *Economic Backwardness in Historical Perspective: A Book of Essays* (Cambridge, MA: Belknap Press of Harvard University Press, 1962).

Gerwarth, Robert, 'The Axis: Germany, Japan and Italy on the Road to War', in Richard J. B. Bosworth and Joe Maiolo (eds), *The Cambridge History of the Second World War*, vol. 2: *Politics and Ideology* (Cambridge and New York: Cambridge University Press, 2015), 21–42.

——, 'The Central European Counter-Revolution: Paramilitary Violence in Germany, Austria and Hungary after the Great War', in *Past & Present* 200 (2008), 175–209.

——, 'Republik und Reichsgründung: Bismarcks kleindeutsche Lösung im Meinungsstreit der ersten deutschen Demokratie', in Heinrich August Winkler (ed.), *Griff nach der Deutungsmacht: Zur Geschichte der Geschichtspolitik in Deutschland* (Göttingen: Wallstein, 2004), 115–33.

Gerwarth, Robert (ed.), *Twisted Paths: Europe 1914–1945* (Oxford and New York: Oxford University Press, 2007).

Gerwarth, Robert, and Erez Manela (eds), *Empires at War, 1911–1923* (Oxford and New York: Oxford University Press, 2014).

Gerwarth, Robert, and John Horne, 'Bolshevism as Fantasy: Fear of Revolution and Counter-Revolutionary Violence, 1917–1923', in Gerwarth and Horne (eds), *War in Peace*, 40–51.

Gerwarth, Robert, and John Horne (eds), 'Vectors of Violence: Paramilitarism in Europe after the Great War, 1917–1923', in *The Journal of Modern History* 83 (2011), 489–512.

——, *War in Peace: Paramilitary Violence after the Great War* (Oxford and New York: Oxford University Press, 2012).

Gerwarth, Robert, and Martin Conway, 'Revolution and Counter-Revolution', in Donald Bloxham and Robert Gerwarth (eds), *Political Violence in Twentieth-Century Europe* (Cambridge and New York: Cambridge University Press, 2011), 140–75.

Geyer, Michael, *Deutsche Rüstungspolitik 1860–1980* (Frankfurt am Main: Suhrkamp, 1984).

Geyer, Michael, '"Endkampf" 1918 and 1945: German Nationalism, Annihilation, and Self-Destruction', in Richard Bessel, Alf Lüdtke and Bernd Weisbrod (eds), *No Man's Land of Violence: Extreme Wars of the 20th Century* (Göttingen: Wallstein, 2006), 37–67.

Giannakopoulos, Giorgos, 'I Ellada sti Mikra Asia: To chroniko tis Mikrasiatikis peripetias', in Vassilis Panagiotopoulos (ed.), *Istoria tou Neou Ellinismou, 1770–2000*, vol. 6 (Athens: Ellinika Grammata, 2003), 84–6.

Gibelli, Antonio, *La Grande Guerra degli italiani 1915–1918* (Milan: Sansoni, 1998).

——, 'L'Italia dalla neutralità al Maggio Radioso', in Audoin-Rouzeau and Becker (eds), *La prima guerra mondiale*, vol. 1, 185–95.

——, *Il popolo bambino: Infanzia e nazione dalla Grande Guerra a Salò* (Turin: Einaudi, 2005).

Gietinger, Klaus, *Der Konterrevolutionär: Waldemar Pabst – eine deutsche Karriere* (Hamburg: Edition Nautilus, 2009).

——, *Eine Leiche im Landwehrkanal: Die Ermordung Rosa Luxemburgs* (Hamburg: Edition Nautilus, 2008).

Gilbert, Martin, *Winston Churchill*, vol. IV, part 3: April 1921–November 1922 (London: Heinemann, 1977).

Gill, Graeme J., *Peasants and Government in the Russian Revolution* (New York: Barnes and Noble, 1979).

Gingeras, Ryan, *Fall of the Sultanate: The Great War and the End of the Ottoman Empire, 1908–1922* (Oxford and New York: Oxford University Press, 2016).

——, *Mustafa Kemal Atatürk: Heir to an Empire* (Oxford and New York: Oxford University Press, 2015).

————, 'Nation-States, Minorities, and Refugees, 1914–1923', in Nicholas Doumanis (ed.), *The Oxford Handbook of Europe 1914–1945* (Oxford and New York: Oxford University Press, 2016).

————, *Sorrowful Shores: Violence, Ethnicity, and the End of the Ottoman Empire 1912–1923* (Oxford and New York: Oxford University Press, 2009).

Giovannini, Elio, *L'Italia massimalista: Socialismo e lotta sociale e politica nel primo Dopoguerra* (Rome: Ediesse 2001).

Gitelman, Zvi Y., *Jewish Nationality and Soviet Politics: The Jewish Sections of the CPSU 1917–1930* (Princeton, NJ: Princeton University Press, 1972).

Glenny, Michael, and Norman Stone (eds), *The Other Russia: The Experience of Exile* (London: Faber and Faber, 1990).

Glenny, Misha, *The Balkans, 1804–1999* (London: Granta Books, 1999).

Goebel, Stefan, 'Re-Membered and Re-Mobilized: The "Sleeping Dead" in Interwar Germany and Britain', in *Journal of Contemporary History* 39 (2004), 487–501.

Goehrke, Carsten, *Russischer Alltag: Geschichte in neun Zeitbildern*, vol. 2 (Zürich: Chronos, 2003).

Golczewski, Frank, *Deutsche und Ukrainer 1914–1939* (Paderborn: Schöningh, 2010).

————, *Polnisch-jüdische Beziehungen 1881–1922: Eine Studie zur Geschichte des Antisemitismus in Osteuropa* (Wiesbaden: Steiner, 1981).

Goldberg, George, *The Peace to End Peace: The Paris Peace Conference of 1919* (London: Pitman, 1970).

Gordeev, Yu. N., *General Denikin: Voenno-istoricheski Ocherk* (Moscow: TPF 'Arkaiur', 1993).

Gould, S. W., 'Austrian Attitudes toward Anschluss: October 1918–September 1919', in *Journal of Modern History* 22 (1950), 220–31.

Goussef, Catherine, *L'Exil russe. La fabrique du réfugié apatride (1920–1939)* (Paris: CNRS Éditions, 2008).

Graebner, Norman, and Edward Bennett, *The Versailles Treaty and Its Legacy: The Failure of the Wilsonian Vision* (Cambridge and New York: Cambridge University Press, 2011).

Graham, Helen, *The Spanish Civil War: A Very Short Introduction* (Oxford and New York: Oxford University Press, 2005).

Gratz, Gusztáv (ed.), *A Bolsevizmus Magyarországon* (Budapest: Franklin-Társulat, 1921).

Grau, Bernhard, *Kurt Eisner, 1867–1919: Eine Biografie* (Munich: C. H. Beck, 2001).

Graziosi, Andrea, *The Great Soviet Peasant War: Bolsheviks and Peasants, 1917–1933* (Cambridge, MA: Harvard University Press, 1996).

Greenhalgh, Elizabeth, *Victory through Coalition: Politics, Command and Supply in Britain and France, 1914–1918* (Cambridge and New York: Cambridge University Press, 2005).

Grenzer, Andreas, *Adel und Landbesitz im ausgehenden Zarenreich* (Stuttgart: Steiner, 1995).

Grosch, Waldemar, *Deutsche und polnische Propaganda während der Volksabstimmung in Oberschlesien 1919–1921* (Dortmund: Forschungsstelle Ostmitteleuropa, 2003).

Groß, Gerhard, 'Eine Frage der Ehre? Die Marineführung und der letzte Flottenvorstoß? 1918', in Jörg Duppler and Gerhard P. Groß (eds), *Kriegsende 1918: Ereignis, Wirkung, Nachwirkung* (Munich: Oldenbourg, 1999), 349–65.

Groueff, Stephane, *Crown of Thorns: The Reign of King Boris III of Bulgaria, 1918–1943* (Lanham, MD: Madison Books, 1987).

Grove, William Remsburgh, *War's Aftermath: Polish Relief in 1919* (New York: House of Field, 1940).

Grozev, Tsvetan, *Voynishkoto vastanie, 1918: Sbornik dokumenti i spomeni* (Sofia: BKP, 1967).

Gruev, Stefan, *Korona ot trani* (Sofia: Balgarski pisatel, 2009).

Guelton, Frédéric, 'Le capitaine de Gaulle et la Pologne (1919–1921)', in Bernard Michel and Józef Łaptos (eds), *Les relations entre la France et la Pologne au XXe siècle* (Cracow: Eventus, 2002), 113–27.

———, 'La France et la guerre polono-bolchevique', in *Annales: Académie Polonaise des Sciences, Centre Scientifique à Paris* 13 (2010), 89–124.

Gueslin Julien, 'Riga, de la métropole russe à la capitale de la Lettonie 1915–1919', in Philippe Chassaigne and Jean-Marc Largeaud (eds), *Villes en guerre (1914–1945)* (Paris: Armand Colin, 2004), 185–95.

Gumz, Jonathan E., *The Resurrection and Collapse of Empire in Habsburg Serbia, 1914–1918* (Cambridge and New York: Cambridge University Press, 2009).

Haapala, Pertti, and Marko Tikka, 'Revolution, Civil War and Terror in Finland in 1918', in Gerwarth and Horne (eds), *War in Peace*, 71–83.

Hagen, Mark von, *Soldiers in the Proletarian Dictatorship: The Red Army and the Soviet Socialist State, 1917–1930* (Ithaca, NY: Cornell University Press, 1990).

———, *War in a European Borderland: Occupations and Occupation Plans in Galicia and Ukraine, 1914–1918* (Seattle, WA: University of Washington Press, 2007).

Hagen, William W., 'The Moral Economy of Ethnic Violence: The Pogrom in Lwów, November 1918', in *Geschichte und Gesellschaft* 31 (2005), 203–26.

Hahlweg, Werner, *Der Diktatfrieden von Brest-Litowsk 1918 und die bolschewistische Weltrevolution* (Münster: Aschendorff, 1960).

Haimson, Leopold, 'The Problem of Stability in Urban Russia, 1905–1917', in *Slavic Review* 23 (1964), 619–42, and 24 (1965), 1–22.

Hall, Richard C., *Balkan Breakthrough: The Battle of Dobro Pole 1918* (Bloomington, IN: Indiana University Press, 2010).

——, 'Balkan Wars 1912–1913', in Ute Daniel et al. (eds), *1914–1918 online. International Encyclopedia of the First World War*.

——, *The Balkan Wars, 1912–1913: Prelude to the First World War* (London and New York: Routledge, 2000).

Haller, Oliver, 'German Defeat in World War I, Influenza and Postwar Memory', in Klaus Weinhauer, Anthony McElligott and Kirsten Heinsohn (eds), *Germany 1916–23: A Revolution in Context* (Bielefeld: Transcript, 2015), 151–80.

Hanebrink, Paul, 'Transnational Culture War: Christianity, Nation and the Judeo-Bolshevik Myth in Hungary 1890–1920', in *Journal of Modern History* (2008), 55–80.

Hanioğlu, M. Sükrü, *Atatürk: An Intellectual Biography* (Princeton, NJ: Princeton University Press, 2011).

——, *A Brief History of the Late Ottoman Empire* (Princeton, NJ: Princeton University Press, 2006).

Harris, J. Paul, *Douglas Haig and the First World War* (Cambridge and New York: Cambridge University Press, 2008).

Hasegawa, Tsuyoshi, 'The February Revolution', in Edward Acton, Vladimir Iu. Cherniaev and William G. Rosenberg, (eds), *Critical Companion to the Russian Revolution 1914–1921* (London: Arnold, 1997), 48–61.

Haslinger, Peter, 'Austria-Hungary', in Gerwarth and Manela (eds), *Empires at War*, 73–90.

Haumann, Heiko, *Beginn der Planwirtschaft. Elektrifizierung, Wirtschaftsplanung und gesellschaftliche Entwicklung Sowjetrusslands, 1917–1921* (Düsseldorf: Bertelsmann, 1974).

Haupt, Georges, *Socialism and the Great War: The Collapse of the Second International* (Oxford: Clarendon Press, 1972).

Hautmann, Hans, *Die Geschichte der Rätebewegung in Österreich 1918–1924* (Vienna: Europaverlag, 1987).

Hawkins, Nigel, *The Starvation Blockades: Naval Blockades of World War I* (Barnsley: Leo Cooper, 2002).

Healy, Maureen, *Vienna and the Fall of the Habsburg Empire: Total War and Everyday Life in World War I* (Cambridge and New York: Cambridge University Press, 2004).

Heifetz, Elias, *The Slaughter of the Jews in the Ukraine in 1919* (New York: Thomas Seltzer, 1921).

Heimann, Mary, *Czechoslovakia: The State that Failed* (New Haven, CT, and London: Yale University Press, 2009).

Hein-Kircher, Heidi, *Der Piłsudski-Kult und seine Bedeutung für den polnischen Staat 1926–1939* (Marburg: Herder-Institut, 2001).

Heinz, Friedrich Wilhelm, *Sprengstoff* (Berlin: Frundsberg Verlag, 1930).

Helmreich, Paul C., *From Paris to Sèvres: The Partition of the Ottoman Empire at the Paris Peace Conference of 1919–1920* (Columbus, OH: Ohio State University Press, 1974).

Herwig, Holger, 'Clio Deceived: Patriotic Self-Censorship in Germany after the Great War', in *International Security* 12 (1987), 5–22.

———, *The First World War: Germany and Austria-Hungary, 1914–1918* (London: Edward Arnold, 1996).

———, *'Luxury Fleet': The Imperial German Navy 1888–1918*, revised edition (London: Ashfield Press, 1987).

Hetherington, Peter, *Unvanquished: Joseph Pilsudski, Resurrected Poland, and the Struggle for Eastern Europe*, 2nd edition (Houston, TX: Pingora Press, 2012).

Hiden, John, *The Baltic States and Weimar Ostpolitik* (Cambridge and New York: Cambridge University Press, 1987).

Hiden, John, and Martyn Housden, *Neighbours or Enemies? Germans, the Baltic, and Beyond* (Amsterdam and New York: Editions Rodopi, 2008).

Hildermeier, Manfred, *Geschichte der Sowjetunion 1917–1991: Entstehung und Niedergang des ersten sozialistischen Staates* (Munich: C. H. Beck, 1998).

Hildermeier, Manfred (ed.), *Der russische Adel von 1700 bis 1917* (Göttingen: Vandenhoeck and Ruprecht, 1990).

Hillmayr, Heinrich, 'München und die Revolution 1918/1919', in Karl Bosl (ed.), *Bayern im Umbruch. Die Revolution von 1918, ihre Voraussetzungen, ihr Verlauf und ihre Folgen* (Munich and Vienna: Oldenbourg, 1969), 453–504.

———, *Roter und Weißer Terror in Bayern nach 1918* (Munich: Nusser, 1974).

Hirschon, Renée, 'Consequences of the Lausanne Convention: An Overview', in idem (ed.), *Crossing the Aegean: An Appraisal of the 1923 Compulsory Population Exchange between Greece and Turkey* (New York: Berghahn Books, 2003), 13–20.

Hitchins, Keith, *Rumania, 1866–1947* (Oxford and New York: Oxford University Press, 1994).

Hitilov, Karl, *Selskostopanskoto nastanyavane na bezhantsite 1927–1932* (Sofia: Glavna direktsiya na bezhantsite, 1932).

Hock, Klaus, *Die Gesetzgebung des Rates der Volksbeauftragten* (Pfaffenweiler: Centaurus, 1987).

Hoensch, Jörg, *A History of Modern Hungary, 1867–1994* (London and New York: Longman, 1995).

Hoensch, Jörg, and Dusan Kovac (eds), *Das Scheitern der Verständigung: Tschechen, Deutsche und Slowaken in der Ersten Republik (1918–1938)* (Essen: Klartext, 1994).

Holquist, Peter, *Making War, Forging Revolution: Russia's Continuum of Crisis, 1914–1921* (Cambridge, MA: Harvard University Press, 2002).

——, 'Violent Russia, Deadly Marxism? Russia in the Epoch of Violence, 1905–21', in *Kritika: Explorations in Russian and Eurasian History* 4 (2003), 627–52.

Hoppu, Tuomas, and Pertti Haapala (eds), *Tampere 1918: A Town in the Civil War* (Tampere: Tampere Museums, 2010).

Horak, Stephan M., *The First Treaty of World War I: Ukraine's Treaty with the Central Powers of February 9, 1918* (Boulder, CO: East European Monographs, 1988).

Horn, Daniel, *Mutiny on the High Seas: Imperial German Naval Mutinies of World War One* (London: Leslie Frewin, 1973).

Horne, John, 'Defending Victory: Paramilitary Politics in France, 1918–26', in Gerwarth and Horne (eds), *War in Peace*, 216–33.

Houlihan, Patrick J., 'Was There an Austrian Stab-in-the-Back Myth? Interwar Military Interpretations of Defeat', in Günther Bischof, Fritz Plasser and Peter Berger (eds), *From Empire to Republic: Post-World War I Austria* (Innsbruck: Innsbruck University Press, 2010), 67–89.

Housden, Martyn, 'When the Baltic Sea was a Bridge for Humanitarian Action: The League of Nations, the Red Cross and the Repatriation of Prisoners of War between Russia and Central Europe, 1920–22', in *Journal of Baltic Studies* 38 (2007), 61–83.

House, Edward M., *The Intimate Papers of Colonel House Arranged as a Narrative by Charles Seymour* (Boston, MA, and New York: Houghton Mifflin, 1926–8).

Howard, N. P., 'The Social and Political Consequences of the Allied Food Blockade of Germany, 1918–19', in *German History* 11 (1993), 161–88.

Hughes-Hallett, Lucy, *The Pike: Gabriele D'Annunzio: Poet, Seducer and Preacher of War* (New York: Fourth Estate, 2013).

Hunt Tooley, T., 'German Political Violence and the Border Plebiscite in Upper Silesia, 1919–1921', in *Central European History* 21 (1988), 56–98.

——, *National Identity and Weimar Germany: Upper Silesia and the Eastern Border, 1918–22* (Lincoln, NB, and London: University of Nebraska Press, 1997).

Huntford, Roland, *Nansen: The Explorer as Hero* (New York: Barnes and Noble Books, 1998).

Hürten, Heinz (ed.), *Zwischen Revolution und Kapp-Putsch: Militär und Innenpolitik, 1918–1920* (Düsseldorf: Droste, 1977).

Ignatieff, Michael, *Isaiah Berlin: A Life* (London: Chatto and Windus, 1998).

Ihrig, Stefan, *Atatürk in the Nazi Imagination* (Cambridge, MA: Harvard University Press, 2014).

Iliev, Andreya, *Atentatat v 'Sveta Nedelya' i teroristite* (Sofia: Ciela, 2011).

Isnenghi, Mario, *L'Italia in piazza. I luoghi della vita pubblica dal 1848 ai giorni nostri* (Milan: Arnoldo Mondadori, 1994).

Isnenghi, Mario, and Giorgio Rochat, *La Grande Guerra 1914–1918* (Milan: La Nuova Italia, 2000).

Jacob, Mathilde, *Rosa Luxemburg: An Intimate Portrait* (London: Lawrence and Wishart, 2000).

Jacobson, Abigail, *From Empire to Empire: Jerusalem between Ottoman and British Rule* (Syracuse, NY: Syracuse University Press, 2011).

Jägerskiöld, Stig, *Mannerheim: Marshal of Finland* (London: Hurst, 1986).

James, Harold, *The German Slump: Politics and Economics 1924–1936* (Oxford and New York: Oxford University Press, 1986).

Jareb, Mario, *Ustaško-domobranski pokret od nastanka do travnja 1941* (Zagreb: Hrvatski institut za povijest – Školska Knjiga, 2006).

Jászi, Oszkár, *The Dissolution of the Habsburg Monarchy* (Chicago, IL: University of Chicago Press, 1929).

———, *Magyariens Schuld: Ungarns Sühne. Revolution und Gegenrevolution in Ungarn* (Munich: Verlag für Kulturpolitik, 1923).

Jędrzejewicz, Wacław, *Pilsudski: A Life for Poland* (New York: Hippocrene Books, 1990).

Jelić-Butić, Fikreta, *Ustaše i Nezavisna država Hrvatska 1941–1945* (Zagreb: Školska Knjiga, 1977).

Jena, Detlef, *Die Zarinnen Rußlands (1547–1918)* (Graz: Styria, 1999).

Jensen, Peter K., 'The Greco-Turkish War, 1920–1922', in *International Journal of Middle East Studies* 10 (1979), 553–65.

Jessen-Klingenberg, Manfred, 'Die Ausrufung der Republik durch Philipp Scheidemann am 9. November 1918', in *Geschichte in Wissenschaft und Unterricht* 19 (1968), 649–56.

Jones, Mark William, 'Violence and Politics in the German Revolution, 1918–19', unpublished PhD thesis, European University Institute, 2011.

Jones, Nigel H., *Hitler's Heralds: The Story of the Freikorps 1918–1923* (London: John Murray, 1987).

Judson, Pieter M., *The Habsburg Empire: A New History* (Cambridge, MA: Harvard University Press, 2016).

Kachulle, Doris, *Waldemar Pabst und die Gegenrevolution* (Berlin: Organon, 2007).

Kallis, Aristotle, *Fascist Ideology: Territory and Expansionism in Italy and Germany, 1922–1945* (London: Routledge, 2000).

Kann, Robert A., *Geschichte des Habsburgerreiches 1526 bis 1918* (Vienna and Cologne: Böhlau, 1990).

———, *The Multinational Empire: Nationalism and National Reform in the Habsburg Monarchy, 1848–1918*, 2 vols (New York: Columbia University Press, 1950).

Kappeler, Andreas, *Rußland als Vielvölkerreich: Entstehung – Geschichte – Zerfall* (Munich: C. H. Beck, 1993).

Karagiannis, Christos, *I istoria enos stratioti (1918–1922)*, ed. Filippos Drakontaeidis (Athens: Kedros 2013).

Karakasidou, Anastasia, *Fields of Wheat, Hills of Blood: Passages to Nationhood in Greek Macedonia, 1870–1990* (Chicago, IL: University of Chicago Press, 1997).

Kasekamp, Andres, *A History of the Baltic States* (New York: Palgrave Macmillan, 2010).

Kaser, Michael Charles, and Edward Albert Radice (eds), *The Economic History of Eastern Europe, 1919–1975*, vol. 1: *Economic Structure and Performance Between the Two Wars* (Oxford: Clarendon Press, 1985).

Kaser, Michael Charles, and Edward Albert Radice (eds), *The Economic History of Eastern Europe, 1919–1975*, vol. 2: *Interwar Policy, the War and Reconstruction* (Oxford: Clarendon Press, 1986).

Kastelov, Boyan, *Bulgaria – ot voyna kam vastanie* (Sofia: Voenno izdatelstvo, 1988).

———, *Ot fronta do Vladaya: Dokumentalen ocherk* (Sofia: BZNS, 1978).

Katkov, George, *The Kornilov Affair: Kerensky and the Breakup of the Russian Army* (London and New York: Longman, 1980).

Katzburg, Nathaniel, *Hungary and the Jews: Policy and Legislation, 1920–1943* (Ramat-Gan: Bar-Ilan University Press, 1981).

———, *Zsidópolitika Magyarországon, 1919–1943* (Budapest: Bábel, 2002).

Katzer, Nikolaus, *Die weiße Bewegung: Herrschaftsbildung, praktische Politik und politische Programmatik im Bürgerkrieg* (Cologne, Weimar and Vienna: Böhlau, 1999).

———, 'Der weiße Mythos: Russischer Antibolschewismus im europäischen Nachkrieg', in Robert Gerwarth and John Horne (eds), *Krieg im Frieden. Paramilitärische Gewalt in Europa nach dem Ersten Weltkrieg* (Göttingen: Wallstein, 2013), 57–93.

Kayali, Hasan, 'The Struggle for Independence', in Reşat Kasaba (ed.), *The*

Cambridge History of Turkey, vol. 4: *Turkey in the Modern World* (Cambridge and New York: Cambridge University Press, 2008).

Kazandjiev, Georgi et al., *Dobrichkata epopeia, 5–6 septemvri 1916* (Dobrich: Matador, 2006).

Kedourie, Elie, 'The End of the Ottoman Empire', in *Journal of Contemporary History* 2 (1968), 19–28.

Keep, John, '1917: The Tyranny of Paris over Petrograd', in *Soviet Studies* 20 (1968), 22–35.

Kelemen, Béla, *Adatok a szegedi ellenforradalom és a szegedi kormány történetéhez* (Szeged: Szerzö Kiadása, 1923).

Kellogg, Michael, *The Russian Roots of Nazism: White Russians and the Making of National Socialism, 1917–1945* (Cambridge and New York: Cambridge University Press, 2005).

Kelly, Matthew J., *The Fenian Ideal and Irish Nationalism, 1882–1916* (Woodbridge: Boydell and Brewer, 2006).

Kennan, George F., *The Decline of Bismarck's European Order: Franco-Russian Relations, 1875–1890* (Princeton, NJ: Princeton University Press, 1981).

Kennedy, David, *Over Here: The First World War and American Society* (Oxford and New York: Oxford University Press, 1980).

Kerekes, Lajos, 'Die "weiße" Allianz: Bayerisch-österreichisch-ungarische Projekte gegen die Regierung Renner im Jahre 1920', in Österreichische Osthefte 7 (1965), 353–66.

Kershaw, Ian, *The End: The Defiance and Destruction of Hitler's Germany, 1944–1945* (London and New York: Allen Lane, 2011).

——, *To Hell and Back: Europe, 1914–1949* (London: Allen Lane, 2015).

——, *Hitler*, vol. 1: *Hubris, 1889–1936* (London: Penguin, 1998).

——, *Hitler*, vol. 2: *Nemesis, 1936–1945* (London: Penguin, 2001).

Kiesel, Helmuth, *Ernst Jünger: Die Biographie* (Munich: Siedler, 2007).

Kimerling Wirtschafter, Elise, *Social Identity in Imperial Russia* (DeKalb, IL: Northern Illinois Press, 1997).

King, Greg, and Penny Wilson, *The Fate of the Romanovs* (Hoboken, NJ: John Wiley and Sons, 2003).

Kingsley Kent, Susan, *Aftershocks: Politics and Trauma in Britain, 1918–1931* (Basingstoke and New York: Palgrave Macmillan, 2009).

Kinross, Patrick, *Atatürk: A Biography of Mustafa Kemal, Father of Modern Turkey* (London: Weidenfeld and Nicolson, 1964).

Király, Béla, 'East Central European Society and Warfare in the Era of the Balkan Wars', in idem and Dimitrije/Đorđević, *East Central European Society and the Balkan Wars* (Boulder, CO: Social Science Monographs, 1987), 3–13.

Király, Béla K., and Nandor F. Dreisiger, (eds), *East Central European Society in World War I* (New York: East European Monographs, 1985).

Kirby, David, *A Concise History of Finland* (Cambridge and New York: Cambridge University Press, 2006).

Kirk, Dudley, *Europe's Population in the Interwar Years* (Geneva and New York: League of Nations, 1946).

Kitchen, James, *The British Imperial Army in the Middle East* (London: Bloomsbury, 2014).

Kitchen, Martin, *The Silent Dictatorship: The Politics of the German High Command under Hindenburg and Ludendorff, 1916–1918* (New York: Holmes and Meier, 1976).

Kitromilides, Paschalis M. (ed.), *Eleftherios Venizelos: The Trials of Statesmanship* (Edinburgh: Edinburgh University Press, 2008).

———, *Exodos*, vol. 3 (Athens: Centre for Asia Minor Studies, 2013).

Klimecki, Michał, *Polsko-ukraińska wojna o Lwów i Wschodnią Galicję 1918–1919 r. Aspekty polityczne I wojskowe* (Warsaw: Wojskowy Instytut Historyczny, 1997).

Klinkhammer, Lutz, Amedeo Osto Guerrazzi and Thomas Schlemmer (eds), *Die 'Achse' im Krieg: Politik, Ideologie und Kriegführung 1939–1945* (Paderborn, Munich, Vienna and Zurich: Schöningh, 2010).

Kluge, Ulrich, 'Militärrevolte und Staatsumsturz. Ausbreitung und Konsolidierung der Räteorganisation im rheinisch-westfälischen Industriegebiet', in Reinhard Rürup (ed.), *Arbeiter- und Soldatenräte im rheinisch-westfälischen Industriegebiet* (Wuppertal: Hammer, 1975), 39–82.

———, *Soldatenräte und Revolution: Studien zur Militärpolitik in Deutschland 1918/19* (Göttingen: Vandenhoeck and Ruprecht, 1975).

Knox, MacGregor, *Common Destiny: Dictatorship, Foreign Policy, and War in Fascist Italy and Nazi Germany* (Cambridge: Cambridge University Press, 2000).

———, *To the Threshold of Power, 1922/23: Origins and Dynamics of the Fascist and National Socialist Dictatorship* (New York: Cambridge University Press, 2007).

Koch, Hannsjoachim W., *Der deutsche Bürgerkrieg: Eine Geschichte der deutschen und österreichischen Freikorps 1918–1923* (Berlin: Ullstein, 1978).

Koenen, Gerd, *Der Russland-Komplex: Die Deutschen und der Osten, 1900–1945* (Munich: C. H. Beck, 2005).

Kopisto, Lauri, 'The British Intervention in South Russia 1918–1920', unpublished PhD thesis, University of Helsinki, 2011.

Kostopoulos, Tasos, *Polemos ke ethnokatharsi, I ksehasmeni plevra mias dekaetous ethnikis eksormisis, 1912–1922* (Athens: Vivliorama, 2007).

Kotowski, Christoph, *Die 'moralische Diktatur', in Polen 1926 bis 1939: Faschismus oder autoritäres Militärregime?* (Munich: Grin, 2011).

Kozhuharov, Kanyu, *Radomirskata republika, 1918–1948* (Sofia: BZNS, 1948).

——, *Reformatorskoto delo na Aleksandar Stambolijski* (Sofia: Fond 'Aleksandar Stambolijski', 1948).

Kozuchowski, Adam, *The Afterlife of Austria-Hungary: The Image of the Habsburg Monarchy in Interwar Europe* (Pittsburgh, PA: University of Pittsburgh Press, 2013).

Kramer, Alan, 'Deportationen', in Gerhard Hirschfeld, Gerd Krumeich and Irina Renz (eds), *Enzyklopädie Erster Weltkrieg* (Paderborn: Schöningh, 2009), 434–5.

——, *Dynamic of Destruction: Culture and Mass Killing in the First World War* (Oxford and New York: Oxford University Press, 2007).

Krämer, Gudrun, *A History of Palestine: From the Ottoman Conquest to the Founding of the State of Israel* (Princeton, NJ: Princeton University Press, 2008).

Kraus, Hans-Christof, *Versailles und die Folgen: Außenpolitik zwischen Revisionismus und Verständigung 1919–1933* (Berlin: be.bra, 2013).

Krause, Andreas, *Scapa Flow: Die Selbstversenkung der Wilhelminischen Flotte* (Berlin: Ullstein, 1999).

Krausz, Tamás, and Judit Vértes (eds), *1919. A Magyarországi Tanácsköztársaság és a kelet-európai forradalmak* (Budapest: L'Harmattan-ELTE BTK Kelet-Európa Története Tanszék, 2010).

Kreis, Georg, *Insel der unsicheren Geborgenheit: die Schweiz in den Kriegsjahren 1914–1918* (Zürich: NZZ, 2014).

Křen, Jan, *Die Konfliktgemeinscbaft: Tschechen und Deutsche, 1780–1918* (Munich: Oldenbourg, 1996).

Krethlow, Carl Alexander, *Generalfeldmarschall Colmar Freiherr von der Goltz Pascha: Eine Biographie* (Paderborn: Ferninand Schöningh, 2012).

Krispin, Martin, *'Für ein freies Russland . . .'. Die Bauernaufstände in den Gouvernements Tambov und Tjumen 1920–1922* (Heidelberg: Winter, 2010)

Krumeich, Gerd (ed.), 'Die Dolchstoß-Legende', in Etienne François and Hagen Schulze (eds), *Deutsche Erinnerungsorte*, vol. 1 (Munich: C. H. Beck, 2001), 585–99.

——, *Versailles 1919: Ziele, Wirkung, Wahrnehmung* (Essen: Klartext Verlag, 2001).

Kucera, Jaroslav, *Minderheit im Nationalstaat. Die Sprachenfrage in den tschechisch-deutschen Beziehungen 1918–1938* (Munich: Oldenbourg, 1999).

Kučera, Rudolf, 'Exploiting Victory, Sinking into Defeat: Uniformed Violence in the Creation of the New Order in Czechoslovakia and Austria 1918–1922', in *Journal of Modern History* (forthcoming).

Kurayev, Oleksii, *Politika Nimechchini i Avstro-Uhorshchini v Pershii svitovij vijni: ukrayinskii napryamok* (Kiev: Inst. Ukraïnskoi Archeohrafiï ta Džereloznavstva Im. M. S. Hrusevskoho, 2009).

Kuromiya, Hiroaki, *Freedom and Terror in the Donbas: A Ukrainian-Russian Borderland 1870s–1990s* (Cambridge and New York: Cambridge University Press, 1998).

Kuron, Hans Jürgen, *Freikorps und Bund Oberland*, unpublished PhD thesis, Munich 1960.

Kusber, Jan, *Krieg und Revolution in Russland 1904–1906: Das Militär im Verhältnis zu Wirtschaft, Autokratie und Gesellschaft* (Stuttgart: Franz Steiner, 1997).

Labanca, Nicola, *La guerra italiana per la Libia, 1911–1931* (Bologna: il Mulino, 2012).

———, 'La guerra sul fronte italiano e Caporetto', in Audoin-Rouzeau and Becker (eds), *La prima guerra mondiale*, vol. 1, 443–60.

———, *Oltremare* (Bologna: il Mulino, 2002).

Lackó, Miklós, 'The Role of Budapest in Hungarian Literature 1890–1935', in Tom Bender (ed.), *Budapest and New York: Studies in Metropolitan Transformation, 1870–1930* (New York: Russell Sage Foundation, 1994), 352–66.

Large, David Clay, *Where Ghosts Walked: Munich's Road to the Third Reich* (New York: W. W. Norton, 1997).

Laschitza, Annelies, *Im Lebensrausch, trotz alledem. Rosa Luxemburg: Eine Biographie* (Berlin: Aufbau, 1996/2002).

———, *Die Liebknechts: Karl und Sophie, Politik und Familie* (Berlin: Aufbau, 2009).

Laschitza, Annelies, and Elke Keller, *Karl Liebknecht: Eine Biographie in Dokumenten* (East Berlin: Dietz, 1982).

Lavery, Jason, 'Finland 1917–19: Three Conflicts, One Country', in *Scandinavian Review* 94 (2006), 6–14.

Lawrence, Jon, 'Forging a Peaceable Kingdom: War, Violence, and Fear of Brutalization in Post-First World War Britain', in *Journal of Modern History* 75 (2003), 557–89.

Le Moal, Frédéric, *La Serbie: Du martyre à la victoire 1914–1918* (Paris: Soteca, 2008).

Leeden, Michael A., *The First Duce: D'Annunzio at Fiume* (Baltimore, MD, and London: Johns Hopkins University Press, 1977).

Leggert, George, *The Cheka: Lenin's Political Police, the All-Russian Extraordinary Commission for Combating Counterrevolution and Sabotage (December 1917 to February 1922)* (Oxford: Clarendon Press, 1981).

Lehovich, Dimitry V., *White against Red: The Life of General Anton Denikin* (New York, W. W. Norton, 1974).

Leidinger, Hannes, 'Der Kieler Aufstand und die deutsche Revolution', in idem and Verena Moritz (eds), *Die Nacht des Kirpitschnikow. Eine andere Geschichte des Ersten Weltkriegs* (Vienna: Deuticke, 2006), 220–35.

Leidinger, Hannes, and Verena Moritz, *Gefangenschaft, Revolution, Heimkehr. Die Bedeutung der Kriegsgefangenproblematik für die Geschichte des Kommunismus in Mittel- und Osteuropa 1917–1920* (Vienna, Cologne and Weimar: Böhlau, 2003).

Leonhard, Jörn, *Die Büchse der Pandora: Geschichte des Ersten Weltkriegs* (Munich: C. H. Beck, 2014).

Levene, Mark, *Crisis of Genocide*, vol. 1: *The European Rimlands 1912– 1938* (Oxford and New York: Oxford University Press, 2014).

——, *War, Jews, and the New Europe: The Diplomacy of Lucien Wolf, 1914–1919* (Oxford and New York: Oxford University Press, 1992).

Lewis, Jill, 'Austria: Heimwehr, NSDAP and the Christian Social State', in Aristotle A. Kallis (ed.), *The Fascism Reader* (London and New York: Routledge, 2003) 212–22.

Lieven, Dominic, *Nicholas II: Emperor of all the Russians* (London: Pimlico, 1994).

——, *Russian Rulers under the Old Regime* (New Haven, CT, and London: Yale University Press, 1989).

Lincoln, W. Bruce, *In War's Dark Shadow: The Russians Before the Great War* (London: Dial Press, 1983).

——, *Passage through Armageddon: The Russians in War and Revolution* (New York: Simon and Schuster, 1986).

——, *Red Victory: A History of the Russian Civil War* (New York: Simon and Schuster, 1989).

Linke, Norbert, *Franz Lehár* (Reinbek bei Hamburg: Rowohlt, 2001).

Lipscher, Ladislav, 'Die Lage der Juden in der Tschechoslowakei nach deren Gründung 1918 bis zu den Parlamentswahlen 1920', in *East Central Europe* 1 (1989), 1–38.

Liulevicius, Vejas Gabriel, *War Land on the Eastern Front: Culture, National Identity and German Occupation in World War I* (Cambridge and New York: Cambridge University Press, 2000).

——, 'Der Osten als apokalyptischer Raum: Deutsche Fronterfahrungen im und nach dem Ersten Weltkrieg', in Gregor Thum (ed.), *Traumland Osten: Deutsche Bilder vom östlichen Europa im 20. Jahrhundert* (Göttingen: Vandenhoeck and Ruprecht, 2006), 47–65.

Lojko, Miklos, *Meddling in Middle Europe: Britain and the 'Lands Between', 1918–1925* (Budapest and New York: Central European University Press, 2006).

Longerich, Peter, *Hitler: Biographie* (Munich: Siedler, 2015).

Lorman, Thomas, 'The Right-Radical Ideology in the Hungarian Army, 1921–23', in *Central Europe* 3 (2005), 67–81.

Lönne, Karl Egon (ed.), *Die Weimarer Republik, 1918–1933: Quellen zum politischen Denken der Deutschen im 19. und 20. Jahrhundert* (Darmstadt: Wissenschaftliche Buchgesellschaft, 2002).

Lösch, Verena, 'Die Geschichte der Tiroler Heimatwehr von ihren Anfängen bis zum Korneuburger Eid (1920–1930)', unpublished PhD thesis, Innsbruck 1986.

Łossowski, Piotr, *Konflikt polsko-litewski 1918–1920*, 2nd edition (Warsaw: Książka i Wiedza, 1996).

Luban, Ottokar, 'Die Massenstreiks für Frieden und Demokratie im Ersten Weltkrieg', in Chajal Boebel and Lothar Wentzel (eds), *Streiken gegen den Krieg: Die Bedeutung der Massenstreiks in der Metallindustrie vom Januar 1918* (Hamburg: VSA-Verlag, 2008), 11–27.

Lüdke, Tilman, *Jihad Made in Germany: Ottoman and German Propaganda and Intelligence Operations in the First World War* (Münster: Lit Verlag, 2005).

Lundgreen-Nielsen, Kay, *The Polish Problem at the Paris Peace Conference: A Study of the Policies of the Great Powers and the Poles, 1918–1919* (Odense: Odense University Press, 1979).

Lupo, Salvatore, *Il fascismo: La politica in un regime totalitario* (Rome: Donzelli, 2000).

Lyttelton, Adrian, 'Fascism and Violence in Post-War Italy: Political Strategy and Social Conflict', in Wolfgang J. Mommsen and Gerhard Hirschfeld (eds), *Social Protest, Violence and Terror* (London: Palgrave Macmillan, 1982), 257–74.

———, *The Seizure of Power: Fascism in Italy 1919–1929* (London: Weidenfeld and Nicolson, 1973).

Lytvyn, Mykola R., *Ukrayins'ko-pol's'ka viyna 1918–1919rr* (Lviv: Inst. Ukraïnoznavstva Im. I. Krypjakevyča NAN Ukraïny; Inst. Schidno-Centralnoï Jevropy, 1998).

Macartney, Carlile A., *The Habsburg Empire, 1790–1918* (London: Weidenfeld and Nicolson, 1969).

———, *National States and National Minorities* (Oxford and New York: Oxford University Press, 1934).

Mace, James E., *Communism and the Dilemmas of National Liberation: National Communism in Soviet Ukraine 1918–1933* (Cambridge, MA: Harvard University Press, 1983).

Machtan, Lothar, *Die Abdankung: Wie Deutschlands gekrönte Häupter aus der Geschichte fielen* (Berlin: Propyläen, 2008).

———, *Prinz Max von Baden: Der letzte Kanzler des Kaisers* (Berlin: Suhrkamp, 2013).

Mack Smith, Denis, *Mussolini's Roman Empire* (London: Longman, 1976).

MacMillan, Margaret, *Peacemakers: The Paris Conference of 1919 and its Attempt to End War* (London: John Murray, 2001).

Maderthaner, Wolfgang, 'Die eigenartige Größe der Beschränkung. Österreichs Revolution im mitteleuropäischen Spannungsfeld', in Helmut Konrad and Wolfgang Maderthaner (eds), . . . *der Rest ist Österreich. Das Werden der Ersten Republik*, vol. 1 (Vienna: Carl Gerold's Sohn, 2008), 187–206.

———, 'Utopian Perspectives and Political Restraint: The Austrian Revolution in the Context of Central European Conflicts', in Günter Bischof, Fritz Plasser and Peter Berger (eds), *From Empire to Republic: Post–World War I Austria* (New Orleans, LA, and Innsbruck: UNO Press and Innsbruck University Press, 2010), 52–66.

Maier, Charles S., *Leviathan 2.0: Inventing Modern Statehood* (Cambridge, MA: Harvard University Press, 2014).

Maier, Michaela, and Wolfgang Maderthaner (eds), *Physik und Revolution: Friedrich Adler – Albert Einstein: Briefe, Dokumente, Stellungnahmen* (Vienna: Locker, 2006).

Malefakis, Edward E., *Agrarian Reform and Peasant Revolution in Spain: Origins of the Civil War* (New Haven, CT, and London: Yale University Press, 1970).

Malinowski, Stephan, *Vom König zum Führer: Sozialer Niedergang und politische Radikalisierung im deutschen Adel zwischen Kaiserreich und NS-Staat* (Frankfurt am Main: Fischer, 2003).

Manela, Erez, *The Wilsonian Moment: Self-Determination and the International Origins of Anticolonial Nationalism* (Oxford and New York: Oxford University Press, 2007).

Mann, Michael, *The Dark Side of Democracy: Explaining Ethnic Cleansing* (Cambridge and New York: Cambridge University Press, 2005).

Mann, Thomas, *Diaries 1919–1939*, trans. Richard and Clare Winston (London: André Deutsch, 1983).

Marantzidis, Nikos, 'Ethnic Identity, Memory and Political Behavior: The Case of Turkish-Speaking Pontian Greeks', in *South European Society and Politics* 5 (2000), 56–79.

Mark, Rudolf A., *Krieg an Fernen Fronten: Die Deutschen in Zentralasien und am Hindukusch 1914–1924* (Paderborn: Ferdinand Schöningh, 2013).

Markov, Georgi, *Bulgaria v Balkanskia sayuz sreshtu Osmanskata imperia, 1911–1913* (Sofia: Zahariy Stoyanov, 2012).

———, *Goliamata voina i bulgarskata strazha mezhdu Sredna Evropa i Orienta, 1916–1919* (Sofia: Akademichno izdatelstvo 'Prof. Marin Drinov', 2006).

——, *Golyamata voina i bulgarskiat klyuch kym evropeiskiat pogreb (1914–1916)* (Sofia: Akademichno izdatelstvo 'Prof. Marin Drinov', 1995).

Marks, Sally, 'The Myths of Reparations', in *Central European History* 11 (1978), 231–9.

Martin, Terry, *The Affirmative Action Empire: Nations and Nationalism in the Soviet Union, 1923–1939* (Ithaca, NY: Cornell University Press, 2001).

März, Eduard, 'Die große Depression in Österreich 1930–1933', in *Wirtschaft und Gesellschaft* 16 (1990), 409–38.

Matsusaka, Yoshihisa Tak, *The Making of Japanese Manchuria, 1904–1932* (Cambridge, MA: Harvard University Press, 2001).

Matthew, James, 'Battling Bolshevik Bogeymen: Spain's *Cordon Sanitaire* against Revolution from a European Perspective, 1917–1923', *Journal of Military History*, 80 (2016), 725–55.

Mavrogordatos, George, 'Metaxi dio polemon. Politiki Istoria 1922–1940', in Vassilis Panagiotopoulos (ed.), *Istoria tou Neou Ellinismou*, vol. 7 (Athens: Ellinika Grammata, 2003), 9–10.

Mawdsley, Evan, 'International Responses to the Russian Civil War (Russian Empire)', in *1914–1918 online. International Encyclopedia of the First World War*.

——, *The Russian Civil War* (Boston, MA, and London: Allen and Unwin, 1987).

——, *The Russian Civil War* (London: Birlinn, 2000).

May, Arthur, *The Passing of the Habsburg Monarchy*, vol. 2 (Philadelphia, PA: University of Pennsylvania Press, 1966).

Mayer, Arno, *The Furies: Violence and Terror in the French and Russian Revolutions* (Princeton, NJ: Princeton University Press, 2000).

——, *Wilson vs. Lenin: Political Origins of the New Democracy, 1917–1918* (Cleveland, OH: World, 1964).

Mazower, Mark, *Dark Continent: Europe's Twentieth Century* (New York: Vintage Books, 1998).

——, *Governing the World: The History of an Idea* (London: Penguin, 2013).

——, *Hitler's Empire: How the Nazis Ruled Europe* (New York and London: Allen Lane, 2008).

——, 'Minorities and the League of Nations in Interwar Europe', in *Daedalus* 126 (1997), 47–63.

——, *Salonica, City of Ghosts: Christians, Muslims and Jews, 1430–1950* (New York: Harper Perennial, 2005).

McAuley, Mary, *Bread and Justice: State and Society in Petrograd, 1917–1922* (Oxford: Clarendon Press, 1991).

McCarthy, Justin, *Death and Exile: The Ethnic Cleansing of Ottoman Muslims 1821–1922* (Princeton, NJ: Darwin Press, 2004).

——, *The Ottoman Peoples and the End of Empire* (London: Arnold, 2005).

McElligott, Anthony, *Rethinking the Weimar Republic: Authority and Authoritarianism, 1916–1936* (London: Bloomsbury, 2014).

McMeekin, Sean, *History's Greatest Heist: The Looting of Russia by the Bolsheviks* (New Haven, CT, and London: Yale University Press, 2009).

McRandle, James, and James Quirk, 'The Blood Test Revisited: A New Look at German Casualty Counts in World War I', in *Journal of Military History* 70 (2006), 667–702.

Meaker, Gerald H., *The Revolutionary Left in Spain 1914–1923* (Stanford, CA: Stanford University Press, 1974).

Melancon, Michael S., *The Lena Goldfields Massacre and the Crisis of the Late Tsarist State* (College Station, TX: Texas A&M University Press, 2006).

Meneses, Filipe de, *Salazar: A Political Biography* (New York: Enigma Books, 2009).

Méouchy, Nadine, and Peter Sluglett (eds), *The British and French Mandates in Comparative Perspective* (Leiden: Brill, 2004).

Meyer, Gert, *Studien zur sozialökonomischen Entwicklung Sowjetrusslands 1921–1923: Die Beziehungen zwischen Stadt und Land zu Beginn der Neuen Ökonomischen Politik* (Cologne: Pahl-Rugenstein, 1974).

Michael, Holger, *Marschall Józef Piłsudski 1867–1935: Schöpfer des modernen Polens* (Bonn: Pahl-Rugenstein, 2010).

Michels, Eckard, 'Die "Spanische Grippe" 1918/19: Verlauf, Folgen und Deutungen in Deutschland im Kontext des Ersten Weltkriegs', in *Vierteljahrshefte für Zeitgeschichte* (2010), 1 –33.

Mick, Christoph, *Lemberg – Lwów – L'viv, 1914–1947: Violence and Ethnicity in a Contested City* (West Lafayette, IN: Purdue University Press, November 2015).

——, 'Vielerlei Kriege: Osteuropa 1918–1921', in Dietrich Beyrau et al. (eds), *Formen des Krieges von der Antike bis zur Gegenwart* (Paderborn: Schöningh 2007), 311–26.

Middlebrook, Martin, *The Kaiser's Battle: The First Day of the German Spring Offensive* (London: Viking, 1978).

Mierau, Fritz, *Russen in Berlin, 1918–1933* (Berlin: Quadriga, 1988).

Mikoletzky, Lorenz, 'Saint-Germain und Karl Renner: Eine Republik wird diktiert', in Konrad and Maderthaner (eds), *Das Werden der Ersten Republik ... der Rest ist Österreich*, vol. 1, 179–86.

Millan, Matteo, 'The Institutionalization of Squadrismo: Disciplining Paramilitary Violence in the Fascist Dictatorship', in *Contemporary European History* 22 (2013), 551–74.

———, *Squadrismo e squadristi nella dittatura fascista* (Rome: Viella, 2014).

Miller, Daniel E., 'Colonizing the Hungarian and German Border Areas during the Czechoslovak Land Reform, 1918–1938', in *Austrian History Yearbook* 34 (2003), 303–17.

Miller, Marshall Lee, *Bulgaria during the Second World War* (Stanford, CA: Stanford University Press, 1975).

Miller, Susanne, *Die Bürde der Macht: Die deutsche Sozialdemokratie 1918–1920* (Düsseldorf: Droste, 1978).

Milow, Caroline, *Die ukrainische Frage 1917–1923 im Spannungsfeld der europäischen Diplomatie* (Wiesbaden: Harrassowitz, 2002).

Milton, Giles, *Paradise Lost: Smyrna 1922: The Destruction of Islam's City of Tolerance* (London: Sceptre, 2008).

Minchev, Dimitre, *Participation of the Population of Macedonia in the First World War* (Sofia: Voenno izdatelstvo, 2004).

Mir, Nejiski, *Vojna enciklopedija* (Belgrade: Vojno-izdavački zavod, 1973).

Mitchell, Allan, *Revolution in Bavaria 1918–19: The Eisner Regime and the Soviet Republic* (Princeton, NJ: Princeton University Press, 1965).

Mitchell, David, *1919: Red Mirage* (London: Jonathan Cape, 1970).

Mitev, Yono, *Fashistkiyat prevrat na deveti yuni 1923 godina i Yunskoto antifashistko vastanie* (Sofia: BZNS, 1973).

Mitter, Rana, *China's War with Japan, 1937–1945: The Struggle for Survival* (London: Allen Lane, 2014).

Mitrofanis, Giorgos, 'Ta dimosia ikonomika. Ikonomiki anorthossi ke polemi, 1909–1922', in Vassilis Panagiotopoulos (ed.), *Istoria tou Neou Ellinismou, 1770–2000*, vol. 6 (Athens: Ellinika Grammata, 2003), 124–7.

Mitrović, Andrej, *Jugoslavija na Konferenciji mira 1919–1920* (Belgrade: Zavod za izdavanje udžbenika SR Srbije, 1969).

———, *Serbia's Great War, 1914–1918* (London: Hurst, 2007).

Mitter, Rana, *A Bitter Revolution: China's Struggle with the Modern World* (Oxford and New York: Oxford University Press, 2004).

Mizov, Nikolay, *Vliyanieto na Velikata oktomvriyska sotsialisticheska revolyutsia varhu Vladayskoto vaorazheno vastanie na voynishkite masi u nas prez septembri 1918 godina* [*The Impact of the Great October Socialist Revolution upon the Vladaya Armed Uprising of the Soldiers' Masses in September 1918*] (Sofia: NS OF, 1957).

Mócsy, István I., *The Effects of World War I: The Uprooted: Hungarian Refugees and their Impact on Hungary's Domestic Politics, 1918–1921* (New York: Columbia University Press, 1983).

Molnár, Miklós, *From Béla Kun to János Kádár: Seventy Years of Hungarian Communism* (New York: St Martin's Press, 1990).

Mommsen, Hans, 'Adolf Hitler und der 9. November 1923', in Johannes Willms (ed.), *Der 9. November. Fünf Essays zur deutschen Geschichte*, 2nd edition (Munich: C. H. Beck, 1995), 33–48.

Montgomery, A. E., 'The Making of the Treaty of Sèvres of 10 August 1920', in *The Historical Journal* 15 (1972), 775–87.

Moral, Juan Díaz del, 'Historia de las agitaciones campesinas andaluzas', in Isidoro Moreno Navarro (ed.), *La identidad cultural de Andalucía, aproximaciones, mixtificaciones, negacionismo y evidencias* (Seville: Fundación Pública Andaluza Centro de Estudios Andaluces, 2008).

———, *Historia de las agitaciones campesinas andaluzas. Córdoba. Antecedentes para una reforma agraria* (Madrid: Alianza, 1995).

Morgan, Philip, *Italian Fascism, 1919–1945* (London: Macmillan, 1995).

Morgenthau, Henry, *I Was Sent to Athens* (Garden City, NY: Doubleday, 1929).

Mosse, George L., *Fallen Soldiers: Reshaping the Memory of the World Wars* (Oxford and New York: Oxford University Press, 1990).

Mroczka, Ludwik, 'Przyczynek do kwestii żydowskiej w Galicji u progu Drugiej Rzeczpospolitej', in Feliksa Kiryka (ed.), *Żydzi w Małopolsce. Studia z dziejów osadnictwa i życia społecznego* (Przemyśl: Południowo-Wschodni Instytut Naukowy w Przemyślu, 1991), 297–308.

Mühlhausen, Walter, *Friedrich Ebert, 1871–1925: Reichspräsident der Weimarer Republik* (Bonn: Dietz Verlag, 2006).

Mulligan, William, *The Great War for Peace* (New Haven, CT, and London: Yale University Press, 2014).

Mussolini, Benito, *Opera omnia*, vols 16 and 29 (Florence: La Fenice, 1955–9).

Nachtigal, Reinhard, 'Die kriegsgefangenen k. u. k. Generalität in Russland während des Ersten Weltkriegs', in *Österreich in Geschichte und Literatur (mit Geographie)* 47 (2003), 258–74.

———, *Kriegsgefangenschaft an der Ostfront 1914–1918: Literaturbericht zu einem neuen Forschungsfeld* (Frankfurt: Peter Lang, 2003).

———, *Russland und seine österreichisch-ungarischen Kriegsgefangenen (1914–1918)* (Remshalden: Verlag Bernhard Albert Greiner, 2003).

Naimark, Norman M., *Fires of Hatred: Ethnic Cleansing in Twentieth-Century Europe* (Cambridge, MA: Harvard University Press, 2002).

Naumov, Georgi, *Aleksandar Tzankov i Andrey Lyapchev v politikata na darzhavnoto upravlenie* (Sofia: IF 94, 2004).

Nebelin, Manfred, *Ludendorff: Diktator im Ersten Weltkrieg* (Munich: Siedler, 2010).

Neck, Rudolf (ed.), *Österreich im Jahre 1918: Berichte und Dokumente* (Vienna: Oldenbourg, 1968).

Nedev, Nedyu, *Aleksandar Stambolijski i zagovorat* (Sofia: BZNS, 1984).

——, *Tsar Boris III: Dvoretsat i tayniyat cabinet* (Plovdiv: IK 'Hermes', 2009).

Nedev, Nikola, and Tsocho Bilyarski, *Doyranskata epopeia, 1915–1918* (Sofia: Aniko/Simolini, 2009).

Negro, Piero del, 'Vittorio Veneto e l'armistizio sul fronte italiano', in Audoin-Rouzeau and Becker (eds), *La prima guerra mondiale*, vol. 2, 333–43.

Neiberg, Michael S., *The Second Battle of the Marne* (Bloomington, IN: Indiana University Press, 2008).

Nello, Paolo, 'La rivoluzione fascista ovvero dello squadrismo nazional rivoluzionario', in *Storia contemporanea* 13 (1982), 1,009–25.

Nettl, Peter, *Rosa Luxemburg* (Frankfurt am Main: Büchergilde Gutenberg, 1968).

Neumann, Wilhelm, *Abwehrkampf und Volksabstimmung in Kärnten, 1918–1920: Legenden und Tatsachen*, 2nd Édition (Klagenfurt: Kärntner Landesarchiv, 1985).

Neutatz, Dietmar, *Träume und Alpträume: Eine Geschichte Russlands im 20. Jahrhundert* (Munich: C. H. Beck, 2013).

Newman, John Paul, 'The Origins, Attributes, and Legacies of Paramilitary Violence in the Balkans', in Gerwarth and Horne (eds), *War in Peace*, 145–63.

——, 'Serbian Integral Nationalism and Mass Violence in the Balkans 1903–1945', in *Tijdschrift voor Geschiedenis*, 124 (2011), 448–63.

——, *Yugoslavia in the Shadow of War: Veterans and the Limits of State Building, 1903–1945* (Cambridge and New York: Cambridge University Press, 2015).

Nicolle, David, *The Italian Invasion of Abyssinia 1935–1936* (Westminster, MD: Osprey, 1997).

Niebrzydowski, Paul, *The American Relief Administration in Poland after the First World War, 1918–1923* (Washington DC: IARO Scholar Research Brief, 2015).

Nikolov, Kosta, *Kletvoprestapnitsite: Vladayskite sabitiya prez septemvri 1918* [*The Oath-breakers: The Vladaya Events in September 1918*] (Sofia: Angoboy, 2002).

Nivet, Philippe, *Les réfugiés français de la Grande Guerre, 1914–1920: Les 'boches du nord'* (Paris: Institut de Stratégie Comparée, 2004).

Norman Davies, *White Eagle, Red Star: The Polish-Soviet War, 1919–20*, 2nd edition (London: Pimlico, 2004).

Noske, Gustav, *Von Kiel bis Kapp: Zur Geschichte der deutschen Revolution* (Berlin: Verlag für Politik und Wirtschaft, 1920).

Nowak, Andrzej, 'Reborn Poland or Reconstructed Empire? Questions on the Course and Results of Polish Eastern Policy (1918–1921)', in *Lithuanian Historical Studies* 13 (2008), 134–42.

Nusser, Horst G., *Konservative Wehrverbände in Bayern, Preussen und Österreich mit einer Biographie von Georg Escherich 1870–1941*, 2 vols (Munich: Nusser, 1973).

O'Brien, Paul, *Mussolini in the First World War: The Journalist, the Soldier, the Fascist* (London: Bloomsbury, 2005).

Ognyanov, Lyubomir, *Voynishkoto vastanie 1918* [*The Soldiers' Uprising*] (Sofia: Nauka i izkustvo, 1988).

Olechnowicz, Andrzej, 'Liberal Anti-Fascism in the 1930s: The Case of Sir Ernest Barker', in *Albion: A Quarterly Journal Concerned with British Studies* 36 (2004), 636–60.

Orga, Irfan, and Margarete Orga, *Atatürk* (London: Michael Joseph, 1962).

Ortaggi, Simonetta, 'Mutamenti sociali e radicalizzazione dei conflitti in Italia tra guerra e dopoguerra', in *Ricerche storiche* 27 (1997), 673–89.

Orzoff, Andrea, *Battle for the Castle* (Oxford and New York: Oxford University Press, 2009).

Osborne, Eric W., *Britain's Economic Blockade of Germany, 1914–1919* (London and New York: Frank Cass, 2004).

Osipova, Taisia, 'Peasant Rebellions: Origins, Scope, Dynamics, and Consequences', in Vladimir N. Brovkin (ed.), *The Bolsheviks in Russian Society* (New Haven, CT, and London: Yale University Press, 1997), 154–76.

Overmans, Rüdiger, 'Kriegsverluste', in Gerhard Hirschfeld, Gerd Krumeich and Irina Renz (eds), *Enzyklopädie Erster Weltkrieg*, 2nd revised edition (Paderborn: Schöningh, 2004), 663–6.

Overy, Richard J., *The Interwar Crisis, 1919–1939* (Essex: Pearson, 1994).

Pallis, Alexandros A., *Greece's Anatolian Venture – and After: A Survey of the Diplomatic and Political Aspects of the Greek Expedition to Asia Minor (1915–1922)* (London: Methuen and Company, 1937).

Palmer, James, *The Bloody White Baron: The Extraordinary Story of the Russian Nobleman who Became the Last Khan of Mongolia* (New York: Basic Books, 2009).

Pasetti, Matteo, *Tra classe e nazione. Rappresentazioni e organizzazione del movimento nazional-sindacalista, 1918–1922* (Rome: Carocci, 2008).

Pastor, Peter, *Hungary between Wilson and Lenin: The Hungarian Revolution of 1918–1919 and the Big Three* (New York: Columbia University Press, East European Monograph, 1976).

Patenaude, Bertrand M., *The Big Show in Bololand: The American Relief Expedition to Soviet Russia in the Famine of 1921* (Stanford, CA: Stanford University Press, 2002).

Pauley, Bruce F., *From Prejudice to Persecution: A History of Austrian Anti-Semitism* (Chapel Hill, NC: University of North Carolina Press, 1992).

——, 'Politischer Antisemitismus im Wien der Zwischenkriegszeit', in Gerhard Botz et al. (eds), *Eine zerstörte Kultur: Jüdisches Leben und Antisemitismus in Wien seit dem 19. Jahrhundert* (Buchloe: Obermayer, 1990), 221–3.

Pavlović, Srdja, *Balkan Anschluss: The Annexation of Montenegro and the Creation of a Common South Slav State* (West Lafayette, IN: Purdue University Press, 2008).

Payne, Stanley, *Franco and Hitler: Spain, Germany, and World War II* (New Haven, CT, and London: Yale University Press, 2008).

Pearson, Raymond, 'Hungary: A State Truncated, a Nation Dismembered', in Seamus Dunn and T. G. Fraser, *Europe and Ethnicity: World War I and Contemporary Ethnic Conflict* (London and New York: Routledge, 1996), 88–109.

——, *National Minorities in Eastern Europe: 1848–1945* (London: Macmillan, 1983).

Pedersen, Susan, *The Guardians: The League of Nations and the Crisis of Empire* (Oxford and New York: Oxford University Press, 2015).

——, 'The Meaning of the Mandates System: An Argument', in *Geschichte und Gesellschaft* 32 (2006), 1–23.

Pentzopoulos, Dimitri, *The Balkan Exchange of Minorities* (Paris and The Hague: Mouton, 2002).

Pereira, Norman G. O., *White Siberia: The Politics of Civil War* (Montreal: McGill-Queen's University Press, 1996).

Perman, Dagmar, *The Shaping of the Czechoslovak State: Diplomatic History of the Boundaries of Czechoslovakia* (Leiden: Brill, 1962).

Petersen, Jens, *Hitler-Mussolini: Die Entstehung der Achse Berlin-Rom 1933–1936* (Tübingen: De Gruyter Niemeyer, 1973).

——, 'Il problema della violenza nel fascismo italiano', in *Storia contemporanea* 13 (1982), 985–1,008.

Petranović, Branko, *Istorija Jugoslavije*, vol. 1 (Belgrade: Nolit, 1988).

Petrov, Ivan Metodiev, *Voynata v Makedonia (1915–1918)* (Sofia: Semarsh, 2008).

Petrov, Viktor, 'The Town on the Sungari', in Stone and Glenny (eds), *The Other Russia*, 205–21.

Petrova, Dimitrina, *Aleksandar Tzankov i negovata partia: 1932–1944* (Sofia: Dio Mira, 2011).

Phillips, Howard, and David Killingray (eds), *The Spanish Influenza Pandemic of 1918–19: New Perspectives* (London and New York: Routledge, 2003).

Piazza, Giuseppe, *La nostra terra promessa: lettere dalla Tripolitania marzo-maggio 1911* (Rome: Lux, 1911).

Pichlík, Karel, 'Der militärische Zusammenbruch der Mittelmächte im Jahre 1918', in Richard Georg Plaschka and Karlheinz Mack (eds), *Die Auflösung des Habsburgerreiches: Zusammenbruch und Neuorientierung im Donauraum* (Munich: Verlag für Geschichte und Politik, 1970), 249–65.

Pipes, Richard, *Russia under the Bolshevik Regime* (New York: Knopf, 1993).

——, *The Russian Revolution 1899–1919* (London: Harvill Press, 1990, 1997)

Pistohlkors, Gert von (ed.), *Deutsche Geschichte im Osten Europas. Baltische Länder* (Berlin: Siedler, 1994).

Pitt-Rivers, George, *The World Significance of the Russian Revolution* (London: Blackwell, 1920).

Plakans, Andrejs, *A Concise History of the Baltic States* (Cambridge and New York: Cambridge University Press, 2011).

——, *The Latvians: A Short History* (Stanford, CA: Hoover Institution Press, 1995).

Plaschka, Richard G., Horst Haselsteiner and Arnold Suppan, *Innere Front: Militärassistenz, Widerstand und Umsturz in der Donaumonarchie 1918*, 2 vols (Vienna: Verlag für Geschichte und Politik, 1974).

Plöckinger, Othmar, *Unter Soldaten und Agitatoren. Hitlers prägende Jahre im deutschen Militär 1918–1920* (Paderborn: Schöningh, 2013).

Plowman, Matthew, 'Irish Republicans and the Indo-German Conspiracy of World War I', in *New Hibernia Review* 7 (2003), 81–105.

Poliakov, Léon, *The History of Anti-Semitism*, vol. 4: *Suicidal Europe, 1870–1933* (Philadelphia, PA: University of Pennsylvania Press, 2003).

Poljakov, Jurij Aleksandrovič et al., *Naselenie Rossii v XX veke: istoričeskie očerki* (Moscow: ROSSPEN, 2000).

Pölöskei, Ferenc, *A rejtélyes Tisza-gyilkosság* (Budapest: Helikon Kiadó, 1988).

Popnikolov, Dimitar, *Balgarite ot Trakiya i spogodbite na Balgaria s Gartsia i Turtsia* (Sofia: n.p., 1928).

Poryazov, Delcho, *Pogromat nad trakijskite bălgari prez 1913 g.: razorenie i etnichesko iztreblenie* (Sofia: Akademichno izdatelstvo 'Prof. Marin Drinov', 2009).

Pourchier-Plasseraud, Suzanne, 'Riga 1905–2005: A City with Conflicting Identities', in *Nordost-Archiv* 15 (2006), 175–94.

Preston, Paul, *The Spanish Civil War: Reaction, Revolution, and Revenge* (New York: W. W. Norton and Company, 2006).

Priestland, David, *The Red Flag: A History of Communism* (London: Penguin, 2009).

Procacci, Giovanna, *Dalla rassegnazione alla rivolta. Mentalità e comportamenti popolari nella Grande Guerra* (Rome: Bulzoni, 1999).

——, *Warfare-welfare: Intervento dello Stato e diritti dei cittadini 1914–18* (Rome: Carocci, 2013).

Prost, Antoine, 'The Impact of War on French and German Political Cultures', in *The Historical Journal* 37 (1994), 209–17.

Prost, Antoine, and Jay Winter (eds), *The Great War in History: Debates and Controversies, 1914 to the Present* (Cambridge and New York: Cambridge University Press, 2005).

Provence, Michael, 'Ottoman Modernity, Colonialism, and Insurgency in the Arab Middle East', in *International Journal of Middle East Studies* 43 (2011), 205–25.

Prusin, Alexander V., *The Lands Between: Conflict in the East European Borderlands, 1870–1992* (Oxford and New York: Oxford University Press, 2010).

Pugh, Martin, *'Hurrah for the Blackshirts!': Fascists and Fascism in Britain between the Wars* (London: Pimlico, 2006).

Pulzer, Peter, *The Rise of Political Anti-Semitism in Germany and Austria*, 2nd revised edition (Cambridge, MA: Harvard University Press, 1988).

Purseigle, Pierre, A '"Wave on to Our Shores": The Exile and Resettlement of Refugees from the Western Front, 1914–1918', in *Contemporary European History*, 16 (2007), 427–44.

Quiroga, Alejandro, *Making Spaniards: Primo de Rivera and the Nationalization of the Masses, 1923–30* (London and New York: Palgrave Macmillan, 2007).

Rabinowitch, Alexander, *The Bolsheviks in Power: The First Year of Soviet Rule in Petrograd* (Bloomington, IN: Indiana University Press, 2007).

Rachaminow, Alan, *POWs and the Great War: Captivity on the Eastern Front* (Oxford and New York: Berg, 2002).

Radzinsky, Edvard, *The Last Tsar: The Life and Death of Nicholas II* (New York: Doubleday, 1992).

Raef, Marc, *Russia Abroad: A Cultural History of the Russian Emigration, 1919–1939* (Oxford and New York: Oxford University Press, 1990).

Rakočević, Novica, *Crna Gora u Prvom svetskom ratu 1914–1918* (Cetinje: Obod, 1969).

Raleigh, Donald J., *Experiencing Russia's Civil War: Politics, Society and*

Revolutionary Culture in Saratov, 1917–1922 (Princeton, NJ: Princeton University Press, 2002).

——, 'The Russian Civil War 1917–1922', in Ronald Grigor Suny (ed.), *The Cambridge History of Russia*, vol. 3 (Cambridge: Cambridge University Press, 2006), 140–67.

Rape, Ludger, *Die österreichischen Heimwehren und die bayerische Rechte 1920–1923* (Vienna: Europa-Verlag, 1977).

Raphael, Lutz, *Imperiale Gewalt und Mobilisierte Nation: Europa 1914–1945* (Munich: C. H. Beck, 2011).

Rappaport, Helen, *Conspirator: Lenin in Exile* (New York: Basic, 2010).

Rauch, Georg von, *The Baltic States: The Years of Independence: Estonia, Latvia, Lithuania, 1917–1940* (Berkeley, CA: University of California Press, 1974).

Rauchensteiner, Manfried, 'L'Autriche entre confiance et résignation, 1918–1920', in Audoin-Rouzeau and Prochasson (eds), *Sortir de la Grande Guerre*, 165–85.

——, *Der Tod des Doppeladlers: Österreich-Ungarn und der Erste Weltkrieg* (Graz: Styria, 1993).

Raun, Toivo U., 'The Revolution of 1905 in the Baltic Provinces and Finland', in *Slavic Review* 43 (1984), 453–67.

Rauscher, Walter, 'Die Republikgründungen 1918 und 1945', in Klaus Koch, Walter Rauscher, Arnold Suppan and Elisabeth Vyslonzil (eds), *Außenpolitische Dokumente der Republik Österreich 1918–1938. Sonderband: Von Saint-Germain zum Belvedere: Österreich und Europa 1919–1955* (Vienna and Munich: Verlag für Geschichte und Politik, 2007), 9–24.

Raymond, Boris, and David R. Jones, *The Russian Diaspora 1917–1941* (Lanham, MD: Scarecrow, 2000).

Read, Anthony, *The World on Fire: 1919 and the Battle with Bolshevism* (London: Pimlico, 2009).

Read, Christopher, *From Tsar to Soviets: The Russian People and their Revolution, 1917–1921* (Oxford and New York: Oxford University Press, 1996).

——, *Lenin: A Revolutionary Life* (Abingdon and New York: Routledge, 2005).

Reichardt, Sven, *Faschistische Kampfbünde: Gewalt und Gemeinschaft im italienischen Squadrismus und in der deutschen SA* (Cologne, Weimar and Vienna: Böhlau Verlag, 2002).

Reinharz, Jehuda, *Chaim Weizmann: The Making of a Statesman*, 2nd edition (Oxford and New York: Oxford University Press, 1993).

Rena, Paul, 'Der christlichsoziale Antisemitismus in Wien 1848–1938', unpublished PhD thesis, Vienna, 1991.

Reulecke, Jürgen, 'Ich möchte einer werden so wie die . . .': Männerbünde im 20. Jahrhundert (Frankfurt am Main: Campus, 2001).

Reynolds, David, The Long Shadow: The Great War and the Twentieth Century (London: Simon and Schuster, 2013).

Reynolds, Michael A., 'The Ottoman-Russian Struggle for Eastern Anatolia and the Caucasus, 1908–1918: Identity, Ideology and the Geopolitics of World Order', PhD thesis, Princeton University, 2003.

——, Shattering Empires: The Clash and Collapse of the Ottoman and Russian Empires, 1908–1918 (Cambridge and New York: Cambridge University Press, 2011).

Rey Reguillo, Fernando del, 'El empresario, el sindicalista y el miedo', in Manuel Pérez Ledesma and Rafael Cruz (eds), Cultura y movilización en la España contemporánea (Madrid: Alianza, 1997), 235–72.

Rhode, Gotthold, 'Das Deutschtum in Posen und Pommerellen in der Zeit der Weimarer Republik', in Senatskommission für das Studium des Deutschtums im Osten an der Rheinischen Friedrich-Wilhelms-Universität Bonn (ed.), Studien zum Deutschtum im Osten (Cologne and Graz: Böhlau, 1966), 88–132.

Riasanovsky, Nicholas Valentine, and Mark Steinberg, A History of Russia (Oxford and New York: Oxford University Press, 2005).

Riccardi, Luca, Alleati non amici: le relazioni politiche tra l'Italia e l'Intesa durante la prima guerra mondiale (Brescia: Morcelliana, 1992).

Rigotti, Francesca, 'Il medico-chirurgo dello Stato nel linguaggio metaforico di Mussolini', in Civiche Raccolte Storiche Milano (ed.), Cultura e società negli anni del fascismo (Milan: Cordani, 1987).

Robinson, Paul, The White Russian Army in Exile, 1920–1941 (Oxford and New York: Oxford University Press, 2002).

Rochat, Giorgio, Gli arditi della grande guerra: origini, battaglie e miti (Milan: Feltrinelli, 1981).

Rodogno, Davide, Fascism's European Empire: Italian Occupation during the Second World War (Cambridge: Cambridge University Press, 2008).

Rogan, Eugene, The Fall of the Ottomans: The Great War in the Middle East, 1914–1920 (London: Allen Lane, 2015).

Rogger, Hans, Russia in the Age of Modernization and Revolution, 1881–1917 (London: Longman, 1983).

Romero Salvadó, Francisco J., The Foundations of Civil War: Revolution, Social Conflict and Reaction in Liberal Spain, 1916–1923 (London: Routledge, 2008).

——, Spain, 1914–1918: Between War and Revolution (London: Routledge, 1999).

Romsics, Gergely, Myth and Remembrance: The Dissolution of the Habsburg

Empire in the Memoir Literature of the Austro-Hungarian Political Elite (New York: Columbia University Press, 2006).

Romsics, Ignác, *A Duna-Tisza Köze Hatalmi Viszonyai 1918–19-ben* (Budapest: Akadémiai Kiadó, 1982).

——, *A trianoni békeszerződés* (Budapest: Osiris, 2008).

Rosenberg, William G., *The Liberals in the Russian Revolution: The Constitutional Democratic Party, 1917–1921* (Princeton, NJ: Princeton University Press, 1974).

Rosenberg, William G., 'Paramilitary Violence in Russia's Civil Wars, 1918–1920', in Gerwarth and Horne (eds), *War in Peace*, 21–39.

Roshwald, Aviel, *Ethnic Nationalism and the Fall of Empires: Central Europe, Russia and the Middle East, 1914–1923* (London: Routledge, 2001).

Rossfeld, Roman, Thomas Buomberger and Patrick Kury (eds), *14/18. Die Schweiz und der Grosse Krieg* (Baden: hier + jetzt, 2014).

Rothenberg, Gunther, *The Army of Francis Joseph* (West Lafayette, IN: Purdue University Press, 1997).

Rubenstein, Joshua, *Leon Trotsky: A Revolutionary's Life* (New Haven, CT, and London: Yale University Press, 2006).

Rudenno, Victor, *Gallipoli: Attack from the Sea* (New Haven, CT, and London: Yale University Press, 2008).

Rudin, Harry Rudolph, *Armistice 1918* (New Haven, CT, and London: Yale University Press, 1944).

Rummel, Rudolph Joseph, *Lethal Politics: Soviet Genocide and Mass Murder since 1917* (Piscataway, NJ: Transaction Publishers, 1990).

Rürup, Reinhard, 'Demokratische Revolution und der "dritte Weg": Die deutsche Revolution von 1918/19 in der neueren wissenschaftlichen Diskussion', in *Geschichte und Gesellschaft* 9 (1983), 278–301.

Rusconi, Gian Enrico, *L'azzardo del 1915: Come l'Italia decide la sua guerra* (Bologna: il Mulino, 2005).

Rust, Christian, 'Self-Determination at the Beginning of 1918 and the German Reaction', in *Lithuanian Historical Studies* 13 (2008), 41–66.

Sabrow, Martin, *Die verdrängte Verschwörung: Der Rathenau-Mord und die deutsche Gegenrevolution* (Frankfurt am Main: Fischer, 1999).

Sagoschen, Christine, *Judenbilder im Wandel der Zeit: die Entwicklung des katholischen Antisemitismus am Beispiel jüdischer Stereotypen unter besonderer Berücksichtigung der Entwicklung in der ersten Republik*, unpublished PhD thesis, Vienna, 1998.

Sakmyster, Thomas, *A Communist Odyssey: The Life of József Pogány* (Budapest and New York: Central European University Press, 2012).

——, 'Gyula Gömbös and the Hungarian Jews, 1918–1936', in *Hungarian Studies Review* 8 (2006), 156–68.

———, *Hungary's Admiral on Horseback: Miklós Horthy, 1918–1944* (Boulder, CO: Eastern European Monographs, 1994).

Salamon, Konrád, 'Proletárditarúra és a Terror', in *Rubicon* (2011), 24–35.

Salaris, Claudia, *Alla festa della rivoluzione. Artisti e libertari con D'Annunzio a Fiume* (Bologna: il Mulino 2002).

Sammartino, Annemarie H., *The Impossible Border: Germany and the East, 1914–1922* (Ithaca, NY, and London: Cornell University Press, 2010).

Sanborn, Joshua, *Drafting the Russian Nation: Military Conscription, Total War, and Mass Politics, 1905–1925* (DeKalb, IL: Northern Illinois University Press, 2003).

———, *Imperial Apocalypse: The Great War and the Destruction of the Russian Empire* (Oxford and New York: Oxford University Press, 2014).

———, 'Unsettling the Empire: Violent Migrations and Social Disaster in Russia during World War I', in *The Journal of Modern History* 77 (2005), 290–324.

Sauer, Bernhard, 'Freikorps und Antisemitismus', in *Zeitschrift für Geschichtswissenschaft* 56 (2008), 5–29.

———, 'Vom "Mythos eines ewigen Soldatentums". Der Feldzug deutscher Freikorps im Baltikum im Jahre 1919', in *Zeitschrift für Geschichtswissenschaft* 43 (1995), 869–902.

Saunders, David, 'The First World War and the End of Tsarism', in Ian D. Thatcher (ed.), *Reinterpreting Revolutionary Russia: Essays in Honour of James D. White* (Basingstoke: Palgrave Macmillan, 2006).

Sayer, Derek, 'British Reaction to the Amritsar Massacre, 1919–1920', in *Past & Present* 131 (1991), 130–64.

Sbacchi, Alberto, *Ethiopia under Mussolini: Fascism and the Colonial Experience* (London: Zed Books, 1985).

Schapiro, Leonard, 'The Role of Jews in the Russian Revolutionary Movement', in *The Slavonic and East European Review* 40:94 (1961), 148–67.

Schivelbusch, Wolfgang, *The Culture of Defeat: On National Trauma, Mourning and Recovery* (New York: Holt, 2003).

Schlag, Gerald, 'Die Grenzziehung Österreich-Ungarn 1922/23', in Burgenländisches Landesarchiv (ed.), *Burgenland in seiner pannonischen Umwelt: Festgabe für August Ernst* (Eisenstadt: Burgenlädisches Landesarchiv, 1984), 333–46.

Schlögel, Karl (ed.) *Chronik russischen Lebens in Deutschland, 1918 bis 1941* (Berlin: Akademie Verlag, 1999).

Schneer, Jonathan, *The Balfour Declaration: The Origins of Arab-Israeli Conflict* (London and Basingstoke: Macmillan, 2014).

Schnell, Felix, *Ordnungshüter auf Abwegen? Herrschaft und illegitime polizeiliche Gewalt in Moskau, 1905–1914* (Wiesbaden: Harrassowitz, 2006).

——, *Räume des Schreckens. Gewalt und Gruppenmilitanz in der Ukraine 1905–1933* (Hamburg: Hamburger Edition, HIS Verlag, 2012).

——, 'Der Sinn der Gewalt: Der Ataman Volynec und der Dauerpogrom von Gajsyn im russischen Bürgerkrieg', in *Zeithistorische Forschung* 5 (2008), 18–39.

Schulman, Jason (ed.), *Rosa Luxemburg: Her Life and Legacy* (New York: Palgrave Macmillan, 2013).

Schulze, Hagen, *Freikorps und Republik, 1918–1920* (Boppard am Rhein: Boldt, 1969).

Schumann, Dirk, 'Europa, der Erste Weltkrieg und die Nachkriegszeit: Eine Kontinuität der Gewalt?', in *Journal of Modern European History* 1 (2003), 24–43.

Schuster, Frank M., *Zwischen allen Fronten: Osteuropäische Juden während des Ersten Weltkriegs (1914–1919)* (Cologne: Böhlau, 2004).

Šedivý, Ivan, 'Zur Loyalität der Legionäre in der ersten Tschechoslowakischen Republik', in Martin Schulze Wessel (ed.), *Loyalitäten in der Tschechoslowakischen Republik 1918–1938: Politische, nationale und kulturelle Zugehörigkeiten* (Munich: Oldenbourg, 2004), 141–52.

Sedlmaier, Alexander, *Deutschlandbilder und Deutschlandpolitik Studien zur Wilson-Administration (1913–1921)* (Stuttgart: Steiner, 2003).

Segré, Claudio G., 'Il colonialismo e la politica estera: variazioni liberali e fasciste', in Richard J. B. Bosworth and Sergio Romano (eds), *La politica estera italiana 1860–1985* (Bologna: il Mulino, 1991), 121–46.

Seipp, Adam, *The Ordeal of Demobilization and the Urban Experience in Britain and Germany, 1917–1921* (Farnham: Ashgate, 2009).

Semov, Mincho, *Pobediteliat prosi mir: Balkanskite voyni 1912–1913* (Sofia: Universitetsko izdatelstvo 'Sv. Kliment Ohridski', 1995).

Service, Robert, *Comrades! World History of Communism* (Cambridge, MA: Harvard University Press, 2007).

——, *Lenin: A Biography* (London: Macmillan, 2000).

——, *Trotsky: A Biography* (Cambridge, MA: Harvard University Press, 2009).

Shapira, Anita, *Ben-Gurion: Father of Modern Israel* (New Haven, CT, and London: Yale University Press, 2014).

Sharp, Alan, *Consequences of the Peace: The Versailles Settlement – Aftermath and Legacy 1919–2010* (London: Haus, 2010).

——, '"The Genie that Would Not Go Back into the Bottle": National Self-Determination and the Legacy of the First World War and the Peace Settlement', in Seamus Dunn and T. G. Fraser (eds), *Europe and Ethnicity: The*

First World War and Contemporary Ethnic Conflict (London and New York: Routledge, 1996), 10–29.

———, 'The New Diplomacy and the New Europe', in Nicholas Doumanis, *The Oxford Handbook of Europe 1914–1945* (Oxford and New York, 2016).

———, 'The Paris Peace Conference and Its Consequences', in Ute Daniel et al. (eds), *1914–1918 online. International Encyclopedia of The First World War*.

———, *The Versailles Settlement: Peacemaking after the First World War, 1919–1923*, 2nd edition (London: Palgrave, 2008).

Sheehan, James, *Where Have All the Soldiers Gone? The Transformation of Modern Europe* (New York: Houghton Mifflin, 2008).

Shimazu, Naoko, *Japan, Race and Equality: The Racial Equality Proposal of 1919* (London: Routledge, 1998).

Siebrecht, Claudia, *The Aesthetics of Loss: German Women's Art of the First World War* (Oxford and New York: Oxford University Press, 2013).

Sieder, Reinhard J., 'Behind the Lines: Working-Class Family Life in Wartime Vienna', in Richard Wall and Jay Winter (eds), *The Upheaval of War: Family, Work and Welfare in Europe, 1914–1918* (Cambridge and New York: Cambridge University Press, 1988), 109–38.

Simeonov, Radoslav, Velichka Mihailova and Donka Vasileva, *Dobrichkata epopeia, 1916* (Dobrich: Ave fakta, 2006).

Simon, Rachel, *Libya Between Ottomanism and Nationalism* (Berlin: Klaus Schwarz, 1987).

Sipos, József, *A pártok és a földrefom 1918–1919* (Budapest: Gondolat, 2009).

Sluga, Glenda, *The Problem of Trieste and the Italo-Yugoslav Border: Difference, Identity, and Sovereignty in Twentieth-Century Europe* (Albany, NY: SUNY Press, 2001).

Smele, Jonathan D., *Civil War in Siberia: The Anti-Bolshevik Government of Admiral Kolchak, 1918–1920* (Cambridge: Cambridge University Press, 1996).

———, *The 'Russian' Civil Wars 1916–1926: Ten Years that Shook the World* (Oxford: Oxford University Press, 2015).

Smith, Canfield, F., 'The Ungernovščina – How and Why?', in *Jahrbücher für Geschichte Osteuropas* 28 (1980), 590–5.

Smith, Douglas, *Former People: The Final Days of the Russian Aristocracy* (London: Macmillan, 2012).

Smith, Jeffrey R., *A People's War: Germany's Political Revolution, 1913–1918* (Lanham, MD: University Press of America, 2007).

Smith, Leonard V., 'Empires at the Paris Peace Conference', in Gerwarth and Manela (eds), *Empires at War*, 254–76.

———, 'Les États-Unis et l'échec d'une seconde mobilisation', in Stéphane

Audoin-Rouzeau and Christophe Prochasson (eds), *Sortir de la Guerre de 14–18* (Paris: Tallandier, 2008), 69–91.

———, 'The Wilsonian Challenge to International Law', in *The Journal of the History of International Law* 13 (2011), 179–208.

Smith, Leonard V., Stéphane Audoin-Rouzeau and Annette Becker, *France and the Great War, 1914–1918* (Cambridge and New York: Cambridge University Press, 2003).

Smith, Michael Llewellyn, *Ionian Vision: Greece in Asia Minor 1919–1922* (London: Allen Lane, 1973).

Smith, Robert E. F. (ed.), *The Russian Peasant, 1920 and 1984* (London: Routledge, 1977).

Smith, Stephen, *Red Petrograd: Revolution in the Factories, 1917–1918* (Cambridge: Cambridge University Press, 1983).

———, *The Russian Revolution: A Very Short Introduction* (Oxford and New York: Oxford University Press, 2002).

Snyder, Timothy, *Bloodlands: Europe between Hitler and Stalin* (New York: Basic Books, 2010).

———, *The Reconstruction of Nations: Poland, Ukraine, Lithuania, Belarus 1569–1999* (New Haven, CT, and London: Yale University Press, 2003).

Solomonidis, Victoria, 'Greece in Asia Minor: The Greek Administration of the Vilayet of Aidin, 1919–1922', unpublished PhD thesis, King's College, University of London, 1984.

Sondhaus, Lawrence, *World War One: The Global Revolution* (Cambridge and New York: Cambridge University Press, 2011).

Sonyel, Salahi, *The Great War and the Tragedy of Anatolia: Turks and Armenians in the Maelstrom of Major Powers* (Ankara: Turkish Historical Society, 2000).

Sprenger, Matthias, *Landsknechte auf dem Weg ins Dritte Reich? Zu Genese und Wandel des Freikorps-Mythos* (Paderborn: Schöningh, 2008).

Stadler, Karl Rudolf, *The Birth of the Austrian Republic 1918–1921* (Leyden: Sijthoff, 1966).

Stamatopoulos, Dimitris, 'I mikrasiatiki ekstratia. I anthropogheografia tis katastrofis', in Antonis Liakos (ed.), *To 1922 ke i prosfighes, mia nea matia* (Athens: Nefeli, 2011), 55–100.

Stanković, Djordje, 'Kako je Jugoslavija počela', in Milan Terzić, *Prvi svetski rat i Balkan – 90 godina kasnije* (Belgrade: Institut za strategijska istraživanja, 2010).

Stead, William, *Tripoli and the Treaties* (London: Bank Buildings, 1911).

Stegmann, Natali, *Kriegsdeutungen, Staatsgründungen, Sozialpolitik: Der*

Helden- und Opferdiskurs in der Tschechoslowakei, 1918–1948 (Munich: Oldenbourg, 2010).

Steiner, Zara, *The Lights that Failed: European International History, 1919–1933* (Oxford and New York: Oxford University Press, 2005).

——, *The Triumph of the Dark: European International History, 1933–1939* (Oxford and New York: Oxford University Press, 2011).

Stephenson, Scott, *The Final Battle: Soldiers of the Western Front and the German Revolution of 1918* (Cambridge and New York: Cambridge University Press, 2009).

Sternhell, Zeev, *Naissance de l'idéologie fasciste* (Paris: Fayard, 1989).

Stevenson, David, *The First World War and International Politics* (Oxford: Oxford University Press, 1988).

——, *With Our Backs to the Wall: Victory and Defeat in 1918* (London: Allen Lane, 2011).

Stewart, Matthew, 'It Was All a Pleasant Business: The Historical Context of "On the Quai at Smyrna"', in *Hemingway Review* 23 (2003), 58–71.

Stone, David, *The Russian Army in the Great War: The Eastern Front, 1914–1917* (Lawrence, KS: University of Kansas Press, 2015).

Stranga, Aivars, 'Communist Dictatorship in Latvia: December 1918–January 1920: Ethnic Policy', in *Lithuanian Historical Studies* 13 (2008), 161–78.

Straub, Eberhard, *Albert Ballin: Der Reeder des Kaisers* (Berlin: Siedler, 2001).

Sullivan, Charles L., 'The 1919 German Campaign in the Baltic: The Final Phase', in Stanley Vardys and Romuald Misiunas, *The Baltic States in Peace and War, 1917–1945* (London: Pennsylvania State University Press, 1978), 31–42.

Sumpf, Alexandre, 'Russian Civil War', in Ute Daniel, Peter Gatrell, Oliver Janz, Heather Jones, Jennifer Keene, Alan Kramer and Bill Nasson (eds), *1914–1918 online. International Encyclopedia of the First World War*.

Sunderland, Williard, *The Baron's Cloak: A History of the Russian Empire in War and Revolution* (Ithaca, NY, and London: Cornell University Press, 2014).

Sundhaussen, Holm, *Geschichte Serbiens: 19.–21. Jahrhundert* (Vienna: Böhlau, 2007).

Suny, Ronald Grigor, 'Explaining Genocide: The Fate of the Armenians in the Late Ottoman Empire', in Richard Bessel and Claudia Haake (eds), *Removing Peoples: Forced Removal in the Modern World* (Oxford and New York: Oxford University Press, 2009), 209–53.

——, *The Structure of Soviet History: Essays and Documents* (Oxford and New York: Oxford University Press, 2014).

——, 'Toward a Social History of the October Revolution', in *American Historical Review* 88 (1983), 31–52.

Swain, Geoffrey, 'Trotsky and the Russian Civil War', in Ian D. Thatcher (ed.), *Reinterpreting Revolutionary Russia: Essays in Honour of James D. White* (Basingstoke: Palgrave, 2006), 86–104.

——, *Trotsky and the Russian Revolution* (London and New York: Routledge, 2014).

Tachjian, Vahé, *La France en Cilicie et en Haute-Mésopotamie: aux confins de la Turquie, de la Syrie et de l'Irak, 1919–1933* (Paris: Editions Karthala, 2004).

Tálos, Emmerich, *Das austrofaschistische Herrschaftssystem: Österreich 1933–1938* (Berlin, Münster and Vienna: LIT, 2013).

Tamari, Salim (ed.), *Year of the Locust: A Soldier's Diary and the Erasure of Palestine's Ottoman Past* (Berkeley, CA: University of California Press, 2011).

Tanchev, Evgeni, *Darzhavno-pravnite vazgledi na Alexandar Stambolijski* (Sofia: BZNS, 1984).

Tankova, V. et al., *Balkanskite voyni 1912–1913: pamet i istoriya* (Sofia: 'Prof. Marin Drinov', 2012).

Tasca, Angelo, *La Naissance du fascisme* (Paris: Gallimard, 1938).

Tasić, Dmitar, 'The Assassination of King Alexander: The Swan Song of the Internal Macedonian Revolutionary Organization', in *Donau. Tijdschrift over Zuidost-Europa* (2008), 30–9.

Taylor, A. J. P., *The Habsburg Monarchy, 1809–1918: A History of the Austrian Empire and Austria-Hungary* (London: Hamish Hamilton, 1948).

Temperley, Harold M. V. (ed.), *A History of the Peace Conference of Paris*, 6 vols (London: Frowde and Hodder and Stoughton, 1921–4).

Teveth, Shabtai, *Ben-Gurion and the Palestinian Arabs: From Peace to War* (Oxford and New York: Oxford University Press, 1985).

——, *The Burning Ground: A Biography of David Ben-Gurion* (Tel Aviv: Schoken, 1997).

Ther, Philipp, 'Deutsche Geschichte als imperiale Geschichte: Polen, slawophone Minderheiten und das Kaiserreich als kontinentales Empire', in Sebastian Conrad and Jürgen Osterhammel (eds), *Das Kaiserreich transnational: Deutschland in der Welt 1871–1914* (Göttingen: Vandenhoeck and Ruprecht, 2004), 129–48.

Theweleit, Klaus, *Male Fantasies*, 2 vols (Minneapolis, MN: University of Minnesota Press, 1987).

Thomas, Ludmilla, *Geschichte Sibiriens: Von den Anfängen bis zur Gegenwart* (Berlin: Akademie-Verlag 1982).

Thompson, Elizabeth F., *Colonial Citizens: Republican Rights, Paternal Priv-*

ilege, and Gender in French Syria and Lebanon (New York: Columbia University Press, 2000).

Thompson, Mark, *The White War: Life and Death on the Italian Front 1915–1919* (London: Faber and Faber, 2009).

Thompson Manning, Roberta, *The Crisis of the Old Order in Russia: Gentry and Government* (Princeton, NJ: Princeton University Press, 1983).

Thoss, Bruno, *Der Ludendorff-Kreis: München als Zentrum der mitteleuropäischen Gegenrevolution zwischen Revolution und Hitler-Putsch* (Munich: Wölfle, 1978).

Thum, Gregor (ed.), *Traumland Osten: Deutsche Bilder vom östlichen Europa im 20. Jahrhundert* (Göttingen: Vandenhoeck and Ruprecht, 2006).

Thunig-Nittner, Gerburg, *Die Tschechoslowakische Legion in Rußland: Ihre Geschichte und Bedeutung bei der Entstehung der 1. Tschechoslowakischen Republik* (Wiesbaden: Harrassowitz, 1970).

Tokes, Rudolf, *Béla Kun and the Hungarian Soviet Republic: The Origins and Role of the Communist Party of Hungary in the Revolutions of 1918–1919* (New York and Stanford, CA: Praeger, 1967).

——, 'Bela Kun: The Man and Revolutionary', in Iván Völgyes (ed.), *Hungary in Revolution* (Lincoln, NB: University of Nebraska Press), 170–207.

Toma, Peter A., 'The Slovak Soviet Republic of 1919', in *American Slavic and East European Review* 17 (1958), 203–15.

Tooze, Adam, *The Deluge: The Great War and the Re-Making of Global Order* (London: Allen Lane, 2014).

Tormay, Cecile, *An Outlaw's Diary*, 2 vols (London: Allan, 1923).

Townshend, Charles, *The Republic: The Fight for Irish Independence 1918–1923* (London: Allen Lane, 2013).

Townson, Nigel, *The Crisis of Democracy in Spain: Centrist Politics under the Second Republic, 1931–1936* (Brighton: Sussex University Press, 2000).

Toynbee, Arnold J., *The Western Question in Greece and Turkey: A Study in the Contact of Civilisations* (Boston, MA: Constable, 1922).

Traverso, Enzo, *Fire and Blood: The European Civil War, 1914–1945* (New York: Verso, 2016).

Troebst, Stefan, *Das makedonische Jahrhundert: Von den Anfängen der nationalrevolutionären Bewegung zum Abkommen von Ohrid 1893–2001* (Munich: Oldenbourg, 2007).

——, *Mussolini, Makedonien und die Mächte 1922–1930. Die 'Innere Makedonische Revolutionäre Organisation', in der Südosteuropapolitik des faschistischen Italien* (Cologne and Vienna: Böhlau, 1987).

Trotnow, Helmut, *Karl Liebknecht: Eine Politische Biographie* (Cologne: Kiepenheuer and Witsch, 1980).

Tunstall, Greyton A., *Blood on the Snow: The Carpathian Winter War of 1915* (Lawrence, KS: University Press of Kansas, 2010).

Üngör, Uğur Ümit, *The Making of Modern Turkey: Nation and State in Eastern Anatolia, 1913–1950* (Oxford and New York: Oxford University Press, 2011).

——, 'Mass Violence against Civilians during the Balkan Wars', in Dominik Geppert, William Mulligan and Andreas Rose (eds), *The Wars Before the Great War: Conflict and International Politics Before the Outbreak of the First World War* (Cambridge and New York: Cambridge University Press, 2015), 76–91.

Ungváry, Krisztián, *A magyar honvédség a második világháborúban* (Budapest: Osiris Kiadó, 2004).

——, 'Sacco di Budapest, 1919. Gheorghe Mârdârescu tábornok válasza Harry Hill Bandholtz vezérőrnagy nem diplomatikus naplójára', in *Budapesti Negyed* 3–4 (2000), 173–203.

Upton, Anthony, *The Finnish Revolution, 1917–18* (Minneapolis, MN: University of Minnesota Press, 1980).

Valli, Roberta Suzzi, 'The Myth of Squadrismo in the Fascist Regime', in *Journal for Contemporary History* 35 (2000), 131–50.

Váry, Albert, *A Vörös Uralom Áldozatai Magyarországon* (Szeged: Szegedi Nyomda, 1993).

Ventrone, Angelo, *La seduzione totalitaria: Guerra, modernità, violenza politica, 1914–1918* (Rome: Donzelli, 2003).

Veremis, Thanos, and Elias Nikolakopoulos (eds), *O Eleftherios Venizelos ke I epochi tou* (Athens: Ellinika Grammata, 2005).

Vincent, C. Paul, *The Politics of Hunger: The Allied Blockade of Germany, 1915–1919* (Athens, OH: Ohio University Press, 1985).

Vivarelli, Roberto, *Storia delle origini del fascismo: L'Italia dalla Grande Guerra alla marcia su Roma* (Bologna: il Mulino, 2012).

Volkmann, Hans-Erich, *Die deutsche Baltikumpolitik zwischen Brest-Litowsk und Compiègne* (Cologne and Vienna: Böhlau, 1970).

Voltan, Vamik D., and Norman Itzkowitz, *The Immortal Atatürk: A Psychobiography* (Chicago, IL: Chicago University Press, 1984).

Vukov, Nikolai, 'The Aftermaths of Defeat: The Fallen, the Catastrophe, and the Public Response of Women to the End of the First World War in Bulgaria', in Ingrid Sharp and Matthew Stibbe (eds), *Aftermaths of War: Women's Movements and Female Activists, 1918–1923* (Leiden: Brill, 2011), 29–47.

——, 'Commemorating the Dead and the Dynamics of Forgetting: "Post-Mortem" Interpretations of World War I in Bulgaria', in Oto Luthar (ed.),

The Great War and Memory in Central and South-Eastern Europe (Leiden: Brill 2016), 162–87.

Wachs, Friedrich-Carl, *Das Verordnungswerk des Reichsdemobilmachungsamtes* (Frankfurt am Main: Peter Lang, 1991).

Wade, Rex A., 'The October Revolution, the Constituent Assembly, and the End of the Russian Revolution', in Ian D. Thatcher (ed.), *Reinterpreting Revolutionary Russia: Essays in Honour of James D. White* (London: Palgrave Macmillan, 2006), 72–85.

——, *Red Guards and Workers' Militias in the Russian Revolution* (Palo Alto, CA: Stanford University Press, 1984).

——, *The Russian Revolution, 1917* (Cambridge and New York: Cambridge University Press, 2000).

Waite, Robert G. L., *Vanguard of Nazism: The Free Corps Movement in Postwar Germany, 1918–1923* (Cambridge, MA: Harvard University Press, 1952).

Walker, Christopher J., *Armenia: The Survival of a Nation*, 2nd edition (London: Routledge, 1990).

Wandycz, Piotr Stefan, *France and her Eastern Allies, 1919–25: French-Czechoslovak-Polish Relations from the Paris Peace Conference to Locarno* (Minneapolis, MN: University of Minnesota Press, 1962).

——, *The Lands of Partitioned Poland, 1795–1918* (Seattle, WA: University of Washington Press, 1974).

Wargelin, Clifford F., 'A High Price for Bread: The First Treaty of Brest-Litovsk and the Break-up of Austria-Hungary, 1917–1918', in *The International History Review* 19 (1997), 757–88.

Wasserstein, Bernard, *The British in Palestine: The Mandatory Government and the Arab-Jewish Conflict 1917–1929* (Oxford: Blackwell, 1991).

Watson, Alexander, *Enduring the Great War: Combat Morale and Collapse in the German and British Armies, 1914–1918* (Cambridge and New York: Cambridge University Press, 2008).

——, *Ring of Steel: Germany and Austria-Hungary at War, 1914–18* (London: Allen Lane, 2014).

Watts, Martin, *The Jewish Legion and the First World War* (London and New York: Palgrave, 2004).

Wawrzinek, Bert, *Manfred von Killinger (1886–1944): Ein politischer Soldat zwischen Freikorps und Auswärtigem Amt* (Preussisch Oldendorf: DVG, 2004).

Weber, Thomas, *Hitler's First War: Adolf Hitler, the Men of the List Regiment, and the First World War* (Oxford and New York: Oxford University Press, 2010).

Wehrhahn, Torsten, *Die Westukrainische Volksrepublik: Zu den polnisch-*

ukrainischen Beziehungen und dem Problem der ukrainischen Staatlichkeit in den Jahren 1918 bis 1923 (Berlin: Weißensee Verlag, 2004).

Weitz, Eric D., 'From the Vienna to the Paris System: International Politics and the Entangled Histories of Human Rights, Forced Deportations, and Civilizing Missions', in *The American Historical Review* 113 (2008), 1,313–43.

Weitz, Eric D., and Omer Bartov (eds), *Shatterzones of Empires: Coexistence and Violence in the German, Habsburg, Russian, and Ottoman Borderlands* (Bloomington, IN: Indiana University Press, 2013).

Werth, Nicolas, 'L'ex-Empire russe, 1918–1921: Les mutations d'une guerre prolongée', in Audoin-Rouzeau and Prochasson (eds), *Sortir de la Grande Guerre*, 285–306.

———, 'The NKVD Mass Secret Operation no. 00447 (August 1937–November 1938)', *Online Encyclopedia of Mass Violence*, published 24 May 2010, last accessed 22 January 2016, URL: http://www.mass violence.org/The-NKVD-Mass-Secret-Operation-no-00447-August -1937.

Wette, Wolfram, *Gustav Noske: Eine politische Biographie* (Düsseldorf: Droste, 1987).

White, James D., 'National Communism and World Revolution: The Political Consequences of German Military Withdrawal from the Baltic Area in 1918–19', in *Europe-Asia Studies* 8 (1994), 1,349–69.

Wiel, Jerome aan de, *The Irish Factor 1899–1919: Ireland's Strategic and Diplomatic Importance for Foreign Powers* (Dublin: Irish Academic Press, 2008).

Wildman, Allan K., *The End of the Russian Imperial Army*, vol. 1: *The Old Army and the Soldiers' Revolt (March–April 1917)* (Princeton, NJ: Princeton University Press, 1980).

———, *The End of the Russian Imperial Army*, vol. 2: *The Road to Soviet Power and Peace* (Princeton, NJ: Princeton University Press, 1987).

Williams, Robert C., *Culture in Exile: Russian Emigrés in Germany, 1881–1941* (Ithaca, NY: Cornell University Press, 1972).

Wilson, Timothy K., *Frontiers of Violence: Conflict and Identity in Ulster and Upper Silesia, 1918–1922* (Oxford and New York: Oxford University Press, 2010).

———, 'The Polish-German Ethnic Dispute in Upper Silesia, 1918–1922: A Reply to Tooley', in *Canadian Review of Studies in Nationalism* 32 (2005), 1–26.

Winkler, Heinrich August, *The Age of Catastrophe: A History of the West 1914–1945* (New Haven, CT, and London: Yale University Press, 2015).

———, *Von der Revolution zur Stabilisierung: Arbeiter und Arbeiterbewegung in der Weimarer Republik, 1918 bis 1924* (Berlin: Dietz, 1984).

——, *Weimar 1918–1933. Die Geschichte der ersten deutschen Demokratie* (Munich: C. H. Beck, 1993).

Winter, Jay, *Sites of Memory, Sites of Mourning: The Great War in European Cultural History* (Cambridge and New York: Cambridge University Press, 1995).

Wirsching, Andreas, *Vom Weltkrieg zum Bürgerkrieg: Politischer Extremismus in Deutschland und Frankreich 1918–1933/39. Berlin und Paris im Vergleich* (Munich: Oldenbourg, 1999).

Wiskemann, Elizabeth, *The Rome-Berlin Axis: A History of the Relations between Hitler and Mussolini* (New York and London: Oxford University Press, 1949).

Wohlgemuth, Heinz, *Karl Liebknecht: Eine Biographie* (East Berlin: Dietz, 1975).

Wróbel, Piotr J., 'The Seeds of Violence: The Brutalization of an East European Region 1917–1921', in *Journal of Modern European History* 1 (2003), 125–49.

Yapp, Malcolm E., *The Making of the Modern Near East: 1792–1923* (London: Longman, 1987).

——, *The Near East Since the First World War: A History to 1995* (London: Longman, 1996).

Yekelchyk, Serhy, 'Bands of Nation-Builders? Insurgency and Ideology in the Ukrainian Civil War', in Gerwarth and Horne (eds), *War in Peace*, 107–25.

Yellin, Eric, *Racism in the Nation's Service: Government Workers and the Color Line in Woodrow Wilson's America* (Chapel Hill, NC: University of North Carolina Press, 2016).

Yianoulopoulos, Yiannis, 'Exoteriki politiki', in Christos Chatziiosif (ed.), *Istoria tis Elladas tou Ikostou eona*, vol. 2, 140–1.

Young, Louise, *Japan's Total Empire: Manchuria and the Culture of Wartime Imperialism* (Berkeley, CA: University of California Press, 1998).

Zabecki, David T., *The German 1918 Offensives: A Case Study in the Operational Level of War* (New York: Routledge, 2006).

Zadgorska, Valentina, *Kragat 'Zveno' (1927–1934)* (Sofia: 'Sv. Kliment Ohridski', 2008).

Zahra, Tara, *Kidnapped Souls: National Indifference and the Battle for Children in the Bohemian Lands, 1900–1948* (Ithaca, NY: Cornell University Press, 2008).

——, 'The "Minority Problem": National Classification in the French and Czechoslovak Borderlands', in *Contemporary European Review* 17 (2008), 137–65.

Zamoyski, Adam, *Warsaw 1920: Lenin's Failed Conquest of Europe* (London: Harper Press, 2008).

Zeman, Zbyněk, *The Masaryks: The Making of Czechoslovakia* (London: I. B. Tauris, 1976).

Ziemann, Benjamin, *Contested Commemorations: Republican War Veterans and Weimar Political Culture* (Cambridge and New York: Cambridge University Press, 2013).

———, *War Experiences in Rural Germany, 1914–1923* (Oxford and New York: Berg, 2007).

Zimmermann, John, *'Von der Bluttat eines Unseligen': Das Attentat Friedrich Adlers und seine Rezeption in der sozialdemokratischen Presse* (Hamburg: Verlag Dr. Kovač, 2000).

Zöllner, Erich, *Geschichte Österreichs: Von den Anfängen bis zur Gegenwart*, 8th edition (Vienna: Verlag für Geschichte und Politik, 1990).

Zorn, Wolfgang, *Geschichte Bayerns im 20. Jahrhundert* (Munich: C. H. Beck, 1986).

Zürcher, Erik Jan, 'The Ottoman Empire and the Armistice of Moudros', in Hugh Cecil and Peter H. Liddle (eds), *At the Eleventh Hour: Reflections, Hopes, and Anxieties at the Closing of the Great War, 1918* (London: Leo Cooper, 1998), 266–75.

———, *Turkey: A Modern History* (London and New York: I. B. Tauris, 2004).

———, *The Young Turk Legacy and Nation Building: From the Ottoman Empire to Atatürk's Turkey* (London: I. B. Tauris, 2010).

Acknowledgements

Writing a book in which appalling levels of mass violence take centre stage can be both solitary and depressing. Yet, despite the grimness of the subject, the research and writing process has been hugely fulfilling and even enjoyable, not least because I have undertaken both tasks in the good company of a large number of inspiring colleagues and friends, who have all contributed to the book's completion in one way or another. Since I first started to think about the themes underpinning this book nearly a decade ago, I have accumulated more debts than I can ever hope to repay. Thanking some of the people who have helped me along the way is no more than a public acknowledgement of those debts.

For the past eight years, I have been fortunate to live and work in Dublin, arguably one of the most dynamic places for the study of the First World War and modern conflict more generally. Countless conversations with my brilliant Dublin-based colleagues and friends – notably John Horne, William Mulligan and Alan Kramer – have helped me enormously to sharpen some of my arguments, and to abandon others. Between 2007 and 2009, John Horne and I led a project on paramilitary violence after 1918, one funded by the Irish Research Council and providing the starting point for a long period of reflection on when exactly the Great War ended. This was followed, between 2009 and 2014, by a project on Europe's 'post-war', funded by the European Research Council and an enterprise that I have had the great privilege to direct. It was very much during this period that the ideas running through the book took shape. This was possible in part because I had the pleasure of working with twelve extremely talented postdoctoral scholars in the Centre for War Studies at University College Dublin – all of them experts on this period, who have since embarked on stellar academic careers: Tomas Balkelis, Julia Eichenberg, Maria Falina, Mark Jones, Matthew Lewis, James Matthews, Matteo Millan, John Paul Newman, Mercedes Peñalba-Sotorrio, Gajendra Singh, Dmitar Tasić and Uğur Ümit Üngör. I could not have written this book without the important empirical research that these scholars undertook on geographical areas as diverse as the Balkans, the Baltic States, Germany, India, Ireland, Italy, the Ottoman Empire, Palestine, Poland and Spain.

In addition to the constant flow of fresh empirical material emanating from their work, we also held a thematic fortnightly seminar series in Dublin, featuring dozens of international experts on European and world history in this period. All of the guest speakers fed directly into our discussions, as did those historians who attended one or more of the several international conferences on the 'post-war' period that were either held in Dublin or at other universities around the world. I am particularly grateful for the hard work that my two research administrators in Dublin, Christina Griessler and Suzanne d'Arcy, put into the organization of these events, and for the generosity of my hosts at the themed workshops and conferences held in Moscow (Nikolaus Katzer), Buenos Aires (María Inés Tato) and Perth, Western Australia (Mark Edele). Most recently, Rudolf Kučera very kindly invited me to open a conference at the Czech Academy of Sciences in Prague with a keynote lecture on 'post-war' violence, followed by a thorough discussion.

I am equally grateful to the Harry Frank Guggenheim Foundation and the European Research Council for funding a significant number of outstanding research assistants, who have provided me with a constant stream of primary documents and translations of recent literature in languages I cannot read. Any author trying to offer a coherent account of the defeated states of Europe at the end of the Great War faces the challenge of writing about vast tracts of land that were home to peoples speaking more languages than any one scholar could possibly master: from Russian to Hungarian, Bulgarian to German, and Ukrainian to Turkish. The list grows even longer when one includes those countries that officially won the war, but felt that they had lost the peace. As much as possible, I have tried to incorporate the often excellent scholarship that has been produced in these various languages – a task that could not have been undertaken without the substantial help of a number of people who assisted me in surmounting linguistic boundaries by translating important scholarship or sources from those languages, or by simply sharing their own important research results with me.

I would particularly like to acknowledge the assistance of Jan Bockelmann in Berlin, Dmitar Tasić in Belgrade, Nikolai Vukov in Sofia, and Spyros Kakouriotis in Athens. The same applies to Ursula Falch, who collated large numbers of documents in various archives in Innsbruck, Vienna and Linz; Eric Weaver (Budapest); and Matteo Pasetti (for offering expert advice and translations of key Italian texts). Meanwhile, Rudolf Mark and Katja Bruisch of the German Historical Institute in Moscow helped to identify key Russian texts and visual sources.

I also benefited immensely from years of close collaboration with Ryan Gingeras and Uğur Ümit Üngör – two of the finest scholars of their generation working on the late Ottoman Empire. In Istanbul, Ayhan Aktar cheerfully provided documents and additional advice on the Greco-Turkish 'population exchange'. Pieter Judson generously sent me the manuscript of his latest book on the Habsburg Empire prior to publication, while Ronald Suny kindly shared large amounts of published and unpublished work with me.

Some of the early conceptual work for this book was done at the Institute for Advanced Study in Princeton, a paradise for any scholar. There I was lucky enough to spend time in the good company of Mustafa Aksakal and William Hagen, with both of whom I had inspiring conversations about our shared interest in the end of the European land empires. In 2014 some initial writing was done at the European University Institute, where I had the good fortune to spend several months as a Fernand Braudel Fellow, benefiting from the intellectual company of Dirk Moses, Pieter Judson, Lucy Riall and Tara Zahra. My sincere thanks to all of them for their hospitality and critical input.

Other colleagues and friends unsparingly gave their time to reading parts of the manuscript: Béla Bodó, Jochen Böhler, Nicholas Doumanis, Roy Foster, John Horne, Stephan Malinowski, Hartmut Pogge von Strandmann, Felix Schnell and Leonard V. Smith all provided extensive feedback on earlier drafts, helped me to weed out mistakes, and strengthen some of the arguments. Needless to say, all remaining errors of fact or judgement in this book are entirely attributable to me.

The research for this book has taken me to various archives across Europe, and I am thankful to the staff of all of them. I am particularly grateful to the Starhemberg family for granting me unrestricted access to the private papers of Ernst Rüdiger Starhemberg, housed in the Oberösterreichisches Landesarchiv in Linz. At the Herder Institut in Marburg, where I had the privilege to spend a semester as an Alexander von Humboldt Senior Research Fellow, I benefited from the expert advice of Dorothee Goeze and Peter Wörster, who provided excellent guidance through the Institute's extensive holdings on the fighting that ensued in the Baltic States after the Great War. My sincere thanks to them, and to my wonderful host in Marburg, the Herder Institut's director, Peter Haslinger.

I am fortunate in having a brilliant literary agent in Andrew Wylie. He and his staff in the Wylie Agency office in London, notably Stephanie Derbyshire, have to take full credit for finding the ideal publishers for this book, not just in the English-speaking world but around the globe. In London, Simon Winder read an earlier draft and made numerous excellent suggestions for further improvement, and I am grateful to him and his team at Penguin for seeing the manuscript through production with such efficiency and good humour. A special word of thanks is due to Richard Mason for doing such a splendid job in copy-editing the typescript. In New York, Eric Chinski and his colleagues at Farrar, Straus and Giroux also provided valuable input and encouragement throughout. I could not have wished for better editors.

My final thanks, as always, go to my family. My parents offered all sorts of support during my frequent visits to Berlin. In Dublin my wife Porscha not only tolerated my long-standing obsession with Europe's violent post-war, but actively shaped my thinking (and writing) on the topic. Despite her own busy schedule, she found time to offer critical feedback and stylistic advice on various occasions. Happy moments away from the desk were usually spent in her company and that of our two sons, Oscar and Lucian, who have lived with this book from

ACKNOWLEDGEMENTS

the day they were born, and who have provided wonderful and plenti-
ful distraction throughout the process. This book is dedicated to them,
in loving memory of the five years we have spent together so far.

Robert Gerwarth
Dublin, Summer 2016

Index

Bolsheviks 193
Lithuanian Soviet Republic 69,
70
Social Democratic Party of Poland
and Lithuania 119
'Little Versailles' Treaty 217
Livonia 39
Lloyd George, David, 2, 156, 171,
172–3, 181, 184, 211, 227,
228, 237, 243
Locarno, Treaty of 248
London, Treaty of 221, 224, 227
Louis XVI 97
Lübeck, Gustav 120
Lübeck (city) 63
Ludendorff, Erich 42, 44, 49,
59–60, 61, 263
Spring Offensive 44–7
Ludwig III 64, 127
Lüttwitz, Walther von 165
Luxemburg, Rosa 118, 119–20,
125, 126, 142
Lvov, Georgy Yevgenyevich 29

Macedonia 50, 51, 52, 115, 208,
210, 228, 261
IMRO 148, 150, 251, 252
Mackensen, August von 52
Magyars 14, 133, 207, 215, 262
See also: Hungary/Hungarians
Makhno, Nestor 78
Malinov, Alexander 53, 113
Manchuria 262
Manisa 241
Mann, Thomas 129, 131–2
Mannerheim, Carl 99, 266
Manuel Calvo 154
Maraş 237
Marie Antoinette 97
Marmaris 227
Marne, Second Battle of the 49

Marx, Karl 21, 78, 118
Communist Manifesto 96
Marxism 20, 33
and the multi-ethnic state 181
Masaryk, Tomáš Garrigue 179–80,
189, 218–19
Masurian Lakes, First Battle of the
49
McMahon, Sir Henry 182
Mehmed VI 57, 59, 115
Mensheviks 22, 30, 78
Mesopotamia 176, 182, 216
Metaxas, Ioannis 229
Michael, Operation 44–6
Middle East 9, 11, 13, 58, 116,
182–6, 210–11, 215
campaigns 56
and the Paris Peace Conference
173, 175–6
Mikhail Alexandrovich of Russia
22
Milan 160
Milev, Geo 151
Miliukov, Pavel 29
Minorities Treaties 216–19, 244,
246
Minsk 193
Mirbach, Wilhelm von 97–8
Mitau (Jelgava) 71, 72
Mogilev 28, 29, 78
Mongolia 88–9
Montenegro 51, 55, 177, 198
Moravia 107–8, 253
Morgenthau, Henry 245
Morocco 175
Moscow 15, 29, 35, 78, 79, 83
Treaty of 253
Mosley, Oswald 253
Mosse, George 12
Moudros / Mudros, Armistice of
55, 57, 115

INDEX